ŚVETĀŚVATAROPANIṢAD

Other books by Devadatta Kālī

In Praise of the Goddess: The Devīmāhātmya and Its Meaning (2003)
The Veiling Brilliance: A Journey to the Goddess (2006)

श्वेताश्वतरोपनिषद्

ŚVETĀŚVATAROPANIṢAD

The Knowledge That Liberates

Translation and Commentary by

DEVADATTA KĀLĪ

Nicolas Hays, Inc.
Lake Worth, FL

Published in 2011 by Nicolas-Hays, Inc.
P. O. Box 540206
Lake Worth, FL 33454-0206
www.nicolashays.com

Distributed to the trade by
Red Wheel/Weiser, LLC
65 Parker St. • Ste. 7
Newburyport, MA 01950
www.redwheelweiser.com

First Edition

ISBN 978-0-89254-166-9

Library of Congress Cataloging-in-Publication Data

Devadatta Kali, 1944–
Svetsvataropanisad : the knowledge that liberates /translation and commentary by Devadatta Kali.—1st ed.
p. cm.
In English and Sanskrit (romanized); includes translation from Sanskrit.
Includes bibliographical references and index.
ISBN 0-89254-166-0 (alk. paper)
1. Upanishads. Svetasvataropanisad—Commentaries. I. Upanishads. Svetasvataropanisad. English. II. Title.
BL1124.7.S846D48 2011
294.5'9218—dc22 2011009046

Cover and text design by David Nelson (Devadatta Kali)

Printed in the United States of America

CONTENTS

PREFACE

As a newcomer to the Vedanta Society of Southern California in the autumn of 1966, I soon became acquainted with the Upaniṣads through an English translation by Swami Prabhavananda and Frederick Manchester. From the beginning I felt a natural compatibility with those ancient texts, and in the case of the Śvetāśvataropaniṣad it was a matter of love at first sight. Perhaps that response was not so unusual: in his preface Manchester had noted that in its latter half the Śvetāśvatara achieves a poetry unequaled by any other Upaniṣad. In the process of translation, he recalled, "it asked for wings," and the resulting flight of eloquence came about more by accident than by design. I found myself captivated by its vision of the transcendent amid a celebration of the immanent, and that impression has never faded. Four decades later this Upaniṣad is no less irresistible than it was on the first encounter.

About the Śvetāśvataropaniṣad

Max Müller, one of the early European translators, found himself intrigued by the Śvetāśvatara's complexities and expressed no small admiration for its distinctive character. Less charitably Paul Deussen, who published a translation soon afterward, criticized the text as a mass of cleverly disguised contradictions. Another translator, Robert Ernest Hume, saw it as a battleground of conflicting doctrines, even while Indian scholars have traditionally viewed it more in terms of reconciliation or synthesis or as a statement of pure Vedantic nondualism. Despite the bewildering assessments there is no question that the Śvetāśvatara has consistently enjoyed respect as one of the most authoritative of the Upaniṣads. The confusion surrounding its interpretation arises from a failure to approach it on its own terms. Accordingly, the introduction to this book, "Text and Context," provides the necessary religious, philosophical, and historical background for a clearer understanding of this remarkable text.

About the translation

For many centuries the Śvetāśvataropaniṣad was passed along orally in Sanskrit from one generation to the next through a process of memorization so exacting that the transmission had nearly the fidelity of a recording. Only much later was it committed to writing. The oldest manuscripts show an occasional variation, but on the whole the teaching has come down in the original language much as the seer Śvetāśvatara configured it. For most readers today, unschooled in India's ancient literary language, acquaintance with the text will be through translation.

To translate literally means "to carry across," and in the broadest sense it entails more than converting an utterance from one language to another. Whenever we communicate through the spoken or written word, even if the exchange takes place through a single common language, we engage in an act of carrying information or ideas across a divide. The purpose of linguistic interaction is to convey information from one mind to another, and with that sharing of information, the question of individual differences and other variables arises. What the speaker or writer intends is not necessarily what the listener or reader will understand. Each participant in the exchange draws on a unique store of experience either in expressing something or in interpreting it, and there is no guarantee that it will come across as intended. Even when two people converse face to face with the additional nuances of tone, mood, rhythm, volume, emphasis, or gesture to reinforce the message, the spoken word may be open to interpretation. On the printed page, without those additional signals, the latitude for interpretation becomes even wider.

Additional layers of complication arise when the message has to be put into another language. Ideally, in carrying meaning across linguistic boundaries, a translation should assure as safe a passage as is humanly possible. The journey can be fraught with difficulty, because each language embodies its own world-view, conditioned by place, time, and culture. The divide can be small and the crossing easy if two languages are closely related; it can be great and fraught with hazard if they are not related at all. In the case of Sanskrit and English the two languages are distantly related and separated by half a world and thousands of years. They speak for very distinct cultures. It is reasonable to ask if the message of the Upaniṣads can be communicated exactly as intended or even sufficiently well.

What makes for a good translation? Obviously fidelity is paramount, but fidelity to the letter of the text all too often produces something lifeless and slavishly literal that paradoxically may obscure rather than clarify. Like a successful original work, a successful translation should speak with clarity and vitality. Translation, as much as original writing, is a creative act.

There can be no such thing as a purely objective translation. In the process of carrying across from one language to another, something is always lost and something else is always added. The losses may be nuances, emphases, associations, esthetic qualities, or even meanings readily evident in the original. These may have to do with the unique qualities of the source language and culture as well as with the personality or outlook of the author. Similarly, for better or worse, the distinctive nature of the second language and the personality and intent of the translator always make themselves felt in some way. As regrettable as the losses may be, so may be the additions if they introduce new colorations and suggestions never intended in the original.

If a translation is to succeed, it must speak naturally in the translator's own voice even while preserving the tone and quality, and above all the meaning, of the original. An expert translator is a discerning listener, sensitive to the moods, colors, and nuances of the source language, to the author's feelings and ideas, and to the conditions that shaped them. Such a translator allows the original text to speak for itself in a different language to a new audience of a different time and place. The aim must be to communicate the message authentically enough across the various divides so that the reader can benefit from it in the manner intended.

The Sanskrit language is unusually rich in vocabulary and astonishing in syntactical virtuosity. It can be lavish in its use of metaphor, and it delights in *double entendre* and other forms of wordplay. Its esthetic qualities are highly refined. Its character differs vastly from that of English and cannot be duplicated. Most Sanskrit words derive from verbal roots, which remain readily apparent even in abstract nouns, and that infuses the language with a characteristic dynamism. Sanskrit conveys a world-view centered not on objects as matter but on objects as process. Even the word for world, *jagat,* means "that which moves." Sanskrit also possesses a directness and a concentration that are difficult to capture in English. Enabled by a highly specialized technical vocabulary, it impresses complex and subtle ideas on the mind with astonishing immediacy, making it the ideal vehicle for the conveyance of Indian philosophical thought.

In any language a given utterance may have more than one level of meaning, and its understanding will be determined by the capacity of the hearer or reader. A metaphor may be taken in more than one way, and even nonmetaphorical language can be ambiguous. The difficulties are compounded in the Upaniṣads, which attempt to express the inexpressible heights of spiritual experience that can only be hinted at and never articulated with razor-sharp definition.

The Śvetāśvataropaniṣad has its own natural flow, arising from the seer's personal enthusiasm and the joy of his spiritual attainment. Each chapter or discourse benefits from being heard or read uninterruptedly. For that reason the entire English translation first appears by itself on pages 69–81. Following that, the main body of the book presents the Upaniṣad verse by verse in Sanskrit and English, accompanied by a detailed commentary.

About the commentary

Belonging originally to an oral tradition, the Upaniṣads are necessarily succinct. Whether composed as prose or poetry, they were designed to be memorized, and each section or verse is pregnant with implications on which a gifted teacher can elaborate. The traditional method of instruction is the threefold process of *śravana, manana,* and *nididhyāsana*—exposure, engagement, and assimilation. *Śravana* means hearing with a receptive attitude. *Manana* means applying one's critical skills and questioning relentlessly until all doubts are resolved. *Nididhyāsana* is a matter of assimilation and the personal transformation that results.

Indian scholarly tradition recognizes several kinds of commentary, each with a specific purpose. Ordinarily a commentary represents or argues for a particular religious or philosophical point of view. In that respect the present commentary differs. Its purpose is to propose the most likely interpretation of Śvetāśvatara's verses across philosophical or sectarian boundaries and also to explain the many nuances, implications, and deeper meanings of the text that do not come across in translation.

Just as the translation aims to be clear, eloquent, and uplifting, the commentary strives for practical relevance. It does not shy away from detailed and sometimes technical explanations when called for, but no effort has been spared to present them lucidly and meaningfully. Wherever a traditionally accepted interpretation does not fit, the commentary offers a solidly argued alternative, most often elegant in its simplicity.

Both the translated text and the supporting commentary aim to convey the vibrant immediacy of the Sanskrit original and the joyful, life-affirming, and sometimes playfully provocative voice of the seer Śvetāśvatara. The purpose is to strip away the many centuries of exegetical accretions in order to make Śvetāśvatara's message heard as he intended—as a statement of profound insight designed to guide, inspire, and enlighten.

Acknowledgements

This book would not be possible without the guidance of many people. First and foremost, deepest gratitude to my revered *guru*, Swami Prabhavananda, Śrī Rāmakṛṣṇa's grand-disciple who taught me both the philosophical and practical sides of Vedānta through his knowledge and example. Heartfelt thanks also to a host of other swamis of the Ramakrishna Order, who have contributed, each in a unique way, to further my spiritual education. Thanks also to the many monastic and householder members of the Vedanta Societies, Kashi Ashram, and Kali Mandir who form my extended spiritual family, and to whom I am indebted for their loving support.

INTRODUCTION: TEXT AND CONTEXT

Tradition and history

"We Indians have a poor sense of history; you see, we live in eternity." Those often spoken words illustrate both the glory of India's eternal religion, the *sanātana dharma,* and the frustration of those who feel the need to take its historical development into account if they are to understand it fully. At a deeper level those same words call attention to the Indian view of the evanescence of worldly affairs against the backdrop of the abiding reality that supports them. In contrast Western religious thought more often rests on the idea of linear progression in which the unfolding events of history signal some greater purpose. For different reasons each approach has much to commend it, and neither should be disregarded for the sake of the other.

The historical approach values knowledge of the chronological development of sacred texts and their ideas as an essential component in proper interpretation. The traditional Indian way of thinking, said to be based in eternity, certainly does not exclude the idea of development but defines it on logical rather than chronological grounds. Indian thought routinely and methodically penetrates the layers of observable existence. Beginning with the experience of human life in the here and now, it acknowledges this as the state of difference or multiplicity (*bheda*), also called duality (*dvaita*). Next, beneath the surface appearance, it discovers a state of identity-in-difference (*bhedābheda*) or unity-in-multiplicity (*dvaitādvaita*). Finally it reaches the ultimate unity of nondifference (*abheda*) or nonduality (*advaita*). The progression is not temporal; all three degrees of experience are eternally present. The recognition of these simultaneous dimensions infused the thought of India's earliest spiritual document, the Ṛgvedasaṁhitā, a collection of more than a thousand hymns that extol the forces of nature, deify them, and finally proclaim an ultimate unity supporting the whole of the perceptible world. These three dimensions of experience have persisted in pervading Indian thought throughout its history, one outlook favored here, another there.

Eventually each came to dominate a discrete branch of the later Vedānta philosophy, but in that historical process the chronological and logical orders do not coincide. Quite the reverse. The original Vedānta of the Upaniṣads expresses the positions of *advaita* and *dvaitādvaita,* reflecting not only that Brahman is the sole reality but that the world is its expression. The earliest systematized Vedānta philosophy, based on the work of Bādarāyaṇa, Gauḍapāda, and Śaṁkara, stressed the nonduality of Brahman and became known as Advaita Vedānta. Two hundred years after Śaṁkara's time, Rāmānuja's school of qualified nondualism, known as Viśiṣṭādvaita Vedānta, promoted a *dvaitādvaita* point of view. Almost two centuries after that Mādhva's Dvaita Vedānta expounded a fully dualistic philosophy.

The chronological and logical outlooks are demonstrably different but equally valid, and the study of sacred texts should not demand a choice of one or the other. Such a choice serves only to limit the would-be interpreter's scope for understanding. Admittedly each approach has its own strengths and weaknesses, and the combined insights of the two together are better than the merits and inadequacies of either one by itself.

The nonhistorical approach takes a sacred text as a timeless and often generalized statement of eternal truth; the historical method seeks to interpret a text on its own terms within a definite context. Of course, the primary purpose of sacred literature is to convey spiritual knowledge, and excessive attention to historical facts can easily eclipse the essential message. But it is equally true that a disregard for the time, place, and circumstances of a text's origin can lead to a misunderstanding of its meaning. Reading a text *sub specie æternitatis,* without considering its intended audience or purpose or the conditions surrounding its composition, has its pitfalls. Either the reading will be so generalized as to miss a specific and often more important point, or the text's removal from the proper context will embolden a commentator to impose on it a meaning that the author might not have intended or could not even have imagined.

Commentators aim to elucidate, of course, but they are not immune to promoting the cherished opinion of a particular philosophical school or spiritual lineage at the expense of others. Even so, it is counterproductive to see their differences as antagonistic rather than complementary. Although Indian thinkers are not immune to disputation, by and large their culture has valued the principles of accommodation and acceptance. Throughout the millennia of Indian religious history, differing views have often been seen as just that—as differing views of a single reality that lies beyond any human power of articulation. The tendency has been to harmonize the sometimes opposing philosophies as distinct parts of a larger whole whose fullness lies well beyond the reach of mere perception or reason. It bears repeating that the primary purpose of sacred literature is to communicate spiritual knowledge, not to fuel intellectual or sectarian debate—or to create confusion.

Conflicting impressions

Still, a great deal of confusion surrounds the Śvetāśvataropaniṣad. The text is a fairly brief work of one hundred thirteen verses, called *mantras,* forming six chapters, lessons, or discourses, designated by the term *adhyāya.* The renowned German Indologist Max Müller wrote in 1884 that he found the Śvetāśvatara one of the most difficult—and interesting—of the Upaniṣads. Considering its dating as highly problematical, he also recognized that knowledge of its place in time was essential for correct interpretation. Müller decided after deliberating carefully that the text was quite old despite its "peculiar features and its peculiar difficulties." Among those "peculiar features" he noted the tendency to personalize the highest Self as Rudra, Hara, Agni, Āditya, and Vāyu, but he dismissed the presence of those names as a reason to consider the Upaniṣad a later sectarian work.[1] To the contrary, the ancient Vedic theonyms, together with the obscurity of many verses and the recognition even by early commentators of a number of variant readings, only convinced Müller of the text's considerable antiquity.[2]

Paul Deussen, a Schopenhauer disciple who published a translation of sixty Upaniṣads in 1887, formed a very different opinion. Noting the Śvetāśvatara's frequent changes of meter and copious quotations from earlier Vedic sources, he concluded that it could not be the work of a single author. He suggested, without any supporting evidence, that this Upaniṣad might have grown from an original core to which members of a particular spiritual community added the Vedic citations along with new material. Deussen criticized the Śvetāśvataropaniṣad for its lack of cohesion and orderly thought. At the same time, he saw emerging in it many important ideas of the later Vedānta philosophy not developed in the earlier Upaniṣads. He ventured to assert that the Śvetāśvatara is the first Upaniṣad to teach the illusory nature of the world. Along with what he perceived as its growing philosophical sophistication, Deussen was troubled by its concurrent tendency to invoke the names of personalized gods, a tendency he tried to dismiss as an "undeserving accommodation" to popular religion.[3] That is a strange conclusion to draw from a text whose opening verse and epilogue leave no doubt that its teachings are intended for a community of advanced ascetics and not for a wider public. Although some of Deussen's findings are valuable to later interpreters, his overall assessment unfairly portrays the Upaniṣad as a compromise that ingeniously masks the contradictions of disparate ideas.[4]

Robert Ernest Hume's translation of thirteen principal Upaniṣads appeared in 1921. Hume, a Congregational minister, missionary, and lecturer who was born in India, meticulously documented the Śvetāśvataropaniṣad's internal cross-references along with citations from other Vedic texts (see Appendix B). He saw this Upaniṣad in terms of doctrinal conflict and assigned it to a period marked by open antagonism between proponents of the Sāṁkhya and Vedānta philosophies. Hume singled out some passages as unmistakably representative of Sāṁkhya and noted a preponderance of verses that impose a Sāṁkhya reading on what appears to be Vedantic content, while he claimed that still other passages refute Sāṁkhya doctrine in favor of Vedānta. He even managed to find in the opening verse of the final chapter a denunciation of Sāṁkhya as "the utterance of deluded men."[5]

In 1937 Swāmī Tyāgīśānanda noted in the introduction to his translation that the Śvetāśvataropaniṣad finds no mention in the *Brahmasūtra,* the earliest known attempt to systematize the teachings of the Upaniṣads. On that basis he determined that the Śvetāśvatara must have been composed later than the fifth century BCE. Nevertheless, he acknowledged this Upaniṣad's authority, noting that commentators on the *Brahmasūtra* frequently cited it to support their doctrines. Tyāgīśānanda felt that the Upaniṣad itself represents no particular point of view but, like the Bhagavadgītā, is the product of a great mind attempting to reconcile the conflicting religious and philosophical views of its time. He considered it a grand synthesis of Vedic, Puranic, Sāṁkhya, and Yoga thought—a work that accordingly harmonizes the disciplines of discriminative knowledge (*jñāna*) and religious devotion (*bhakti*).[6]

Swami Nikhilananda, writing in 1952, also emphasized the spiritual authority of the Śvetāśvataropaniṣad, acknowledging its frequent citation by ancient commentators to support various doctrines, including those of the later Vedānta philosophy. Despite the sometimes markedly theistic character that distinguishes it from most of the other principal Upaniṣads, Nikhilananda concluded that the Śvetāśvatara adheres to the purely nondualistic teaching of the singular reality of Brahman.[7]

In contrast, a year later Sarvepalli Radhakrishnan underscored this same Upaniṣad's theistic and devotional character, noting that the text's emphasis falls not on the impersonal Brahman but on the personal Īśvara (Rudra), the manifest deity who is omniscient and omnipotent. At the same time, the Upaniṣad does not deny the unity of souls and the world within one supreme reality. Like Tyāgīśānanda, Radhakrishnan felt that the text attempted to reconcile the different philosophical and religious views of its time.[8]

In the second edition of *Classical Sāṁkhya*, Gerald Larson wrote in 1979 that it is difficult to assign even an approximate date to the Śvetāśvataropaniṣad but that some scholars place it around the third century BCE. Larson emphasized its predominant theism. Calling attention also to its frequent use of Sāṁkhya terminology and its detailed account of yogic practice, he saw a clear indication of the proto-Sāṁkhya and proto-Yoga tendencies that would crystallize some six or seven hundred years later into the classical systems defined by Īśvarakṛṣṇa's *Sāṁkhyakārikā* and Patañjali's *Yogasūtra*. Larson noted that the Śvetāśvataropaniṣad is directed to an "elite group of initiates," a fact which accounts for its "rather puzzling style and presentation."[9]

Swāmī Gambhīrānanda, whose translation dates from 1986, thought it wrong to consider the Śvetāśvataropaniṣad a devotional text, even though its grandeur clearly expresses a harmony of devotion and knowledge. Instead he viewed it as an unambiguous statement of Vedantic nondualism.[10]

Eight years later Swami Lokeswarananda's exposition agreed with Gambhīrānanda's and Nikhilananda's assessment that the world-view infusing this Upaniṣad is Śaṁkara's *vivartavāda*—the doctrine that the created universe with all its multiplicity is nothing more than a false superimposition on Brahman, the ultimate reality.[11]

Patrick Olivelle, commissioned by Oxford University Press for a 1996 edition of the major Upaniṣads, described the Śvetāśvatara as a late text reflecting the influence of the Sāṁkhya-Yoga schools and the theistic tendencies of the emerging devotional sects. Olivelle blamed its "somewhat chaotic" presentation on an attempt to integrate an array of disparate cosmologies and theologies into a framework whose primary idea is the unity of God. Noting the Upaniṣad's technical disposition and complex philosophical arguments, he proposed that the many quotations from older Vedic sources were employed by the author as proof-texts and that those quotations often appear newly interpreted.[12]

Swami Vedananda's edition from 2001 is based on notes detailing an earlier exposition by Swami Bhaskareshwarananda in the light of Advaita Vedānta. This interpretation emphasizes the creation as the divine play of Brahman (*brahmalīlā*). Vedananda characterized the seer Śvetāśvatara's teaching as unique in its clarity regarding intricate philosophical points on the nature of reality. Additionally he held the orthodox opinion that all the Upaniṣads are undatable and at least four thousand years old.[13]

To the contrary, in a translation of the major Upaniṣads commissioned by Penguin Books India and revised in 2003, Valerie Roebuck assigned a very late date to the Śvetāśvataropaniṣad, believing it to contain early references to the Sāṁkhya, Yoga, and Vedānta philosophical schools and to the devotional (*bhakti*) movement of sectarian Hinduism. She saw in this text an implied plurality of individual souls (*puruṣas*), consistent with classical Sāṁkhya, but conceded nevertheless that the dualistic principles of nontheistic Sāṁkhya are subordinated to the singular person of "the god" (*deva*).[14]

Félix G. Ilárraz and Òscar Pujol, the editors of a Spanish translation of the major Upaniṣads that appeared in 2003, declared that the ascetics whom Śvetāśvatara addressed were unaffiliated with any particular Vedic or Brahmanic lineage (*sampradāya*). Noting the very eclectic character of the text, they called attention to its abundant citations from earlier Vedic literature as well as to the ample treatment of Sāṁkhya and Yoga themes and the emphasis on a personal God (Īśvara) capable of elevating the spiritual aspirant to the experience of ultimate reality.[15]

The astonishing breadth of contradictory impressions demonstrated in this brief overview raises more questions than it answers. Does the Śvetāśvataropaniṣad date from more than four thousand years ago or less than two thousand or from some time in between? Is it the work of a single author or of multiple contributors? Is it sectarian or without sectarian affiliation? Is it primarily theistic and devotional, or is its theism an unfortunate concession to popular religion? Is it philosophical, and if so, which school does it represent—the Sāṁkhya, the Yoga, or the Vedānta? Is it eclectic or puzzling or somewhat chaotic, or is it unique in its clarity? Is it a compromise that cleverly masks its internal contradictions, or is it the attempt of a great mind to synthesize the many religious and philosophical trends of its time? Could the Śvetāśvataropaniṣad just possibly be a coherent statement in its own right? The answers to all these questions depend on knowing something about its place in Indian religious history.

A question of history

The starting point of any inquiry must be the dating of India's most ancient sacred texts, the Vedas. Again the question of tradition and history comes to the fore, because there are two views of how the Vedas originated.

Orthodox Hinduism holds that the Vedas are beginningless, eternal, and of nonhuman origin (*apauruṣeya*). At the beginning of every cycle of cosmic manifestation, they are revealed to the creator god, Brahmā, in his deepest contemplation. From the indescribable light in the lotus of his heart the sound of *Oṁ* first emerges, and from *Oṁ* are born all the other sounds—the vowels, the consonants, the entire alphabet of creation from which the Vedas take shape. The Vedas are the revealed knowledge (*śruti*) that Brahmā then imparts to the seers (*ṛṣis*), who in turn teach others from generation to generation.

Understood historically, the origin of the Vedas is somewhat different. As in any society of any time or place, within the Vedic culture there were men and women whose vision extended beyond the limits of everyday life. They pondered the great questions of existence: Where did this world come from? Who, or what, created it? Who are we, and where are we headed? The answers were revealed internally to the divinely inspired seers and poets who composed the Vedic texts. In all likelihood those seers were historical figures, and like many such figures whose achievements long outlive them, the Vedic *ṛṣis* took on larger than life stature in the minds of succeeding generations and became mythologized as semidivine beings.

The traditional account of the Vedas deals primarily with meaning, and the historical account deals with fact. The two are not antithetical but complementary. Knowing the historical circumstances surrounding the composition of the Vedas in no way undermines their spiritual truth but rather helps to clarify it.

From the beginning the Vedas were memorized and transmitted orally from one generation to the next, but because an oral tradition leaves no written documents, the knowledge of when, how, and in what order the texts took shape will remain ever hazy. Still, an approximate idea of their origination is essential to comprehending the long continuum of Indian religious and philosophical thought that follows in their wake.

Although there is much to admire in Max Müller's pioneering efforts to make the teachings of the East available to the West, his attempt to date the Vedas turned out to be a blunder with far–reaching consequences. Even today many scholars accept his hypothesis, published in 1859, that the Vedas were composed around 1200–1000 BCE. To arrive at such a date Müller began with a seven hundred-year-old collection of stories, Somadeva's *Kāthāsaritasāgara*, which contains a tale of one Kātyāyana Vararuci, a minister in the court of King Nanda. On the dubious assumption that this Kātyāyana must have been the author of a famous mathematical treatise, the *Kātyāyanasūtra*, Müller turned to India's mythologized religious histories, the Purāṇas, in order to determine a date for King Nanda's reign. Placing Kātyāyana around the fourth century BCE, he then dated the *sūtra* period of Indian literature to around 600–200 BCE. Next Müller proposed, for whatever reason, that Sanskrit literature regularly changed its form every two hundred years, even though by his own reckoning the *sūtra* period lasted four hundred. With his arbitrary formula in place, it was a simple matter of calculating backward to the time of the ancient Vedic hymns, which he assigned to the period of 1200–1000 BCE.[16]

Müller's colleagues were aghast. W. D. Whitney envisioned that the hymns of the Ṛgveda were sung as early as 2000 BCE,[17] and Martin Haug dated them to 2400 BCE.[18] In 1891 Müller yielded to the objections of Theodore Goldstücker, W. D. Whitney, H. H. Wilson, and others, conceding that no power on earth could ever determine whether the Vedic hymns were three or four or five thousand years old. Much to his dismay, the date of 1200–1000 BCE stuck as if engraved in stone. It remains an article of faith among many historians and academics today, even though the method that produced it is questionable at best, even though Müller admitted later that it was purely hypothetical,[19] and even though Hindu traditionalists have been insisting all along that the Vedas are much older.

Fortunately present-day researchers have more to rely on than Müller's whim. Even so, in trying to make sense of the prodigious volume of new data, they run the gamut from tenacious "late-daters" who uphold Müller's outmoded calculations to extremists in the other direction who make extravagant claims for the Vedas' antiquity. Still, a clearer picture of ancient India is beginning to emerge from the weighing of literary and archeological data against the findings of the physical sciences, including geology, hydrology, astronomy, paleobotany, and genetics. The combined evidence of these disciplines provides compelling support for Martin Haug's and W. D. Whitney's proposed dating of the Ṛgvedic hymns to the third millennium BCE.

The Saṁhitā, or liturgical portion, of the Ṛgveda constitutes the most ancient Vedic literature. It consists of 1028 hymns, composed over hundreds of years and arranged in ten books, called *maṇḍalas.* For a long while scholars have recognized that the second through seventh *maṇḍalas* are the oldest, each being the work of a single *ṛṣi* or members of his clan. On the basis of authorship the sixth *maṇḍala,* ascribed to the family of Bhāradvājas, appears to be the oldest.[20] It is also the one with the most references to the Sarasvatī River, a crucial factor in dating the Vedic texts.

Bharadvāja Bārhaspatya's hymn to Sarasvatī (6.61) describes the river as more majestic than any other—swift-moving, flowing with a tempestuous roar, and carving a course through the landscape. In the slightly later seventh *maṇḍala,* the seer Vasiṣṭha also describes the deified Sarasvatī as surpassing all other rivers in majesty and might as it flows from the mountains to the ocean (7.95.1–2). In a second hymn he acknowledges the people dwelling along the river's grassy banks (7.96.2). In total the Ṛgvedasaṁhitā mentions the Sarasvatī River sixty-eight times, with the greatest frequency in the earliest *maṇḍalas.*[21] The hymns invariably portray the Sarasvatī as flowing in full majesty.[22]

Around the middle of the third millennium BCE something happened. Data from the physical sciences confirm that tectonic upheavals refashioned the topography of Vedic India. According to one theory, the flow of the Śutudrī River (the present-day Sutlej) was diverted from the Sarasvatī into the Indus system. The flow of the Yāmunā, which also had fed the Sarasvatī, was redirected to the Gangetic system.[23] Deprived of a large volume of water, the mighty Sarasvatī began to dry up. The upper or northeast part of the river was affected immediately, and the lower or southwest stretch ran dry around 1900 BCE, causing the settlements along its banks to be abandoned. The ancient Vedic homeland, called Saptasindhu—the Land of Seven Rivers—could no longer claim that name. Today part of that region is called Punjab, meaning "five waters."

The drying up of the Sarasvatī provides an important historical marker between the early and late Vedic periods. The Ṛgvedasaṁhitā, which consistently describes the Sarasvatī as flowing in full majesty, clearly belongs to the early period before 1900 BCE. The rest of the Vedic texts—the Saṁhitās of the Sāmaveda, Yajurveda, and Atharvaveda along with the Brāhmaṇas, Āraṇyakas, and Upaniṣads—are products of the late Vedic period, which began when the dessication was well under way if not already complete.

The oldest texts of the later Vedic period, along with the post-Vedic Mahābhārata, preserve memories of the devastating hydrological events that refashioned the landscape described in the hymns of the Ṛgveda. The Ṛgvedasaṁhitā lauds the mighty Sarasvatī River as seven-sistered, but the Vājasaneyisaṁhitā (34.11) of the Śukla Yajurveda gives the number of tributaries as five, reflecting the loss of the Sutlej and the Yāmunā.[24] Passages found in the Brāhmaṇas also chronicle the drying up of the Sarasvatī. The Śatapathabrāhmaṇa (14.1.1.8) of the Śukla Yajurveda clearly refers to the desertification of the land, and two portions of the Sāmaveda—the Pañcaviṁśabrāhmaṇa (25.10.6) and the Jaiminīyopaniṣadbrāhmaṇa (4.26)—report that the holy river disappeared under the desert sands at a place called Vinaśa.[25] For a long while scholars regarded these stories as no more than fanciful myths, but in the 1970s satellite photos revealed the dry river bed of the Sarasvatī, three and a half miles wide on average, exactly where the Vedic hymns said this once mightiest of rivers flowed.

In line with Müller's calculations, scholars commonly date the Vedic Saṁhitās to 1500–1000 BCE and assign the Brāhmaṇas to the period of 1000–650 BCE. The Brāhmaṇas are large compendia concerned primarily with the performance and meaning of Vedic ritual. Undoubtedly composed over many centuries, they might not have reached their final form until the early first millennium BCE, but their origin clearly belongs to the preceding millennium.

Lying midway between the Brāhmaṇas and the Upaniṣads, the Āraṇyakas are transitional texts in content and tone. Named after ascetics (*araṇas*) who retired to the seclusion of the forest (*araṇya*) to follow a contemplative life, these "forest treatises" are more esoteric than the Brāhmaṇas and explore the inner spiritual significance of the Vedic rituals.

The Upaniṣads form the completion or end (*anta*) of the Veda and are accordingly called the Vedānta. They contain the teachings of ancient seers on the identity of the Self (*ātman*) and the ultimate reality (Brahman) and the means to liberation (*mokṣa*) through knowledge. Western scholars generally assign the twelve principal Upaniṣads to the period of 700–200 BCE, but the dates of the early and middle-period texts should probably be pushed back a few centuries. The earliest Upaniṣads are the Bṛhadāraṇyaka and the Chāndogya, and both are large compilations that quote from earlier sources and contain parallel passages and stories drawn from a common, and considerably older, stock of teachings. The Bṛhadāraṇyakopaniṣad, which contains the dialogues and teachings of the great *ṛṣi* Yājñavalkya, forms the final section of the Śatapathabrāhmaṇa. The other early Upaniṣads are the Taittirīya, Aitareya, Kauṣītaki, and Īśa, and they too show close ties to older Vedic texts. Forming the middle period, the Kena, Kaṭha, Śvetāśvatara, and Muṇḍaka Upaniṣads share many common features and anticipate the development of later Hindu philosophy. The latest of the principal Upaniṣads are the Praśna and the Māṇḍūkya.

Although Vedic literature is often presented in terms of straightforward development, the distinctions between Saṁhitā, Brāhmaṇa, Āraṇyaka, and Upaniṣad are not always clear. Far from being chronological markers, they relate more often to the kind of text and its purpose than to the order of composition.

Admittedly the timeline for the Vedic texts is vague, but it would not be unreasonable to place the Śvetāśvataropaniṣad around 500 BCE. That date finds support in Moti Lal Pandit's confident assertion that it belongs to the sixth or fifth century BCE[26] and in the nearly coinciding opinions of N. N. Bhattacharyya[27] and Jan Gonda[28] that place it around the same time.

Is this Upaniṣad the work of a single author or of several? Deussen alone suggests that it is the product of collective endeavor but then concedes that it must have grown out of an earlier core that had a single author called Śvetāśvatara. Who was he? Unlike many of the other great Upaniṣadic seers, for whom at least some information survives, Śvetāśvatara left few traces apart from the work that bears his name—a rather curious name that appears to be more of an epithet. It means "he who has white mules," a metaphor for a person of purified senses, qualified to teach the highest knowledge. The name appears only once in the Upaniṣad (6.21), in an epilogue that may be a later addition.[29] The seer's followers, the Śvetāśvataras, are mentioned in Śaunaka's *Caraṇavyūha* as forming a particular Vedic school (*śākhā*), one of eighty-six belonging to the Yajurveda, but apart from the Śvetāśvataropaniṣad no other text of theirs is known.[30]

The many Vedic quotations that led Deussen to consider this Upaniṣad a composite work impressed Olivelle as proof-texts cited by the seer in support of his teaching. Quoting sacred texts is a time-honored method of imparting spiritual instruction. Even the earliest Upaniṣads, the Bṛhadāraṇyaka and the Chāndogya, have their great *ṛṣis* quote passages from still earlier works, now lost, that were considered ancient and authoritative at the time.

Do the frequent citations make the Śvetāśvataropaniṣad an eclectic work as Deussen and others suggested? The quotations themselves can answer the question best. The Upaniṣad contains thirty verses that are quoted from older sources. The quoted verses may be common to as many as four earlier sources or as few as one. Usually they are completely faithful to the source; in just under a quarter of the cases they show minor variations. From their comparison some conclusions can be tentatively drawn. The thirty verses actually constitute twenty-two passages, and their most likely sources are as follows: seven are from the Ṛgvedasaṁhitā; six from the Vājasaneyisaṁhitā; five from the Kaṭhopaniṣad; two from the Taittirīyasaṁhitā; and one each from the Atharvaveda and the Bṛhadāraṇyakopaniṣad. As for transmission, the data suggest that seven passages entered the Śvetāśvataropaniṣad directly from the Ṛgveda, seven each from the Kṛṣṇa and Śukla recensions of the Yajurveda, and one from the Atharvaveda (see Appendix B, Table 1). Since the Śvetāśvataropaniṣad belongs to the Yajurvedic lineage, the preponderance of material from that source is not surprising.

This analysis demonstrates that far from indicating a chaotic eclecticism, this Upaniṣad's wealth of quotations underscores its unified outlook and its place in the school of the Taittirīyas, followers of the *ṛṣi* Vaiśampāyana, traditionally the original teacher of the Yajurveda. The Taittirīya heritage will prove highly revealing later on, but for now we must address the claim that the Śvetāśvataropaniṣad expresses the views of the Sāṁkhya philosophy.

Sāṁkhya

The alleged connection with Sāṁkhya rests primarily on the presence of certain words that are deemed characteristic of that philosophy and on the occasional presentation of ideas in terms of enumerated principles. Not all scholars agree that either vocabulary or enumeration is enough to place the Śvetāśvataropaniṣad in the Sāṁkhya fold. As Max Müller observed, "No doubt there are expressions in this Upaniṣad which remind us of technical terms used at a later time in the Sāṁkhya system of philosophy, but of Sāṁkhya doctrines, which I had myself formerly suspected in this Upaniṣad, I can on closer study find very little."[31] Müller even questioned the propriety of labeling certain terms as Sāṁkhya since the Śvetāśvataropaniṣad was composed long before the classical Sāṁkhya philosophy existed.[32] As for the enumerations, he noted that numbers such as one, two, three, five, eight, sixteen, twenty, forty-eight, and fifty coincide with those found in the later Sāṁkhya and Yoga systems, and he doubted that the similarities were accidental, but he also observed that attempts to explain the meaning of earlier enumerations in the light of later philosophical systems were generally "forced and unsatisfactory."[33]

Deussen was initially puzzled by the frequency of Sāṁkhya terms in an Upaniṣad whose Vedantic philosophy represents the antithesis of Sāṁkhya doctrine. He concluded that this Upaniṣad predates Sāṁkhya but also marks an important stage in its development. He saw no antagonism in the text between the Vedānta and the Sāṁkhya for the simple reason that the Sāṁkhya had not yet solidified into a philosophical system.[34]

Disregarding Müller's and Deussen's findings, Hume assigned the Śvetāśvataropaniṣad to a period after the emergence of the Sāṁkhya system and saw the text in terms of clashing theologies. Later writers, such as Tyāgīśānanda, Radhakrishnan, Olivelle, and Roebuck also accepted the presence of Sāṁkhya (or at least proto-Sāṁkhya) elements but portrayed the Upaniṣad's tone as syncretistic rather than antagonistic.

What is the relationship between the Śvetāśvataropaniṣad and Sāṁkhya, and can that philosophy serve as a standard for interpretation? These are questions that cry out for answers, and answers first require some knowledge of the history and nature of the Sāṁkhya philosophy itself.

In modern Hinduism Sāṁkhya is one of six orthodox (*āstika*) philosophical systems or *darśanas* ("ways of seeing"). The six are paired as Nyāya-Vaiśeṣika, Sāṁkhya-Yoga, and Mīmāṁsā-Vedānta. Of these the Sāṁkhya is generally recognized as the oldest. About its origin very little can be said with certainty. According to all the Sāṁkhya texts, its founder was the sage Kapila, whom tradition places in the late seventh or early sixth century BCE, one or two hundred years before the Buddha. If Kapila was a historical figure, his life is at best shrouded in the mists of legend. According to the Sāṁkhya specialist Gerald Larson, Kapila is a purely mythical figure.[35]

The Sāṁkhya philosophy has not been preserved in its original form, nor can scholars agree on what that form was. The earliest surviving text is Īśvarakṛṣṇa's *Sāṁkhyakārikā,* but this collection of seventy-two verses is the definitive statement of the fully formed classical system. It dates from around the third to the fifth centuries CE, about a thousand years after the lifetime of Sāṁkhya's reputed founder. In the traditional lineage of Sāṁkhya preceptors, beginning with Kapila, Īśvarakṛṣṇa is the twenty-sixth. Anything said to be Sāṁkhya before the appearance of his *Sāṁkhyakārikā* is, properly speaking, proto-Sāṁkhya or Sāṁkhya-in-the-making.

The claim that Sāṁkhya is originally pre- or non-Vedic can neither be substantiated nor disproven. Śaṁkara, the greatest exponent of Advaita Vedānta, wrote in his commentary (*bhāṣya*) on the *Brahmasūtra* that the Sāṁkhya system is anti-Vedic and has no legitimate claim to orthodoxy; instead he referred to it as a Tantra.[36] The origins of Tantra appear to lie outside of the Brahmanical "great tradition,"[37] but despite the Vedic-Tantric dichotomy, much in the ancient Vedic texts themselves must certainly be pre- or non-Aryan in origin. Very early on a variety of myths, practices, and philosophical speculations from widely diverse sources were absorbed into the Brahmanical religion.[38] Of course, all that took place so long ago that tracing any of it with certainty is next to impossible.

If the hard facts are elusive, the general process of assimilation affords a vivid picture of the currency of ideas in ancient India. Out of a common source, let us say the instruction of a great seer, the first disciples would develop individual lineages exhibiting parallel presentations of the original teachings. With each new generation some divergence of expression or interpretation would enter in. Because nothing was written down until after the Vedic period had come to a close, for many centuries knowledge was transmitted exclusively through human contact, and in the same way religious and philosophical doctrines evolved. Wandering ascetics and other travelers would carry ideas from one region to another, from remote forest retreats to royal courts and centers of population. It was common practice in the Vedic age for scholars and sages to engage in religious discourse and debate, and in such a way ideas met and clashed and merged and diverged, and the terms and doctrines that enshrined them evolved over time.

In Larson's opinion Sāṁkhya is most likely a "derivative and composite" system produced over many centuries from a wide variety of orthodox and heterodox sources.[39] Its components include ancient creation myths; the observation of the mind in states of waking, dreaming, and deep sleep; older and later yogic techniques, including the regulation of the breath; and concepts from Buddhism and Jainism.[40] Sāṁkhya's cosmogonical views relate to the Ṛgveda's great speculative hymn, the Puruṣasūkta (10.90), and the Sāṁkhya views on the Self, knowledge, and liberation grew out of the teachings and practices detailed in the Brāhmaṇas and the early Upaniṣads. None of this yet reveals a Sāṁkhya system or even a clear Sāṁkhya terminology[41]—only developing doctrines and trends of thought. According to Larson the first clear indications of Sāṁkhya-like speculation and vocabulary emerged in the yogic environment of the Kaṭhopaniṣad[42] and developed further in the Śvetāśvataropaniṣad and Bhagavadgītā.[43]

The Śvetāśvataropaniṣad makes one possible reference to Sāṁkhya in the compound *sāṁkhyayoga* (6.13). Not all scholars agree with Larson that this grammatical pairing is evidence of a single tradition that later split into two separate systems. In the context of the Upaniṣad it is unlikely that *sāṁkhyayoga* refers to any philosophical tradition at all. Many commentators believe that it simply advises the spiritual aspirant to engage in intellectual analysis (*sāṁkhya*) and its practical application (*yoga*).

In Larson's reading this verse indicates that a division has not yet taken place within a single Sāṁkhya-Yoga tradition. The separation is evident in the Mokṣadharma section of the Mahābhārata (12.168–353), where one passage (349.64–68) lists Sāṁkhya and Yoga as two separate religions. The Mokṣadharma cannot be dated any more precisely than to the period between the fifth century BCE and the first century CE, and its several descriptions of Sāṁkhya principles and vocabulary show considerable variation, indicating that Sāṁkhya was still a work in progress at that time.[44]

Some centuries later, between 300 and 500 CE, the distinct doctrines of various proto-Sāṁkhya lineages were assimilated and synthesized by Īśvarakṛṣṇa in his *Sāṁkhyakārikā,* the work that defines classical Sāṁkhya. At roughly the same time, or perhaps a little earlier, Patañjali made a comparable and definitive synthesis of Yoga in his classic *Yogasūtra.*[45] The important point is that the Sāṁkhya philosophy as it is understood today did not exist when the Śvetāśvataropaniṣad was composed but solidified as a philosophical system only eight hundred or more years later.

Of course, evidence points to the existence of some form or perhaps many forms of proto-Sāṁkhya doctrine at the time of the middle-period Upaniṣads, but few details are known. This proto-Sāṁkhya interacted over hundreds of years with other currents of Indian thought, influencing them and in turn being influenced. It contributed several basic concepts, such as that of three universal energies (*guṇas*), to other philosophical systems, which redefined them and employed them in their own ways.

The word *sāṁkhya* has to do with enumeration. It aptly describes a world-view based on categorizing phenomena in a rational manner and tracing a systematic evolution from an ultimate cause. As a dualistic system, classical Sāṁkhya recognizes *two* ultimate realities—*puruṣa* and *prakṛti*. They are the first two of twenty-five categories of existence, called *tattvas*. *Puruṣa* is the passive, unchanging conscious principle, but it is not singular; there are as many *puruṣas* as there are sentient beings, and these *puruṣas* beyond number remain ever separate and distinct from one another. In that sense Sāṁkhya is not only a dualistic philosophy but a pluralistic one. *Prakṛti* is the active principle that, in its original state, exists as unmanifest materiality. It is one—there are not multiple *prakṛtis*—but through the activation of its potential energies, the *guṇas*, it becomes the many. *Prakṛti* cannot be experienced in itself, but its existence is inferred through its manifestations.

Similarly, the *guṇas*—the universal energies of *sattva, rajas,* and *tamas*—cannot be perceived in their pure, unevolved state but only inferred from their effects. *Sattva* manifests as light, clarity, calm, goodness, peace, and so on. It is the energy that reveals. *Tamas* manifests as darkness, ignorance, dullness, heaviness, inertia, and density. It is the concealing force. *Rajas* is the restless, active, and passionate energy in between that allows *sattva* and *tamas* to interact.

Puruṣa is sentient but inactive spirit; *prakṛti* is insentient matter. These two realities are irreconcilably different and absolutely separate.[46] Their sole commonality is that both are eternal.[47] Although they never come into actual contact, they engage in some sort of interaction through proximity, which initiates the process of cosmic manifestation within *prakṛti*.[48] The universe evolves somehow through a relationship that is no more real than that between an object and its shadow.[49]

The cosmos does not come into existence through divine volition, because classical Sāṁkhya is nontheistic and sees no need for a creator. Rather, its manifestation can be explained through the theory of inherent causality (*satkāryavāda*). *Prakṛti*, through the activation of its inherent *guṇas*, evolves into twenty-three additional categories of mind and matter (*tattvas*). It is not that something is created out of nothing or that anything new is ever added. It is a matter of the cause changing into the effect, which already exists in potentiality. The classic illustrations of this principle are the fire latent in wood and the curd potential in milk. The transformation (*pariṇāma*) of undifferentiated *prakṛti* into the manifest universe is a change of state from the unevolved (*avyakta*) to the evolved (*vyakta*). The doctrine of transformation, called *pariṇāmavāda*, holds that the change is actual and not apparent, so from the Sāṁkhya point of view the world is real. Sāṁkhya is quick to point out that the universe comes forth from *prakṛti*, not from *puruṣa*, and that the suffering inherent in human existence arises from the erroneous entanglement of spirit with matter. Accordingly, the goal of human life is to free consciousness (*puruṣa*) from the fetters of materiality (*prakṛti*), a goal achievable through understanding the very structure of human experience.[50]

Although the arguments for the Śvetāśvataropaniṣad's Sāṁkhya orientation rest primarily on vocabulary and enumeration, neither of these, on closer scrutiny, proves as persuasive as it first appears. As for vocabulary, we may believe that philosophical or spiritual truth is immutable, but the language that attempts to express it is demonstrably mutable. Words can have multiple nuances, and sometimes they even change their basic meaning over time. At any given moment a word can convey different shades of meaning in different environments or be ambiguous in a single environment. Too much has been made of the Śvetāśvataropaniṣad's so-called Sāṁkhya terminology. The words most often singled out include *puruṣa, prakṛti, pradhāna, guṇa, avyakta, vyakta,* and *kṣetrajña*. However, none of these words occur with compelling frequency, and some are either generic or common to the works of other philosophical systems, where they do not necessarily have the same technical definitions assigned to them in classical Sāṁkhya.

The word *puruṣa* is a case in point. Sometimes it simply means "person." In the Ṛgveda's famous hymn known as the Puruṣasūkta (10.90) it denotes a unitary, primordial, transcendental being as the source of the universe. In the Upaniṣads and later religious texts, *puruṣa* is often used interchangeably with *ātman* ("self"), either in a universal or individual sense. The Upaniṣads, including the Śvetā-śvatara, stress the absolute unity of *ātman:* the Self or *puruṣa* is the ultimate consciousness, one and indivisible. It is known also as Brahman. Although classical Sāṁkhya also defines *puruṣa* as the pure consciousness that is the true Self, it holds that there are as many *puruṣas* as there are individual beings, and each is an eternally distinct reality.

The term *prakṛti* appears in no Upaniṣad before the Śvetāśvatara, but its usage there (4.10) marks the antithesis of its later classical Sāṁkhya definition. Moreover, the single instance of this word in this Upaniṣad should not be taken as a sign of Sāṁkhya leanings. The term *prakṛti* occurs twenty-one times in the Bhagavadgītā, but far from being labeled a Sāṁkhya work, the Bhagavadgītā is celebrated as one of the three cornerstones (*prasthānatraya*) of Vedānta.

The evidence of other so-called Sāṁkhya terms is hardly more convincing and often dismissable on similar grounds. Meanwhile, the Śvetāśvataropaniṣad abounds in terms associated with another system, not yet mentioned, which will claim our full attention later.

As for enumeration, it too cannot be taken as specially emblematic of Sāṁkhya. At the most basic level, enumeration is a mnemonic device universally characteristic of oral cultures. Its employment in the Śvetāśvataropaniṣad is hardly surprising and merely follows the example of the Ṛgvedasaṁhitā and early Upaniṣads such as the Bṛhadāraṇyaka, Aitareya, and Taittirīya.[51]

As for the numbers themselves, their similarity often can be traced to observable facts and general ideas and not necessarily to a specific philosophy. The concept of *one,* for example, relates to a basic cosmogonical question common throughout the ancient world: how does the One give rise to the many? *Two* reflects the polarization common to all human experience, with its dualities of happiness and misery, beauty and ugliness, good and evil, light and dark, and all the rest. *Three* is similarly pervasive in the empirical world. Time has three facets—past, present, and future. Matter exists in three states—solid, liquid, and gaseous. Objects have height, width, and depth. Language has three grammatical persons to denote the speaker, the one spoken to, and the one spoken about. Living beings and inanimate objects are classified as masculine, feminine, or neuter. Living beings experience three states of consciousness—waking, dreaming, and deep sleep. Everything has a beginning, a middle, and an end. *Five* likewise has many empirical associations. Various groupings of five occur in the earliest Upaniṣads to describe physical and mental phenomena. The Taittirīyopaniṣad (1.7) lists six such pentads, three pertaining to the physical universe and three to the embodied self. These latter three enumerate five vital airs or metabolic functions (*prāṇa, vyāna, apāna, udāna, samāna*), five sensory-intellectual faculties (sight, hearing, mind, speech, touch), and five constituents of the physical body (skin, flesh, muscle, bone, marrow).

One, two, three, five. In this series each number is the sum of the preceding two. If the series is extended, *eight* and *thirteen* also figure in the Indian philosophical enumerations. Moreover, this mathematical pattern is pervasive in the structure of the natural world and reflected further in the human arts and sciences. Wherever it occurs, this numerical principle represents and underlies order, intelligence, and creativity.

Clearly enumeration is more than a simple (but undeniably useful) mnemonic device that people of ancient times employed to transmit and perpetuate knowledge. It is also more than a matter of superficial observation. At a deeper level enumeration affords a way of elaborating on a collection of objects or concepts in a rational and systematic way in order to explore their connections and interactions and ultimately to discover their meaning. In that way the understanding of our empirical experience can become a means to transcendence.

That kind of teaching is explicit in the Bṛhadāraṇyakopaniṣad, where Yājñavalkya instructs his beloved wife Maitreyī on the nature of phenomenal existence. Just as everything has been breathed forth from the Self (4.5.11), everything returns to it. Just as all waters have the ocean as their center of union (*ekāyana*), each of the five physical sensations has its center of absorption in an organ of perception, and each of five physical activities relates to a bodily organ (4.5.12). Likewise, intention (*saṅkalpa*) is concentrated in the mind (*manas*), and knowledge (*vidyā*) has its center in the heart (*hṛdaya*).

Seventeen of the twenty-two items catalogued in Yājñavalkya's dialogue found their way into the later Sāṁkhya enumeration of cosmic principles (*tattvas*) that explain the structure and functioning of the mental-material universe. As this scheme developed over the course of centuries and the number of principles fluctuated, its basic outline was readily adopted by the teachers of other philosophical persuasions and adapted to suit their own purposes. According to the definitive statement of the *Sāṁkhyakārikā,* classical Sāṁkhya recognizes twenty-five *tattvas*, beginning with *puruṣa* (1), the eternally passive principle of pure consciousness, and *prakṛti* (2), the potentially active principle of unconscious materiality. Together these two represent an irreconcilable duality of opposites, but through some sort of proximity *prakṛti* becomes activated and generates twenty-three additional categories of existence. The triad of *buddhi* (3), *ahaṁkāra* (4), and *manas* (5) constitutes the internal organ (*antaḥkaraṇa*) that functions as intellect (the conative-determinative faculty), ego (the sense of personal identity), and mind (the capacity of ordinary perception and thinking that bridges the internal and external worlds). In the Sāṁkhya scheme of evolution *buddhi* generates *ahaṁkāra,* which in turn produces not only *manas* but also five *buddhīndriyas* (6–10) or sensory faculties, five *karmendriyas* (11–15) or faculties of action, and five *tanmātras* (16–20) or subtle elements, from which the five *mahābhūtas* (21–25) or material elements evolve.

The classical Sāṁkhya *tattvas* describe a fundamentally dualistic reality in which consciousness (*puruṣa*) is eternally distinct from matter (*prakṛti* and its evolutes). Returning to the question of whether or not the Śvetāśvataropaniṣad is a Sāṁkhya text, Max Müller will have the last word: "Whatever Sāṁkhya philosophers of a later date may have imagined that they could discover in that Upaniṣad in support of their theories, there is not one passage in it which, if rightly interpreted, not by itself, but in connection with the whole text, could be quoted in support of a dualistic philosophy such as the Sāṁkhya, as a system, decidedly is."[52]

Vedānta

Of all the Indian philosophies the Vedānta would seem to have the strongest claim for legitimacy in interpreting the Śvetāśvataropaniṣad, for in one sense the term *vedānta* signifies the Upaniṣads themselves as the embodiment of the highest spiritual knowledge. However, the Upaniṣads do not present a unified philosophy but preserve instead the revelations and teachings of many seers and sages in texts that are highly varied in content and style, composed over many centuries across a wide expanse of northern India. In the single instance when the Śvetāśvataropaniṣad uses the term *vedānta* (6.22), it does not refer to the philosophical system of that name—that was a later development. It signifies instead the collective wisdom of great teachers who had attempted, each with a distinctive voice, to express the same direct experience of transcendence.

Although not presenting a consistent or methodical philosophy, all the Upaniṣads share the same general point of view. All proclaim that there is a single reality, Brahman, which is pure consciousness. Although absolutely One and unconditioned, this reality of realities expresses itself through the diversity of the manifest universe even while remaining absolutely One, infinite, and transcendent. Ever beyond the categories of time, space, and causality, Brahman creates, sustains, and dissolves the whole of phenomenal existence. In the nondualistic view of the Upaniṣads, the world and the individual are manifestations of the one Brahman, and there is no unbridgeable divide between nature, humanity, and divinity. The universe arises out of Brahman's own self-concealment, effected by the veiling power of *māyā*. Here *māyā* does not carry the connotation of illusion, employed by some later philosophers to deny the reality of the temporal, finite world. The Upaniṣads regard *māyā* as the creative magic of the Absolute through which the finite realm comes into existence. If *māyā* is to be taken as illusion in any sense, it is only an illusion of separation from the unity of Brahman, whose nature is unlimited joy (*ānanda*). Once separated from the inherent joy of nondual consciousness, the individual undergoes a diversity of experience that encompasses enjoyment and suffering. Because each soul becomes caught up in an ongoing chain of cause and effect, the highest aim of human life is a search for release (*mokṣa*) from finitude and duality—a search for permanence amid the impermanence of an ever-changing world and for the infinite Absolute amid the perplexities and limitations of relative existence. Boundless being, consciousness, and joy (*saccidānanda*) are ultimately one, and they are the very nature of Brahman—the same reality that is the individual's own true Self (*ātman*). Liberation consists in recognizing the identity of *ātman* and Brahman. This supreme teaching of the Upaniṣads can be summed up in four great sayings (*mahāvākyas*): "Pure consciousness is Brahman" (*prajñānaṁ brahma*) (Aitareyopaniṣad 3.1.3); "This Self is Brahman" (*ayam ātmā brahma*) (Bṛhadāraṇyakopaniṣad 2.5.19; Māṇḍūkyopaniṣad 2); "You are that" (*tat tvam asi*) (Chāndogyopaniṣad 6.8.7); and "I am Brahman" (*ahaṁ brahmāsmi*) (Bṛhadāraṇyakopaniṣad 1.4.10).

These revelations came through direct knowledge, but it fell to later generations of thinkers to organize them into coherent systems of thought. Of the six classical *darśanas*, Vedānta is the most important, the most widely known, and the most influential. In the broader sense Vedānta is as old as the Upaniṣads, but as a formal system it is somewhat younger. Its oldest surviving document is the *Brahmasūtra* (or *Vedāntasūtra*) of Bādarāyaṇa, who lived some time between the fifth and first centuries BCE.

The framework that Bādarāyaṇa created rests on the thinking of the early seers, especially Uddālaka Āruṇi, a famous teacher in the Chāndogyopaniṣad, and Yājñavalkya, a central figure of the Bṛhadāraṇyakopaniṣad.[53] Although the *Brahmasūtra* lays out a structure for systematizing the teachings of the Upaniṣads, it announces the basic ideas in the form of brief aphorisms (*sūtras*) that present the topics to be expanded upon by qualified teachers or commentators. By themselves the *sūtras* are unintelligible. The *sūtra* literature belongs to a time when spiritual knowledge was not yet committed to writing but transmitted orally, and the extremely condensed format allowed for easier recall of basic principles, which could then be developed into comprehensive expositions. Because of their extreme brevity, *sūtras* can be elaborated upon in different ways. Not surprisingly, the many and diverse commentaries on the *Brahmasūtra*, beginning with Śaṁkara's *Brahmasūtrabhāṣya*, coincide with the eventual proliferation of different philosophical schools, each expressing a distinct point of view.

After Bādarāyaṇa, the next major figure to emerge in the Vedantic lineage was Gauḍapāda, who lived in the sixth or seventh century CE. Acknowledged as the founder of the nondualistic philosophy known as Advaita Vedānta, Gauḍapāda developed a rigorous monism, possibly to counter a contemporary tendency to interpret the Upaniṣads dualistically. His intention was to restore their original, monistic vision and to present it in a clear, systematic way. Gauḍapāda might also have reacted to Buddhistic thought, which was widespread throughout India at the time. Without question he was intimately acquainted with the ideas of the Buddhist philosophers Vasubandhu and Nāgārjuna and drew upon them in order to deny the reality of the external world and to show that its origination was impossible from the nondualistic standpoint.[54] But far from promoting any sort of nihilism, Gauḍapāda refashioned Buddhist doctrine in accord with his own Vedantic ideas to demonstrate the absolute reality of *ātman*, the nondual Self.[55]

His only known work, the verse commentary (*kārikā*) on the Māṇḍūkyopaniṣad, is the first systematic exposition of Advaita Vedānta on a purely philosophical and rational basis. Its dominant theme is the reality of Brahman, the nondual, unborn Self. At the heart of the argument stands the idea that only that which is self-existent and uncreated is real. *Ātman*, which is pure consciousness, is absolutely real. On the other hand, the world only *appears* to be created but has no more reality than the illusory circle of light produced by the flame of a whirling torch. The external world arises through the Self's own power of *māyā*, which veils the essential unity and projects the multiplicity of the phenomenal universe, but in truth the many are only illusory manifestations of the changeless One. In Gauḍapāda's usage, *māyā* moves away from its original Vedic connotation of magical power and begins to take on its later philosophical import as the principle of cosmic nescience or illusion. Accordingly the individuation of the Self as multiple, finite selves is a misconception, and empirical existence is a dream that will be dispelled on awakening to the knowledge of the unchanging reality of consciousness-in-itself. Ultimately even *māyā*, the Self's own power, has to be relegated to the realm of unreality.[56] Gauḍapāda's philosophy, known as the doctrine of nonorigination (*ajātivāda*), represents the loftiness of nondual realization, summarized succinctly in the *Māṇḍūkyakārikā* (2.32): "There is neither dissolution nor origination; there are none bound and none striving, none longing for liberation, and none liberated. This is the absolute truth."

Gauḍapāda's doctrine of the world as illusion marked a turning point in the development of Vedantic thought, and his revolutionary philosophy of Advaita Vedānta would reach its height soon afterward with the advent of one of India's greatest thinkers. Śaṁkara, also known as Śaṁkarācārya or Ādi Śaṁkara, was a brilliant philosopher, mystic, and saint who built on Gauḍapāda's teaching, moderating and refining its views and raising Advaita Vedānta to preeminence.

Śaṁkara

According to tradition Gauḍapāda's disciple Govindapāda was Śaṁkara's *guru*, although that relationship may be more symbolic than historical. Exactly when Śaṁkara lived is far from certain. The monastic traditions he established at Dvārakā, Purī, and Kañcīpuram give the year of his birth as 509 BCE, but the one at Śṛṅgerī claims that he was born in 44 BCE. Modern Indian and Western scholarship, beginning with K. B. Pathak's research in 1882, has tried to correlate historically datable people, places, and events with references in Śaṁkara's *Brahmasūtrabhāṣya* and other literary works. Those efforts have produced a range of possible dates anywhere from the fifth to the ninth centuries of the Common Era. Most specifically, K. B. Pathak deduced that Śaṁkara lived from 788 to 820 CE. While other scholars have argued that he flourished a century or two earlier, Pathak's dating is widely accepted as reasonable, albeit with some reservation.[57]

Because Śaṁkara was one of the most influential figures in the history of Indian thought, he inspired a number of biographies, written long after his lifetime. These traditional accounts sometimes disagree among themselves over the details and often magnify the philosopher-saint's earthly existence with colorful legends and miraculous events. But there can be little doubt that Śaṁkara was born in Kerala, in the village of Kālaḍi, to pious *brāhmaṇa* parents who conferred on him one of the names of the god Śiva. He left home at an early age to pursue an ascetic life and joined a hermitage on the bank of the river Narmadā, where he became Govindapāda's disciple. In his thirty-two years of life (thirty-eight by one reckoning)[58] Śaṁkara traveled the length and breadth of the subcontinent, establishing monasteries in the east, west, north, and south. He also produced some of the most brilliant texts in the history of Indian thought, among them the earliest known commentary on Bādarāyaṇa's *Brahmasūtra.* He is credited with more than three hundred literary works, a staggering and impossible number. Their sheer volume apart, their wide variance in subject matter, point of view, style, and intellectual acuity marks them as the products of many authors, probably of later monks who assumed the honorific title *Śaṁkarācārya* when heading the monasteries at Śṛṅgerī in Mysore, Dvārakā in Gujarat, Badrīnāth in the Himālayas, Purī in Orissa, and Kāñcīpuram in Tamil Nadu.[59] The German scholar Paul Hacker noted that the colophons of the works generally deemed genuine designate their author by the term *Bhagavat*, never by the name or title *Śaṁkarācārya*. After stringent analysis, Hacker concluded that because the *Brahmasūtrabhāṣya* can be authenticated beyond doubt, it must serve as the measure by which all the other texts attributed to Śaṁkara are evaluated. On the basis of Hacker's and other scholars' research, Karl H. Potter concluded in his *Encyclopaedia of Indian Philosophies* that only eight texts are without question the work of Śaṁkara: the *Brahmasūtrabhāṣya, Upadeśasahasri,* and the commentaries (all designated as *bhāṣya*) on the Bṛhadāraṇyaka, Taittirīya, Aitareya, Chāndogya, Muṇḍaka, and Praśna Upaniṣads. Whatever opinions other scholars may hold about any particular text, most concur that greater or lesser degrees of doubt surround the authenticity of many works, both major and minor.[60]

The quintessence of Śaṁkara's philosophy can be found in the often-quoted twentieth verse of the *Brahmajñānāvalīmālā*, a minor text of unconfirmed authorship: "Brahman is real, the world is false, and the individual soul is none other than Brahman" (*brahma satyaṁ jagan mithyā jīvo brahmaiva nāparaḥ*). Unfortunately this sweeping pronouncement is liable to misunderstanding and has served to mischaracterize Śaṁkara's Advaita Vedānta as an illusionist or world-denying philosophy. To take it at face value is to do a great disservice to one of India's supreme thinkers. Behind these words lies a world-view that is astoundingly rich and subtle.

What did Śaṁkara really mean by these words? The answer lies in defining his terms. By *real* he meant permanent and unchanging; by *false* he meant impermanent and subject to change. But that is only the beginning. His distinctive philosophy proposes a principle known as *bādha,* which means "invalidation" or "sublation." In plain language, sublation means that whatever is experienced appears true only until an experience of a higher order disproves it. While we are dreaming, the dream seems real, but when we awaken, we recognize it as only a dream. The dream state is sublated by waking consciousness. In the same way, the entire universe of our waking existence vanishes with the knowledge of the nondual Brahman. In this experience, called *nirvikalpa samādhi,* the world dissolves; its relative truth is sublated by something higher. And so, Śaṁkara's philosophy proposes a three-tiered ordering of experience. The *pāramārthika* is the absolutely real, the eternally changeless Brahman, which is pure being-consciousness-bliss (*saccidānanda*). The *vyāvahārika* denotes the here and now, our everyday existence which is impermanent and subject to change; it is neither totally real nor totally unreal. The *prātibhāsika* is the inherently unreal; this term refers to a dream, a mirage, a hallucination, or a logical impossibility such as "a square circle" or "the son of a barren woman." According to Śaṁkara the world is neither real nor illusory, but somewhere in between. As long as it is a matter of our own experience, it cannot be denied, but it is proven insubstantial by the knowledge of the Absolute. Brahman alone is the ultimate reality, because it cannot be sublated by anything else. It is consciousness in its unconditioned state, experienced in *nirvikalpa samādhi* as "no-thingness"—not nothingness but a positive reality of which nothing can be said or thought.

Advaita Vedānta agrees with Sāṁkhya that creation is a transition from a potential to a manifest state, but after that the two philosophies part company. The Sāṁkhya doctrine, called *pariṇāmavāda,* regards the transformation as real. Advaita Vedānta regards it as a mere appearance; this doctrine is called *vivartavāda.* The ever-changing world-appearance is overlaid on the unchanging reality of Brahman. It is a superimposition (*adhyāsa*), a misperception like a rope seen in semidarkness and mistaken for a snake. Although the snake *seemed* very real at the time, it existed only as an idea in the mind of the perceiver. It's not that there was nothing there; there *was* something, but just not what the perceiver thought. In the same way, we mistake the appearance of the world for the reality of Brahman and ascribe permanence where there is none. In that sense Śaṁkara called the world false (*mithyā*). As in Sāṁkhya, we can blame our ignorance, our not knowing the truth. The fault lies in the semi-darkness that obscured the real nature of the rope and caused us to mistake it for a snake. Vedānta calls that semidarkness *māyā.*

Vivartavāda, the doctrine of appearance, holds that the world is not the product of Brahman but of *māyā,* which is Brahman's causal potency. Unlike the *prakṛti* of Sāṁkhya, *māyā* is not an independent principle but an indefinable something totally dependent on Brahman.[61] In Śaṁkara's nondualism the rope does not cause the snake; the semidarkness causes the misperception of the rope as a snake. Actual change can never take place in the immutable Brahman,[62] and Brahman, being absolute, can have no causal relationship with anything else. If it did, it would be relative and not absolute. So the obvious conclusion is that even the causal relationship is apparent and belongs to the realm of *māyā.*[63]

Finally, the knowledge of Brahman is Self-knowledge. In fact, Brahman and *ātman* are two words for the same reality. The empirical self (*jīva*) is a composite of Self and not-self, a simple matter of wrong identification brought on by the superimposition of finite qualities on the Infinite. Liberation comes through the knowledge of one's true nature. Consider Śaṁkara's memorable dictum once more, paying special attention this time to the last part: "Brahman is real, the world is false, and the individual soul is none other than Brahman." In the end his statement affirms the reality of who we truly are. That is why the knower of Brahman says, "I am Brahman," the imperishable reality of absolute consciousness.

Owing to its origin in the Upaniṣads, the Vedānta philosophy would appear to be a reliable standard for their interpretation. Although Max Müller rightly concluded that nontheistic Sāṁkhya dualism does not make for a comfortable fit with the Śvetāśvataropaniṣad's theistically inclined nondualism, he accepted rather uncritically that the Advaita Vedānta version of nondualism provides the correct insight into Śvetāśvatara's teachings. This is not surprising, given the information available to him at the time. After the ascendence of Advaita Vedānta, this philosophy and its later permutations served for hundreds of years as the lens through which almost every religious or philosophical text was read regardless of the tradition it represented. When Vedānta's main rival, the Sāṁkhya system, experienced a renaissance in the sixteenth century, even it bore the marked influence of Vedānta.[64] It is not unusual that after centuries of philosophical dominance interpretations based on classical Vedānta would go unquestioned.

In the notes accompanying his translation of the Śvetāśvataropaniṣad, Müller acknowledged his reliance on three ancient commentaries, one purported to be the work of Śaṁkarācārya, and all three belonging to the Advaita Vedānta school, even though differing widely among themselves.

The *Śvetāśvataropaniṣadvṛtti,* bearing the name of Śaṁkarācārya, is obviously the work of someone else. This commentary resembles none of Śaṁkara's six (or ten) authentic commentaries on other Upaniṣads and departs from them in significant ways. To begin with, it is called a *vṛtti* (gloss) and not a *bhāṣya* (explanatory exposition) like the others. It abounds in long quotations from the Bhagavadgītā and the Purāṇas, but the genuine commentaries quote mostly from the Vedas and other Upaniṣads.[65] Unlike the authentic commentaries, the *Vṛtti* lacks an accompanying secondary commentary (*ṭīkā*) by the fourteenth-century Vedantic scholar Ānandagiri. Śaṁkara's genuine work scrupulously elucidates the meanings of words and phrases, but the *Vṛtti* fails in that respect also.[66] Overall it shows no evidence of the dignity and penetrating insight characteristic of Śaṁkara's own *bhāṣyas.*[67] Its unknown author is possibly a later monk who bore the title of Śaṁkarācārya.[68] In any case, the *Vṛtti* is spurious and its date is unknown.

The earlier of the two datable commentaries is the *Śvetāśvataropaniṣadvivaraṇa* of Vijñānabhagavat, whose *guru,* Jñānottamapujyapāda, lived from 910 to 954. Because Jñānottama had composed a subcommentary on Śaṁkara's *Brahmasūtrabhāṣya,* we might suspect that Śaṁkara's vigorous refutation of Sāṁkhya doctrine in that work would have influenced Vijñānabhagavat. Not so. Although the *Vivaraṇa* at times goes out of its way to avoid any suggestion of Sāṁkhya cosmology, curiously its overall interpretation is strongly oriented toward spiritual practice and reflects the influence of the Sāṁkhya-related Yoga system. The other two commentaries do not.

The third ancient commentary, the *Śvetāśvataropaniṣaddīpikā,* was composed by Śaṁkarānanda, who lived from 1228 to 1333.[69] A prolific writer on Advaita Vedānta, he produced commentaries on one hundred eight Upaniṣads and was the teacher of the great Vedic commentator Sāyaṇācārya.

Some commentators, in their zeal to prove the superiority of their own views, have been known to overlook or disregard or distort a text's original intent. Even the great Śaṁkara, who produced outstanding commentaries on the Upaniṣads, is not without fault. Swami Prabhavananda, whose monastic roots trace back to the

Śaṁkara lineage of Purī, observed tactfully that "Śaṁkara never directly contradicts the Upaniṣads, although sometimes he appears to interpret them to suit his own views."[70] In the case of the Śvetāśvataropaniṣad, the *Vṛtti* attributed to Śaṁkarācārya carries an unjustified weight of authority and has distorted the import of some passages, creating serious misunderstandings that subsequent translators and commentators have perpetuated.

In 1886 the American Sanskritist W. D. Whitney called attention to this problem in his review of Max Müller's edition of the Upaniṣads: "If the non-Sanskrit-reading public is to have these obscure treatises placed in its hands at all for study, it ought first of all to know just what they say and what they do not say. Thus far it has had no means of doing this; no simple philological translation, none that was not filled in and tinged throughout with the later Hindu comment, has been given to the world."[71]

For now, it is enough to say that some of the doctrines of Advaita Vedānta (or of Sāṁkhya for that matter), followed a thousand years and more after the Śvetāśvataropaniṣad and do not reflect the text's original intent. Müller, Deussen, and others all too often overlooked the disparity between later philosophical doctrine and the positions implied or clearly set forth in this Upaniṣad, but they also overlooked a more obvious clue hidden in plain sight: most of its names for the deity are names of the god Śiva.

Rudra and *yoga*

The divine names unequivocally place the Śvetāśvataropaniṣad in a Śaiva environment. Most immediately apparent is the frequency of the name *Rudra,* which occurs in this Upaniṣad six times (3.2, 3.4, 3.5, 4.12, 4.21, 4.22). Rudra, later known as Śiva, was the storm god of the ancient Ṛgvedic hymns. The word *śiva* occurs seven times (3.5, 3.6, 3.11, 4.14, 4.16, 4.18, 5.14), not yet as a proper name but as an adjective indicating Rudra's auspicious, benevolent, and gracious qualities. Another Śaiva name, *Hara,* can be found once (1.10). Having strong Śaiva associations, the term *īśa,* meaning "lord," "ruler," or "master," appears seven times (1.8, 1.9, 3.7, 3.20, 4.7, 5.3, 6.17), either as a common noun or a divine epithet, and the related *īśāna* has four occurrences (3.12, 3.15, 3.17, 4.11). *Maheśvara,* later a common epithet of Śiva meaning "Great Lord," can be found twice (4.10, 6.7)

Śiva may well represent one of India's earliest conceptions of divinity. When an exquisitely carved stone seal, some forty-five centuries old, was discovered in 1931 at Mohenjo-daro in the Indus Valley, the archeologist Sir John Marshall identified it as a prototypical representation of Śiva. Because the seal portrays a naked, ithyphallic figure seated in a yogic posture on a dais, Marshall based his identification on Śiva's age-old association with *yoga*. The figure, who appears to be meditating, has three faces, looking left, right, and ahead. Bangles cover his arms, a series of necklaces adorns his chest, and he is crowned with a headdress of long, curving buffalo horns. Six animals surround him—a tiger, an elephant, a rhinoceros, a buffalo, and below the dais two deer or antelope. Their presence led Marshall to dub the artifact the "Paśupati" seal, since another name of Śiva is Paśupati, the Lord of Beasts.

Seventy years later the archeologist Shereen Ratnagar contested Marshall's opinion, pointing out that the Vedic Paśupati is the lord of the domesticated animal (*paśu*), not of the wild beast (*mṛga*).[72] She suggested that the buffalo-horn headdress and the wild animals might identify the mysterious figure as a shaman, who would have retreated to the seclusion of the forest, naked and without shelter.[73] Other archeologists and scholars before Ratnagar had also put forward dissenting theories that identified the figure variously as Indra, Agni, Varuṇa, an unnamed goddess, the buffalo demon Mahiṣa, and so on. S. P. Singh, agreeing more or less with Marshall, identified the meditating figure as Rudra on the tenuous evidence of a Ṛgvedic hymn (1.64) that extols the Maruts, Rudra's sons, as bulls of heaven who consume the forests like elephants, roar like lions, and display the beauty of antelopes.[74]

Since the discovery of the first "proto-Śiva" seal, two others have come to light at Mohenjo-daro and Harappa along with several molded terracotta tablets depicting the same figure. These tablets provide a possible link between ancient India's archeological and textual records, because some of them illustrate the cross-legged "proto-Śiva" watching another male figure kill a water buffalo by pinning its head underfoot and thrusting a spear into its shoulder.[75] The Mahābhārata (3.221) records an identical scene, in which Śiva's son Skanda kills the buffalo demon, Mahiṣāsura. That is the oldest known verbal account of a famous myth which reached definitive form around the fifth century CE in the Devīmāhātmya, celebrating the goddess Durgā as Mahiṣāsura's slayer. The older version in the Mahābhārata indicates the story's Śaiva origin and suggests a possible link to the enigmatic, meditating figure portrayed on the artifacts from the third millennium BCE.[76]

Whoever that figure may be, without question yogic practice has a very long history and early connections with Rudra-Śiva. Along with the ancient Indus Valley images suggesting rigorous physical and mental disciples, the Ṛgvedasaṁhitā provides textual evidence in a hymn (10.136) that describes the ascetic who practices them. He is long-haired (*keśin*), silent (*muni*), and naked (literally, "girdled with the wind"). This wanderer "has his home in both the eastern and western sea" and treads "the path of sylvan beasts, where the gods have gone before." A "sweet and most delightful friend," the long-haired ascetic engages in "the holy work of every god" and drinks from the same cup as Rudra.[77]

By the time of the Upaniṣads, communities of monk-like ascetics (*śramaṇas*) had become numerous. Possibly the *śramaṇas* were successors to the *keśins*.[78] In any case, their presence affirms the widespread practice of disciplines involving body and mind. Although the early Upaniṣads speak of such practices as an interiorization of the Vedic rituals, the word *yoga* appears only once, in the Taittirīyopaniṣad (2.4.1). In explaining the five sheathes that encase the Self (the physical, vital, mental, intelligent, and causal bodies), the word *yoga* arises in connection with the next-to-innermost sheath, which consists of right apprehension (*vijñānamayaḥ*)—the certitude that begins with faith (*śraddhā*) in the efficacy of the Vedic sacrifices. According to Śaṁkara's commentary *yoga* denotes the conjunction or concentration that forms the central part or torso or self (*ātmā*) of the intelligence-body (*vijñānamayakośa*).[79]

The middle-period Kaṭhopaniṣad offers a more developed account of yogic practice by way of the instruction that Yama, the king of death, imparts to the boy Naciketas. In Gerald Larson's opinion the Kaṭha is the first Upaniṣad that clearly refers to Sāṁkhya ideas and terminology,[80] and it presents them in the context of *yoga*. Here the Sāṁkhya-like enumerations of principles appear mostly in regard to the practice of meditation, aiming to define and give order to various states of consciousness.[81]

The trend toward systematic presentation becomes more apparent in the second chapter of the Śvetāśvataropaniṣad, but its version of *yoga* still represents a rudimentary stage of development compared to Patañjali's classical formulation, which would not appear until six or seven hundred years later. Nevertheless, like Patañjali's *Yogasūtra,* the middle-period Upaniṣads encompass a wide range of traditional practices based on self-discipline, concentration, and meditation.[82]

Among the later Upaniṣads of the Kṛṣṇa Yajurveda, the Maitrī, or Maitrāyaṇīya, describes *yoga* as a sixfold process, consisting of breath-control (*prāṇāyāma*), sensory withdrawal (*pratyāhāra*), meditation (*dhyāna*), concentration (*dhāraṇā*), contemplative inquiry (*tarka*), and absorption (*samādhi*).[83] This methodology may represent an alternative to Śvetāśvatara's formulation and Patañjali's Sāṁkhya-oriented *aṣṭāṅga* ("eight-limbed") *yoga.*

Larson's study, which consistently links *yoga* to dualistic Sāṁkhya doctrine[84] does not take into account the formulation of another eight-limbed *yoga* found in the *Pāśupatasūtra,* a work attributed to the the Śaiva saint Lakulīśa, who lived from around 100–150 CE.[85] The *Pāśupatasūtra* devotes the third of its five chapters to an exposition of a highly complex and highly structured *yoga* with eight limbs or means. The first four pertain to outward practice characterized by physical activities (*kriyālakṣaṇa*). They are *niyama* (daily observances), *yama* (abstentions), *āsana* (sitting), and *prāṇāyāma* (breathing). The remaining four apply to inward practice limited to mental concentration (*kriyoparamalakṣaṇa*). They are *pratyāhāra* (mental withdrawal from empirical stimuli), *dhyāna* (concentration with an objective reference), *dhāraṇā* (concentration without an objective reference), and *samādhi* (involuntary concentration due to grace, resulting in a state of identification with Śiva). The technical terms for the eight limbs are the same ones used by Patañjali in the *Yogasūtra,* but the older *Pāśupatasūtra* places them in a slightly different order and applies them to somewhat different practices or differently defined states of awareness.[86]

Around the second or third century CE, Patañjali compiled his *Yogasūtra,* a masterly exposition of *aṣṭāṅga yoga* that remains the definitive manual of classical Yoga philosophy and practice. It was this formalized system that became paired with Sāṁkhya in the scheme of the six *darṣanas* of orthodox Hindu thought.

There are too many gaps in the historical record to allow the evolution of *yoga* to be traced with any degree of certainty, and many questions remain unanswered. In general the diverse theories and practices characterized as *yoga* must have developed over thousands of years through multiple lines of transmission, describable as pre- or non-Vedic, Vedic, Vedantic, proto-Sāṁkhya, and so on. Thus *yoga* was universally valued for the efficacy of its methods independent of any philosophical position or sectarian leaning. What is certain is that its roots reach back very far. The archeological evidence appears to connect the first stirrings of *yoga* to the Śiva-like deity of the Indus Valley artifacts, and the Ṛgveda's hymn to the *keśin* demonstrably links yogic practice to the deity known as Rudra.

Rudra-Śiva

The name *Rudra* opens a window to the remote past, to an age of seers who sensed divinity in the sky and weather and soil and celebrated its inspiration in the rapturous Ṛgvedic hymns. In the rumbling thunder they heard the voice of Indra, king of the gods. In the lightning they saw the flash of his thunderbolt that pierced the clouds that held the rain that caused plants to sprout and flourish and yield food. They saw the rain as the sacred union of the sky father and the earth mother, whose coupling brought forth and sustained all life. In fire's heat and light they sensed the power of Agni, who alone among the gods traveled freely throughout the three worlds of heaven, atmosphere, and earth. In the high heaven Agni's light blazed forth as the sun, through the sky it flashed as lightning, and on earth it burned as the sacrificial fire that consumed the worshipers' offerings and sent them in the rising smoke to the gods on high. For the Vedic worshipers every force of nature was deified and personified, often in an overlapping profusion and confusion of names and functions.

The word *rudra* is first found in the Vedic hymns as an adjective applied to various members of the pantheon: to Agni, Indra, Mitra, Varuṇa, and others. Most likely it means "crying," "howling," "roaring," "dreadful," or "terrible." As it became a proper name, meaning "Howler," *Rudra* signified a powerful, destructive deity most often associated with storms.[87] Because the Vedic people regarded all the forces of nature as interconnected, Rudra represented not only the awesome, destructive fury of the tempest but also the beneficence of fertility, healing, and welfare. He had two sides, one fierce (*ugra*) and one gentle (*saumya*). A second possible derivation of his name links it to the adjective *rudhira,* meaning "red," "blood-red," or "bloody." This connection to the English words *red* and *ruddy* supports a positive, life-promoting view of Rudra's power, associated with health and vigor.[88]

Divine powers were seen to be many, but divinity was essentially one. In a well-known verse of the Ṛgveda (1.164.46), the seer observed that this divinity is called Indra, Mitra, Varuṇa, Agni, Yama, Garutmān, and Mātariśvan; yet that truth, that being, is One; the wise call it by various names (*ekaṁ sad viprā bahudhā vadanti*). Despite a proliferation of gods and goddesses, the illumined seers understood the unity underlying them all. Thus any deity, Rudra included, represents the whole of divinity, and the nature of divine power is both reassuring of well-being (*vayas*) as well as fear-inspiring (*tveṣa*).

The Ṛgveda's four hymns addressed to Rudra (1.43, 1.114, 2.33, 7.46) consistently celebrate him as the lord of healing. The magnificent hymn composed by the seer Gṛtsamada (2.33) portrays him as the "best of all physicians," who possesses the "most saving medicines" and "strengthening balms." His gracious hand bestows health and comfort. Gṛtsamada praises Rudra as the blissful god of all created beings, the mightiest of the mighty, who rests in his own glory. In him, the sovereign (*īśāna*) of this world, the power of divinity (*asurya*) is inherent; from him it never departs. The hymnist asks the god to "transport us over trouble to well-being,"[89] and in a particularly beautiful passage he prays, "As one who finds shade in blazing sunlight, may I, unharmed, win Rudra's grace (2.33.6)."

As for Rudra's fierce power, all four hymns mention it, sometimes beseeching him not to visit his wrath upon his human subjects, at other times asking that he ward off evil and afford protection against malevolent forces. In one hymn (7.46) the seer Vasiṣṭha extols the wise and compassionate Rudra as possessing a firm bow and swift arrows. Their function, disclosed in a verse from a much later hymn (Ṛgveda 10.125.6), is to chasten the unrighteous. Even when wrathful, Rudra, as the upholder of the moral order, is a force for good and the protector of his devotees.

The Vedas often express Rudra's auspicious side by the epithet *śiva,* which was not yet a proper name but an adjective meaning "auspicious," "propitious," "benevolent," or "gracious." In the later age of the Purāṇas, around the second century BCE, an interesting reversal took place: *rudra* became the epithet while *Śiva* became the primary name of this great deity.[90] By then Rudra-Śiva was no longer viewed merely as a storm god or even as an abstracted force of nature but as the overarching philosophical principle of disintegration and reintegration.[91]

The Vedic texts suggest that most worshipers of this great, benevolent-destructive deity either belonged to the lower orders of Vedic society, existed at its margins, or had the status of outsiders. That may account in part for the longstanding connection between Rudra-Śiva and ascetics or *yogins,*[92] such as those extolled in the Ṛgveda's already mentioned hymn to the *keśin* (10.136). That ancient text, composed before 1900 BCE, describes a sect of long-haired, seminaked, ochre-clad wanderers whose appearance is remarkably close to that of present-day Śaiva *saṁnyāsins.*[93]

When the name *Rudra* is invoked in the Śvetāśvataropaniṣad, it is not with the same sense as in the Vedic hymns; rather, it represents the Supreme Being, both as the personal God (*deva*) or Lord (*īśa*) and the impersonal Brahman. It would be wrong to think of Rudra here as a sectarian deity, even as the supreme Śaiva God, because there is only one Supreme Being, who (or which) manifests in various forms and is called by a multitude of names. In the nondualistic view of the Śvetāśvataropaniṣad, everything emerges from the one Brahman, exists within it, and merges back into it.

Śaivism

If gaps in historical continuity and a web of complex interactions bedevil our understanding of how Sāṁkhya developed, our knowledge of Śaivism's long evolution is even less certain and more problematic. The texts of the late Vedic period—most notably the works of the Taittirīya school and also the Śaunakasaṁhitā of the Atharvaveda—contain Śaiva elements. The Taittirīyabrāhmaṇa, the Taittirīyāraṇyaka, and the Taittirīyopaniṣad are the source of most of the quotations in the Śvetāśvataropaniṣad (see p. 13). It is this same

Upaniṣad that Jan Gonda of the University of Utrecht called the "oldest document of rising Śivaism [*sic*]"[94] and one that exerted an unmistakable influence on the development of subsequent Śaiva thought.[95] All these texts, together with the Ṛgveda's much older hymns to Rudra, attest to the existence of some sort of Vedic proto-Śaivism that extended over a long period of time and displayed the whole range of philosophical possibilities from dualistic (*dvaita*) to dualistic-nondualistic (*dvaitādvaita*) to nondualistic (*advaita*).

Notwithstanding the textual indications of an incipient and evolving Vedic Śaivism, most scholars believe that Śiva was originally a non-Vedic deity who became absorbed into the Vedic pantheon in the distant past. If the earliest form of Rudra worship and the Brahmanical religion were originally separate and possibly antagonistic, the cult of Rudra became integrated into the Vedic fold by the time of the Taittirīyasaṁhitā.[96] What the original Śaiva religion or philosophy might have been like is anyone's guess, and complicating the picture, Śaivism has always had a large number of independent practitioners. Certainly Śaivism evolved over many centuries, but its evolution is not a matter of simple linear development.[97] The two earliest documented forms of sectarian Śaivism, both dating from around the fourth century BCE, represent two distinct streams of thought. These are the dualistic Pāśupata and the nondualistic Nāndikeśvara schools. In the absence of more precise dating or of any older documentation, the logical assumption is that both forms of Śaivism coexisted and developed side by side.[98]

In all likelihood the members of various Śaiva lineages and their subsects interacted, debated, exchanged ideas, and influenced one another. One indication of such interaction is the rise of a reformed Śaivism in the second century CE. Its founder, Lakulīśa, transformed the dualistic Pāśupata outlook into one characterized as *dvaitādvaita,* recognizing that multiplicity exists within an ultimate unity. A further distinction also appeared: whereas the dualistic Pāśupata system was considered non-Vedic, the reformed Lākulīśa Pāśupata Śaivism was Vedic-oriented and drew its fundamental tenets from the Taittirīyāraṇyaka.[99]

Around the same time as Lākulīśa Pāśupata Śaivism arose, a large body of texts known as the Śaivāgama probably began to take shape. The many texts of the Śaivāgama represent the whole logical range of Indian philosophy. Among them the nondualistic Āgamas

(Tantras) and those that lend themselves to such an interpretation constitute the scriptural foundation of the nondualistic school of Kashmir Śaivism.

This highly developed school, also known as the Trikaśāstra ("triadic teaching") or Trikadarśana appears to have historical and philosophical roots in the earlier nondualistic school of Nāndikeśvara Śaivism[100] although it attributes its formal beginning to a seminal text of the early ninth century CE, the *Śivasūtra* of Vasugupta. Some two hundred years later Trika Śaivism reached its apogee with the brilliant philosopher-mystic Abhinavagupta, the Śaiva counterpart to Vedānta's Śaṁkara.

With this brief outline of Vedic and non-Vedic, dualistic and nondualistic forms of Śaivism in place, a more detailed look at some of their features will demonstrate their relevance to the proper understanding of the Śvetāśvataropaniṣad.

The Taittirīya tradition

The beginnings of the Taittirīya tradition (*śākhā*) lie in a distant past where history and legend intertwine. A story recorded in the Viṣṇupurāṇa (3.5.1–29) tells that Yājñavalkya was the nephew and disciple of the original teacher of the Yajurveda, the great sage (*mahāmuni*) Vaiśampāyana. On one occasion the young and perhaps overly confident Yājñavalkya incurred the displeasure of his *guru,* who took offence at his audacity and ordered him to give back everything that he had been taught. Yājñavalkya immediately disgorged all the sacred verses (*mantras*), which fell to the ground in tangible form, whereupon Vaiśampāyana commanded his other disciples to pick them up. Each disciple, taking the form of a partridge (*tittiri*), eagerly devoured them. Because this collection of *mantras* had been soiled, it was thenceforth called the Taittirīyasaṁhitā of the Kṛṣṇa ("black") Yajurveda. Yājñavalkya, resolving to have no further human preceptor, began to worship the sun god, Sūrya, whom the Śatapathabrāhmaṇa (6.1.3.17) identifies with Īśāna, the highest form of Rudra. Pleased with Yājñavalkya's ardor, Sūrya assumed the form of a horse (*vājin*) and taught him previously undisclosed portions of the Yajurveda. This fresh knowledge came to be known as the Vājasaneyisaṁhitā of the Śukla ("white") Yajurveda.[101] In later years

Yājñavalkya grew to be one of the greatest of the ancient *ṛṣis*, one whose teachings form the basis of much subsequent Indian thought.

The Taittirīyasaṁhitā of the Kṛṣṇa Yajurveda is the second-oldest of all the Vedic texts. It contains a hymn known as the Rudrādhyāya (4.5, 4.7), a powerful invocation consisting of epithets of Rudra as the immanent face of the universal Brahman. This same litany of divine names and prayers forms two sections of the Vājasaneyisaṁhitā (16, 18), where it is known as the Śatarudrīya. Both versions confirm that the ongoing worship of Rudra, first indicated in the Ṛgvedasaṁhitā, continued into the late Vedic period. Some centuries later, when eighteen verses from the Taittirīya and Vājasaneyi texts reappeared in the Śvetāśvataropaniṣad, three of them (3.5, 3.6, 4.22) were drawn from the Rudrādhyāya and Śatarudrīya hymns.

These scriptural citations are compelling, but they are not the only evidence linking the Śvetāśvataropaniṣad to the Taittirīya lineage. In his commentary on the ninth verse of the Īśopaniṣad Śaṁkara refers to a *śvetāśvatarāṇāṁ mantropaniṣad*, an "Upaniṣad [consisting] of the *mantras* of the Śvetāśvataras." According to Śaunaka's *Caraṇavyūha*, a fairly early text of the post-Vedic period, the Śvetāśvataras were members of a particular Vedic school (*śākhā*), one of eighty-six belonging to the Yajurveda. What little evidence there is indicates that the Śvetāśvataropaniṣad occupies a position somewhere between the Vedic proto-Śaiva Taittirīya lineages and the appearance of the first identifiable Śaiva sects, the Nāndikeśvara and the Pāśupata.

Nāndikeśvara Śaivism

The nondualistic Nāndikeśvara school takes its name from its founder, Nandikeśvara, the author of a brief work entitled *Nandikeśvarakāśikā*. Literary tradition strongly suggests that the sage was an older contemporary of the grammarian-philosopher Pāṇini,[102] who lived around the fourth century BCE. In fact, the second verse of the *Kāśikā* clearly was intended to guide Pāṇini in constructing his theory of grammar. The other twenty-five verses preserve the earliest known formulation of a nondualistic Śaiva philosophy.[103] The *Kāśikā* has only one commentary, Upamanyu's *Tattvavimarśinī*, composed much later, around the late eleventh or early twelfth century CE.[104]

The fact that Nāndikeśvara Śaivism has attracted little attention in no way diminishes its importance. Many of its distinctive features are remarkably close to the doctrines of the fully developed, non-dualistic Trika Śaivism of Kashmir that reached its height some fifteen centuries later. In fact, many of the ideas expressed with enigmatic brevity in the *Kāśikā* become meaningful only in the light of Kashmir's later Śaiva thinkers—Kallaṭa, Somānanda, Utpala, and Abhinavagupta.[105]

Nāndikeśvara Śaivism is a school that emphasizes the practice of austerities with the aim of knowing the single reality beyond all categories of phenomenal existence. That transcendental reality is, of course, Brahman, the Self, the ultimate "I" (*aham*), the all-graceful Śiva. Significantly, the *Nandikeśvarakāśikā* speaks of Brahman, the all-pervading source of everything, as *prakāśa,* the undifferentiated radiance of pure consciousness. *Prakāśa* expresses itself spontaneously as the universe through its own power, called *citkalā*—literally, "an aspect of consciousness." Brahman, thus manifesting itself as the creator, is known as Īśvara, the Lord. *Citkalā,* the energy of consciousness, is also known as *māyā,* but here *māyā* is not the indefinable principle of ignorance or illusion as defined by the Vedānta, nor is it strictly the Trika notion of the principle of limitation, conceptualized as a *tattva* distinct from Śakti. In Nandikeśvara's understanding, *māyā* and *śakti* are one and the same—the very energy of consciousness, inseparably related to *prakāśa.* Nandikeśvara's concept of *māyā* is identical to what the Trika philosophy calls *vimarśa.* Other Trika synonyms for *vimarśa* include *citi* (consciousness conceived of as feminine and dynamic) and *svātantrya,* absolutely free will.[106] Most important, the Nāndikeśvara and Trika ideas concerning *māyā* can be found adumbrated even earlier in the Śvetāśvataropaniṣad.

The Nāndikeśvara is the first Śaiva system to propose the philosophy of voluntarism, the theory that will is the fundamental principle or primary factor in universal or individual experience. The term *voluntarism* in the Śaiva context does not signal determinism; quite the opposite. A better term would be *volitional spontaneity*—the idea that the universe comes about through the spontaneous and joyful expression of boundless divine freedom (*svātantrya*). This doctrine, called *svātantryavāda* in the Trika system, is already present some thirteen centuries earlier in Nandikeśvara's philosophy.[107] But even before that, it appears in embryonic form in Śvetāśvatara's teachings.

Nandikeśvara defines Brahman as the universal mind and speaks of *māyā* as *manovṛtti*, "the mind's activity."[108] Thus *māyā* is cosmic ideation, and the world is its product, the overflow of Brahman's own spontaneous joy. There is no separation between the Divine and its own self-expression. Nandikeśvara uses the beautiful analogy of the moon and moonlight, later invoked by the Śākta poet of the Devīmāhātmya (5.10) to express the identical teaching in terms of the Divine Mother: "Salutation to her always who is moonlight (*jyotsnāyai*), who has the form of the moon (*indurūpiṇyai*) and is blissful (*sukhāyai*)."[109] Like later Śaivism and Śāktism, the Nāndikeśvara system regards the divine reality as both the source and its manifestation. It does not consider the relationship between creator and creation in terms of a potter and a pot, to use a classic example. The manifest is not different in essence from that which manifests it. Whereas dualism envisions that the potter (the efficient cause) and clay (the material cause) are separate and dissimilar entities that together produce the pot, Brahman for Nandikeśvara is both consciousness-in-itself and its expression as the world.

All categories of existence are nothing other than manifestations of consciousness, and according to this early nondualistic Śaivism, these manifestations can be explained as thirty-six principles (*tattvas*) beyond which abides Paraśiva, the transcendental reality. The *tattvas* are Śiva (1), Śakti (2), Īśvara (3), the twenty-five *tattvas* of Sāṁkhya (4–28) with some differences in conception, the five vital airs (*prāṇa, apāna, samāna, vyāna, udāna*) (29–33), and the three *guṇas* (*sattva, rajas,* and *tamas*) (34–36). Similarly Trika Śaivism places the supreme unity of consciousness, called Paramaśiva, above the thirty-six categories of existence, but the details of its *tattvas* differ in many respects.[110]

Pāśupata Śaivism

The original form of Pāśupata Śaivism, distinct from Lakulīśa's later reformed version, dates from around the fifth or fourth century BCE and appears to be contemporary with Nandikeśvara's nondualistic school.[111] No texts of the dualistic Pāśupata Śaivism survive, but its philosophical positions can be reconstructed from other sources.

One early reference can be dated to some time between the fifth century BCE and the first century CE. It occurs in one of the oldest portions of the Mahābhārata, known as the Mokṣadharma (12.168–353).[112] This text lists five well established doctrinal systems: Veda, Sāṁkhya, Yoga, Pañcarātra (a Tantric form of Vaiṣṇavism), and Pāśupata. Notably the latter four are presented as distinct from Vedic tradition. Nevertheless, the Mokṣadharma (12.349.64–68) affirms the divine origin of the Pāśupatajñāna, naming Śrīkaṇṭha (Śiva), consort of Umā, as its first teacher. Elsewhere (12.285.194–195), emphasizing its anti-Vedic character, this same text has Śrīkaṇṭha declaring himself opposed to the Brahmanical caste rules and stages of life (*varṇāśramadharma*) and asserting that the religion he ordained is recognized by the wise as superior.[113]

Śaṁkara, in his *Brahmasūtrabhāṣya* (2.2.37 and immediately preceding remarks), refutes Sāṁkhya, Yoga, Pāśupata, and other Śaiva tenets as outside the Vedic pale. The Pāśupata system that he criticizes is the original, dualistic form and not Lakulīśa's reformed version,[114] a fact substantiated by later commentators on the *Brahmasūtra*.[115] Haribhadra Sūri's and Rājaśekhara's detailed compendia of Indian philosophies, dating from the eighth and early tenth centuries, further indicate that the dualistic Pāśupatajñāna forms the common basis of two of the six orthodox *darśanas,* the Nyāya and the Vaiśeṣika. These twin systems, concerned respectively with logic and phenomenology, arose around the third century BCE. Their founders, Gautama and Kaṇāda, were known to be devotees of Śiva, and their doctrines clearly followed an existing Śaiva tradition. In fact, the Nyāya school was designated as Śaiva, and the Vaiśeṣika school as Pāśupata. The older Pāśupatajñāna, apart from being the common basis of these two *darśanas,* appears to have contributed also to the dualistic Śaivāgama texts that took shape in Kashmir in the early centuries of the Common Era.[116] Through these texts the teachings of the original Pāśupata Śaivism survive in the present-day dualistic Śaiva Siddhānta of South India.[117]

The old Pāśupata dualism has its roots in the Vedic worship of Paśupati, the benevolent form of Rudra. From what can be deduced, its teachings center on five major topics: cause (*kāraṇa*), effect (*kārya*), union (*yoga*), ritual (*vidhi*), and the cessation of suffering (*duḥkhānta*).

Kāraṇa is also called *pati* ("lord"), and *kārya* is called *paśu* (the individual soul, under his control). Pati, the Lord, is the uncaused cause, but only the efficient cause, likened to a potter and independent of the material cause, *pradhāna,* likened to clay. It appears that Pāśupata dualism accepted the proto-Sāṁkhya categories of existence (*tattvas*) at some stage of their development that cannot be determined exactly. Like the orthodox Vaiśeṣika philosophy that evolved from it, the Pāśupata regarded individual souls as coeternal with the efficient and material causes and defined liberation (*mokṣa*) as nothing more than the end of suffering (*duḥkhānta*).[118]

Lākulīśa Pāśupata Śaivism

The Mokṣadharma portion of the Mahābhārata defined the earlier dualistic Pāśupatajñāna as outside the Vedic fold even while recognizing the Vedic religion as one among several. No doubt it also recognized that the non-Vedic forms of worship and practice had large popular followings. For the continuing survival of the Brahmanical religion and the restoration of its prestige in the face of the growing Śaiva, Vaiṣṇava, Gāṇapatya, and Śākta cults (not to mention Buddhism), it would have been of strategic benefit somehow to integrate the non-Vedic majority into the Brahmanical fold.[119] The move to Sanskritize or Aryanize popular religion led to the reinterpretation of ancient Upaniṣadic teachings in a more popular light by incorporating many non-Vedic myths, legends, personalities, and deities into a synthesized "history" chronicled in the Purāṇas. At the same time as Vedic religion absorbed non-Vedic elements, the extra-Vedic (*vedabāhya*) sectarian religions not surprisingly saw Vedic influences flowing into them as well. Conceivably this was the historical process at work in the formation of the reformed branch of Pāśupatism that properly should be called Lākulīśa Pāśupata Śaivism.

An inscription found on a stone pillar near Mathurā indicates that Lakulīśa, the reputed founder of this sect, lived in the first half of the second century CE, a date that correlates well with archeological and textual references to the pupils of his lineage.[120] Later texts, namely the Purāṇas and Āgamas, clearly distinguish between Pāśupatas and Lākulīśas and identify Lakulīśa as the twenty-eighth incarnation of Śiva. He obviously had precursors, just as Gautama Buddha was one in a long line of Buddhas and Mahāvīra was the twenty-fourth *tīrthaṅkara* in the Jain lineage. And just as Gautama Buddha and Mahāvīra rose to such pre-eminence that they are sometimes considered founders of their respective religions, Lakulīśa, by virtue of his outstanding qualities, became known, incorrectly, as the founder of Pāśupata Śaivism, even though he was the reformer of a pre-existing and somewhat different sect. Since the Purāṇas and sectarian texts alike portray him as a member of the *brāhmaṇa* caste, he might well have wanted to modify some of the more questionable Pāśupata practices to bring them closer in line with the approved norms of Vedic orthodoxy. Even so, he seems not to have gone far enough; his ideas still display a curious mixture of Brahmanical orthodoxy and transgressive practices.[121]

The oldest known text of Lākulīśa Pāśupata Śaivism is the *Pāśupatasūtra.* Although some scholars attribute it to Lakulīśa,[122] in truth nothing is known of its authorship[123] or its date. Rāśikara Kauṇḍinya's commentary, the *Pañcārthabhāṣya,* can be assigned to the fourth or fifth century CE,[124] but as for the *sūtra* text itself, its many archaic traits (most notably its identification of Paśupati with Prajāpati and the Vedic Rudra) indicate considerable antiquity.[125]

Lākulīśa Pāśupatism represents a confluence of elements from the Vedic Taittirīya tradition and the original Pāśupatism. From the Taittirīyāraṇyaka (Mahānārāyaṇopaniṣad, sections 17–21 of the Āndhra recension) Lakulīśa adopted five *mantras* that depict the five faces of Rudra—Sadyojāta, Vāmadeva, Aghora, Tatpuruṣa, Īśāna—and made them the basis of his philosophy and practice. Meditation on these different aspects of Rudra marks the progression through five stages of the Lākulīśa spiritual path (*sādhanāmārga*).[126] From the teachings of the dualistic Pāśupatism Lakulīśa adopted the five topics of cause (*kāraṇa, pati*), effect (*kārya, paśu*), union (*yoga*), injunction (*vidhi*), and the cessation of suffering (*duḥkhānta*).[127]

Cause (*kāraṇa*) concerns the nature of Pati, the Lord, as eternal and uncaused. As the ultimate cause, the Lord, also called Mahādeva, is playful by nature, manifesting the created universe and divine grace alike through this playfulness.[128] It is the failure to recognize him as the simultaneous creator, sustainer, and destroyer of all phenomena that results in human bondage.[129] This failure of recognition is, of course, the lack of right knowledge.

Effect (*kārya*) concerns the conditions of temporal existence and their problems, especially those relating to the human being (*paśu*). It presents human evolution along the lines of Sāṁkhya and holds that the soul remains fettered as long as it is conditioned by the *tattvas* (intellect, ego, mind, senses, and so on).[130] *Kārya*, or effect, is threefold, consisting of *vidyā*, *kalā*, and *paśu*. *Vidyā* is the sentiency of the individual subject that distinguishes it from *kalā*, or matter, which is deemed insentient (*jaḍa*). *Kalā* is the psychophysical limitation of the individual subject. In the Lākulīśa system *kalā* is roughly comparable to the Sāṁkhya *pradhāna* or *prakṛti*, although the twenty-three additional categories contained within it do not correspond exactly. *Paśu* is the unliberated individual, endowed with limited sentiency (*vidyā*) and bound by the constraints of mental and physical attributes in the realm of matter (*kalā*). Nevertheless, *kalā* is subservient to *vidyā*, just as a chariot with horses is under the control of the charioteer.[131]

Connection (*yoga*) refers to the union of the soul (*paśu*) with God (Pati) through the activity of the individual's conceptual faculty (*citta*).[132] Despite the similarity of terms, Lakulīśa defines *yoga* not in Patañjali's later sense of restraining the rise of activity in the mind (*yogaś cittavṛttinirodhaḥ—Yogasūtra* 1.2) but in the sense of union with the Lord. This union is not the result of the aspirant's efforts alone—which are likened to a bird's alighting on a rock—but of a human-divine reciprocity, likened to two fighting rams. As much as the *paśu* may aspire, union cannot be achieved without the Lord's grace.[133] As for actual practice, mental effort is both active (*sātmaka*) and passive (*nirātmaka*). Active endeavor includes *pūjā* (worship), *japa* (*mantra* repetition), and *dhyāna* (one-pointed meditation).[134] The *Pāśupatasūtra* instructs the *yogin* to meditate in the heart (*hṛdi kurvīta dhāraṇām*), an injunction that the commentator Kauṇḍinya understands as focusing the whole of one's attention on the *ātman*.[135] In contrast, the passive form of spiritual endeavor consists not of any such practices, but purely of intense feeling.[136]

Injunction (*vidhi*) lays out further means to spiritual attainment that may be undertaken only by advanced aspirants. These controversial practices include feigning madness in public, disruptive behavior in temples, discourtesy toward women, and other transgressions of religious and societal norms that will call down disapproval. To invite abuse is to gain purification, because public disgrace will hasten the conquest of the aspirant's ego. It will also result in the transference of good *karma* from those who condemn or abuse the practitioner.[137] These practices, while appearing antinomian, are in fact strictly regulated by the spiritual preceptor and are not a license for willful misbehavior. Union with Śiva (*rudrasāyujya*) comes through intense asceticism on the part of the near-naked, ash-besmeared, celibate Pāśupata Śaivas,[138] whose provocative customs pale before some of the more extreme practices of later and more radically transgressive Śaiva sects such as the Kāpālikas and Kālāmukhas.[139]

Cessation of suffering (*duḥkhānta*) is the ultimate spiritual goal. The Sāṁkhya would agree, but here the theistic character of Lakulīśa's doctrine shines through with the declaration that freedom ultimately comes through the Lord's grace (*īśaprasādāt*).[140] Then Lakulīśa broaches another idea: that *mokṣa* is more than freedom from suffering and even more than freedom from all kinds of wrong knowledge (*Pāśupatasūtra* 4.49). In accord with the Taittirīyāraṇyaka, he says that *mokṣa* is total establishment (*pratiṣṭhā*) in Brahman, defined by the commentator Sāyaṇa as firmness in the thought of one's identity with Brahman.[141] For Lakulīśa *mokṣa* is the attainment of divine perfection,[142] a state of ultimate realization that comes complete with the divine powers of knowledge and action.[143] That same position seems fairly evident in the Śvetāśvataropaniṣad (1.11), which declares that the aspirant who has cast off all fetters and gone beyond the sense of individuality "attains the third state, that of universal lordship (*viśvaiśvaryam*)," adding that "in the One all desires are fulfilled."

Except for *vidhi* the topics codified in the *Pāśupatasūtra* have much in common with the themes of the Śvetāśvataropaniṣad. A cursory look reveals that Śvetāśvatara's opening *mantra* (1.1) poses the question, What is the cause? The same question and its answer figure prominently in the sixth and final chapter (6.1–2, 6.5, 6.9, 6.13, 6.16–17). Suffering or affliction appears in several *mantras* (1.2, 1.4, 1.5, 1.11, 3.10, 4.7). The idea of the individual soul conditioned by *tattvas* occurs at least three times (1.4, 1.5, 6.3). There is also the triad of God, soul, and bondage (1.9, 1.12), known to the Lākulīśas as Pati, *paśu*, and *pāśa*. Rudra is the ultimate cause, nevertheless present in all created things (4.1–4; 4.10, 5.4–5, 6.3); he is the soul's own source (2.7), and failure to recognize that is the cause of human bondage (1.6). If lack of right knowledge is the cause of bondage, then it is knowledge itself that liberates or confers immortality (1.6, 1.9, 1.11, 3.7–8, 3.13, 4.15, 4.17, 4.20, 5.6), and liberation is articulated as the release from fetters (*pāśaiḥ*) (1.8, 2.15, 4.16, 5.13, 6.13). How is the goal to be attained? First through active mental effort (1.13–16; 2.5), and then through the particulars of *yoga* (2.6–14) along with meditation in the heart (4.20). The goal is to unite with Rudra, whom the third chapter glorifies as the nondual but theistic Supreme Being and the bestower of grace (3.11, 3.20). Knowing him and uniting with him, one achieves the cessation of all illusion (1.10).

There can be little doubt that the teachings of the *Pāśupatasūtra* derive from those of the Taittirīyāraṇyaka, which they closely resemble.[144] Sāyaṇa's understanding of the nature of Brahman as expressed in the Taittirīyāraṇyaka coincides in large part with the *Pāśupatasūtra*'s configuration of the Supreme Being as Pati. In fact, in the Śaiva text the terms *pati, kāraṇa,* and Brahman are synonymous.[145] Another point in common is that both texts define *māyā* as Brahman's power, having no independent existence. Both texts refer to Brahman as *māyin*[146] ("the artful one," "the conjurer"), implying that he is the lord of *māyā*. Significantly, this term occurs nowhere in the Upaniṣads except in the Śvetāśvatara (4.9–10). The intimate connection between Brahman and *māyā,* or between Śiva and Śakti in Śaiva terms, has very ancient roots. The Taittirīyāraṇkaya declares that Rudra is the Self of all living beings. He is being itself. Transcending all, he is all that ever had, has, or will have existence.[147] This statement mirrors an earlier passage from the Ṛgvedasaṁhitā (1.89.10), which uses similar ideas to praise Aditi, the ancient Vedic concept of the Divine Mother as infinity and the prototype of Śakti: "Aditi is the heaven; Aditi is the atmosphere; Aditi is the mother, the father, the son. / All the gods are Aditi, and the five peoples; Aditi is that which is born; Aditi is that which will be born."

Sāyaṇa understands the Taittirīyāraṇyaka's underlying philosophy as *dvaitādvaitavāda*. From his Vedantic standpoint the absolute Brahman is *nirguṇa,* without attributes or qualifications; Brahman associated with *māyā* is *saguṇa,* with attributes. *Saguṇa* Brahman is also known as Īśvara, the personal God. Sāyaṇa comments that the inherent nature (*svabhāva*) of *nirguṇa* Brahman is the unity of being-consciousness-bliss (*saccidānanda*), and the nature of *saguṇa* Brahman is the activity of creating, sustaining, and dissolving the universe. The limited senses of the embodied self and the objective world they perceive are the effects of Brahman qualified by *māyā*, and as effects they have no being apart from the cause. *Dvaitādvaitvāda* in Vedantic terms can be summarized as a doctrine that views duality as a manifestation or evolved state of a basic nonduality.[148] Lākulīśa Pāśupatism also subscribes to the *dvaitādvaita* doctrine. Sometimes referred to by the term *bhedābhedavāda*, this doctrine proposes that difference (*bheda*) and identity (*abheda*) are not contradictory. Rather, identity describes the nondual Brahman in its essence, and difference describes its multiple forms of expression.[149] Unlike the *advaita* doctrine, the *dvaitādvaita* or *bhedābheda* accepts both the reality of dualism in the empirical experience and the reality of nondualism in the transcendental. It is in the latter experience that the individual soul (*jīva*) attains union with Śiva.[150]

Apart from the Śvetāśvataropaniṣad's many quotations from the Taittirīya texts and the obvious links between the Taittirīyāraṇyaka and the *Pāśupatasūtra*, is there any demonstrable link between the *ṛṣi* Śvetāśvatara and Lakulīśa's sect? The Kurmapurāṇa, composed some time after the Mahābhārata, devotes a passage (1.13.48–49) to the story of King Suśīla, who makes a pilgrimage to the Himālayas and there praises Śiva with Vedic hymns. When he has finished his devotions, there appears to him *a great Pāśupata*—Śvetāsvatara—who initiates the king in the Pāśupata path with a Vedic *mantra*. Now entering the renunciate's stage of life (*saṁnyāsa*), the king smears himself with ashes, a requisite sign of the Śaiva ascetic, and dedicates himself thenceforth to the study of the Vedas.[151] Of course, this Purāṇa, following the Śvetāśvataropaniṣad by nearly a thousand years, does nothing to confirm Śvetāśvatara's historicity or religious affiliation. Nevertheless, it links Śvetāśvatara to a Vedic form of Pāśupatism and identifies him as an earlier figure whom the later sectarians revered as a spiritual ancestor.

Elsewhere in the Kurmapurāṇa Śiva repeatedly stresses the importance of the Vedic Pāśupata vow as the way to liberation. In one passage (2.37.140–142) he exhorts his devotees—described as tranquil, of controlled mind, naked but for a loincloth, ash-besmeared, and celibate—to follow the supreme Pāśupata vow, which he himself created in ancient times. That vow, he says, is the essence of the Vedas, and its purpose is the attainment of liberation. But three verses later (2.37.145–146) Śiva condemns the paths of both the Pāśupatas and the Lākulīśas as outside the Veda (*vedabāhya*) and not to be followed![152] The troubling inconsistency makes sense only if we entertain the notion that the Kūrmapurāṇa is dealing with *three* forms of Pāśupata Śaivism—the subversive sect of dualists described as non-Vedic in the Mokṣadharma, Lakulīśa's less subversive and somewhat Vedicized sect, and a slightly different Purāṇic sect allied more closely to contemporary Vedic (*smārta*) practice. It is pure speculation, of course, but perhaps the approved form of Vedic Śaivism belongs to the lineage of the Taittirīyas and Śvetāśvataras, not by way of Lakulīśa. If this be the case, when the Kūrmapurāṇa extols Śvetāśvatara as "a great Pāśupata," perhaps it does so in the broader sense of a great Śaiva *ṛṣi* rather than in the sense of a sectarian figure. The Purāṇa seems to promote the worship of Śiva-Paśupati according to acceptable Vedic norms, a practice it heartily endorses even while denouncing the dualistic Pāśupata and reformed Lākulīśa paths as non-Vedic. In fact, when Śiva extols the follower of the Pāśupata vow, he describes a practitioner little different from the Ṛgveda's ascetic devotee of Rudra, portrayed so vividly in the hymn to the *keśin* (see p. 32).

The Śaivāgama

Historically the Śaiva sects had grown numerous and diverse by the Puranic age. Besides the Vedic-oriented Śaivas of the Taittirīya and Śvetāśvatara lineages, there were the dualistic Pāśupatas and their various descendants along with four additional subsects of the reformist Lākulīśas, each following one of the the founder's direct disciples. Besides these, Śaivism as a whole no doubt embraced practitioners from other unaffiliated lineages as well.

Around this time a vast corpus of texts known as the Śaivāgama appeared on the horizon, probably after long centuries of oral transmission and evolution. Scholars generally assign them to the early centuries of the Common Era,[153] even though the oldest preserved manuscripts date only from the eighth or ninth centuries.[154] It can be established that before the time of Śaṁkara (788–820), these texts had already achieved an authoritative status. The *Saundaryalaharī* and *Dakṣiṇāmūrtistotra,* both attributed to Śaṁkara, along with the writings of his disciple Sureśvara, reveal specific knowledge of the nondualistic Śaivāgama texts and their teachings.[155]

Although the Śaivāgama is classified as Tantric and not Vedic, one of its texts, the Mṛgendratantra, invokes the Rudra hymns of the Taittirīyasaṁhitā and the Vājasaneyisaṁhitā to demonstrate that the Śaiva tradition existed since Vedic times.[156] Unlike a heterodox system such as Buddhism, which rejected the authority of the Vedas, the Śaivāgama neither opposed nor fully allied itself to the Vedic tradition. Instead it acknowledged whatever Vedic teachings agreed with its own doctrines and sometimes even declared itself to be the essence of the Veda (*vedasāraḥ śivāgamaḥ*).[157] At the same time it recognized both the Lākulīśas and the Pāśupatas as legitimate sources of Śaiva teaching.[158] In the late tenth or early eleventh century Abhinavagupta affirmed those connections, writing in the *Tantrāloka* (36.13–17) that the Śaivāgama has two main divisions, one stemming from Lakulīśa and a larger one from Śrīkaṇṭha,[159] presumably meaning Śiva himself. Neither, he insisted, can be dissociated from the nondual Trikaśāstra.[160]

In general the texts of the Śaivāgama follow a four-part structure, each part centering on one of four traditional topics: *jñāna* (higher knowledge), *yoga* (practices and techniques), *kriyā* (ritual action and its requirements), and *caryā* (proper comportment in religious observances).[161]

The many works that constitute the Śaivāgama represent the entire logical range of Indian thought. These individual Āgamas, or Tantras, belong to three classes, designated *dvaita, dvaitādvaita,* and *advaita.* This triple classification, based on the logical progression from duality to nonduality, also correlates to the Taittirīyāraṇyaka's portrayal of Rudra-Śiva as five-faced (*pañcavaktra*). The same quintuple imagery that underlies the structure of Lakulīśa's school here serves to assert the divinely revealed nature of the Āgamas. The ten *dvaita* (or Śiva) Āgamas proceed from those aspects of Śiva known as Īśa, Tatpuruṣa, and Sadyojāta; the eighteen *dvaitādvaita* (or Rudra) Āgamas proceed from Vāma and Aghora; and the sixty-four *advaita* (or Bhairava) Āgamas proceed from the union of Śiva and Śakti.[162] Traditionally each of these ninety-two texts represents a separate lineage and a particular stage of spiritual development from the purely dual to the absolutely nondual.[163] The *advaita* texts and those that lend themselves to nondualistic interpretation constitute the primary scriptural foundation of the nondualistic Śaivism of Kashmir.

The Trikaśāstra

In the middle of the ninth century CE, a distinct branch of nondualistic Śaivism developed in the fertile valley of Kashmir, a renowned center of learning where spiritual and secular knowledge had flourished for many centuries among Hindus and Buddhists alike. Just when the worship of Śiva was established in Kashmir is anybody's guess, but in all likelihood the oral transmission of Śaiva teaching from *guru* to disciple began in Vedic times. In succeeding centuries this Śaiva teaching acknowledged the entire logical range of philosophical positions from dualism to nondualism.

The specific nondualistic school popularly known as Kashmir Śaivism traces its formal beginning to the middle of the ninth century CE when the *Śivasūtra* was revealed to the sage Vasugupta. Along with the already existing Śaivāgama, this text quickly attained the status of scripture and provided the foundation for what would become the most highly developed form of Śaiva nondualism. The divine revelation from Śiva himself was seen as a response to the dualism then prevalent in Kashmir, which taught an eternal distinction between God and the soul, God and the world, and the soul and the world. Arranged in three chapters, the *Śivasūtra*'s seventy-seven aphorisms deal with four topics: ultimate reality, the world-process, bondage, and liberation. Practically speaking, the *Śivasūtra* is a comprehensive manual on the *yoga* of realizing the supreme identity—that of the individual soul and ultimate consciousness.

The inseparability of consciousness (*cit, saṁvid*) and its energy (*śakti*), already articulated some twelve centuries earlier by Nandikeśvara (see pp. 39–41), forms a basic tenet of nondual Kashmir Śaivism. Accordingly, either Vasugupta or, by some accounts, his disciple Kallaṭabhaṭṭa, composed a companion work to the *Śivasūtra* that elaborates on its principles and emphasizes the dynamic aspect of consciousness, the pulsation or vibration known as *spanda.* The *Spandakārikā* [Stanzas on vibration] and the *Śivasūtra*, together with further commentaries on both of them, constitute a body of literature known as the Spandaśāstra.

Somānanda, possibly a disciple of Vasugupta, composed the first philosophical treatise of nondualistic Kashmir Śaivism, entitled *Śivadṛṣṭi* [Vision of Śiva]. Whereas the *Śivasūtra* prescribes a complex course of yogic practices, *Śivadṛṣṭi* proposes that self-realization is a simple matter of *recognizing* one's true being as divine. This doctrine of recognition (*pratyabhijñāvāda*) forms the philosophical basis of nondualistic Kashmir Śaivism. Owing to the extreme difficulty of Somānanda's text, it fell to his disciple Utpaladeva to make the teaching more accessible. In his *Īśvarapratyabhijñākārikā* [Stanzas on the recognition of God], Utpaladeva popularized the doctrine that the individual *paśu* is in essence Pati, or Śiva, who has forgotten his divine nature through (mis)identification with the limitations of mind and body. Enlightenment is the recognition of one's own authentic nature as Śiva himself. As a systematic theology and a philosophy of consciousness-as-the-Absolute, the Pratyabhijñā system represents the fullest expression of Śaiva nondualism. Somānanda's *Śivadṛṣṭi*, Utpaladeva's *Īśvarapratyabhijñākārikā*, and treatises by later writers form a body of texts known as the Pratyabhijñāśāstra.

Together the Śaivāgama, the Spandaśāstra, and the Pratyabhijñāśāstra form the vast literary corpus of nondualistic Kashmir Śaivism. They do not represent individually defined schools so much as different lines of *guru*-disciple transmission and different tendencies within the overall aggregate of lineages, with frequently overlapping theoretical views and practical techniques. Among them, Vasugupta's and Kallaṭabhaṭṭa's innovative Spanda teachings, further developed by Somānanda and Utpaladeva as the Pratyabhijñā philosophy, took their place alongside earlier nondualistic traditions of Kashmir, based on the Śaivāgama.[164]

It was the brilliant Abhinavagupta who synthesized all those currents of nondualistic thought into a system of encyclopedic scope, fully encompassed within the Trika.[165] Because the term *Kashmir Śaivism* properly embraces lineages from dualistic to nondualistic,[166] we have adopted the terms *Trikaśāstra* and *Trikadarśana* as convenient designations for nondualistic Kashmir Śaivism as a whole. The term *trika* ("triad") refers to the threefold nature of experience, conceptualized in terms of Śiva-Śakti-*nara* (divine consciousness, its power, and the human being) or in terms of *para-parāpara-apara* (the supreme nondual state, the state of identity-in-difference, and the state of difference or duality) or in terms of *paśu-pati-pāśa* (the bound soul, the Lord, and the bondage that is phenomenality). The word *śāstra* means teaching not only in the sense of an exposition of principles and ideas but also in the sense of a discipline to be followed and an ideal to be pursued. *Śāstra* is not only a way of thinking but also a way of living. Likewise *darśana,* often translated as "philosophy," indicates a world-view that infuses every aspect of one's existence.

Abhinavagupta was born sometime between 940 and 975 and lived until around 1025. His intense religious devotion and lifelong love of learning led him to thoroughgoing study in the fields of religion, philosophy, poetics, drama, language, and esthetics. He was more than an intellectual giant, however. He was a saintly ascetic and a fervent devotee who came to be recognized as an illumined soul (*jīvanmukta*). In the course of his life he studied with many *gurus* and had direct knowledge of several Śaiva traditions, including the Krama, Trika, Kula, Spanda, and Pratyabhijñā.[167] The Krama is an esoteric teaching centering on the internalized worship of Kālī, leading to self-identification with the ultimate reality of consciousness.[168] Together the Krama, the Kula, and the original Trika derive directly from the Śaivāgama tradition, which itself has roots in the Pāśupata and Lākulīśa Pāśupata lineages.[169] In contrast the Spanda-Pratyabhijñā teachings are native to Kashmir. They are strongly reminiscent of early Vedāntic tenets[170] but also represent a unique innovation in nondualistic thought.[171] Abhinavagupta brought together these many ideas and practices under the existing name of Trika. Writing prolifically in elegant Sanskrit, he produced a large body of works, crowned by the *Tantrāloka* [Light of the Tantras], a massive compendium of all aspects of his Trika Śaivism's philosophy and practice.

Like Śaṁkara's Advaita Vedānta, the Trikadarśana is nondualistic. In many respects the two philosophies agree, in other ways they complement each other, and on some points they hold divergent or even opposing views. Nevertheless, both recognize that there is one ultimate reality. The Vedānta calls this Brahman; the Trika calls it Paramaśiva, Śiva, or *saṁvid* ("consciousness"). Whatever it is called, the ultimate reality is infinite, unconditioned, nonrelational consciousness.

Advaita Vedānta understands Brahman as eternally unchanging. For Śaṁkara immutability and reality are synonymous, and Brahman is ever inactive and devoid of attributes (*nirguṇa*). Associated somehow with *māyā* or nescience (*avidyā*), Brahman appears to take on qualities and become *saguṇa*. Then it is known as Īśvara, the personal God who creates, sustains, and dissolves the universe.

Nevertheless, the power of activity belongs entirely to *māyā* and not to Brahman. For that reason the adherents of the Trikaśāstra sometimes refer to Śaṁkara's Vedānta as *śāntabrahmavāda* ("doctrine of the inactive [or peaceful] Brahman").

In contrast the Trika or Pratyabhijñā philosophy is known as *īśvarādvayavāda* ("doctrine of the Lord's nonduality").[172] Whereas the *nirguṇa* Brahman of Vedānta is inactive and impersonal, the Paramaśiva of the Trika system has activity as its inherent power (*śakti*). It also has its own sense of identity as the ultimate I (*pūrṇāhaṁtā*). For this reason the term *īśvarādvayavāda* is sometimes translated as "doctrine of theistic absolutism." Śiva is the eternal, immutable radiance of pure consciousness (*prakāśa*)—the impersonal, absolute Brahman of the Vedānta—as well as its own self-referential capacity and power of self-expression (*vimarśa*). In the Trika philosophy there is no dichotomy of Brahman and *māyā* as in Vedānta, but the recognition of a single consciousness that is both at rest and active. It is both *prakāśa* and *vimarśa,* both Śiva and Śakti. Simply put, Śakti without Śiva has no being, and Śiva without Śakti has no expression.[173] Śiva is at once the unchanging, absolute, transcendental consciousness *and* the supreme God endowed with the powers of omniscience, omnipotence, and activity.[174] To speak of God as formless and with form is not to speak of two separate deities or even two separate aspects of a single deity. Instead, Paramaśiva is one indivisible reality that the human mind mistakenly thinks of as two.

On that point Śrī Rāmakṛṣṇa, the great Bengali seer of the nineteenth century, was particularly emphatic. "Brahman and Śakti are identical," he said, elaborating that it is not possible to accept one without accepting the other, any more than it is possible to conceive of the sun's rays without the sun or the sun without its rays. The same holds true of the Absolute and the relative; neither is conceivable without the other.[175] Śrī Rāmakṛṣṇa taught that the transcendental Brahman is also Kālī, the primal energy (*ādyāśakti*). When inactive, it is called Brahman, and when creating, preserving, and destroying, it is called Śakti. Brahman can be compared to still water; the same water, moving in waves, is comparable to Śakti.[176] But, whether moving or still, water is water and nothing else.[177]

Advaita Vedānta holds that *māyā* is indefinable (*anirvacanīyā*), and so is its relationship with Brahman. If one accepts that *māyā* is relative and Brahman is absolute, there can be no real relationship between the two, for any relationship would relativize the Absolute—a logical absurdity. Therefore any causal relationship between Brahman and *māyā* is only apparent and belongs to *māyā* alone.[178] For that reason, Advaita Vedānta views *māyā* as an indefinable causal potency totally dependent on Brahman in some indefinable way.

If one accepts that Brahman is the sole reality, then *māyā* and its effects are something less than real—*apart from* Brahman and not *a part of* it. Śaṁkara characterized the world as *mithyā*—false, misleading, ever mutable, and not what it appears to be. He regarded the world as a mere appearance (*vivarta*), superimposed by *māyā* on the reality of Brahman. The doctrine of appearance (*vivartavāda*) employs the classic analogy of the rope and the snake to make its point. The rope (Brahman) does not cause the snake (the world); the semidarkness (*māyā*) causes the misperception (the *adhyāsa* or superimposition) in the perceiver, who then mistakes the rope for a snake. All the while, the rope remains unchanged. Similarly, no change can take place in the immutable Brahman.

Trika Śaivism, on the other hand, views *māyā* as Śiva's own self-assumed power of limitation by which he, the infinite One, experiences his creation through innumerable finite centers of consciousness, the individual *jīvas.* Consciousness (Śiva, *cit, saṁvid*) is the sole reality, and nothing exists apart from it. The Trikaśāstra rejects the Vedānta's doctrine of superimposition as retaining traces of dualism: *māyā,* superimposing the world-appearance (*vivarta*), is something other than Brahman. The Śaiva philosophy regards the world-appearance (*ābhāsa*) as a display of divine glory, an aspect or expression of Paramaśiva himself as his own ideation. The *ābhāsa* is not real in Śaṁkara's sense of eternal immutability and permanence, but it is real in the sense that it exists as experience within the reality of divine consciousness. Unlike Advaita Vedānta, the Trikaśāstra does not exclude *māyā* but accepts it as an aspect of Śiva and integrates it into one, all-embracing reality.[179]

The ideas surrounding liberation (*mokṣa*), discussed previously in relation to Sāṁkhya and earlier forms of Śaivism, differ somewhat in relation to both Advaita Vedānta and the Trikaśāstra. For the dualistic Sāṁkhya, *mokṣa* is the freedom from suffering (*duḥkha*) that arises on realizing the distinction (*viveka*) between consciousness (*puruṣa*), and matter (*prakṛti*). Sāṁkhya defines liberation as *puruṣa* abiding in its true, original nature, in complete isolation (*kaivalya*) from *prakṛti.* Pāśupata Śaivism similarly views *mokṣa* as the cessation of suffering (*duḥkhānta*). When Lakulīśa enacted his reforms, he extended the definition of *mokṣa* beyond the cessation of suffering to include the positive attainment of divine omniscience and omnipotence. In agreement with the Upaniṣads, Gauḍapāda's Advaita Vedānta views liberation as the result of dispelling the ignorance of *māyā* and knowing the Self (*ātman*) to be the ever blissful, nondual Brahman beyond empirical existence. Śaṁkara, following the Upaniṣads and Gauḍapāda, likewise defines *mokṣa* as realizing the identity of *ātman* and Brahman. In the transcendental (*pāramārthika*) knowledge of Brahman, the lower experience of the empirical (*vyāvahārika*) universe vanishes into the absolute oneness of *saccidānanda*. The Trika-śāstra agrees that liberation (*mokṣa, mukti*) is the recognition (*pratyabhijñā*) of one's true nature as the divine Infinite. To recognize the *jīva* as Śiva is to experience the original I-consciousness (*akṛtrimāhaṁvimarśa*), which is immediate, nonrelational awareness. This is the attainment of *cidānanda,* the bliss of universal consciousness. The Trika teaching adds that the highest bliss is *jagadānanda,* the state in which the world does not vanish but appears as nothing other than the singular divine consciousness.[180]

Śrī Rāmakṛṣṇa repeatedly used a simple analogy to explain this view of liberation, and it is one that reconciles the teachings of the Advaita Vedānta and the Trika. First he would present the Vedāntin's method of negation. By saying that Brahman is "not this, not this" (*neti neti*), the practitioner arrives at the understanding that Brahman is not living beings, not the material universe, not the twenty-four *tattvas.* The world becomes dreamlike and insubstantial, then vanishes in *nirvikalpa samādhi.* This realization of the Self is known as *jñāna.* But there is another state, known as *vijñāna,* which is a fuller knowledge. After the negation comes the affirmation that God himself has become all this. Śrī Rāmakṛṣṇa would explain that while ascending the stairs to the roof of a house, one is aware of both the stairs and the roof and negates the stairs as not being the roof. But on reaching the roof, one realizes that the stairs and the roof are made of the same materials—brick, lime, and brick-dust. After that, how is it possible to accept the roof and reject the stairs? Śrī Rāmakṛṣṇa used the term *vijñānin* for one who has been to the roof and back, who experiences the *nirguṇa* and the *saguṇa* as the same reality, and who knows that Brahman itself has become the universe and all living beings.[181]

The thiry-six *tattvas* of Trika Śaivism

Like the Sāṁkhya and the Vedānta, the Trika rejects the idea of *creatio ex nihilo* as logically untenable. Simply put, something cannot come out of nothing. According to the Trikaśāstra everything pre-exists potentially in the wholeness of undifferentiated consciousness. Properly speaking, creation is a process of emanation (*sṛṣṭi*), not a process of making something out of nothing or of making something out of something else. The universe is the self-expression of the supreme Śiva, who assumes the finitude of mind and matter even while remaining infinite in the undifferentiated wholeness of pure awareness. The doctrine of consciousness-as-cause (*cetanakāraṇavāda*) holds that the world comes into existence through divine ideation and employs the imagery of thirty-six *tattvas* or principles of mind and matter to explain how the one reality expresses itself as the multiplicity of sentient beings and insentient objects that make up the universe. It would be incorrect to think of these principles as separate entities or indeed as *things* of any kind. They are only points on the continuum of awareness, like places on a rainbow that can be identified as red or yellow or blue.

Sāṁkhya, after centuries of evolution, settled on a scheme of twenty-five *tattvas,* headed by *puruṣa* and *prakṛti*—ultimate consciousness and ultimate materiality. The Vedānta refashioned this scheme to suit its own nondualistic view. Equating *puruṣa* with the absolute Brahman and elevating it above the list of categories, it retained the twenty-four remaining *tattvas* that belong to the realm of phenomenality. In contrast Trika Śaivism added eleven more *tattvas* to Sāṁkhya's twenty-five, allowing a closer look at the more rarefied levels of consciousness and the specific workings of *māyā.* This expanded scheme reveals a penetrating observation of the natural world, of the human mind that experiences it, and of the essential awareness that illuminates the experience.

Trika's thirty-six *tattvas* fall into three groups, called the pure order (*śuddhādhvan*), the pure-impure order (*śuddhāśuddhādhvan*), and the impure order (*aśuddhādhvan*). The word *adhvan* means "course" or "journey" and suggests the movement of consciousness through three phases of experience—nonduality, self-imposed limitation, and plurality. These phases mirror the other triple classifications already encountered in Indian thought (see pp. 1–2).

The pure order is the universal experience of divine unity. It consists of five *tattvas,* designated *śiva* (1), *śakti* (2), *sadāśiva* (3), *īśvara* (4), and *sadvidyā* or *śuddhavidyā* (5). The pure-impure order consists of the principles of subjective limitation, called *māyā* (6), *kalā* (7), *vidyā* (8), *rāga* (9), *kāla* (10), and *niyati* (11). The impure order comprises the remaining twenty-five *tattvas,* which bear the same names as their Sāṁkhya counterparts, although their conceptualization differs in some respects (see p. 21).

Paramaśiva, the supreme reality-in-itself, is nonrelational. Also called *anuttara*—that beyond which there is nothing else—it transcends even the highest *tattva.* Though One and absolute, it has the potentiality for polarization. Simply abiding in its own infinite radiance, consciousness is called Śiva or *prakāśa*—the first *tattva.* Because its very nature is energy, it is also called Śakti or *vimarśa*—the second *tattva. Prakāśa* is self-luminous consciousness, and *vimarśa* is its self-referential or reflective capacity—consciousness reflected in consciousness. *Prakāśa* and *vimarśa* are one and indivisible—the Supreme Being's own self-awareness, known as *pūrṇāhaṁtā* ("I-ness-in-full"). Śiva-Śakti is the Absolute experiencing itself as pure Self. This has nothing to do with ego, which is based on the premise of I and other.

In the universal experience (*śuddhādhvan*) there is no other, and the Supreme Being enjoys only absolute freedom and boundless joy. At this stage of unified consciousness no manifestation has taken place. Nevertheless, the *śuddhādhvan* contains the gradations conceived of as the first five *tattvas.* These correspond to the five divine powers (*śaktis*). *Śiva* (1) and *śakti* (2) respectively represent the essential nature of consciousness as awareness (*cicchakti*) and spontaneous joy (*ānandaśakti*). *Sadāśiva* (3), *īśvara* (4), and *sadvidyā* (5) represent the powers of divine activity, consisting of will (*icchāśakti*), knowledge (*jñānaśakti*), and action (*kriyāśakti*). They represent consciousness in the initial phases leading to cosmic manifestation.

The Chāndogyopaniṣad (6.2.3) relates that the One, seeing itself alone and without a second, observed, May I become many; may I procreate (*bahu syāṁ prajāyeyeti*). This initial creative urge is conceptualized as *sadāśiva.* Out of the pure subjectivity of *aham* ("I") arises an indistinct idea of *idam* ("this"), the initial stirring of objectivity. The *sadāśiva* state is characterized by the Sanskrit formula *aham idam* ("*I* am this"), with emphasis on *I* and only a vague idea of a *this* within it.

The *īśvaratattva* should not be confused with Īśvara, the personal deity of Vedānta. Each presents a somewhat different concept of divine creativity. In the *īśvara* state the power of knowledge (*jñānaśakti*) predominates and effects the ideation of the universe. Attention shifts from the subjective *aham* to the objective *idam,* so the *īśvara* state is described as *idam aham* ("*this* am I"). *This,* now emphasized, becomes the definite plan of the universe.

In the *sadvidyā* state the aspects of subjectivity and objectivity become more clearly defined, held in reciprocal balance like the two pans of a scale but close to splitting apart. Predominant here is the divine power of action (*kriyāśakti*), the ability to assume any and every form. This is the state of *ahaṁ ca idaṁ ca* ("I am and this is"). Even so, there is no duality. Subjective and objective awareness remain together in the unity of the universal experience.

In the *śuddhādhvan* divine consciousness shades from the absolute oneness of *pūrṇāhaṁtā* into the still unified stages of *aham idam, idam aham,* and *ahaṁ ca idaṁ ca.* After awareness has passed through the veils of the pure-impure order (*śuddhāśuddhādhvan*), the potential split of subjectivity and objectivity will become actual in the realm of duality or multiplicity. This experience will be characterized as *aham ahaṁ ca idam idaṁ ca* ("I am I, and this is this").

Cosmic manifestation (*ābhāsa*) results from the self-limitation or contraction (*saṁkoca*) of Śiva's infinite consciousness into the finite experience of countless sentient *jīvas.* Accordingly the first *tattva* of the pure-impure order is *māyā* (6), consciousness functioning as its own limiting and differentiating power. Working in five different ways, *māyā* generates five *kañcukas* ("coverings" or "cloaks"), the *tattvas* of subjective limitation that conceal in turn Śiva's omnipotence, omniscience, self-satisfaction, eternality, and omnipresence.

Kalā (7), the principle of partialness or aspect, negates the divine wholeness and makes possible the many and separate components of phenomenal existence. Through division and fragmentation, *kalā* apportions Śiva's effortless omnipotence (*sarvakartṛtva*) among the countless *jīvas,* reducing it to *prayatnatva,* a condition in which everything requires effort. Similarly *vidyā* (8) shrinks divine omniscience (*sarvajñātṛtva*) to the individual's greatly restricted, specific, and imperfect awareness.

The universal experience of Śiva is one of wholeness, perfection, and complete fulfillment (*pūrṇatva*). *Rāga* (9), which means "desire" or "passionate attraction," negates that inherent satisfaction, leaving a sense of incompleteness or lack that the *jīva* ever seeks to assuage in every possible way. Of course, no form of mundane or temporal satisfaction can compensate for this existential deficiency. As the seer Sanatkumāra observes in the Chāndogyopaniṣad (7.23–25), there is no lasting happiness (*sukha*) in the finite (*alpa*), but only in the infinite Brahman, the supreme Self.

In its changeless perfection Śiva is imperishable and eternal. Eternity is not a limitless extension of time but a state of utter timelessness. *Kāla* (10), the principle of time, negates divine eternality (*nityatva*), finitizing it as past, present, and future and reducing the divine experience of timeless imperishability to the finitude of human mortality.

Niyati (11), translated as "necessity" or "determinism," is the principle that negates divine omnipresence (*vyāpakatva*) and restricts individual experience to a particular place. Together with *māyā's* four other *kañcukas, niyati* also creates the rules by which the universe works. For example, *kāla* contracts eternality into time, and *niyati* establishes its irreversible direction. Giving rise to causality, *niyati* reduces the unfettered freedom of divine action (*kriyā*) to the binding action (*karma*) that keeps the *jīva* caught up in the ever-repeating round of birth, death, and rebirth known as *saṁsāra.*

Unitary consciousness, having passed through the veils of *māyā* and entered the realm of phenomenality (*aśuddhādhvan*), appears split into *puruṣa* (12) and *prakṛti* (13)—subjective individuality and objective materiality. In the Trika definition *puruṣa* is not the ultimate conscious principle of Sāṁkhya. As in Sāṁkhya, there are as many *puruṣas* as there are sentient beings, but the Trikaśāstra likens them to the myriad individual rays of the one sun, because consciousness is ultimately One. Here *puruṣa* is consciousness experiencing itself as the condition of limited individuality but not yet as an individual person. The further conditioning of mind, personality, and body has yet to evolve in *prakṛti.*

Unlike Sāṁkhya, for which *prakṛti* is a single principle, the Trikaśāstra accepts multiple *prakṛtis,* each an extension (*prasāra*) of a *puruṣa.* As unevolved materiality, *prakṛti* holds in perfect balance the three energies (*guṇas*) of creation, the forces of *sattva, rajas,* and *tamas* (see p. 17). Once their equilibrium has been disturbed, they combine and recombine, evolving into the twenty-three remaining categories of mind and matter. Trika teaching regards the *guṇas* as scaled down versions of the divine powers of will, knowledge, and action. Through *māyā, jñānaśakti* contracts into *sattva, icchāśakti* into *rajas,* and *kriyāśakti* into *tamas.* These three *śaktis* also contract into the three *tattvas* of mental operation—*buddhi* (14), *ahaṁkāra* (15), and *manas* (16), which together form the *antaḥkaraṇa* ("inner instrument"), commonly referred to as the mind.

Buddhi is the highest manifestation of human consciousness. Often called "intelligence" or "intellect," it is the mental function whereby knowledge becomes certain or determinate. *Buddhi* is a contracted form of *jñānaśakti,* now restricted to the individual's capacity for knowledge.

Ahaṁkāra ("I-maker") conditions the *puruṣa*-consciousness as the ego, with a subjective sense of self as *I,* an objectified sense of self as *me,* and an appropriative impulse expressed through *mine.* By identifying the Self with things that are not-self—with mind, emotions, body, and their associated experiences—*ahaṁkāra* reduces Śiva's unfettered freedom and joy to the ego-defined condition, held hostage both to external circumstances and to the mind's restless thoughts and ever-shifting moods. The Trikaśāstra regards *ahaṁkāra* as a finite expression of *icchāśakti,* the unbounded divine will.

To *manas* (16) belong the functions of perceiving, conceptualizing, and reasoning. *Manas* receives sensory information from the surrounding world but does not come to a final determination. It can be called the faculty of indeterminate knowledge, in distinction to *buddhi,* the faculty of determinate knowledge. *Manas* is a reduced version of *kriyāśakti,* the divine power to assume any form at will for its own enjoyment. According to Indian theories of epistemology, *manas* assumes the forms and attributes of whatever it perceives through the five sensory faculties (*jñānendriyas*).

The *jñānendriyas* are not the physical sense organs but the powers of perception that work through them. From subtler to grosser, the five principles of perception are hearing (*śrotra*) (17), touch (*tvak*) (18), sight (*cakṣu*) (19), taste (*rasanā*) (20), and smell (*ghrāṇa*) (21). Because they gather perceptual information from the exterior world and transmit it to *manas*, their function can be described as one of "data in."

The function of "response out" belongs to the five capacities of activity (*karmendriyas*). These again are not the physical organs but the powers that work through them and enable the embodied soul to interact with the external world. They are speech (*vāc*) (22), handling (*pāṇi*) (23), locomotion (*pāda*) (24), excretion (*pāyu*) (25), and procreation (*upastha*) (26).

Five subtle elements (*tanmātras*), sharing the characteristics of both the subjective and objective sides of experience, act as the interface between the senses and the material world. Imperceptible in themselves, these primary elements are the stimuli for perception: sound (*śabda*) (27) for hearing, touch (*sparśa*) (28) for feeling, form and color (*rūpa*) (29) for seeing, taste (*rasa*) (30) for tasting, and odor (*gandha*) (31) for smelling.

From the *tanmātras* evolve the five gross elements (*mahābhūtas*)—space (*ākāśa*) (32), air (*vāyu*) (33), fire (*tejas*) (34), water (*ap*) (35), and earth (*pṛthivī*) (36). Their order reflects the number of sensory faculties that can perceive them. *Ākāśa* can be inferred on the basis of sound. *Vāyu* can be heard and felt. *Tejas* can be heard, felt, and seen. *Ap* can be heard, felt, seen, and tasted. *Pṛthivī* can be heard, felt, seen, tasted, and smelled.

The thirty-six *tattvas* explain how the universe and the individual being alike come into existence, how they are constituted, and how they function. From Śiva's standpoint manifestation is a process of contraction (*saṁkoca*). At every stage consciousness contracts itself further and grows denser, finally congealing into solid matter. From the *jīva's* standpoint, various spiritual practices can reverse the process and retrace the course. As human consciousness expands, it encounters subtler and subtler states until finally reaching the recognition of its true identity as the infinite Śiva.

Trika Śaivism and *yoga*

If the "proto-Śiva" artifacts recovered from Mohenjo-daro and Harappa represent a figure engaged in yogic practice, the tradition of *yoga* can be documented as far back as four and a half millennia. If that figure is the deity now known as Śiva, the link between *yoga* and Śaivism is equally old. From the earliest indications *yoga* appears to be an essential component of Śaiva thought and practice.

Tracing the joint development of *yoga* and Śaivism in an unbroken trajectory is impossible, owing to large gaps in the historical record. Moreover, the association of *yoga* and Śaivism is by no means exclusive. The Sāṁkhya also demonstrates a longstanding connection with *yoga* that precedes the formulations of the separate but closely related classical Yoga and Sāṁkhya *darśanas*. A passage in the Mokṣadharma section of the Mahābhārata (12.349.64–68), composed between the fifth century BCE and the first century CE, names the Veda, the Sāṁkhya, the Yoga, the Vaiṣṇava Pañcarātra, and the Śaiva Pāśupata as five distinct religions, but as a spiritual technology *yoga* figures in all of them.

In the much earlier Vedic tradition, the Ṛgveda's hymn to the *keśin* (1.136) celebrates the long-haired ascetic wanderer, intimate with Rudra, and provides the oldest known literary link between *yoga* and Śaivism. In the lineage of the Kṛṣṇa Yajurveda, the Taittirīyopaniṣad (2.4.1) employs the word *yoga* for the first time—in an analytical inquiry into the five sheathes encasing the innermost Self. In the same lineage the Kaṭhopaniṣad presents a more developed account of yogic practice. A still more systematic presentation follows in the Śvetāśvataropaniṣad's second chapter. Still later the Maitryopaniṣad (6.18–19) defines *yoga* as a sixfold practice, somewhat closer to Patañjali's definitive statement in the *Yogasūtra.* But even before Patañjali's final systematization of an eightfold (*aṣṭāṅga*) methodology, the Śaiva *Pāśupatasūtra* is found already to contain an exposition of a highly complex and highly structured *yoga* with eight limbs or means.

Yoga continues to make its presence felt in the Śaivāgama. A case in point is the Vijñānabhairava, a classic nondualistic treatise that describes one hundred twelve methods for uniting human consciousness with the divine reality. This Tantric *yoga* also infuses the thought and practices of nondualistic Kashmir Śaivism through its foundational scripture, the *Śivasūtra,* best described as a manual on the *yoga* of the supreme identity of *jīva* and Śiva.

Abhinavagupta, as a practitioner of *yoga,* was familiar with a wide variety of Śaiva yogic traditions as well as Patañjali's system.

However, he discounted the value of Patañjali's first three limbs—*yama, niyama,* and *āsana*—saying that they relate to the body and are only indirect aids to concentration. Abhinavagupta's favored methodology, presented in the *Tantrāloka* (3.101), consists of the six disciplines specified in the Maitryopaniṣad—control of the breath (*prāṇāyāma*), withdrawal of the senses (*pratyāhāra*), meditation (*dhyāna*), concentration (*dhāraṇā*), contemplative inquiry (*tarka*), and absorption (*samādhi*). These are, of course, Patañjali's remaining five limbs plus *tarka*. In regard to *tarka* ("logic"), Abhinavagupta contends that *sattarka* ("true logic") is the most important aspect of *yoga*—the "only direct means for realization of the Ultimate." Unlike ordinary logic, *sattarka* does not deal with empirical knowledge but with spiritual awareness. Only when *buddhi* has risen above concern with anything phenomenal does *sattarka* emerge; its unique capacity is to "uproot the apparent distinction between subject and object." Accordingly Abhinavagupta equates *sattarka* to the *sadvidyātattva,* that level in the ascent or expansion of consciousness where *aham* and *idam* become reunited.[182] In his analysis *sattarka* brings one to apprehend the identity of the individual with the universal; it is therefore the true logic that enables consciousness to pierce the veil of ignorance through which it has appeared in objective manifestations and to recognize its own nature as purely subjective.[183] Finally, consistent with Trika's theistic absolutism (*īśvarādvayavāda*), Abhinavagupta not only defines *sattarka* as the knowledge of universal oneness (*sattarkaḥ śuddhavidyaiva*) but adds that it results from divine grace (*sā cecchā parameśituḥ*).[184]

Interpreting the Śvetāśvataropaniṣad

Certain items of vocabulary, already discussed, are often cited to demonstrate the Śvetāśvataropaniṣad's Sāṁkhya leanings, but their evidence has proven less than persuasive (see pp. 18–19). The term *puruṣa,* for example, occurs frequently throughout the Upaniṣads and earlier Vedic texts with a broad range of meaning. It appears nine times in the Śvetāśvataropaniṣad, variously denoting the individual soul, the human being, and the Supreme Being in both transcendental and immanent aspects, but no usage accords with the later technical definition of classical Sāṁkhya. *Prakṛti,* that other characteristic Sāṁkhya term, occurs only once, and then in the generic sense of "nature," which is then equated with the Vedantic *māyā*. The results for other "Sāṁkhya" terms—*avyakta, kevala, guṇa, tattva, pradhāna,* and *sāṁkhya* itself—are no more conclusive. Most often these words occur in a context far removed from Sāṁkhya doctrine. A few shared terms cannot reconcile Sāṁkhya's nontheistic dualism with the Upaniṣad's theistic nondualism.

Other items of vocabulary point more convincingly toward the Śvetāśvataropaniṣad's Śaiva character. Apart from the decisive evidence of the theonyms already discussed (see pp. 30–31), the text makes use of several terms with decidedly Śaiva associations. To mention only three, the word *śakti* appears in no Upaniṣad until the Śvetāśvatara, where it is present both by itself and in compounds. The adjective *śiva* also marks its first usage in any Upaniṣad, occurring seven times. *Pāśa,* a common Śaiva term for a fetter that binds the soul, appears eight times in the course of the text.

Kṣetrajña ("knower of the field") occurs once as a metaphor for the individual sentient soul. Often cited as a proto-Sāṁkhya term that was replaced by *puruṣa* in the classical philosophy,[185] it continued long afterward to be part of the Trika vocabulary.[186] A word such as this invites us to consider that throughout the millennia of Indian history, many strands of ritualistic action, interior contemplation, and metaphysical speculation have converged, intertwined, cross-fertilized, and again diverged, continually weaving an ever richer tapestry from the inexhaustible breadth and depth of religious, spiritual, and philosophical possibility. The Vedānta, Sāṁkhya, Yoga, Śaiva, and other systems are all products of that vibrant spiritual environment. It is that environment which gave birth to the Śvetāśvataropaniṣad and also provides the context in which it should be appreciated.

The text is a middle-period Upaniṣad that can be assigned reasonably to the sixth or fifth century BCE. Its authorship is attributed to the *ṛṣi* Śvetāśvatara, about whom almost nothing is known. His historicity can neither be confirmed nor denied. The text that bears his name belongs to a lineage firmly grounded in the early Ṛgvedic tradition and the slightly later, Śaiva-leaning Taittirīya texts of the Kṛṣṇa Yajurveda. The Upaniṣad's Śaiva orientation clearly shines forth not only through its names for the Divine, all associated with the deity later called Śiva, but also through its distinctive philosophical point of view, an emerging theistic nondualism that anticipates the unique *īśvarādvayavāda* of the later Trika Śaivism. At the same time, as a major and authoritative Upaniṣad, it embodies the Vedānta in the broadest sense of that term and serves as a foundational text of the later philosophical system of the same name.

We must keep in mind that the Vedānta, Yoga, and Sāṁkhya *darśanas* as well as the Trikaśāstra were formalized a thousand or more years after the *ṛṣi* Śvetāśvatara articulated his spiritual vision and prescribed the means for others to attain it. Neither he nor any other seer would give voice to the most intimate and sacred dimension of spiritual experience with the idea that others should misunderstand it or make it a matter of contention. As we approach our text, our method should be neither to accept any one of the philosophies as the singular guide nor to exclude any other but to consider which provides the best fit in a given instance. The best fit is the one that produces the greatest clarity and insight with the greatest simplicity of means. No doubt the Vedānta, the Sāṁkhya, the Yoga, and the Trika *darśanas* all have a role to play in elucidating Śvetāśvatara's teachings, but none can claim exclusivity.

For several centuries the Vedānta has been the dominant voice in the exegesis of this Upaniṣad, with contentious notes added here and there by the Sāṁkhya. Now Śaiva teaching can add a new frame of reference and afford a fresh look at a text that for too long has been branded puzzling, eclectic, even incoherent. The perspective of the Trikaśāstra brings much-needed clarity, insight, and simplicity to difficult passages, where other interpretations have failed to convince. It silences the unjust charge that this Upaniṣad is a patchwork of disparate ideas and contradictions. In the light of Śaiva tradition the text becomes a coherent, crystal-clear exposition of nondualistic thought and yogic practice, expressed with elegant simplicity.

The Śvetāśvataropaniṣad is at once highly conservative and radically innovative. It quotes liberally from the ancient Saṁhitās of the Ṛgveda and Yajurveda even while containing the seeds of later Sāṁkhya, Yoga, and Vedānta thought and anticipating some unique features of Trika Śaivism. From its opening verse, bursting with the perennial questions of human existence, it sets a tone of lively inquiry. In the course of six lessons, the *ṛṣi* Śvetāśvatara eloquently articulates an entirely workable approach to spiritual life and tells his listeners what to expect. He celebrates the divine presence in and through all of creation and portrays the world as the manifest glory of the even greater divine reality from which it comes. The hallmark of his world-view is the simultaneous immanence and transcendence of that divine reality, which he sometimes chooses to call God. Śvetāśvatara's message is the joyous utterance of a soul who has known "beyond all darkness this great Person, effulgent like the sun." It is an experience he wishes passionately to share.

ŚVETĀŚVATAROPANIṢAD

CHAPTER ONE

1 *Oṁ*. [The sage Śvetāśvatara said:] Seekers of the higher knowledge ask: What is the cause [of this universe]? Is it Brahman? From what are we born? By what do we live? In what is our permanence? O knowers of Brahman, what law governs us, whose lives run their course through happiness and all the rest?

2 Time, the inherent nature of things, design, chance, the elements, primordial matter, individual awareness—these are to be considered as the cause. But not even a combination of these can be the cause, for they are themselves effects. Nor can the individual soul [be the cause], for that also is not sovereign but subject to happiness and misery.

3 Entering into deep meditation, the seekers realized within themselves the power of the effulgent Self that lies hidden by its own effects. It is he who presides, purely One, over all those possible causes from time to the individual soul.

4 Him [they envisioned as a wheel] with a single rim and three bands, sixteen ends, fifty spokes, twenty counterspokes, and six octads. Bound [to its axle] by a single fastener of manifold forms, it moves along three different roads, driven by a single delusion with a twofold cause.

5 [Or, they said,] we think of him [as a river] with five currents. Its sharp bends are the five elements, its waves are the five vital forces, and its origin is the mind—the source of fivefold perception. It has

five whirlpools, and its tumbling rapids are the five kinds of misery. Flowing around five obstructions, it takes on countless aspects.

6 On this vast wheel of Brahman, wherein everything lives and dies, the soul revolves, thinking itself different from the animating force. Yet blessed by the knowledge of that very Brahman, it attains immortality.

7 What they praise is indeed the supreme Brahman, the firm support, the imperishable One. In it exists the universe. Here, realizing it within, the knowers of Brahman become merged in Brahman. Intent on it as their highest goal, they are freed from rebirth.

8 The Lord supports all this universe, wherein the perishable and the imperishable, the manifest and the unmanifest, are joined together. Forgetful of his lordship and thinking himself the enjoyer, the Self becomes bound. Knowing that effulgent being, one is freed from all fetters.

9 The two, the [all-]knowing [Lord] and the not-knowing [soul], are unborn [from all eternity]; the ruler and the ruled are both unborn. There is one other without beginning, intent on relating the enjoyer to that which is to be enjoyed, even while the infinite Self, though appearing as the universe, acts not at all. When this triad is fully known, it is seen to be Brahman.

10 That which is perishable is matter. That which is immortal and imperishable is Hara, the one God [who] rules over perishable matter and the soul. By constantly meditating on him, uniting with him, and becoming that reality, one at last attains the cessation of all illusion.

11 When God is known, all fetters fall away. When life's afflictions waste away, birth and death come to an end. By constantly meditating on him and going beyond the sense of individuality, one attains the third state, that of universal sovereignty; in the One alone all desires are fulfilled.

12 This is to be known as abiding eternally within oneself. Beyond this there is nothing further to be known. When the enjoyer rightly understands the enjoyed and the means of enjoyment, all this is declared to be the threefold Brahman.

13 As fire's visible flame lies latent and unseen in wood, never absent and ever poised to shine forth when two kindling sticks are rubbed together, likewise with the friction of *Oṁ*, the Self within the body is revealed.

14 By making one's own embodied awareness the lower kindling stick and *Oṁ* the upper, and by generating friction through constant meditation, one should see God as one sees the once-hidden fire.

15 As oil in sesame seeds, as butter in milk, as water beneath a dry riverbed, and as fire in wood, so also is this Self grasped in the self of one who discerns it through sincerity and ardor.

16 As butter in milk, [one discerns] the Self as all-pervading [when it is] fixed upon, firmly fixed upon through the ardor for Self-knowledge. Concerning Brahman, that is the highest teaching.

CHAPTER TWO

1 First joining the mind and holy thoughts for the sake of reaching the truth, Savitṛ perceived the light of fire and brought it forth from the earth.

2 With mind intent, we [are inspired] by Savitṛ, who shines in the sun, to attain the highest bliss through his power.

3 Those who would aspire to supreme bliss, the bright-shining Savitṛ impels heavenward, harnessing their senses with the mind and thought.

4 They concentrate the mind and harness the thoughts, those wise ones, inspired by the great wise One. He alone, who knows the way, has ordained the means. Great be the praise of the effulgent Savitṛ!

5 With adoration I join [mind and thought] to the most excellent Brahman; may my praise thus go forth along the path of the wise. Hear, all you children of immortal bliss, who have ascended to heavenly abodes!

6 Where fire is kindled, where breath is controlled, where bliss overflows, there true understanding arises.

7 Through Savitṛ, who sets all things in motion, may one delight in the eternal Brahman. Make your abode there; your fulfillment will not bind you at all.

8 Holding the body steady with chest, neck, and head aligned, then mentally directing the senses into the heart, one who is wise may cross over every fear-laden current on the raft of Brahman.

9 Holding the movements of the limbs in check and controlling the vital forces in the body, one should breath gently through the nostrils. The wise one, always attentive, should restrain his mind as he would a chariot yoked to unruly horses.

10 In a clean and level place, free of pebbles, fire, and dust, free of noise and dampness, calming to the mind, and not displeasing to the eye—here, sheltered from the wind and retiring into solitude, one should concentrate the mind.

11 Mist, smoke, the sun, wind, fire, fireflies, lightning, crystals, and the moon—these apparitions precede the revelation of Brahman in *yoga*.

12 When the subtle essences of the five elements—earth, water, fire, air, and space—are revealed in the perception of *yoga*, then one attains a body made of the fire of divine union; for him there is neither sickness, old age, nor death.

13 They say that the first signs of progress in *yoga* are a sense of bodily lightness, health, freedom from craving, a clear complexion, a beautiful voice, a pleasant odor, and scant excretions.

14 Just as a mirror, coated with dirt, again gleams brightly when well cleaned, so the embodied soul, perceiving its own true nature, becomes One—completely fulfilled and free from sorrow.

15 Through the reality of the Self, radiant as a lamp within the heart, one who is established in meditation knows the reality of Brahman as unborn [and ever being], constant, and untouched by anything within the creation; knowing that effulgent being, one is freed from all fetters.

16 This same divine being pervades all directions, everywhere; he himself is the first born, yet he abides within the womb. It is he that

is born, he that will be born. He stands turned toward [all] living beings, facing in all directions.

17 To the effulgent being who is in fire and water, who has entered into all of creation, who is in the plants and trees, to that deity, salutations again and again!

CHAPTER THREE

1 He who is One, the master of [*māyā's*] net, rules by his sovereign powers; by his sovereign powers he rules over all the worlds at their coming forth and throughout their existence, he who is One alone. They who know this become immortal.

2 Rudra is surely One! They stand present before no second who would rule these worlds by sovereign powers; he stands turned toward [all] living beings. Having projected all the worlds, he withdraws them at the end of time—he, the guardian.

3 His eyes everywhere and his faces everywhere, his arms everywhere and his feet everywhere, the one God forges with arms and bellows, causing heaven and earth to be born.

4 He who is the source and substance of the gods is Rudra, lord of the universe and great seer. In the beginning he brought forth Hiraṇyagarbha. May he endow us with clear understanding!

5 The gracious form that is yours, O Rudra, neither terrifies nor bodes any ill. With that most beneficent form, O Mountain-Dweller, shine brightly upon us!

6 The arrow that you hold ready in hand, O Mountain-Dweller, make it propitious. Protector of the Mountains, do not injure man or beast.

7 Higher than that is the supreme Brahman, who expands forth as every kind of creature, yet remains hidden in all beings. He alone encompasses the universe; those who know the Lord become immortal.

8 I know beyond all darkness this great Person, effulgent like the

sun. Knowing him alone, one goes beyond death. There is no other way by which to go.

9 There is nothing higher or lower than he; there is no one smaller or greater than he. Like a tree, immovable, the One abides in his own glory. By that Person is all this world filled.

10 Far higher than the creator is the formless One, beyond affliction. They who know this become immortal, but the rest get only misery.

11 All faces, heads, and necks belong to him who dwells deep in the heart of all beings. Therefore the glorious Lord is all-pervading, universally present, and gracious.

12 Truly the great Lord is the innermost Person, who inspires the mind to attain to this absolute purity; he is the ruler and the imperishable light.

13 This Person, the size of a thumb, is the inner Self, ever established in the hearts of living beings—the lord of humankind, corresponding within to the heart and mind. They who know this become immortal.

14 Having a thousand heads, a thousand eyes, and a thousand feet, and surrounding the earth on all sides, this Person extends beyond it by ten fingers' breadth.

15 What has been and what will be and what grows up by food, the Person is truly all this—and the lord of immortality as well.

16 With hands and feet on every side, with eyes and heads and faces everywhere, possessing ears on every side, it stands in the world, encompassing all.

17 Resplendent with the qualities of all the senses, from all the senses [it stands] removed—the power ruling over all, the great refuge of all.

18 The spirit embodied in the city of nine gates moves outward, to and fro—the master of the whole world, of the immovable and the moving.

19 Grasping and moving swiftly though without hands and feet, he sees without eyes, he hears without ears. Whatever is to be known, he knows; yet of him there is no knower. They call him the foremost, the great Person.

20 Smaller than small, greater than great, the Self is established in the heart of every creature. Beholding him who is untouched by desire, one becomes free of sorrow; by the creator's grace he beholds the glory that is the Lord.

21 I know this ageless, primordial Self of all, diffused everywhere by its power of all-pervasiveness, whom the expounders of Brahman declare birthless, whom they indeed declare eternal.

CHAPTER FOUR

1 He who is One and without color brings forth many colors in many ways by his own power and by his own design: in the end the universe comes apart—and in the beginning the effulgent God. May he endow us with clear understanding!

2 That indeed is Agni, that is Āditya, that is Vāyu, that is also Candramās; that is indeed the brightness, that is Brahman, that is the Āpaḥ, that is Prajāpati.

3 You are woman, you are man, you are youth and maiden too; aged, you totter along with a staff; taking birth, you face in every direction.

4 You are the dark blue butterfly, the green parrot with red eyes, the thundercloud, the seasons, and the seas. Without beginning you simply *are,* pervading all, you from whom all worlds are born.

5 Coupling with a she-goat of red, white, and black who gives birth to many offspring like herself, a he-goat takes his pleasure. From her whose purpose is enjoyment another he-goat abstains.

6 Two fair-winged birds, inseparable companions, cling fast to the very same tree. One of them eats the sweet fruit while the other, not eating, looks on.

7 On that same tree the individual soul, overwhelmed by powerlessness and bewildered, grieves. When it beholds the other—the contented master and his glory—it is freed from sorrow.

8 He who knows not in which syllable of the sacred verse all the gods in highest heaven repose, what will he do with the sacred verse? They alone who know it, they themselves abide in it.

9 The sacred verses, the sacrifices, the rituals, the observances, what has been, and what will be, and what the Vedas declare, [all these abide in this syllable]. From this the lord of *māyā* sends forth all this world in which the soul is confined by *māyā*.

10 One should know nature surely to be *māyā* and the Great Lord to be the lord of *māyā*, but also this whole world to be filled with beings who are his parts.

11 The One in whom all this world comes together and dissolves, the One who dwells in every kind of being—realizing that beneficent, resplendent, and praiseworthy Lord, one fully and forever goes to peace.

12 He who is the source and substance of the gods is Rudra, lord of the universe and great seer. He saw Hiraṇyagarbha being born. May he endow us with clear understanding!

13 He who is the ruler of the gods, in whom the worlds rest, he who rules over the two-footed and the four-footed creatures—what [other] god shall we worship with oblation?

14 He is subtler than the subtlest, in the midst of the unformed the creator of everything, assuming many forms. He alone encompasses the universe; knowing that auspicious being, one fully and forever goes to peace.

15 He is surely the protector of the world in time, the lord of the universe, in all beings hidden, in whom the seers and gods are absorbed in meditation. Knowing him alone, one cuts through the bonds of death.

16 Knowing the auspicious one hidden in all beings like the most subtle essence of clarified butter, knowing that effulgent being who alone encompasses the universe, one is freed from all fetters.

17 This god, the maker of all things, the great Self, is ever established in the hearts of living beings, corresponding within to the heart, intelligence, and mind. They who know this become immortal.

18 When the darkness of ignorance is no more, then there is neither day nor night, neither existence nor nonexistence, only the auspicious One alone. That is the imperishable, that is the glory of Savitṛ, and from that the ancient wisdom has come forth.

19 Not above, not across, not in the middle has anyone fully grasped him; there is no measure of him whose name is great glory.

20 His form stands not in the range of sight; no one sees him with the eye. They who with the heart and mind know him as abiding in the heart, they become immortal.

21 Because you are unborn, one who is fearful takes refuge in you. O Rudra, by that which is your benevolent face protect me always!

22 Harm us not in respect to our children and grandchildren, our lives, our cattle, our horses. Slay not our heroes in anger, O Rudra. Bearing oblations, we invoke you always!

CHAPTER FIVE

1 In the imperishable, infinite, and absolute Brahman, wherein both knowledge and ignorance lie hidden, surely ignorance is the perishable and knowledge is the immortal; but he who presides over knowledge and ignorance is [yet] another.

2 The One who dwells in every kind of being, in all visible forms and in all their sources, is he who in the beginning contains the red-gold seer, begotten by his thoughts, and witnesses him being born.

3 Spreading out every single net, each one differently, into this field of action, this God [then] gathers them in. Moreover, having issued forth [all this by acting as] the lords of creation, thus the Lord, the great Self, holds sovereignty over all.

4 Just as the sun shines above, below, and across, illuminating all

directions, so the glorious God, worthy of worship, presides as One over all his manifestations.

5 And just as he who is the source of everything develops his own nature and transforms all that is potential, he it is who presides as One over this entire universe and distributes all its [diverse] qualities.

6 That [Brahman] is hidden in the Upaniṣads, which among the Vedas are to be kept secret; Brahmā knows it as the source of expansion. The gods and seers of old who knew it became absorbed in it and truly immortal.

7 [But when] possessed of qualities, he who becomes the doer of action that bears fruit experiences the results of whatever he has done. That living soul, of manifold form and three qualities and three paths, roams about according to his own deeds.

8 He who is the size of a thumb and brilliant like the sun becomes endowed with intention and a sense of individuality. Through the attributes of mind and body as well is he seen as distinct, in fact as no larger than the point of an awl.

9 The individual soul should be recognized as a fraction of the hundredth part of the tip of a hair, again divided a hundred times—yet it partakes of infinity.

10 It is neither female nor male, nor is it even neuter; whatever body it assumes, with that is it associated.

11 [As] the body lives and grows through an abundance of food and drink, [so] the dweller in the body, through its intentions, involvements, outlooks, and delusions, assumes a succession of forms and conditions according to its actions.

12 Indeed many forms, gross and subtle, does the embodied soul choose according to its own merits. Driven by its involvement with the effects of its actions and their particular qualities, it is seen as greatly inferior.

13 [But the Self is] without beginning or end, in the midst of the unformed the creator of everything, assuming many forms. He

alone encompasses the universe; knowing that effulgent being, one is freed from all fetters.

14 [The Self] who is to be grasped intuitively, who is called bodiless, the auspicious maker of existence and nonexistence, the effulgent being who brings forth the creation and its parts—they who know him lay aside the smallness of individuality.

CHAPTER SIX

1 Some thinkers speak of the inherent nature of things [as the cause of the universe]; others, of likewise muddled mind, speak of time. But it is the power and glory of the effulgent God here in the world by which this wheel of Brahman revolves.

2 Ever enveloping all this world, he is the intelligent maker of time, the omniscient possessor of the forces of creation. At his direction this work of creation surely unfolds. It is to be reflected upon as earth, water, fire, air, and space.

3 After effecting the work of creation—having joined together with each stage of manifestation by one, two, three, or eight, and with time and the trifling qualities of mind and body—he again turns away from it.

4 He who undertakes the activities associated with conditions [again] undoes all the states of creation. When they are no more, what he has wrought is destroyed; when his handiwork perishes, he endures, different from it, in his true nature.

5 When he who has the universe as his form, who is to be glorified as the essence of existence, has first been revered as the effulgent being abiding in one's own consciousness, he, the beginning and the conjoiner of elements, is himself seen as beyond the three times and without parts.

6 When the lord of blessedness, who brings goodness and drives away evil, is known to abide in oneself as the immortal support of all, he by whom this expansive universe revolves is seen as higher and other than the parts of the world-tree and the aspects of time.

7 May we know the effulgent lord of the world who is to be adored, the Great Lord supreme among lords, the God supreme among gods, the Sovereign supreme among sovereigns.

8 He has no need to act, nor any instrument of action; no one is seen as his equal or superior. It is heard that his supreme power is indeed manifold, a natural expression of his intelligence and might.

9 He has no master in the world nor ruler nor any distinctive mark. He is the cause, the Lord of the lord of the senses, and he has neither progenitor nor overlord.

10 Like a spider with the filaments of its web, the one God surrounds himself with the things produced spontaneously from his unevolved nature. May he grant us entry into Brahman!

11 The one God, hidden in all beings and pervading everything, is the soul of all creatures. Overseeing the universe, dwelling in all beings, he is the witness, the perceiver, and the Absolute devoid of qualities.

12 He who makes manifold the single seed is the one master of the actionless many. Steady are they who discover him abiding in themselves; to them belongs constant happiness and not to others.

13 He who fulfills all desires is the Eternal among the eternals, the Intelligent among the intelligent, the One among the many, the cause to be discovered through observing and directing the mind. Knowing that effulgent being, one is freed from all fetters.

14 There the sun shines not, nor the moon and stars, nor does the lightning illumine, much less this earthly fire. He alone shining, everything shines after him. By his light all this universe shines.

15 The one supreme Self in the midst of this world, he alone is the fire submerged in water. Knowing him alone, one goes beyond death. There is no other way by which to go.

16 He, the all-doing, the all-knowing, is the self-originated one; he is the intelligent maker of time, the omniscient possessor of the forces of creation, the master of the natural world and the human

soul. He is the cause of bondage to continuing existence and of release from the soul's wandering.

17 As such, he, the immortal, abiding as lord, is the all-knowing and everywhere-present guardian of this world; there is no other cause for his ruling [than he himself] who is the master of this world forever and ever.

18 Longing for liberation, I take refuge in that very God who shines by his own intelligence, who creates Brahmā in the beginning and who indeed bestows on him the Vedas.

19 [I take refuge in him], the supreme bridge to immortality, who is undivided, actionless, tranquil, faultless, and untainted, like a fire that has ceased its blazing.

20 Apart from knowing the effulgent God, there will be an end to misery only when humankind can roll up the sky like a piece of leather.

21 Śvetāśvatara, knowing Brahman itself by the power of his austerities and by the grace of God, thus imparted to the ascetics the highest means of purification, in which the multitude of seers rightly take delight.

22 The supreme secret, imparted in the Vedānta in a former age, is not to be given to one of unsubdued passions nor, again, to one who is neither a son nor a disciple.

23 To the one who has supreme devotion to God, and as to God so to the teacher, to that great-souled one shine forth these matters that have been related; to that great-souled one they shine forth!

प्रथमोऽध्यायः

CHAPTER ONE

1

ॐ ॥ ब्रह्मवादिनो वदन्ति ।

किं कारणं ब्रह्म कुतः स्म जाता

जीवाम केन क्व च सम्प्रतिष्ठा ।

अधिष्ठिताः केन सुखेतरेषु

वर्तामहे ब्रह्मविदो व्यवस्थाम् ॥ १ ॥

Oṁ. brahmavādino vadanti /
kiṁ kāraṇaṁ brahma kutaḥ sma jātā jīvāma kena kva ca sampratiṣṭhā /
adhiṣṭhitāḥ kena sukhetareṣu vartāmahe brahmavido vyavasthām //

1. [The sage Śvetāśvatara said:] Seekers of the higher knowledge ask: What is the cause [of this universe]? Is it Brahman? From what are we born? By what do we live? In what is our permanence? O knowers of Brahman, what law governs us, whose lives run their course through happiness and all the rest?

Imagine the scene. About two and a half thousand years ago, in the forest, under the shade of a tree, a sage sits amid a small group of disciples who have gathered to hear him speak on the nature of reality. He is called Śvetāśvatara, not a name but an epithet meaning "he who has superior white mules." As a metaphor for a person of purified senses, it indicates that the holy man is qualified to teach the higher spiritual knowledge.

Śvetāśvatara explains that it is natural human curiosity to wonder where we come from, what we are doing here, where we are headed, and if our lives really mean anything. These are, of course, profound questions, the bigger questions of life that especially interest the thinkers and spiritual seekers among us. How did the world come into existence? Why are we born? Do our lives have any meaning beyond what we do from day to day? Amid the constant changes we witness and undergo along our journey from birth to maturity, through decline to inevitable death, do we ourselves have any permanence? As long as we live in this world, must we remain in the grip of the never-ending fluctuation between happiness and misery and everything in between? Is there something that governs life's ups and downs?

We are little different from the people who lived thousands of years ago and asked those very questions. They too observed each new dawn and day's inevitable fading into night. They witnessed the passing seasons and the ongoing cycles of life and felt all the joy and sorrow that we also feel. Beyond the natural forces of thunder, fire, sunlight, water, and wind, beyond the majesty of the vaulted sky and the expansive earth, beyond their emotional and intellectual responses to the world around them, they recognized that there lay a profound mystery. The universe itself *must* hold a greater meaning.

The early observers noticed that all activity appears linked in an endless chain of cause and effect. Logically, every effect has a cause, and every effect becomes the cause of something further. Beyond this seemingly unending succession, they wondered if the universe itself can be traced back to a single first cause which is itself uncaused.

What is the cause? This opening question posed by the seer immediately hints at the Śaiva character that will become explicit in the Upaniṣad's names for the Divine. Although this Upaniṣad is older than any known sectarian form of Śaivism, it belongs to a Vedic tradition with Śaiva leanings and appears to have been composed not long before the earliest Śaiva sect arose. That sect, the Pāśupata, takes its name from Paśupati, the Lord of Beasts, an earlier name of Śiva that harks back to the Atharvaveda. The two components, *paśu* and *pati*, signify in turn the bound soul and the controlling Lord. More abstractly these terms represent the effect (*kārya*) and the cause (*kāraṇa*)—the first two categories of Pāśupata Śaivism, *kāraṇa* being the first.[1] It is significant that Śvetāśvatara's initial utterance concerning the mystery of our existence is *kiṁ kāraṇam*—What is the cause? The idea of an uncaused cause played a very important role in Pāśupata metaphysics.[2] That is not to imply that Śvetāśvatara anticipated the non-Vedic Pāśupatajñāna or would have subscribed to its dualistic views. In fact, his Upaniṣad expounds the philosophy of nonduality (*advaita*). Later, when Pāśupata doctrine was reformed by Lakulīśa and brought closer to acceptable Vedic norms, it became a philosophy of unity-in-multiplicity (*dvaitādvaita*), retaining cause and effect as its first two categories and using the terms *pati, kāraṇa,* and Brahman synonymously to signify the divine reality.[3] Similarly in the Śvetāśvataropaniṣad, where immediately after broaching the matter of cause (*kāraṇa*), the seer asks, Is it Brahman?

Could the uncaused cause be Brahman? The seers whose teachings have come down to us in the form of the Upaniṣads most often speak of Brahman as absolute oneness—the self-existent and indefinable unity of consciousness to be attained through right knowledge. The basic meaning of the word *brahman* is "growth, expansion, a swelling of the spirit or soul."[4] The expansion of the individual soul toward the transcendental One was for the ancient seekers a matter not just of philosophical pondering but of their own experience. Similarly the self-expression of Brahman as the universe was an accepted part of their world-view, as the Chāndogyopaniṣad (3.14.1) so effectively states: "All this [universe] is truly Brahman (*sarvaṁ khalv idam brahma*); from that all things originate, in that they dissolve, by that are they sustained; in tranquility one should meditate on that." This pronouncement tells us that the highest thought on which the human mind can be fixed is that of a being which is the cause, the goal, and the support of the universe. That is Brahman, the eternal subject apart from which the universe has no existence.

Śvetāśvatara will build on the teaching of his revered forebears, often speaking of Brahman as the Absolute, just as the older *ṛṣis* did. At other times his idea of Brahman will take on a personal warmth, and we will sense that he is describing a glorious sovereign whom he also calls God (*deva*), Lord (*īśa, bhagavān*), Hara, or Rudra. That God can be reached not only by right knowledge (*jñāna*) but also through devotion (*bhakti*) and divine grace (*prasāda*).

If the opening *mantra* hints at this Upaniṣad's Śaiva character, it also indicates some distance from the later Sāṁkhya view of life. The clue is subtle, most often overlooked, but nevertheless powerful. The seer asks, What law governs us, whose lives run their course through happiness and all the rest? The phrase "through happiness and all the rest" (*sukhetareṣu*) has been translated previously as "in pain or in pleasure,"[5] "in ... joy and sorrow,"[6] "in pains and pleasures,"[7] "of happiness and misery,"[8] "of happiness and its opposite,"[9] "in pleasure or in pain,"[10] "in pleasures and other than pleasures (pains),"[11] "joy and its opposite,"[12] "about pain and pleasure,"[13] "in pleasure and in pain,"[14] "in joy and sorrow,"[15] "in joys and their opposite."[16] All but three of the cited translations employ the words *pain, misery,* or *sorrow,* but in fact no such word appears in the Sanskrit. *Sukhetareṣu* means "in happiness"—or more broadly, "in existential well-being" (*sukha*)—"and in all the rest (*itareṣu*)." This phrase bears important implications. It does not mention suffering (*duḥkha*) explicitly, and that in itself distances Śvetāśvatara's teachings from the Sāṁkhya tendencies of his time. Sāṁkhya, like Buddhism, emphasizes the suffering inherent in life, so much so that its definitive text, Īśvarakṛṣṇa's *Sāṁkhyakārikā,* opens with the word *duḥkha* and presents its philosophy as a way to permanent release from this universal, pain-laden human condition. Śvetāśvatara's world-view, grounded in that of the earlier Upaniṣads, is more life-affirming. That is not to say that the seer denies the presence of suffering in the world. It is implied in the compound *sukhetareṣu,* literally "happiness (joy, pleasure, well-being) *and all the rest.*" But the seer assures us that life is not a polarized experience of two extremes. That idea would be more clearly expressed by the term *sukhetarayoḥ,* which Śvetāśvatara does not use. Human life involves both happiness and misery, to be sure, but embraces the entire range of experience in between. There is no pessimism in Śvetāśvatara's phrasing, rather an acknowledgement of the richness and wonder of existence. That richness and wonder are of no concern to Sāṁkhya. Although that system provides an incisive analysis of our experience in the world, it has little interest in satisfying human curiosity or in making the world meaningful in its own right. Sāṁkhya's sole purpose is to release the conscious being (*jña, puruṣa*) from the inherent and inevitable suffering of embodied existence.[17]

Clearly the language, emphasis, and tone of Śvetāśvatara's opening series of questions do not suggest any Sāṁkhya leanings but instead intimate the seer's Śaiva disposition, which will soon become readily apparent. His is no pessimistic view of the universe but one that embraces all sorts of experience. His attitude is closer to that of the later, nondualistic Kashmir Śaivas, who aspire to experience the Divine in totality—in its own nature as well as in its own self-expression, which is the world and everything it holds.

2

कालः स्वभावो नियतिर्यदृच्छा
भूतानि योनिः पुरुष इति चिन्त्या ।
संयोग एषां नत्वात्मभावा-
दात्माप्यनीशः सुखदुःखहेतोः ॥ २ ॥

kālaḥ svabhāvo niyatir yadṛcchā bhūtāni yoniḥ puruṣa iti cintyā /
saṁyoga eṣāṁ na tv ātmabhāvād ātmāpy anīśaḥ sukhaduḥkhahetoḥ //

2. Time, the inherent nature of things, design, chance, the elements, primordial matter, individual awareness—these are to be considered as the cause. But not even a combination of these can be the cause, for they are themselves effects. Nor can the individual soul [be the cause], for that also is not sovereign but subject to happiness and misery.

The seven possible causes that Śvetāśvatara mentions in passing were all proposed and debated by philosophers before him and one time or another formed part of the fabric of Indian thought.[18] He dismisses them quickly with a single observation.

Certainly time (*kāla*) is a powerful force, unstoppable in its ever-forward motion and bringing constant change. Indeed, it struck some philosophers as the animating force in and through everything. If we could imagine time standing still, everything, even our thoughts, would come to a screeching halt—frozen, silent, and immobile. Without time, existence as we know it would not be possible. We think of time as continuous and going on forever; simultaneously we perceive it as divided into past, present, and future. But in our observation, every moment of time comes into existence and then vanishes like any other created thing. As Śvetāśvatara says, time is an effect. How can it be the cause?

When we consider the inherent nature (*svabhāva*) of anything, we reason that any inseparable characteristic, such as the wetness of water, has no existence apart from the thing in which it inheres. But we do not say that wetness is the cause of water. On a broader scale the inherent nature of the manifest universe has no separate existence apart from the manifest universe itself and therefore cannot precede it as its cause. Like time, the inherent nature of anything—its size, shape, color, texture, or any other quality—is only an observable, and therefore created, phenomenon. Interestingly inherent nature (*svabhāva*) plays a part in the classical Sāṁkhya theory of manifestation,[19] but here Śvetāśvatara rejects it outright.

Is the universe caused either by design (*niyati*) or by chance (*yadṛcchā*)? The universe appears to be a coherent whole that functions according to some sort of natural law or determination (*niyati*). Everywhere we observe organization, pattern, regularity, and regulation. The ripe mango does not float away in the breeze but falls to the ground. The mango seed produces a mango tree, not wheat or sesame. The sun rises and sets daily, right when expected. Since the universe operates according to reliable laws, we can rule out randomness or chance (*yadṛcchā*) as the cause of the creation. With all its predictability and dazzling, orderly complexity, the universe cannot be a mere accident. But whether we are talking about order or chaos, we must keep in mind that all the governing principles of the physical universe—as well as the occasional, seemingly random events we cannot explain—are based on our perceptions of how objects behave. Neither design nor chance are more than abstract principles created by reason, and so they also cannot be the underlying cause of our existence.

What about the elements that form the physical universe—space (*ākāśa*), air (*vāyu*), fire (*agni*), water (*ap*), and earth (*pṛthivī*)? We can easily refute this materialistic view by objecting that the elements are observable, created phenomena; and because they are only parts of the whole, none of them, either separately or together, can possibly be its cause. Moreover, how can the awareness of beings who feel, think, and act arise from insentient matter?

Up to this point the *mantra* presents few difficulties. The first five words name as possible causes time (*kāla*), inherent nature (*svabhāva*), determinism or design (*niyati*), chance or randomness (*yadṛcchā*), and the physical elements (*bhūtāni*). Their meanings are clear, but now serious difficulties arise. The meanings of the two remaining terms, *yoni* and *puruṣa*, are far from certain in the present context. Some translations exclude *yoni* from the series of seven possibilities, asking instead if one of the other six is not the source (*yoni*) of the universe.[20] Other translations count *yoni* as one of seven possible causes.[21] Either reading is possible, but the straightforward listing is simple, and removing *yoni* from the series of causes is syntactically strained.

The greater problem lies in the interpretation of the words *yoni* and *puruṣa*. The translators who include *yoni* as one of seven possible causes fail to agree on what the term means, suggesting "a [female] womb,"[22] "energy,"[23] "primal energy,"[24] "the womb,"[25] "the source of birth,"[26] "a womb,"[27] or "primal matter."[28] Among all the translators there is no more agreement surrounding the intended meaning of *puruṣa,* variously rendered as "the person,"[29] "the spirit,"[30] "a [male] person,"[31] "intelligence,"[32] "the living self,"[33] "the individual soul,"[34] "the individual self,"[35] "the Person,"[36] or "a person."[37]

The use of these two terms in other Upaniṣads, especially those closely related to the Śvetāśvatara, likewise fails to clarify their intended meaning. Most often *yoni* simply means "source" and only in a few specific instances refers to the female generative organ. In the Śvetāśvataropaniṣad *yoni* means "source" (2.7), implies latency (1.13), and twice occurs doubled in the idiomatic expression *yoniṁ yonim* (4.11, 5.2), meaning "every kind of." In other Upaniṣads *puruṣa* embraces several meanings: man, human being, spirit, the immanent aspect of the Supreme Being, the principle of universal consciousness from which creation proceeds, or Brahman. The *ṛṣi* Śvetāśvatara similarly employs *puruṣa* to indicate an ordinary human being (3.6), the individual soul (4.7), and the Supreme Being in both immanent and transcendent aspects (3.8, 3.9, 3.12, 3.14, 3.15, 3.19). Comparing the various translations reveals that the common denominator for *yoni* is some kind of creative energy, materiality or matrix—still a wide range. For *puruṣa* it is some kind of awareness. The definitions are vague, but Śvetāśvatara provides a clue in the second half of the present verse when he dismisses all seven possible causes as impossible, "for they are themselves effects."

If *yoni* and *puruṣa* were beginning to sound like Sāṁkhya's *prakṛti* and *puruṣa,* the two ultimate realities of materiality and consciousness, Śvetāśvatara quickly corrects that impression. Simply put, ultimate principles cannot be effects. Is there another philosophical system that recognizes entities akin to *puruṣa* and *prakṛti* not as ultimate principles but as part of the created realm? Yes. The doctrine set forth in the *Pāśupatasūtra* and known as Lākulīśa Pāśupata Śaivism (see pp. 43–49) recognizes a principle of insentient materiality roughly equivalent to *prakṛti,* which it calls *kalā.* This same system conceives of the conscious principle, elsewhere called *puruṣa,* as consisting of the individual subject (*paśu*) and its limited sentience (*vidyā*). This doctrine places both principles, corresponding to *prakṛti* and *puruṣa,* in the category of effect (*kārya*). *Kārya* thus consists of the insentient (*acit*) and the sentient (*cit*), the known object and the knowing subject. But *kārya,* as an expression of divine will—and therefore an effect—has its origin and dependence in the Divine itself, otherwise known as the cause (*kāraṇa*).[38]

The teaching attributed to Lakulīśa is an offshoot of the older, non-Vedic Pāśupata sect, reformed to bring it closer to Brahmanical orthodoxy. To that end it may well have drawn on ideas already set forth in the Śvetāśvataropaniṣad. In any case, the *Pāśupatasūtra*'s definition of categories, although later than this Upaniṣad, is nearer to it in time than any of the philosophies customarily invoked in its interpretation. Regarding the meaning of *yoni* and *puruṣa* in the present context, the philosophical outlook of the *Pāśupatasūtra* easily clarifies an otherwise intractable question.

With a clearer idea of what *yoni* and *puruṣa* mean, we can go on to the second half of the *mantra.* The elements (*bhūtāni*) emerge from an undifferentiated, unevolved primordial matter or matrix (*yoni*). The philosophers of the Sāṁkhya school teach that this matter (*prakṛti* or *pradhāna*) is by itself insensate and incapable of acting on its own. Therefore they link it in some indefinable way to an intelligent principle or conscious spirit (*puruṣa*) and say that the proximity sparks the cosmic evolution. Śvetāśvatara, already having rejected the view that Sāṁkhya came to embrace, asks if *puruṣa* by itself can be the cause. So far, every cause we have considered—and rejected—is something existing in its own individual state and therefore observable. To be observed requires an observer, and the entire universe can quite simply be reduced to a triad of the knowing subject, the known object, and the means of knowing that relates them. In the Śaiva view, *puruṣa,* the perceiving individual subject, belongs to the universe as much as the perceived object does; neither the knower nor the known exists apart from the other, and therefore *puruṣa* in that sense cannot be the cause.

When we understand *puruṣa* as the embodied self (*ātman*), here meaning the individual soul, we recognize immediately that it is subject to the effects of happiness and misery. Far from being free and self-ruling, the individual soul is bound by the law of cause and effect. It too is a created being that must itself have a cause.

Śvetāśvatara, like Lakulīśa after him and the still later philosophers of nondualistic Trika Śaivism, regards *puruṣa* and *prakṛti* (*yoni*) not as Sāṁkhya's two ultimate principles but as effects—as manifest forms within the universe. Neither can be the cause he seeks. In the spirit of the earlier Upaniṣads, Śvetāśvatara's Vedantic nondualism recognizes that the ultimate cause has to be an uncompounded something in its own right, free from any other force, influence, delineation, or limitation. The ultimate cause has to be itself uncaused. What it is the seer will reveal in the *mantra* that follows.

3

ते ध्यानयोगानुगता अपश्यन्

देवात्मशक्तिं स्वगुणैर्निगूढाम् ।

यः कारणानि निखिलानि तानि

कालात्मयुक्तान्यधितिष्ठत्येकः ॥ ३ ॥

te dhyānayogānugatā apaśyan devātmaśaktiṁ svaguṇair nigūḍhām /
yaḥ kāraṇāni nikhilāni tāni kālātmayuktāny adhitiṣṭhaty ekaḥ //

3. Entering into deep meditation, the seekers realized within themselves the power of the effulgent Self that lies hidden by its own effects. It is he who presides, purely One, over all those possible causes from time to the individual soul.

The cause of the universe—and of our existence—is not to be found in anything "out there," not to be discovered by observing phenomena or by reasoning about our observations. Śvetāśvatara now draws our attention away from the initial, external inquiries of the spiritual seekers and past philosophers to the redirection of their awareness inward—beyond the senses, mind, ego, and intellect. In a state of profound quietude they discovered a self-luminous power that remains hidden during the ordinary states of waking, dreaming, and dreamless sleep. Śvetāśvatara calls this power *devātmaśakti,* the energy (*śakti*) of the effugent Self (*devātman*).

Of all the major Upaniṣads only this one uses the term *śakti,*[39] and its appearance in *mantras* 1.3, 2.2, 4.1, and 6.8 is highly significant. The term is not unknown in earlier Vedic literature. It occurs even in the Ṛgvedasaṁhitā but there means "power" or "ability" in a general sense. In the Brāhmaṇas *śakti* designates more specific abilities, but it is not employed in the mythological imagery of those texts, even where certain goddesses associated with male gods suggest the incipient concept of consort-as-power.[40] Only later does *śakti* acquire the meaning we are most likely to associate with it today—that of the singular feminine power principle. Of course, archeological evidence reveals that the idea of an all-powerful Mother Goddess is even older, much older, than the Vedic tradition, and the eloquent evidence of some Ṛgvedic hymns demonstrates that the profoundly ancient idea of feminine divinity entered the Vedic consciousness at an early date. Even so, the concept of *śakti* as the dynamic feminine principle is all but absent from later Vedic literature. A notable exception is the Śvetāśvataropaniṣad.

That dynamic feminine principle figures prominently, though, in early Śaiva religion and thought. Although few traces of the dualistic Pāśupata teaching survive, the nondualistic philosophy of Nandikeśvara is preserved in a single text, probably a century or two younger than the Śvetāśvataropaniṣad (see pp. 39–41). The *Nandikeśvarakāśikā* (verse 11) presents *śakti* as inseparable from Śiva, just as moonlight is from the moon or as meaning is from language (*candracandrikayor yad vad yathā vāgarthayor iva*).[41] Brahman, or consciousness in its undifferentiated radiance (*prakāśa*), expresses itself spontaneously as the creation through its own power (*citkalā*, literally "an aspect of consciousness"). Śvetāśvatara expresses this same concept of consciousness and its inseparable energy by the term *devātmaśakti*—the power of the effulgent Self.

Likewise, in the second century CE Lakulīśa appears to have been influenced by the Śvetāśvataropaniṣad. His *dvaitādvaita* revisioning of the older dualistic Pāśupata doctrine holds that effect (*kārya*) exists within cause (*kāraṇa*) as its power, no different from it than heat is from fire.[42] According to the *Pāśupatasūtra* (verse 58), the manifest triad of *vidyā*, *kalā*, and *paśu*, which constitutes *kārya* (see p. 90), lies in the potentiality (*śakti*) of the Lord (Pati) that is his very being.[43]

Even while affirming Śvetāśvatara's distinctly Śaiva outlook, the concept of *devātmaśakti* distances his Upaniṣad from the Sāṁkhya view of reality. Classical Sāṁkhya holds that the two ultimate principles—creative power (*prakṛti*) and conscious spirit (*puruṣa*)—are completely independent of each other. The Śaiva philosophies see the two not only as united in a mutually and necessarily connected relationship (*avinābhāvasambandha*) but ultimately as one reality.

In a theistic sense *devātmaśakti* can mean the inherent power (*ātmaśakti*) of the effulgent deity (*deva*), or God.[44] In the nondualistic sense, because reality is purely One (and divine), *devātmaśakti* can mean the effulgent (*deva*) power of the Self (*ātmaśakti*), "the self-conscious power present in everyone."[45] Either reading is valid according to Śvetāśvatara's understanding, which anticipates the Trikaśāstra's doctrine of a simultaneously theistic and nondual God.

The shining reality, revealed in deep meditation, remains hidden in the three ordinary states of consciousness, which are waking (*jāgrat*), dreaming (*svapna*), and dreamless sleep (*suṣupti*). Through its own veiling power, called *māyā*, the cause that is Brahman conceals its own infinite nature behind the dazzling multiplicity of its own effects—those same effects that appear to us as all the names and forms and qualities that fill the universe.

We may not have noticed that, very quietly, Śvetāśvatara has answered his initial question. Is Brahman the cause? The owner of this self-luminous consciousness hidden by its *own* effects logically has to be the cause of those effects. Not only does it lie concealed within all that it creates, but, the seer tells us, it actively presides over every aspect of the creation. Unlike the individual soul, which is subject to the duality of enjoyment and suffering, this innermost, shining One is the autonomous ruler, untouched by anything else.

4

तमेकनेमिं त्रिवृतं षोडशान्तं
शतार्धारं विंशतिप्रत्यराभिः ।
अष्टकैः षड्भिर्विश्वरूपैकपाशं
त्रिमार्गभेदं द्विनिमित्तैकमोहम् ॥ ४ ॥

tam ekanemiṁ trivṛtaṁ ṣoḍaśāntaṁ śatārdharaṁ viṁśatipratyarābhiḥ / aṣṭakaiḥ ṣaḍbhir viśvarūpaikapāśaṁ trimārgabhedaṁ dvinimittaika-moham //

4. Him [they envisioned as a wheel] with a single rim and three bands, sixteen ends, fifty spokes, twenty counterspokes, and six octads. Bound [to its axle] by a single fastener of manifold forms, it moves along three different roads, driven by a single delusion with a twofold cause.

The first three *mantras* deal with cause (*kāraṇa*), the first primary category of Pāśupata and Lākulīśa Pāśupata metaphysics. Now attention shifts to effect (*kārya*), the second primary category.

This *mantra* is immediately arresting because of its exuberant enumeration and enigmatic symbolism, all relating to the imagery of the cosmic wheel. It lists no fewer than one hundred forty-five items but gives little clue as to what these carefully inventoried symbols represent. Commentators generally follow the interpretation found in the *Śvetāśvataropaniṣadvṛtti*, an undatable commentary attributed to Śaṁkarācārya but undoubtedly the work of a lesser figure writing from the scholastic standpoint of later Advaita Vedānta. Since the *Vṛtti* draws heavily on the *Sāṁkhyakārikā*, the situation is extremely complicated: the interpretation of a *mantra* composed by a Vedic Śaiva around the sixth or fifth century BCE is based on a Sāṁkhya text written a thousand years later, reinterpreted by an unknown author of the rival Advaita Vedānta school! To recover the original meaning of Śvetāśvatara's symbolism may be well nigh impossible.

Max Müller wondered if this difficult verse represented a summary of the existing philosophical ideas of its time or if it was merely a product of the author's fancy.[46] Tending toward the former view, he followed "Śaṁkara's" commentary, as most others after him have done and as we also shall do for lack of a better model.

The metaphor of the wheel of Brahman (*brahmacakra*) would have been readily understood by Śvetāśvatara's listeners, so readily that the seer finds no need even to mention the word *wheel*. One can assume it from the enumeration of its constituent parts—the rim, the spokes, and so on. In the same way, human beings can infer the single divine reality through its manifestations, the many and varied facets of life in the universe. If there is doubt about what Śvetāśvatara means, rest assured: he will employ the term *brahmacakra*—a term unique to this Upaniṣad—in two later verses (1.6, 6.1).

His listeners would have been familiar with the imagery of the cosmic wheel from earlier Upaniṣads. The Bṛhadāraṇyaka (2.5.15) teaches that just as the spokes of a wheel are held together by the rim and hub, so all the worlds and their creatures are held together in the Self (*ātmani*), who is the lord of all beings (*bhūtānām adhipatiḥ*). An extended prose paragraph in the Ṛgveda's Kauṣītakyupaniṣad (3.8) employs the same imagery in a richly detailed exhortation that one should seek to understand neither the physical nor the mental constituents of the manifest universe but only the reality behind them. That reality is more than the intelligent Self (*prajñātmā*) and lord of the world (*lokādhipatiḥ*): "he is myself—one should know that" (*sa ma ātmeti vidyāt*).

The revolving wheel is an apt metaphor for the constant motion and cyclical processes of the universe. We witness the circular motion of the stars in the night sky, the passing seasons, and the ever-repeating round of birth and death (*saṁsāra*). Life is a journey, and in the age of the Upaniṣads the wheel represented the technology that allowed people to travel over long distances in a short time. Its construction required great knowledge and skill, because all its parts had to work together as one well-functioning system.

According to "Śaṁkara's" *Vṛtti,* the wheel's rim represents *māyā* or *prakṛti,* two terms that Śvetāśvatara will declare in a later verse (4.10) to be identical. As a wheel's circumference defines its limits, *māyā* is the Divine's own limiting power. *Prakṛti* is primordial matter or nature in its unevolved state, holding latent within itself the three universal energies, the *guṇas,* here visualized as the rim's three encircling bands or hoops. When the undifferentiated energy of *prakṛti* moves from potentiality to actuality, it divides into the three *guṇas,* which then combine and recombine in increasingly complex patterns to produce everything in the universe from fleeting thoughts to solid matter.

The *guṇas* ("threads") represent the strands of energy from which the manifest universe is woven. They are called *tamas, rajas,* and *sattva,* and each has a distinctive character and function. *Tamas* conceals; it manifests variously as denseness, heaviness, solidity, inertia, resistance, dullness, darkness, ignorance, and error. *Sattva* reveals; it manifests as light, clarity, purity, calmness, goodness, and wisdom. *Rajas* operates intermediately between darkness and light; it manifests as activity, restlessness, impurity, aggression, urgency, and passion. It is through *rajas* that *tamas* and *sattva* interact.

The sixteen ends are the end-products of *prakṛti,* and with their evolution the creation becomes complete. The author of the *Vṛtti* explains them as mind (*manas*), the five faculties of perception (*jñānendriyas* or *buddhīndriyas*), the five faculties of action (*karmendriyas*), and the five physical elements (*mahābhūtas*). These are intimately connected, and all have to do with knowledge and action. Knowledge of the outer world streams in through the five faculties of sight (*cakṣu*), hearing (*śrotra*), smell (*ghrāṇa*), taste (*rasanā*), and touch (*sparśa*). The senses are the instruments of knowing that link us to the external objects known to the mind as perceived sensations. Just as knowledge of the outer world enters our awareness through the five *jñānendriyas,* our responses stream out through the five faculties of action—the capacities for grasping (*pāṇi*), moving from place to place (*pāda*), speaking (*vāc*), excreting (*pāyu*), and procreating (*upastha*). The faculties of perception and action cannot be separated. The former allow information about the physical world to enter into our awareness, and the latter carry out our responses. The *jñānendriyas* and *karmendriyas* work together, enabling us to interact with the exterior world.

Just as a wheel's spokes bear its weight and support its motion, the *brahmacakra's* fifty spokes represent the psychophysical dispositions that keep us revolving on the wheel of *saṁsāra*. To interpret this metaphor, the author of the *Vṛtti* relies on the *Sāṁkhyakārikā* (verse 46), which classifies the fifty dispositions under the four headings of misconception, disability, satisfaction, and perfection.

Misconception (*viparyaya*) takes five forms: obscurity (*tamas*), delusion (*moha*), extreme delusion (*mahāmoha*), gloom (*tāmisra*), and utter darkness (*andhatāmisra*). An alternative reading correlates the five forms of misconception with the five afflictions (*kleśas*) specified in Patañjali's *Yogasūtra* (2.3) as ignorance (*avidyā*), egoity (*asmitā*), attachment (*rāga*), aversion (*dveṣa*), and the clinging to life or habituality (*abhiniveśa*). In either case these errors in thinking arise when the infinite Self identifies with the finite mind, intellect, ego, and the five natural elements.[47]

Disability (*aśakti*) assumes twenty-eight forms. The *Sāṁkhyakārikā* (verse 49) observes that eleven relate to the malfunctioning, impairment, frustration, or failure of the mind and the ten sensory and motor faculties. The other seventeen concern the intellectual capacity (*buddhi*) as it relates to the nine forms of satisfaction and the eight kinds of perfection.

The nine forms of satisfaction (*tuṣṭi*) arise in two ways, either from attaining worldly objects and objectives or in successfully renouncing the desire for them.[48] The first four, deemed internal, are better characterized by the word *complacency*. The *Sāṁkhyakārikā* (verse 50) lists them as contentment with the experience of the natural world (*prakṛtituṣṭi*); contentment with one's limited understanding of it (*upadānatuṣṭi*); complacency that proper knowledge will arise in due time (*kālatuṣṭi*), otherwise known as incuriosity; and the willingness to leave everything up to fortune (*bhāgyatuṣṭi*). In contrast, the five external forms of satisfaction arise from turning away from the objects of the senses.

Perfection (*siddhi*) is eightfold and manifests as different forms of knowledge. The *Sāṁkhyakārikā* (verse 51) details the *siddhis* as natural knowledge that arises without instruction as a result of good tendencies (*ūha*), spontaneous comprehension that comes without study (*śabda*), the knowledge that arises from scriptural study (*adhyayana*), the removal of suffering (*duḥkhavighāta*) which is threefold (*traya*), the knowledge gained from friendly and well-intended discussion (*suhṛtprāpti*), and generosity of spirit (*danā*).[49]

The fifty spokes elaborate on the many ways we interact with the world through our behavior, our knowledge, or our lack of knowledge. In human experience the positive qualities defined as the eight *siddhis* are hindered by the dispositions of the previously enumerated categories—by all our misconceptions, incapacities, and complacencies.

The spokes are reinforced by twenty counterspokes, or wedges, which again are thought to symbolize the five organs of perception (*jñānendriyas*) and the five organs of action (*karmendriyas*) along with their ten corresponding objects. The repeated use of the same principles to explain the different features of the metaphorical wheel is one of the troubling aspects of this traditional interpretation. That said, the five faculties of hearing, touch, sight, taste, and smell have as their corresponding objects the five subtle elements (*tanmātras*)—the pure sensations of sound (*śabda*), touch (*sparśa*), form and color (*rūpa*), taste (*rasa*), and odor (*gandha*). The *tanmātras* are the sensory stimuli of the corresponding gross elements (*mahābhūtas*), which are space, air, fire, water, and earth. In perception the *tanmātras* function as an interface between mind and matter. In action the *karmendriyas* relate to the physical world, made of the *mahābhūtas,* as the capacities of grasping, movement, speech, excretion, and reproduction.

Other manifestations of mind and matter form six additional categories of eight components each. Neither the *Sāṁkhyakārikā* nor the Śvetāśvataropaniṣad itself gives any clue as to what these "six sets of eight" represent, and the word *aṣṭaka* ("octad"), apart from its usage in the present verse, occurs nowhere else in the Upaniṣads.[50] As interpreted in the *Vṛtti,* these octads are a loose miscellany scarcely reflective of Sāṁkhya's rigorous logic. This traditionally accepted interpretation is troubling also because some of the explanations duplicate those already given to other symbols. There is considerable overlap, for example, in the interpretation of the sixteen ends, the twenty counterspokes, and the octad of nature, where the same *jñānendriyas, karmendriyas, mahābhūtas,* and other principles show up time and again.

According to the *Vṛtti*, the octad of nature (*prakṛtyaṣṭaka*) consists of the five gross elements plus the inner organ (*antaḥkaraṇa*), formed of the mind (*manas*), the intellect or determinative faculty (*buddhi*), and the ego-sense (*ahaṁkāra*).

The octad of substances (*dhātvaṣṭaka*) constitutes the physical body, made of skin (*carma*), internal tissue (*tvac*), muscle (*māṁsa*), blood (*asṛk*), fat (*medas*), bone (*asthi*), marrow (*majjā*), and semen (*śukra*).

The eight forms of mastery (*aiśvaryāṣṭaka*) are extraordinary abilities gained through yogic practice, but these are to be avoided as obstacles to liberation. They are the ability to make oneself as minute as an atom (*aṇimā*) or as light as air (*laghimā*), to reach anything that is desired (*prāpti*), to have any desire fulfilled at will (*prākāmya*), to make oneself as huge as a mountain (*mahimā*), to dominate over others (*īśitva*), to influence others irresistibly (*vaśitva*), and to control or suppress desires (*kāmāvasāyitā*).[51]

The eight states of mind (*bhāvāṣṭaka*) are righteousness (*dharma*), unrighteousness (*adharma*), knowledge (*jñāna*), ignorance (*ajñāna*), dispassion (*vairāgya*), attachment (*avairāgya*), a sense of empowerment (*aiśvarya*), and a sense of powerlessness (*anaiśvarya*).

The eight kinds of supernatural beings (*devāṣṭaka*), either divine or demonic, are Brahmā, Prajāpati, gods (*devas*), celestial musicians (*gandharvas*), harmless ghosts (*yakṣas*), malevolent demons (*rākṣasas*), deceased ancestors (*pitṛs*), and the vilest of ogres (*piśācas*).

Finally, the eight virtues (*guṇāṣṭaka*) are compassion (*dayā*), patience (*kṣamā*), absence of ill-will (*anasūya*), purity (*śauca*), ease (*anāyāsa*), goodness (*maṅgala*), magnanimity (*akārpaṇya*), and contentment (*aspṛhā*).[52]

Binding the wheel to the axle is a leather strap (*pāśa*), a metaphor for desire. Since *pāśa* is also the Śaiva term for existential bondage, the simultaneous concrete and abstract meanings make for delightful wordplay while revealing profound wisdom. Although desire (*kāma*) is a single impulse, it expresses itself in countless ways that keep the individual soul tied to worldly existence.

The embodied soul may follow one of three different paths, characterized by righteousness (*dharma*), unrighteousness (*adharma*), or knowledge (*jñāna*). The first two concern the duality of proper and improper conduct in this world; the third transcends the other two and leads to liberation.

Underlying this state of worldly existence is a single delusion (*ekamoha*), defined in Vijñānabhagavat's *Śvetāśvataropaniṣadvivaraṇa* as the individual's constructed identity, the confounding sense of selfhood that results from the identification of infinite Self with not-self.[53] When the infinite consciousness that is *ātman* or Brahman or *pati* identifies with its own finite projections, it experiences itself as an individual being (*paśu*), possessed of body, mind, intellect, and ego. It falls into the delusion of separateness and limitation that is the human condition. This single delusion of the One taking itself to be one among many is described here as *dvinimitta*—a term whose translation and interpretation are difficult, owing to an ambiguity in the Sanskrit. Does *dvinimittaikamoha* mean "a single delusion (*ekamoha*) arising from (or having) two causes (or a twofold cause) (*dvinimitta*)"? That is the majority opinion.[54] But a minority opinion discerns an opposite meaning—"a single delusion which is the cause of [the] two."[55]

The first step is to determine what "the two" are. Are they good and evil actions,[56] happiness and misery,[57] either of those possibilities,[58] or maybe *puruṣa* and *prakṛti*?[59]

Since there have been strong indications already that the nontheistic dualism of Sāṁkhya does not form a comfortable fit with the theistic nondualism of this Upaniṣad, we can rule out *puruṣa* and *prakṛti*, at least in the classical Sāṁkhya sense. Then, can good and evil actions be the cause of delusion? Not if *delusion* means primal nescience (*avidyā*)—and that is certainly what it seems to mean here. Śvetāśvatara is describing the *aiśvaryasarga*, the manifestation from the standpoint of the creator, wherein the duality of virtue and vice arises from the cosmic delusion and not the other way around. Of course, in the *pāśavasarga*, the world experienced by the bound soul (*paśu*), good and evil actions perpetuate *karma* and are the cause of continuing bondage, but this *mantra* does not speak from that point of view. Likewise happiness and misery (*sukha* and *duḥkha*) cannot be the cause of delusion. Delusion is *their* cause.

We can deduce that Śvetāśvatara is speaking of a single delusion whose cause is twofold, but what is that twofold cause (*dvinimitta*)? The three ancient Advaita Vedānta commentaries fail to give a definitive answer. They were written hundreds of years after the Upaniṣad. The *Vṛtti*, falsely attributed to Śaṁkara, has to be later than his time, but how much later we cannot say. The earliest datable commentary is Vijñānabhagavat's *Śvetāśvataropaniṣadvivaraṇa,* which belongs to the tenth century, and the other Vedānta commentary, Śaṁkarānanda's *Śvetāśvataropaniṣaddīpikā,* is three or four centuries younger.

Perhaps clarification lies elsewhere, such as in Utpaladeva's *Īśvarapratyabhijñākārikā* [Stanzas on the recognition of God]. Composed around the beginning of the tenth century,[60] it is contemporary with Vijñānabhagavat's *Vivaraṇa* and has the added advantage of stemming from a rich Śaiva heritage partly shared with the Śvetāśvataropaniṣad. In the *Kārikā* (2.4.7) Utpaladeva writes that cause (*kāraṇa*) is only the knowing subject who, in two modes of manifestation, remains unchanged in his unity. The two modes are the internal and external realities of the empirical universe (2.4.6). Experienced by the creator as *aham* and *idam* (see p. 59) and by the *paśu* as I and other, this may well be the twofold cause—the division of consciousness into the two modes of subjectivity and objectivity on which the single delusion of individual selfhood rests, and from which relativization and limitation arise.

Through the metaphor of the wheel, Śvetāśvatara produced a meticulously detailed and, for its time, scientifically rational plan of the universe. Over the centuries the precise meaning of his complex symbolism was lost, and the traditional interpretation, devised perhaps a millennium and a half later, is laced with uncertainty. There can be no doubt that the seer intended to illustrate how the phenomenon of physical and mental experience is put together and how it works. Even though understood imperfectly today, his model affords insight into how we perceive, feel, think, and act.

5

पञ्चस्रोतोम्बुं पञ्चयोन्युग्रवक्रां
पञ्चप्राणोर्मिं पञ्चबुद्ध्यादिमूलाम् ।
पञ्चावर्तां पञ्चदुःखौघवेगां
पञ्चाशद्भेदां पञ्चपर्वामधीमः ॥ ५ ॥

pañcasrotombuṁ pañcayony ugravakrāṁ pañcaprāṇormiṁ
pañcabuddhyādimūlām /
pañcāvartāṁ pañcaduḥkhaughavegāṁ pañcāśadbhedāṁ pañcaparvām
adhīmaḥ //

5. [Or, they said,] we think of him [as a river] with five currents. Its sharp bends are the five elements, its waves are the five vital forces, and its origin is the mind—the source of the fivefold perception. It has five whirlpools, and its tumbling rapids are the five kinds of misery. Flowing around five obstructions, it takes on countless aspects.

Another way to think of the manifest Brahman is through the imagery of a river. The idea of divine power as a river has captivated the Indian imagination ever since the ancient *ṛṣis* who composed the hymns of the Ṛgveda deified the Sarasvatī River and extolled it above all others (see pp. 10–11). In what may be the earliest of the those hymns (6.61), the seer Bharadvāja asks the graciously inclined Sarasvatī to further her worshipers' thoughts with might and to guide them to the glorious treasure of spiritual knowledge. From the beginning the Sarasvatī was regarded not only as a holy river but also as a personified deity. Beyond that she came to be recognized as the shining stream of consciousness, prompting the composer of a later hymn (1.3.12) to rhapsodize, "A mighty stream is Sarasvatī; with her light she lightens, illuminates, all pious minds."[61]

A river is always different, yet ever the same. The imagery of a dynamic flow of water along a determined course reflects that the universe too is a spontaneous flow of constant change within an unchanging unity. As water evaporates from the sea, falls as rain, and flows back again into the sea, the creation emanates from and returns to Brahman, taking on and then relinquishing countless forms and qualities along the way. And just as the water of the river is not different from the water of the sea, the universe is ultimately not different from its divine source.[62]

Like the preceding description of Brahman's manifestation as the wheel of the universe, the metaphor of the river also deals with the philosophical category of effect (*kārya*). In Max Müller's opinion its imagery represents Brahman as having the nature of both cause and effect (*kāryakāraṇātmaka*). For the details of his interpretation

Müller relied for the most part on the *Śvetāśvataropaniṣadvṛtti* but noted that it leaves some of the symbolism unexplained.[63] Overall, modern commentators also have followed the *Vṛtti,* with occasionally divided opinions and their own attempts to fill in the blanks, but as with the preceding *mantra* the exact meaning of some details remains elusive.

The river of consciousness is one whose water flows in five currents (*pañcasrotombu*). There is general agreement that these represent the five sensory faculties (*jñānendriyas*). Their flow is "wild and winding"[64] or "fierce and crooked,"[65] owing to the sharp bends (*ugravakra*) that symbolize the five physical elements (*mahābhūtas*). Because these give shape to the material universe that the mind perceives, the metaphor of "five sharp bends" is particularly effective. This description also evokes a river fraught with many dangers to those who would navigate its course or live along its banks, just as existence is ever filled with the potential for danger or misery. But we must not forget that the river's flow also provides sustenance for living creatures and an avenue for transport and communication. In the same way, the universe can be experienced positively as a place of benevolence and joy for those who have acquired some measure of wisdom.[66]

The author of the *Vṛtti* equates the river's waves with the five faculties of action (*karmendriyas*), even though the literal meaning of *pañcaprāṇormi* is "whose waves (*ūrmi*) are the five vital breaths (*pañcaprāṇa*)." Some translators accept the *Vṛtti*'s interpretation,[67] some see no reason not to take the word *prāṇa* at face value,[68] and others admit the possibility of either meaning.[69] The five breaths or vital airs (*prāṇas* or *vāyus*) are *prāṇa, apāna, samāna, udāna,* and *vyāna.* On the gross (*sthūla*) or physiological level, *prāṇa* is the outgoing breath and the force that governs respiration; *apāna* is the incoming, downward breath, responsible for elimination; *samāna* is the internal breath that governs digestion, assimilation, and circulation; *vyāna* presides over the nervous system, speech, and conscious action; and *udāna* promotes growth, maintains bodily heat, and aids the soul in leaving the body at death.[70]

According to the Trikaśāstra, the five *prāṇas* also function on the subtle (*sūkṣma*) level and relate to various states of consciousness. In deep meditation, when mind and body are calm and the need for oxygen is reduced, the outward movement of *prāṇa* and the inward movement of *apāna* balance each other and resolve into the unified state of *samāna*.[71] When *udāna* rises internally, the meditator attains *turīya* ("the fourth"), the state of consciousness beyond the three ordinary states of waking, dreaming, and dreamless sleep.[72] Finally, *vyāna* leads to the experience of unconditioned consciousness known as *turyātīta* ("beyond the fourth"), the ultimate Oneness.[73]

After the uncertainty over the meaning of *pañcaprāṇa*, there is almost unanimous agreement on what the next three metaphors represent. Because the existence of the universe depends upon the mind's experience of it, the universe is said to have its origin in the mind, which perceives through the five senses. That is the meaning of *pañcabuddhyādimūla*. Perception, as expressed by the Sāṁkhya and Yoga systems, is merely the modification of mind (*citta*)—the medium of consciousness—in the form of distinct waves (*vṛttis*). Advaita Vedānta concurs that fivefold perception (*pañcabuddhi*) is only a modification of the mind.[74] This view is borne out by Gauḍapāda's *Māṇḍūkyakārikā* (3.31), which explains, "This duality (*idaṁ dvaitam*), together with all that is moving and unmoving (*yat kiṁcit sacarācaram*), is perceived by the mind (*manodṛśyam*); when the mind ceases to be the mind (*manaso hy amanībhāve*), duality surely is not perceived (*dvaitaṁ naivopalabhyate*)." While Gauḍapāda intended this to be an argument for the insubstantiality of the phenomenal universe, it can equally be taken as a statement that the world of our experience is a manifestation resulting from the activity of consciousness.

As already noted, the river of shining consciousness does not always flow smoothly. Neither does the human experience that it represents. Along its course we encounter five whirlpools, which symbolize the *tanmātras*—all the stimuli of sound, touch, sight, taste, and smell that draw us in and threaten to engulf us. Whether attractive or repulsive, these sensory experiences command our attention and impel us to react accordingly.

Five rapids also disrupt the water's smooth flow. They are almost always explained as the five miseries of human life, said to consist of being in the womb, being born, growing old, falling prey to illness, and dying.

The commentary attributed to Śaṁkarācārya does not attempt to explain the meaning of the last two metaphors. *Pañcaparva*, which occurs at the very end, refers to some sort of obstruction, perhaps fallen branches that disrupt the current or a dam that impedes its flow or submerged boulders that pose a threat. There is no agreement. Commentators and translators either remain silent[75] or propose that *pañcaparva* stands for the five afflictions (*kleśas*) enumerated in Patañjali's *Yogasūtra* (2.3).[76] These are ignorance (*avidyā*), egoity (*asmitā*), attachment (*rāga*), aversion (*dveśa*), and habituality or the clinging to life (*abhiniveśa*). Ignorance, the primary obstacle, can be defined as a misreading of reality, based on the erroneous identification of the eternal, indwelling Self with the transient body-mind complex, composed of elements that are not-self. Expressed as the ego, this basic ignorance engenders further misconceptions in the paired obstacles of attachment and aversion. Attachment is "that which dwells upon pleasure," and aversion is "that which dwells upon pain."[77] Just as the mind is captivated by what it desires or loves, it is equally bound by what it fears or hates, if only by its attempts at avoidance. Progressing toward enlightenment, we slowly free ourselves from the attractions and aversions that constantly clamor for our attention and impel us to act. Life is a chain—or better, a web—of cause and effect in which we become enmeshed, and the task of liberation is made all the more difficult by the fifth obstacle, the intentional clinging to life, or our ingrained habits. Either interpretation of *abhiniveśa* is possible. We cling to life out of fear of death, but this clinging is nothing more than holding fast to the nonrecognition of our own true nature—the birthless, deathless, infinitely conscious Self, free of the constraints and qualities on which we build the smallness of our personal identities and rest in the comfort (or discomfort) of their familiarity.

More than any other of this *mantra's* symbols, the penultimate metaphor defies interpretation. *Pañcāśadbheda* means "having fifty divergences," but what those are, few commentators or translators are prepared to say. Among the early Vedantic commentaries, the *Vṛtti* remains silent, and Śaṁkarānanda's *Dīpikā* argues unconvincingly that the verse enumerates not seven but ten (!) groups of five, which together account for the river's fifty characteristics (*bhedas*).[78] The modern scholars who venture a guess agree that *pañcāśadbheda* may refer to the fifty psychophysical dispositions already detailed as the fifty spokes of the cosmic wheel.[79]

Since the word *bheda* can signify any kind of divergence—breaking, splitting, separation, partition, bursting, sprouting, or blossoming, to mention only a few—its fifty manifestations need not allude only to existential woe but to the entirety of life's experiences, the "all the rest" of the Upaniṣad's opening verse. And *fifty* may not literally mean "fifty." Perhaps it means that the river of phenomenal existence has *innumerable* ramifications.[80]

The arresting feature of this *mantra's* enumerations is that they all consist of pentads, groups of five, with the single exception of one aggregate of fifty, a multiple of five. Apart from the natural observation that there are five senses, five elements, and so on—principles accepted by all schools of Hindu philosophy—enumerations of five are generally common in early Vedic thinking, and they are especially prevalent in Śaiva thought.[81] The Vedic Taittirīya lineage, which has decided Śaiva leanings (see pp. 38–39), was the first to teach that the embodied human being consists of five sheathes that successively envelop the Self. These, originally suggested in the Taittirīyopaniṣad (2.4.1), came to be delineated by the Vedānta as the causal sheath (*ānandamayakośa*), the intelligent sheath (*vijñānamayakośa*), the mental sheath (*manomayakośa*), the vital sheath (*prāṇamayakośa*), and the physical sheath (*annamayakośa*).

Although the earliest recognized form of sectarian Śaivism, the Pāśupata, has no surviving texts, its world-view, spiritual practices, and ultimate goal seem to have been presented systematically according to five topics: cause (*kāraṇa*), effect (*kārya*), union (*yoga*), ritual (*vidhi*), and the cessation of suffering (*duḥkhānta*). When Lakulīśa reformed Pāśupatism to bring it closer to Vedic norms, he retained the older system's five topics but altered them in significant ways. He also taught that the mind of the bound individual (*paśu*) is subject to five impurities (*malas*). These he named as the wrong knowledge (*mithyājñāna*) that includes error, doubt, and base emotions; as demerit (*adharma*), which comprises the accumulated effects of past and present misdeeds; as attachment and its cause (*saktihetu*), which concern identification with the body, life-force, and intellect and holding to their objects; as the inclination of the mind to empirical objects (*cyuti*); and as subjective individuality (*paśutva*), the bound state characterized by the absence of divine omniscience and omnipotence—the *paśu* having forgotten its true identity as Pati, the all-knowing, all-powerful Lord.[82]

Additionally Lakulīśa formulated his *yoga* as a practical path (*sādhanāmārga*) with five stages, each based on and corresponding to one of Rudra's five faces, called Sadyojāta, Vāmadeva, Aghora, Tatpuruṣa, and Īśāna. These aspects are named in the Mahānārāyaṇopaniṣad (Āndhra recension, sections 17–21), a late supplement (*khila*) forming the tenth and final book of the Taittirīyāraṇyaka.[83]

The mouths of the five-faced (*pañcavaktra*) Śiva are by tradition the sources of the Śaivāgama in all its aspects (see p. 50). As an outgrowth of the nondualistic portion of the Śaivāgama, the Trikaśāstra speaks of Paramaśiva as formless and unmanifest (*niṣkala*), the ultimate unity that nevertheless has a ceaseless, fivefold cosmic activity (*pañcakṛtya*). Each of the five actions corresponds to one of the five faces named in the Taittirīyāraṇyaka: emanation (*sṛṣṭi*) to Sadyojāta, maintenance (*sthiti*) to Vāmadeva, resorption (*saṁhṛti*) to Aghora, self-concealment or bondage (*nigraha*) to Tatpuruṣa, and self-revelation or grace (*anugraha*) to Īśāna.[84]

In the present *mantra,* with its seven pentads, Śvetāśvatara evokes the imagery of a river to explain how the unmanifest One expresses itself as all the multiplicity of the universe. Writing some fourteen centuries afterward, Abhinavagupta's disciple Kṣemarāja also employs a scheme of seven pentads in his *Pratyabhijñāhṛdaya* [The essence of Self-recognition]. Composed in the form of *sūtras* with Kṣemarāja's own commentary, the text is a simplified exposition of Utpaladeva's Pratyabhijñā philosophy. The seventh *sūtra* and its commentary elucidate that at the level of unmanifest unity, Śiva—the one Self (*ātman*)—has consciousness (*cit*) as his essential nature. That consciousness, though infinite and undifferentiated, forms a pentad of awareness (*cit*), bliss (*ānanda*), will (*icchā*), knowledge (*jñāna*), and action (*kriyā*). Through his absolutely spontaneous free will (*svātantrya*) Śiva enters into nescience (*akhyāti,* meaning *māyā*) and through its five coverings (*kalā, vidyā, rāga, kāla,* and *niyati*) assumes limitation in the form of another pentad. There, rendered finite, Śiva's five powers assume the corresponding forms of limited subjectivity (*puruṣa*), limited objectivity (*prakṛti*), egoity (*ahaṁkara*), intelligence (*buddhi*), and mind (*manas*). From *ahaṁkāra* evolve the five faculties of perception (*jñānendriyas*), the five faculties of action (*karmendriyas*), and the five subtle elements (*tanmātras*). The *tanmātras* in turn produce the five gross elements (*mahābhūtas*), with the last—earth (*pṛthivī*)—marking the terminal point of cosmic evolution (see pp. 58–62).

According to Kṣemarāja the initial pentad of the *cit, ānanda, icchā, jñāna,* and *kriyā śaktis,* which constitute Śiva's essential nature, belongs to the pure course of consciousness (*śuddhādhvan*) above *māyā,* in which there is no difference between knower and known. The six other pentads belong to the impure course (*aśuddhādhvan*), which runs from *puruṣa*—where difference begins—all the way down to earth.[85] The seven sets of five, together with *māyā* account for the thirty-six *tattvas* of Trika Śaivism in its fully developed form.

Although it is possible to impose Kṣemarāja's ideas on Śvetāśvatara's verse, that reading would be no more definitive than those of the traditionally accepted commentators, who fail to clarify and sometimes stop short of trying. Parts of a Trika-based reading work very well, but other parts form an uncomfortable fit. It is unlikely that an exact parallel exists between the meaning that Śvetāśvatara intended by his seven pentads and the scheme set forth by Kṣemarāja in the *Pratyabhijñāhṛdaya.* Still, both texts belong to the Śaiva fold, and though we may never know how closely their details match, their overall outlooks are probably rather similar.

Finally, it should be noted that the previous verse (1.4) dealt with the metaphor of the wheel of Brahman, and the following verse (1.6) returns to it. Śvetāśvatara's interpolation of the river hardly seems accidental, since its fivefold imagery occupies the chapter's fifth *mantra.* It undoubtedly interrupts the logical flow of thought, but such spontaneous playfulness would not be entirely unexpected from a gifted Śaiva teacher or indeed from an illumined soul.

6

सर्वाजीवे सर्वसंस्थे बृहन्ते
अस्मिन् हंसो भ्राम्यते ब्रह्मचक्रे ।
पृथगात्मानं प्रेरितारं च मत्वा
जुष्टस्ततस्तेनामृतत्वमेति ॥ ६ ॥

sarvājīve sarvasaṁsthe bṛhante asmin haṁso bhrāmyate brahmacakre /
pṛthag ātmānaṁ preritāraṁ ca matvā juṣṭas tatas tenāmṛtatvam eti //

6. On this vast wheel of Brahman, wherein everything lives and dies, the soul revolves, thinking itself different from the animating force. Yet blessed by the knowledge of that very Brahman, it attains immortality.

In the cosmic drama everything comes into existence, remains for a while, then merges back into the source. The image of the individual soul spinning around on the revolving wheel of the universe illustrates the repeating cycle of birth, death, and rebirth.

Haṁsa, the term for soul, is a commonly recognized metaphor. It literally denotes a migratory aquatic bird such as a swan or a goose. Since Vedic times the term has symbolized either the individual soul, as it does here, or the universal spirit.[86] When *haṁsa* refers to the individual soul, it evokes the bird's long migratory flights in order to symbolize the transmigration from lifetime to lifetime. When it refers to the universal spirit dwelling in the midst of creation, *haṁsa* is a metaphor for Brahman, the unity at the heart of all manifestation.[87] The white color of the swan or of the Indian goose (*Anser indicus*)[88] represents the inherent purity of the indwelling spirit. Traditionally the elegant swan has been a practical symbol of spiritual discrimination (*viveka*) because of the belief that its beak possesses the abililty to separate milk from water. While the infinite, ever-perfect Self (*haṁsa*) appears to participate in the experience of the world, it nevertheless remains unentangled, unlike the bound soul (*paśu*). In Vedantic terms, the immanent Brahman, Īśvara, is the master of his *māyā,* while the soul is its captive.

In the Upaniṣads *haṁsa* is a widely accepted image of the supreme spirit or of the liberated Self, freely moving about.[89] This ancient image occurs in the earliest Upaniṣad, the Bṛhadāraṇyaka (4.3.11–12), where the seer Yājñavalkya delivers a discourse to King Janaka on the nature of the Self. He prefaces his teaching by saying, "Regarding this subject, there are the following verses," and then quotes the still older teaching: "Overcoming by sleep what belongs to the body, the ever-wakeful one contemplates the sleeping senses; withdrawing his light, he goes back to his abode—he, the golden one (*hiraṇmayaḥ*), the solitary swan (*ekahaṁsaḥ*). Guarding with his breath (*prāṇena*) the nest below (*avaraṁ kulāyam*), the immortal one (*amṛtaḥ*) roams outside; the immortal one goes wherever he wishes—he, the golden one, the solitary swan." Yājñavalkya says that even while the attributes, sensations, and activities of the body rest in the inertia of sleep, the luminous Self (*hiraṇmaya ekahaṁsaḥ*) remains awake. It keeps the body alive by means of the vital forces ("guarding with his breath the nest below") while it, by nature ever free, moves about at will.

As long as the individual soul identifies with the phenomena of body, mind, personality, attachments, and aversions, it remains bound by them. Failing to recognize its true identity as the supreme Self behind all such appearances, it remains separated from its own inconceivably grander reality. But through proper inquiry and spiritual practice, the individual can dissolve the sense of separation and reach the knowledge that the indwelling *ātman* is not different from the ultimate reality of Brahman. *Blessed* by this knowledge, the freed soul merges into the ineffable, self-luminous Oneness beyond time, space, and causation. Two important facets of Śvetāśvatara's teaching first appear in this *mantra*. One, to be repeated often, is that knowledge frees one from all fetters; the other is that knowledge is a blessing that comes through divine grace.

7

उद्गीतमेतत्परमं तु ब्रह्म
तस्मिंस्त्रयं सुप्रतिष्ठाक्षरं च ।
अत्रान्तरं ब्रह्मविदो विदित्वा
लीना ब्रह्मणि तत्पराः योनिमुक्ताः ॥ ७ ॥

udgītam etat paramaṁ tu brahma tasmiṁs trayaṁ supratiṣṭhākṣaraṁ ca /
atrāntaraṁ brahmavido viditvā līnā brahmaṇi tatparāḥ yonimuktāḥ //

7. What they praise is indeed the supreme Brahman, the firm support, the imperishable One. In it exists the universe. Here, realizing it within, the knowers of Brahman become merged in Brahman. Intent on it as their highest goal, they are freed from rebirth.

This (*etat*), which has been presented as the cosmic wheel (1.4, 1.6) and as the river of consciousness (1.5), is proclaimed, sung forth, and celebrated (*udgītam*) by the Vedic seers as the supreme Brahman (*paramaṁ brahma*). And not only as the supreme Brahman but also as the firm support, the immovable foundation (*supratiṣṭhā*), of the universe, for Brahman is that which is imperishable (*akṣaram*).

Speaking from direct knowledge of the singular, self-luminous power within, the seers have proclaimed that Brahman, the cause, presides over this universe, purely One (1.3). That raises one of the most fascinating questions of philosophy. How does the One become many? Or, how does the Infinite become finite? How can the divine reality be both beyond the universe and active within it? These are matters that will become clear in the course of the Upaniṣad. For now it will suffice to accept that Brahman is both transcendent and immanent.

In Brahman (*tasmin*) the universe (*trayam*) exists. The word *traya* literally means "triad" or something threefold, and its use to represent the universe may seem puzzling at first. But if we observe the surrounding world and our own selves, we often encounter the threefold nature of manifest phenomena. We look at the space around us and the objects it contains and experience them through the three dimensions of height, breadth, and depth. Looking closer, we understand that physical matter exists in three states—solid, liquid, and gaseous. Perceiving all these objects, inert and animate, insentient and sentient, ourselves included, we speak of them in terms of three grammatical persons (*I*, the speaker; *you*, the spoken to; *he*, *she*, *it*, the spoken of). The pronouns also reflect that we recognize three genders—masculine, feminine, and neuter. All of this pertains to the observation of things in space. Then there is time. We perceive it as divided into past, present, and future. Accordingly, everything seems to have a beginning, a middle, and an end. We witness the cosmic functions of creation (*sṛṣṭi*), maintenance (*sthiti*), and dissolution (*saṁhāra*) taking place everywhere. At a higher level of abstraction the philosophers teach that the building blocks of the universe are three *guṇas* or universal energies. The universe itself is based on a triad of time, space, and causality. Everything exists on three planes—the causal (*kāraṇa*), which is the state of potentiality or latency; the subtle (*sūkṣma*), which is the realm of thought and mental activity; and the gross (*sthūla*), which is the plane of physical matter. These principles are not mere abstractions. They are borne out every day in our own experience, because we live our lives in the corresponding gross, subtle, and causal states of waking, dreaming, and dreamless sleep. Our experience of this world is purely a matter of experience in consciousness.

That last point is what Śvetāśvatara intends to convey by the word *traya*—that the universe is a matter of our experience in consciousness. He wants us to understand that the single consciousness that is Brahman appears to assume a threefold division as the enjoying subject (*bhoktṛ*), the object to be enjoyed (*bhogya*), and the inciting power (*preritṛ*) that brings about the enjoyment. Lest there be any doubt about his meaning, the seer will name the constituents of the triad outright in a later *mantra* (1.12) and declare that they, in reality, are nothing but Brahman.

So, we are able to experience the existence of the world, to relate to it, and to act in it because of the threefold split of consciousness into subject, object, and cognitive act. To use another set of terms, we can say that for the world to be experienced there must be the knower (*pramātṛ*), the known (*prameya*), and the knowing that connects them, the means of knowledge (*pramāṇa*).

According to Śaiva nondualism, everything that appears as manifest has the radiant pulsation of consciousness (*sphurattā*) as its essential nature. This same power of one's own true nature (*svabala*) is what Śvetāśvatara calls *devātmaśakti*. Also known in the Trikaśāstra as *spanda*, the "apparent motion in the motionless Śiva,"[90] this vibration of consciousness is his own blissful, self-expressive freedom (*svātantryaśakti*), responsible for all the appearances and experiences at the lower level of the individual soul (*jīva*).[91]

Of course, every distinction of the perceptible universe is based on the underlying principle of difference (*bheda*). So is the very experience of the universe. Śvetāśvatara made that clear when he said that the individual soul (*haṁsa*) revolves on the wheel of Brahman, thinking itself different (*pṛthak*) from the animating force (*preṛtāram*), the *devātmaśakti* (1.6). In ordinary awareness we perceive *bheda* in all the features and activities of the world and see ourselves, although involved, as somehow distinct from them. In contrast, the enlightened *yogin*, established in nondual Self-knowledge, sees the oneness (*abheda*) of it all.

That is the next point. Śvetāśvatara says that here (*atra*), in the here and now, one can realize the imperishable reality within (*antaram*). The knowers of Brahman (*brahmavidaḥ*), by making Brahman the sole focus of the heart and mind (*tatparāḥ*), become merged in Brahman (*līnā brahmaṇi*) and thus freed from rebirth (*yonimuktāḥ*). As the Muṇḍakopaniṣad (3.2.9) also teaches, "Whoever knows the supreme Brahman becomes Brahman."

8

संयुक्तमेतत् क्षरमक्षरं च
व्यक्ताव्यक्तं भरते विश्वमीशः ।
अनीशश्चात्मा बध्यते भोक्तृ-
भावाज् ज्ञात्वा देवं मुच्यते सर्वपाशैः ॥ ८ ॥

saṁyuktam etat kṣaram akṣaraṁ ca vyaktāvyaktaṁ bharate viśvam īśaḥ /
anīśaś cātmā badhyate bhoktṛbhāvāj jñātvā devaṁ mucyate sarvapāśaiḥ //

8. The Lord supports all this universe, wherein the perishable and the imperishable, the manifest and the unmanifest, are joined together. Forgetful of his lordship and thinking himself the enjoyer, the Self becomes bound. Knowing that effulgent being, one is freed from all fetters.

Now, for the first time Śvetāśvatara speaks of the divine reality as the Lord (Īśa). This distinctly Śaiva term is one of the seer's most frequent ways of referring to the Divine (see p. 30). It derives from the verbal root *īś*, meaning "to command," "to rule," "to reign," "to be master of," and designates here the supreme Lord, who holds within himself all this vast and varied universe.

The Absolute is the sole support of all that is momentary and all that is enduring, of that which perishes (*kṣaram*) and that which does not (*akṣaram*). In it exist the manifest (*vyaktam*) and the unmanifest (*avyaktam*). All that we perceive and perceive not, the visible and the invisible, the apparent and the hidden, the effect and the cause—all these are mingled together (*saṁyuktam*) in the play of creation.

According to the nondualistic teaching of the Spandaśāstra, in the transcendental state Śiva has the knowledge of himself as absolute fullness. In that fullness of unitary consciousness—in Śiva's own infinite sense of I (*pūrṇāhaṁtā*)—reside the powers of lordship (*īśvaratā*), of creative knowledge (*jñātṛtva*), and of creative activity (*kartṛtva*). United in the Divine, these same powers manifest diversely as the universe, bringing together and moving apart the multiple elements of creation.[92]

From his divine standpoint the Lord views the universe as an expression of his own sovereignty (*aiśvaryasarga*). Īśa, knowing his essential nature to be pure consciousness, ever free of differentiation, is himself ever free. It is through that very power of his own free will, his *svātantryaśakti*, that the ruling Self (*ātmā*) may wish to relinquish his lordship, to become bereft of power (*anīśaḥ*), in order to engage in the play of the universe. This idea of the infinite One wishing to express itself by becoming the finite many finds support in Upaniṣads far older than the Śvetāśvatara.

A passage in the Chāndogyopaniṣad (6.2.1–3) relates that Brahman, purely One without a second (*ekam evādvitīyam*), thought (*aikṣata*), May I be many, may I grow forth (*bahu syāṁ prajāyeyeti*). The verb *aikṣata*, meaning "saw," "saw in the mind," "beheld," considered," prompted the great Śaṁkara to comment that the highest Lord (*parameśvara*), abiding as the Self of the various elements, produces the manifold effects of creation by his power of thought.[93] The verb *prajāyeya* means "may I cause myself to propagate, to bring forth." Since there is only the oneness of consciousness, that itself is the only possible source for what is to be brought forth.

A parallel passage occurs in the Taittirīyopaniṣad (2.6.1) and is of special relevance, belonging to the same preceptorial lineage as the later Śvetāśvataropaniṣad. Here Brahman desired (*akāmayata*), May I be many, may I grow forth (*bahu syāṁ prajāyeyeti*). The verb *akāmayata* hints at a voluntaristic philosophy, one which posits that will is either the fundamental principle of reality or the primary factor in experience. Interestingly, voluntarism emerges slightly after Śvetāśvatara's time in Nandikeśvara's nondualistic Śaivism (see p. 40) and later passes into the nondualistic Trikaśāstra of Kashmir. According to the Taittirīyopaniṣad, Brahman, having willed, next performed austerity (*sa tapo 'tapyata*), meaning he deliberated,[94] and then emitted (*asṛjata*) all this (*idaṁ sarvam*). Śaṁkara's commentary on this verse equates the performance of austerity with the exercise of knowledge (*tapa iti jñānam ucyate*). Śaṁkara adds that Brahman willed, thought, and created.[95] Any student of Śaivism cannot fail to notice the parallel with Śiva's powers of will (*icchā*), knowledge (*jñāna*), and action (*kriyā*).

The protovoluntaristic position of the Taittirīyopaniṣad comes across also in the Śvetāśvataropaniṣad. In the imagery of the cosmic wheel (1.4) the metaphor of a leather strap (*pāśa*) expresses Brahman's desire (*kāma*) as the single impulse whose countless expressions keep the play of creation going.

The supreme Brahman, now thinking himself to be the enjoyer (*bhoktṛ*) or experient of the phenomenal world, regards things in a different light. Viewing the universe not as his self-willed emission (*aiśvaryasarga*) but as a bondage-laden phenomenon (*pāśavasarga*), he thinks himself bound. Simply put, Śiva becomes *jīva*—divinity expresses itself through the individual soul.

But how? The cosmic emanation comes about through the power of *māyā*. And what, exactly, is *māyā?* Advaita Vedānta defines it as Brahman's inscrutable power, sometimes called the power of ignorance (*avidyāśakti*). It is neither wholly real nor wholly unreal but somehow dependent on Brahman and inseparable from it, just as the power to burn is inseparable from fire. That said, Brahman ever rests in its own perfection as absolute being-consciousness-bliss (*saccidānanda*) and does not actively create. Instead Advaita Vedānta teaches that the apparent world, with all its objects and individual souls, is superimposed on Brahman through this mysterious power of *māyā*.

In contrast, the Trikadarśana teaches that the universe becomes manifest when the Absolute, called Paramaśiva or simply Śiva, freely and willingly engages in sportive self-limitation (*krīḍā* or *līlā*) through his power of *māyā*. According to this philosophy the creation is not a superimposition on reality but the Absolute's own self-projection. As for *māyā*, the Trika philosophers were not content to regard it as a single, homogeneous principle. Taking a closer look, they discovered deeper insights into what *māyā* is and how it works to shroud the oneness of the Absolute in the veils of creation. Śiva's pure unity is lost, or so it seems, in the manyness of his own projections. Through his *māyā* the Lord enters into every name and form. In this state of finite experience, he dilutes his lordship among souls beyond number, and the light of the Self, no longer surpassing even the sun in brilliance, is diffused here and there like the dimness of myriad fireflies. Each soul, finding itself in the thrall of worldly experience, thinks itself bound.

Advaita Vedānta declares that *nirguṇa* Brahman, being beyond all qualities, is utter perfection. The Trikadarśana also holds that the Absolute is perfection itself but allows that divine perfection is all-powerful, all-knowing, complete in itself, eternal, and all-pervading. Hence Śiva's five perfections are omnipotence (*sarvakartṛtva*), omniscience (*sarvajñātṛtva*), fullness or self-satisfaction (*pūrṇatva*), eternality (*nityatva*), and omnipresence (*vyāpakatva*).

Māyā, in contrast, is Śiva's power of limitation, with five restricting conditions (*kañcukas*) corresponding to his fivefold perfection. The *kañcukas* give rise to a fivefold sense of difference (*bheda*) within the undifferentiated unity (*abheda*) of the Absolute, effectively reducing the infinite One to the finitude of space-time.[96] Through *māyā* the all-pervading Self assumes limited individuality. The effulgent oneness of consciousness, now obscured, appears instead as the separate lights of innumerable finite souls—the multiple self-expressions of the one supreme Lord. As Śvetāśvatara puts it, the Self grows forgetful of his lordship.

From the divine perspective the ever-perfect Īśa engages playfully in the game of his own creation, experiencing it through countless individual souls. From the human perspective, we experience our individuality as a sense of difference, separateness, and even alienation from other living beings and insensate objects. We become acutely aware of our limitations. As the grammarian Pāṇini, a Śaiva, pointed out, *māyā's* veils (*kañcukas*) exist inside human thought and perception as the components of existential ignorance (*pauruṣa ajñāna*). The Trikaśāstra takes a more positive view in speaking collectively of the *kañcukas* as *dhāraṇā:* apart from the restrictions they impose, they are also the *support* that makes human existence possible. The Lord (Īśa) and his power are one and the same, so consciousness itself is the support of its own creativity (*īśvara*). In the same way, the *kañcukas* support the manifestation of the phenomenal world. Or, phrased in the manner of Advaita Vedānta, *īśa* here stands for Brahman, the support of both Īśvara (the cause) and his effects (the world).[97]

In the Trika system *māyā* and the five *kañcukas* form the mixed or pure-impure order (*śuddhāśuddhādhvan*), the level of consciousness intermediate between the transcendental unity of Śiva and the multiplicity experienced by the *jīva* (see pp. 57–58). Forming a distinctive feature of Śaiva cosmology, the *kañcukas* are five in number. They are called *kalā, vidyā, rāga, kāla,* and *niyati.*

Two of these terms, *kāla* and *niyati,* have already figured in Śvetāśvatara's discourse (1.2) as the possible cause of the universe and human existence. The seer was quick to dismiss them, pointing out that they themselves are effects. Neither can be the ultimate cause—that was subsequently shown to be the power of consciousness itself (*devātmaśakti*) (1.3). This power within the divine unity arises as the initial urge to manifest, bearing out the declaration of earlier Upaniṣads, "May I be many, may I grow forth" (*bahu syāṁ prajāyeyeti*). Elaborated in Trika nondualism as *icchāśakti,* it is the power inherent in the pure subjectivity of consciousness that first engenders a vague idea of objectivity within itself. In the Trika system cosmic evolution is conceptualized as a causal chain of thirty-six principles (*tattvas*), each principle that emerges being the source and becoming the cause of the next. As the tenth and eleventh *tattvas, kāla* and *niyati* are two of *māyā's* five differentiating and limiting capacities. Each is the effect of something preceding as well as the cause of something further. It is through the five *kañcukas* of *māyā* that the single reality of consciousness appears to assume two separate aspects in the phenomenal or impure creation (*aśuddhādhvan*)—the individualized subjective experient (*puruṣa*) and the objectivity (*prakṛti*) that are the twelfth and thirteenth *tattvas* of the Trika system.

The first of *māyā's* five *kañcukas* or limiting capacities is *kalā. Kalā,* meaning "part," "particle," or "aspect," is the factor that reduces divine omnipotence (*sarvakartṛtva*) to the individual's limited and particularized capacity for action (*kiñcitkartṛtva*).[98] The absolute freedom (*svātantrya*) and boundless power (*kriyāśakti*) of its original, divine nature forgotten, the Self appearing as the *jīva* mistakes itself as the finite doer. What for the Lord is pure, spontaneous, and motiveless action (*kriyā*) becomes for the bound soul the impure, limited, and binding action (*karma*) that unfolds in a world of multiplicity, relationship, and relativity. In this world human action cannot be motiveless, and *karma* is binding because it involves the ethical choices of virtue or merit *(puṇya)* and vice or demerit (*pāpa*) as well as expectation and consequence.

Ordinarily *vidyā* means "knowledge," but the *kañcuka* of that name is the power to compromise divine omniscience (*sarvajñātṛtva*) and reduce it to the impure knowledge (*aśuddhavidyā*) of the finite being. Limited consciousness understands itself not as the infinite One but as the individual knower, endowed no longer with that supreme knowledge by which all else is known, but with an incomplete and fragmentary understanding that is faulty, unreliable, and misleading. Because of this *kañcuka* the bound soul (*paśu*) forgets its true, all-knowing nature and lives instead in existential ignorance (*pauruṣa ajñāna*), wherein is rooted the paltry sense of ego (*asmitā*). The *tattva* known as *vidyā* produces the impurity of duality in regard to the sense of selfhood; each *jīva* recognizes itself as a lone experient in a sea of otherness. In distinction, the Lord alone recognizes the world as his own projection.[99]

Rāga ("passion") obscures the fullness or self-satisfaction (*pūrṇatva*) of our original divine nature. This imperfection of *rāga* stems from *vidyā's* differentiation of self and other, creating a sense of lack. Distracted by all the finite objects of sense, the bound soul is incapable of comprehending its original, unbounded wholeness. Seeking satisfaction outside itself, the *paśu* becomes reduced to a state of dependency. A sense of lack leads to dissatisfaction and the urge for enjoyment and the desire for possession. Possession, in turn, breeds attachment, and attachment inevitably carries with it the fear of loss. Also, the unavoidable companion of desire (*rāga*) is its mirror-image, aversion (*dveṣa*), and this inseparable pair again reflects consciousness in a state of duality, marked by attraction, craving, clinging, avoidance, and selfishness. When the impurity of *rāga* dissolves, there remains in its place a feeling of oneness with all creation (*sarvātmabhāva*), also characterised as universal love (*viśvaprema*).[100] The reason is simple: one who maintains an attitude of neither attachment nor aversion becomes free of both and attains the equanimity of *brahmabhāva*, the state in which the nature of divine consciousness, or the essential Self, is revealed.[101]

The Self is eternal, but *kāla* ("time") is the apparent limitation on the eternality (*nityatva*) of the Divine. While the true Self remains unconditioned by time (*akāla*), the individual soul is bound by it. Out of timelessness the deluding power of *kāla* creates the sense of "I was, I am, I shall be," and leads us to perceive everything in terms of past, present, and future.[102] Time is not an objective reality, but only a concept that the finite mind imagines to be real. Time does not exist apart from the finite knower, on whom its restrictions bear down heavily. It restricts in not allowing us to conceive of anything except in temporal terms. *Kāla* generates a sense of before and after, which suggests the idea of sequence (*krama*). Even though time seems to pass as an unbroken flow, we divide its span into segments, measured as seconds, minutes, hours, days, weeks, months, years, centuries, and millennia. Within this flow we perceive constant change and become painfully aware of the impermanence of life. In this way *kāla* reduces the boundless eternality of the Divine to the finitude of human mortality.

If the Lord's fifth perfection is omnipresence (*vyāpakatva*), it follows that its restriction is physical space. Bound as we are by time, we are also constrained by space. But *niyati* is more: it is determinism, destiny, natural law, or causality.[103] *Niyati* ties the human soul and all other created things to "the law of nature that establishes the order of succession in the appearance of all phenomena."[104] For example, it determines how a seed develops into a tree, and only into the same kind of tree that produced the seed. Such determinism limits the divine power of infinite possibility. *Niyati* also determines the manner in which created things interact and the sequentiality (*krama*) by which all events unfold.[105] No embodied being can fulfill its desires through the mere force of will, but only by following the logical steps dictated by how things work in the natural world.[106] In distinction the Lord is not bound by *niyati*; in fact, it is Śiva who, through his *jñānaśakti*, determines or designs the very laws that operate throughout nature, including the law of *karma* that holds the *paśu* captive and causes it to reap the sweet and bitter fruits of its actions.[107]

It should be evident by now that the *kañcukas*, *māyā's* limiting powers, do not operate independently of one another but work together to produce the phenomenal universe. *Māyā* is the *devātma-śakti*, the power of the effulgent Self to express itself as, in, and through the universe and all its individual beings. The *kañcukas* are that power's five basic modes of limitation by which the infinite Self experiences itself as finite. That Self (Śiva), as the creator, is the master of his own *māyā*; the individual self (*jīva*, *paśu*) is *māyā's* captive. But in the end the *jīva* is Śiva, only appearing diluted and deluded by *māyā*. When the separate soul at last awakens to the resplendent wholeness of its true divinity, all the limiting impurities fall away, and unbounded Oneness shines in absolute freedom. That is the gist of Śvetāśvatara's concluding thought: "Knowing that effulgent being [the Lord, Brahman, as one's own true Self], one is freed from all fetters." That utterance, so succinct in the original Sanskrit (*jñātvā devaṁ mucyate sarvapāśaiḥ*), underscores the Upaniṣad's dominant theme of liberation through knowledge, an idea explicit in nearly a third of the verses overall. These exact words will become a refrain that resounds four more times in the course of the seer's teaching (2.15, 4.16, 5.13, 6.13).

9

ज्ञाज्ञौ द्वावजावीशनीशावजा
ह्येका भोक्तृभोग्यार्थयुक्ता ।
अनन्तश्चात्मा विश्वरूपो ह्यकर्ता
त्रयं यदा विन्दते ब्रह्ममेतत् ॥ ९ ॥

jñājñau dvāv ajāv īśanīśāv ajā hy ekā bhoktṛbhogyārthayuktā /
anantaś cātmā viśvarūpo hy akartā trayaṁ yadā vindyate brahmam etat //

9. The two, the [all-]knowing [Lord] and the not-knowing [soul], are unborn [from all eternity]; the ruler and the ruled are both unborn. There is one other without beginning, intent on relating the enjoyer to that which is to be enjoyed, even while the infinite Self, though appearing as the universe, acts not at all. When this triad is fully known, it is seen to be Brahman.

Continuing with the theme of knowledge, the present *mantra* is highly significant. Unfortunately a good deal of confusion surrounds it, partly because of its terseness, partly because of syntactical and grammatical irregularities,[108] partly because it reverts twice to the archaic style of the older Vedic language,[109] partly because its symbolism is obscure, partly because the word *aja* ("unborn" or "goat") presents the possibility of a *double entendre* (unlikely here, but fully intended later on in *mantra* 4.5), and partly because commentators attempt to read the verse according to doctrines of classical Sāṁkhya or Advaita Vedānta that were formulated centuries later. It would be fruitless to detail the wide-ranging interpretations and their ramifications here, because our purpose is simply to seek insight into what the text actually says.

Essential to understanding this *mantra* is the acknowledgement, all appearances to the contrary, that life in this world is less a matter of being than of knowing, because everything depends on awareness. Somehow human attention becomes focused on the existence of objects and events rather than on the knowledge of their existence. But Abhinavagupta, writing in the *Tantrāloka* (3.57), explains that it is the knowledge that is essential. All the phenomena of this world are dependent on knowledge (*jñānasāpekṣa*), because whatever is known to the mind is known not as the thing-in-itself but as the *knowledge* of that thing.[110]

In trying to clarify the experience of the world, this *mantra* probes deeply into the nature and functioning of consciousness itself. First Śvetāśvatara speaks of something knowing (*jña*) and something unknowing (*ajña*). The word *jña* here means not just "knowing" or conscious, but more properly "all-knowing," and it refers to the Lord (Īśa) as personal God, creator, and ruler.[111] In the same way, *ajña* here does not mean "unknowing" in the sense of insentient (*jaḍa*); rather it describes the condition of the individual soul as limited in the capacity to know. The *jīva* is not devoid of consciousness but only unaware of its own original nature. Its ignorance or not-knowing (*ajñāna*) masks its true infinitude and causes it to see itself as finite, separate, and identified with any number of objective, perceivable qualities that belong to body, mind, and personality. Again, this not-knowing is not an absence of consciousness but only a reduction of consciousness. Certainly the *jīva* experiences life in this world as a sentient being—of that there can be no doubt—but its knowledge is imperfect because it is only partial.

In the Trika understanding, human awareness is no more than a contraction (*saṁkoca*) of divine omniscience (*sarvajñātṛtva*) into the particularized awareness (*kiñcitjñātṛtva*) of the individual experient. In the same way, divine omnipotence (*sarvakartṛtva*) contracts into the individual's particularized ability (*kiñcitkartṛtva*), and that is the point Śvetāśvatara makes by qualifying this pair of *jña* and *ajña* as *īśa* and *anīśa.* The Lord is all-powerful and sovereign (*īśa*), and the individual soul is restricted and bereft of power (*anīśa*). Put another way, whereas the Lord is the master of *māyā,* the soul is its subject, fettered by the inescapable duality of enjoyment and suffering. Significantly, the paired terms *jña-ajña* and *īśa-anīśa* refer directly to consciousness and its inseparable power, whether they are called Brahman and *māyā,* Śiva and Śakti, *prakāśa* and *vimarśa,* or anything else. Moreover, in nondualistic Śaiva thought the two—consciousness and its power—are not only inseparable but identical.

The all-knowing Īśa and the partially knowing *jīva* are both unborn (*aja*). The word *aja* means "unproduced," "unoriginated," and "being from all eternity." It is fairly obvious that the absolute Brahman, the ultimate reality, is unborn, but how can the same be said of the active, creating-ruling God and of the individual soul bound by time and space? The answer is simple: they too have consciousness as their essential nature.

And there is one other unborn (*ajā*). Note that it is grammatically feminine. This third unborn is intent on relating the enjoyer to that which is to be enjoyed (*bhoktṛbhogyārthayuktā*). Here it is important to understand that the Sanskrit words for *enjoyer* and *enjoyed* carry more than the idea of pleasure. They derive from the verbal root *bhuj,* meaning to enjoy in a general sense, especially to enjoy food and drink, to consume, to use, to possess, and in the broadest sense to experience even that which causes suffering—in other words, to experience life in "happiness and all the rest" (*sukhetareṣu*), as Śvetāśvatara phrased it in his opening statement (1.1).

What is this third unoriginated entity (*ajā*)? Scholars following the Vedantic *Śvetāśvataropaniṣadvṛtti*[112] or the Sāṁkhya explanation[113] understand *ajā* to mean *prakṛti,* but the doctrines of either philosophy do not fit well with the *mantra* overall and raise technical difficulties that have to be explained away. From what Śvetāśvatara says about it, *ajā* cannot be classical Sāṁkhya's *prakṛti,* an entity eternally separate from *puruṣa*. Nor can it be Advaita Vedānta's *māyā* or *prakṛti,* a dependent and lesser entity that is unexplainable, being not real though not wholly unreal either. Max Müller took this unborn feminine to be *devātmaśakti*,[114] the effulgent Self's power of creation already mentioned in the text (1.3), the essential capability of consciousness itself to bring about the manifestation of the cosmos. Śvetāśvatara refers to the three unborn principles as a triad (*traya*) and says that when known in its true nature this triad is seen to be the singular reality of Brahman.

The interpretation of the triad according to Advaita Vedānta teaches that everything in the universe appears to exist because of the radiance of an all-pervading, self-luminous consciousness. That view finds support in a verse common to three Upaniṣads—the Kaṭha (2.3.15), the Śvetāśvatara (6.14), and the Muṇḍaka (2.2.10)—which declares, "He alone shining, everything shines after him. By his light all this universe shines." In the light of consciousness the universe becomes manifest through the threefold distinction of the knower (*pramātṛ*), the known (*prameya*), and the knowing (*pramiti*)—a distinction that rests, however, on the unity of Brahman, the eternal witness (*sākṣin*). That single consciousness, reflected in the mind (*antaḥkaraṇa*), then appears as the individual soul (*jīva*), the finite percipient or cognizer (*pramātṛ*) to whom the phenomenal world becomes apparent in all its variation.[115] Thus, pure consciousness dwells in every sentient being both as the infinite witness (*sākṣin*) and the finite knower (*pramātṛ*). The object known (*prameya*) is nothing but a modification of the mind (*antaḥkaraṇavṛtti*), and the process of cognition (*pramiti*) also is a manifestation of consciousness.[116] So far, so good. However, possibly referring to the above-cited verse (6.14 in the present Upaniṣad), Śaṁkara's disciple Sureśvara observes that only the immutable consciousness (*kūṭastha caitanya*), shining as the witness, is self-luminous and claims that the members of the triad are themselves devoid of consciousness, shining only by the reflected light of the Self.[117] For the Śaiva the implications will be somewhat different.

The ramifications of the Vedantic interpretation of *traya* as the triad of knower, knowing, and known do not quite correspond to the Śaiva view or even, exactly, to what Śvetāśvatara's triad of Īśa, *jīva*, and *devātmakśakti* indicates. Lest there be any doubt, the seer will make clear in a later *mantra* (1.12) that his triad consists of the enjoyer (*bhoktṛ*), the enjoyed (*bhogya*), and the inciting power of consciousness (*preritṛ*). *Bhoktṛ* signifies the Lord (*jña*, Īśa), *bhogya* his enjoyment of experiencing the universe through the individual souls, and *preritṛ* the impelling power of consciousness that sets everything in motion. Founded on the text's own internal evidence, this explanation of the triad as consisting of the Lord, the individual soul, and the divine creative (or binding) power resembles the triad of *pati, paśu,* and *pāśa* expressed in the *Pāśupatasūtra,* an idea refined to the fullest extent in the later Trika doctrine of the three orders of creation.

The Trika system presents the manifestation of the phenomenal universe as a flow, a course or a journey (*adhvan*) of consciousness out of the primal divine light, or Śiva. To explain the process the Trikaśāstra proposes a model of thirty-six cosmic principles (*tattvas*) grouped into three orders. The pure order (*śuddhādhvan*) is the divine experience within the Lord Śiva's unitary consciousness. The pure-impure order (*śuddhāśuddhādhvan*) is Śiva's own power of creativity through differentiation and limitation. The impure order (*aśuddhādhvan*) is the fully diversified universe of name, form, and quality, or consciousness in its manifest aspect. The pure order corresponds to the all-knowing Lord (*jña,* Īśa), who becomes the individual experient (*ajña, anīśa*) of the impure order, which is nothing but the free expression of his own being through the creative or projecting power of his own shining consciousness (*devātmaśakti*), filtered through the pure-impure order, known as *māyā.* In this way the supreme Śiva (Brahman) becomes the enjoyer (*bhoktṛ*) of that which is to be enjoyed (*bhogya*)—the manifest universe with all its individual experients.

Even while *māyā,* the inciting power (*preritṛ*), perpetuates the round of existence for the bound soul, the Self (*ātman*) remains pure consciousness-in-itself, a nonagent (*akartṛ*), ever-blissful in its own absolute freedom (*svātantrya*). What, then, is the difference between the Lord and the soul? Śvetāśvatara has already told us. It is the difference of divine omniscience and human unknowing, of divine omnipotence and human frailty. It cannot be a difference of essence, because both Īśa and *jīva* have consciousness as their essence. Whether consciousness is at rest (*viśrānti*) as Brahman-Paramaśiva or in motion as the world-creating *devātmaśakti* (and the innumerable souls it projects), either way it is consciousness. The difference is one of purity and impurity, meaning of oneness and multiplicity. Śiva, being absolute subjectivity, is attributeless (*nirguṇa*) and perfect. The *jīvā,* being consciousness tainted with the limitations of objectivity, is imperfect. But when the *jīva*, in deepest meditation, divests itself of *māyā's* limiting veils, it realizes its essential identity with the unbounded Self. When all is known as Brahman, the triple distinction of subject, object, and their relationship melts into pure oneness, and the Absolute alone remains.

The directness and power of Śvetāśvatara's utterance invites us at this point to review what he has taught thus far in the discourse that forms this first chapter. The inquirers of the opening verse (*brahmavādinaḥ*), like all spiritual aspirants, begin by studying the surrounding world and their interactions with it. Śvetāśvatara summarily dismisses various philosophies that propose this or that as the ultimate cause of the universe and human existence (1.2). Next he directs our attention inward, invoking the seekers who in deep meditation discovered the indwelling power of consciousness that belongs to the effulgent Self who presides, purely One, over all of creation (1.3). Śvetāśvatara glosses over their highly complex vision of the cosmos as the wheel of Brahman (1.4), not elaborating on the symbolism either because its meaning would have been readily apparent to his listeners or because its complexity betokens the effect rather than the cause. He is only slightly more explicit on the imagery of the river of consciousness (1.5), although we are left with the impression of its innumerable aspects uppermost in our minds. Certainly as the One becomes the many, greater and greater complexity arises. The seers attest to that in their detailed analyses of the phenomenal universe. But that is not Śvetāśvatara's point. The deeper we penetrate into our own awareness, the simpler our view of reality becomes. It is as if he is urging us to stop wondering about the untold manyness of the wheel's unexplained parts, to leave behind the puzzling enumerations of the river's flow, and simply to *wonder* at the simplicity behind it all.

Now he reduces the whole of existence to a triad within consciousness, and that triad in turn to nothing other than the singular reality of Brahman. Of course, we can never be certain of the subtlest nuances that these ancient verses may or may not convey or of the seer's precise intention in every instance, but perhaps the point he wishes to impress on us is that in trying to understand our existence, we begin by making it unnecessarily complicated. After all, it should be clear from the sixth *mantra* onward that he is attempting to draw us away from all that and toward the ultimate simplicity.

10

क्षरं प्रधानममृताक्षरं हरः
क्षरात्मानावीशते देव एकः ।
तस्याभिध्यानाद्योजनात्तत्त्व-
भावात् भूयश्चान्ते विश्वमायानिवृत्तिः ॥ १० ॥

kṣaraṁ pradhānam amṛtākṣaraṁ haraḥ kṣarātmānāv īśate deva ekaḥ / tasyābhidhyānād yojanāt tattvabhāvāt bhuyaś cānte viśvamāyānivṛttiḥ //

10. That which is perishable is matter. That which is immortal and imperishable is Hara, the one God [who] rules over perishable matter and the soul. By constantly meditating on him, uniting with him, and becoming that reality, one at last attains the cessation of all illusion.

In the previous *mantra* Śvetāśvatara drew a distinction between the bound soul and the boundless Self. Then he alluded to the inciting power of consciousness as their connector. Together the three form a triad. To make his meaning clear beyond a doubt, in a future *mantra* the seer will define this triad as consisting of the enjoyer or experient (*bhoktṛ*), the to-be-enjoyed or experienced (*bhogya*), and the inciting power that relates them (*preritṛ*).

Continuing, Śvetāśvatara elaborates methodically on the foregoing verse. Whatever is made of matter (*pradhānam*) is perishable (*kṣaram*). The objective world of nature, produced by *māyā,* is ever-changing and therefore destructible. That which changes does not and cannot endure forever. But beyond nature there is a reality that is deathless (*amṛtam*) and imperishable (*akṣaram*)—the eternal subject, or Brahman, here called Hara. The author of the *Śvetāśvataropaniṣadvṛtti* explains that the name *Hara* means "destroyer" or "remover" in the sense that the Lord is the destroyer or remover of ignorance. That observation is semantically accurate, of course, but it fails to reveal the true breadth and depth of what Śvetāśvatara wants to convey. By this name he clearly refers to the Absolute[118] and then characterizes this Absolute, Hara, as ruling over perishable matter and the soul. This is highly significant, because the philosophical outlook it presents found its way into the *Pāśupatasūtra,* a subsequent Śaiva text that parallels the Upaniṣad's teaching by speaking of the cause (*kāraṇa,* Brahman, *pati*) as ruling over the effect (*kārya*) that consists of matter and the individual soul. Hara is the one God (*deva ekaḥ*) who rules (*īśate*) over impermanent matter and the restless soul. Although human lives are always in flux, the Divine abides, peaceful and unchanging, in every heart. The verb *īśate* is also significant, because it belongs to the same source as the theonyms *Īśa, Īśāna,* and *Īśvara* and also the word *aiśvarya* ("sovereignty"), an important theme in the next *mantra.*

The many ways in which this Upaniṣad refers to God raise a profound question. It is only natural that *Brahman,* a neuter noun, is grammatically associated with the neuter pronouns *it* and *its.* By the same logic, the masculine designations of the divine reality (*īśa, deva,* Hara, Rudra, *ātman,* and others) take the masculine pronouns *he, him,* and *his.* In the course of Śvetāśvatara's teaching, there is a fairly free mixing of the two sets of pronouns, suggesting one of two conclusions. Either this Upaniṣad, as Paul Deussen proposed, has failed to synthesize adequately the differing points of view it encompasses, or it offers us a surprising new way of looking at the divine reality, a very fluid way that moves easily between a transpersonal "it" and a theistic "him."

In its own way, although with very different philosophical conclusions, Advaita Vedānta recognizes Brahman in those same two aspects. Without attributes, *nirguṇa* Brahman is the unchanging ground of existence. With attributes, *saguṇa* Brahman is Brahman associated with *māyā,* the active personal God known as Īśvara, who creates, sustains, and dissolves the universe. Nevertheless, Advaita Vedānta considers *nirguṇa* Brahman alone as the absolute and ultimate reality, which it sees as impersonal.

The Trikaśāstra, although every bit as nondualistic as Advaita Vedānta, would disagree with the term *impersonal.* As a prelude, let us consider the great dictum (*mahāvākya*) of the Bṛhadāraṇyakopaniṣad (1.4.10): "I am Brahman" (*ahaṁ brahmāsmi*). Notice that there is a declarer who says, "*I* am Brahman." We cannot leave the *I* out of the identity equation even when the declared identity is that of the highest reality. And so, the Vedantic characterization of the Supreme

Being as impersonal seems at odds with the *mahāvākya*. In the Trika teaching Paramaśiva is likewise nondual and absolute, but far from being a remote and impersonal principle, he (or it) is extremely personal. In fact, Paramaśiva is the ultimate and absolute I. This view, central to nondual Kashmir Śaivism, is embodied in the doctrine of the Lord's nonduality (*īśvarādvayavāda*).

That doctrine, also known as theistic absolutism, theistic monism, or monistic theism, was first articulated in Somānanda's *Śivadṛṣṭi* [Vision of Śiva], the foundational statement of the Pratyabhijñā philosophy.[119] *Īśvarādvayavāda* is the doctrine of the absolute but personal God who is the sole reality and in essence the highest level of consciousness.[120] Like the nondualistic teaching of the Upaniṣads, *īśvarādvayavāda* is said to be founded on experience, in this case the experience of the ancient Kashmiri Śaiva sages who chose not to rely on mere logic and intellectual speculation but who "discovered the Absolute within themselves and found they were one with it." They experienced the reality of the Self as divine creative energy. For them God was neither a remote ruler nor an inert mass of consciousness (the *cidghana* of the Vedānta) but rather the animating force within everything—consciousness giving expression to the whole of creation even while remaining ever pure, infinite, and transcendent.[121] Notice how closely this account parallels Śvetāśvatara's description of ancient seekers discovering within themselves the power of the effulgent Self (*devātmaśakti*) (1.3). That effulgent Self, according to the Trikaśāstra, is not an impersonal principle but the ultimate Person.[122]

What is the one quality that makes a person a person? It is the awareness of self. And it follows that there cannot be a conscious self without the sense of I. What we ordinarily understand by *I* is the confining sense of ego (*asmitā*), which distinguishes and separates the individual soul from all other souls and indeed from the rest of creation. This ego-based I has little to do with the divine reality's own sense of self (*ahaṁtā*); the ego offers at best only a dim glimmer of absolute subjectivity amid the welter of objective qualities by which it identifies and defines itself. To the contrary, Śiva's luminous sense of I is boundlessly whole and One without a second (*advitīya*). There is no other. Unlike the individual ego-sense (*asmitā*), founded on division, Śiva's I-ness (*ahaṁtā*) is the perfection of wholeness (*pūrṇatva*), or I-ness in full (*pūrṇāhaṁtā*).

Our human self-awareness as separate beings is determined and colored by all the attributes of body, mind, personality, and external objects with which we mistakenly identify and bind ourselves, forgetful of our true nature. We may wonder, then, how the Absolute, which is free of all such defining limitations, can have a sense of self-awareness. On what could infinite self-awareness possibly be based if there is nothing other than the One? According to the Trikaśāstra, self-radiant consciousness (*prakāśa*) has an inherent self-referential energy (*vimarśa*), which Abhinavagupta defined as "the capacity of the Self to know itself in all its purity."[123] Thus, the consciousness that is the supreme Śiva eternally vibrates with its own pure awareness of I.

When the Absolute wills, imagines, and projects the creation out of its own consciousness, that pure knowledge of I (*aham*) becomes the differentiated knowledge of "I am this" (*aham idam*) (see pp. 58–59). Nevertheless, even in the state of universal manifestation and multiplicity, God's own awareness of "I am" remains an ever-present and indispensable part of the equation. In other words, the supreme reality, eternally resting in its own transcendence (*aham*), can simultaneously appear at will as the ruling Lord (Īśa, Pati) and the world he rules over (*idam*), consisting of perishable matter and the individual soul (*pāśa* and *paśu*).

In the light of this understanding, the boundary between transcendental reality, personal God, individual soul, and created universe is a fluid one, if in fact there is any boundary at all. Along the continuum of consciousness, the Divine can never be separate but is identical to the self in every being. We cannot deny that in our everyday lives, going about our mundane business, we are always aware of our own existence. That is a natural reflection of the Self within, whose being is absolute and ever-present.

The purpose of spiritual practice (*sādhanā*) is to recognize our identity with that shining reality. The Absolute may be beyond the reach of the limited mind and unattainable through any relative form of knowledge, such as cognizing or reasoning. It cannot be expressed through the concepts of thought and language, which at best are only distant approximations of its seeming beyondness. The Absolute can be known, however, through direct revelation (*darśana*). By looking inward and reaching the state of deepest contemplation, the spiritual aspirant (*sādhaka*) transcends every individual limitation and discovers the ultimate truth that God and Self are one.

In the Bhagavadgītā (6.29), Śrī Kṛṣṇa says, "He who is established in *yoga* beholds the vision of sameness everywhere, the Self present in all beings and all beings in the Self." One whose consciousness is released (*mukta*) from false identification with the manifold qualities of body, mind, personality, habits, interests, and possessions identifies with awareness alone. That awareness, while pervading all qualities, is not confined by them. Echoing the teaching of the Bhagavadgītā, the *Śivasūtra* (1.14) declares in two words (*dṛśyaṁ śarīram*) that all phenomena, internal and external, are like the *yogin's* own body—as Abhinavagupta's disciple Kṣemarāja explains, identical with oneself and not different.[124] Of course *body* here does not refer to one's physical body, because this state of expanded awareness results from no longer identifying with the physical form (or even with mental qualities) but with consciousness alone. The Sanskrit word for *body* derives from a root meaning "to support" (*śri*), and the point here is that consciousness is the very support of the universe. When this mystical vision opens up, whatever is seen (*dṛśyam*) is intuited to be one's own substance, not separate or different. This state of unitary awareness is known as *sarvātmabhāva,* the experience of all existence as one's own Self, to which nothing can be external. Just as the experience of the *sadāśiva-tattva* is "I am this [entire universe]" (*aham idam*), so is the experience of the *yogin* in the ecstasy of universal consciousness.[125]

Spiritual attainment rarely comes spontaneously and most often involves sincere commitment and diligence to bring about a progressive unfoldment. The *sādhanā* that Śvetāśvatara describes here has three stages. The first consists of focusing the mind (*abhidhyāna*) on the object of meditation to the exclusion of all other thoughts, but along with purposeful direction of the mind, *abhidhyāna* also entails a sense of intense longing. When concentration grows deep enough, the meditator passes into the second stage, that of yoking or harnessing or holding fast (*yojana*), and comes face to face with the object of meditation. The two are joined together in the contemplative union (*samādhi*) described by the Sāṁkhya as *samprajñāta* ("differentiated") and by the Vedānta as *savikalpa* ("with concepts")—a visionary state in which the very idea or concept of soul and Self is all that remains as the final obstacle dividing consciousness. Beyond that lies the third stage, which Śvetāśvatara refers to as "becoming the reality" (*tattvabhāva*). This nondual experience is the *samādhi* known as *asamprajñāta* ("undifferentiated") or *nirvikalpa* ("free of differentiated conception"), in which all distinction melts away and the soul merges with the supreme Self in complete identity,[126] that ultimate identity proclaimed by the *mahāvākya* "I am Brahman" (see p. 23).

11

ज्ञात्वा देवं सर्वपाशापहानिः
क्षीणैः क्लेशैर्जन्ममृत्युप्रहाणिः ।
तस्याभिध्यानात्तृतीयं देहभेदे
विश्वैश्वर्यं केवल आप्तकामः ॥ ११ ॥

jñātvā devaṁ sarvapāśāpahāṇiḥ kṣīṇaiḥ kleśair janmamṛtyuprahāṇiḥ / tasyābhidhyānāt tṛtīyaṁ dehabhede viśvaiśvaryaṁ kevala āptakāmaḥ //

11. When God is known, all fetters fall away. When life's afflictions waste away, birth and death come to an end. By constantly meditating on him and going beyond the sense of individuality, one attains the third state, that of universal sovereignty; in the One alone all desires are fulfilled.

When God is known (*jñātvā devam*)—that is, when the effulgent reality is experienced—the result is the falling away of all fetters (*sarvapāśāpahāṇiḥ*). This initial quarter (*pāda*) of the verse emphasizes that the way to liberation is through knowledge—knowledge of the self-luminous being at the heart of all existence.

It will be instructive here to distinguish between the English words *being* and *existence*. In common speech the verb *to exist* means "to be" or "to have reality," but this word derives from the Latin *existere,* which literally means "to step forth" or "to emerge." In a strict sense, *to exist* means "to be in a given condition or state or place, to manifest in a specific way." The distinction carries over into the nouns *being* and *existence*. Being simply *is;* existence is being in a conditioned state.

The knowledge of one's true, unconditioned being deepens one step at a time through diligent spiritual practice (*sādhanā*). In the previous *mantra* Śvetāśvatara described the gradual process leading to liberation as threefold, citing *abhidhyāna* (constant, purposeful meditation infused with longing), *yojana* (holding fast or yoking oneself to the ideal), and *tattvabhāva* (becoming that, identifying with the reality of the Self). With spiritual practice the mental fetters that once bound so tightly first loosen and then lose their hold. The individual soul (*paśu*) who can identify with the divine Self (*pati*) is no longer bound; it experiences the falling away of all fetters.

The fetters can be many and varied according to individual experience, but the Kulārṇavatantra, Yoginīhṛdayatantra, and other texts generally recognize eight as basic, with some variation. The enumeration found in the Paraśurāmakalpasūtra (10.70), written some time before 1300 CE, lists the eight as hate (*ghṛṇā*); shame (*lajjā*); fear (*bhayā*); suspicion, distrust, or hesitation (*śaṅkā*); arrogance of family or ancestry (*kula*); concern over proper conduct (*śīla*), a sense of superiority based on caste (*jāti*), and disgust or secrecy (*jugupsā*). Any of these, by themselves or in combination, can keep the mind in perpetual turmoil, and turmoil is bondage. Every fetter (*pāśa*) exists in the mind as a negative modification of consciousness. All are effects of the limiting and obscuring powers (*kañcukas*) of *māyā*, which impose their particular influences and impinge on the essential freedom of the Self (see. pp. 59–60).

The permutations are innumerable, but a few examples will suffice. Hate (*ghṛṇā*) arises from a sense of difference joined to a lack of right understanding. The sense of difference is caused by *māyā's* power of *kalā,* which veils the wholeness of being and allows the infinite One to manifest as the multifarious and finite many. Not knowing that reality is One comes about through *māyā's* power of *vidyā,* which reduces divine omniscience to the poverty of human (mis)understanding. Śiva's joyful sense of difference is no longer recognized as essential to the divine play; in the *jīva's* ignorance it can become venomous.

Hate is closely linked to fear (*bhayā*). Of course some fears are legitimately grounded in natural impulses of self-protection and survival, but the kind of fear that fetters is not a spontaneous reaction to danger; rather it is a cultivated delusion that manifests as animosity and malevolence toward anything perceived as different, unfamiliar, or threatening. That kind of fear is based on the misunderstanding of difference. Recalling from the Upaniṣads that Brahman thought, "May I be many, may I grow forth," we can recognize that diversity is the whole point of the creation (see pp. 114–115). God creates all this out of his own fertile imagination for his own delight.

When the infinite One expresses itself as the finite many, another of *māyā's* veils comes into play. *Rāga* is the veiling of divine wholeness and perfection (*pūrṇatva*). The individual soul, having forgotten its original nature, experiences a state of existential imperfection (*apūrṇatva*) and lack. It continually seeks satisfaction in any number of ways, but no amount of finite enjoyment can permanently fill the void. Wherever there is momentary gain, there is also the fear of loss, and that fear is closely tied to *māyā's* veil of time (*kāla*), which brings constant change, impermanence, and the specter of mortality.

As for the here-and-now feelings of inadequacy, there are two more fetters. Pride of caste (*jāti*) relates to one's position in society, and pride of family (*kula*) concerns the vanity of personal lineage. Both forms of pride aim at setting oneself above others, but their effect is negative and divisive, reinforcing a sense of difference and leading to alienation.

A third form of pride is *śīla*, the concern over acting in what will be seen as the proper way and presenting the right image of oneself. This pride of conduct further objectifies one's sense of self, only strengthening the sense of bondage. Moreover, it has little to do with what is morally right but is a surrender to convention based on what others think and expect. It is a fetter that reduces life to role-playing and drains it of spontaneity.

The failure to live up to expectations, along with regret over past mistakes or feelings of personal inadequacy, plays out through another fetter, the sense of shame (*lajjā*). Like pride of conduct, shame is a powerful social mechanism that can drive one's thoughts and actions. The need to keep up appearances can involve sustaining a deception, which in turn entangles one in the fetter of secrecy (*jugupsā*). Always having to be on guard and ever fearful of slipping up consumes a vast amount of mental energy, all the while draining life of openness and integrity.

One who has something to hide tends to think the same of others. In that way shame and secrecy breed distrust, and one becomes bound by the fetter of suspicion (*śaṅkā*). This outward projection of one's own faults serves no purpose other than to sully the experience of human life and to sow the seeds of discord.

Because the universe functions according to *māyā's* veil of determinism or natural law (*niyati*), the *jīva* becomes caught up in an intricate web of cause and effect. Instead of directing attention toward the goal of Self-knowledge, the mind and heart instead become tied into a monstrous mass of knots made of the interacting fetters of hatred, fear, pride of birth, pride of family, concern over appearances, secrecy, suspicion, and shame. Thus are we bound.

After the fetters, the next *pāda* draws our attention to life's inherent afflictions. This passage marks the only occurrence of the term *kleśa* in the principal Upaniṣads, and although Śvetāśvatara does not specify what the *kleśas* are, some centuries later Patañjali identified them in the *Yogasūtra* (2.3) as five pain-bearing dispositions. They are ignorance (*avidyā*), the ego-sense (*asmitā*), attraction (*rāga*), aversion (*dveṣa*), and habituality (*abhiniveśa*) (see p. 105). Because the mind is constantly active and ever-changing, the *Yogasūtra* (2.4) goes on to observe that the *kleśas* exist in various degrees of manifestation. At a given moment the condition of any one of them can be latent (*prasupta*), attentuated (*tanu*), interrupted (*vicchinna*), or, as the focus of attention, steadily operative (*udāra*). As long as consciousness remains in a state of activity (*cittavṛtti*), it engages with phenomenality and is bound. Only when this activity stills does the *jīva* recognize its own true being. Only then does the repeated round of birth, death, and rebirth come to an end. From the vantage point of one who has attained this highest state of consciousness, liberation is simply the recognition (*pratyabhijñā*) that one was always free and never bound.

In the third stage (*tṛtīyam*) of the process of liberation, which Śvetāśvatara calls "becoming the reality" (*tattvabhāva*), the aspirant experiences *dehabheda.* This Sanskrit term is usually translated as "the dissolution of the body,"[127] "the break-up of the body,"[128] "the fall of the body,"[129] or simply "death,"[130] but in fact *dehabheda* means a great deal more and has been rendered also as "going beyond the consciousness of the body,"[131] or "transcend[ing] physical consciousness."[132] *Deha* means not only "body" in the physical sense but also "form," "shape," "appearance," "manifestation," "individual," or "person."[133] *Bheda* likewise has a wide range of meanings, including "breaking," "splitting," "separation," "partition," "distinction," difference."[134] Although *deha* can apply to the physical body alone, the context here suggests the broader sense of the whole embodied person. Rather than signifying physical death, *dehabheda* simply means a change in consciousness—a dissociation in the here and now from the strictures of individuality.

Liberation is, of course, the subject of this entire *mantra,* and Śvetāśvatara's views are highly significant, because they anticipate and infuse later Śaiva doctrines. The seer defines liberation not only as freedom from bondage (*pāśa*) and affliction (*kleśa*) and finite individuality (*deha*) but also as identification with the divine Self (*deva*), which is inseparable from its power (*devātmaśakti*). This identification (*tattvabhāva*) is tantamount to universal sovereignty (*viśvaiśvarya*).

Unlike Śvetāśvatara's view, that of the roughly contemporaneous, dualistic Pāśupata sect defined *mokṣa* only as the cessation of suffering (*duḥkhānta*).[135] This is the same view clearly articulated at the outset of classical Sāṁkhya's defining text, Īśvarakṛṣṇa's *Sāṁkhyakārikā*. But Lakulīśa's reformed version of Pāśupatism redefined the older Śaiva doctrine of liberation and brought it closer to the views that Śvetāśvatara had expressed. The redefinition of liberation was not original to Śvetāśvatara, however. Lakulīśa drew upon the Taittirīyāraṇyaka[136] when he explained that besides freedom from all miseries, *mokṣa* also entails the positive attainment of the divine powers of knowledge and action,[137] otherwise known as supreme lordship (*pāramaiśvaryāvāpti*).[138] Śvetāśvatara's similar view, expressed some six or seven centuries before Lakulīśa's, may also have drawn on the Taittirīya tradition but took a somewhat different turn.

Śvetāśvatara's teaching is nondualistic (*advaita*), and Lakulīśa's is one of unity-in-multiplicity (*dvaitādvaita*). Lakulīśa considered *yoga* as union with the Divine, subtly distinct from Śvetāśvatara's idea of what that means, and radically distinct from Patañjali's classic definition that "yoga is the cessation of activity in the medium of consciousness" (*yogaś cittavṛttinirodhaḥ*), resulting in the disengagement of *puruṣa* from *prakṛti*.[139] Conversely in Lakulīśa's *dvaitādvaita* philosophy the individualized consciousness (*citta*) becomes united (*yukta*) with Maheśvara (Śiva), and in the matter of *yoga* as union Śvetāśvatara had gone still further, boldly proclaiming that *mokṣa* means not only an absorptive joining (*sāyujya*) but also "becoming that reality" (*tattvabhāva*)—complete identification.

Regarding liberation the present *mantra* expresses a decidedly Śaiva point of view that differs in several ways from the tenets of either Sāṁkhya-Yoga or Advaita Vedānta. Most of the differences revolve around the three terms of the final *pāda* (*viśvaiśvaryaṁ kevala āptakāmaḥ*), which hold radically different implications for the followers of the three philosophies.

Viśvaiśvarya is a compound of *viśva*, signifying the universe or totality, and *aiśvarya*, derived from the same source as *īśa* ("lord") and meaning "lordship," "rulership," "sovereignty." After Śvetāśvatara and Lakulīśa, the doctrine of *mokṣa* that includes the divine powers of knowledge and action and universal sovereignty developed further under the philosopher-seers of the Trikadarśana.

To understand the implications, we must first consider how Advaita Vedānta and the Trikaśāstra view the divine reality. Both systems agree on the nonduality of the Self. For both, the ultimate Self is consciousness, and the essence of that consciousness is self-luminosity (*prakāśa*). After that the opinions diverge. Advaita Vedānta considers that Brahman is only *prakāśa*—a static, eternally immutable principle. Moreover, Brahman is impersonal and inactive (*niṣkriya*), leading the Śaiva nondualists to call the Vedānta philosophy *śāntabrahmavāda* ("doctrine of the quiescent Brahman"). In contrast, the Śaiva *īśvarādvayavāda* ("doctrine of the Lord's nonduality") teaches that Śiva, the supreme Self, although utterly transcendental, is personal and has the capacity for action.[140]

Note here that along with *inactive* and *active* two additional terms have entered the discussion: *impersonal* and *personal*. In Trika teaching the essence of ultimate consciousness is not only transcendental self-luminosity (*prakāśa*) but also dynamic self-awareness (*vimarśa*). The light of consciousness (*prakāśa*) and its activity (*vimarśa*) are not different from each other; they are one and the same.[141] A synonym for *vimarśa* is *svātantrya*, one of the Trikaśāstra's many names for dynamic consciousness. Thus *vimarśa* also signifies absolute freedom, unconditioned autonomy, and hence the power of joy (*ānandaśakti*) beyond any imperfection or limitation.[142] That said, the self-referential capacity of *vimarśa*, the divine I-ness (*ahaṁtā*), is not like the *jīva's* limited I-am-ness (*asmitā*), which is predicated on difference and separation. Rather, the divine I includes everything *within* itself, and in that sense Śiva is alone (*kevala*) in a state of pure nonduality.[143]

The term *kevala* can mean "alone," "sole," "excluding others," "isolated," "absolute," "simple," "pure," "uncompounded," or "whole." In the technical sense of classical Sāṁkhya, it means "isolated." Its abstract derivative, *kaivalya,* expresses the Sāṁkhya view that *mokṣa* is the isolation of *puruṣa* from *prakṛti.* The idea that freedom results from separation is the ultimate affirmation of duality. In contrast, for Advaita Vedānta *kevala* means "alone" in the sense of "absolute" or "One without a second," and *kaivalya* means "absolute nonduality," for the liberated Self *is* the sole reality.[144]

Śvetāśvatara equates the absolute freedom of Self-knowledge with universal sovereignty (*viśvaiśvarya*), implying that the power of sovereignty is inherent to the supreme Self. This poses a challenge to some commentators, who are hard put to reconcile the seer's affirmation with Advaita Vedānta's view of an inactive Brahman. Max Müller and others,[145] following the *Śvetāśvataropaniṣadvṛtti* attributed to Śaṁkarācārya, dismiss *viśvaiśvarya* as a blissful, after-death state in the highest heaven (*brahmaloka*), falling short of full liberation.

To deal with this problematic passage, some authors go beyond editorial comment and interpolate qualifying phrases into the text itself. One such translation reads, "the aspirant, transcending that state also [universal sovereignty], abides in the complete bliss of Brahman." The accompanying commentary adds that only with the renunciation of all powers does one rest satisfied in union with Brahman.[146] Another translator makes a similar interpolation: "[Renouncing those powers] he attains to absolute self-fulfillment."[147] The idea of renunciation comes from a quotation in the *Vṛtti,* drawn from the Śivadharmottara, an Upapurāṇa (secondary Purāṇa) datable to no later than the tenth century CE. The quoted passage makes a distinction between meditation (*dhyāna*) and knowledge (*jñāna*), saying that *dhyāna* leads to lordship but *jñāna* confers liberation.

Other translator-commentators leave Śvetāśvatara's text intact but elaborate on this same point. In one instance the freed individual becomes a "co-worker" with the personal Lord for as long as the cosmic process continues and only merges into the Absolute thereafter.[148] Another commentator repeats that meditation and knowledge lead respectively to the acquisition of incomparable divine power (*aiśvaryam atulam*) or to liberation (*muktim*) and claims that power is to be rejected if one aspires to be free.[149]

Such a dichotomy is not even suggested by Śvetāśvatara's actual words. The text of his Upaniṣad offers no support for such an interpretation; rather, it presents a clear and uncomplicated exposition of a doctrine of the Taittirīya lineage that was in turn taken up by Lakulīśa and later developed to its fullest by the philosopher-seers of Kashmir.

Finally, Śvetāśvatara proclaims, "In the One all desires are fulfilled" (*kevala āptakāmaḥ*). When the absolute unity of the Self is experienced, the fulfillment of all desire results. In truth, desire fulfilled is desire that no longer exists. The state that Trika Śaivism defines as Śivahood is the unified consciousness of the One enjoying the perfection of its own being, free of any lack and therefore free of any desire.

Śvetāśvatara was not the first seer to associate infinite satisfaction and universal sovereignty with liberation. Many centuries earlier Yājñavalkya had made the same connection in his dialogue with King Janaka, and even those thoughts were not Yājñavalkya's own. As recorded in the Bṛhadāraṇyakopaniṣad (4.4.7, 12–14) Yājñavalkya begins, "There is a verse regarding this (*tad eṣa śloko bhavati*)." He continues, "When all desires that are fixed in the heart are let go, then the mortal becomes immortal and attains Brahman *here* [in the body or in this world] .... If a person discerns the Self, saying "I am this" (*ayam asmīti*), then why should the body be troubled (*śarīram anusaṁjvaret*) by willing what (*kim icchan*) for the desire of what (*kasya kāmāya*)? Whoever has discovered and awakened to the Self that has entered into the abyss that is the body (*saṁdehye gahane*), he is the creator of the universe (*sa viśvakṛt*), for he is the maker of everything (*sa hi sarvasya kartā*). His is the world (*tasya lokaḥ*); indeed he is the world itself (*sa u loka eva*). Truly now, being right here (*ihaiva santo 'tha*), we [can] know that (*vidmas tad vayam*)."

The gist is that divinity can be experienced in the here and now (*iha*) as one's own being (*ayam asmīti*, "I am this") apart from the body. Why, then, should the body be a source of distress? The all-powerful Self (or I-ness) is the creator of the universe and its sovereign and even the universe itself (*sa u loka eva*). Interestingly, *u loka* is an archaic figure of speech considered by some authorities to signify freedom of space, motion, or scope.[150] If so, the statement "his is the world (*tasya lokaḥ*); indeed he is the world itself (*sa u loka eva*)" suggests the Lord's own freedom to act (*svātantrya*) throughout the manifest universe, embracing everything from the innermost space of the human heart and mind to the unfathomable reaches of the cosmos. The ideas cited by Yājñavalkya in his discourse to King Janaka anticipate the much later Trika doctrine that the absolute Self is not different from the universal Lord or even from the world he rules over.

The association of universal sovereignty, perfect fulfillment, and liberation is a vision of ultimate unity. Far from being a radical departure on Śvetāśvatara's part, it has its origin in the oldest tradition of the Vedānta, already old when it was preserved in the Bṛhadāraṇyakopaniṣad.

As articulated much later in Trika teaching, it is through Śiva's own capacity of self-limitation (*māyā*) that he willingly expresses himself as innumerable finite souls. Then, as Śvetāśvatara explains in *mantra* 1.8, "Forgetful of his lordship…, the Self becomes bound." But the bondage is only apparent, and with the dawning of Self-knowledge the *jīva* recognizes that it has never been anything other than Śiva, possessed of omnipotence (*sarvakartṛtva*), omniscience (*sarvajñātṛtva*), omnipresence (*vyāpakatva*), eternality (*nityatva*), and perfection (*pūrṇatva*).

12

एतज्ज्ञेयं नित्यमेवात्मसंस्थं
नातः परं वेदितव्यं हि किञ्चित्।
भोक्ता भोग्यं प्रेरितारं च मत्वा
सर्वं प्रोक्तं त्रिविधं ब्रह्ममेतत्॥ १२ ॥

etaj jñeyaṁ nityam evātmasaṁsthaṁ nātaḥ paraṁ veditavyaṁ hi kiñcit /
bhoktā bhogyaṁ preritāraṁ ca matvā sarvaṁ proktaṁ trividhaṁ brahmam etat //

12. This is to be known as abiding eternally within oneself. Beyond this there is nothing further to be known. When the enjoyer rightly understands the enjoyed and the means of enjoyment, all this is declared to be the threefold Brahman.

The Sanskrit language has several words for "this," and the one that begins the twelfth *mantra* denotes the utmost degree of nearness. "This"—the ultimate realization described in the previous verse—is total identification with the universal Self. "This is to be known" (*etaj jñeyam*) not as anything external, not as anything to be attained, but as the pure essence of one's own being, ever-present and ready to be realized within. The nondual Self is nearer than the nearest, and beyond its experience there is nothing more to be known. Abhinavagupta condensed that thought into a single word, which he used to designate the ultimate truth. He called it *anuttara,* meaning "that beyond which there is nothing else."

In connection with *mantra* 1.8 we considered how the individual soul emerges in the process of cosmic evolution through the supreme Lord's voluntary donning of *māyā's* five cloaks (*kañcukas*) along with the corresponding limitations they impose on his five intrinsic perfections (see pp. 116–119). As consciousness forgets its wholeness, it becomes diminished in terms of its ability to know and act and finds itself subject to the restrictions of time, space, and causality. Śiva, manifest as *jīva,* sports as innumerable finite souls, experiencing the world projected out of his own awareness and subject to all manner of ups and downs. In Vedantic terms, the Self, in identifying with all that is not-self, forgets its infinite, eternal nature and thinks itself bound.

What matters most for spiritual aspirants is that the process is reversible. When the individualized consciousness-as-subject, otherwise known as the experient (*bhoktṛ*), regains the knowledge of its own infinite and unconditioned subjectivity (*ahaṁtā*), it understands that the true nature of what is experienced (*bhogya*) is consciousness also—consciousness-as-object—and that the dichotomy of knower and known is the product of the inciter (*preritṛ*), the power of consciousness to express itself through the capacity of *māyā*. The three components of phenomenal awareness—*bhoktṛ, bhogya* and *preritṛ*—are the triad alluded to in *mantra* 1.9 and fully disclosed here. When enlightenment dawns, all three are recognized to be a single reality—Brahman—in three interacting modes.

13

वह्नेर्यथा योनिगतस्य मूर्तिर्न
दृश्यते नैव च लिङ्गनाशः ।
स भूय एवेन्धनयोनिगृह्य-
स्तद्वोभयं वै प्रणवेन देहे ॥ १३ ॥

vahner yathā yonigatasya mūrtir na dṛṣyate naiva ca liṅganāśaḥ /
sa bhūya evendhanayonigṛhyas tad vobhayaṁ vai praṇavena dehe //

13. As fire's visible flame lies latent and unseen in wood, never absent and ever poised to shine forth when two kindling sticks are rubbed together, likewise with the friction of *Oṁ*, the Self within the body is revealed.

The analogy of kindling a fire illustrates how the Self, abiding eternally in everyone, can be realized through meditation. Fire, the latent energy ever present in combustible materials, requires only the proper conditions to be actualized. Until then, it remains but a hidden potentiality. The process of igniting the Vedic sacrificial fire involves a lower kindling stick (*araṇi* or *adharāraṇi*) that has a depression into which the upper stick (*uttarāraṇi*) is fitted and then twirled vigorously until the heat of the friction ignites the surrounding tinder and the flame bursts forth.

In the same way as fire lies latent in wood, the glory of the Self remains unperceived in the ordinary state of human awareness. That embodied state, indicated here by the word *deha,* means not only the limitation of the physical form but of the entire mind-body complex and the sense of individual identity it confers. By the "friction" of intensive meditation on the sacred syllable *Oṁ*, it is possible to subdue the myriad sensory impressions and thoughts swirling about in human awareness and to reach a one-pointedness of concentration conducive to higher states of knowledge, culminating in the revelation—the bursting forth, so to speak—of the Self.

To appreciate the significance and utility of the present verse, we need to know more about the syllable *Oṁ*. Both the Vedic and Tantric traditions recognize certain holy words or syllables as seeds (*bījas*) of spiritual consciousness. They represent the differentiated expressions of the sound-energy that projects itself through the names and forms of the universe. First and foremost among the *bījas* is *Oṁ*, the great seed (*mahābīja*) that is the source of all else. It is the supreme verbal symbol of Brahman both as the Absolute and as the personal God (Īśvara).[151] The seer Pippalāda confirms this latter point in the Praśnopaniṣad (5.2) when he tells his disciple Satyakāma, "That which is the syllable *Oṁ* (*oṁkāra*) is truly the higher (*param*) and the lower (*aparam*) Brahman."

The unnamed seer of the Māṇḍūkyopaniṣad goes even farther, proclaiming in the first two verses of that work: "This syllable *Oṁ* (*om ity etad akṣaram*) is all this (*idaṁ sarvam*, a common expression meaning "the universe"). ... All that was, is, and will be is only the syllable *Oṁ* (*oṁkāra eva*); whatever else is beyond threefold time, that too is surely *Oṁ*. Therefore all this is Brahman (*sarvam hy etad brahma*); this Self is Brahman (*ayam ātmā brahma*); this very Self has four quarters (*so 'yam ātmā catuṣpāt*)."

The technical term for *Oṁ* is *praṇava*. This is a very ancient term, used in the Ṛgvedasaṁhitā as well as in the Yajurveda's Taittirīyasaṁhitā and Vājasaneyisaṁhitā, texts that loom large in Śvetāśvatara's preceptorial lineage (see p. 13). *Praṇava* means "sounding" or "reverberating" and refers to the vibration of consciousness itself, inaudible to our physical ears but "heard" by *yogins* in states of deep meditation and described as the unstruck (*anāhata*) sound. When we think of the syllable *Oṁ* or pronounce it, we are not directly experiencing the reality of the transcendental *praṇava* but only its approximation at the lower levels of conceptual thought and articulated speech. As we experience it at the phenomenal level, the sacred syllable is said to be compounded of four quarters or sounds, but in reality the primordial *praṇava* is uncompounded and indivisible, for it is the vibration of the nondual Brahman itself. What we perceive and conceptualize as the four sonic constituents arise from this primordial vibration of consciousness.[152]

What are these four parts or quarters of which the Māṇḍūkyopaniṣad speaks? From the standpoint of Sanskrit phonetics, the *praṇava* consists of three measurable elements (*mātras*)—the phonemes *a, u,* and *m*—and the indefinitely prolonged and immeasurable nasal resonance represented by the dot (*bindu*) written over the *m* in both the Devanāgarī script and Roman transliteration (*ṁ*).[153] The vowel *a* (*akāra*) originates deep in the throat, and the vowel *u* (*ukāra*) carries the vibration forward to the closed lips, which then articulate the consonant *m* (*makāra*). Thereupon follows the nasal resonance, the "after-sound" (*anusvāra*). The *oṁkāra* or *praṇava* thus encompasses the entire range of speech production.

Various meanings have been ascribed to *Oṁ* and its constituents. Two interpretations, the ontological and the epistemological, relate in turn to existing and knowing. Though different, they are not antagonistic; rather, they offer two distinct frames of reference for the same question. Their complementarity is borne out by the Vedantic "definition" of the indefinable Brahman as *saccidānanda*—being (*sat*), consciousness (*cit*), and bliss (*ānanda*). But Brahman is indivisibly One, and such designations as *being* and *consciousness* are no more than approximations of a single, inexpressible reality.

Ontologically speaking, the three *mātras* of *Oṁ* symbolize the beginning, middle, and end of all things. They represent the lower (*apara*) or active Brahman as the creator, sustainer, and dissolver of the universe through the divine powers of emanation (*sṛṣṭi*), maintenance (*sthiti*), and resorption (*saṁhāra*). The *bindu* symbolizes the condensed state of power immediately before the actualization of the universe, the point of all possibility from which the creation proceeds.

The Māṇḍūkyopaniṣad (verses 3–5, 7) correlates the sounds *a, u,* and *m* with the three ways in which the universal Self experiences its own collective cosmic embodiment. These are the same states of consciousness that we as individuals experience as waking, dreaming, and dreamless sleep. *Akāra* represents Vaiśvāṇara, the universal experient in the waking state (*jāgrat*); *ukāra* stands for Taijasa, the universal experient in the dream state (*svapna*); and *makāra* represents Prājña, the universal experient in deep sleep (*suṣupti*). In the waking state consciousness relates to gross, external objects; in dream it relates to subtle, internal objects; in deep sleep it is free of awareness of any objects at all, undifferentiated and blissful, yet clouded by the sense of individuality. Beyond these three states of ordinary awareness, yet pervading them all, is a fourth (*turīya*), represented by the *anusvāra*. Marked by the cessation of all phenomena (*prapañcopaśamam*), unchanging (*śāntam*), auspicious (*śivam*), and nondual (*advaitam*), that is the Self and that, the Māṇḍūkyopaniṣad instructs, is to be known (*sa ātmā sa vijñeyaḥ*).

Gauḍapāda's commentary, the *Māṇḍūkyakārikā* (1.24–25), advises the aspirant to contemplate the meaning of the sacred syllable quarter by quarter and to think of nothing else. One should fix total awareness on the *praṇava* (*yuñjīta praṇave cetaḥ*), for *Oṁ* is Brahman (*praṇavo brahma*). The *Kārikā* continues (1.26–28): "The *praṇava* is surely the beginning, the middle, and the end of everything. Knowing *Oṁ* in this way, one attains that which is eternal (*tad anantaram*). One should surely know *Oṁ* to be God (*praṇavaṁ hīśvaraṁ vidyāt*), seated in the hearts of all (*sarvasya hṛdi saṁsthitam*)."

About a thousand years before Gauḍapāda wrote those words, Śvetāśvatara taught that one could attain the cessation of all illusion by constantly meditating on God, uniting with him, and becoming that reality (1.10). Meditation on *Oṁ*, the supreme *mantra* not different from God himself, is a means to that end.

Why is meditation on *Oṁ* so efficacious? It all has to do with sound and meaning as explained by the theory of *sphoṭa*. The word *sphoṭa* denotes a bursting open, an expansion, a blossoming, or a disclosure. As a technical term it signifies the capacity of meaning (*artha*) to burst forth from the sound (*śabda*) of a word. The concept of *sphoṭa* was explored by the grammarian-philosopher Bhartṛhari, who lived around the fifth century CE, sometime between Patañjali and Gauḍapāda. Bhartṛhari explained in his great treatise, the *Vākyapadīya* [On the saying and the word] (1.83), that *sphoṭa* is not a gradual process but a sudden flashing, a single internally illumined act.[154] This idea of sudden bursting reminds us of the analogy that Śvetāśvatara had drawn much earlier between kindling a fire and meditating on the sacred syllable *Oṁ*. The analogy does not owe its aptness to mere chance; far from being a casual comparison, it penetrates deeply, suggesting the commonality of light bursting forth, be it the physical brightness of fire igniting from dull wood or the spiritual radiance of enlightenment flashing forth from the murk of ordinary awareness.

Bhartṛhari was a *brāhmaṇa* and probably a Maitrāyaṇīya, a member of a Vedic lineage (*śākhā*) belonging, like Śvetāśvatara's, to the Kṛṣṇa Yajurveda. Besides that he was strongly influenced by the Vaiśeṣika philosophy, whose founder, Kaṇāda, was a devotee of Śiva and a Pāśupata. Although Bhartṛhari is considered to be an important predecessor of Śaṁkara, not all of his ideas were destined to survive in the emerging mainstream of Advaita Vedānta. Some of them passed directly into various schools of nondualistic Kashmir Śaivism[155] and deeply impressed themselves on the great Abhinavagupta.[156]

Pre-Śaṁkara Vedānta, reaching back to an ancient and venerable grammatical tradition, laid great importance on the power of the word. Through linguistic analysis Bhartṛhari sought to penetrate the nature and the workings of consciousness, convinced that such knowledge would lead to liberation. He thought of Brahman and its creative activity in terms of speech (*vāc*) or the word (*śabda*). Like Gauḍapāda, he needed no convincing of the eternal immutability and homogeneity of Brahman, but he also posited that the seeds of apparent differentiation are deeply latent in the ultimate unity of consciousness. Brahman, ever One and the same, lies beyond the mind's ability to grasp—except through symbols and approximations. As the Upaniṣads had declared, the supreme symbol of Brahman is the *praṇava,* and this is the seed (*bīja*) of the entire creation. So, for Bhartṛhari the concept of the *praṇava* implies not just a nameless, formless, eternally quiescent Brahman but one that is simultaneously powerful, dynamic, and active—a God who manifests this world by releasing his own energy through the word.[157]

Just as any ordinary word has the power to call forth the idea it embodies, so does the supreme word. In the case of *Oṁ* the idea is the emanation, sustenance, and withdrawal of the entire universe, all taking place within the Absolute. As "the immediate source of the creation"[158] or "the seed-force that evolves into the universe,"[159] the *praṇava* represents the vibratory motion (*spanda*) of consciousness, which is also described as the creative word (*vāc*) or the Lord's own creative ideation.

How does this relate to the concept of *sphoṭa?* In the fourteenth century CE Mādhava, the brother of the renowned Vedic commentator Sāyaṇa, identified *sphoṭa*, Brahman, and the *praṇava* as one and the same. His great compendium of religious systems, the *Sarvadarśanasaṁgraha* (13.6), defines *sphoṭa* as Brahman itself and calls it the eternal, undivided word that is the source and cause of the world—the beginningless, endless, and indestructible essence of all speech, shining out in the meaning of all things.

We have already seen how the constituent quarters of *Oṁ* apply to the manifestation of the universe as well as to states of consciousness. There is another way in which they can be applied to awareness: the phonemes *a, u,* and *m* correspond to the gross, subtle, and causal levels of experience. The *akāra* stands for perceptual knowledge, the sensory experience of physical objects. The *ukāra* represents conceptual knowledge, the mental or intellectual experience of ideas and abstractions. The *makāra* signifies intuitive knowledge, which flashes with an immediacy free of any progression and betokens our oneness with the universe. Beyond those three levels of lower awareness lies the higher knowledge of the transcendental Self, symbolized by the *anusvāra*. When the mind succeeds in making *Oṁ* the sole object of concentration and becomes saturated in it, then in this state of deep meditation the gross, subtle, and causal sounds (*śabda*) evaporate in turn until only the meaning (*artha*), the ineffable radiance itself, remains.

When speaking of the *oṁkāra* and its meaning, philosophers of various persuasions resort to a confusing array of synonymous or sometimes overlapping technical terms. When Śrī Rāmakṛṣṇa, who professed little book learning, spoke of the *praṇava*, he said simply that his understanding arose from his own experience. As he explained it, the spontaneous (*anāhata*), self-sustained sound of *Oṁ* *is* Brahman, eternally vibrating with the pulsation of *emerging* and *merging*. These two words are important, because they direct our attention back to questions posed in the first *mantra* of this Upaniṣad: Where did we come from, and where are we headed? Śrī Rāmakṛṣṇa likened the sound of *Oṁ* to a heavy weight falling into the ocean and generating waves. In this "ocean of consciousness without limit" (*cidākāśa*), the waves represent the relative rising out of the Absolute. Everything that exists—whether in causal, subtle, or gross manifestation—emerges from the great cause that is Brahman and then subsides into it again. The sound of Brahman, this *Oṁ*, as Śrī Rāmakṛṣṇa explained, is heard by *yogins* in states of high mystical awareness, but what is to be gained from that? The answer is quite simple. Hearing the ocean's roar from a distance, one is guided by the sound to the ocean itself, because where the roar is, there the ocean also must be. The *yogin* who follows the *praṇava's* sound back to its source merges into the limitless ocean of consciousness.[160]

14

स्वदेहमरणिं कृत्वा प्रणवं चोत्तरारणिम् ।
ध्याननिर्मथनाभ्यासाद्देवं पश्येन्निगूढवत् ॥ १४ ॥

svadeham araṇiṁ kṛtvā praṇavaṁ cottarāraṇim /
dhyānanirmathanābhyāsād devaṁ paśyen nigūḍhavat //

14. By making one's own embodied awareness the lower kindling stick and *Oṁ* the upper, and by generating friction through constant meditation, one should see God as one sees the once-hidden fire.

Śvetāśvatara's graphic image of kindling sticks represents a way for us to manage our own awareness, to direct the movement (*vṛtti*) within the mind toward the goal of Self-knowledge. The upper kindling stick represents the higher Self, the knowledge that "I am Brahman" (*ahaṁ brahmāsmi*) as the Bṛhadāraṇyakopaniṣad (1.4.10) proclaims. The context of that most ancient of *mahāvākyas* is highly instructive, because it first presents the great dictum in terms of Brahman's own Self-awareness: "It knew itself only as 'I am Brahman' (*tad ātmānam evāvet, ahaṁ brahmāsmīti).* Therefore [through this power of knowledge] it [Brahman] became all (*tasmāt tat sarvam abhavat*)." Then this passage continues, "Whoever knows that 'I am Brahman' (*ya evaṁ veda ahaṁ brahmāsmīti*) becomes all this (*sa idaṁ sarvaṁ bhavati*)." In other words, for the one who attains the highest knowledge, the sense of self expands (or bursts forth like a flame) into the radiance of divine universality, the fullness of identity known in the Trikaśāstra as the pure order (*śuddhādhvan*) or universal consciousness.

Just as the two kindling sticks are of one substance—wood—the higher Self and the lower self are of one substance—consciousness. The difference is that divine consciousness is infinite and unconditioned, whereas human consciousness, until it realizes its true nature and shines forth in full glory, is finite and conditioned.

It is only the thick veiling of ordinary awareness that prevents us from recognizing our true nature, the higher Self. The veiling is only partial, of course, for without a glimmer of light we could not even be aware of our own existence. Even though only the illumined soul experiences the supreme Self in the incomprehensible fullness of being (*sat*), nevertheless we experience the same reality of consciousness as our own restricted and conditioned existence (*bhāva*). The light of Brahman is ever familiar to us but only dimly as the sense of I that sees itself encumbered by all the trappings of individual identity.

Whereas the previous *mantra* dealt more with theory, the present one emphasizes practice. Of course theory and practice go hand in hand, ultimately relating to two powers of consciousness, those of knowledge (*jñāna*) and action (*kriyā*). The third power of consciousness, that of will (*icchā*), also figures in. Even as Śiva's manifestation of this universe comes about through the exercise of those three divine powers, our individual efforts toward enlightenment involve the use of those same powers as they are manifest in our everyday experience. Śvetāśvatara tells us to combine our understanding and our doing with our firm intention.

Contemplation on the identity of the lower self with the higher Self must be done with the utmost diligence, as the phrase *dhyānanirmathanābhyāsād* instructs us. *Nirmathana* means "rubbing" or "churning" and refers to the friction that produces fire from wood. *Dhyāna* means "meditation" in the sense of unwavering attenion to a single object of contemplation. *Dhyānanirmathana* thus means the process of creating a flashing forth of insight through holding the mind fast to a single thought, in this case the identity of the lower self (*ātman*) and the higher Self (*paramātman*). The metaphor of the kindling sticks thus echoes another *mahāvākya:* "This self is Brahman" (*ayam ātmā brahma*). Finally, *ābhyāsa* indicates repeated exercise, discipline, and practice that becomes constant and habitual. By the phrase *dhyānanirmathanābhyāsād* Śvetāśvatara instructs us that if we would know the effulgent truth of our being, we must repeatedly, diligently, unwaveringly, and consistently direct the mind toward the awareness that the essence of our embodied selfhood is none other than the supreme Self that expresses itself through everything.

By visualizing the embodied self as the lower kindling stick and Brahman as the upper one, symbolized by *Oṁ*, and then by mentally repeating the *oṁkāra*, the meditator generates intense concentration or spiritual "heat" (*tapas*). This practice is known as meditation on I-consciousness (*ahaṁgrahopāsanā*).[161] In greater detail, it consists of first focusing the mind on I-am-ness (*asmitā*), the individual sense of self, tinged with objectivity. Next the meditator associates that self-awareness with the continually repeating sound of *Oṁ*, all the while regarding the *praṇava* as the reality itself. In that intense and holy atmosphere, the lower self gains a sense of its own divinity. Self-awareness becomes gradually divested of the impurities of the objectified ego-sense (*asmitā*) and comes to recognize its own essential subjectivity (*ahaṁtā*)—the same shining consciousness that is *paramātman* or Brahman. Then, as the *mantra* concludes, "one should see God (*devaṁ paśyet*)." From practice, that is the result we can surely expect.

15

तिलेषु तैलं दधिनीव सर्पिरा-
पः स्रोतःस्वरणीषु चाग्निः ।
एवमात्माऽत्मनि गृह्यतेऽसौ स-
त्येनैनं तपसा योऽनुपश्यति ॥ १५ ॥

tileṣu tailaṁ dadhinīva sarpir āpaḥ srotaḥsv araṇīṣu cāgniḥ /
evam ātmā 'tmani gṛhyate 'sau satyenainaṁ tapasā yo 'nupaśyati //

15. As oil in sesame seeds, as butter in milk, as water beneath a dry riverbed, and as fire in wood, so also is this Self grasped in the self of one who discerns it through sincerity and ardor.

All four analogies here imply divine immanence[162] and suggest that something valuable is to be brought forth from that which contains it. Each case calls for earnest and unflagging effort to produce the desired results. Sesame seeds must be crushed to extract the clear oil that permeates them. Coagulated milk must be churned to separate the butter pervasive in it. Where a dry riverbed conceals an underground spring, the water can be reached only by digging. Kindling sticks release their latent fire only through vigorously applied friction.

In the same way, spiritual progress requires genuine effort. The examples of extracting pure oil from sesame seeds and butter from milk indicate that *sādhanā* is a process of refinement—the ongoing refinement of our own awareness. Discovering life-giving water in a dry riverbed suggests the bliss that comes with the revelation of the indwelling Self. The image of the flame bursting forth from dry tinder symbolizes the light of infinite consciousness flashing through the veils of *māyā* and consuming them by its brilliance.

Śvetāśvatara employs an equally strong image in saying that the Self is grasped (*gṛhyate*) in the self. Of course he does not mean the act of physically taking hold but, more subtly, of mentally taking hold. In Sanskrit and English alike, *to grasp* can mean "to understand." The infinite Self (*ātmā*) is to be recognized in the finite self (*ātmani*) and understood as our true being.

This mental grasping comes about when the aspirant discerns (*anupaśyati*) the Self after attentive observation carried out with sincerity (*satyena*) and ardor (*tapasā*). The first of these conditions, *satya,* encompasses the ideas of truth, reality, honesty, goodness, and virtue. A Sanskrit maxim reminds us that there is no virtue higher than truth (*satyān nāsti paro dharmaḥ*). Utter sincerity is the *sine qua non* of spiritual life.

The word *tapas* embraces a wide range of meaning and has no exact English equivalent. In translations of the present *mantra* it has been rendered as "penance,"[163] "austerity,"[164] "asceticism,"[165] "self-restraint,"[166] "concentration,"[167] or "meditation."[168]

Penance, a term reeking of sin and expiation, says more about the religious and cultural background of Max Müller and Paul Deussen, who employ this word, than about Śvetāśvatara's own world-view. *Austerity* is hardly a better choice if taken to mean long-faced self-denial. Śvetāśvatara is not averse to celebrating the joys of creation, as we shall see in the fourth chapter. Overall, penance and self-denial do not fit well with the Śaiva mentality, and the experience of life as God's own self-expression is not something to run away from but something to be embraced, refined, and transformed through spiritual practice.

By *austerity* one translator means "subject[ing] ourselves to certain disciplines,"[169] but a more precise and helpful definition is "fixing the mind and sense-organs one-pointedly on Ātman."[170] That definition goes back to the Mahābhārata (12.250.4), where Vyāsa instructs that the highest *tapas* (*paramaṁ tapaḥ*) is one-pointedness (*aikāgryam*) of the mind (*manasaḥ*) and perceptive faculties (*indriyāṇām*) on a single object. From that definition it is easy to understand how *tapas* can be translated as "self-restraint," "concentration," or "meditation."

In the earliest Upaniṣad, the Bṛhadāraṇyaka (1.2.6), *tapas* is the heated concentration by which Brahman (as Hiraṇyagarbha) creates the world. *Tapas* is literally the heat of mental endeavor through which all creation is effected.[171] Nowhere is this creative function of *tapas* more tellingly expressed than in an already cited passage from the Taittirīyopaniṣad (2.6.1) (see pp. 114–115). This passage describes, step by step, how after desiring to become many the supreme Self performed *tapas*, emitted all this (*idaṁ sarvam asṛjata*), and indeed entered (*evānuprāviśat*) into the realm of duality with its rich variety of distinctions.

Conversely *tapas* is also the mental endeavor that directs the spiritual aspirant back to the original, unmanifest state. How can that be? Consciousness is One, merely flowing in two directions. The Bṛhadāraṇyakopaniṣad (4.4.22) teaches that it is Brahman, "this great unborn Self" (*eṣa mahān aja ātmā*) that one seeks to know through *tapas* and other disciplines.

The question naturally arises that if *tapas* literally means "warmth" or "heat," don't terms such as *austerity* and *self-control* imply something very different? The idea of austerity conjures up images of coldness, renunciation, and lack of involvement. Self-control also can be thought of in terms of self-denial and asceticism, but in the broader sense it means withdrawing the mind from any distracting object or thought and redirecting it toward a single, chosen object of contemplation. To repeat the Mahābhārata's definition, the highest *tapas* is one-pointed concentration. Such one-pointedness is impossible without ardor. And what is ardor? Warmth, passion, eagerness, enthusiasm, zeal, and more literally intense heat. The word *ardor*, identical to the Latin word for "flame," seems the closest English equivalent of the Sanskrit *tapas*.

To bring forth the radiance of the Self in full glory requires passionate discipline—sustained, fully directed concentration on the identity of the lower self and the supreme Self. The sense of individuality (*asmitā*) is to be refined into divine Self-awareness (*ahaṁtā*), and this is possible only because the essence of both is the same self-luminous consciousness. Returning once more to Śvetāśvatara's analogies, the way to enlightenment is a process of refining, extracting, digging, and igniting, all designed to strip away the obscuring distractions of phenomenality until the brilliance and majesty of the higher Self alone remains.

16

सर्वव्यापिनमात्मानं क्षीरे सर्पिरिवार्पितम् ।
आत्मविद्यातपोमूलं तद्ब्रह्मोपनिषत् परम् ॥ १६ ॥

sarvavyāpinam ātmānaṁ kṣīre sarpir ivārpitam /
ātmavidyātapomūlaṁ tad brahmopaniṣat param //

16. As butter in milk, [one discerns] the Self as all-pervading [when it is] fixed upon, firmly fixed upon through the ardor for Self-knowledge. Concerning Brahman, that is the highest teaching.

In the original Sanskrit this *mantra* and the preceeding one form a single utterance that concludes Śvetāśvatara's first discourse.

At the outset the seer posed a series of questions, beginning with What is the cause [of this universe]? and ending with What law governs us, whose lives run their course through happiness and all the rest? (1.1).

He lost no time in revealing that the cause of the universe and of our phenomenal existence is to be found within ourselves in deepest meditation. That ultimate, uncaused cause is the power of the effulgent Self (*devātmaśakti*) that lies hidden by its own effects (1.3). It is the limitless power of divine consciousness to express its own inherent joy in and through the manifest universe. The supreme Self is ever-present throughout the vast cosmos and in the more immediate world of our personal experience, which unfolds "in happiness and all the rest" (*sukhetareṣu*). The Self is the consciousness driving our every perception, thought, word, and action; and although it remains unnoticed in our ordinary, distracted state, it is as present as the invisible butter pervasive in milk.

Looking inward, the aspiring soul asks, Who am I? The answer, in the highest sense, is *ahaṁtā,* the divine I-ness. But having forgotten that true, original nature, unconditioned and absolutely free, the individual soul instead experiences *asmitā,* the conditioned ego-self, ever subject to the limitations of *māyā* that keep it in bondage. And what is that bondage? Simply put, identification with the body-mind complex. Even so, the light of consciousness itself—the essence of the divine Self—is never absent from human experience but only dimmed by mistaken identification with the veils of body, mind, and personality.

By removing what we are not, we recognize what we are. To that end Śvetāśvatara recommended meditation on *Oṁ* as a means of reintegrating our apparent selfhood with the true Self beyond duality (1.13–14). Now, in the final two *mantras* he seeks to impress on us the total commitment we must make. The thought of the divine Self must become fixed (*arpitam*) in the mind at all times and firmly rooted (*mūlam*) in the ardor (*tapas*) for Self-knowledge (*ātmavidyā*).

Self-knowledge is both the means and the goal, or as the Muṇḍakopaniṣad (3.2.9) puts it, "Whoever knows the supreme Brahman becomes Brahman." Nothing exists apart from the sole reality of consciousness, not even bondage and freedom. They exist in the mind, and the mind is only consciousness in a particular form. The same power of consciousness that expresses itself as the individual's experience of the universe, when reversing its direction, assumes the form of ardent concentration and turns back to its own self-luminous unity. The Self is the means to its own realization. To know the Self is to become the Self, and this Self is Brahman. There is no teaching higher than this.

द्वितीयोऽध्यायः

CHAPTER TWO

1

युञ्जानः प्रथमं मनस्तत्त्वाय सविता धियः ।
अग्नेर्ज्योतिर्निचाय्य पृथिव्या अध्याभरत् ॥ १ ॥

yuñjānaḥ prathamaṁ manas tattvāya savitā dhiyaḥ /
agner jyotir nicāyya pṛthivyā adhyābharat //

1. First joining the mind and holy thoughts for the sake of reaching the truth, Savitṛ perceived the light of fire and brought it forth from the earth.

The beginning of Śvetāśvatara's second discourse has an archaic ring, and his listeners, well versed in tradition, would have recognized the first five *mantras* as quotations of parallel passages from the Taittirīyasaṁhitā (4.1.1.1–5) and the Vājasaneyisaṁhitā (11.1–5). These same verses appear quoted also in the Śatapathabrāhmaṇa (6.3.1.12–17), where they fulfill a liturgical function in accompanying offerings to the solar deity Savitṛ. Like the present Upaniṣad, all three of the older texts belong to the preceptorial lineages of the Yajurveda (see pp. 13, 39). Additionally, the fourth and fifth *mantras* can be traced back to the Ṛgvedasaṁhitā (5.81.1, 10.13.1), the oldest source of all (see Appendix B, Table 1).

In citing the ancient Vedic texts Śvetāśvatara draws from a growing literary corpus that originated ages before his time and was soon to reach completion. Consisting of Saṁhitās, Brāhmaṇas, Āraṇyakas, and Upaniṣads, it is a body of revealed knowledge (*śruti*) that culminates in the teaching of the indwelling Self (*ātman*) and its identity with the transcendental reality of Brahman (see pp. 11–12). That truth, experienced directly by great seers and sages, was passed down orally from *guru* to disciple for hundreds, if not thousands, of years and became codified as the Vedas. Because the Vedas are designated as *śruti,* they remain the ultimate authority of the *sanātana dharma,* India's eternal religion.

To regard the Vedas as spiritually authoritative is not the same as to subscribe to an authoritarian doctrine. The *sanātana dharma* requires no one to accept any set of beliefs but only to experience the divine reality for oneself. When Śvetāśvatara teaches, he is urging his disciples to discover the truth of their own being; he does not want them merely to take his word for it. He may reverently quote the teachings of enlightened souls from the distant past, but he himself is also an enlightened soul who speaks from his own experience and with the conviction that achieving Self-knowledge is his disciples' practical goal as well. Thus the Upaniṣad that bears his name belongs to the Vedic canon and is revered as *śruti,* or revealed knowledge.

We may be puzzled by the *mantra* just uttered and the four that follow. The words are simple enough, but on the surface they make little sense. Max Müller took the first seven *mantras* of this chapter to be nothing more than an invocation drawn from older hymns to Savitṛ, an ancient Vedic deity who represents the rising sun. He contended that the verses held no deeper meaning and that the *Svetāśvaropaniṣadvṛtti,* which he accepted uncritically as Śaṁkara's own work, had twisted them to the point of nonsensicality in order to make them reflect the teachings of the later Yoga *darśana.*[1] Müller's assessment should be taken with a grain of salt.

As we shall see, the opening *mantras* form an integral part of Śvetāśvatara's instruction and carry a great deal of meaning. Their true significance would have been known only to the more erudite of the seer's listeners, for even at that time the archaic Vedic language was becoming more and more difficult to understand. As the language evolved, simultaneously the meaning of many of its colorful figures of speech was being forgotten. For that reason, around the time of Śvetāśvatara, a scholar named Yāska compiled his treatise, the *Nirukta,* in order to insure that the keys to understanding the Vedas would not be lost.

To complicate matters, Śvetāśvatara presents the first five *mantras* in a new context wherein ritual activity is internalized and reinterpreted to signify the goal of attaining union with Brahman. Such an interpretation hardly seems forced, given that each of the verses begins with a form of the verb *yuj* ("to yoke" or "to join"), which is also the source of the noun *yoga.* From the earliest times yogic practice had been intimately associated with Śaiva religion (see pp. 30–34), and by the time of the Pāśupata sect it had been formalized as the third of that school's five principal topics. Naturally excluding the transgressive *vidhi* (see pp. 42, 45–46), Śvetāśvatara's first discourse centers on the other four, discussing cause (*kāraṇa*) (1.1–3, 7, 9, 10), effect (*kārya*) (1.4–6, 8–10), union (*yoga*) (1.3, 10, 12–16), and liberation (*duḥkhānta*) (1.7–8, 10–11).

Now the seer is ready to devote his entire second discourse to the topic of *yoga.* Symbolically the first *mantra* describes the preliminary step of achieving purity of mind through the observance of proper moral conduct (*dharma*) and the practice of self-control.[2] As the instrument of experience, the mind (*manas,* here meaning the entire *antaḥkaraṇa*) must be made pure in regard to both its internal workings and its interaction with the outer world. In the most literal reading of this verse, purification is a matter of joining the mind to holy thoughts (*dhiyaḥ*). The usual translation of *dhiyaḥ* varies from "thought"[3] or "thoughts,"[4] to "reason,"[5] "senses,"[6] "organs" (of perception),[7] or "intellectual powers."[8] A comparison of these renderings shows that translators of the Advaita Vedānta tradition, following the *Vṛtti,* take *dhiyaḥ* to mean the outgoing senses or the sensory and motor organs (*jñānendriyas* and *karmendriyas*). However, the word *dhī* means "thought," especially religious thought, reflection, meditation, understanding, and even devotion. In earlier Vedic times the plural form (*dhiyaḥ*) expressed the specific idea of holy thoughts, and that is most likely what Śvetāśvatara intends. That said, whichever interpretation one chooses to accept, the idea is first to harness the activity of the mind.

Pursuant to that thought, it is important to understand the seer's purpose in invoking the solar deity Savitṛ. Because the sun is the brightest light in the sky and a light that shines by its own power, it is the primary symbol of Brahman in the Vedas. Savitṛ is not the sun's visible orb, though; that is the sun god Sūrya. The word *savitṛ* means "rouser" or "vivifier" or "one who brings forth or inspires,"[9] and it connotes Sūrya's power or, put another way, the *śakti* of Brahman. As the power of consciousness, Savitṛ expresses himself through the outgoing activity of the mind and sense organs, paradoxically keeping the true Self hidden. Conversely Savitṛ also draws the mind in toward knowledge of the effulgent Self.[10] He is thus the guiding principle in the heart that leads one to higher and higher states of awareness.

The phrase "the light of fire" (*agner jyotiḥ*) disproves Müller's assertion that the quoted verses are nothing more than an invocation without deeper meaning. If we consider fire to represent ordinary consciousness, then its light is its essence—pure consciousness-in-itself. Discerning (*nicāyya*) the pure light means distinguishing it from the impurity and limitation of individual awareness. Savitṛ brings the light of fire out from the earth; consciousness itself has the power to release the individual's awareness from the obscuring and binding physicality of matter and its attractions.[11] Bringing the light out of the earth is another metaphor along the lines of extracting oil from sesame seeds, churning butter from milk, or manifesting fire from kindling sticks. Far from serving no purpose other than invocation, the present *mantra* is well integrated and felicitously takes up exactly where Śvetāśvatara's first discourse left off.

In summary, the seer instructs that in order to attain Self-knowledge and liberation, we must first direct the activity of the mind to holy thoughts, then meditate on the light of pure consciousness in the heart as distinct from the fire of ordinary awareness in the intellect. In that way the Self, the inner reality behind all physical appearances, will be revealed.[12]

2

युक्तेन मनसा वयं देवस्य सवितुः सवे ।
सुवर्गेयाय शक्त्या ॥ २ ॥

yuktena manasā vayaṁ devasya savituḥ save /
suvargeyāya śaktyā //

2. With mind intent, we [are inspired] by Savitṛ, who shines in the sun, to attain the highest bliss through his power.

No spiritual practice can be done without first setting ourselves to the task. We must begin with the mind (*manas*) joined (*yukta*) to our intention. The word *yukta,* related to the English word *yoked,* means "joined," "fixed upon," "engaged in," "intent upon," "attentive," "concentrated," or "controlled." These words carry different shades of meaning, yet all imply that managing the mind does not come without conscious effort.

In the original Sanskrit this *mantra* lacks a verb, leaving us to supply one. The pronoun *we (vayam)* tells us that we ourselves are the subject of the phantom verb, but what we are to do is left unsaid. It seems logical to assume that at one time the missing verb was so obvious that there was no need to utter it. What would make it so obvious?

The most sacred prayer of the Ṛgveda and one known to all Hindus concerns Savitṛ. It is the great Gāyatrī *mantra* (3.62.10): *tat savitur vareṇyaṁ bhargo devasya dhīmahi dhiyo yo naḥ pracodayāt*— "May we meditate upon the splendor of the divinity, the supreme effulgence, and may That inspire our thoughts."[13] May Savitṛ inspire our thoughts. May we, with our minds intent on attaining the highest bliss, *be inspired* by Savitṛ. There is the missing verb.

Savitṛ shines in the sun (*save*). The word *sava* literally means "one who sets in motion" or "one who stimulates." Each day the rising sun rouses earthly creatures from their sleep and sends them to their appointed tasks. Yet behind the sun's radiant orb, indeed behind everything made manifest by its light, Savitṛ is the inner power who brings forth or inspires. We are to be inspired by that spiritual light shining in and through our own awareness.

The opening phrase "with mind intent" (*yuktena manasā*) points out the need for self-effort. The verse ends with the phrase "through his power" (*śaktyā*), reminding us that our attainment of spiritual knowledge and bliss ultimately rests on divine grace. In our present state of limitation, we have no other choice but to make the initial effort toward Self-knowledge; but in reality, the finite can never embrace the Infinite and must be embraced by it. Put another way, spiritual life begins with self-effort and ends in self-surrender.

3

युक्त्वाय मनसा देवान् सुवर्यतो धिया दिवम् ।
बृहज्ज्योतिः करिष्यतः सविता प्रसुवाति तान् ॥ ३ ॥

yuktvāya manasā devān suvaryato dhiyā divam /
bṛhaj jyotiḥ kariṣyataḥ savitā prasuvāti tān //

3. Those who would aspire to supreme bliss, the bright-shining Savitṛ impels heavenward, harnessing their senses with the mind and thought.

To emphasize the point just made, illumination comes through the power of grace. It is Savitṛ, the immanent God, who impels us heavenward, meaning toward knowledge of the supreme Self (*paramātman*).[14] It is he who directs us away from the distractions of the outer world by turning our naturally outgoing senses inward.

Those facets of our awareness that are engaged in experiencing the external creation are spoken of symbolically here as *devas,* literally "gods" or "shining ones," owing to the consciousness that operates through them. As Savitṛ withdraws these "gods" (*devān*) from the materiality of the earth, he sends them to heaven or the sky (*divam*). The sky has served since the earliest Vedic times as a visible, shining symbol of infinity; internalized, it signifies our own interior "sky of consciousness" (*cidgagana*), the infinitude of Brahman to be realized in deepest *samādhi.*

Knowledge of Brahman can be achieved only by turning the flow of awareness away from the ever-moving world and back to its unchanging, ever-blissful source. Of course, since everything is God's own expression, as Śvetāśvatara will make clear in his fourth discourse, the world and our interactions with it are nothing but consciousness, although in modified, restricted, or veiled forms. The outward motion of consciousness produces diversification and the sense of multiple individualities; its inward motion leads toward unification or the knowledge of Brahman. Through his own self-revealing luminosity Savitṛ harnesses our perceptions and mental activities and turns them inward and Godward.

4

युञ्जते मन उत युञ्जते धियो
विप्रा विप्रस्य बृहतो विपश्चितः ।
वि होत्रा दधे वयुनाविदेक
इन्मही देवस्य सवितुः परिष्टुतिः ॥ ४ ॥

yuñjate mana uta yuñjate dhiyo viprā viprasya bṛhato vipaścitaḥ /
vi hotrā dadhe vayunāvid eka in mahī devasya savituḥ pariṣṭutiḥ //

4. They concentrate the mind and harness the thoughts, those wise ones, inspired by the great wise One. He alone, who knows the way, has ordained the means. Great be the praise of the effulgent Savitṛ!

The first five *mantras,* centering on Savitṛ, the rouser or vivifier, emphasize the dynamic aspect of divine consciousness. In this verse the wise ones (*viprāḥ*) are those who have felt the inner stirring of the supreme Self, which is itself stirred (*vipraḥ*). The word *vipra,* like its English cognate, *vibrate,* expresses an internal movement, in this case the inherent pulsation, vibration, or shimmering of consciousness (*spanda*). Nowadays the term *spanda* is emblematic of nondualistic Kashmir Śaivism in general and associated especially with the Spanda school, based on Vasugupta's *Śivasūtra* and the *Spandakārikā.* According to this school, Śiva—the single reality of consciousness known to the Vedānta as Brahman—expresses itself in every subject, object, and action in the manifest world through its own inherent dynamism (*spanda*).

Although appearing nowhere in the Upaniṣads, the word *spanda* is not absent from the lexicon of pre-Śaṁkara Vedānta, nor is the concept it represents. The term figures prominently in Bhartṛhari's *Vākyapadīya*. The synonym *spandita* and the verb *spand* occur in five verses of Gauḍapāda's *Māṇḍūkyakārikā*. Gauḍapāda observed that both in the waking state and in dream the mind vibrates (*spandate*) as though appearing in two aspects (*dvayābhāsam*), the knowing subject and the known object (3.29). Later he elaborated on this point. After affirming that consciousness (*vijñānam*) is itself unoriginated, unmoving, nonmaterial, quiescent, and nondual, he then added, two verses later, that even as the motion of a firebrand (*alātaspanditam*) appears as straight or curved or otherwise configured (*ṛjuvakrādikābhāsam*), the vibration of consciousness (*vijñānaspanditam*) likewise appears as the perception and the perceiver (*grahaṇagrāhakābhāsam*) (4.47).

But wait! After saying that consciousness is unmoving (*acalam*), Gauḍapāda expounds on its vibration, quivering, or movement (*spanditam*). He seems to contradict himself—unless one understands *spanda* not as physical motion but as something subtler, even beyond subtlety. This can be explained, at least on the phenomenal level, by the example of a simple drawing that can appear either as the image of a white goblet on a black background or of two facing profiles in silhouette. At first the mind perceives one or the other of the two possibilities. Then either through conscious effort or perhaps spontaneously, the perception of the image shifts and the mind cognizes the other possibility. What has changed? Not the object, not the conditions of the perception. Nothing has changed externally, but clearly there has been a change in awareness, what we might call a "movement" in consciousness, independent of any actual motion.

Gauḍapāda continues that when the firebrand moves (*alāte spandamāne*), the created appearances do not come from anywhere else (4.49). Likewise, when consciousness vibrates (*vijñāne spandamāne*), appearances do not come to it from anywhere else either (4.51), simply because other than consciousness there is nothing else. Finally he asserts that duality (*dvayam*), possessed of cognized object and cognizing subject (*grāhyagrāhakavat*) is "surely this vibration of consciousness" (*cittaspanditam evedam*) (4.72).

Returning to what Śvetāśvatara most likely intends to convey, the divine Self is said to be stirred because it enjoys the vibrant radiance of its own awareness, and the individual soul, once touched by God, naturally longs to know that blissful vibrancy ever more fully.

In its original context (Ṛgveda 5.81.1) this *mantra* begins an ecstatic hymn to Savitṛ, wherein "they" are his worshipful priests. Here in a context divorced from ritual, "they" are those who aspire to enlightenment. Śvetāśvatara's intention is to tell us that though we may engage in the practice of *yoga,* God alone is familiar with all the ways of the spirit (*vayunāvit*) and directs us in our efforts to attain him. That is an allusion to divine grace. The Lord himself has established all the means of turning our minds Godward, through the outer observances of ritual worship and the interior methods of prayer and meditation. Therefore, let us praise the great God, Savitṛ!

5

युजे वां ब्रह्म पूर्व्यं नमोभि-
विश्लोक एतु पथ्येव सूरेः ।
शृण्वन्तु विश्वे अमृतस्य पुत्रा
आ ये धामानि दिव्यानि तस्थुः ॥ ५ ॥

yuje vāṁ brahma pūrvyaṁ namobhir viśloka etu pathy eva sūreḥ /
śṛṇvantu viśve amṛtasya putrā ā ye dhāmāni divyāni tasthuḥ //

5. With adoration I join [mind and thought] to the most excellent Brahman; may my praise thus go forth along the path of the wise. Hear, all you children of immortal bliss, who have ascended to heavenly abodes!

This fifth *mantra* first occurs in the Saṁhitā of the Ṛgveda (10.13.1), where it forms the opening verse of a hymn directly concerned with the performance of ritual.

The first two words (*yuje vām*) literally mean "I join the two of you." The two of what? we wonder. The original hymn is dedicated to the pair of oblation carts (*havirdhānas*) in which offerings of the sacred *soma* plant were conveyed to the ritual site. For the singer of that hymn, "the two of you" meant the sacred vehicles.[15]

With the decline and eventual disappearance of certain Vedic rites, a *mantra* such as this has acquired different meanings over the course of the millennia. As quoted by Śvetāśvatara, this *mantra* no longer applies to a sacrificial ritual; its meaning is now concerned with the practice of meditation.

"I join the two of you" can no longer refer to oblation carts but has to have another meaning. Looking back over the preceding four *mantras,* we find in three of them that two words occur paired. Those words are *mind* (*manas*) and *thought* (*dhī*). We can deduce that here "I join the two of you" means "I join mind and thought." *Mind* indicates the instrument of awareness, and *thought* represents the content of that awareness.

Another question arises, this one concerning Brahman. In the very early context of the Ṛgvedasaṁhitā, it is by no means certain that the term *brahman* meant the nondual supreme reality that it signifies in later Vedantic thought. *Brahman* originally meant "pious effusion or utterance, outpouring of the heart in worshipping the gods, prayer."[16] In the ancient Vedic liturgy, the first part of this *mantra* might well have meant something like, "With adoration (*namobhiḥ*) I join the most excellent (*pūrvyam*) outpouring of my heart (*brahman*) to the two of you (*vām*, the holy oblation carts)."

By Śvetāśvatara's time, this utterance necessarily had taken on a different meaning, expressing the idea of turning the mind and its thoughts reverently and devotedly toward the divine reality that is Brahman. And just as the practices and prayers of the wise have been conveyed Godward, so also may ours.

The opening words of the second line, "Hear, all you children of immortal bliss" (*śṛṇvantu viśve amṛtasya pūtrāḥ*), have likewise acquired a new connotation in the present age—as the Hindu response to the doctrine of original sin and eternal damnation, prevalent in the West. At the World's Parliament of Religions, held in Chicago in 1893, Śrī Rāmakṛṣṇa's disciple, Swami Vivekananda, decried that doctrine by addressing his audience as "children of immortal bliss." In soaring rhetoric he pointed out the hopefulness of that name and boldly declared that the Hindu refuses to call anyone a sinner, seeing all people as children of God, as "heirs to immortal bliss," as "holy and perfect beings," indeed as "divinities on earth." To call anyone a sinner, he added, is itself a sin, "a standing libel on human nature."[17]

"Children of immortal bliss"—we cannot know how that eloquent phrase fell on the ears of its first hearers nearly four thousand years ago, but there is every reason to believe that it was then, as now, an unequivocal proclamation of humankind's innate divinity.

6

अग्निर्यत्राभिमथ्यते वायुर्यत्राधिरुध्यते ।
सोमो यत्रातिरिच्यते तत्र सञ्जायते मनः ॥ ६ ॥

agnir yatrābimathyate vāyur yatrādhirudhyate /
somo yatrātiricyate tatra sañjāyate manaḥ //

6. Where fire is kindled, where breath is controlled, where bliss overflows, there true understanding arises.

This *mantra,* seeming to belong to an earlier, unidentified source, describes a portion of the Vedic *soma* sacrifice that was no longer performed by Śvetāśvatara's time. Translated literally it reads, "Where fire is kindled through friction, where air is controlled, where the *soma* juice overflows, there the mind is born." The words are open to widely differing interpretations, and though many commentators are often at odds with one another in the details, they all agree that the *mantra* describes some sort of gradual process of purification that leads to spiritual awakening.

Most plausibly, the verse metaphorically describes various phases of yogic practice.[18] Fire (*agni*) here represents the heat of spiritual ardor (*tapas*) engendered by mental one-pointedness, such as the meditation on *Oṁ* described previously (1.14). The purposeful effort of kindling by friction is essential to success, and once ignited, this metaphoric fire burns away ignorance and its effects from the aspirant's consciousness.[19] In short, *where* refers to consciousness itself, because nothing takes place outside of consciousness.

In the original context, the control of the air or breath (*vāyu*) probably referred to blowing on the kindling sticks during the igniting process. Here, in the context of *yoga*, it refers to the practitioner's control of the breath (*prāṇāyāma*), the mindful attention to the three phases of breathing: exhalation (*recaka*), inhalation (*pūraka*), and suspension (*kumbhaka*). When the flow of the breath becomes regular, quietude of the mind naturally results.

The use of *soma* was widespread in earlier Vedic rituals, and the entire ninth *maṇḍala* of the Ṛgvedasaṁhitā consists of hymns to this intoxicant, derived from a plant that can no longer be identified conclusively. With declining use, *soma* came to be associated in the Brāhmaṇas with the moon, thought to be the receptacle of *amṛta*, the nectar of immortality. In yogic terms *soma* most likely represents an internally experienced bliss, poetically described as "the wine of divine love."[20] In other words, *soma* becomes the metaphor for a certain level of blissful absorption achieved during meditation.

As used here, the final word, *manas*, has the broader connotation of "understanding," a meaning found in the Ṛgvedasaṁhitā. Overall, this *mantra* indicates that when ordinary awareness is guided, first through the proper observance of external ritual and then through increasingly internalized techniques of self-direction, it progresses toward the recognition of the indwelling spiritual reality. True knowledge is revealed to the aspirant when illumination bursts forth (*sañjāyate*) like a kindled flame.

7

सवित्रा प्रसवेन जुषेत ब्रह्म पूर्व्यम् ।
तत्र योनिं कृणवसे न हि ते पूर्तमक्षिपत् ॥ ७ ॥

savitrā prasavena juṣeta brahma pūrvyam /
tatra yoniṁ kṛṇavase na hi te pūrtam akṣipat //

7. Through Savitṛ, who sets all things in motion, may one delight in the eternal Brahman. Make your abode there; your fulfillment will not bind you at all.

God is both the immanent Savitṛ, the active power of consciousness that has manifested this world, and the transcendental Brahman, the underlying truth of all existence, which is unalloyed bliss. The meaning of the first half of this *mantra* is clear.

The second half presents great difficulties. Its last six words (*kṛṇavase na hi te pūrtam akṣipat*) originally straddled two verses of the Ṛgvedasaṁhita (6.16.17–18) and belonged to two separate sentences. Appended here to *tatra yonim,* they can scarely be considered a quotation in a strict sense, and whatever they meant in the original context, that meaning does not apply here. The meaning is far from clear even in the original setting, the seer Bharadvāja's hymn to the fire god Agni in what may be the oldest part of the Ṛgveda.[21] In the very different environment of the Upaniṣad the words are no less puzzling. Moreover, their insertion here accounts for the awkward pronominal shift from *one* in the first half of the *mantra* to *you* in the second half. Originally *you* referred to Agni; here it refers to the spiritual aspirant or *yogin*.

Attempts to interpret the elliptical clause *tatra yoniṁ kṛṇavase* have produced divergent opinions. The majority view takes *tatra* ("there") to represent Brahman and *yonim* also to stand for the ultimate abode or goal of spiritual endeavor, which is establishment in Brahman. The majority view also takes the Vedic subjunctive *kṛṇavase* in either a conditional or exhortatory sense: "if thou make [*sic*] thy dwelling there,"[22] "when there you take your place,"[23] "be absorbed, through samādhi, in the eternal Brahman,"[24] "you should generate steadfastness [self-absorption] in That,"[25] "concentrate on meditating on that eternal Brahman,"[26] "concentrate and get absorbed in that Brahman."[27] A smaller contingent takes *yoni* to mean "source": "if there thou make [*sic*] thy source,"[28] "there make your source,"[29] and the enigmatic "make there a source of birth for yourself."[30] One translator hedges his bet with "make your source (dwelling) there."[31]

Diverging somewhat, a pair of translators impute new meaning to the verb *kṛṇavase* ("[may you] make"): "if there you cipher [solve the mystery of] your origin."[32] Then comes a wildly divergent reading: "attaining whom [Brahman] (*tatra*) thou destroyest (*kṛṇavase*) the source (*yonim*) [the mind that gives rise to the phenomenal world],"[33] and that is echoed in another translation: "thus will the source of ignorance be destroyed."[34]

In the interest of not adding unintended meaning to this ambiguous passage, we suggest simply, "make your abode there," *there* referring to the eternal Brahman mentioned in the preceding line. This Brahman is, of course, both the source *and* the ultimate abode—two legitimate meanings of the word *yoni*.

The translation of what follows (*na hi te pūrtam akṣipat*) likewise requires explanation. Everything hinges on the meaning of the word *pūrtam*. Previous translators have rendered it as "path,"[35] "earlier deed,"[36] "former [work],"[37] "results of past actions,"[38] "karma,"[39] "work,"[40] "action sanctified by the Smṛtis,"[41] "public welfare activities,"[42] "the gifts you have given,"[43] "scriptural work,"[44] "good deeds,"[45] and "what you have done."[46] The great variance is problematic, but the problem is not insurmountable.

The first point to clarify is that *pūrta* does not mean just any action, but only a meritorious work or act of pious liberality.[47] We can thus rule out any interpretation of *pūrta* as *karma* in general. Of course, *any* action, meritorious or not, is binding. The acts of charity and piety enjoined by the ancient Vedas were fully intended to yield positive results such as abundance, progeny, and heavenly beatitude. It was all a matter of cause and effect, but in the philosophical thinking that arose from the Upaniṣads, a finite cause can only produce a commensurately finite effect. Even heavenly reward is temporary and thus bounded by temporality. No action, unless performed with complete selflessness and without any desire for its results, can be anything other than binding. Why, then, would this *mantra* single out only virtuous, religiously prescribed actions and then say that they will not bind? Perhaps it doesn't. Perhaps *pūrta* indicates something entirely different.

Taken at face value, *pūrta* means two things. First, it means "fulfilling," the fulfilling of some wish or obligation. And second, it means "fulfillment," the reward that follows.[48] When Śvetāśvatara says, "Your fulfillment will not bind you at all," he is not speaking of fulfillment in the relative sense, where one duty fulfilled or one desire satisfied still belongs to a chain of further thoughts, feelings, and events. Rather, the fulfillment of which he speaks is different. Even though it is the result of actions performed, they are the actions of spiritual practice, and specifically the efforts of directing the mind in meditation. The point is that the effort of spiritual endeavor is qualitatively different from all other forms of action. That is why "your fulfllment will not bind you at all" (*na hi te pūrtam akṣipat*). *Pūrta* here stands for the unique satisfaction that comes only with the knowledge of Brahman. Unlike all lesser fulfillments, this one is the satisfaction of ultimate freedom.

The ancient verses quoted thus far dealt originally with ritual action, and Śvetāśvatara has presented them anew in the light of internalized yogic practice. In the present *mantra,* the meaning of the term *pūrta* has shifted from fulfilling a religious obligation to the fulfillment of Self-knowledge. No doubt the pleasure of this *double entendre* was not lost on our seer, for this is not his first engagement in wordplay (see pp. 99, 121), nor will it be his last. Now, on this stunning cadence, he is ready to pursue the teaching of *yoga* in his own words.

8

त्रिरुन्नतं स्थाप्य समं शरीरं
हृदीन्द्रियाणि मनसा सन्निवेश्य ।
ब्रह्मोडुपेन प्रतरेत विद्वान्
स्रोतांसि सर्वाणि भयावहानि ॥ ८ ॥

trirunnataṁ sthāpya samaṁ śarīraṁ hṛdīndriyāṇi manasā sanniveśya / brahmoḍupena pratareta vidvān srotāṁsi sarvāṇi bhayāvahāni //

8. Holding the body steady with chest, neck, and head aligned, then mentally directing the senses into the heart, one who is wise may cross over every fear-laden current on the raft of Brahman.

Yogic practice has so long a history in India that its origins are untraceable today. All that can be said for certain is that the evidence known to us indicates a very great antiquity (see pp. 31–34).

For serious students of Indian philosophy and spiritual practice the word *yoga* immediately brings to mind the *Yogasūtra* of Patañjali, an unexcelled manual on the management of consciousness. It was compiled probably around the fourth century CE,[49] eight or nine hundred years after the Śvetāśvataropaniṣad, but because there is no firm conclusion regarding who Patañjali was, and because some authorities identify him with the grammarian Patañjali, who lived around 400 BCE, the *Yogasūtra*'s dating remains uncertain.

In any case, its content consists of elements already well known from the Upaniṣads.[50] Patañjali makes clear at the outset that what he is about to present is nothing new but rather the cumulative knowledge of an ancient tradition. That is the import of the opening aphorism: "Now, instruction in *yoga*" (*atha yogānuśāsanam*) (1.1). The exact meaning of *anuśāsana* is not just teaching or instruction but a presentation of teaching that has previously been given by others.

The next *sūtra* defines *yoga* as "the restraint of activity in the medium of individualized consciousness" (*yogaś cittavṛttinirodhaḥ*) (1.2). This, of course, is the same idea that Śvetāśvatara means to convey with the ancient Vedic quotations that begin his second chapter. Being an earlier formulation than the *Yogasūtra,* Śvetāśvatara's discourse presents its ideas in a less developed and less rigorously logical manner. In contrast, the *Yogasūtra*'s first two chapters present an astonishingly detailed examination of the mind's functions and the means to master them. They observe every state of ordinary awareness with scientific precision and then prescribe the methods that lead the prospective *yogin* to successively higher states of awareness. Thoroughly practical, they also advise of the inevitable obstacles along the way until the indescribable, ultimate state of consciousness-being is reached. Based on the Sāṁkhya philosophy, the *Yogasūtra* explains the transcendental experience as the disengagement of consciousness (*puruṣa*) from materiality (*prakṛti*). Once released, the *puruṣa* abides in its own original nature, a state defined as *kaivalya* ("isolation"), or total freedom from existential woe (*duḥkha*).

The *Yogasūtra*'s second chapter, given over to practice (*sādhanā*) presents a logically ordered and comprehensive system consisting of eight "limbs" (*aṣṭāṅgayoga*). These are called *yama, niyama, āsana, prāṇāyāma, pratyāhāra, dhāraṇā, dhyāna,* and *samādhi* (2.29).

Patañjali's eight-step process begins with how an aspirant relates to the outer world. Śvetāśvatara's less systematic and differently ordered exposition alludes to something similar in the opening line of his second discourse: "First joining the mind and holy thoughts for the sake of reaching the truth..." (2.1). This suggests that the preliminary step toward achieving enlightenment is observing proper moral conduct and self-control. Patañjali expands upon and systematizes those matters of moral conduct and self-control in the first two steps of his eight-limbed *yoga*, the precepts known as *yama* and *niyama*.

As defined in the *Yogasūtra* (2.30), *yama* ("restraint") consists of five ethical precepts: noninjury to others (*ahiṁsā*), truthfulness (*satya*), non-stealing (*asteya*), chastity (*brahmacarya*), and abstention from greed (*aparigraha*). These precepts, being universal, constitute the Great Vow (*mahāvrata*) (2.31). Their purpose is to rid the aspirant of the negative tendencies and behavior that create disharmony with the surrounding world. How can there be tranquility within, if there is disharmony without? The Great Vow is to be practiced in thought, word, and deed at all times, in all places, and in all circumstances.

With the second limb, called *niyama* ("observance"), the aspirant cultivates the five positive qualities of physical and mental purity (*śauca*), contentment (*saṁtoṣa*), austerity (*tapas*), study (*svādhyāya*), and devotion to God (*īśvarapraṇidhāna*) (2.32).

The virtues of *yama* have enormous practical value. Practicing non-injury (*ahiṁsā*) in thought, speech, and action leads to benevolence toward the natural and human environment; all sense of discord and strife evaporates. Observing truthfulness (*satya*) at all times gives rise to complete moral integrity. In the broadest sense non-stealing (*asteya*) means noncovetousness. Letting go of mental cravings banishes the sense of existential lack and incompleteness, which runs contrary to the true fullness (*pūrṇatva*) of the Self. *Brahmacarya* in the broadest sense means freedom from the human preoccupation with sex; the absence of sexual desire frees the mind to pursue the spiritual goal wholeheartedly. *Brahmacarya* is not repression but rather the redirection of mental energy toward the goal of Self-realization. *Aparigraha* is the nonacceptance of anything that would impose an obligation on the receiver; this term is also taken to mean not accepting more than one needs. Either way it results in a freedom from compromise conducive to spiritual growth.

The observances of *niyama* are similarly pragmatic. When the body is regarded as the dwelling-place of the *ātman*, the *sādhaka* logically feels the need to treat it with respect. Purity (*śauca*) involves the entire mind-body complex. Physical and mental cleanliness are necessary as well as the purity of physical and mental nutrition. In Indian thought, *food* refers not only to what is consumed through the mouth but also to what is taken in through any of the sense organs. As one thinks, so one becomes. Accordingly the would-be *yogin* must be highly discerning in the choice of interests, entertainment, and company kept. Contentment (*saṁtoṣa*) means acceptance and gratitude—letting go of both resistance and dissatisfaction. That practice helps to focus the attention on the moment and frees one from regrets over the past and worries about the future. Austerity (*tapas*) should not be taken in the negative sense of self-denial or mortification (see pp. 150–152), because that would only contravene the sense of respect for body and mind as the vehicles of divine consciousness. Rather, *tapas* should be understood in the positive light of ardor for self-mastery. Enthusiasm is further invigorated by study (*svādhyāya*)—reading and thinking about sacred texts and holy teachings as well as mentally repeating a *mantra.* Such practices help to engender devotion (*praṇidhāna*), which is pure love. Even as true love for another human being places the greater good of the beloved first and foremost, devotion to the divine ideal leads to selflessness. And even as the passionate love for another person draws the mind constantly to the object of love, so does religious devotion (*bhakti*) lead to constant recollectedness of the divine beloved.

After discussing the details of *yama* and *niyama,* Patañjali introduces the third limb of *yoga,* the proper posture (*āsana*) for sitting in meditation (2.46). His only requirement is that it be steady and unforced. It is with this matter of *āsana* that Śvetāśvatara begins the present *mantra,* instructing in greater detail how the body should be firmly positioned but relaxed, with the chest, neck, and head held erect. This is the posture already indicated in the ancient representations of the "proto-Śiva" figure from the Indus Valley. Such a posture is essential when the spiritual energy within the body becomes aroused, but until then the main purpose of *āsana* is to forget the physical body altogether while the mind remains alert.

Śvetāśvatara describes this alertness as "mentally directing the senses into the heart." This is, in fact, Patañjali's fifth limb of *yoga,* which the *Yogasūtra* (2.54) calls *pratyāhāra,* the withdrawal of the mind from the objects of the senses. Śvetāśvatara presented this practice earlier in mythic terms, quoting that Savitṛ, the power of consciousness, directs the mind inward, away from the distractions of the outer world (2.3). As the naturally outgoing senses (*devas*) are withdrawn from materiality, consciousness turns back upon itself.

The place wherein consciousness turns back upon itself is the heart. Śvetāśvatara uses the word *heart* here for the first time, and that word (*hṛd* or *hṛdaya*) will occur six more times in the course of the Upaniṣad, twice each in *mantras* 3.13, 4.17, and 4.20. Additionally he alludes to the heart once by the word *iha* ("here, in this place") (2.15) and twice by the metaphor of a cave or hidden place (*guha*) (3.11, 3.20).

The heart has played a major role in Indian religious thought ever since the time of the Ṛgvedasaṁhitā. It can convey a variety of meanings on different levels, sometimes referring to the physical organ but more often indicating the interior of the body or the middle or center of anything, often as its best part or essence. More significantly, as the seat of feeling and thinking, the heart signifies the mind or soul. Finally it becomes identified with consciousness itself.

Even in the Ṛgvedic age the penetration of profound mysteries was said to come through the heart. It was there that a person would find the light of higher insight, would experience the One, and would become a seer (*ṛṣi*). Accordingly the heart was said to see what the eye cannot.[51] Śvetāśvatara will give voice to this very idea later on, declaring of Brahman: "His form stands not in the range of sight; no one sees him with the eye. They who, with the heart (*hṛdā*) and mind, know him as abiding in the heart (*hṛdistham*), they become immortal" (4.20).

In the ritualistic context of the Śatapathabrāhmaṇa (3.8.3.8) the heart is declared to be the Self and the mind (*ātmā vai mano hṛdayam*) as well as the receptacle of life-breath (*prāṇa*). A later passage of the same text (8.5.4.3) observes that a human being "thinks with the heart and mind" (*hṛdayena manasā cetayate*). Considered together, these verses highlight the intimate connection between selfhood and consciousness.

The earliest Upaniṣad, the Bṛhadāraṇyaka, is also the one richest in references to the heart. In a dialogue between King Ajātaśatru of Kāśi and the learned Gārgya Bālāki, the heart is treated as the locus of consciousness in which all sensory perceptions are gathered and united (2.1.17–19). In the famous debate at King Janaka's court, Yājñavalkya told the renowned teacher Vidagdha Śākalya that visible appearances are founded on the heart, because it is by the heart that one recognizes them (3.9.19). When Śākalya inquired on what the heart is founded, Yājñavalkya berated him, asking, "How could it be founded on anything other than ourselves? ... As for the Self, one can only say 'not this, not this' (*neti nety ātmā*)" (3.9.25–26). On another occasion, during a royal audience, King Janaka asked Yājñavalkya if what Śākalya had said is true, that the heart is Brahman. Yājñavalkya assented to what he considered a self-evident truth and then elaborated that the heart is stability itself, the abode and support of all beings. The heart, he affirmed resoundingly, is truly the supreme Brahman (*hṛdayaṁ vai ... paramaṁ brahma*) (4.1.7).

The Chāndogyopaniṣad (8.1.1–3) speaks of a dwelling-place in the body, shaped like a small lotus (*daharaṁ puṇḍarīkam*), and in it an interior space (*antarākāśaḥ*) wherein abides something that one should desire to understand or recognize (*vijijñāsitavyam*). This inner space within the heart (*antarhṛdaye*) contains the entire universe and beyond that the sum total of reality, for that heart-space is none other than Brahman.[52] Another passage in the same Upaniṣad (3.13.1–5) describes five openings of the heart and gives the instruction to meditate on them and their corresponding energies, faculties, elements, and deities. Both passages suggest yogic and proto-Sāṁkhya affinities.

The connection between the heart and *yoga,* already present in the early Chāndogyopaniṣad, becomes clearer and more recognizable in the middle-period Kaṭhopaniṣad, which contains several verses involving the heart. Variants of those verses occur in the present Upaniṣad as well, altered to reflect its Śaiva character (see Appendix B, Table 1).

There is good reason to believe that the passages in the Upaniṣads dealing with the heart may account for the central and exalted position that its symbolism occupies later in nondualistic Kashmir Śaivism, even though that system rests not on the authority of the Vedas but on that of the Śaivāgama.[53] It is certainly true that some of the Śaivāgama's ideas, practices, and verbal symbols have much in common with those of the Upaniṣads. For example, two themes—the Chāndogyopaniṣad's image of the space within the lotus of the heart and the Śvetāśvataropaniṣad's instruction to join the mind and thought to Brahman—reappear in the Vijñānabhairava, a major treatise on *yoga* belonging to the Śaivāgama. The Vijñānabhairava, probably dating from the seventh century CE, was held in such esteem that Abhinavagupta dubbed it the Śivavijñānopaniṣad [The hidden teaching on the realization of the Absolute].[54] In verse 49 we read that one who has merged the mind with the other senses in the interior space of the heart (*hṛdyākāśe*) and has entered into the center between the two hemispheres of the lotus (*padmasampuṭamadhyagaḥ*), attentive to nothing else, reaches supreme felicity (*paramaṁ saubhāgyam*). Through this symbolic language the text, in the words of Śiva himself, explains that by directing the mind and its various faculties inward to the heart with no other thought, the aspirant achieves the unification of consciousness. The center of the heart symbolizes consciousness (*cit*) in its purest state as the supreme knower or subject (*pramātṛ*), and the two hemispheres of the lotus represent that same consciousness modified as the object known (*prameya*) and the act or means of knowing (*pramāṇa*). The *yogin* who has gone to the center (*madhyagaḥ*) merges with the Self and attains the highest freedom.[55]

Śvetāśvatara concludes the present *mantra* by affirming that "one who is wise may cross over every fear-laden current on the raft of Brahman." The ancient image of a raft or boat taking one safely across the river or ocean of human existence is first recorded in the Ṛgvedasaṁhitā (10.63.10). There the Infinite as the Divine Mother, Aditi, is praised first as the shining totality of the manifest creation. Then lauded as well-protecting, granting secure refuge, and guiding safely, she is likened to a divine ship, well-fitted with oars, free of defects, and admitting no water. The hymnist exhorts, "Let us board this ship for our well-being."[56] Śvetāśvatara, citing the common metaphor of temporal existence as a river (1.5), reconfigures the vessel as a raft, which the author of the *Śvetāśvataropaniṣadvṛtti* interprets as the *praṇava*. One who is wise (*vidvān*) knows the meaning of *Oṁ* and the means of meditating on it. This same idea resurfaces later in the *Yogasūtra* (1.28), where Patañjali emphasizes constant repetition of *Oṁ* together with meditation on its meaning (*taj japaḥ tadarthabhāvanam*). This is the very practice that Śvetāśvatara advocates—mental repetition of the supreme *mantra* along with the knowledge of its meaning. This practice takes one across the river of mundane existence (*saṁsāra*) with all its fear-laden currents, safely across the mind's tumultuous flow of ignorant and bondage-creating thoughts.[57]

9

प्राणान् प्रपीड्येह संयुक्तचेष्टः
क्षीणे प्राणे नासिकयोच्छ्वसीत ।
दुष्टाश्वयुक्तमिव वाहमेनं
विद्वान् मनो धारयेताप्रमत्तः ॥ ९ ॥

prāṇān prapīḍyeha saṁyuktaceṣṭaḥ kṣīṇe prāṇe nāsikayocchvasīta /
duṣṭāśvayuktam iva vāham enaṁ vidvān mano dhārayetāpramattaḥ //

9. Holding the movements of the limbs in check and controlling the vital forces in the body, one should breath gently through the nostrils. The wise one, always attentive, should restrain his mind as he would a chariot yoked to unruly horses.

After settling comfortably into a posture that will not draw the mind's attention to the body, the meditator should sit motionless. In this state of physical quietude the metabolic functions governed by the five aspects of the vital force (*prāṇa*) naturally slow down. Here it is important to remember that *prāṇa*, outwardly visible as the breath, encompasses the entire range of physiological functions and extends beyond that into the subtler realm of spiritual awareness (see pp. 103–104).

At the metabolic and the subtler levels the various forms of *prāṇa* can be regulated indirectly through the control of the physical breath. Śvetāśvatara alluded to this earlier in the phrase "where breath is controlled" (2.6). This practice is Patañjali's fourth limb of *yoga*, known as *prāṇāyāma*. Because of potential danger to the nervous system, the various exercises of inhalation, suspension, and exhalation involved in the practice of *prāṇāyāma* are best avoided and should be undertaken, if at all, only under the watchful guidance of a qualified teacher. They are not necessary, because when the activities of the body and the mind are quieted, the volume of breath involuntarily diminishes and a state conducive to deeper contemplation should arise naturally.

Actual practice does not always bear that out. All too often, sitting quietly only heightens awareness of the internal chatter of the mind. Still, *prāṇāyāma* is like putting the cart before the horse, and speaking of horses, that is just what Śvetāśvatara does next. He compares the mind to a chariot yoked to unruly horses.

The simile bears some resemblance to a passage in the Kaṭhopaniṣad (1.3.3–9), which likens the body (*śarīra*) to a chariot, the Self (*ātman*) to the lord of the chariot, the intellect (*buddhi*) to the charioteer, and the mind (*manas*) to the reins. The sensory faculties (*indriyāṇi*) are the horses, and the objects that they perceive are the paths traveled. One who has no control over the mind lacks right understanding and fails to reach the goal, but one who is possessed of right understanding, with the mind ever harnessed (*yuktena manasā sadā*), reaches the end of the journey and the highest state of the all-pervading Brahman.[58]

Śvetāśvatara's point, similarly, is that the unruly thoughts of the mind can be managed only by determined direction and unwavering attention. The meditator's mental wandering often begins with the swirling about of recent thoughts, but even when the matters of immediate concern have been successfully put to rest, long-buried memories or impressions may surface randomly and in turn initiate a chain of free association. After some time the meditator becomes aware of how far the mind has strayed. This will happen countless times, but little by little, with increasing vigilance, the meditator learns at the first sign of wandering to bring the attention back to the object of meditation.

This process is exactly what Śrī Kṛṣṇa describes in the Bhagavadgītā: "When the mind is completely controlled and rests in the Self alone, then one who is free from longing and all desires is called steadfast (*yuktaḥ*). As the light of a lamp does not flicker in a windless place, so is [the mind of] the *yogin* of controlled thought, meditating on the Self" (6.18–19). "Whenever the unsteady mind goes astray, from here to there, it should be brought back to rest in the Self" (6.26).

Mental waywardness is a universal and persistent phenomenon. Even in the light of Śrī Kṛṣṇa's wise counsel, Arjuna complains, "Restless indeed is this mind, O Kṛṣṇa, troubling, powerful, unyielding—as difficult to tame, I think, as the wind" (6.34). And therein lies the need for continuing practice.

10

समे शुचौ शर्करावह्निवालुका-
विवर्जिते शब्दजलाश्रयादिभिः ।
मनोनुकूले न तु चक्षुपीडन
गुहानिवाताश्रयणे प्रयोजयेत् ॥ १० ॥

same śucau śarkarāvahnivālukāvivarjite śabdajalāśrayādibhiḥ /
manonukūle na tu cakṣupīḍane guhānivātāśrayaṇe prayojayet //

10. In a clean and level place, free of pebbles, fire, and dust, free of noise and dampness, calming to the mind, and not displeasing to the eye—here, sheltered from the wind and retiring into solitude, one should concentrate the mind.

Śvetāśvatara next stipulates the conditions of a suitable environment for meditation. The floor must be level and smooth in order to provide a firm base, free of pebbles, gravel, dampness, and any other distracting irritant. The air too must be unpolluted and free of dust and smoke. There must be nothing to offer visual distraction, and no sounds should intrude, nor should the wind make itself felt. Accordingly, the seer recommends retiring to a solitary place.

This and the two preceding *mantras* address the themes of posture, breath control, and withdrawal of the mind from sensory objects. Together they anticipate a similar passage in the Bhagavadgītā (6.10–13), where Śrī Kṛṣṇa counsels Arjuna to practice concentration in solitude and in a clean spot. He intimates that *āsana* refers not only to posture but also to the place where the *yogin* sits. Then he instructs Arjuna to hold the body firm with the head and neck erect, adding that the gaze should be fixed on the tip of the nose. Thus situated, the *sādhaka* is to make the mind one-pointed.

When Śvetāśvatara advises retiring to a solitary place, he uses the word *guha,* which literally means "cave." *Guha* must be taken here in a figurative sense, and indeed it refers to the heart. To understand what *heart* really means, we must penetrate yet another layer of symbolism (see pp. 173–175). In Śaiva usage the heart signifies the deepest consciousness—the heart or center of reality.[59] Retiring to such a "place" is both the means and the goal of meditation.

11

नीहारधूमार्कानिलानलानां
खद्योतविद्युत्स्फटिकशशीनाम्।
एतानि रूपाणि पुरःसराणि
ब्रह्मण्यभिव्यक्तिकराणि योगे ॥ ११ ॥

nīhāradhūmārkānilānalānāṁ khadyotavidyutsphaṭikaśaśīnām /
etāni rūpāṇi puraḥsarāṇi brahmaṇy abhivyaktikarāṇi yoge //

11. Mist, smoke, the sun, wind, fire, fireflies, lightning, crystals, and the moon—these apparitions precede the revelation of Brahman in *yoga*.

In the course of practice a meditator, with eyes closed, may "see" certain forms. These are not the same as physical objects seen with the eyes open but are phenomena of consciousness "seen" with the mind.[60] For different people and at different times, such experiences may vary, but as Śvetāśvatara indicates, most are manifestations of light, resembling either the soft glow of mist or smoke, the sparkling of fireflies, the glitter of a crystal, the flash of lightning, the serene radiance of the moon, or the brilliance of the sun. Such manifestations of the inner light of consciousness are common to mystics of every tradition the world over.[61]

There can be no doubt that these experiences are signs of progress, but it is important to remember that they are only signs. It is equally important to keep in mind that not everyone experiences them, and a truer and better indicator of spiritual progress is the change that takes place in the aspirant's character along the path to knowledge of Brahman.[62]

12

पृथ्व्यप्तेजोऽनिलखे समुत्थिते
पञ्चात्मके योगगुणे प्रवृत्ते ।
न तस्य रोगो न जरा न मृत्युः
प्राप्तस्य योगाग्निमयं शरीरम् ॥ १२ ॥

pṛthvyaptejonilakhe samutthite pañcātmake yogaguṇe pravṛtte /
na tasya rogo na jarā na mṛtyuḥ prāptasya yogāgnimayaṁ śarīram //

12. When the subtle essences of the five elements—earth, water, fire, air, and space—are revealed in the perception of *yoga*, then one attains a body made of the fire of divine union; for him there is neither sickness, old age, nor death.

Eventually the mind achieves a breakthrough from the perception of physical matter to a subtler state of awareness. It is one thing to experience a subtler dimension directly and quite another to attempt its description. To explain something as rarefied as Śvetāśvatara presents here requires language that is both technical and deliberative, even though the experience described is natural and spontaneous. The experience is immediate; its definition is an afterthought. Still, to understand the passage from the gross to the subtle plane requires some knowledge of how matter and mind are constituted.

The process of creation is essentially the movement from unity (*abheda*) to difference (*bheda*), from the absolute oneness of consciousness itself (*advaita*) to the prodigal diversity of all things mental and material (*dvaita*). The created realm reflects this basic fact everywhere through a hierarchical arrangement from subtler to grosser, from nonmaterial to material, from inner to outer.

Every material object in the cosmos, including the human body, is made of the five physical elements. These are space (*ākāśa* or *kha*), air (*vāyu* or *anila*), fire (*tejas* or *agni*), water (*ap*), and earth (*pṛthivī*). Because each gross element (*mahābhūta*) possesses a specific dominant property, physical matter is said to be of five kinds according to how it is perceived. The five gross elements are classified in an order that reflects the number of sensory faculties that can perceive them. *Ākāśa* is inferred on the basis of sound. *Vāyu* is heard and felt. *Tejas* is heard, felt, and seen. *Ap* is heard, felt, seen, and tasted. *Pṛthivī* is heard, felt, seen, tasted, and smelled. It is through the senses that we first experience the phenomenal world, and each sense has the power to reveal something about that world in a specific way.

Behind each gross element (*mahābhūta* or *sthūlabhūta*) there is a corresponding subtle element (*tanmātra* or *sūkṣmabhūta*). The subtle elements are sound (*śabda*), touch (*sparśa*), form and color (*rūpa*), taste (*rasa*), and smell (*gandha*). Just as the physical body (*sthūla-śarīra*) is composed of the five gross elements, the subtle or mental body (*sūkṣmaśarīra*) is composed of the five subtle elements.[63]

There is a significant difference between the gross and the subtle elements. The gross, perceptible in ordinary states of consciousness, are compounded from the subtle, which are simple, rudimentary, and imperceptible in themselves.[64] Those are in fact the sensory stimuli inherent in perceptible matter, and the term *tanmātra* ("that alone") indicates their homogeneous nature. Still, each *tanmātra* consists of the pure energy of the *guṇas* and therefore displays sattvic, rajasic, and tamasic aspects. Within each *tanmātra* the three *guṇa* energies remain inseparable, but one always overpowers the others by varying degrees in order to produce different manifestations.[65]

Each gross element is compounded of the five subtle elements in a process known as *pañcīkaraṇa* ("quintuplication"). One half of each *mahābhūta* consists of the corresponding *tanmātra*; the other half is made of equal parts of the other four. For example, space (*ākāśa*) is one half *śabda* and one eighth each *sparśa, rūpa, rasa,* and *gandha.* Air consists of one half *sparśa* and one eighth each of the others, and so on. In this way, each of the five subtle elements is dominant in its corresponding gross element, but the other four are also present.

The gross elements are composed of the tamasic aspects of the five subtle elements, so it follows that *tamas* predominates in physical matter,[66] including the human body. Similarly the rajasic aspects of the subtle elements form the vital force (*prāṇa*), which animates the body and governs the biological and metabolic processes.[67] The sattvic aspects of the subtle elements form the inner organ of consciousness (*antaḥkaraṇa*),[68] through which the embodied individual experiences the phenomenal world.

From a practical standpoint the purpose of meditation is to harness the mind's own power to concentrate and then to direct it toward the goal of Self-knowledge. In doing so, we actually begin to retrace the steps through which the cosmos has evolved from pure consciousness all the way down to solid matter. Along the spiritual quest the outer will be dissolved into the inner, the gross into the subtle, the material into the nonmaterial.

Along the way various experiences may arise, as Śvetāśvatara mentioned in the previous *mantra*. Now he speaks of the passage of awareness wherein the meditator's mind breaks through the barriers of ordinary sensory knowledge by which the outer world is revealed and reaches the level of the *tanmātras*.

Certain practices produce certain results. By concentrating on the tip of the nose, the *yogin* experiences a "heavenly" fragrance outside the realm of ordinary perception. By concentrating on the tip of the tongue, the *yogin* experiences a supersensory awareness of taste. Similarly, concentration on the hard palate reveals a supersensory experience of color, concentration on the middle of the tongue produces a supersensory awareness of touch, and concentration on the root of the tongue reveals a heavenly sound beyond the range of ordinary sense perception.[69] Not all meditators will experience every one of these states of awareness, but even one such experience is a sure sign of progress.[70]

Nevertheless, such powers have little value in themselves and should not be given much attention.[71] The true value of the states described here is expressed in Patañjali's *Yogasūtra* (1.35): "An engrossing concentration that leads to extraordinary perceptions encourages the mind to persevere." Yogic experience of the subtle elements steadies and redirects the mind. Gaining a sense of its own strength and ability,[72] the mind will no longer be attracted by outward objects.[73] Sensuous enjoyment of material objects leads to craving for more of the same, but the rarefied beauty of the subtle elements inspires one to reach even beyond them to the ineffable source from which all creation flows.

At this stage the *yogin* achieves the "fruit of conquest over the physical elements" (*bhūtajayaphala*), described as the burning away of bodily imperfections in the metaphorical fire of *yoga*. Now understanding that the Self is separate from the body, the *yogin* will no longer be affected by sickness, old age, or death.

13

लघुत्वमारोग्यमलोलुपत्वं
वर्णप्रसादः स्वरसौष्ठवं च ।
गन्धः शुभो मूत्रपुरीषमल्पं
योगप्रवृत्तिं प्रथमां वदन्ति ॥ १३ ॥

laghutvam ārogyam alolupatvaṁ varṇaprasādaḥ svarasauṣṭhvaṁ ca /
gandhaḥ śubho mūtrapurīṣam alpaṁ yogapravṛttiṁ prathamāṁ vadanti //

13. They say that the first signs of progress in *yoga* are a sense of bodily lightness, health, freedom from craving, a clear complexion, a beautiful voice, a pleasant odor, and scant excretions.

Because the yogic journey begins from the point of engrossment in the material world, it is only natural that the first signs of progress relate to outwardly observable changes, such as the physical benefits described here. At this early stage the aspirant must be cautioned that it is all too easy to mistake the experience of something out of the ordinary for something greater than it is, and also that attachment to such experiences will impede further advancement. Any sign of progress should not be an enticement to stay contentedly in one place but an encouragement to press on.

14

यथैव बिम्बं मृदयोपलिप्तं
तेजोमयं भ्राजते तत् सुधान्तम् ।
तद्वाऽऽत्मतत्त्वं प्रसमीक्ष्य देही
एकः कृतार्थो भवते वीतशोकः ॥ १४ ॥

yathaiva bimbaṁ mṛdayopaliptaṁ tejomayaṁ bhrājate tat sudhāntam /
tad vā 'tmatattvaṁ prasamīkṣya dehī ekaḥ kṛtārtho bhavate vītaśokaḥ //

14. Just as a mirror, coated with dirt, again gleams brightly when well cleaned, so the embodied soul, perceiving its own true nature, becomes One—completely fulfilled and free from sorrow.

In ancient times, mirrors were highly polished, shining discs made of copper, bronze, or silver. It is to such a mirror that Svetāśvatara likens the true Self, pointing out that both have the inherent capacity to shine and to reflect. Still, the light of either one can be obscured—the material light of the mirror by dirt or dust and the spiritual light of the *ātman* by the impurity defined as ignorance of the nondual Self.

Fundamental to the verb *bhrājate* ("gleams," "shines," "glitters," or "sparkles") is the idea of light. The nature of light is to shine of its own accord; if it did not shine, it would not be light. In both the Vedānta and the Trikaśāstra that effulgent nature of consciousness is called *prakāśa,* and according to the Vedānta Brahman is only *prakāśa* (see p. 136). But the function of light is to illuminate, to shine on something else and reveal it. The Trikaśāstra calls that function *vimarśa.* Because Trika teaching recognizes no reality other than consciousness itself, what can *vimarśa* possibly reveal? Being the self-referential or self-reflective power of consciousness, *vimarśa* makes *prakāśa* known to itself. The two are in fact one, and that One is the supreme identity that the *yogin* seeks.

Together the nature and function of consciousness operate throughout the manifest universe, which is in Trika teaching the divine reality's own self-expression. On the gross plane, physical light shining on an object makes it visible and knowable to the individual experient. On the subtle plane, the light of consciousness shining through the mind illuminates all perceptions and thoughts and brings understanding to the experience.

In the case of the mirror, the quality of shining is not caused by the act of cleaning but only revealed by it, because the capacity to shine was there all along, merely hidden beneath the dirt. Similarly the self-luminous radiance of consciousness is ever present, even though we rarely think about it owing to the myriad distractions of perception and conceptualization that constantly occupy the mind.

Of course, the example of the mirror barely hints at the boundless brilliance of the light of the *ātman* that goes unrecognized in our present state of unknowing.

That unknowing (*ajñāna*) is, according to the Vedānta, the impurity that soils the mirror, and it arises through the *ātman's* apparent association with *māyā*. Somewhat differently the Trika-śāstra views the finite soul as a contracted form of the infinite Self and considers the impurity (*mala*) to be the contraction or finitude produced by *māyā's* limiting power. *Mala* takes three forms. *Āṇava-mala* is the contraction of universal consciousness into limited individuality; it is the root impurity that gives rise to the other two. *Māyīyamala* is the impurity of duality or difference that perceives everything in terms of I and other. *Kārmamala* is the impurity of action performed out of necessity or compulsion, impelled by the sense of imperfection or lack inherent in *āṇavamala*.

The *yogin's* awareness is to be purified of all ignorance or limitation. Once the impurity is removed, the embodied soul (*dehī*) recognizes its own true nature (*ātmatattvam*) as undivided, self-luminous consciousness and experiences that in its absolute purity. In the dazzling, nondual awareness beyond all difference, the individual self, which formerly regarded itself as separate, loses all distinction of I and other and in the reintegration of consciousness becomes completely fulfilled (*kṛtārthaḥ*). In the supreme identity of I-ness in full (*pūrṇāhaṁtā*), every objective has been attained, every purpose has been accomplished, and there is complete satisfaction in divine perfection (*pūrṇatva*). Thus is the *yogin* freed from all sorrow (*vītaśokaḥ*).

15

यदात्मतत्त्वेन तु ब्रह्मतत्त्वं
दीपोपमेनेह युक्तः प्रपश्येत्।
अजं ध्रुवं सर्वतत्त्वैर्विशुद्धं
ज्ञात्वा देवं मुच्यते सर्वपाशैः॥ १५॥

yadātmatattvena tu brahmatattvaṁ dīpopameneha yuktaḥ prapaśyet /
ajaṁ dhruvaṁ sarvatattvair viśuddhaṁ jñātvā devaṁ mucyate sarvapāśaiḥ //

15. Through the reality of the Self, radiant as a lamp within the heart, one who is established in meditation knows the reality of Brahman as unborn [and ever being], constant, and untouched by anything within the creation; knowing that effulgent being, one is freed from all fetters.

The example of the mirror in the previous *mantra* shows that the key to enlightenment is not found in anything external but is inherent within the spiritual seeker. The pure spirit (*ātman*) within the embodied human being (*dehin*) is identical to the transcendental reality known as Brahman. The individual soul is nothing other than spirit in its embodied state. In Vedantic teaching that same Brahman, as related to the manifest universe, is personalized as the universal Lord and called *deva*, or God.[74]

Each of these terms—*ātman*, Brahman, and *deva*—expresses a definite concept according to the limitations of human awareness; yet they should be thought of not as discrete entities but rather as one indefinable reality regarded from different points of view. All three express the same unity of the ever blissful being-consciousness.

The word *iha* means "here" or "in this place," and the place is the meditator's heart, the center of consciousness. Again evoking the imagery of light, Śvetāśvatara says that the true essence of the individual self (*ātmatattva*) is radiant like a lamp. Because nothing can be known but by the light of consciousness, the revealing luminosity of the *ātman* within, which is one's one awareness, is none other than the self-luminosity (*prakāśa*) that is Brahman. The two are identical even as the light of a flame is inseparable the flame itself. One of the four *mahāvākyas* likewise reveals that identity: quoting the ancient *ṛṣi* Dadhyac Ātharvaṇa, the Bṛhadāraṇyakopaniṣad (2.5.19) declares, "This Self is Brahman" (*ayam ātmā brahma*)."

Perfection in *yoga* is the knowledge of Brahman, and that knowledge is in fact the complete identification of *ātman* and Brahman.[75] In the words of the Muṇḍakopaniṣad (3.2.9), "Whoever knows the supreme Brahman becomes Brahman." On the way to this state of identification with the Absolute, the *yogin* sheds all fetters one by one, relinquishes all ties to the external circumstances and internal attitudes that have perpetuated the appearance of difference and separation and have kept the soul in bondage to worldly existence.

Between this verse and the previous one a subtle but momentous shift has taken place. *Mantra* 2.14 referred to the *yogin* as an embodied soul (*dehin*), still aspiring. Now that same *yogin* is called *yukta*, indicating that the goal of union with the supreme reality has been reached. From the standpoint of the unenlightened soul, it is natural to think of the path to Self-knowledge or God-realization as a quest, and the aspirant is likely to begin with the idea that the goal is something to be attained. But from the standpoint of realization, there is nothing to be attained; the shining perfection of pure consciousness is the very nature of the questing self and has been so all along. This reality of one's being (*ātmatattva*) only dawns when difference vanishes and the One alone shines in the ultimate radiance of *nirvikalpa samādhi*.[76] Only then does one recognize that the self and Brahman, *jīva* and Śiva, never were different. The enlightened being (*yuktaḥ*) realizes its own true nature as unborn (*ajam*) from all eternity, ever unchanging (*dhruvam*), and untouched by anything (*sarvatattvair viśuddham*). Nothing has been achieved or attained other than the recognition of one's true identity.

With this verse Śvetāśvatara's exposition of *yoga* in his own words comes to an end. It seems fitting to conclude this portion of our study with an epilogue.

We began with the observation that tracing the ancient origins of *yoga* is impossible. Following the many lines of its development is hardly less challenging. That said, a few items in the textual evidence appear crucial to even the briefest of summaries. The Ṛgvedasaṁhitā offers the earliest recorded account of yogic practice in its hymn to the ascetic, a long-haired, silent, marginalized wanderer associated with the proto-Śiva god Rudra (see p. 32). Also belonging to the early Vedic literature, the passages from the Yajurveda's Taittirīyasaṁhitā and Vājasaneyisaṁhitā quoted by Śvetāśvatara to introduce his presentation of *yoga* speak of yoking or harnessing the mind. The three oldest Upaniṣads (the Bṛhadāraṇyaka, Chāndogya, and Taittirīya) teach a contemplative discipline leading to knowledge of the transcendental Self, and in the Taittirīya, for the first time, the process is called *yoga*.[77] Two middle-period Upaniṣads, the Kaṭha and the Śvetāśvatara, employ the compound *sāṁkhyayoga*, which indicates not the two classical *darśanas* of a later age but the close association of theory and practice. Even so, the Kaṭhopaniṣad (2.3.11) also gives a definition of *yoga* that clearly anticipates Patañjali's *yogaś cittavṛttinirodhaḥ*: "This they consider as *yoga*, the steady holding back of the senses" (*taṁ yogam iti manyante sthirām indriyadhāraṇām*). The Śvetāśvataropaniṣad goes even further, leading one scholar to cite verses 2.8–13 as the earliest systematic account of yogic techniques.[78]

In his second discourse Śvetāśvatara indeed specifies some of the limbs of *yoga*, albeit in a form that is far earlier and less developed than Patañjali's. The seer perhaps only alludes to *yama* and *niyama* (see pp. 170–171), but he definitely describes *āsana*, *prāṇāyāma*, and *pratyāhāra*, even if not by those names. Likewise he does not use the term *dhāraṇā*, even while clearly stressing the "holding" of attention expressed by various derivatives of the root *yuj* ("to yoke," "to harness," or "to fix"). These figure in five quoted *mantras* (2.1–5) and three of his own (2.9, 2.10, 2.15), and the actual term *yoga* appears outright in three additional verses (2.11, 2.12, 2.13). As for *dhyāna*, Śvetāśvatara employs the word twice (1.3, 1.14), not as a specific step in the yogic process but in the sense of meditation in general. The word *samādhi* is entirely absent from the Upaniṣad, even though what it signifies is central to the text and spoken of in many different ways.

Five of Patañjali's eight terms appear together, perhaps for the first time, in the late and notoriously eclectic Maitryupaniṣad (6.18), which adds another term, *tarka*, to form a sixfold (*ṣaḍaṅga*) *yoga* (see p. 33). The greatest Śaiva nondualist, Abhinavagupta, preferred the sixfold *yoga* of the Maitryupaniṣad over Patañjali's eightfold path (see pp. 63–64).

Interestingly, an eightfold (*aṣṭāṅga*) *yoga* described by the same eight terms as Patañjali's appears in a Śaiva text well before the *Yogasūtra*'s composition. That text is the *Pāśupatasūtra*, attributed to Lakulīśa (see p. 44), who appears to have been strongly influenced by Śvetāśvatara's teaching (see pp. 46–47). The *Pāśupatasūtra* in turn exerted no small influence on the nondualistic Śaivism of Kashmir, which has as its foundational document Vasugupta's *Śivasūtra*, a treatise on the *yoga* of supreme identity (see p. 51). The *Śivasūtra* differs in many ways from Patañjali's earlier *Yogasūtra*, in no small part because it rests philosophically on theistic nondualism rather than on Sāṁkhya dualism. The terms *yama* and *niyama* appear nowhere in the *Śivasūtra*, and the meaning of *āsana* is entirely reconfigured in the text (3.16). Instead of a physical posture, it denotes a mental disposition—that of being "seated" or firmly established in *śakti*, the power of divine consciousness.[79] Here *āsana* represents a higher state than *prāṇāyāma, dhāraṇā, pratyāhāra,* and *samādhi,* all of which this text defines differently, designates by other terms (3.5), and characterizes as the means to acquire and maintain *dhyāna.* In Vasugupta's text *dhyāna* stands for the realization that the knower (*pramātṛ*), the known (*prameya*), and the knowing (*pramāṇa*) are aspects of *saṁvid,* or supreme consciousness. The *Śivasūtra* thus takes an epistemological principle widespread in Indian philosophy and places it within a yogic context, exactly as Śvetāśvatara had done centuries before when teaching the triadic nature of Brahman in *mantras* 1.7 and 1.9 (see pp. 112, 123–124).

This brief overview of isolated moments in the development of *yoga,* from its primordial association with proto-Śiva or Rudra to its sophisticated formulation in the *Śivasūtra*—with the Śvetāśvataro-paniṣad figuring somewhere in between—serves as a reminder of the countless strands of thought and practice that have met, intertwined, and then diverged over three and a half millennia, producing an inexhaustible wealth for the scholar and spiritual aspirant alike. The historical details may continue to elude us, but the teachings ever remain to light the way.

16

एष ह देवः प्रदिशोऽनु सर्वाः
पूर्वो ह जातः स उ गर्भे अन्तः ।
स एव जातः स जनिष्यमाणः
प्रत्यङ्‌ जनांस्तिष्ठति सर्वतोमुखः ॥ १६ ॥

eṣa ha devaḥ pradiśo 'nu sarvāḥ pūrvo ha jātaḥ sa u garbhe antaḥ /
sa eva jātaḥ sa janiṣyamāṇaḥ pratyaṅ janāṁs tiṣṭhati sarvatomukhaḥ //

16. This same divine being pervades all directions, everywhere; he himself is the first born, yet he abides within the womb. It is he that is born, he that will be born. He stands turned toward [all] living beings, facing in all directions.

Śvetāśvatara ends his discourse on *yoga* as he began, by reciting verses that were ancient even in his time. Of the two that conclude this chapter, the first is identical to Vājasaneyisaṁhitā 32.4.

That effulgent God (*eṣa ha devaḥ*), the indwelling radiance so eloquently portrayed in the preceding verse, is everywhere present. His reach extends to the four quarters of the sky (*pradiśaḥ*) and pervades them through and through (*anu sarvāḥ*). There is no place where he is not.

He is "the first born" (*pūrvo ha jātaḥ*). Commentators traditionally refer here to a verse of the Ṛgvedasaṁhitā (10.121.1): "In the beginning there appeared Hiraṇyagarbha, born the one lord of all that exists." The hymn to which this verse belongs later calls him Prajāpati, the Lord of Creatures (10.121.10). Elsewhere the Ṛgveda (4.53.2) identifies Prajāpati with Savitṛ. So, by invoking "the first born," Śvetāśvatara comes full circle, back to Savitṛ, a form of the sun god who represents the light of consciousness shining within all beings (see pp. 157–161).

In Vedic mythology *hiraṇyagarbha* is the golden womb or egg, "resplendent as the sun, out of which the self-existent Brahma[n] was born as Brahmā the Creator."[80] By extension the term *hiraṇyagarbha* came to be another name of Brahmā, the creative aspect of the Divine.

Apart from the mythological dimension of earlier Vedic texts, the present *mantra* can be appreciated in terms of the philosophical systems that developed later. According to Śaṁkara's Vedānta, the attributeless (*nirguṇa*) Brahman, in association with its dependent power of *māyā* (its causal potency), appears with attributes. This *saguṇa* Brahman is known as Īśvara. In other words, the impersonal, transcendental reality, viewed through the veil of *māyā*, appears as the personal God,[81] the all-encompassing efficient and material cause of the universe, having both the will to create and the wherewithal to do so.[82] In Vedantic teaching the name *Īśvara*, derived from *īś* ("to command," "to rule," "to reign"), means "Lord" and denotes the highest concept of divinity conceivable by the human mind.

In the philosophical system of the Vedānta, Hiraṇyagarbha is the first to emerge from Īśvara in the cosmogonic process, hence the epithet "first born." As the cosmic soul, Hiraṇyagarbha is the first self-conscious being, the first manifestation of subject as distinct from object.[83] This view differs considerably from that of the Trikaśāstra, which considers the ultimate reality, Paramaśiva, as supremely self-conscious, and the initial distinction of subjectivity and objectivity (not yet subject and object, however) taking place within the universal and still unified awareness of the *sadāśivatattva* (see pp. 58–59, 129).

As the Vedānta explains it, Hiraṇyagarbha's subtle body is the universal mind or cosmic intelligence (*mahātattva*), and his gross body is the physicality of the universe.[84] According to Dharmarāja's *Vedāntaparibhāṣā* (verse 7), an Advaita text from the seventeenth century, the manifestation of Hiraṇyagarbha's subtle and gross bodies and of the subtle bodies of all individual souls (*jīvas*) is the direct action of Parameśvara, the Supreme Lord; all subsequent creation—the gross bodies of the *jīvas* and the remaining forms of the physical universe—is effected indirectly through the agency of Hiraṇyagarbha.[85] When thought of as presiding over the physical universe, Hiraṇyagarbha is called Virāj.[86] In the Vedantic view, Virāj, meaning "shining far and wide" as well as "ruling," is the single awareness pervading the totality of created things.

Having declared the effulgent reality (*deva*) to be the first born, the present *mantra* adds the qualification "yet he abides within the womb" (*sa u garbhe antaḥ*). This statement is less paradoxical than it seems. Because Brahman is the sole reality, its manifestation and its essence are of necessity the same consciousness. As Śrī Rāmakṛṣṇa said of the relative and the Absolute, neither is conceivable without the other.[87] The relative is active, like water moving in waves; the Absolute is like still water;[88] but whether moving or still, water is water and nothing else.[89]

According to Trika understanding, the manifestation (*sṛṣṭi*) and dissolution (*saṁhāra*) of the universe are nothing other than the "descending" contraction and the "ascending" expansion of a single consciousness. In explaining how the One becomes many, the Trika conceptualizes the descent—the manifestation and structure of the universe—in terms of cosmic principles (*tattvas*). It was some proto-version of Sāṁkhya that first described the nature and operation of the *tattvas;* later the classical system laid out by the *Sāṁkhyakārikā* recognized twenty-five such principles. The first, *puruṣa,* is the ultimate reality of consciousness or spirit, and the second, *prakṛti,* is the ultimate reality of materiality. From *prakṛti* the remaining twenty-three *tattvas* evolve (see p. 21). The Vedānta adopted the framework of the *tattvas* with one major modification. *Puruṣa,* equated with Brahman, remains above (or apart from) the cosmic scheme, and the remaining *tattvas* are the twenty-four cosmic principles operative in the realm of *māyā.* In contrast to the Vedānta, the Nāndikeśvara, Lākulīśa, and Trika schools of Śaivism accept the twenty-five Sāṁkhya *tattvas* with only minor adjustments and add eleven more for a tally of thirty-six. The genius of the Trika system is to acknowledge the Sāṁkhya scheme as representating the dualistic mode of consciousness and to integrate it into the larger framework of absolute nondualism (*parādvaita*) (see pp. 57–62).

We have seen already how the *tattvas* provide a rational basis for understanding the evolution of the universe. Now we shall consider how they can clarify our understanding of the *yogin's* spiritual ascent. Of course, the roles of *prakṛti* and its evolutes have been thoroughly examined by the Sāṁkhya and Yoga *darśanas* and by every school of Vedānta through their inquiries into the nature and functioning of matter, mind, intellect, and ego, all designed to help the aspirant reach the goal of illumination. Our attention will turn instead to the Trikaśāstra's subtle gradations of consciousness that lie above the barrier of *māyā.*

These gradations are the Trika's first five *tattvas,* called *śiva* (1), *śakti* (2), *sadāśiva* (3), *īśvara* (4), and *sadvidyā* (5). Transcending *māyā,* they belong to the category of the pure experience (*śuddhādhvan*) or pure creation (*śuddhasṛṣṭi*). When considered from the Divine's own standpoint—that is, from the process of cosmic manifestation—they are marked in descending order by increasing objectivity. Their division, it must be stressed, does not indicate discrete levels so much as points along a continuum. Each stands for a particular stage of awareness in an unbroken flow. Considered from the standpoint of the *yogin,* who is intent on transcending the multiplicity of the universe, these same five *tattvas* are marked, in ascending order, by increasing subjectivity.

Pure subjectivity, or Self-knowledge, is the complete unification or reintegration of consciousness. That is what Śvetāśvatara meant when he said that "the embodied soul, perceiving its own true nature, becomes One" (2.14).

In the overall panorama of existence-being, the Trikaśāstra delineates seven grades of experience from the bound state of a *paśu* to the nondual realization of Śivahood. In each the experient or knower (*pramātṛ*) is designated by a particular term, the distinction resting on the aspirant's degree of spiritual purity. The journey (*adhvan*) is in fact a gradual attenuation of existential impurity (*mala*), and when that progressively thins,[90] the light of the Self shines through ever more brightly.[91]

The first three experients (*pralayākala, sakala,* and *vijñānākala*) belong to the impure creation (*aśuddhasṛṣṭi*). Only two of them concern us here. The *sakalapramātṛ* is the individual bound soul, or *paśu*. The term *sakala* means "consisting of parts" and in the Śaiva context specifically means "affected by the elements of the material world."[92] It denotes the everyday state of dualistic existence in which we experience ourselves and all facets of the perceivable universe as separate entities. In this state, driven by *rajas*, the soul is bound by the three impurites of individuality (*āṇavamala*), duality (*māyīyamala*), and causality (*kārmamala*) (see p. 185). The *vijñānākala* is the experient who has shed the fetters of *kārmamala* and *māyīyamala* but remains bound by *āṇavamala,* the sense of individuality. The *yogin* of this attainment is a saintly man or woman, saturated in *sattva* and poised to cross over into the pure experience (*śuddhādhvan*) or pure creation (*śuddhasṛṣṭi*).

As mentioned earlier, from Śiva's divine standpoint the evolution or descent through the *tattvas* is an unbroken flow of awareness. From the soul's human standpoint, the ascent has an apparent disjunction. From the *paśu's* perspective the *tattvas* from *pṛthivī* to *māyā* (that is, from the physical and mental creation through the causal agency of Śiva's own self-limiting power), constitute the experience of impure or diversified awareness. Penetrating *māyā's* veils, the *yogin* enters the realm of the pure experience, or universal consciousness. In two successive verses Śvetāśvatara alludes to just such a boundary crossing. We observed earlier that between *mantras* 2.14 and 2.15 a subtle but momentous shift occurs. The former verse refers to the *yogin* as a still-aspiring, embodied soul (*dehin*), and the latter calls that same *yogin* a *yukta,* one who experiences union with the supreme reality.

Śvetāśvatara says no more about the transition. Beyond the succinctly formulated verses of the Upaniṣad, there is no way for us to know how fully he might have expounded on this phase of the spiritual journey to those who actually heard his discourses. Although mildly speculative, it seems fully in keeping with the spirit of his teaching to supplement it here with the insights of the Trikaśāstra. After all, Śvetāśvatara exerted an unmistakable influence on the development of later Śaiva ideas.[93]

Regarding this transitional area, the Trikaśāstra provides exquisitely detailed insight in tracking the movement of consciousness through the five *tattvas* of the pure creation. That movement has already been explained in terms of Śiva's descent, or self-expression, as the universe and its myriad souls (see pp. 58–59). Now, from the *yogin's* perspective it will be revealed as the ascent of consciousness to its ultimate purity. The ascent through the *śuddhādhvan* has four stages, in which the experient (*pramātṛ*) is successively designated as *mantra, mantreśvara, mantramaheśvara,* and *śiva.*

The term *mantra* in this usage indicates one who ideates. For the experient of the three states in which this term figures (the *sadvidyā, īśvara,* and *sadāśiva tattvas*), the material creation is no longer perceived as material but only as an ideation within the divine consciousness.[94] Beyond these three states the term *mantra* disappears, for in the purely subjective experience of the *śakti-śiva* state, there is no longer any ideation of objectivity at all.

As the *mantra*-experient (*mantrapramātṛ*), the *yogin* has penetrated the layers of *māyā* and its *kañcukas* and has reached awareness of the *sadvidyātattva,* the category of pure knowledge, so-called because it is a unified experience beyond duality. This experience offers the first inkling of the aspirant's own true nature as Śiva-consciousness, but such realization is not yet lasting. At first it comes and goes; it is not stable but flickering. The content of this experience is "I am Śiva (*śivo 'ham*)—the universe (*idam*) is not an objective reality—I am Śiva—the universe is not an objective reality," and so on.[95] Even though a distinct awareness of subject (*pramātṛ*) and object (*prameya*) remains, both the knower and the known are recognized as existing solely within the experient's awareness and in that sense are unified. The universe (*idam*) is no longer experienced as the seemingly solid product of *māyā,* as in the impure creation, but as the nonmaterial, internal effect of conscious self-projection.[96] Here the *mantrapramātṛ* experiences within consciousness the power of activity (*kriyāśakti*) that allows ideated objects to assume external appearance (*ābhāsa*) in the impure creation lying below the level of *māyā*.[97]

When awareness rises from here to the greater subjectivity of the *īśvaratattva*, the experient is known as the *mantreśvarapramātṛ*. Now the universe appears not even as a projection in consciousness but purely as one's own expansion. This knowledge is epitomized by the words "*this [universe]* am I" (*idam aham*). Here the divine power of knowledge (*jñānaśakti*) dominates the *yogin's* awareness.

Ascending to the still purer subjectivity and the near-unification of consciousness in the *sadāśivatattva*, the *yogin* is known as the *mantramaheśvarapramātṛ*, whose awareness is summed up by the statement, "*I am* this [whole universe]" (*aham idam*). Here the divine will to create (*icchāśakti*) is dominant.[98]

Subjectivity becomes Self-realization when it reaches its ultimate purity in the two highest states of consciousness—*śaktitattva* and *śivatattva*. Calling them "two" only underscores the impotence of the mind to penetrate the ultimate mystery, for all human thought exists within duality. Though we tend to think of the *śivatattva* and the *śaktitattva* as separate, Abhinavagupta cautioned in the *Parātrīśikā-vivaraṇa* that Śakti should not be considered distinct from Śiva (*na hi śaktiḥ śivād bhedam āmarśayet*).[99] Consciousness and its power are the same reality, an inconceivable unity devoid of difference. The *śivaśaktitattva* is therefore transcendental (*parā*).[100] Reaching it, the *yogin*, now called *śivapramātṛ*, experiences the supreme beatitude of *cicchakti* and *ānandaśakti*, the highest power(s) of consciousness.[101] Put another way, the *śivapramātṛ* experiences only the nondual awareness of the infinite Self (*aham*),[102] devoid of the slightest trace of objectivity.[103]

Philosophy is only an afterthought to experience, but it is the experience itself in which the present *mantra* exults. The ancient seer quoted by Śvetāśvatara proclaims his direct vision of the effulgent divinity that pervades everything. That reality is the very God (*deva*) who manifests as this universe and witnesses the world of his own making even while abiding in his own infinite perfection. Ever reposing in the radiance of his own oneness, he has been born and will continue to be born as every creature, looking out at the world of his own making through innumerable faces turned in every direction. The *yogin's* goal is to realize him. Having done so, the liberated soul attains the supreme identity summed up as "I am Brahman" (*ahaṁ brahmāsmi*) or "I am Śiva" (*śivo 'ham*).

17

यो देवो अग्नौ योऽप्सु
यो विश्वं भुवनमाविवेश ।
य ओषधीषु यो वनस्पतिषु
तस्मै देवाय नमो नमः ॥ १७ ॥

yo devo agnau yo 'psu yo viṣvaṁ bhuvanam āviveśa /
ya oṣadhīṣu yo vanaspatiṣu tasmai devāya namo namaḥ //

17. To the effulgent being who is in fire and water, who has entered into all of creation, who is in the plants and trees, to that deity, salutations again and again!

Having declared the supreme Self to be the transcendental reality (2.14) as well as an immanent presence throughout creation (2.15–16), Śvetāśvatara ends his second chapter on a note of praise.

This *mantra* is not original with him but rather a variant of Taittirīyasaṁhitā 5.5.9.3 and Atharvaveda 7.87.[104] In those texts, along with other variations, the name *Rudra* occurs in place of the word *deva* (*yo rudro 'gnau yo 'psu ya oṣadhīṣu / yo rudro viśvā bhuvanāviveśa tasmai rudrāya namo 'stu*). Although Śvetāśvatara chooses not to invoke the name of Rudra at this moment, it is a name he will speak six times in the next two chapters.

This *mantra* expresses reverence and adoration not in the usual dualistic sense of a devotee's praise for an external and separate God but as the seer's outpouring of joy and wonder on experiencing the ultimate union. Since the *ṛṣi* is established in the all-pervading One, there is no longer any question of one praising another but only of the Self exulting in the bliss of the Self.

तृतीयोऽध्यायः

CHAPTER THREE

1

य एको जालवानीशत ईशनीभिः
सर्वाँल्लोकानीशत ईशनीभिः ।
य एवैक उद्भवे सम्भवे च
य एतद् विदुरमृतास्ते भवन्ति ॥ १ ॥

ya eko jālavān īśata īśanībhiḥ sarvāṁ llokān īśata īśanībhiḥ /
ya evaika udbhave sambhave ca ya etad vidur amṛtās te bhavanti //

1. He who is One, the master of [*māyā's*] net, rules by his sovereign powers; by his sovereign powers he rules over all the worlds at their coming forth and throughout their existence, he who is One alone. They who know this become immortal.

In his first discourse Śvetāśvatara expounded on four topics—the cause of existence (*kāraṇa*), the nature of the phenomenal world (*kārya*), the means of knowing the fullness of reality (*yoga*), and the nature of liberation. In his second lesson he elaborated on the third topic, the practice of *yoga*, emphasizing its great antiquity by framing it in Vedic terms. It is significant that the topics are four of the five on which the non-Vedic Pāśupata sect, roughly contemporary with Śvetāśvatara, based its teaching. Those five topics also form the framework of the later *Pāśupatasūtra,* ascribed to Lakulīśa. Equally significant is the absence from Śvetāśvatara's Upaniṣad of the fourth topic (*vidhi*), which centers on the transgressive Śaiva practices unacceptable to Vedic orthodoxy (see pp. 45–47). This omission underscores the prevailingly Vedic nature of Śvetāśvatara's Śaivism, a Śaivism that will shine unmistakably in the language and ideas of the third chapter.

At the outset of his third discourse, dealing with the nature of the Divine, two thoughts are uppermost in the seer's mind. The first is unity. Śvetāśvatara begins, "He who is One, the master of [*māyā's*] net..." (*ya eko jālavān*), then emphasizes, "he who is One alone" (*ya evaikaḥ*). The One remains ever so, even while issuing the worlds out of himself and engaging with them (*udbhave sambhave ca*). What a typically Śaiva vision of God and creation! The Lord is One in a oneness that simultaneously embraces its own transcendental immutabilty, its own ever-changing manifestation, the soul who experiences it, and the master who rules over it. These last three, in Śaiva terminology, are the triad of *pāśa, paśu,* and *pati.*

Along with the idea of divine unity, the second thought to which Śvetāśvatara gives equal importance is that of divine sovereignty. The master is the "possessor of the net" (*jālavān*). Commenting on this verse, the author of the *Śvetāśvataropaniṣadvṛtti* takes the net (*jāla*) to mean *māyā,* defined in Vedantic terms as Brahman's inscrutable causal potency. *Māyā* is like a net because of its ability to ensnare the individual soul in the travails of worldly existence. When the soul is thus entangled, *māyā* confounds and controls it. In distinction, the possessor of the net is in no way under *māyā's* spell. It is he who controls *māyā* and rules this universe, all the while remaining untouched by it. Who is this lord of *māyā?* According to the Vedānta it is not the supreme Brahman, devoid of qualities (*nirguṇa*), for that is immutable and incapable of action. Rather, it is the Brahman that, in association with *māyā,* only appears qualified (*saguṇa*). *Saguṇa* Brahman is also known as Īśvara, a name that means "Lord" or "Master" and denotes the personal God. The master of the net rules by his own sovereign powers (*jālavān īśate īśanībhiḥ*). The Sanskrit language makes clear the inherent connection between the Lord (Īśvara) who rules (*īśate*) by his ruling powers (*īśanībhiḥ*). The words all derive from a common source, the verbal root *īś,* meaning "to own," "to be master of," "to command," "to rule," "to reign."

The word *īśanībhiḥ* demands closer scrutiny. Although what follows may seem like linguistic hairsplitting, it signals that the present *mantra* marks a major development in Indian thought. *Īśanībhiḥ* would be the instrumental plural of a feminine noun (**īśanī*) that is not found in Monier-Williams's monumental *Sanskrit-English Dictionary.* Only a neuter form (*īśana*) is given, which means "a commanding" or "a reigning." The instrumental plural is *īśanaiḥ.* A concordance to the Upaniṣads cites the word in question as *īśinībhiḥ,*[1] the instrumental plural of the feminine noun *īśinī,* meaning "supremacy."[2] Not only is "ruling by his supremacies" awkward, but every Sanskrit edition of the text known to us reads *īśanībhiḥ* and not *īśinībhiḥ.*[3] A plausible explanation is that the questionable **īśanī* is "a feminine derivative of *īś-,* 'to rule', a power appropriate to Rudra-Śiva (*īśa* or *īśvara*): cf. *śakti.*"[4] In fact, it is well known that the Śvetāśvataropaniṣad represents an early example of the emerging doctrine of Śakti. The curious *īśanībhiḥ* may very well be making the point that Śvetāśvatara conceived of divine power as feminine and deliberately expressed it in that way.

Of course the idea of feminine power is not without precedent in India, not even in the ancient, masculinely inclined Vedic religion. Indra, who headed the pantheon, had as his consort the goddess Indrāṇī, who was also known as Śacī, signifying "might,"[5] and specifically the might to render assistance, kindness, or favor.[6] Similarly Prajāpati was paired with Vāc, the goddess who represents the creative power of speech.[7] In other cases as well, the goddess or female consort suggests the concept of energy. In the Brāhmaṇas we find that her union with the male god effects the creation of the world. What the earlier portions of the Vedas express mythologically assumes greater abstraction in the Śvetāśvataropaniṣad, where one supreme God (*deva,* Īśa, Īśāna, Rudra) manifests and rules the world through his own power (*devātmaśakti*) or powers (*īśanībhiḥ*), conceptualized as feminine.[8]

What are these powers? This *mantra* specifies the capacities of sending forth and sustaining the universe. The next *mantra* will again mention them and add the power of dissolution to complete the triadic cosmic cycle of *sṛṣṭi, sthiti,* and *saṁhāra.*

As already shown, the Vedānta and the Trikaśāstra offer two different philosophical perspectives on divine power (see pp. 53–54, 136). According to Advaita Vedānta, Brahman can only act as Īśvara—that is, in association with *māyā,* whose powers are concealment (*āvaraṇaśakti*) and projection (*vikṣepaśakti*). The power of concealment hides the unity of Brahman, and the power of projection creates the appearance of multiple phenomena. Just as, from an earthly vantage point, a tiny cloud can obscure the mighty sun, so does *āvaraṇaśakti* veil the infinitude of Brahman; yet as the sun, unaffected, continues to shine, so *nirguṇa* Brahman is eternally immutable in its own nature[9] and apart from the events of the manifest universe. To use another analogy, Brahman is not affected by *māyā* any more than a cobra is poisoned by its own venom.[10] Brahman, being pure consciousness, remains untouched by any action.[11]

In one important respect Trika teaching disagrees. Advaita Vedānta sets up an unbridgeable gulf between *nirguṇa* Brahman and the power of *māyā,* which is dependent on Brahman but indefinably so. The Trikadarśana teaches that in reality there is no difference between the possessor of power (*śaktimat*) and the power (*śakti*) it possesses. The word *śaktimat* recalls the present *mantra's* parallel term *jālavat* ("possessor of the net"). Consciousness without the power of awareness would be insentiency. One cannot possibly speak of consciousness as unconscious. Śiva is consciousness itself, and Śakti is his own Self-awareness, his natural and inseparable creative pulsation (*spanda*), and his inherent power to manifest the universe, to maintain the manifestation, and to withdraw it. Because the Trika admits no difference between Śiva and Śakti, it is the supreme, nondual divinity itself that is the cause of the universe.[12]

Just as it is a child's nature to play, it is Śiva's nature to create playfully—not out of compulsion or necessity but only out of unbounded, spontaneous freedom (*svātantrya*). The creation, which is divine play (*krīḍā* or *līlā*), arises out of the absolute freedom to act (or not to act), independent of any conditions. The power of absolute freedom (*svātantryaśakti*) is also intrinsically joyful.[13] Significantly this typically Śaiva doctrine of a joyful creation, so different from the world-denying illusionism of the post-Śaṁkara scholastics, nevertheless has its roots in the original Vedānta, which is to say in the Upaniṣads. In the Taittirīyopaniṣad (3.6.1)—an ancient and highly authoritative text of a Yajurvedic lineage related to Śvetāśvatara's—

we read: "For truly, from joy alone all beings are born (*ānandādd hy eva khalv imāni bhūtāni jāyante*); once born, by joy they live (*ānandena jātāni jīvanti*); toward joy they move, and into joy they merge (*ānandaṁ prayanty abhisaṁviśanti*).

Śvetāśvatara declares not once but twice that the master of the net rules by his sovereign powers. Every force at work in the universe functions by divine command, as he alone wills.[14] In Trika teaching sovereignty (*aiśvarya*, another derivative of *īś*) is inherent in the Supreme Being, a point already anticipated by Śvetāśvatara in *mantra* 1.11 but dismissed by the writers of later Vedantic commentaries (see pp. 137–138).

The Trikaśāstra ascribes five primary powers (*śaktis*) to the supreme Lord Śiva. These are *cicchakti* (the power of consciousness), *ānandaśakti* (the power of bliss, synonymous with *svātantryaśakti*), *icchāśakti* (the power of will), *jñānaśakti* (the power of knowledge), and *kriyāśakti* (the power of activity). These five powers fall into two separate categories. The powers of consciousness and bliss are the power of Śiva's very nature (*svarūpaśakti*) beyond any act of creation. The powers of will, knowledge, and activity have to do with the manifestation of the cosmos and arise at the first stirrings of creation in the *sadāśiva, īśvara,* and *sadvidyā tattvas.*

Even during cosmic manifestation, as Śvetāśvatara reminds us, the supreme reality that is God remains One (*ekaḥ*) and ever the same.[15] "They who know this (*etat*) become immortal." The pronoun *etat* refers to extreme proximity: "this" is a matter of the seer's own inner experience. The truth of divine unity is not mere theoretical knowledge but an experience of the most intimate sort. And just as the manifestation of the cosmos is the Lord's experience of his own conscious self-expression, the *yogin's* practice aims at a conscious reversal of that process.

The means to spiritual knowledge rests on the practice of joining the mind to the object of meditation by withdrawing attention from the categories (*tattvas*) of phenomenal experience that stand in the way. The meditator begins by withdrawing the mind from outward perceptions and works back, *tattva* by *tattva,* through increasingly subtler aspects of awareness, progressing all the while toward their ultimate source. The process is a matter of directing consciousness back upon itself to encounter and dissolve the increasingly subtler forms of its content until only its essence remains.[16]

It is no accident that the present *mantra* associates the themes of knowledge and divine powers. Although Śvetāśvatara does not elaborate here on the meditative process beyond what he has already outlined in the second chapter, we can look to the much later Trika system for further details. With ever-increasing concentration the *yogin* ascends gradually through the twenty-five *tattvas* of phenomenal experience from *pṛthivī* to *puruṣa,* from the perception of solid matter and its qualities to the abstraction of materiality itself (*prakṛti*) and its difference from the individualized conscious experient (*puruṣa*). Above this highest (or initial) manifestation of duality hover the six *tattvas* of *māyā,* like obscuring layers of cloud. The *yogin* who penetrates them enters into an awareness of universality, embodied in the five highest *tattvas* that constitute the *śuddhādhvan* (see pp. 192–195). Having transcended the duality of *puruṣa* and *prakṛti,* the *yogin* reaches the state of unity-in-difference (*bhedābheda* or *dvaitādvaita*) which characterizes the *sadvidyā, īśvara,* and *sadāśiva tattvas.* At these three levels of unified and increasingly subjective awareness, the *yogin* experiences in turn the divine powers of *kriyā, jñāna,* and *icchā.* Beyond them the *yogin's* awareness rises to the still higher state of nonduality (*abheda* or *advaita*).

An authoritative *yogaśāstra* of the Śaivāgama, written around twelve centuries after Śvetāśvatara's lifetime, explains this sublime experience of nonduality. Calling it the highest form of worship, the Vijñānabhairava (verse 151) reads: "Absorption into Rudra's powers (*rudraśaktisamāveśaḥ*) is the [true] place of pilgrimage (*tat kṣetram*), the highest contemplation (*bhāvanā parā*); apart from that reality (*anyathā tasya tattvasya*), what worship (*kā pūjā*) [is there] and who [is there] to be pleased (*kaś ca tṛpyati*)?" In the supreme fulfillment of nondual realization,[17] the *yogin* experiences the highest divine powers, *ānandaśakti* and *cicchakti.* These are the powers of the *śakti* and *śiva tattvas* and are, in truth, not two but one. They are *svarūpaśakti,* the power of the Divine's own essence. In the experience of this singularity the very idea of *tattva* vanishes, and all that remains is eternal, immutable, and essential Self-consciousness (*svasaṁvedana*)—consciousness that is conscious of itself only. This is the recognition (*pratyabhijñā*) of one's true, original nature.[18] This supreme state of oneness beyond all *tattvas* is *anuttara,* the ultimate "beyond which there is nothing else," the state of Paramaśiva, or consciousness resting in its absolute purity.

Śvetāśvatara's closing thought is that "they who know this become immortal." *This* (*etat*) is a neuter pronoun that refers not to the masculine deity (*ekaḥ, jālavān*) but to his sovereign unity. He who supports existence and rules over all existence by his sovereign powers remains ever One. Experiencing that nonduality, we become immortal (*amṛtāḥ*), or deathless in nature.[19] This does not mean that we will live forever as individuals in our present, particularized forms. Rather, we will abide in the timeless immortality of Self-realization, in the absolute reality of our true being. Moreover, that supreme state can be experienced here and now.

2

एको हि रुद्रो न द्वितीयाय तस्थु-
य इमाँल्लोकानीशत ईशनीभिः ।
प्रत्यङ् जनांस्तिष्ठति सञ्चुकोचान्तकाले
संसृज्य विश्वा भुवनानि गोपाः ॥ २ ॥

eko hi rudro na dvitīyāya tasthur ya imāṁ llokān īśata īśanībhiḥ /
pratyaṅ janāṁs tiṣṭhati saṅcukocāntakāle saṁsṛjya viśvā bhuvanāni gopāḥ //

2. Rudra is surely One! They stand present before no second who would rule these worlds by sovereign powers; he stands turned toward [all] living beings. Having projected all the worlds, he withdraws them at the end of time—he, the guardian.

This *mantra* and the preceding one form a single utterance, and the archaic features of the language suggest that the passage may be drawn from an older, unidentified source. Again the two verses bring together the themes of oneness and lordship, of the divine unity and sovereignty that later become the hallmarks of Trika Śaivism's unique theistic nondualism, known as *īśvarādvayavāda*.

God is indeed One (*eko hi rudraḥ*). They who know this know that they stand present before no other power, no second (*na dvitīyāya*) that rules or even witnesses their existence. This is a variant of the common Vedantic locution that Brahman is One without a second (*advitīya*).

Besides repeating what the first *mantra* said so emphatically, the second adds something else of the utmost significance. For the first time in the Upaniṣad we encounter the name *Rudra,* a name that will occur again five more times (3.4, 3.5, 4.12, 4.21, 4.22). Known from the hymns of the Ṛgvedasaṁhitā, it represents one of the oldest Indian conceptions of the Supreme Being, who by virtue of his auspiciousness later came to be known as Śiva (see pp. 34–36).

In fact every name for God in the Śvetāśvataropaniṣad reveals its Śaiva character. Earlier the seer used the name *Hara* ("seizer," "destroyer") to refer to the deity (1.10). He also used the term *īśa,* meaning "lord," "ruler," or "master" (1.8, 1.9) and will use it again (3.7, 3.20, 4.7, 5.3, 6.17). Either as common nouns or theonyms, *īśa*/Īśa and the related *īśāna*/Īśāna (3.12, 3.15, 3.17, 4.11) have strong Śaiva associations. So does the name *Maheśvara* (4.10, 6.7), later a common epithet of Śiva meaning "Great Lord."

Even in the ancient Ṛgvedasaṁhitā Rudra represents the whole of divinity; so do Indra, Mitra, Varuṇa, Agni, and other members of the pantheon. The reality is One, whatever name it goes by (1.164.46). Accordingly, all powers belong to the One, so it is only natural that the Vedic hymns should extol Rudra's powers as either fear-inspiring (*tveṣa*) or supportive of well-being (*vayas*). In this second respect the texts frequently employ the adjective *śiva* ("auspicious," "propitious," "benevolent," or "gracious"), and the practice continues even in the Śvetāśvataropaniṣad (3.5, 3.6, 3.11, 4.14, 4.16, 4.18, 5.14). Not until three or four centuries later does the adjective become the name *Śiva.*[20]

In the Ṛgvedasaṁhitā the name *Rudra* signifies a deity surprisingly close to the one portrayed in the opening *mantras* of the present chapter. An eloquent hymn (2.33) composed by the Vedic *ṛṣi* Gṛtsamada praises Rudra as the blissful god of all created beings, the mightiest of the mighty, resting in his own glory. He is the sovereign (*īśāna*) of this world, in whom the power of divinity (*asurya*) is inherent and from whom it never departs.

In the Śvetāśvataropaniṣad the name *Rudra* bears a range of associations and connotations. *Mantra* 4.22, a quotation of Ṛgveda

1.114.8 (which also figures in the Taittirīyasaṁhitā's Rudrādhyāya hymn and the Vājasaneyisaṁhitā's Śatarudrīya hymn) is clearly propitiatory toward Rudra and designed to avert divine wrath. In contrast *mantra* 3.5, also a quotation from the Rudrādhyāya and Śatarudrīya hymns, speaks only of the god's gracious beneficence. Likewise, Śvetāśvatara's *mantra* 4.21 emphasizes the eternal deity's benevolent face. Not traced to any earlier source, *mantra* 3.4 and its variant, 4.12, portray Rudra as the ultimate principle that is the source and substance of the gods, the eternal witness to the birth of the creator god; even so, this same Rudra is the universal Lord to whom humans may appeal for the gift of right understanding. Together these references demonstrate that the seer's view of the Supreme Being serves as a link between the ancient Vedic conception of Rudra and the later, highly developed doctrine of the Lord's nonduality, unique to the Trikadarśana.

The previous *mantra* mentioned the coming forth (*udbhava*) and the continuing existence (*sambhava*) of the universe. The present *mantra* completes the cosmic cycle: "Having projected all the worlds (*saṁsṛjya viśvā bhuvanāni*), he withdraws them (*saṅcukoca*) at the end of time (*antakāle*)—he, the protector (*gopāḥ*)." The emphasis here is on the final word, making the point that the transcendent deity is also immanent. He stands facing all living beings (*pratyaṅ janāṁs tiṣṭhati*) (see also 2.16). Always and under all conditions God, Rudra, is the universal guardian and protector.

3

विश्वतश्चक्षुरुत विश्वतोमुखो
विश्वतोबाहुरुत विश्वतस्पात् ।
सं बाहुभ्यां धमति संपतत्रै-
र्द्यावाभूमी जनयन् देव एकः ॥ ३ ॥

viśvataścakṣur uta viśvatomukho viśvatobāhur uta viśvataspāt /
saṁ bāhubhyāṁ dhamati saṁpatatrair dyāvābhūmī janayan deva ekaḥ //

3. His eyes everywhere and his faces everywhere, his arms everywhere and his feet everywhere, the one God forges with arms and bellows, causing heaven and earth to be born.

This widely quoted *mantra* originated in the Ṛgveda (10.81.3) and appears in a number of later texts (see Appendix B, Table 1). It comes from a hymn to Viśvakarman (the "all-creating"), the Supreme Being conceptualized as the architect of the universe. In the later mythology of the Purāṇas, Viśvakarman is identified with Tvaṣṭṛ, the artisan and lord of all skills, the smith who fashioned Indra's thunderbolt.[21] The present *mantra* foreshadows that identity with its vivid picture of a smith laboring at his forge. Although the language is obscure and early commentators managed to read a wide range of meanings into its symbolism, at the most concrete level it evokes an all-knowing, omnipresent, all-powerful, and all-animating deity who excites (*saṁdhamati*) the flames of his forge by working the bellows (most likely a series of fans made of feathers)[22] with his two arms in the process of fashioning heaven and earth.

Viśvakarman is the Vedic conception of creative power personified. He is the subject of two hymns of the Ṛgvedasaṁhitā (10.81, 10.82), both belonging to the very late stratum and characteristically rich in metaphysical abstraction. The hymns inform us that the One, wishing (*icchamānaḥ*), creates the vast treasure of this universe (10.81.1).[23] The participle *icchamāna* and the broader idea it suggests lay the foundation for a voluntaristic philosophy and anticipate both the Trika term *icchāśakti* and the Trika doctrine of the absolute freedom of the divine will (*svātantryavāda*) (see pp. 40–41). The Vedic hymns also declare that Viśvakarman's greatness defies all powers of human comprehension (10.81.2,4; 10.82.7); the one God, who himself names the gods, remains unknown (10.82.3), unborn (*aja*), older than earth and heaven, and earlier than the gods themselves (10.82.5–6).

Behind the graphic imagery of a superhuman smith who fans the flames of his forge, the present *mantra* carries deeper implications. Just as the smith fashions objects from metal, Viśvakarman-Tvaṣṭṛ, the divine craftsman, creates forms from formlessness; according to the Atharvaveda (12.3.33) that is his special power.[24] Clearly the doctrine of *creatio ex nihilo,* the idea that God brings forth the world out of nothing, is neither a Vedic, a Vedantic, nor a Śaiva concept. Here, strictly speaking, *creation* is a misleading term; what is really meant is a manifestation of what already exists in potentiality. The world results only from a change of name and form (*nāmarūpa*),[25] *nāma* being the archetypal idea and *rūpa* its material expression. In the nondualistic view the world does not exist apart from its source. The dualist likens God merely to a potter (the efficient cause), who fashions clay (the material cause) into a pot (the effect); but the nondualist sees the Divine as both the efficient and the material cause[26] as well as the effect. Rudra is One without a second; there is nothing else. As the Chāndogyopaniṣad (3.14.1) puts it, "All this is indeed Brahman" (*sarvaṁ khalv idaṁ brahma*).

Although no analogy can explain perfectly the inexplicable mystery of creation, the example of a seed comes close. A mighty banyan tree grows from a tiny seed. Every component of the tree—roots, trunk, branches, leaves, blossoms, fruits—is latent within that seed, unseen and unmanifest, but already present in the power of becoming. In the same way, everything emerges from Brahman. Even this analogy is imperfect, though, because the seed, once it has developed into the tree, cannot withdraw the tree back into itself, whereas Brahman can and does project and withdraw the universe in an unending cycle.[27]

The word *saṁdhamati* ("blows together," "excites") describes the action of Viśvakarman's bellows or fans in directing air into the creative fire. Its imagery recalls another passage in the Ṛgveda involving the movement of air. In the great hymn known as the Devīsūkta, the creative energy, personified as Vāc, the goddess of speech, proclaims, "I breathe forth like the wind, setting all the worlds in motion" (Ṛgveda 10.125.8).[28] The similarity is more than a coincidence, because one of the two earlier hymns to Viśvakarman invokes him as Vācaspati, the Lord of Speech (Ṛgveda 10.81.7), and links him directly to the feminine creative power.

If that were not enough, the second hymn to Viśvakarman provides another link. After lauding him as the unborn One, wherein all existing things abide, the seer cautions: "You will not know him who produced all these; another has risen up in your midst. Fog-enshrouded they go about, those who sing his praises, chattering and devoted to worldly pleasures" (Ṛgveda 10.82.7). This appears to be a poetic description of *māyā* as the divine power of self-concealment, later termed *āvaraṇaśakti*. Sāyaṇa, the fourteenth-century commentator, takes this verse to mean that people who are engaged in temporal enjoyment and who sing praises for the sake of felicity in the world to come know nothing of God. Another commentator, Mahīdhara, takes a similar view, saying that such people have no knowledge of truth and are instead subject to false knowledge or ignorance[29]—in other words, to *māyā*. Reinforcing this view, Viśvakarman, as the divine craftsman Tvaṣṭṛ, is noted for his powers of *māyā*.[30]

Like the two preceding verses, the present one, cited from the Ṛgveda, associates divine unity with sovereignty. Rudra is the one God (*deva ekaḥ*) and the god who is One. Possessed of superhuman powers, he is all-knowing (*viśvataścakṣuḥ*, "having eyes everywhere"), omnipresent (*viśvatomukhaḥ*, "facing in every direction"), omnipotent (*viśvatobāhuḥ*, "having arms everywhere"), and all-animating (*viśvataspāt*, "having feet [the powers of movement] everywhere"). Projecting this universe, he sees through every pair of eyes, hears through every pair of ears, speaks through every mouth, and experiences his creation through every faculty of every sentient being.

4

यो देवानां प्रभवश्चोद्भवश्च
विश्वाधिपो रुद्रो महर्षिः ।
हिरण्यगर्भं जनयामास पूर्वं
स नो बुद्ध्या शुभया संयुनक्तु ॥ ४ ॥

yo devānāṁ prabhavaś codbhavaś ca viśvādhipo rudro maharṣiḥ /
hiraṇyagarbhaṁ janayāmāsa pūrvaṁ sa no buddhyā śubhayā saṁyunaktu //

4. He who is the source and substance of the gods is Rudra, lord of the universe and great seer. In the beginning he brought forth Hiraṇyagarbha. May he endow us with clear understanding!

Rudra, the highest reality, is the source, the cause, and the creator. All those meanings are inherent in the word *prabhava*. Yet even while the nondual reality remains ever in repose as the unchanging support of all manifestation, he (or it), through the will to manifest (*icchāśakti*), is also the process by which the gods themselves become manifest. He is their coming forth, their becoming visible, their very existence. All those meanings belong to the word *udbhava*. The phrase *prabhavaś codbhavaś ca* implies that the eternally immutable reality of consciousness gives rise to manifestation and is the essence, the process, and the product all at once. From the initial desire to manifest, which takes shape first as concept (*nāma*) and then as materialization into form (*rūpa*), this process of emanation (*sṛṣṭi*) is a seamless flow within the single reality of consciousness.

Abhinavagupta writes that it cannot be otherwise. In the *Īśvarapratyabhijñāvivṛtivimarśinī* he explains how the ultimate cause can appear as the effect without ever changing at all. In an ordinary or actual transformation (*pariṇāma*), such as the change of milk into butter, the original form of the causal factor becomes lost when replaced by the form of the effect. Milk is no longer milk but butter. However, the ultimate cause, which is the light of consciousness, has no form other than its own. Were the light of consciousness to be transformed into anything else, it would no longer be the light of consciousness, and in its absence the experience of the effect (the empirical universe) would not be possible. By the same token, if the effect (the universe) were anything other than the light of consciousness, albeit seemingly transformed, how could it appear? Again, the experience of it would not be possible.[31]

The Upaniṣads provide textual support for Abhinavagupta's reasoning. A well known verse that occurs in three of the principal Upaniṣads—the Kaṭha (2.3.15), the Śvetāśvatara (6.14), and the Muṇḍaka (2.2.10)—declares: "There the sun shines not, nor the moon and stars, nor does the lightning illumine, much less this earthly fire. He alone shining, everything shines after him. By his light all this universe shines."

That divine light is the inner light of the Self. A brief treatise on Advaita Vedānta attributed to Śaṁkara puts it eloquently. The penultimate verse (67) of *Ātmabodha* [Self-knowledge] reads: "Risen in the space of the heart, the Self, the sun of knowledge, dispels the darkness (*hṛdākāśodito hy ātmā bodhabhānus tamopahṛt*); pervading all and supporting all, it shines and causes everything to shine" (*sarva-vyāpī sarvadhārī bhāti bhāsayate 'khilam*).

In trying to fathom this divine mystery, we must distinguish between consciousness and its contents. The ever immutable light of consciousness is the *sine qua non* for the experience of its own content, a content that is its own ever-changing manifestation (*ābhāsa*).

When Śvetāśvatara says that Rudra is the source and substance of the gods (*devānām prabhavaś codbhavaś ca*), he is implying something well beyond mythological imagery. More profoundly the gods, the "shining ones," signify the senses, the outward-flowing functions of awareness through which the Supreme Being and all sentient creatures experience the creation. The difference is that we as individuals experience it through our own human limitations, whereas Rudra as the universal ruler (*viśvādhipaḥ*) and omniscient seer (*maharṣiḥ*) enjoys it as divine universality.

According to Vedic tradition, in the process of cosmic manifestation Rudra first engenders Hiraṇyagarbha, the "golden womb" from which the rest of creation emanates in turn (see pp. 190–191). Rudra is therefore Brahman, anterior to all manifestation.

"May he endow us with clear understanding!" The English "clear understanding" is a pale reflection of the Sanskrit *buddhyā śubhayā*. "Clear" is only one of the many meanings of *śubha,* which also means "bright," "splendid," "fit," "good," auspicious," and "virtuous." *Buddhi,* translated here as "understanding," also means "intelligence," "reason," "mind," or "intellect." Previous renderings include "good thoughts,"[32] "good thoughts [the power to discriminate],"[33] "noble insight,"[34] "clear intellect,"[35] "clear understanding,"[36] "good understanding,"[37] "lucid intelligence,"[38] "right intuitive understanding,"[39] and "clear intelligence."[40]

Śvetāśvatara's fine-sounding prayer has an obvious model in the Gāyatrī *mantra's* "may that [effulgent being] inspire our thoughts" (*dhiyo yo naḥ pracodayāt*). To appreciate its profundity we need only consider the meaning of *buddhi* as indicated by an often-cited passage from the Kaṭhopaniṣad (1.3.3–12). This passage likens the individual self (*ātman*) to the master of a chariot (*ratha*). The chariot is the embodied soul's vehicle of experience. The senses (*indriyāṇi*) are the horses that pull it along, the reins are the mind (*manas*), and the charioteer is the intelligent faculty (*buddhi*) that holds the reins. The ordinary human being, with a chronically uncontrolled mind (*ayuktamanasā sadā*), is like the unfortunate rider who is dragged and jerked erratically along the roads of worldly experience by unruly horses. All the while, the charioteer, representing the *buddhi,* has the capacity to take control. As the highest manifestation of consciousness in the human being and as the soul's ruling power,[41] the *buddhi* can seize the reins and direct the mind to increasingly higher states of awareness beyond sensory perception and conceptual knowledge and even beyond the idea of a creator God (*ātmā mahān,* meaning Hiraṇyagarbha). It can direct the mind to the Unmanifest (*avyakta*) and finally to the purity of consciousness-in-itself (*puruṣa* in the Vedāntic sense of Brahman), the unchanging light[42] beyond which there is nothing higher (*na paraṁ kiñcit*). That is the true Self, hidden in all beings but recognized only by seers of subtle things (*sūkṣmadarśibhiḥ*) through a closely attentive and keen intelligence (*agryayā buddhyā sūkṣmayā*).

In light of the Kaṭhopaniṣad's teaching, Śvetāśvatara's noble prayer invites us to aspire to a condition of clear, attentive, and morally excellent awareness that will direct us toward realization of the all-pervading divinity who is not only the source and support of all our experience but is indeed our very being.

5

या ते रुद्र शिवा तनूरघोराऽपापकाशिनी ।
तया नास्तनुवा शन्तमया गिरिशन्ताभिचाकशीहि ॥ ५ ॥

yā te rudra śivā tanūr aghorā 'pāpakāśinī /
tayā nas tanuvā śantamayā giriśantābhicākaśīhi //

5. The gracious form that is yours, O Rudra, neither terrifies nor bodes any ill. With that most beneficent form, O Mountain-Dweller, shine brightly upon us!

This *mantra* and the one that follows occur also in the Taittirīya-saṁhitā (4.5.1c–d) and the Vājasaneyisaṁhitā (16.2–3) in the context of the ancient Śaiva hymns known respectively as the Rudrādhyāya and the Śatarudrīya. The hymns incorporate motifs from the still older Ṛgvedic hymns to Rudra.

The present *mantra* addresses the personified deity as Rudra while the term *śivā* occurs as an adjective to qualify his benign aspect. The mention of his form as benevolent and non-terrifying (*aghorā*) is a reminder that Rudra also has his fierce aspect, but here we are assured that he bodes no ill or harm. *Apāpakāśinī* can be analyzed in two ways: either as revealing (*kāśinī*) virtue, purity, holiness, or goodness (*apāpa*), or as *not* revealing (*a-kāśinī*) evil or harm (*pāpa*). Either way, the meaning is similar, although the emphasis on not displaying harm (as opposed to showing goodness) seems more in keeping with some of the apotropaic passages in Rudra's Ṛgvedic hymns.

The second half of the *mantra* is purely positive, extolling the deity's most beneficent (*śantama*) aspect. The first syllable, *śaṁ*, carries the idea of auspiciousness, happiness, and well-being. It also forms the first part of two common names of Śiva: Śaṁkara ("he who causes prosperity or well-being")[43] and Śambhū ("existing for, causing, or granting happiness and well-being").[44] The idea of benevolence accords well with the Ṛgveda's frequent and consistent praise of Rudra as a kind protector and healer.

Giriśanta, an epithet meaning "mountain-dweller," stems from Śiva's traditional association with the Himālayas, and with one mountain in particular—Kailāsa, his sacred abode. The epithet evokes the popular imagery of the white, ash-besmeared deity with matted locks, seated atop the holy mountain and absorbed in meditation. This is Śiva, the ascetic, ever-blissful lord of *yogins.* Because his form is turned auspiciously to the south, he is described as *dakṣinamūrti,* and we can visualize him gazing graciously on the world below.

Grace is just what the imperative verb *abhicākaśīhi* asks him to bestow. *Abhikāś* means "to look upon," "to shine upon," or "to illuminate," and the intensive or frequentative form (with *us* as the direct object) means "look upon us always," "shine brightly upon us," or "illuminate us through and through." Since the root of the verb is *kāś* ("to be visible," "to shine," "to be brilliant"), the readings that involve light seem closer to the full import. Rudra, whose nature is pure effulgence, is asked to shine brightly upon his devotees, to bestow his blessings of material bounty and mental well-being. And beyond that, he is asked to light us through and through, to grant us spiritual illumination.

6

यामिषुं गिरिशन्त हस्ते बिभर्ष्यस्तवे ।
शिवां गिरित्र तां कुरु मा हिंसीः पुरुषं जगत् ॥ ६ ॥

yām iṣuṁ giriśanta haste bibharṣy astave /
śivāṁ giritra tāṁ kuru mā hiṁsīḥ puruṣaṁ jagat //

6. The arrow that you hold ready in hand, O Mountain-Dweller, make it propitious. Protector of the Mountains, do not injure man or beast.

For the seer's listeners familiar with Rudra's ancient Vedic hymns, this *mantra* evokes the image of the copper-complexioned archer whose bow and arrow serve a benign, protective, and evil-destroying purpose.

Apart from taking this verse at face value as a simple appeal for divine favor, we can look deeper into its symbols. Several commentators have done just that, with widely differing results. The arrow, taken by one to suggest the terrible aspect of God,[45] represents for another the *praṇava* (*Oṁ*), or one of the Vedic *mahāvākyas*—sacred utterances that are the "weapons" to empower the spiritual aspirant in conquering ignorance.[46] Since this verse originally predates the Upaniṣads, the arrow as a symbol of the *mahāvākyas* is dismissible on chronological grounds, but the idea of the arrow as the *praṇava* has merit. Moreover, the vivid image of Rudra, holding the arrow in readiness, ever willing to make his knowledge available to those who seek it,[47] suggests a deity who is kindly rather than wrathful. A verse of the Devīsūkta (Ṛgveda 10.125.6) that describes Rudra's arrow as aimed at the "hater of devotion" confirms that its purpose is to keep us safe from the unrighteous and their actions. The epithet *Giritra*, which means "Protector of the Mountains," reinforces the deity's role as a guardian.

The injunction "do not injure man (*puruṣam*) or beast (*jagat*)," is perfectly clear on the surface. In the original context of the Rudrādhyāya and Śatarudrīya hymns, "man" and "beast" are the most logical renderings of the multivalent words *puruṣa* and *jagat*, because they agree with the Vedic portrayal of Rudra as the protector of humankind and livestock. As the older Vedic language gradually evolved into classical Sanskrit, some words acquired multiple, even contradictory, meanings. *Jagat*, with its basic sense of "that which moves or is alive," early on signified any animate being, human or animal. It also denoted an animal as distinct from a human being, as in the present instance. In the later language the term became more likely to signify the world or the earth,[48] this entire realm of phenomenality, which is ever in motion. The meaning of "do not injure man or beast" can be expanded to "do not injure humankind or the world." Either way, this verse and the preceding one are a supplication to a God conceived in personal terms.

7

ततः परं ब्रह्म परं बृहन्तं
यथानिकायं सर्वभूतेषु गूढम् ।
विश्वस्यैकं परिवेष्टितार-
मीशं तं ज्ञात्वाऽमृता भवन्ति ॥ ७ ॥

tataḥ paraṁ brahma paraṁ bṛhantaṁ yathānikāyaṁ sarvabhūteṣu gūḍham / viśvasyaikaṁ pariveṣṭitāram īśaṁ taṁ jñātvā 'mṛtā bhavanti //

7. Beyond that is the supreme Brahman, who expands forth as every kind of creature, yet remains hidden in all beings. He alone encompasses the universe; those who know the Lord become immortal.

The phrase "beyond that" (*tataḥ param*) refers to the personal aspect of God just invoked and signals a return to the main theme of the discourse, which is the nature of divine reality. Reaffirming what he has already presented in the first four *mantras,* Śvetāśvatara announces dramatically that there is something higher than our understanding of the creator god and anterior to him. That is the supreme Brahman, abiding in its own essence.

In fact the supreme Brahman and the personal God are one; they are the same divinity in transcendent and immanent aspects.[49] Accordingly this *mantra* employs both the words *Brahman* and *Īśa* ("Lord") to refer to the singular divine being, whom Śvetāśvatara also calls Rudra. The use of that name in the two preceding verses to denote the personalized deity follows right after the seer had applied it to the One without a second in *mantra* 3.2; his usage suggests the singularity of the Śaiva concept of God, who remains the transcendent, nondual Self and ultimate I even while expressing himself as the creator and sovereign Lord whose presence pervades and illumines the whole of creation.

That conception of God is the primary theme of the Upaniṣad's third chapter. Excluding *mantras* 3.5 and 3.7, which have the character of a rhetorical interpolation, ten of the verses refer to transcendence and immanence together, three to transcendence alone, and six to immanence, with constant juxtaposition and alternation. Woven into this structure, two additional themes stand out. Six *mantras* speak of divine sovereignty (3.1, 3.2, 3.4, 3.7, 3.12, 3.18), and five link knowledge to immortality (3.1, 3.7, 3.8, 3.10, 3.13).

The highest reality is Brahman, consciousness itself, that "expands forth as every kind of creature." The word *bṛhantam* ("expanding," "increasing") also suggests radiating, as light radiates from a luminous source. This raises an interesting question. If Brahman is already infinite, how can it expand? If there is nothing other than Brahman, where, except in Brahman itself, can the expansion take place? Here the definition of *bṛhanta* as "increasing" is useful, and it is the very idea found in the already cited passage from the Chāndogyopaniṣad (6.2.1–3) in which Brahman, purely One without a second (*ekam evādvitīyam*), thought, May I be many, may I grow forth (*bahu syāṁ prajāyeyeti*).

Growing from one to many is simultaneously an act of increase and division. While the One is ever infinite and undivided, the many are necessarily finite and separate from one another. Finitude and separation are, of course, forms of limitation. Śaṁkara accepted limitation as a causal factor, and Vācaspati Miśra, who founded the post-Śaṁkara Bhāmatī ("lustrous") school of Advaita Vedānta in the ninth century, formalized it into the doctrine of limitation (*avaccheda-vāda*). Just as space is one and unlimited but appears divided when contained in a multitude of pots, so does the infinite Brahman appear divided as innumerable *jīvas* when associated with the delimiting adjuncts of mind and body. Limitation is a matter of ignorance (*avidyā*), of mistakenly associating the Self with that which it is not. When the limitations are removed, the nondifference of Brahman and *jīvātman* is realized. As part of the often quoted statement attributed to Śaṁkara goes, "The individual soul is none other than Brahman" (*jīvo brahmaiva nāparaḥ*).

The Trikaśāstra also has a well-developed doctrine of cosmic manifestation as limitation. It defines *māyā* as Śiva's own limiting power and meticulously analyzes its functioning and effects (see pp. 115–119). The individual soul (*jīva*) is nothing other than Śiva experiencing phenomenal existence through his own self-imposed and seemingly divisive limitations. Because consciousness is Śiva's own nature, his manifestation is sometimes described as a "coagulating" or "thickening" of consciousness. As ideation moves from concept (*nāma*) to form (*rūpa*), the energy of consciousness "condenses" or "becomes [increasingly] dense."[50] Interestingly, another meaning of *bṛhanta* is "becoming compact, solid, or thick." The denseness of the manifestation also explains why Śvetāśvatara was led earlier to describe the Supreme Being's shining causative power (*devātmaśaktim*) as lying "hidden by its own effects" (*svaguṇair nigūḍhām*) (1.3). Now rephrasing that thought, he says that the supreme Brahman who expands forth as every kind of creature (*bṛhantaṁ yathānikāyam*) remains hidden in all beings (*sarvabhūteṣu gūḍham*). All things that exist are but God's diverse forms of self-expression, each with its own level of awareness. The same divine consciousness is present everywhere in varying degrees of transparency and never absent.

Indian philosophy recognizes three successive levels of human experience. The ordinary state is the experience of duality (*dvaita*). Duality is in fact a plurality with a threefold difference of God, the individual soul, and material phenomena. Moreover, their relationships create a fivefold structure based on the difference (*bheda*) between God and the soul, God and matter, the soul and matter, one soul and another, and one material object and another.[51] In the dualistic view God and the devotee are intrinsically separate. The next level of experience recognizes unity in diversity (*dvaitādvaita* or *bhedābheda*) and comprehends the underlying unity of God, soul, and the world. Still higher, the level of nondual awareness (*advaita*) is the experience of nondifference (*abheda*) wherein everything melts into the unconditioned reality of the Self as pure consciousness.

Trika Śaivism teaches that in the highest state consciousness expands into the experience of limitless being and absolute unity. It views the ultimate realization as the knowledge that everything is divine, just as the Upaniṣads declare time and again. This totally monistic view in which the very distinction of relative and absolute vanishes is known as *pratyakṣādvaita* ("nonduality present before the eyes") or *parādvaita* ("supreme nonduality").[52] The experient sees the sacred unity even in phenomenal perceptions, knowing that they are not phenomena at all but the single reality of shining consciousness.

It bears repeating here that Śrī Rāmakṛṣṇa, whose experience transcended all sectarian and philosophical divides, called this state *vijñāna*. He spoke of Self-realization as *jñāna* and added that *vijñāna* is a fuller knowledge. After the *jñānin's* negation of the phenomenal world through the discriminative process of *neti nety ātmā* ("the Self is not this, not this") comes the affirmation that God himself has become the universe and all living beings. He explained that a person ascending the stairs to the roof of a house negates the stairs as not being the roof but on reaching the roof realizes that the stairs and the roof are made of the same materials—brick, lime, and brick-dust. After that, how is it possible to accept the roof and reject the stairs? The *vijñānin*, having been to the roof and back, experiences the Absolute and the relative as the same reality.[53]

Śrī Rāmakṛṣṇa, whose teaching lies at the heart of the modern Vedānta movement, affirmed that in the ultimate unity of consciousness, the final distinction of relative and absolute melts away. As for the many and sometimes contentious philosophical positions of the *paṇḍits*, he would simply reply from his own experience that God is both with and without form and can be known either way. To that we can add Śvetāśvatara's concluding thought, which is a recurring theme in his teaching: by knowing the one supreme Lord (*ekam īśam*) who encompasses and contains the entire universe, the knowers of Brahman become immortal.

8

वेदाहमेतं पुरुषं महान्त-
मादित्यवर्णं तमसः परस्तात् ।
तमेव विदित्वाऽतिमृत्युमेति
नान्यः पन्था विद्यतेऽयनाय ॥ ८ ॥

vedāham etaṁ puruṣaṁ mahāntam ādityavarṇaṁ tamasaḥ parastāt /
tam eva viditvā 'timṛtyum eti nānyaḥ panthā vidyate 'yanāya //

8. I know beyond all darkness this great Person, effulgent like the sun. Knowing him alone, one goes beyond death. There is no other way by which to go.

The Upaniṣads owe their glory to the simple fact that they are not philosophical musings but records of direct experience and thus authentic revelation (*śruti*). The present *mantra* exemplifies outstandingly the immediacy of a seer's own declaration of what he has realized. All appearance to the contrary, this sublime utterance did not originate with Śvetāśvatara. He is quoting the words of an earlier *ṛṣi* recorded in the Vājasaneyisaṁhitā (31.18). His citation of that sublime utterance makes it no less forceful or memorable but underscores that the ancient pronouncement was already well recognized even in Śvetāśvatara's time.

The words *I know* link the verse to the previous *mantra's* closing thought that they who know the Lord attain immortality (*īśaṁ taṁ jñātvā 'mṛtā bhavanti*). The linkage indicates in all likelihood that the quoted verse serves as a proof text, a citation of scriptural authority.

Its archaic Vedic language conveys a richness of nuance impossible to convey in English by mere word-for-word translation. The phrase *I know,* for example, makes the case at the outset. The verb *veda* represents an older form of the perfect tense ("I have known") but carries a present meaning. "I have known and continue to know" is the idea it expresses. Having realized divinity, the seer becomes established in that knowledge.

At the heart of the declaration lies the word *puruṣa*, a term with no single equivalent in English and a broad range of meanings in Sanskrit. This word probably derives from the verbal root *pṝ* ("to fill," "to inflate").[54] At a basic level *puruṣa* can mean "man" or "person" or "human being." Appearing often in the early Vedic texts and the Upaniṣads, it also designates the animating principle in all sentient beings—in other words, the soul or spirit. When meaning the individual soul, it is often used interchangeably with *ātman* ("self"). In the great hymn of the Ṛgveda known as the Puruṣasūkta (10.90) it signifies the primordial Person as the source and soul of the universe.[55] The word *puruṣa* occurs nine times in the Śvetāśvataropaniṣad, variously indicating the ordinary human being (3.6), the individual soul (1.2, 4.7), and the universal Supreme Being who is both immanent and transcendent (3.8, 3.9, 3.12, 3.14, 3.15, 3.19).

In the philosophical systems that developed many centuries after the composition of the Upaniṣads, *puruṣa* serves as a technical term with highly specific meanings that vary from one system to another. In the Sāṁkhya and Yoga *darśanas,* it indicates the eternal conscious principle and inactive witness within each individual; there are as many *puruṣas* as there are sentient beings. In contrast, Advaita Vedānta equates *puruṣa* with *ātman*-Brahman and insists on its utter singularity. The Trikadarśana agrees with the Sāṁkhya in admitting a plurality of *puruṣas* but defines them not as the ultimate reality of consciousness but as consciousness divided and individualized by *māyā's* limiting veils. In the Trika understanding *puruṣa* is the individual experient of duality.[56]

The term *puruṣa* thus poses a difficulty for translators, even in the present context when modified as *etaṁ puruṣaṁ mahāntam.* Translation alone cannot communicate the full intent of the original Sanskrit. This phrase has been rendered variously as "that great person,"[57] "that Purusha, the great one,"[58] "this mighty Person,"[59] "this Great Being,"[60] "that Great Person,"[61] "the great Purusha,"[62] "the Supreme Person,"[63] "this great Person,"[64] "that Great Being [that Cosmic Self],"[65] "that immense Person,"[66] "this great being,"[67] "this great person,"[68] and "that great *puruṣa.*"[69] All agree that *puruṣa* signifies the singular divinity, but what they fail to convey is the many and vital nuances inherent in the original language.

First, there are the implications of the pronoun *etam* ("this"). It implies the greatest degree of proximity to the speaker: *this* divine being is the nearest of the near. Moreover, the pronoun is emphatic in suggesting something known to the listener as well either through perceptual or conceptual experience.[70] *This* divine being is the nearest of the near to speaker and listener alike, all-pervading as the indwelling Self of each individual and as the single essence of the entire cosmos.

For understanding the intended meaning of *puruṣa* in the present context the Puruṣasūkta (10.90) is our most reliable guide. That hymn, which Paul Deussen considered the Ṛgveda's culminating philosophical statement,[71] portrays *puruṣa* as the primal Person, the unitary Supreme Being who is the source of the universe as its efficient and material cause. Although the word *puruṣa* came to mean something very different in the Trikaśāstra, that later system shares a basic understanding of the Supreme Being with that found in the ancient Vedic text. Trika Śaivism teaches that Śiva is the "material" from which and within which the universe becomes manifest as well as the motivating or efficient cause. The "material" cannot be external to the single reality of consciousness but is only its self-expression.[72] We can be sure that the Puruṣasūkta's view of divine reality coincides with Śvetāśvatara's, for in this discourse on the nature of God the seer will quote two verses from that very hymn. Those verses (3.14–15) will tell us that the Supreme Being is all that has been, all that is, and all that will be. Said to have a thousand heads, eyes, and feet, it is the single consciousness experiencing the multiplicity of its own creation through the individualized and embodied awareness of countless sentient creatures.[73] Śvetāśvatara made the same point in the previous *mantra* (3.7) when he identified the reality of which he speaks as "the supreme Brahman, who expands forth as every kind of creature" (*brahma paraṁ bṛhantaṁ yathānikāyam*).

"This great Person" is experienced as great (*mahāntam*) in terms of space, time, quantity, degree, and eminence. Moreover, *mahāntam*, as the present participle of the verbal root *mah,* also carries the ideas of arousing, exciting, gladdening, rejoicing, and delighting in. All of this fits well with the Śaiva concept of God as the eternal and ultimate I that simultaneously enjoys its own spontaneous overflow of creative freedom through all the glorious diversity of the multiform universe.

In summation, the present *mantra* seeks to convey that "this great Person" is nearer than the nearest. It cannot be otherwise, for who is nearer than the Self? It is immensely expansive (*mahāntam*), and there can be nothing apart from it. Knowing no end—no limit whatever—it is the infinite One. To know God is to experience the awareness of universality that causes everything to be seen in a new light, in an awareness "colored like the sun" (*ādityavarṇam*) and infusing everything with a vibrant brilliance. Even brighter than the solar radiance, this great Person is *prakāśa,* the radiance of consciousness itself. Self-luminous and illuminating all things, it is beyond all darkness (*tamasaḥ parastāt*). When the denseness of name and form dissolves, consciousness alone shines forth in its essential and perfect clarity. The illumined soul, entering into the light of Self-knowledge, transcends the limitations of mortality and is established in timeless, luminous imperishability. There is no other way. That is a simple statement of fact, based on the experience of reality in its full glory.

9

यस्मात् परं नापरमस्ति किंचिद्य-
स्मान्नाणीयो न ज्यायोऽस्ति कश्चित् ।
वृक्ष इव स्तब्धो दिवि तिष्ठत्येक-
स्तेनेदं पूर्णं पुरुषेण सर्वम् ॥ ९ ॥

yasmāt paraṁ nāparam asti kiṁcid yasmān nāṇīyo na jyāyo 'sti kaścit /
vṛkṣa iva stabdho divi tiṣṭhaty ekas tenedaṁ pūrṇaṁ puruṣeṇa sarvam //

9. There is nothing higher or lower than he; there is no one smaller or greater than he. Like a tree, immovable, the One abides in his own glory. By that Person is all this world filled.

Continuing to speak of the self-luminous divine being, Śvetāśvatara declares that there is nothing higher (*param*) or lower (*aparam*). There is no one more minute (*aṇīyam*) and no one greater (*jyāyaḥ*) than he who is smaller than an atom (*aṇu*) yet surpassing every existing thing in every respect.

"There is no one smaller or greater than he." This statement invites comparison to a passage in the Kaṭhopaniṣad (1.2.18–20). There, after describing the Self as uncreated (*ajaḥ*), constant (*nityaḥ*), and ever aware (*vipaścit*), Yama tells Naciketas that the Self (*ātmā*), established in the heart of every creature, is "smaller than small and greater than great" (*aṇoraṇīyān mahato mahīyān*). Echoing this same thought, Śvetāśvatara intends to convey that no limitation can be set on the shining Person that pervades all and lies beyond all. No matter what quality the mind can perceive or entertain, the Self transcends it. The divine Person is therefore unknowable by ordinary means and knowable only by direct, unmediated experience (*anubhava*).

Transcending every category (*tattva*) of experience and even thought itself, the *ātman* is described five times in the Bṛhadāraṇyakopaniṣad as "not this, not this" (*neti neti*). The Śaivāgama expresses the same idea with the term *anuttara* ("that beyond which there is nothing else"), a synonym for supreme consciousness (*parā saṁvid*).[74] Abhinavagupta extols the supreme state in a poetic work, *Anuttarāṣṭikā* [Eight verses on the Transcendent], which celebrates the Self as abiding in its own nature, going nowhere, doing nothing, only *being*. In this ultimate realization there is no difference between worshiper, worshiped, and worshiping, for all division comes from *māyā*. In truth there is nothing apart from the nonduality of consciousness (*cidadvāya*), wherein everything is pure in the true essence of its own experience (*sarvaṁ svānubhavasvābhāvavimalam*).

Evoking a primal image, Śvetāśvatara now likens the Ultimate to the *aśvattha* tree (*Ficus religiosa*). Known also as the pipal, this tree has been held sacred in India for thousands of years. Its heart-shaped leaves, often in groups of three, figure prominently as decorative motifs on pottery crafted as early as the mid fourth millennium BCE, a thousand years before the rise of urban civilization along the Indus and Sarasvatī Rivers. More elaborate representations of the tree, often in a religious context, adorn various objects recovered from the Bronze Age cities throughout the Indus-Sarasvatī cultural complex.[75] Terracotta tablets from Mohenjo-daro invariably depict a deity residing in a pipal tree, and similar artifacts from Harappa show a divine figure framed by an arch of pipal leaves.

Indian villagers even today believe that the deity resides in the pipal tree,[76] and as further evidence of cultural continuity one of the epithets of Tārā, a personified form of *śakti,* is Vṛkṣamadhyanivāsinī, "the [female] dweller in the midst of the tree." Among the ancient Indus-Sarasvatī stone seals and terracotta tablets that depict ritual scenes, one illustrates human figures bowing with water jars before the holy tree. In today's India it is customary to offer water at the base of a pipal tree in order to insure fertility or long life.[77]

In the ancient representations a deity often wears a horned headdress topped by a triad of pipal leaves. An outstanding example of this iconography is the well known "proto-Śiva" figure. Although that figure's identity remains unresolved (see pp. 31–32), the traditional Hindu custom of installing a stone *liṅga* at the base of either the pipal tree or the closely related banyan (*Ficus indica*)[78] offers more evidence of the pipal's connection to Śiva.

To what can we attribute the pipal's sacredness? The earliest textual clues may be found in the Vedic literature. Side-stepping the question of the relationship (or identity) of the Vedic people and the inhabitants of the Indus-Sarasvatī cities, we can note that the early poet-seers who composed the Ṛgveda's hymns had a keen appreciation of nature, which they regarded as infused with divine power. No doubt they would have concurred with a modern observer[79] who notes that the *aśvattha* tree provides sanctuary for all manner of living creatures. Birds, insects, snakes, and rodents find homes in its lush foliage, in the hollows of its trunk, and in its roots. Bees make honey from the nectar of its blossoms, and monkeys and deer feed on the figs that sprout from its trunk. Perhaps, like another present-day observer,[80] the ancients were impressed by the *aśvattha's* independence, self-sufficiency, and majesty.

One verse of a Ṛgvedic hymn (10.97.5) names the *aśvattha* tree as the growing-place or source (*niṣadanam*) of certain healing plants. In a highly metaphorical passage dealing with disciplined study of the sacred knowledge (*brahmacarya*), the Chāndogyopaniṣad (8.5.3) mentions the *aśvattha* as showering the nectar of immortality (*somasavanaḥ*). In context the symbolism clearly refers to some sort of inner experience. In another hymn of the Ṛgvedasaṁhitā the *ṛṣi* Śunaḥśepa speaks of a tree whose trunk, sustained by the great god Varuṇa, is rooted high above, with rays that stream downward to sink within us and be hidden (1.24.7).[81] Here two ideas stand out.

First, the tree is upside down. Second, the downward-streaming rays that sink within us and become hidden (1.24.7) are strongly suggestive of Śvetāśvatara's earlier reference to *devātmaśakti,* the power of the effulgent Self that lies hidden by its own effects (*svaguṇair nigūḍhām*) (1.3).

Although not identified specifically, this upside-down tree is in all likelihood the prototype for a vibrant passage in the Kathopaniṣad (2.3.1): "This is the eternal *aśvattha* tree with its root above and branches below. That indeed is resplendent; that is Brahman; that alone is called immortal. In that all worlds are contained, and no one goes beyond it. This [nearest One which is the source of all light] truly is That [Brahman]."

As in the Kaṭhopaniṣad, the tree described by Śvetāśvatara takes on cosmic proportions, having its roots above in the Unmanifest and its branches and leaves extending downward as the manifest universe. In keeping with the primary theme of the seer's third discourse, the tree symbolizes both the transcendent and immanent aspects of the Divine.

Like a tree (*vṛkṣa iva*), immovable (*stabdhaḥ*), the One (*ekaḥ*) stands (*tiṣṭhati*) in heaven (*divi*)." This vivid imagery likewise means more than what is immediately apparent, and the commentator who composed the *Śvetāśvataropaniṣadvṛtti* advances the metaphor one step further, taking the physical sky or heaven to symbolize divine glory. The One who "stands in heaven" signifies the One who "remains firm in his own brilliance and glory" (*divi dyotanātmani sve mahimni tiṣṭhati*).[82]

By that Person (*puruṣa*) of sunlike effulgence all this world is filled (*pūrṇaṁ puruṣena sarvam*). The Sanskrit suggests more than any translation can convey. Since the adjective *pūrṇa* and the noun *puruṣa* both derive ultimately from the same verbal root *pṝ* ("to fill"), this final thought brings to mind two related terms commonly used in the Trikaśāstra. One is *pūrṇatva,* the Divine's own infinite and absolute fullness, and the other is *pūrṇāhaṁtā,* the Divine's own ultimate sense of Self. All this hints, of course, at unfathomable unity.

Just as the great seer Śvetāśvatara quoted earlier texts in the presentation of his teaching, he in turn was quoted by later teachers. The present *mantra,* presumably original to this Upaniṣad, appears again in the later Mahānārāyaṇopaniṣad (12.13), which forms the tenth book of the Taittirīyāraṇyaka (see Appendix B, Table 2).

10

ततो यदुत्तरतरं तदरूपमनामयम् ।
य एतद्विदुरमृतास्ते भवन्ति अथेतरे दुःखमेवापियन्ति ॥ १० ॥

tato yad uttarataraṁ tad arūpam anāmayam /
ya etad vidur amṛtās te bhavanti athetare duḥkham evāpiyanti //

10. Far higher than the creator is the formless One, beyond affliction. They who know this become immortal, but the rest get only misery.

Returning to the point made so dramatically in *mantra* 3.7, Śvetāśvatara reaffirms that there is a reality far higher than the personal God who projects, maintains, and ultimately reabsorbs the universe. This transcendental One beyond all phenonema remains ever free. It is *arūpam,* free of form and its limitations; it is *anāmayam,* free of any sort of affliction. They who know this (*etat*) are bound no more by the temporal, spatial, and causal limitations of human existence. Released from the bonds of temporal finitude, they become immortal. As for the rest (*itare*), they who do not know the supreme reality remain entangled in phenomenal existence and all its attendant woes. Their inescapable lot is the misery of finitude.

The experience of suffering is universal, of course, but the Upaniṣads rarely express it by the word *duḥkha.* Before the Śvetāśvatara, this term appears only in the Bṛhadāraṇyakopaniṣad (4.4.13–14). There the *ṛṣi* Yājñavalka instructs King Janaka in the necessity of discovering and awakening to the Self that has penetrated the body-mind complex, "this perilous and inaccessible place," vulnerable to every sort of danger and ill and clogged with obstacles to Self-realization. But, as Yājñavalkya says, it is possible in this very body (*ihaiva*) to know that [Brahman]. Then he adds, "They who know it become immortal, but the rest get only misery" (*ye tad vidur amṛtās te bhavanti athetare duḥkham evāpiyanti*). Except for Śvetāśvatara's substitution of *etat* for *tat*, the words are identical.

The word *duḥkha* can mean what we ordinarily think of as pain, misery, or suffering, but here it means something broader. It signifies the entirety of existential discomfort, the imperfection of the human condition. Of course life is not a constant state of physical agony or mental anguish or profound unhappiness, but everything is not entirely right either.

To illustrate this point, early Buddhist teaching employed one possible derivation of the word *duḥkha*. The pejorative prefix *duḥ* implies evil, difficulty, hardship, or inferiority. The noun *kha* can refer to any opening, space, or vacuity. It is also the word for the hole at the center of a wheel. The image of an off-center wheel demonstrates the nature of *duḥkha*, for such a wheel guarantees a bumpy ride. As surely as life has its ups, it has its downs, one following the other. Life is not exclusively suffering, but as long as the ride remains bumpy, we do not experience the uninterrupted joy and peace that are inherent in our true being.

Unlike the Buddhist and Sāṁkhya teachers, Śvetāśvatara does not dwell on *duḥkha*. He mentions it only four times in the course of this Upaniṣad (1.2, 1.5, 3.10, 6.20), and nowhere does he elaborate on its characteristics. As for the present *mantra*, one modern commentator brings up the traditional threefold classification of suffering as *ādhidaivika*, *ādhibhautika*, and *ādhyātmika*.[83] These terms can be found in commentaries on the opening verse of Īśvarakṛṣṇa's *Sāṁkhyakārikā*, which begins, "Because of the affliction of the threefold misery..." (*duḥkhatrayābhighātāt*). Of course, the *Sāṁkhyakārikā* belongs to a philosophical tradition distinct from Śvetāśvatara's; moreover, it was composed a thousand or so years after the Upaniṣad, and the commentaries were written even later. Although there is no guarantee that any of these texts reflect Śvetāśvatara's views, the rational analysis they offer is helpful in understanding human suffering.

To the category of *ādhidaivika* belong the calamities brought on by the forces of nature—earthquakes, fires, floods, droughts, excessive heat or cold, violent storms, and the rest. Those natural events and conditions are beyond human control.[84] Human strength is limited to evading them or to mitigating their full effect.

The suffering classified as *ādhibhautika* includes every sort of pain or injury inflicted by other living beings as well as insensate physical objects.[85] It encompasses wars, assaults, attacks by animals, and any other misery perpetrated by others through word or deed.

Suffering classified as *ādhyātmika* arises from the mind-body complex itself.[86] Physical illness is considered *ādhyātmika* even though we recognize today a wide range of disease-causing agents external to ourselves. In the classical Sāṁkhya view the causes of mental distress are separation from that which holds attraction (*rāga*) and contact with that which provokes aversion (*dveṣa*).[87] We recognize today that the suffering called *ādhyātmika* includes any kind of self-inflicted harm, either physical or psychological. Allowing negative thoughts and destructive emotions to misguide us is *ādhyātmika;* so are seeking escape through addictions or compulsive behavior and holding to the denial that keeps us mired in often preventable or reversible misery.

Of course, any painful circumstance may have more than one cause, and that is why the *Sāṁkhyakārikā* refers to *duḥkha* as threefold. In the complex web of existence, the three kinds of suffering are interwoven, and the three-way categorization invites us to analyze our unease in order to uncover its roots, however deep and tangled they prove to be. We are to examine our patterns of response, which are *ādhyātmika*, in the face of whatever befalls us, whether *ādhidaivika* or *ādhibhautika* in origin, and to cultivate a rational approach to life's difficulties.

The present *mantra* makes a bold contrast between human imperfection and divine perfection, and when it tells us that the supreme Brahman is *anāmayam* ("having no disease"), we are to take that in the broadest sense as meaning inherently free of every imperfection and impurity of phenomenal existence. In our unenlightened state we believe that happiness depends on factors outside of ourselves, but knowledge of the supreme Self brings freedom from dependence on anything external.[88]

The supreme Self is not just beyond (*uttaram*), but far beyond (*uttarataram*)—one might say even "beyond the beyond."[89] At the same time this (*etat*) Self is also nearmost because all distinction of otherness has vanished. They who know the Self experience the absolute unity of consciousness-bliss, the pure nondifference (*abheda*) that is infinite plenitude and perfect joy.

Joy is our true nature, and not the state of contraction that we call human existence. In the Chāndogyopaniṣad (7.23–24.1) Sanatkumāra tells Nārada, "The Infinite (*bhūmā*) alone is happiness (*sukham*); there is no happiness in the finite (*alpe*). ... Where one sees nothing else, hears nothing else, discerns nothing else, that is the Infinite. But where one sees something else, hears something else, discerns something else, that is the finite. Truly, what is infinite is immortal, but what is finite is mortal."

11

सर्वाननशिरोग्रीवः सर्वभूतगुहाशयः ।
सर्वव्यापी स भगवांस्तस्मात् सर्वगतः शिवः ॥ ११ ॥

sarvānanaśirogrīvaḥ sarvabhūtaguhāśayaḥ /
sarvavyāpī sa bhagavāṁs tasmāt sarvagataḥ śivaḥ //

11. All faces, heads, and necks belong to him who dwells deep in the heart of all beings. Therefore the glorious Lord is all-pervading, universally present, and gracious.

Whereas the previous *mantra* drew a firm line of demarcation between the Infinite and the finite, this one blurs that distinction. Returning to his primary thesis, Śvetāśvatara declares that Rudra is the sole reality, simultaneously beyond and within everything, at once possessed of formlessness and form. The Absolute, God as creative power, and God as present in the world are not three separate entities but a single being that from our unenlightened perspective appears to have the distinction of three logical phases, aspects, or facets.

The present *mantra* follows in the spirit of two verses from the Ṛgvedasaṁhitā, leading one translator[90] to regard it as a paraphrase of 10.81.3, already quoted verbatim as *mantra* 3.3, and of 10.90.1, which will be quoted as *mantra* 3.14. Rooted in the ancient Vedic hymns, Śvetāśvatara's thinking conceives of Rudra (or Brahman) both as the transpersonal conscious reality that dwells deep in the heart of all beings (*sarvabhūtagūhaśayaḥ*) and as "the glorious Lord" (*bhagavān*), the personal God who is gracious (*śivaḥ*). As noted previously, this theology is highly suggestive of the later Trika doctrine of the Lord's nonduality (*īśvarādvayavāda*). Significantly, the British scholar H. H. Wilson, writing in 1828, reported that the present *mantra* was cited by Śaivas as Vedic authority for their teaching.[91]

Reflecting on Śvetāśvatara's central thesis of God's simultaneous transcendence and immanence, one can say that Brahman-in-itself (*brahmasvarūpa*) is beyond all things even while, as its own power (*brahmaśakti*), it *is* all things.[92] Water, rising in the form of a wave, does not cease to be water, nor can the wave ever be apart from the water. There can be no place where the Divine is not. There is one Self, one consciousness (*cit*) that is the eternal subject, and the entire universe is nothing but *cit* appearing as its own object.[93] Although ultimately beyond any limitation of form, the formless One is ever free to experience the life of the universe through every form and through the intelligence present in every heart and mind. "All faces, heads, and necks" are his, we are told in imagery suggestive of superhuman grandeur. Serene beyond any human affliction, free from every flaw of phenomenality, the divine Self shines forth as consciousness, its awareness present everywhere, experiencing everything.

The supreme *cit* is the changeless principle beyond, in, and through all experience. It is all-pervading (*sarvavyāpī*) and omnipresent (*sarvagataḥ*). While these two terms may appear redundant, they are not. In its expression of all-pervasiveness, *sarvayāpī* contains the idea of inherent invariability, suggesting the immutable reality of consciousness-in-itself (*citsvarūpa*). *Sarvagataḥ,* "gone everywhere," implies motion and suggests an equally infinite but somehow more dynamic reality (*cicchakti*).

To describe the divine Self as the personal deity, Śvetāśvatara employs the term *bhagavat,* translated here as "the glorious Lord." Frequently applied to Viṣṇu or Kṛṣṇa in the Bhagavadgītā and Bhāgavatapurāṇa, this title occasionally occurs elsewhere in connection with Rudra-Śiva. It conveys the overall impression of a resplendent, venerable, and holy being who possesses all wealth and happiness and who is to be adored.[94] In the *Vṛtti* attributed to Śaṁkara, the commentator defines *bhagavat* as the possessor of six divine glories: sovereignty or lordship (*aiśvarya*), righteousness or virtue (*dharma*), splendor or beauty (*yaśas*), prosperity or majesty (*śrī*), wisdom or knowledge (*jñāna*), and nonattachment or dispassion (*vairāgya*).[95] These are, of course, qualities that inspire our respect and devotion. If they are qualities of the all-pervading divine

Self (*paramātman*), then they are inherent in every *jīvātman*, in each of us, merely waiting to shine forth. Moreover, because the word *bhagavat* derives from the root *bhaj* ("to divide," "to distribute," "to share with," "to partake of"), the personal God who bears this title is by nature the embodiment of all goodness and abundance. *Bhagavān* is benevolent, auspicious, and ever-gracious (*śivaḥ*).

12

महान् प्रभुर्वै पुरुषः सत्त्वस्यैष प्रवर्तकः ।
सुनिर्मलामिमां प्राप्तिमीशानो ज्योतिरव्ययः ॥ १२ ॥

mahān prabhur vai puruṣaḥ sattvasyaiṣa pravartakaḥ /
sunirmalām imāṁ prāptim īśāno jyotir avyayaḥ //

12. Truly the great Lord is the innermost Person, who inspires the mind to attain to this absolute purity; he is the ruler and the imperishable light.

The innermost Person (*puruṣaḥ*), the conscious principle within every living being, is the great master or Lord (*mahān prabhuḥ*) who is great in every sense of the word, who is unimaginably powerful, expansive, and exalted. He dwells within as the impelling or inspiring force (*pravartakaḥ*) of every mind (*sattvasya*). Here the term *puruṣa* does not carry the specific (and mutually distinct) meanings of the later philosophical systems, and *sattva* does not indicate the *guṇa* of that name. By *sattva* the Upaniṣad means a general sense of mind, marked by a positive disposition that includes strength of character, self-direction, and right resolution. It is the presence of this nearmost (*eṣaḥ*) divine being that causes us to aspire to this (*imām*) absolutely pure attainment (*sunirmalāṁ prāptim*), our own inherent perfection beyond all human misery, which is described in *mantra* 3.10. To achieve such purity is to know the *ātman*[96] and to abide simply in one's own true being.[97]

The indwelling Self (*puruṣaḥ*), reigning (*īśānaḥ*) over all else because of its superiority to all else, is the uncreated, self-luminous, and imperishable light (*jyotir avyayaḥ*) of pure consciousness.[98] The purpose of *sādhanā* is to regain that original state of awareness, totally free of impurity (*sunirmala*). This is Self-knowledge beyond all ignorance.

The idea of ignorance as impurity is fully developed in the Trikaśāstra. In its scheme of thirty-six *tattvas*, the five highest states of consciousness (*śiva, śakti, sadāśiva, īśvara, sadvidyā*) represent the pure (*śuddha*) creation. At this level the ideation of an objective "this" (*idam*) has begun, but it remains within the unity, or purity, of the divine experience. Śiva is fully aware that "this" is nothing more than his own ideation, yet to be projected as the universe. Separating the pure from the impure creation are six intermediary (*śuddhā-śuddha*) *tattvas*, consisting of *māyā* and its five limiting functions (*kañcukas*) (see pp. 117–120). Only through *māyā* and its *kañcukas* does the division of *aham* and *idam* into subject-object duality become actualized. Tainted by the impurity of *māyā*, Śiva experiences himself as *jīva*, who mistakes *idam* as distinct and separate from *aham* even while, paradoxically, entertaining a sense of individuality (*asmitā*) based on self-identification with the objective manifestations that constitute the mind and body and their experiences. Those objective manifestations are the remaining twenty-four *tattvas* from *prakṛti* to *pṛthivī*, which constitute the impure (*aśuddha*) creation.

Māyā produces three conditions of contraction designated by the term *mala* ("impurity"). To recall Śvetāśvatara's earlier example (2.14), the *malas* sully the perfection of divine luminosity just as dirt blocks the reflectivity of a mirror. Or we can say that the *malas* hide the imperishable light of the Self just as clouds obscure the radiant face of the sun.

Āṇavamala, the impurity of individuation, is the fundamental impurity and root cause of the other two *malas*. It reduces the Divine's own sense of infinitude to the limited awareness of individual selfhood. This basic sense of individuality is the ground or cause of the ego-sense.[99] In short, *āṇavamala* is the imperfection related to a diminished sense of self.

As this sense of individuality or separation evolves into the more fully defined sense of I and other, a further condition of impurity known as *māyīyamala* arises. *Māyīyamala* produces the separation of subject and object and the distinction of one object from another—in other words, the awareness of plurality. Through a process of contrast, comparison, and exclusion, *māyīyamala* directs consciousness to focus on diversity rather than on the unity that is its original nature.[100]

It is only natural that with the sense of an individual I (*āṇavamala*), followed by the sense of I and other (*māyīyamala*), the next step would be the interaction of the limited I and the multiple other. This state of affairs is the impurity of action, known as *kārmamala*. It produces bondage (*karma*) sustained by an erroneous sense of finitude and the individual's continuing interaction with a deceptive dualism of self and not-self. Unlike the divine power of action (*kriyāśakti*), which is the spontaneous overflow of divine fullness,[101] the restricted and restrictive power of human action (*karma*) attempts to satisfy those desires arising out of a fundamental sense of lack (the result of *āṇavamala*) or to deal with a continual misreading of reality (the result of *māyīyamala*). In truth the *malas*, like every other feature of manifestation, are nothing more than modifications of consciousness. As modifications of the singular *cit* they are not discrete entities so much as different movements within a reality that is by nature One and undivided.

Along with the forgetfulness of our essential nature comes the loss of freedom. Because freedom (*svātantrya*) is the absence of limitation, it follows that the removal of limitation restores the essential freedom of the Self. The Śaiva philosopher-mystic Utpaladeva expresses this memorably in his *Īśvarapratyabhijñākārikā* (3.2.4), when he observes that because of the impurity of individuality (*āṇavamala*) there is neither freedom of consciousness nor consciousness of freedom. The two occur simultaneously and are reciprocal.[102] This double-edged existential predicament arises directly out of the forgetfulness of one's true nature; it can be resolved through recognition (*pratyabhijñā*) of our own original perfection, the innermost Person that Śvetāśvatara here calls "the great Lord."

13

अङ्गुष्ठमात्रः पुरुषोऽन्तरात्मा
सदा जनानां हृदये सन्निविष्टः ।

हृदा मन्वीषो मनसाभिक्लृप्तो
य एतद् विदुरमृतास्ते भवन्ति ॥ १३ ॥

aṅguṣṭhamātraḥ puruṣo 'ntarātmā sadā janānāṁ hṛdaye sanniviṣṭaḥ /
hṛdā manvīśo manasābhiklpto ya etad vidur amṛtās te bhavanti //

13. This Person, the size of a thumb, is the inner Self, ever established in the hearts of living beings—the lord of humankind, corresponding within to the heart and mind. They who know this become immortal.

"This Person, the size of a thumb," a description found three times in the slightly earlier Kaṭhopaniṣad (2.1.12, 2.1.14, 2.3.17), is not to be taken literally, because the infinite *ātman* knows no such limitation.[103] The image is intended only as a practical aid to concentration, instructing the meditator to visualize one-pointedly a luminous presence in the heart. Here it bears repeating that the word *heart* does not mean the physical organ or even its location in the chest; rather, it means the deepest consciousness, which is the center, or "heart," of reality (see pp. 172–175). The light of consciousness in the individual heart is the same light of consciousness that is the heart or essence of the entire universe.[104] According to the nondualism of Advaita Vedānta and Trika Śaivism alike, there is one *ātman* and one only; *ātman* does not exist in the plural. The innermost Self (*antarātmā*) of one being is the same as that of all others. Although ever present in every creature, the supreme Self remains One and undivided.

This ultimate unity of being is expressed collectively in the *mahāvākyas,* the great pronouncements of the Upaniṣads on the supreme identity (see p. 23). *Ahaṁ brahmāsmi* ("I am Brahman"); *tat tvam asi* ("you are that"); *ayam ātmā brahma* ("this Self is Brahman"); *prajñānaṁ brahma* ("pure consciousness is Brahman")—each *mahāvākya* reveals the same truth from the perspective of a different grammatical person. *I* am Brahman, *you* are Brahman, *he* (*she*, *it*) is Brahman.[105]

"Ever established in the hearts of living beings" means that wherever we go and whatever we do at any time, we are never apart from the Divine. In fact, it is the supreme Self that experiences the universe through every creature. The consciousness that is *ātman*, as the indwelling ruler or lord of all humankind (*manvīśaḥ*) functions in the individual through the intelligence of the heart (*hṛdā*) and mind (*manasā*).

"They who know this become immortal" (*ya etad vidur amṛtās te bhavanti*). This pronouncement, traceable to the *ṛṣi* Yājñavalkya (see p. 225), functions as a leitmotif in Śvetāśvatara's third discourse (3.1, 3.10, 3.13) and recurs twice again in the fourth, once verbatim (4.17) and once slightly varied (4.20). The same idea is phrased somewhat differently in *mantra* 3.7 (*taṁ jñātvā 'mṛtā bhavanti*), but the meaning is identical: they who know the supreme Self in all its radiant boundlessness realize their own imperishability.

It should be apparent by now that knowledge is a recurring theme of Śvetāśvatara's teaching. Thirty-six verses of his Upaniṣad—nearly a third of the total—refer to knowledge or knowing in some way. That is hardly surprising, considering that the essential nature (*svabhāva*) of the Self is consciousness. The seer's primary point, made a dozen times, is that knowledge of the Self leads to immortality (1.6, 3.7, 3.8, 3.10, 3.13, 3.21, 4.15, 4.17, 4.20. 5.1, 5.6, 6.15). Self-knowledge frees one from all fetters (1. 8, 1.11, 2.15, 4.16, 5.13, 6.13). Knowing, one lays aside the limitations of individuality (5.14), sees an end to misery (6.20), experiences timelessness (6.6), goes to peace forever (4.14), abides in Brahman (4.8), attains freedom from rebirth and merges in Brahman (1.7).

How can knowledge lead to immortality or liberation? First it is essential to understand just what Śvetāśvatara means by knowledge. In the Muṇḍakopaniṣad the *ṛṣi* Aṅgiras informs the householder Śaunaka that "the knowers of Brahman (*brahmavidaḥ*) declare that two kinds of knowledge (*dve vidye*) are to be known, the higher (*parā*) and the lower (*aparā*)" (1.14). In the next verse he identifies the lower knowledge as the Vedic texts and other branches of learning; in contrast the higher knowledge is that by which the imperishable reality (*akṣaram*) is apprehended.

The later schools of Indian thought developed this basic idea into a rich array of epistemologies, each with its own point of view and distinctive vocabulary. Underlying the profusion of varying details, however, is the basic understanding that knowledge (*vidyā*, *jñāna*) is either lower (*aparā*) or supreme (*parā*). This does not mean that the former is to be disparaged. Far from it. First, it is the same consciousness that is essential to all forms of knowledge; second, the aspirant disciplined in the lower knowledge gains proper direction to strive for the supreme knowledge.[106] The Vedānta enriches the vocabulary by speaking of the lower knowledge as mediate (*parokṣa*) and empirical (*vyāvahārika*) and the supreme knowledge as unmediated (*aparokṣa*) and transcendental (*pāramārthika*). The Śaiva nondualists interpret *vyāvahārika* as "functional," emphasizing the active nature of ordinary experience in the here and now. They also employ the terms *laukika* ("worldly") and *bauddha* ("intellectual") to underscore an objective environment and the mental awareness of it. Conversely, because transcendental knowledge lies beyond the limitation of sensory perception or intellectual exercise,[107] the Śaivas call it nonworldly (*alaukika*) or pertaining to consciousness alone (*pauruṣa*). Other Śaiva terms are *pratyabhijñājñāna* ("recognitive knowledge") and *śivānubhūti* ("experience of Śiva").[108]

Because empirical knowledge requires an object, it is dependent on name and form (*nāmarūpa*). Accordingly it is confined to awareness of phenomenal manifestation. The Indian schools of philosophy have developed theories of how it operates within this circumscribed sphere. First and foremost, they all recognize a triadic arrangement consisting of a knowing subject (*pramātṛ*), a known object (*prameya*), and a process of knowing (*pramāṇa*). The whole of creation is made of this triad.[109] Long before the philosophical theories took shape, Śvetāśvatara laid their foundation in his first discourse. In two *mantras* (1.9, 1.12) he speaks of a triad (*traya*) of experient (*bhoktṛ*), the experienced (*bhogya*), and the impelling force (*preritṛ*) that relates the one to the other. All three, he declares, are Brahman. That same idea finds expression much later in Abhinavagupta's *Īśvarapratyabhijñāvivṛtivimarśinī*, where the seer-philosopher writes that nothing perceived can be independent of perception and that perception cannot be independent of a perceiver; therefore, he concludes, the empirical universe is, in essence, the perceiver, the one universal consciousness[110] whose own diversification and assumption of forms account for the experience of an objective, phenomenal world.

Mediate knowledge (*parokṣajñāna*) can be either perceptual or conceptual, and the two are interrelated. According to Sāṁkhya, perception (*dṛṣṭa*) involves the senses (*indriyas*), the mind (*manas*), the ego (*ahaṁkāra*), and the intellect (*buddhi*), this last and highest function of human awareness making the final determination. Advaita Vedānta distinguishes between external and internal perception. In external perception (*indriyapratyakṣa*) the awareness of an object comes through the sensory faculties, and this experience is the primary means of knowing the physical world. Internal perception concerns sensations that are perceived independent of external sensory stimulation,[111] for example, feelings of well-being (*sukha*) and distress (*duḥkha*), empowerment or limitation, and the full array of human emotions. Perceptions, acted on by the mind, serve as the basis for reflection, reasoning, and abstract thought. Here the focus shifts from the gross (*sthūla*) to the subtle (*sūkṣma*), from material objects to the knowledge derived from them in the form of mental objects or ideas. In other words, perceptual knowledge is the basis of conceptual knowledge.

The philosophical schools have detailed theories that explore every possible intricacy of mediate knowledge (*parokṣajñāna*) and set the guidelines for determining its validity or error. Their conclusions go well beyond the present topic, but it is worth mentioning that they differ among themselves over how many methods of knowing (*pramāṇas*) there are. The number ranges from two to ten, but broadly speaking the means of knowing can be reduced to three. They are perception (*pratyakṣa*), inference (*anumāna*), and reliable authority (*śabda, āgama*).

The first two relate in turn to perceptual knowledge and conceptual knowledge. The third *pramāṇa* is verbal testimony or reliable authority. Sāṁkhya calls this *āptavacana* and defines it as the teaching of scripture and sages.[112] Other systems, including the Vedānta, call it *śabda* or *āgama.* In the Vedantic definition *āgama* is the principle medium of formal instruction. The knowledge of some things cannot be experienced through perception—for example, a historical event or something taking place in a distant location. Other knowledge cannot be inferred on one's own, owing to lack of information, training, or intellectual capacity—for example, acquiring a foreign language or discovering an advanced mathematical principle. But such knowledge can be gained through a reliable teacher, in person or through writings. *Śabda* or *āgama* is thus acknowledged as a valid supplement to perception and inference.[113]

Although the three *pramāṇas* are valid sources of empirical knowledge that allow us to function in the world, as lower knowledge they remain dependent on name and form and restricted to the realm of phenomenality. They cannot confer liberation or immortality. The reason is simple. The culmination of knowledge lies neither in perceptual nor conceptual awareness but in intuitional experience. Empirical knowledge is mediate (*parokṣa*), requiring a means or process to relate a knowing subject to an object to be known. Intuitional experience (*aparokṣānubhūti*) is direct and immediate. Having no distinction of subject and object and no need for relating, it is the reintegration of consciousness into its ultimate unity. In the absence of intermediaries such as perception, thought, and reason, all that remains is consciousness itself—at once self-luminous (*svayamprakāśa*) and self-aware.

This single consciousness is, of course, the essence of all knowledge, higher or lower, and as the sole reality it is the ground of all experience. It is self-revealing and also revealing of itself as its own manifestations.[114] In Yājñavalkya's counsel to Maitreyī, immortalized in the Bṛhadāraṇyakopaniṣad (2.4.5), "The Self being known, all this [universe] is known" (*ātmano … vijñānenedaṁ sarvaṁ viditam*).

In summary, the lower knowledge, based on the experience of this world, is relative, because it involves the knower, the object to be known, and the process of knowing. It presupposes a difference between the subject (*aham*) and the object (*idam*) along with the relational process that defines them as the knower and the known. We can gain knowledge of the surrounding world through sense perception; we can engage in our own process of inquiry, reasoning, speculation, and determination; and we can accept facts or ideas as true on the basis of reliable authority. Still, all forms of empirical knowledge are restricted to the realm of ordinary experience and cannot liberate.

In contrast, the higher knowledge is immediate. It does not depend on any process. Because there is no relating activity, the distinction of knower, known, and knowing vanishes. This supreme knowledge is the fullness of consciousness wherein I and other are merged in undifferentiated unity. The state of the Self resting in its own nature (*svarūpaviśrānti*), in the joy of self-recognition (*pratyabhijñā*), is the most intimate and the most blissful of experiences.

How do we know that this inner experience, which we cannot describe to others or even formulate in thought, is real when there is nothing about it that can be quantified or qualified, measured or described? That is just the point. There is no object and no objectivity, because knower and known have merged into perfect oneness. To know so fully and so intimately is to become what is known.

14

सहस्रशीर्षा पुरुषः सहस्राक्षः सहस्रपात्।
स भूमिं विश्वतो वृत्वा अत्यतिष्ठद्दशाङ्गुलम्॥ १४ ॥

sahasraśīrṣā puruṣaḥ sahasrākṣaḥ sahasrapāt /
sa bhūmiṁ viśvato vṛtvā aty atiṣṭhad daśāṅgulam //

14. Having a thousand heads, a thousand eyes, and a thousand feet, and surrounding the earth on all sides, this Person extends beyond it by ten fingers' breadth.

This and the following *mantra* are identical to Ṛgveda 10.90.1–2, the first two verses of the Puruṣasūkta, a highly significant hymn that extols the Supreme Being as the primordial reality and omnipresent, life-giving consciousness.

This transcendent-yet-immanent universal Self is said to have a thousand heads, a thousand eyes, and a thousand feet. The ancient metaphor means that it possesses innumerable organs of thinking, perceiving, and acting. It is a single consciousness that experiences the untold vastness and variety of its own creation, refracted through the awareness of countless individual creatures.

However far we look across the broad expanse of this earth, in whichever direction, there is no place where the divine presence is not. It encompasses the whole world and saturates it through and through. Yet we must not forget that this ever-present, shining reality is not limited to the forms of creation. Here the verse reveals an extraordinary truth, although the language that expresses it may strike us at first as puzzling: this divine presence (*puruṣa*) extends beyond the earth by ten fingers' breadth.

The Ṛgvedasaṁhitā is replete with such figures of speech, and the meanings of many are lost to us today. In the present instance we are fortunate to have in the *Śvetāśvataropaniṣadvṛtti* an interpretation that is not only convincing but compellingly so. In the human body the heart lies at a distance of ten fingers' breadth above the navel. This is the heart of awareness, the center of consciousness described in the previous *mantra.* By making the fragmented awareness of ordinary experience one-pointed—by uniting all the mental powers, directing them inward, and merging them in the single inner light of the heart that is their source—the meditator can reach beyond the multiplicity of the world and enter into the ineffable peace of the pure Self. Miraculously that blissful core of reality is but the breadth of ten fingers away.

15

पुरुष एवेदं सर्वं यद् भूतं यच्च भव्यम्।
उतामृतत्वस्येशानो यदन्नेनातिरोहति ॥ १५ ॥

puruṣa evedaṁ sarvaṁ yad bhūtaṁ yac ca bhavyam /
utāmṛtatvasyeśāno yad annenātirohati //

15. What has been and what will be and what grows up by food, the Person is truly all this—and the lord of immortality as well.

Past, present, and future—all these are divine. All this universe of our experience (*idaṁ sarvam*) is nothing but divine consciousness in one form or another. The past is what has been (*yad bhūtam*), and the future is what will be (*yad bhavyam*). The present is literally "what grows up by food" (*yad annenātirohati*). Life depends on what is consumed (*anna*), and whatever is alive now exists in the present. The word for food (*anna*) can itself be taken figuratively to mean the lowest, or most observable, form in which the *puruṣa* is manifested, its outermost covering.[115] In that sense, the present consists of the state in which spirit is clothed in matter and through it (*annena*) enacts (*atirohati*) the play of the universe.

Even so, the indwelling Person ever remains the ruler (*īśānaḥ*), reigning over not only the mortal realm but even over immortality (*amṛtatva*) itself. What does this mean? Simply that the supreme Self is subordinate to nothing. He, or it, is in no way restricted by time, neither by its fleetingness nor its duration. He is everything that ever was, is, and will be; but he also transcends time altogether. That is the true meaning of immortality—transcending time. And then he transcends even the *idea* of immortality, because no concept can limit him. His sovereignty is absolute.

How the One becomes the many or at least appears to become the many is a perennial theme of Indian thought, addressed even by the *ṛṣis* of Ṛgvedic times. The Puruṣasūkta, of which the present *mantra* and the preceding one are quotations, begins with the solid, graspable imagery of the divinity's heads, eyes, and feet beyond number; then it rapidly shifts to the idea of transcendence. The universal being extends beyond the physical realm "by ten fingers' breadth." This figure of speech, already explained as signifying the inherent nearness of the *ātman* in the heart, at the same time signifies the world-transcending infinitude of Brahman. "Ten fingers' breath" signals divine immanence and transcendence alike, and the author of the *Śvetāśvataropaniṣadvṛtti* proposes both interpretations.

Along with the idea of a transcendental Absolute, the Puruṣasūkta presents the conception of the Divine as personal. Although this being expresses his power and glory through all the universes of past, present, and future by becoming them, he is in no way limited by them. The primordial, universal being freely evolves himself into the universe of our experience, and the hymn couches this in the language of ritual. Symbolically *puruṣa* is both the sacrificer and the sacrificed, which is to say the subject (*aham*) and the object (*idam*). But according to the hymn, the cosmos is made of only a fourth of his being. The world is not a complete self-expression of divine glory, because divine glory in its fullness is inexpressible.[116] In his own being (*svabhāva*) the supreme Self transcends his own expression, because any manifestation, however grand and glorious, is by nature partial and ever-changing, while that from which it arises remains ever whole and immutable.[117]

Still, we must keep in mind that the partial and the whole, the changing and the unchanging, are different aspects of a single reality. That is a core tenet of the Trikaśāstra. Even in the restriction of our limited, dualistic understanding, the manifestation cannot be entirely separated from that which manifests it. If the world were competely cut off from the light of consciousness, it would be imperceptible, as Abhinavagupta explains (see p. 209). In so far as the finite mind is capable of grasping it, consciousness-as-subject and consciousness-as-object coexist in a relationship of mutual necessity (*avinābhāvasambandha*).

Besides the Puruṣasūkta, the Ṛgveda contains other hymns that foreshadow the metaphysics of the Upaniṣads. One of the best-known is the Hymn of Creation. The Nāsadīyasūkta (Ṛgveda 10.129) evokes the Absolute as inutterably beyond duality, beyond even existence (*sat*) and nonexistence (*asat*). Because there is nothing apart from the One (*tad ekam*), there is nothing to act upon it, and creation can only be a spontaneous, self-activated process. This hymn too anticipates the later Trika doctrine of manifestation. Even while resting in the indescribable perfection of its own being, the One, through its own intrinsic power (*tapas*, literally "warmth," "heat") first brings forth desire (*kāma*), or an aspiration to existence. Through its own cosmic will (*icchā* in Śaiva parlance), the undifferentiated One appears as the creator and the created. This act of will is an act of self-definition, and it is also an act of self-limitation (see pp. 116–120), because to define is to limit.[118] In reality there is nothing other than the One. *From* that One and *by* that One the universe is made. The singular Self is both the material and the efficient cause of a cosmos that cannot possibly exist apart from it.[119]

The Trikaśāstra affirms that the state of ignorance (*avidyā*) in which we live is nevertheless a state of consciousness—but consciousness in contraction (*saṁkoca*). The human mind cannot encompass infinity but turns its attention instead to the countless details of objectified and finite diversity that make up the empirical universe. In and through this ignorance, consciousness is ever-present although appearing as limited. To repeat a point already made, without consciousness no perception, knowledge, experience, or awareness of any kind would be possible. In our state of contracted consciousness (*aparajñāna*), we are aware only to a degree and remain unaware of the true unity of being, which is revealed as the Self by the higher knowledge (*parajñāna*). As long as the individual remains bound, the lower knowledge, based on the model of "I (*aham*) know this (*idam*)," obscures the higher, which is the Self's own recognition of its true nature (*svasvabhāva*) as Paramaśiva, the essence of everything.[120] This last point finds support in the Bṛhadāraṇyakopaniṣad (4.4.13), where Yājñavalkya tells King Janaka, "Whoever has discovered and directly awakened to the Self (*ātmā*) that has entered into this dense body, he is the maker of the universe, for he is the maker of everything. The world is his—indeed he is the world itself" (*tasya lokaḥ sa u loka eva*).

As if in a single breath the present *mantra* speaks of the *puruṣa* as the ultimate, transpersonal reality, calling him "the lord of immortality" (*amṛtatvasyeśānaḥ*), and as the embodied individual who lives dependent on material sustenance (*yad annenātirohati*). A subsequent verse of the Puruṣasūkta (Ṛgveda 10.90.4), which Śvetāśvatara does not quote, speaks of the *puruṣa's* ascent and descent—its resting in changeless eternality and its striding forth *here* in every direction to experience the world in all its animate and inanimate diversity. Just as the universal, divine consciousness becomes contracted as individualized human awareness, that same human awareness may expand into the boundless joy of its original freedom.

16

सर्वतः पाणिपादं तत् सर्वतोऽक्षिशिरोमुखम् ।
सर्वतः श्रुतिमल्लोके सर्वमावृत्य तिष्ठति ॥ १६ ॥

sarvataḥ pāṇipādaṁ tat sarvato 'kṣiśiromukham /
sarvataḥ śrutimal loke sarvam āvṛtya tiṣṭhati //

16. With hands and feet on every side, with eyes and heads and faces everywhere, possessing ears on every side, it stands in the world, encompassing all.

This *mantra,* quoted later in the Bhagavadgītā (13.13), continues the theme of divine immanence. The Self, here referred to by the neuter pronoun *tat,* stands in the world (*loke tiṣṭhati*), encompassing everything (*sarvam āvṛtya*). *Tiṣṭhati* can also mean "stations [itself]" or "remains engaged in," and *sarvam āvṛtya,* meaning "encompassing all," likewise suggests an active participation in the life of the cosmos. Here is a divine being that is involved in its own creation as the single subject or knower of all objects of experience, and those objects are nothing but its own projections.

Accordingly the world can be understood as an outward reflection of divine glory. As Abhinavagupta puts it, creation is nothing other than the materialization of Lord Śiva's will, overflowing from his ever-blissful fullness (*paripūrṇatā*).[121] In harmony with that view, the present *mantra* portrays phenomenality as an inconceivably magnificent and present sacredness, vibrant in and through every human perception, thought, and deed.

17

सर्वेन्द्रियगुणाभासं सर्वेन्द्रियविवर्जितम् ।
सर्वस्य प्रभुमीशानं सर्वस्य शरणं बृहत् ॥ १७ ॥

sarvendriyaguṇābhāsaṁ sarvendriyavivarjitam /
sarvasya prabhum īśānaṁ sarvasya śaraṇaṁ bṛhat //

17. Resplendent with the qualities of all the senses, from all the senses [it stands] removed—the power ruling over all, the great refuge of all.

The first half of this *mantra,* both here and as it reappears in the Bhagavadgītā (13.14), forms a single grammatical utterance with the preceeding verse. It continues to describe the Supreme Being that participates in its own creation, shining resplendently through the diversified qualities of the sensory faculties (*sarvendriyaguṇābhāsam*), even while standing removed from them (*sarvendriyavivarjitam*). How can that be? There are several ways to resolve the apparent contradiction, and each of the different philosophical systems has its own solution.

The passage first presents an image of the indwelling conscious Self experiencing the life of the universe through every faculty of perception and action, through every *jñānendriya* and *karmendriya* (see pp. 96–97). To some degree every living creature is a vehicle of that conscious Self, which is most fully manifest in human beings. Our human awareness enables us to know that every sensory impression is fleeting. Our life's experience consists of a steady stream of discrete, instantaneous impressions, configured as the surrounding realm of time and space. Through the medium of the senses, countless impressions flash before the inner organ of consciousness (*antaḥkaraṇa*), within which the cognitive, conative, and affective processes produce the sense of an individual experient and the world it experiences.

This stream of diversified and ever-changing awareness would not be possible without an underlying or all-pervading constant. And so Śvetāśvatara says that apart from the dazzling sensory array through which the created realm is revealed, there lies something utterly removed or "twisted off" (*vivarjitam*). That something is, of course, the supreme Self, who stands (*tiṣṭhati*) amid the panoramic play of the cosmos but, established in his own power, remains ever serene while witnessing it.

The divine Self, who is the ruling power over all (*sarvasya prabhum īśānam*), resides at the center of all experience. Ever blissful, he is the refuge of all beings (*sarvasya śaraṇaṁ bṛhat*). This portrayal of the Divine as the ultimate in strength, peace, and benevolence accords well with the ancient hymns to Rudra in the Ṛgveda, which extol him as the protective, compassionate lord of healing and well-being. At this point in the text some editions of the Upaniṣad replace "the great refuge of all" (*sarvasya śaraṇaṁ bṛhat*) with "the refuge and friend of all" (*sarvasya śaraṇaṁ suhṛt*),[122] an even more personal characterization of a kind-hearted God whose love is unconditional.

As already noted, the six lines forming *mantra* 3.16 and the first half of 3.17 reappear in the Bhagavadgītā (13.13–14). There they are followed by a philosophical elaboration not found in Śvetāśvatara's older discourse. The Gītā's extended passage is rich with typical Sāṁkhya terminology and philosophical concepts, but it also expresses some ideas that are decidedly Vedantic. Because the Gītā predates the fully developed classical *darśanas,* it cannot be expected to conform to any one of them entirely, and its teachings are open to interpretation. Regarding this very passage Abhinavagupta notes in his commentary, the *Gītārthasaṁgraha,* that the essential message of the Supreme Lord, Parameśvara, is the nondifference underlying all the particular types of knowledge defined by the various philosophical systems. The Śaiva philosopher then goes on to make the point that knowledge of nondifference is essential to knowing the nondual Brahman.[123]

From the standpoint of Advaita Vedānta, the interpretation of the passage in question, either as it occurs in the Śvetāśvataropaniṣad or in the Bhagavadgītā, takes the grammatical (and epistemological) subject (*tat*) to be *saguṇa* Brahman, endowed with innumerable hands, feet, eyes, heads, faces, and ears. These sensory and operative faculties (*indriyas*) are the mere adjuncts of name and form (*nāmarūpa*), a superimposition (*vivarta*) by the deluding power of *māyā* on the sole reality of the ultimately uninvolved *nirguṇa* Brahman.[124] In this way Advaita Vedānta resolves the apparent contradiction of a Supreme Being that is said to be both involved and removed by considering the manifest world, and therefore any involvement with it, as ultimately unreal.

In contrast the Trikaśāstra rejects the doctrine of superimposition (*vivartavāda*). The idea that something (the world-appearance) can be superimposed on something else (Brahman) by something that is ultimately not Brahman (*māyā*) retains traces of dualism. Accordingly to distinguish the monistic Trika position Abhinavagupta employed the term *parādvaita* or *paramādvaya* ("supreme nondualism").[125] This doctrine holds that the reality of the eternal Śiva does not exclude his own self-expression as the phenomenal universe. The Trika philosophy does not regard the world as an illusory superimposition (*vivarta*) lacking reality but as a phenomenal appearance (*ābhāsa*) within the singular reality of consciousness.

Whatever has its being in reality is not illusory. In the present *mantra* the phrase "resplendent with the qualities of all the senses" (*sarvendriyaguṇābhāsam*) marks the only instance of the word *ābhāsa* in the major Upaniṣads. This word means "splendor," "light," "color," or "appearance." Gauḍapāda's *Māṇḍūkyakārikā*, the oldest known text of Advaita Vedānta, employs *ābhāsa* to express that the unitary consciousness *appears* divided into subject and object (see p. 162). By the sixteenth century, in Sadānanda Yogīndra's *Vedāntasāra* [The quintessence of Vedānta], *ābhāsa* means a mere appearance or even a fallacious one.

This usage stands in sharp contrast to the Trikaśāstra's already well established use of the term to define its own theory of manifestation, called *ābhāsavāda,* as the doctrine of appearance-in-reality. Here *ābhāsa* retains the basic meanings of the verbal root *bhās,* from which it derives: "to shine," "to be bright," "to appear," "to occur to the mind," "to be conceived or imagined," "to become clear or evident."[126] As a technical term of the Trikaśāstra *ābhāsa* can mean any manifestation,[127] the projection of consciousness,[128] the phenomenality of sensory experience,[129] the reflection of thought external to the [individual] mind,[130] and even a "luminous display."[131] It suggests a positive world-view without the sense of illusion.[132]

Śvetāśvatara declares here that the One, which he began by calling Rudra (3.1), remains unchanged even in the midst of manifestation, and his view agrees with that of the later Śaiva nondualists. Conversely, whatever appears to exist actually and externally has its being potentially and eternally within divine consciousness. Śiva, through the creative power of his own free will (*svātantryaśakti*), can appear in any form he wishes, and whatever forms he conceives are already latent within him.[133] Blissful and playful by nature, Śiva accomplishes his divine play (*krīḍā* or *līlā*) without any outside influence, for there is nothing other than he.

Returning to Abhinavagupta's *Gītārthasaṁgraha,* we find that he concludes his commentary on the thirteenth chapter with a summary verse (*saṁgrahaśloka*) that resolves the apparent contradiction of the present passage from the Trika point of view: "This difference (*bhedaḥ*) between *puruṣa* and *prakṛti* [between the knowing subject and the manifest object] belongs to those of bewildered mind (*saṁmūḍhacetasām*), but those who are completely fulfilled (*paripūrṇāḥ*) [perfected in *yoga* and knowing their own wholeness] understand this world (*manyante ayaṁ jagat*) to be the taintless Self (*nirmalātmam*)." The knotty problem of a simultaneously transcendent and immanent reality lies not in the nature of God and the world but in the inadequacy of human understanding.

18

नवद्वारे पुरे देही हंसो लेलायते बहिः ।

वशी सर्वस्य लोकस्य स्थावरस्य चरस्य च ॥ १८ ॥

navadvāre pure dehī haṁso lelāyate bahiḥ /
vaśī sarvasya lokasya sthāvarasya carasya ca //

18. The spirit embodied in the city of nine gates moves outward, to and fro—the master of the whole world, of the immovable and the moving.

The previous *mantra* emphasized the serene detachment of the divine Person, without whose consciousness the cosmos could not function. Now the emphasis shifts to his active involvement in the universe through the vehicle of the human body.

As Śvetāśvatara has already said, the conscious principle works through the differentiated powers of the five senses in order to make the universe knowable. The one consciousness is the source and foundation of all its own modifications, such as sensory stimuli and the mind's processes and responses. Throughout the universe, the same consciousness presides also over everything material, whether it be immovable as a mountain and stationary as a tree or moving as a living creature.

The term *indriya* in the previous verse focuses on the sensory faculties (*jñānendriyas*), but now, when Śvetāśvatara says that the embodied spirit "moves outward, to and fro" (*lelāyate bahiḥ*), he clearly refers to the faculties of action (*karmendriyas*). Through these capacities of grasping, locomotion, speech, excretion, and reproduction, the *jīva* interacts physically with the material world, where the divine creative ideation has become "frozen" into form, into the immovable and moving forms that represent the utmost externalization or objectification of consciousness.

Although the Divine is present in everything, it is most clearly manifest in human form. The supreme Person becomes embodied (*dehī*) in "the city of nine gates" (*navadvāre*)—a common metaphor for the human body with its nine apertures, seven in the head and two below. The body, as the dwelling-place of the spirit (*haṁsa*), is its vehicle for the experience of the world.

As previously discussed, the term *haṁsa* in the Vedic tradition symbolizes either the individual soul or the universal spirit (see pp. 109–110). In the Trikadarśana *haṁsa* indicates also the energy of Śiva's creative and dissolving breaths.[134] Some texts identify the syllable *haṁ* as the in-breath (*apāna*) and *sa* as the out-breath (*prāṇa*);

others reverse the roles, so there is textual support for either characterization. If we take *haṁ* as the in-breath, it represents the contraction of consciousness into finitude. Paradoxically, this contraction is the emanation (*sṛṣṭi*) of the universe. It follows that *sa,* as the out-breath, represents the expansion of consciousness and the resorption (*saṁhāra*) of differentiation into pure unity. Accordingly, *haṁ* is Śakti, and *sa* is Śiva. If we assign the opposite functions to the two syllables, then *haṁ* as the out-breath symbolizes the expansion to infinite oneness (and the dissolution of the universe), while *sa* as the in-breath stands for the contraction of the infinite One into the finite many. Either way, when the relative world is experienced, the Absolute disappears; and when the Infinite is known, the finite world vanishes.[135]

Abhinavagupta's disciple Kṣemarāja writes in his commentary on the Svacchandatantra (7.29) that with the out-breath (*ha*) Śiva gives out the universe and with the in-breath (*sa*) he takes it back. Whatever happens on the cosmic scale happens also at the individual level. When the divine breath becomes minutely reduced as the individual's life-force (*prāṇa*), *haṁsa* is none other than the ever-luminous Śiva pulsating in the heart of living creatures.[136]

The Dhyānabindūpaniṣad (verses 60–61) agrees that *ha* is the exhalation and *sa* is the inhalation, and it observes that through the act of breathing one recites the *haṁsa mantra* continually.[137] The Vijñānabhairava (verse 155), an early Śaiva Tantra dating from around the seventh century CE, elaborates on this theme, but here, conversely, *ha* is the in-breath, representing Śakti, and *sa* is the out-breath, representing Śiva. *Ha* and *sa* are joined by the *anusvāra,* the nasalized *ṁ,* which stands for the soul (*jīva*). *Ha* plus *ṁ* plus *sa(ḥ)* form *haṁsaḥ,* also known as the Trika *mantra,* because it consists of three elements—divine power, the human soul, and God. A human being breathes in and out 21,600 times per day, all the while unknowingly repeating this *mantra* in a process of automatic recitation (*ajapājapa*). This *mantra, haṁsaḥ,* means "I am he [Śiva]"; with repetition it seems to become *so 'ham,* which means "He [the Absolute] am I."[138] Either way the meaning is the same. According to the Jñānārṇavatantra (10.6–7)—where *ha* represents Śiva, the imperishable, undifferentiated reality, and *sa* stands for Śakti, the cause of creation—the utterance of this *mantra,* the affirmation that "I am he," brings the *yogin* to Self-realization.[139]

19

अपाणिपादो जवनो ग्रहीता
पश्यत्यचक्षुः स शृणोत्यकर्णः ।
स वेत्ति वेद्यं न च तस्यास्ति वेत्ता
तमाहुरग्र्यं पुरुषं महान्तम् ॥ १९ ॥

apāṇipādo javano grahītā paśyaty acakṣuḥ sa śṛṇoty akarṇaḥ /
sa vetti vedyaṁ na ca tasyāsti vettā tam āhur agryaṁ puruṣaṁ mahāntam //

19. Grasping and moving swiftly though without hands and feet, he sees without eyes, he hears without ears. Whatever is to be known, he knows; yet of him there is no knower. They call him the foremost, the great Person.

Through his own divine play the supreme Self appears as all objects moving and unmoving and as all sentient beings. Yet even while immanent, he remains distinct from the creation, and the reason is simple: although the multiplicity of phenomena depends on division and limitation, the Self is indivisible and unlimited in every way. Being the source, essence, and support of all, the Divine cannot possibly be dependent on anything.[140] Although he is said to grasp, move, see, and hear, he does so without the need of hands, feet, eyes, or ears.

Śvetāśvatara's examples imply the entire range of motor and sensory capacities. The point is that the faculties of action (*karmendriyas*) and perception (*jñānendriyas*) are finite and dependent on difference. Grasping involves one who grasps, the act of grasping, and the object grasped. Locomotion involves an entity that moves and the act of moving from one place to another. Speech, elimination, and procreation similarly involve an agent, an action, and something acted upon. In the same way, the sensory organs function because of the differentiation of subject and object and a particular process that relates them. Wherever actions are performed or sensations perceived, there is difference, division, and relation. Empirical experience is finite and relative, but the source of such experience—consciousness itself—remains undivided and absolute.

"Whatever is to be known, he knows; yet of him there is no knower." Beyond our limited, individual experience, the indwelling Self, through every being, experiences all. Still, we wonder why the knower cannot be known. There are several reasons. Because the Self is limitless, it cannot be described. Why not? Because to describe is to limit. The Self cannot be known, because it is not an object. The Kenopaniṣad (2.3) teaches that whoever thinks he has known Brahman (as an object of perception) has not known Brahman. Yet this same Self is the limitless consciousness that makes all the limited, or relative, forms of knowledge possible.[141] The Self knows everything because it is knowledge itself—the supreme knowledge in which knower, knowing, and known have all merged into oneness. In the transcendental unity of consciousness, who is there to know whom? According to Śaṁkara's commentary on the Kenopaniṣad, Self-knowledge is not knowledge in the ordinary, relative sense but absolute knowledge; it is direct, intuitive realization (*saṁyagdarśanam*).[142]

The Infinite embraces the finite, but the finite can never comprehend the Infinite. In the Bṛhadāraṇyakopaniṣad's scene of the great debate at King Janaka's court, after a long exposition concerning the seer who is never seen, the perceiver who is never perceived, the thinker who is never thought of, Yājñavalkya concludes that there is no other than that: "This is your Self, the inner controller, the immortal" (*eṣa ta ātmāntaryāmy amṛtaḥ*) (3.7.2). Śaṁkara, commenting on this passage, observes that Brahman is like a thread on which all creatures are strung like flowers in a garland.[143]

Śvetāśvatara concludes by calling the universal spirit (*puruṣam*) foremost (*agryam*) because it is the primordial, first cause;[144] he calls it great (*mahāntam*) because it is not limited, as its creations are.

20

अणोरणीयान् महतो महीया-

नात्मा गुहायां निहितोऽस्य जन्तोः ।

तमक्रतुं पश्यति वीतशोको
धातुः प्रसादान्महिमानमीशम् ॥ २० ॥

aṇor aṇīyān mahato mahīyān ātmā guhāyāṁ nihito 'sya jantoḥ /
tam akratuṁ paśyati vītaśoko dhātuḥ prasādān mahimānam īśam //

20. Smaller than small, greater than great, the Self is established in the heart of every creature. Beholding him who is untouched by desire, one becomes free of sorrow; by the creator's grace he beholds the glory that is the Lord.

The Self (*ātmā*), who is the innermost essence of every created being (*jantoḥ*), is smaller than an atom and greater than the entire expanse of the universe. These examples from either end of the spectrum are a way of saying that the *ātman* both pervades and encompasses all. The supreme Self transcends every possible boundary. Being established or fixed (*nihitaḥ*) in the heart of every living creature (*guhāyām asya jantoḥ*) does not limit him but signals that he is the essence of all that exists.

As the creator and support of everything, the supreme Self is also conceived of here as the all-powerful God. With that in mind Śvetāśvatara says that by the creator's grace (*dhātuḥ prasādāt*) the illumined soul beholds the great and majestic glory (*mahimānam*) that is the Lord (*īśam*). In the fullness of his own glory the Lord is free of desire (*akratum*), and the one who knows him becomes likewise untroubled (*vītaśokaḥ*). The correspondence is clear: the Muṇḍakopaniṣad (3.2.9) explains that "whoever knows the supreme Brahman becomes Brahman."

The present *mantra* is a variant of a verse from the Kaṭhopaniṣad (1.2.20), and Śvetāśvatara's altered version is in turn quoted later in the Mahānārāyaṇopaniṣad (12.1), a late addition to the Taittirīyāraṇyaka. Comparison of the original and emended versions will reveal a great deal about the theological convictions that led Śvetāśvatara to make the changes. On the surface they may appear minor, but their implications are great.

In the Kaṭhopaniṣad the text runs as follows: *aṇor aṇīyān mahato mahīyān ātmāsya jantor nihito guhāyām / tam* **akratuḥ** *paśyati vītaśoko*

dhātuprasādān *mahimānam* **ātmanaḥ**. Svetāśvatara changes this to: *aṇor aṇīyān mahato mahīyān ātmā guhāyāṁ nihito 'sya jantoḥ / tam* **akratuṁ** *paśyati vītaśoko* **dhātuḥ prasādān** *mahimānam* **īśam**. The differences in the verse's second quarter (*ātmāsya jantor nihito guhāyām* versus *ātmā guhāyāṁ nihito 'sya jantoḥ*) concern only a change in word order; the meaning is exactly the same. The variants in bold-face type signal a difference in philosophical outlook.

The translation of the Kaṭhopaniṣad's version reads: "Smaller than small, greater than great, the Self is established in the heart of every creature; one who is untouched by desire (*akratuḥ*) and free of sorrow, through the tranquility of the senses (*dhātuprasādāt*), beholds the glory of the Self (*ātmanaḥ*)."

The meaning of this verse conforms to the Kaṭhopaniṣad's emphasis on yogic practice. Here Yama, instructing the boy Naciketas, says that Self-knowledge has two preconditions. First the *aspirant* must be untouched by desire (*akratuḥ*). *Akratu,* often translated as "desireless," means a great deal more; it signifies a state of consciousness over which desire has no hold whatsoever, an imperturbable state over which desire is completely powerless to exert its influence. Second, in the absence of desire, the aspirant's mind becomes untroubled (*vītaśokaḥ*)—devoid of any sort of affliction, sorrow, or grief. Thus, through the stilling of the mental processes (*dhātuprasādāt*)—which Patañjali's *Yogasūtra* calls *cittavṛttinirodhaḥ*—the one whose awareness can no longer be disturbed sees (*paśyati*) the supreme glory of the Self (*mahimānam ātmanaḥ*).

Why does Śvetāśvatara change this verse? He certainly is not averse to *yoga.* In fact, his second discourse goes beyond the Kaṭhopaniṣad in its detailing of yogic practice (see pp. 187–188). The answer lies in his choice here to emphasize the Śaiva idea of the Divine. In Yama's instruction the adjective *akratuḥ* is in the nominative case and refers to the aspiring *yogin.* It is the human being who must become untouched by desire. Śvetāśvatara's *akratum,* in the accusative, modifies him (*tam*), the Lord (*īśam*) who is untouched by desire because he abides in the fullness of his own perfection. His glory does not derive from any qualities or attributes but is his own absolute nature.[145] That explains why Śvetāśvatara says "the glory that is the Lord" and not "the glory of the Lord." In the Śaiva view Parameśvara is his own glory, for consciousness and its power are identical. Unlike Śvetāśvatara's restatement, suggestive of the Trikaśāstra's later theological absolutism (*īśvarādvaya-vāda*), the Kaṭhopaniṣad's older version merely reads "the glory of the Self" (*mahimānam ātmanaḥ*). Of course, that glory of the *ātman* is nothing but the *yogin's* own divine nature, "seen" in direct, nondual experience.[146] Although the two Upaniṣads may appear to differ, the ultimate goal they describe is one and the same.

Along with the idea that Rudra is at once the supreme reality (Brahman), the supreme Self (*paramātman*), and the supreme Lord (Parameśvara), Śvetāśvatara introduces the idea of divine grace. He does so by a very subtle alteration to the Kaṭhopaniṣad's text. He changes the original *dhātuprasādāt*, a grammatical compound of *dhātu* and *prasād* to *dhātuḥ prasādāt*. *Dhātu* in the compound means "senses" or "mental operations," and *prasād* can be taken in the sense of "tranquility" or "clarity." The *yogin* attains Self-realization through the stilling of the mind. In Śvetāśvatara's version *dhātuḥ* is the genitive of *dhātṛ* ("creator"), and *prasād* means "grace." "By the creator's grace" (*dhatuḥ prasādāt*) imparts a theistic flavor absent from the original. In view of the seer's previous indulgence in wordplay (see pp. 99, 121, 169), the cleverness of his emendations once again confirms a lively spirit eager to express a particular point of view in an engaging way. Where the Kaṭhopaniṣad emphasizes the need for management of the mind, Śvetāśvatara's reworking brings out the idea of God's grace or self-revelation.

Throughout his teaching the seer has emphasized the liberating role of knowledge, and we might think that this knowledge comes through our own efforts. But now he says that God is the cause of liberation. Is he contradicting what he said earlier, or is it we who fail to understand him fully?

The question of self-effort versus grace runs like a persistent thread through the fabric of Indian religious thinking. Some doctrines, especially those emphasizing knowledge (*jñāna*), opt for self-effort. Such a view predominates in religions of the ancient *śramaṇa* tradition. The word *śramaṇa* ("making an effort") denotes the ascetic who does so, and religions such as Jainism and Buddhism leave the task of enlightenment to the aspirant. Within the Vedic and Tantric folds of Hinduism, sects such as the Vaiṣṇava and Śaiva accept the role of grace as well,[147] especially when the emphasis is on religious devotion (*bhakti*). The nondualistic Trikaśāstra reconciles the two positions simply and elegantly. Grace, or self-revelation (*anugraha*), is as natural a divine function as are self-concealment (*nigraha*) and the manifestation (*sṛṣṭi*), sustenance (*sthiti*), and dissolution (*saṁhāra*) of this universe. Śiva's grace (*anugraha*) is spontaneous, ever present, and unconditional. But just as a covered vessel cannot accumulate any rainwater, the individual *jīva,* covered by impervious layers of ignorance, does not permit the light of divine consciousness to shine through. The rain falls equally on every vessel, but only those that are uncovered have the capacity to receive it. In the same way divine grace showers equally on all, but only those who open themselves to it through self-purification—through spiritual practice, devotion, or self-surrender—receive it. In accord with this view, Śvetāśvatara's teaching, taken as a whole, reveals that liberation involves more than our own efforts, because without the constant presence of grace, those efforts would come to nought. The intensity of the grace may be commensurate with the amount of effort, but grace and self-effort most definitely work hand in hand.[148]

Finally, this *mantra* reminds us that the single reality that we refer to as God, Brahman, or *ātman* can be thought of in all those ways. The main point of this discourse is that the impersonal reality and the personal God, transcendent and immanent, are not different entities, but two aspects of the One.[149] The difference in terminology arises from different degrees of experience. Thus we give the unnamable various names. It is God from the theological point of view, Brahman from the philosophical, and *ātman* from the experiential. If the relationship of these terms is still hard to grasp, it can be clarified in the following Vedantic summation: "God is personalized Brahman. God's Self and my Self [*ātman*] are the same."[150]

21

वेदाहमेतमजरं पुराणं सर्वा-
त्मानं सर्वगतं विभुत्वात् ।
जन्मनिरोधं प्रवदन्ति यस्य
ब्रह्मवादिनो हि प्रवदन्ति नित्यम् ॥ २१ ॥

vedāham etam ajaraṁ purāṇaṁ sarvātmānaṁ sarvagataṁ vibhutvāt /
janmanirodhaṁ pravadanti yasya brahmavādino hi pravadanti nityam //

21. I know this ageless, primordial Self of all, diffused everywhere by its power of all-pervasiveness, whom the expounders of Brahman declare birthless, whom they indeed declare eternal.

Like *mantra* 3.8, which it resembles, the concluding verse of the third discourse gives voice to the direct experience of the divine reality. This ecstatic glimpse into the nature of our own true being proclaims that the Self is primordial (*purāṇam*), exempt from birth (*janmanirodham*), and ageless (*ajaram*). Unborn and never growing old, it is not subject to change; not subject to change, it is imperishable and eternal (*nityam*). Before and apart from any beginning of time and space, the supreme Self has never not been and never will not be. Although all phenomenal existence proceeds from it, it remains ever in its own perfection.

"This Self of all (*etaṁ sarvātmānam*)" is the nearest of the near. Everywhere present (*sarvagatam*) by reason of its all-pervasiveness, omnipresence, omniscience, and sovereignty (all meanings of *vibhutvāt*), it lies hidden in every human heart. Every human being has the potential for Self-knowledge, which is the realization of its own divinity. This is the supreme knowledge (*parāvidyā*) that has been proclaimed by the illumined preceptors of past and present generations (*brahmavādinaḥ*).[151] The one who hears this revelation is not to accept it on faith but to verify its truth through experience.

चतुर्थोऽध्यायः

CHAPTER FOUR

1

य एकोऽवर्णो बहुधा शक्तियोगाद्
वर्णाननेकान् निहितार्थो दधाति ।
वि चैति चान्ते विश्वमादौ स देवः
स नो बुद्ध्या शुभया संयुनक्तु ॥ १ ॥

ya eko 'varṇo bahudhā śaktiyogād varṇān anekān nihitārtho dadhāti /
vi caiti cānte viśvam ādau sa devaḥ sa no buddhyā śubhayā saṁyunaktu //

1. He who is One and without color brings forth many colors in many ways by his own power and by his own design: in the end the universe comes apart—and in the beginning the effulgent God. May he endow us with clear understanding!

The six chapters of this Upaniṣad are separate discourses in which the *ṛṣi* Śvetāśvatara imparts his insights on a variety of topics. The first lesson begins with the perennial questions of human existence and teaches that the answers are revealed in deepest contemplation. We need only know the supreme reality, the divine Self that lies hidden by its own effects. Consequently the second lesson turns to the practical means for revealing this divine Self. The third lesson examines its nature and concludes that the transcendent Brahman and the immanent God ruling over all creation are a single and singular reality which is also the innermost consciousness of every being. Whoever knows that becomes liberated and immortal.

The fourth discourse takes as its point of departure a *mantra* of the previous chapter (3.15), which is in turn a quotation of the second verse of the Ṛgveda's Puruṣasūkta (10.90.2): "What has been and what will be and what grows up by food, the Person is truly all this—and the lord of immortality as well." That, in essence, is the outline of Śvetāśvatara's fourth discourse. The divine reality is also the world around us. Roughly the chapter's first half (4.1–10) centers on divinity manifest as the multicolored world of natural forces, human beings, animals, birds, weather, and vegetation. The whole panorama of nature is nothing other than Rudra's own self-expression. The chapter's second half (4.11–22) reminds us that as dazzling as the temporal creation may appear, the infinite, eternal source from which it springs is immeasurably more glorious.

Śvetāśvatara starts by saying that the One (*ekaḥ*), who is colorless (*avarṇaḥ*), brings forth many colors (*varṇān anekān*) in many ways (*bahudhā*). In the beginning (*ādau*) the One creates the incalculable diversity of the surrounding world and all the wonders of the vast heavens that lie beyond this earth. He accomplishes this through the exercise of his own power (*śaktiyogāt*) and by his own design (*nihitārthaḥ*). Then, at the end the universe all comes apart (*vi caiti cānte viśvam*).

God purposefully brings forth the universe, and then it all comes apart? That is how it appears to us. If we watch a seed sprout and eventually grow into a mature plant, we see the process of creation unfold steadily in a predictable, purposeful way. Everything happens as it should, and we find that reassuring. On the other hand, destruction, dissolution, or death can come suddenly and unexpectedly. The finality is disquieting, and it can sow the seeds of futility and meaninglessness in our minds.

Is Śvetāśvatara's matter-of-factness calculated to disquiet? Perhaps, or perhaps not. We know from history that provocation is not foreign to the Śaiva tradition; it can be an effective way of getting an idea across. If God creates the universe, it follows that he also brings it to an end, but why didn't Śvetāśvatara say that? Having seized our attention, he invites us to look deeper into what he is trying to tell us.

There can be no doubt that this *mantra* is highly problematic. Max Müller observed that the third quarter "does not construe" grammatically and found the corruption unaccountable. He pointed out a parallel passage in *mantra* 4.11 and based his translation on it.[1] Later scholars have suggested emendations to correct the faulty syntax and to clarify the meaning,[2] but is that really necessary? Perhaps the solution has been elusive in its startling simplicity. Paradoxically, it will take a technical analysis to reveal it, but this detailed inquiry will pay handsome dividends.

Together with a number of other verses of this Upaniṣad that are not identified as quotations from older sources (for example, 1.9, 1.10, 1.12, 2.7, 2.14, 3.21, 4.11 6.17), this one displays features of the archaic Vedic language that predate the usage of classical Sanskrit established by Pāṇini around the fourth century BCE. This stylistic evidence suggests that the Śvetāśvataropaniṣad dates from around the sixth or fifth century BCE. Being able to place it in a historical context helps to clarify the intended meaning of enigmatic passages such as the verse at hand.

On the whole, the first half of the *mantra* is straightforward enough. God is One (*ekaḥ*). The unity of the Supreme Being has been stressed many times throughout this and other Upaniṣads. What does it mean to say that God is colorless (*avarṇaḥ*)? Here color means differentiation. Colorlessness implies something that is undifferentiated and without qualities (*nirguṇa*). A common Śaiva simile compares the Absolute to the fluid of a peahen's egg. Before fertilization it is clear and colorless; yet from that unconditioned unity the multicolored peacock takes form. So it is with Paramaśiva, in whom all the dazzling variety of the creation lies latent.

The idea of color more specifically refers to the *guṇas*, the three differentiated energies of divine power that Śvetāśvatara will discuss in *mantra* 4.5. Each of these energies is conventionally identified with a color—*tamas* with black, *rajas* with red, and *sattva* with white. The world of our experience is composed of the energies of the *guṇas*, combined and recombined in patterns of ever-increasing complexity to create everything from the subtlety of thought to the denseness of a stone. So, Śvetāśvatara says that at the beginning of a cycle of manifestation, God, by his own design (*nihitārthaḥ*), produces the full spectrum of colors (*varṇān anekān*) in manifold ways (*bahudhā*) through the application of his own power (*śaktiyogāt*).

The difficulty comes in the third quarter (*pāda*) of the verse. It displays an archaic feature known as tmesis, the separation of the verbal prefix (in this case *vi*) from the verb proper (*eti*). As we shall see, this single verb holds the key not only to the entire verse but to Śvetāśvatara's entire world-view. The text reads *vi caiti cānte viśvam ādau sa devaḥ*. A literal translation is "in the end the universe comes apart—and in the beginning the effulgent God." Something seems to be missing. As already mentioned, Max Müller noted the similarity to the second quarter of *mantra* 4.11, which qualifies the One (*ekaḥ*) as he "in whom all this world comes together and dissolves" (*yasminn idaṁ saṁ ca vi caiti sarvam*). He used that to clarify the present *mantra*.

In the same spirit a later scholar has suggested emending the third *pāda* to read *vi cānta eti viśvam ādau saṁ caiva*.[3] This spells out that there are two functions: in the end the universe comes apart—*vi eti*—and in the beginning it comes together—*sam* [*eti*]. The verbs *vi eti* and *sam eti* are intransitive: it is the universe that comes apart at the end and comes together at the beginning. But that creates a problem of what to do with the leftover *sa devaḥ*. Grammatically the nominative *sa devaḥ* cannot be accommodated; God in the nominative case plays no role in this passage. What to do with him? The translator who accepts this emendation simply leaves him out.[4]

Two pioneering translators, Max Müller and Paul Deussen, consider *sa devaḥ* as beginning the fourth quarter,[5] even though that disturbs the metrical scheme and in the original Sanskrit seems unnaturally emphatic. The most common solution is to regard *sa devaḥ* as the grammatical subject of the entire *mantra*,[6] but that leaves the rest of the third quarter in a muddle. It seems that any solution for one part of the verse creates a new problem somewhere else. The grammatical ins and outs are enough to fill many paragraphs and are as fascinating as they are technically complex, but the point is not what is wrong with any given translation. The point is what Śvetāśvatara intends to convey—and if he succeeds.

As logical and meritorious as the argument may be that the third *pāda* implies that the universe comes together (*sam eti*) along with stating outright that it comes apart (*vi eti*), the place of *sa devaḥ* remains an insoluble problem if it is related grammatically to the fourth *pāda* or to the verse as a whole. In fact, *sa devaḥ* is an integral part of the third *pāda,* and any other "solution" misses the point.

The third *pāda* is exactly as it should be. The construction is elliptical, but not in the way one might think. There are two grammatical subjects here—the universe (*viśvam*) and the effulgent God (*sa devaḥ*)—and one intransitive verb (*vi eti*) that does double duty for both. Śvetāśvatara's economy rests on the fact that this verb expresses *two opposite actions,* or *a single action considered from two points of view.* Given his propensity for linguistic playfulness, it seems that the seer is trying to express, in a startlingly memorable way, something very profound and elusively simple.

To repeat, the text reads *vi caiti cānte viśvam ādau sa devaḥ*—"in the end the universe comes apart—and in the beginning the effulgent God." Recast in classical Sanskrit, without ellipsis, the passage would read *viśvam ante vyeti ca sa deva ādau vyeti ca*—"in the end the universe comes apart, and in the beginning God comes apart." Now it is an even more perplexing and provocative statement, to be sure, and to make sense of it requires an understanding of what the verb *vyeti* really means. In early texts such as the Ṛgveda, it can mean "goes apart," "goes in different directions," "diverges," "is diffused, scattered, distributed, divided, extended." In the Upaniṣads and the Mahābhārata it can also mean "perishes," "disappears," or "is lost."[7] In the end (*ante*) everything (*viśvam*) comes apart; the universe dissolves and disappears (*vi eti*). In the beginning (*ādau*) that effulgent God (*sa devaḥ*) comes apart; the divine oneness becomes divided and extended (*vi eti*). *He expands into diversity.* At the end of a cosmic cycle the phenomenal universe, with all its intricate diversity and all its artful order, comes apart. At the beginning of the cycle, it is the unity of the Absolute that comes apart. The supreme, nondual consciousness diverges into the modes of subjectivity (*ahaṁtā*) and objectivity (*idaṁtā*) and thus initiates the process of cosmic manifestation. God "comes apart" in the sense that the original unity becomes hidden—as Śvetāśvatara expressed it earlier (1.3), "hidden by its own effects."

The verb *vi eti* is expressed not twice but only once in this *pāda* for a very good reason. It speaks of one process, experienced from two perspectives, the human and the divine. One other point is noteworthy. Normally one would expect to hear of the beginning and the end in that order, but the text reverses them, putting the end first and then the beginning. This reversal of logical order has a definite purpose. The cycle of creation and dissolution is ongoing: every end is followed by a new beginning.

Emanation and withdrawal constitute two phases of a single process, and this process takes place within the sole reality of divine consciousness. What Śvetāśvatara intimates here in seminal form grew into the later teaching known to Kashmir's nondualist Śaivas as Spandaśāstra, especially in its early state of development. *Spanda* is the pulsation of consciousness, the universal rhythm infusing the ebb and flow of all perception, thought, feeling, and action.[8] It is not movement in the sense of physical motion in space but a shift of modality within consciousness itself, two phases of a pulsation from nondifferentiation (*abheda*) to differentiation (*bheda*), from uncreated and purely subjective *being* to the created and objectified condition of *becoming*. The two phases are called *unmeṣa* and *nimeṣa*. With *unmeṣa* ("opening the eyes") Śiva manifests the phenomenal universe; with *nimeṣa* ("closing the eyes") he withdraws it. The two pulses are also called *vikāsa* ("expansion") and *saṁkoca* ("contraction").

In the *Spandanirṇaya*, a commentary on the *Spandakārikā*, Kṣemarāja makes a startling observation rather in the spirit of Śvetāśvatara's. He writes that the contraction or withdrawal (*nimeṣa*) of previously expressed diversity is simultaneously the expansion (*unmeṣa*) of consciousness into its essential unity; conversely the expansion (*unmeṣa*) into diversity is also a contraction (*nimeṣa*) of the infinite, unitary consciousness into finitude.[9]

Simply put, the contraction of the universe is the expansion of consciousness, and the expansion of the universe is the contraction of consciousness—that sums up Śvetāśvatara's laconic statement (*vi caiti cānte viśvam ādau sa devaḥ*) and its deep-reaching implication. *Spanda* is the life-pulse of consciousness, so it follows that being and becoming are inseparably cooperative. Being is itself perpetually becoming (*satatodita*),[10] and becoming cannot exist apart from being. As Śvetāśvatara's poetic fourth discourse will teach us, God is in the creation and the creation is in God. God *is* the creation, and the creation *is* God.

One additional problem remains, and that is the translation of a term in the *mantra's* second quarter. Depending on the translation, the term has two diametrically opposed meanings. The grammatical compound *nihitārthaḥ*, modifying the One (*ekaḥ*), has to do with how

God exercises his own power. It is translated here as "by his own design," but that is at odds with the majority view and calls for an explanation. The second element of the compound (*arthaḥ*) means "whose purpose is," and the first element (*nihita*) qualifies it. The confusion arises over the meaning of *nihita.* Ordinarily the word is rendered as "hidden,"[11] "inscrutable,"[12] "unknown,"[13] or "incomprehensible."[14] Alternatively it is translated as "set"[15] or "definite."[16]

Among the translators who follow the first alternative, one (a rigorous Vedāntin who here curiously adopts a Śaiva mode of expression) writes that the divine purpose is beyond human comprehension, being absolutely spontaneous, voluntary, and free from any external compulsion.[17] Another translator explains similarly that the divine purpose, remaining unknown, is therefore independent.[18] Yet another characterizes it as motiveless and lacking in personal interest,[19] and a fourth finds the divine intention purposeless, because purpose would imply an imperfection in the perfect Brahman; therefore the universe is nothing but divine play (*līlā*) devoid of any real purpose.[20]

On the other hand, Müller opts for the reading "with set purpose,"[21] and Deussen proposes "with a definite aim."[22] In their support, Monier-Williams's dictionary shows no connection between the participle *nihita* and the idea of hiddenness or inscrutability. Rather, *nihita* means "laid," "placed," "fixed," and sometimes "resolved" or "determined."[23]

Why should a word be ascribed a meaning it does not have, particularly one that implies the opposite? To make sense of this perplexing verse, Müller relies on the *Śvetāśvataropaniṣadvṛtti,* noting that this commentary explains the meanimg of *nihitārthaḥ* as "with set purpose" (*gṛhītaprayoganaḥ svārthanirapekṣaḥ*). He then observes that some Vedāntins read *gṛhītaprayoganaḥ* as *agṛhītaprayoganaḥ,* taking it as "without any definite object." That, he says, conforms to the philosophical position of a world-appearance superimposed by *māyā* rather than one self-generated by *devātmaśakti.*[24]

Advaita Vedānta holds that the world is not the creation of Brahman, for Brahman is eternally inactive. The world is the result of Brahman's infinite perfection being hidden from our awareness by the inscrutable power of *māyā.* In contrast, nondualistic Śaivism teaches that Śiva—absolute consciousness—by the power of his own will (*icchāśakti*) forms an intention to manifest. By the power of his own knowledge (*jñānaśakti*)—that is, by his own design, a design that rests in complete freedom (*svātantrya*)—he ideates what the manifestation will be like. Then by his capacity to act (*kriyāśakti*)—that is, by the exercise of his own power (*śaktiyogāt*)—he sets the process in motion. Whereas Advaita Vedānta sees the universe as a mere appearance (*vivarta*) and a superimposition (*adhyāsa*) on the changeless reality of Brahman, the Trikaśāstra regards the world as an active process of self-expression arising out of Śiva's own absolute freedom. Where Advaita Vedānta sees the world as blanketed in unknowing, Trika Śaivism sees divine will, intelligence, and power shining through everything.

Finally, after intimating so much about the generation and dissolution of the universe by a purposeful God, Śvetāśvatara prays, "May he endow us with clear understanding!" Clear understanding alone removes the uncertainty, doubt, and fear attendant on our worldly existence and allows us to see the world as an ever-changing expression of divinity. With clear understanding we recognize also who *we* truly are, for absolute clarity of consciousness is the pure awareness that is Self-knowledge.

2

तदेवाग्निस्तदादित्यस्तद्वायुस्तदु चन्द्रमाः ।
तदेव शुक्रं तद् ब्रह्म तदापस्तत् प्रजापतिः ॥ २ ॥

tad evāgnis tad ādityas tad vāyus tad u candramāḥ /
tad eva śukraṁ tad brahma tad āpas tat prajāpatiḥ //

2. That indeed is Agni, that is Āditya, that is Vāyu, that is also Candramās; that is indeed the brightness, that is Brahman, that is the Āpaḥ, that is Prajāpati.

The last quarter of the preceding *mantra*—"May he [the effulgent God] endow us with clear understanding!"—is an obvious allusion to the closing words of the Ṛgveda's Gāyatrī *mantra,* (3.62.10), "May that [divine effulgence] inspire our thoughts." Now Śvetāśvatara quotes a verse from the Vājasaneyisaṁhitā (32.1) that gives voice to the older Vedic vision of divinity spread out before us as the sweeping vista of the natural world (see p. 34). Coming on the heels of his powerful opening statement of God's motivation and creative capacity, this verse celebrates the Supreme Being personified as the forces of nature. Although humans conceive of him in many different ways, calling him Mitra, Indra, Varuṇa, Agni, or any other name, the Ṛgveda proclaims that "truth is One; the wise call it variously" (*ekaṁ sad viprā bahudhā vadanti*) (1.164.46). Divine manifestations are to be understood philosophically as particularized self-expressions of a single, indefinable principle. The *mantra* from the Vājasaneyisaṁhitā repeatedly refers to this principle as *it* (*tat*), a shift in gender from the masculine *he* of the previous *mantra,* referring to *sa devaḥ*. This fluidity of gender reflects the all-inclusive yet incomprehensible nature of the Divine, which no pronoun—neither *he, she, it,* nor any other—can adequately represent.

The Vedic deities are not separate entities at all but are more like rays of light emanating from the sun of infinite consciousness. The idea of light is prominent among those named here. Agni (fire), Āditya (the sun), Candramās (the moon), and *śukram* ("brightness," "clarity") all represent some form of light. Light radiates, and with the idea of radiation come the related ideas of emanation, expansion, and all-pervasiveness. Vāyu (wind) suggests omnipresence. Brahman, in its original sense, means "growth" or "expansion." Āpaḥ, the waters, are the primordial womb, and Prajāpati, the Lord of Creatures, is the divine progenitor personified. Śvetāśvatara quotes this ancient *mantra* to support what he said immediately before. God, although One and only One, manifests in many ways and brings into existence all the glories of the perceivable universe.

3

त्वं स्त्री त्वं पुमानसि त्वं कुमार उत वा कुमारी ।
त्वं जीर्णो दण्डेन वञ्चसि
त्वं जातो भवसि विश्वतोमुखः ॥ ३ ॥

tvaṁ strī tvaṁ pumān asi tvaṁ kumāra uta vā kumārī /
tvaṁ jīrṇo daṇḍena vañcasi tvaṁ jāto bhavasi viśvatomukhaḥ //

3. You are woman, you are man, you are youth and maiden too; aged, you totter along with a staff; taking birth, you face in every direction.

Divinity manifests not only as natural forces but also as every human being. Here we are tempted just to enjoy the beauty of the word-pictures, to savor the joyous wonder that prompted an earlier seer to utter them. The words come from the Atharvaveda (10.8.27), and as Śvetāśvatara recites them here, their few carefully chosen images conjure up the scope of human existence and then tell us that it is God himself who lives through all human life. In the rhapsodic outpouring that follows next, Śvetāśvatara's own words celebrate the divine presence in other living creatures.

4

नीलः पतङ्गो हरितो लोहिताक्ष-
स्तडिद्गर्भ ऋतवः समुद्राः ।
अनादिमत्त्वं विभुत्वेन वर्तसे
यतो जातानि भुवनानि विश्वा ॥ ४ ॥

nīlaḥ pataṅgo harito lohitākṣas taḍidgarbha ṛtavaḥ samudrāḥ /
anādimat tvaṁ vibhutvena vartase yato jātāni bhuvanāni viśvā //

4. You are the dark blue butterfly, the green parrot with red eyes, the thundercloud, the seasons, and the seas. Without beginning you simply *are*, pervading all, you from whom all worlds are born.

From the One who is without color (*avarṇa*) comes an explosion of color. The seer, overwhelmed by nature's beauty, transports us into the deep forest, where the jewel-like blue butterfly silently floats on the breeze and the red-eyed parrot sits perched amid the profusion of greenery. We sense the gray-black darkness of the storm cloud overhead, literally pregnant with golden flashes of lightning (*taḍidgarbhaḥ*), and know that the rain it releases will soon cool the earth. We contemplate the passing seasons, each painting the landscape at the appointed time with its own distinctive colors—the tender green of spring, the deeper shades of summer, the gold of the harvest, and the somber hues of the fallow months. We behold the vastness of the open sea; we feel its bracing winds and sense the power of its tides. Throughout the changing moods we acknowledge nature's constant grandeur. All this beauty reminds us at every turn of the immeasurably greater something from which all this comes forth—the supreme, self-existent One.

Still, the world is bound to elicit many different responses from those who experience it. Along with the exultation of the poet-seers whose insights are embodied in the Upaniṣads comes the questioning of the philosophers, who generally speak not from intuitive experience but from reasoning over the experiences of others. Although the focus of their philosophies is the higher, unmediated knowledge (*parāvidyā*), the philosophies themselves belong to the realm of the lower, mediate knowledge (*aparāvidyā*). So it is that the many systems of thought that claim the authority of the Upaniṣads to support their widely differing views sometimes draw contradictory conclusions from the same texts. Simply put, the ultimate truth can be experienced but not explained, and even the most brilliant attempts fall short.

The Sanskrit term for any philosophical thesis, proposition, or doctrine is *vāda* ("speaking about"). A doctrine is a systematic teaching based on carefully thought out principles, held to be correct by its advocates. That said, any doctrine should be held as a matter of opinion and not as a statement of absolute truth. The many *vādas* are simply diverse approaches to something that lies beyond all definition.

The topic announced at the outset of this chapter is the emanation of phenomenality out of unconditioned consciousness or, as Śvetāśvatara puts it, God appearing as the universe. So far the seer has informed us that God (*sa devaḥ*), who is One (*ekaḥ*) and purposeful (*nihitārthaḥ*), has brought forth this universe of dazzling color out of his own undifferentiated colorlessness. In the end it all dissolves, and in every new beginning it comes together again. The two philosophical traditions commonly invoked in the study of this Upaniṣad are the Sāṁkhya and more often the Advaita Vedānta. How do their positions on the questions of cosmic origination, causality, and the reality or unreality of the world compare to Śvetāśvatara's poetic vision?

The Sāṁkhya was still in a formative stage when Śvetāśvatara lived and taught. Its philosophical positions were still in flux and would not reach definitive form until eight to ten centuries later in Īśvarakṛṣṇa's *Sāṁkhyakārikā*. The classical Sāṁkhya portrayed there is a nontheistic philosophy, holding that there is no God and therefore no divine purpose. The manifestation of the universe comes about through an unexplainable proximity of two eternally antithetical realities—one insensate, material, and singular (*prakṛti*), the other conscious, spiritual, and plural (*puruṣa*). Although sparked by the proximity of the conscious but inactive *puruṣa*, cosmic evolution proceeds from the unconscious but active *prakṛti*. It is the involvement of consciousness with matter that accounts for phenomenal existence, defined in the opening verse of the *Sāṁkhyakārikā* as suffering (*duḥkha*). The goal of human life is to disentangle, or to liberate, consciousness from matter and to regain knowledge of one's true, original being.

This is a far cry from Śvetāśvatara's celebration of the wonders of a universe that comes together and then comes apart through the intention of a self-luminous God. When Śvetāśvatara celebrates God—the supreme reality—as sun and moon, woman and man, youth and maiden, butterfly and parrot, raincloud and lightning, passing seasons, and surging seas, his meaning is fairly obvious. It is God that has become this universe.

This world-view is dramatically unlike the Sāṁkhya's in several respects and significantly different from Advaita Vedānta's as well. There is nothing in this Upaniṣad to suggest that Śvetāśvatara regards the world as anything other than a divine manifestation. It follows that whatever emanates from the divine reality partakes of that reality. That is the same view set forth in the Bṛhadāraṇyakopaniṣad (2.3.1–2), where Brahman is said to have just two aspects (*dve vāva brahmaṇo rūpe*). One is formed (*mūrtam*) and mortal (*martyam*); the other is unformed (*amūrtam*) and immortal (*amṛtam*). Later in the same text (2.5.18–19) we read that this Supreme Being created all two-footed and four-footed bodies and entered into them. There is nothing he does not envelop and nothing he does not pervade.

Like the original Vedānta of the Upaniṣads, the Sāṁkhya maintains that the world, for all its faults, is real. In contrast the later Advaita Vedānta philosophy teaches that Brahman alone is real and the world is at best something less. The Sāṁkhya and the Vedānta agree that the universe exists in latency before its manifestation and that creation is only a transition from a potential to an actual state. This idea, widespread in Indian thought, is known as the doctrine of pre-existent effect (*satkāryavāda*). Sāṁkhya regards the transformation (*pariṇāma*) as actual, like the change of milk into curd, but Advaita Vedānta sees it as only apparent.[25] Rejecting the Sāṁkhya's *pariṇāmavāda,* Advaita Vedānta regards the ever-changing world as a mere appearance (*vivarta*), superimposed on the never-changing reality of Brahman. This superimposition (*adhyāsa*) is like a snake seen in semidarkness but revealed in the light to be a rope. The snake exists only in the perceiver's misperception. The Vedantic *vivartavāda* maintains that the world is nothing more than a misperception superimposed by *māyā* on the reality of divine consciousness. Because change can never take place within the immutable Brahman, any transformation from cause to effect occurs only in the realm of phenomenality.[26] The universe is therefore not the product of Brahman but of *māyā.* This doctrine, referred to (sometimes pejoratively) as *māyāvāda,* defines *māyā* as the power to create error, but only at the empirical level. Brahman, being absolutely transcendental and absolutely One, can have no causal relationship. The only possible conclusion is that the causal relationship itself is apparent and exists only in *māyā.*[27]

Neither real nor totally unreal, this mysterious *māyā,* according to Vedānta, is nevertheless Brahman's causal potency. Unlike the Sāṁkhya's *prakṛti,* it is not an independent principle but an indefinable something totally dependent on the sole reality of Brahman.[28] *Nirguṇa* Brahman—the unconditioned Absolute—through an apparent association with *māyā,* becomes *saguṇa,* and it is this *saguṇa* Brahman or Īśvara that Vedānta regards as God. This personal yet formless God is both the material and the efficient cause of the superimposed universe, while the supreme Brahman (*parabrahman*) remains its eternally unchanging substratum.

There can be no question that Śvetāśvatara's deepest convictions are also nondualistic. His repeated declaration of the One as the highest truth makes that abundantly clear. Still, his view of the world, common to the Upaniṣads, differs from the later permutations of the Advaita Vedānta philosophers, who lived many centuries later. At the same time his thinking reveals distinctive Śaiva tendencies. Some of his ideas on the nature of God, *māyā,* and cosmic manifestation appear a century or two afterward in Nandikeśvara's monistic Śaivism (see pp. 39–41) and still later in the nondualistic Śaiva thinking of Kashmir.

Unlike the post-Śaṁkara scholastics, who reduced their great predecessor's subtle and nuanced observations (see pp. 26–27) to a denunciation of the world as mere illusion, the Trika seers affirmed a joyful astonishment (*camatkāra*) at the wonders of creation.[29] They declared that this world is neither an illusion to be dismissed or a simulacrum to be despised. Granted, the world is an appearance, but this appearance (*ābhāsa*) is a manifest form of the Absolute.[30] As an objective reality in consciousness,[31] the world is true and not illusory. Accordingly the Trika doctrine, distinct from the Vedantic *vivartavāda,* is called *ābhāsavāda.* Significantly, the sole instance of the word *ābhāsa* in the Upaniṣads occurs in Śvetāśvatara's third discourse (3.17), where it indicates the divine resplendence pervading our experience of the world (see pp. 245–246).

Abhinavagupta's encyclopedic *Tantrāloka* [Light of the Tantras] explains that every object experienced through perception and thought is a self-projected manifestation (*ābhāsa*) or an emanation (*unmeṣa*) of divine consciousness.[32] At the same time the world is *not* a material reality, independent of consciousness.[33] In Trika thinking, objectivity and materiality are not the same and must not be confused. Objectivity exists within consciousness, but materiality would have to be something outside of consciousness—an impossibility, because there is nothing other than consciousness. Even though the universe *appears* as an independent material reality, what we call matter is a projection of, by, and within consciousness itself.[34] Therefore, the Trika doctrine of internality, called *antarārthavāda,*[35] holds that everything exists only within consciousness (*saṁvid*), which is to say within the singular Śiva. The only "reality" that matter can lay claim to is the reality of consciousness *appearing* as matter.[36] The whole of phenomenality, in which we have our existence, shines within divine ideation.[37] Abhinavagupta writes in his *Īśvarapratya-*

bhijñāvimarśinī [A consideration of the recognition of God] (2.2–3) that ideation (*saṁvṛti*) is the basis of all phenomena. Phenomena are therefore a reality—a specific kind of reality, to be sure, but most definitely not a falsehood.[38]

Because it is the ideation that appears as objects, ideation itself is a form of *ābhāsa* or manifestation and not absolute, unconditioned consciousness. This last thought—that ideation itself is a form of *ābhāsa*—led Abhinavagupta to distinguish two different kinds of truth or reality (*satya*). One he calls *paramārthasatya*—absolute reality; the other, *saṁvṛtisatya*—the reality of the phenomenal world, based on ideation. This principle, recalling Śaṁkara's distinction of the *pāramārthika* and the *vyāvahārika,* concedes that in this world-as-appearance, everything is not equal. There are successive levels of manifestation, the "higher" or "fuller" ones being more real than the "lower" ones, which are farther removed from the center of consciousness.[39] Of the Trikaśāstra's thirty-six *tattvas* only two are absolutely real—the *śivatattva* and the *śaktitattva*—and these two are in fact one. Beginning with the *sadāśivatattva,* the rest are *ābhāsas*—but that is not to deny their reality. They are entirely real in that they exist eternally within Paramaśiva as his divine potency, but to their objective manifestation we must assign a lesser degree of reality simply because all created things have a beginning and an end.[40]

The Trikaśāstra, like Sāṁkhya and Advaita Vedānta, accepts the doctrine of the pre-existent effect (*satkāryavāda*) as its theory of cosmic evolution, but in its own way. In the "descending" movement from *tattva* to *tattva,* the energy (*śakti*), making manifest at each step what was already potential in the preceding step, flows in an unbroken current but remains inseparable from the *śivatattva* that is its ultimate source.[41] Abhinavagupta makes that point clear in the opening sentence of his *Parātrīśikāvivaraṇa.* He writes, "Śakti [energy] surely should not be considered as different from Śiva" (*na hi śaktiḥ śivāt bhedam āmarśayet*). Thus, every objective appearance in the universe is rooted in the divine reality itself and shines forth as its visible expression.

The Trikaśāstra rejects the Sāṁkhya theory of actual transformation (*pariṇāmavāda*), agreeing with Advaita Vedānta that the change from cause into effect is only apparent. But there is an important difference. In Vedantic teaching, *vivarta* signifies an appearance of something that has no true being, such as the often cited snake superimposed on the rope. Trika teaching objects that the doctrine of superimposition (*adhyāsavāda*) implies an external imposing agent and therefore retains a trace of dualism. The Vedānta replies that Brahman and *māyā* are inseparable, to which the Trika counters that inseparable is not identical. The concept of superimposition remains problematical for the Śaiva nondualist. In fact, to distinguish the Trikaśāstra's rigorous nondualism from that of Advaita Vedānta, Abhinavagupta used the term *parādvaita*, "absolute nondualism."[42] This point of view, rejecting the Vedantic superimposition (*adhyāsa*), instead teaches that the world is Śiva's own self-projection (*ābhāsa*), and that everything in the universe, even that which appears inert (*jaḍa*), is consciousness.

Abhinavagupta observes further that knowledge of the world is dependent on knowledge itself. This may seem unnecessarily obvious, but it is a profound statement. As Abhinavagupta explains, whenever an object is known to the mind, it is known as the *knowledge of the object* and not as the object itself. He rightly points out that even if a material object were real, it could not enter the mind as a material object but only as a sensory impression or ideation. Thus, any object is known only as it appears to the mind.[43]

Being at once theistic and nondualistic, the Trika *īśvarādvayavāda* maintains that there is no real separation—just an apparent one—between God and his creation. Abhinavagupta expresses this elegantly in the *Tantrāloka* (3.268): "In the Self, which is consciousness, all this apparent multitude of existence shines forth as a reflection, and it is truly the Self who is the lord of the universe."[44] He compares the world-appearance to an image reflected in a mirror, using *pratibimba* ("reflection") as a synonym for *ābhāsa*.

Śaṁkara, also citing the idea of reflection, explains that the individual soul (*jīva*) is none other than Brahman reflected in the mirror of ignorance (*avidyā*). He suggests that the prototype (*bimba*) and its reflection (*pratibimba*) are equally real. The last part of his famous dictum says as much: "the individual soul is none other than Brahman" (*jīvo brahmaiva nāparaḥ*). Śaṁkara's disciple Sureśvara further developed the theory of reflection (*pratibimbavāda*) and made it the position of his Vivaraṇa ("explanation") school of Advaita Vedānta. Retitled *ābhāsavāda*, it differs from Śaṁkara's teaching in one respect. Sureśvara maintains that the reflection is less real than the prototype. He makes the further distinction that consciousness reflected in ignorance manifests as Īśvara and consciousness reflected in the *buddhi* manifests as the *jīva.*

Developed in the mid ninth century, the Vedantic *ābhāsavāda* became with some modification the basis of the Trika world-view, but the modification makes a major change. Whereas the Vedantic version maintains that the world is a reflection of consciousness (*prakāśa*) in the mirror of ignorance (*avidyā*), the Trika version sees the world as a reflection of consciousness in the mirror of consciousness, in its own self-reflective capacity (*vimarśa*).

Of course the mirror analogy, like any analogy for the ineffable, is imperfect, and Abhinavagupta is aware of its shortcomings. He points out that in the ordinary world an object reflected in a mirror exists outside of the mirror and that the mirror is unaware of the reflection. In contrast, the object reflected in consciousness has no existence outside of consciousness, and even the mirror that reflects it is that same consciousness in its reflective mode. Śiva, the ultimate reality, actively creates the reflection within himself and is fully aware of it.[45]

The individual *jīva* or *paśu* experiences the world in an entirely different light, unable to recognize that Śiva's self-imposed finitization as the world-appearance takes place entirely within the infinitude of consciousness itself. When Śiva "descends" to the level of the individual subject (*puruṣa*), that individual mistakes the *ābhāsa* for an exterior, objective world having material substance. The limited knower perceives the world as something separate, even though the separation is in truth only apparent.[46]

Because the Trikaśāstra regards the universe as consciousness in a state of manifestation (*ābhāsa*), it is sometimes called a doctrine of realist idealism. Regarding philosophical idealism, there are two kinds. One is subjective idealism (*dṛṣṭisṛṣṭivāda*), and the other is absolute idealism (*sṛṣṭidṛṣṭivāda*). Subjective idealism holds that the world-appearance is the projection of an individual mind. The Trikaśāstra does not accept this as its theory of manifestation because it negates the necessity of God. Instead it embraces a philosophy of absolute idealism. The world is an ideation of the supreme consciousness (*parāsaṁvid*) that is the universal Self. Despite a tangle of *vādas* and isms, we should recall that the quest for spiritual knowledge should not be a vain, speculative exercise. Abhinavagupta reminds us that the Trikaśāstra is a tradition of experience (*anubhava-*

sampradāya), based on the direct spiritual insight of seers and sages and intent on bringing its followers to that same realization.[47]

Śaṁkara's teaching on sublation, with its three-tiered scheme of experience, likens the world to a dream from which the enlightened soul awakens to the reality of Brahman (see pp. 26–27). The dream analogy can also be instructive in explaining the merits of *sṛṣṭidṛṣṭivāda* over *dṛṣṭisṛṣṭivāda*. Though rejecting subjective idealism as a theory of creation, Trika teaching nevertheless acknowledges its limited operation at the individual level. A dream is something we all experience, and what is it other than a state in which consciousness appears as phenomena? A dream may contain all the same elements as our waking life—places, people, objects, situations, and events—either in a "realistic" configuration as in our waking state or in fantastic, impossible ways. As in the waking state, dream-consciousness is dichotomized into the awareness of subject and object. The dreamer is the subject, and everything else is the object, but the individual experient does not know it is dreaming and mistakes the dream for reality. Unaware that the dream is the creation of his or her own mind, the dreamer fails to recognize that the elements of the dream rise up unbidden out of the storehouse of subconscious impressions. The dreamer lacks the freedom to direct the dream in a desired way, and in the absence of conscious control the dream can turn into a nightmare.[48]

While awake we can exercise a modicum of free will in imagination or daydreaming. No longer in the thrall of sleep, we can use the power of ideation to create a world exactly to our liking, and because we are awake, we know that a daydream is a daydream and nothing more. The daydream analogy comes closer to the cosmic ideation (*sṛṣṭikalpanā*) of Śiva, who is not subject to the deluding power of *māya* but is its master. But there is one important difference. A daydream remains a reflection or idea in the individual mind; it cannot be perceived by anyone else. The universe, being a product of Śiva's ideation and not that of any individual mind, is experienced by all sentient creatures. For this reason the world is for Śiva a subjective reality, but to the *jīva* the same world appears as an objective reality with a clearly drawn distinction of self and other. Upon that distinction follow all the attendant colorations and consequences of the human condition.

There is yet another reason why the world cannot be a product of individual ideation. Individual souls come into this world and depart from it, and all the while the world goes on for the simple reason that it is the creation of Śiva's mind and not of theirs. Thus, following observation and logic, the Trikaśāstra adopts the position of absolute, rather than subjective, idealism.

The world exists as long as Śiva sees it in his mind's eye, so to speak. With the closing of his eyes (*nimeṣa*) the universe dissolves. Time, space, and causality evaporate, and Śiva rests in his own perfection. Then again, with the opening of his eyes (*unmeṣa*) Śiva initiates anew the cosmic play.[49] The Trika teaching echoes Śvetāśvatara's statement of everything (*viśvam*) coming apart in the end and of God bringing forth all things at the beginning.

It goes without saying that Vedānta also acknowledges the alternation between manifest and nonmanifest states, but the Trikaśāstra uniquely develops this idea into the concept of *spanda*, the eternal pulsation of consciousness. Originating with Vasugupta's *Śivasūtra*, the Spandaśāstra holds that Śiva manifests through his inherent dynamism. *Spanda* is not movement in any usual sense but a pulsation of the modalities of consciousness-as-subject and consciousness-as-object. It is the all-inclusive reality experiencing itself in two different ways. As *aham* Śiva rests in the integral self-awareness of consciousness in its ultimate simplicity (*akhaṇḍānubhava*). As *idam* he is actively engaged in expressing his own overflowing joy through the multiform conditioning of that same consciousness as manifestation. Neither mode negates the other; the two are simultaneous.[50]

This spontaneous pulsation is said to move outward and inward, although those terms belong to the temporal-spatial order of existence and cannot even approximate the reality. The outward movement imposes self-limitation. It is sometimes described as a "coagulating" (*śyānatā*) or "thickening" (*ghanatā*) of consciousness. Through ideation, which appears first as concept (*nāma*) and then as form (*rūpa*), the energy of consciousness is said to condense or to become dense. With the loss of transparency and the dimming of its light, its freedom is likewise diminished. Even so, the manifestation never becomes entirely disconnected from the ultimate reality of Śiva, without which there could be no existence at all.[51] Śiva—consciousness itself—remains the ever whole, infinite, timeless, and inviolable perfection.[52] When the energy that creates the world-appearance reverses, it becomes the so-called inward pulsation that effects a dissolution of all the projected names and forms and a return to pristine clarity.

The outward movement is a "descent" into an increasingly conditioned state, subject to *niyati, māyā's* function of causal determination. Conversely the inward movement is an "ascent" to absolute freedom. In our ignorance we perceive the two pulses as separate, but the illumined soul knows that both modes of consciousness are Śiva, despite the conventional thinking that distinguishes them as lower (*apara*) and supreme (*para*).[53] In truth our empirical awareness is a product of Śiva's radiant pulsation (*sphurattā* or *ullāsa*), and the capacities of cognition and action through which we live out our own existence are nothing but specialized aspects of this same vibrating consciousness.[54]

Any philosophical world-view has practical consequences for the spiritual aspirant. For the Vedantic *advaitin* the goal is the withdrawal (*nivṛtti*) from the finite order of sensory experience and a return to the oneness of the infinite Brahman. For the Śaiva nondualist the involution of consciousness is only half of the picture, because *nivṛtti* is necessarily balanced by *pravṛtti*. Both movements are integral to the eternal pulsation.[55] The Śaiva's goal is to participate fully in the universal vibration of the Absolute, both in its creative surge into multiplicity and in its subsiding dissolution into unity. While Śaṁkara extols the virtue of dispassion (*vairāgya*) Abhinavagupta, in the *Mālinīvijayavārtika* (1.240–242), instructs that there is a supreme dispassion (*paravairāgya*). By this he means not shrinking from the world in ascetic denial but realizing the world itself as a manifestation of the Absolute—recognizing that the Divine is both the finite many and the infinite One.[56] *Spanda* is both Śiva's passion for self-expression (*rāga*) and his urge for withdrawal (*virāga*) from the sensory universe that he projects. The reality of neither can be denied.[57]

The Vedānta counters that the unity of the changeless Brahman alone is true and real and that the changing world is false. To this Abhinavagupta responds that both belong to an inconceivably greater nonduality (*mahādvaya*) beyond diversity *and* unity. Both duality and unity, either separate or together, are equally present in the ultimate consciousness, and therein lies the supreme secret.[58]

In the words of the Chāndogyopaniṣad (3.14.3), "All this world is Brahman" (*sarvaṁ khalv idaṁ brahma*). With declarations such as this, the ancient *ṛṣis* spoke on the question of the reality or unreality of the world from their own direct realization. The experience of a modern seer, Śrī Rāmakṛṣṇa, bears them out. The *Śrī Śrī Rāmakṛṣṇa Kaṭhāmṛta* records a scene that took place one Sunday afternoon in the winter of 1883. One of the visitors to the Dakṣiṇeśvar temple had expounded on Vedānta, causing Rāmakṛṣṇa's disciple, Mahendranath Gupta, to fall into a pensive mood. After the guests had left he queried, "Is the world unreal?"

"Why should it be unreal?" the holy man countered, adding that the reality or unreality of the world is a matter for the speculation of philosophers. Later that evening, perhaps sensing his disciple's continuing disquiet, Śrī Rāmakṛṣṇa asked again, "Why should the universe be unreal?" Then he made an extraordinary disclosure.

Once, in the Kālī temple the Divine Mother had revealed to him that it was she who had become everything. He described seeing everything as full of consciousness—the image of the Goddess, the altar, the worship vessels, the door-sill, the marble floor. Everything was consciousness; everything was saturated in bliss; everything vibrated with the Mother's power. In that state Śrī Rāmakṛṣṇa fed a cat with the food that was to be offered to the Mother. He realized that she herself had become everything.[59]

Śrī Rāmakṛṣṇa often declared that Brahman and Śakti are identical. If you accept one, you must accept the other. Can you conceive of the sun's rays without the sun, or of the sun without its rays? The Absolute (*nitya*) and the relative (*līlā*) belong to one and the same reality.[60] When consciousness is inactive, it is called Brahman; when it creates, preserves, and destroys, it is called Śakti. Brahman is like still water; Śakti is the same water, moving in waves.[61] Whether moving or still, water is water.[62] Interestingly Abhinavagupta made the identical point in the *Tantrāloka* (4.181–188), evoking the same imagery of the ocean and its waves.[63]

5

अजामेकां लोहितशुक्लकृष्णां

बह्वीः प्रजाः सृजमानां सरूपाः ।

अजो ह्येको जुषमाणोऽनुशेते
जहात्येनां भुक्तभोगामजोऽन्यः ॥ ५ ॥

ajām ekāṁ lohitaśuklakṛṣṇāṁ bahvīḥ prajāḥ sṛjamānāṁ sarūpāḥ /
ajo hy eko juṣamāno 'nuśete jahāty enāṁ bhuktabhogām ajo 'nyaḥ //

5. Coupling with a she-goat of red, white, and black who gives birth to many offspring like herself, a he-goat takes his pleasure. From her whose purpose is enjoyment another he-goat abstains.

After the images of people, butterflies, and parrots, the picture of three goats is imagery with a difference. Śvetāśvatara, who has demonstrated a cleverness with language several times already, is not about to overlook a *double entendre* that so felicitously suits his purpose. The word *ajā* means either "she-goat" or something feminine and unborn, and the word *ajaḥ* means either "he-goat" or something masculine and unborn. The pun is just too good to pass up, because it so brilliantly shifts the discourse from the imagery of living creatures and the physical world to the cosmogonic and ontological abstractions that are the seer's real topic. At face value the goats and their dalliances add little more to his colorful panorama of creation, but the deeper meaning behind the pun takes us to the heart of his world-affirming philosophy.

Little could the seer have known what his innocent delight would lead to. Max Müller notes that for a long while this verse was "a bone of contention" between Sāṁkhya and Vedānta philosophers who were intent on finding scriptural support for their particular ideas.[64] Even Śaṁkara invokes the verse in the *Brahmasūtrabhāṣya* (1.4.8–10) to refute the Sāṁkhya doctrine of an independent material reality and multiple *puruṣas*.

According to the Sāṁkhya reading, this *mantra* supports the idea that there are two ultimate principles, the singular *prakṛti* and the pluralistic *puruṣa.* The she-goat represents *prakṛti,* also called *pradhāna,* and her red, white, and black stripes symbolize the three *guṇas*, her inherent energies. When one *puruṣa,* the male goat lying beside her, falls under her seductive spell, he forgets that his true nature is pure consciousness and becomes engrossed in the play of the *guṇas*. In taking his delight, he discovers that where there is enjoyment there is also its inescapable companion, suffering. Eventually, having had his fill, he is ready to let go. As he abandons the she-goat, another he-goat waits, ready to take his place beside her. And so the world goes on and on. The one *prakṛti* first captivates, then releases, *puruṣas* without end.[65]

Śaṁkara, contending that this *mantra* does not represent the dualistic Sāṁkhya point of view, dismisses the talk of goats. He claims instead that *ajā* denotes the unborn feminine principle which springs from the supreme Lord and becomes the material source of living beings. The red, white, and black stripes, rather than representing the Sāṁkhya's *guṇas,* allude to a passage in the Chāndogyopaniṣad (6.4.1–4), where the seer Uddālaka Āruṇi instructs his son Śvetaketu that everything is composed of three elements. The red is fire; the white is water; the black is earth.

In the original context of the Chāndogyopaniṣad the quoted passage implies a great deal more. In the beginning the divine being (*sat*) that is One without a second (*ekam evādvitīyam*) (6.2.2) willed or thought (*aikṣata,* "saw"), May I be many, may I grow forth (*bahu syāṁ prajāyeyeti*); then it produced (*asṛjata,* "emitted") fire, water, and earth (6.2.3–4). Having produced the elements, which are thrice declared real, the One entered into them and effected all further creation through their modification as names arising from speech (*vāc*) (6.4.1–3). Similarly the Bṛhadāraṇyakopaniṣad (1.6.1), which analyzes the world as a triad of name, form, and action (*trayaṁ vā idaṁ nāma rūpaṁ karma*), claims that all three are expressions of *vāc,* their commonality and source, literally "their Brahman" (*eṣāṁ brahma*). Even before the Upaniṣads the Śatapathabrāhmaṇa (7.5.2.21) observed that "*vāc* is truly the unborn one (*vagvai ajā*), and from *vāc* the maker of the universe brought forth living beings" (*vāco vai prajāḥ viśvakarmā yajāna*). The still older Ṛgvedasaṁhitā (10.114.8) declares that the word is coextensive with Brahman (*yāvad brahma viṣṭhitaṁ tāvatī vāk*). On the basis of Vedic authority (*śruti*) we can establish that the unborn feminine principle is *vāc,* the creative word and source of the triadic manifestation.

Returning to the *Brahmasūtrabhāṣya* (1.4.9), we find that Śaṁkara next cites the Śvetāśvataropaniṣad (1.1–3) to support his position that Brahman, not *pradhāna,* is the cause of the universe. But where Śvetāśvatara calls this cause *devātmaśakti,* the power (*śakti*) of the effulgent Self (*devātma*), Śaṁkara departs from the letter of the text and reads *devātmaśakti* as "the power of the supreme Lord." This signals a profound difference of opinion, which will soon become evident. However, the two men agree that the cause is some sort of divine power and not a second, independent principle as the Sāṁkhya would have it. For Śvetāśvatara *devātmaśakti* is the causal unity that gives rise to the breathtaking diversity of the world. To our ordinary perception the unity remains hidden by the very qualities it manifests (*svaguṇair nigūḍhām*). Consciousness is inherently dynamic, and *devātmaśakti* is the inherent power of consciousness itself. But for Śaṁkara, whose doctrine does not allow for any movement or change within Brahman, *devātmaśakti* must be reconfigured to signify something else.

That poses a problem for Śaṁkara. He cannot deny Brahman as the cause, for that would be a contradiction of Vedic authority. The above-cited passages from the *śruti* make little or no distinction between Brahman and its creative power (*vāc*). Here in the present Upaniṣad *devātmaśakti* is synonymous with *vāc*. How does Śaṁkara get around this? By making the distinction that *devātmaśakti* is only the material (and not the efficient) cause of the universe, even though no such distinction exists in the *śruti* passages cited above. To support this distinction he takes some latitude in reading *devātmaśakti* as "the power of the supreme Lord" rather than as "the power of the effulgent Self." Of course the effulgent Self signifies the supreme reality of Brahman, but in Śaṁkara's philosophy reality is immutable. Advaita Vedānta allows for no activity or change in the absolute (*nirguṇa*) Brahman. And so Śaṁkara interprets *devātmaśakti* as *saguṇa* Brahman—as Īśvara, the supreme Lord. Īśvara is Brahman associated with *māyā*—qualified by *māyā*—and so his quality of creative power is no more than a limiting adjunct (*upādhi*). Thus, Īśvara himself is only an apparent aspect of *nirguṇa* Brahman, this latter being the sole reality according to Advaita Vedānta.[66]

By not acknowledging *devātmaśakti* as the inherent and essential power of consciousness as the Śaivas do, Śaṁkara preserves the immutability, which is for him the reality, of Brahman. At the same time, if the world is the creation of a creator who is himself only apparent, what does that say about the reality, or the value, of the world that Śvetāśvatara celebrates so glowingly in this chapter? Śaṁkara's interpretation seems no closer to the spirit of Śvetāśvatara's teaching than the Sāṁkhya doctrine that he is so eager to disprove.

Philosophical wrangling is certainly not Śvetāśvatara's intention, and if we want a clear idea of this verse's meaning, we need look no farther than the Śvetāśvataropaniṣad itself. The seer has already made clear exactly what he is talking about. The text provides its own frame of reference in *mantras* 1.7, 1.9, and 1.12. The key lies in the word *traya* ("triad").

In *mantra* 1.7 *traya* signifies the universe, and there the point is that the universe is a matter of our experience in consciousness. The unitary, formless consciousness that is Brahman appears as the threefold form of the enjoying subject (*bhoktṛ*), the object to be enjoyed (*bhogya*), and the inciting power (*preritṛ*) that relates them. The triad signifies a three-way split of consciousness into subject, object, and cognitive act—into the knower (*pramātṛ*), the known (*prameya*), and the process of knowing (*pramāṇa*).

Two verses later Śvetāśvatara approaches the triad from a slightly different angle and invests additional meaning in the three members. The first is the all-knowing (*jña*) universal experient (*bhoktṛ*), described also as the ruling Lord (Īśa), commonly called Pati in Śaiva texts. The second member, which is only partially aware (*ajña*) and ruled over (*anīśa*), is that which is to be experienced (*bhogya*) by the ruling Lord. *Bhogya* includes not only the individual soul (*jīva* or *paśu*) but also the world that appears as the individual's object of awareness. The individual experient (*paśu*) itself consists of individualized subjective awareness (*puruṣa* in the Trika sense) identified with objective principles of *prakṛti*, such as ego (*ahaṁkāra*), intellect (*buddhi*), and mind (*manas*). The individual's self-awareness is an objectified self-awareness, limited in its capacities of knowing and acting. That is why the *paśu* is only partially aware (*ajña*) and ruled over (*anīśa*). The third member is the feminine principle, whose purpose is to relate the enjoyer to that which is to be enjoyed (*bhoktṛbhogyārthayuktā*). This binding principle (*pāśa*) completes the triad, which the Trikaśāstra often describes as *pati-paśu-pāśa*. "When this triad is fully known," says Śvetāśvatara, "it is seen to be Brahman." Again in *mantra* 1.12 the seer declares, "When the enjoyer (*bhoktā*) rightly understands the enjoyed (*bhogyam*) and the means of enjoyment (*preritāram*), all this is declared to be the threefold Brahman."

In *mantra* 1.9 the word *aja* is intended in its literal sense of "unborn" or "unproduced" or "having eternal being." It has the same intent in the present verse also, all punning aside. Why would Śvetāśvatara say that the Lord, the bound soul, and the process that relates them are all unborn? That statement contradicts various points of the Sāṁkhya and the Vedānta alike. The Sāṁkhya recognizes no Lord, and the Vedānta does not acknowledge the eternal reality of the bound soul, since bondage or ignorance is merely apparent, admittedly having no beginning but most decisively having an end. One answer would be that Śvetāśvatara is speaking from the level of a realized soul, having transcended all concepts of God (Īśvara), individual soul (*jīvātman*), and *māyā*. That is the idea developed later by Gauḍapāda in his doctrine of nonorigination (*ajātivāda*). That seems a plausible argument until we remember that Gauḍapāda denies the reality of the world that Śvetāśvatara so joyfully celebrates. Fortunately, there is a simpler explanation. The members of the triad are eternal in that each has consciousness as its essence. When this is fully known (1.9) and rightly understood (1.12), all three are experienced as the single reality of Brahman.

For further insight we need to look closely at the final quarter of the verse. Śvetāśvatara's exact words are, "From her whose purpose is enjoyment another he-goat abstains" (*jahāty enāṁ bhuktabhogām ajo 'nyaḥ*). The term *bhuktibhogām* ("who is to be enjoyed") is feminine and modifies *enām* ("her"), the feminine principle. Almost every translator reads it as if it were *bhuktibhogaḥ* ("having enjoyed her pleasures"), modifing the masculine principle who, having enjoyed the female's delights and presumably grown tired of them, subsequently rejects her (*jahāty enām*).[67] However, the text unequivocally reads *bhuktibhogām*. This is a grammatical compound to be read as "whose *bhoga* is *bhukti*." Among several meanings of *bhoga* the one that works best here is "use" or "utility,"[68] and the meaning of *bhukti* is "enjoyment."[69] *Bhuktibhogām* describes the feminine principle as her "whose purpose is enjoyment." This straightforward reading agrees with Śvetāśvatara's earlier statement (1.9) that the one unborn feminine principle (*ajā*) is "intent on relating the enjoyer to that which is to be enjoyed" (*bhoktṛbhogyārthayuktā*).

By the power of consciousness, variously called *preritṛ*, *māyā*, or *devātmaśakti*, the world is to be enjoyed through the individual experient (*jīva*), the active he-goat, while Śiva, the other he-goat, abstains (*jahāti*), merely witnessing the play of creation even while resting in the immeasurable bliss of his own transcendence. To support the Sāṁkhya and Vedānta positions the verb *jahāti* is usually translated as "abandons," "gives up," "relinquishes," or "lays side." It should be obvious that all those meanings require previous involvement, but for Śvetāśvatara, for whom the first he-goat represents the Lord (Īśa, Pati), there can be no involvement; God is never enchanted or deluded or held captive by *māyā* but is always *māyā's* lord, as the seer will soon make clear (4.9–10). Here *jahāti* is better rendered as "abstains from" or "refrains from."[70] As the seer has already made clear (1.9), while *māyā* relates the enjoyer to the enjoyed, the infinite Self, though appearing as the universe (*viśvarūpaḥ*), acts not at all (1.9). For Śvetāśvatara the triad of *bhoktṛ*, *bhogya* and *preritṛ* is a threefold differentiation of a single reality. Because the three are but different aspects of the one consciousness, for the illumined soul there is nothing but Brahman.

We have seen that the Sāṁkhya interprets the active he-goat as the bound *puruṣa*, the other he-goat as the liberated *puruṣa*, and the she-goat as the captivating *prakṛti*. *Puruṣa* and *prakṛti* are the two eternally distinct realities of consciousness and matter. A *puruṣa's* bondage arises from its conjunction (*saṁyoga*) or involvement with *prakṛti*. Liberation is *kaivalya*, the dissociation of consciousness from matter, wherein the *puruṣa* regains the knowledge of its true, original nature. Whether the *puruṣa* is bound or free, an eternal plurality of *puruṣas* and a single *prakṛti* remain. This cannot be reconciled with Śvetāśvatara's teaching that to the enlightened, all three members of the triad are known to be the one Brahman.

Advaita Vedānta sees the triad as consisting of the bound soul (*jīvātman*), the soul that is liberated (*mukta*), and the binding *māyā*. While recognizing that the soul is Brahman—"this Self is Brahman" (*ayam ātmā brahma*), as the Bṛhadāraṇyakopaniṣad proclaims, and "the individual soul is none other than Brahman" (*jīvo brahmaiva nāparaḥ*), as Śaṁkara repeats—Advaita Vedānta does not equate Brahman and *māyā*. It forces a disconnect between consciousness and its power, saying that Brahman alone is real, and *māyā* is neither real nor unreal and exists only in an indefinable (*anirvacanīya*) dependence. Again, it is hard to reconcile this with Śvetāśvatara's teaching that all three members of the triad are the one Brahman.

Is there another system of philosophy with which Śvetāśvatara's teaching is compatible? There is, if we observe that by his own definition in *mantra* 1.9 the triad signifies the Lord, the bound soul, and the inciting power. In the goat analogy the seer intends *bhoktṛ* (the onlooking goat) as the supreme experient or Lord and *bhogya* (the enjoying goat) as both the objectified individual soul and the world of its experience. That is the key.

This unique formulation shows up again in another philosophical system that is closer in time and in spirit to Śvetāśvatara's teaching than are either classical Sāṁkhya or Advaita Vedānta. That system is Lakuliśa's version of Pāśupata Śaivism (see pp. 43–49). Like Śvetāśvatara, whose two he-goats represent in turn the uninvolved, which is to say the completely subjective, Lord (Īśa) and the objectified *jīva,* Lakuliśa makes the same distinction. In his philosophy the first primary category is *kāraṇa* ("cause"), meaning the Lord (Pati), also called Brahman.[71] The second category is *kārya* ("effect"), which includes *paśu* (consisting of *puruṣa,* the individual subject, and *vidyā,* its sentiency) along with *kalā,* the insentient (*jaḍa*) object of its experience. *Kalā,* in Lakulīśa's system, corresponds to the Sāṁkhya *prakṛti,* or *pradhāna,* and contains the same twenty-three *tattvas.* This conception, so different from that of India's other philosophical systems,[72] has its basis in the Śvetāśvataropaniṣad. It is but one of many instances where this Upaniṣad influenced Lakulīśa and through him left its mark on the later nondualistic Śaivism of Kashmir.

Śvetāśvatara's words anticipate the later nondualistic Śaiva stand that the material world is to be enjoyed as Paramaśiva's own expression. That acceptance is what drives the seer's eloquent celebration of nature's beauty. Lord Śiva's divine play is to create this world for his own pleasure and to experience it through each *jīva.* But the finite *jīva,* endowed with only veiled awareness, experiences this play as the duality of pleasure (*sukha*) and misery (*duḥkha*). Even so, the Śaiva path is not one of ascetic withdrawal (*nivṛtti*) but of attunement to the divine light sparkling in and through all manifestation. As the Chāndogyopaniṣad (3.14.1) declares, all this world is divine (*sarvaṁ khalv idaṁ brahma*). Śaiva nondualism is not about spirit and matter or about Brahman and *māyā* but about the oneness of everything, and whether we experience reality in its pristine perfection or in the conditioned state of the world, it is to the illumined soul One and only One.

6

द्वा सुपर्णा सयुजा सखाया
समानं वृक्षं परिषस्वजाते ।
तयोरन्यः पिप्पलं स्वाद्वत्त्य-
नश्नन्नन्यो अभिचाकशीति ॥ ६ ॥

dvā suparṇā sayujā sakhāyā samānaṁ vṛkṣaṁ pariṣasvajāte /
tayor anyaḥ pippalaṁ svādv atty anśnann anyo abhicākaśīti //

6. Two fair-winged birds, inseparable companions, cling fast to the very same tree. One of them eats the sweet fruit while the other, not eating, looks on.

Śvetāśvatara evokes the natural world in yet another memorable image, this time quoting from the Ṛgvedasaṁhitā (1.164.20). This verse may be older still than the ancient hymn in which it occurs. Literary analysis suggests that this stanza and the two that follow it in the Ṛgveda might have been unconnected originally and placed together merely because they have the word *suparṇa* ("fair-winged") in common. Collectively the three do not form a clear or unified meaning, and even in the time of Sāyaṇa, the eminent commentator, their interpretation was fraught with difficulty.[73] By itself the present verse seems clear enough, and because of its effective symbolism it was sufficiently well known in Upaniṣadic times to be incorporated also into the Muṇḍakopaniṣad (3.1.1).

According to Sāyaṇa's commentary, the two birds represent the embodied soul (*jīva*) and the supreme Self (*paramātman*). They are inseparable companions (*sayujā sakhāyā*), because they dwell in the same body, symbolized by the tree. *Jīva* and *paramātman* are inseparable for another reason as well. Their essence—consciousness—is one and the same. Their intrinsic relationship can be illustrated through the analogy of reflection.

Advaita Vedānta and the Trikaśāstra have their own versions of the doctrine of reflection (*pratibimbavāda*) (see pp. 272–273). For the former, *jīva* is an image of *paramātman* reflected in the *buddhi.*[74] According to Trika teaching Śiva appears as the individual soul (*jīva*), reflected in the mirror of consciousness itself. Just as a mirror remains untouched by the reflections that shine from it, the supreme Self, who is Śiva, remains untransformed. At the same time, the subjective, objective, and instrumental phenomena (the threefold *bhoktṛ-bhogya-preritṛ* or *pramātṛ-prameya-pramāṇa*) shine as a reflection of Śiva's divine powers within his own self-luminous awareness.[75] Between the prototype that is reflected (*bimba*) and its reflection (*pratibimba*) or appearance (*ābhāsa*) there exist both non-difference (*abheda*) and difference (*bheda*). *Paramātman* and *jīva* are identical in that both are essentially consciousness.[76] They are different in that *paramātman* is consciousness in its infinite, unconditioned purity and the *jīva* is that same consciousness limited and conditioned by *māyā.* And so, the two selves are in truth one, merely appearing as higher (*para*) and lower (*apara*). The "tree" of temporal existence is a meeting-place of the transcendent and the empirical facets of a single reality. The two are seemingly different, one entirely free and resting in its own purity, the other not free but conditioned by the impurities or limiting factors of *māyā*—but still pure in essence.[77]

The lower self eats the sweet fruit of the tree. This is a metaphor based on the close connection between the ideas of eating, consuming, and experiencing. In all likelihood, in the earlier context of the Ṛgveda the idea of "eating the sweet fruits" carried the positive message of celebrating nature's bounty, conferred on humankind through the beneficence of the deities of earth and sky. The worldview is a positive one, and nothing in this verse suggests otherwise. The sweet fruit represents the rewards of past actions, of which the bound soul partakes while the ever free Self, the second bird, looks on as a witness.[78]

However, in the context of the verse that follows in both the Śvetāśvataropaniṣad and the Muṇḍakopaniṣad (3.1.2), commentators are justified in taking the consumption of the sweet fruits in the broader sense of experiencing the full range of "the pleasant or unpleasant fruits of action,"[79] "the sweet and bitter fruits,"[80] "the consequences, good as well as bad,"[81] or "the fruit of action, having the characteristics of joy and sorrow."[82] In the opening *mantra* of this Upaniṣad Śvetāśvatara, who takes an overall positive view of creation, speaks of human life as running its course "through happiness and all the rest" (*sukhetareṣu*). And now the verse he has chosen to quote says that while the lower soul experiences all the phenomena of embodied existence, the higher Self looks on, unattached (*anśnan,* "not eating"), as a witness of the cosmic play.

But the verse also says that both birds cling fast to the tree. If the second bird is unattached, how can it cling, let alone cling fast? The intensive form of the verb (*pariṣasvajāte*) indicates that the clinging is tenacious and persistent. It indicates that both the lower self and the higher Self have an intimate connection to the body. In the case of the lower self the connection is fairly obvious. The *jīva* clings out of the sense of individual identity that the body confers, but what about the *paramātman*? It "clings fast" in the sense that physical matter is actually its manifestation. Where is the line of demarcation where matter ends and spirit begins?[83]

The supreme Self looks on continuously (*abhicākaśīti*). Again, the verb is in the intensive or frequentative form. *Paramātman* is the constant and eternal witness (*sākṣin*) to the ever-changing play of creation. Does that mean that it is passive? No, because to be passive means to be acted upon. Brahman cannot be acted upon for the simple reason that it is One without a second. Who or what is there to act upon it? This is a lesson that Yājñavalkya imparted to King Janaka in the following passage from the Bṛhadāraṇyakopaniṣad (4.3.31–32): "'When there seems to be another, one might see the other, smell the other, taste the other, speak to the other, hear the other, think of the other, touch the other, know the other. The seer who is free from duality becomes One and as clear as water. This is the state of Brahman, your Majesty.' Yājñavalkya instructed him thus: 'This is his highest goal; this is his highest fulfillment; this is his supreme state; this is his supreme bliss. All other creatures live in a fraction of this bliss.'"

7

समाने वृक्षे पुरुषो निमग्नोऽ-

नीशया शोचति मुह्यमानः ।

जुष्टं यदा पश्यत्यन्यमीश-
मस्य महिमानमिति वीतशोकः ॥ ७ ॥

samāne vṛkṣe puruṣo nimagno 'nīśayā śocati muhyamānaḥ /
juṣṭaṁ yadā paśyaty anyam īśam asya mahimānam iti vītaśokaḥ //

7. On that same tree the individual soul, overwhelmed by powerlessness and bewildered, grieves. When it beholds the other—the contented master and his glory—it is freed from sorrow.

This *mantra,* found also in the Muṇḍakopaniṣad (3.1.2) but not in the Ṛgveda, leaves no question that the experience of the *jīva* is marked by misery as well as pleasure.

Separation and limitation define the state of the individual soul (*puruṣa*). That soul exists in a state of dualistic awareness, having forgotten its true identity as the ultimate oneness of the supreme Self (*paramātman*). It thinks itself to be *jīva,* forgetting that it is Śiva. It owes its perplexity to *māyā,* through whose veiling power nothing in the world is as it seems to be. All appearance comes about through *māyā's* five limiting "cloaks" (*kañcukas*). Divine omnipotence (*sarvakartṛtva*) appears reduced to the individual's limited power. Divine omniscience (*sarvajñātṛtva*) manifests as paltry human understanding. The perfection of divine fullness (*pūrṇatva*) shows itself as the imperfection of individual lack. Divine imperishability (*nityatva*) shrinks to human mortality. And divine omnipresence (*vyāpakatva*) seemingly gives way to the restrictions of relativity and causality. Thus bewildered or confused in its thinking (*muhyamānaḥ*), the embodied soul laments (*śocati*), overwhelmed or engulfed (*nimagnaḥ*) by feelings of helplessness (*anīśayā*) that can and do arise in response to life's changing and challenging circumstances.

Unlike the individual soul, subject to all the bondages of *māyā,* the other (*anyam*) is the higher Self, contented (*juṣṭam*) because it is eternally free. Unconditioned by *māyā's* limitations, it rules over them as their master (*īśam*). When the individual soul rises to knowledge of its own true being—which is *paramātman,* resting in the blissful radiance of its own glory (*mahimānam*)—it is freed from sorrow (*vītaśokaḥ*).

Depending on the interpreter's point of view, the word *īśa* ("lord," "master," "ruler") reveals different philosophical nuances, inclined to express theism,[84] transcendental Selfhood,[85] or either possibility.[86] The *mantra* again calls to mind this Upaniṣad's fluid boundary between the personal God and the absolute Self, anticipating the seamless view of the Trikaśāstra's doctrine of the Lord's nonduality (*īśvarādvayavāda*). This invites us to ponder if the continuity of consciousness really allows for any boundary at all.

The image of the two birds illustrates that the purpose of spiritual life is to remove the misconception that we are what in fact we are not. Knowledge of the *paramātman*, whose essence is identical to the essence of every living being—the ever present, all-pervading consciousness—has the power to transform our vision of life. When the divine light begins to penetrate the murk of our mundane affairs, we begin to have intimations of its glory—of our own inherent glory—and our sorrow is lifted. Through Self-knowledge we regain our own long-forgotten sovereignty—another distinctly Śaiva teaching (see pp. 46, 135–136). We realize that the higher Self, though dwelling in the body, can never be conditioned by it. As *paramātman* we remain unaffected and unafflicted by the travails of *saṁsāra*, immune to the pangs of hunger, thirst, grief, infirmity, and inevitable death.[87] Through the identification of *jīva* with Śiva, we overcome the constraints of ignorance and rejoice in the freedom of our true being.

8

ऋचो अक्षरे परमे व्योमन्
यस्मिन्देवा अधि विश्वे निषेदुः ।
यस्तं न वेद किमृचा करिष्यति
य इत्तद्विदुस्त इमे समासते ॥ ८ ॥

ṛco akṣare parame vyoman yasmin devā adhi viśve niṣeduḥ /
yas taṁ na veda kim ṛcā kariṣyati ya it tad vidus ta ime samāsate //

8. He who knows not in which syllable of the sacred verse all the gods in highest heaven repose, what will he do with the sacred verse? They alone who know it, they themselves abide in it.

This verse, quoted from the same hymn of the Ṛgveda (1.164.39) as *mantra* 4.6, illustrates the longstanding connection in Indian thought between the divine reality and the word (*vāc*) as creative power.

The term *akṣara* holds the key to what Śvetāśvatara intends to convey. Like *aja,* it has two meanings. Besides "imperishable," *akṣara* also means "syllable" and more specifically the syllable *Oṁ.* In the original Ṛgvedic verse, *akṣara* symbolizes *Oṁ,*[88] and that meaning is confirmed when the same verse reappears in the Taittirīyāraṇyaka (2.11.6).[89] Regarding its quotation in the present context, the *Śvetāśvataropaniṣadvṛtti* takes *akṣara* to stand for *paramātman,*[90] but the ultimate import is the same. Imperishability is permanence, permanence is the nature of Brahman, and Brahman is the higher Self.

This verse emphasizes knowing, specifically knowing in which syllable (*yasminn akṣare*) of the sacred verse (*ṛcaḥ*) "all the gods in highest heaven repose." To know that is to recognize the power of the *praṇava,* the sound-symbol of the transcendent and immanent Brahman (see pp. 142–144). As for those gods in highest heaven, are they poetic symbols or abstractions or principles of a higher order? When Śvetāśvatara spoke of them earlier (2.3), we learned that they, the *devas* ("gods" or "shining ones"), represent the sensory faculties (*jñānendriyas*), those facets of consciousness that are engaged in experiencing the external creation. When awareness withdraws from the phenomenal realm, as in yogic practice, these "gods" (*devāḥ*) return to "heaven" (*vyoman*), the shining sky of infinite consciousness that is their true abode.

From the time of the Ṛgvedasaṁhitā, the connection between supreme reality and the creative word fascinated the Indian mind. The Upaniṣads continued to explore this theme, and still later, around the middle of the fifth century CE, the grammarian Bhartṛhari formulated a philosophy of language, set forth in his *Vākyapadīya.* According to this treatise (1.120) the world preexists in a state of involution within the sacred word (*vāc* or *śabda*) and by means of utterance evolves into its empirical form. The entire cosmos is therefore an evolution of the word (*śabdasya pariṇāmaḥ*). So say the knowers of sacred tradition.[91] This word, *Oṁ,* is the divine unity that remains ever indissoluble and unchangeable (*akṣara*). It is the matrix that holds in potentiality all the multiplicity of the cosmos that is to emerge from it; it is also the power that impels the emergence. The *praṇava* is the sound-symbol of consciousness-in-itself (*parabrahman*) and of its potentiality of becoming (Īśvara). It thus links the transcendental unity of the ultimate Self to the plurality of its own self-expression. Through the power of the word, the world comes into existence. Through this same power, when the outward flow is reversed, the individual experient (*jīva* or *paśu*) regains its original state of unity.

That is why, apart from its philosophical significance, the present verse has great practical value. It urges us to act in order to know. The Vedic *ṛṣi* who first chanted it and the later sages who quoted it convey the vision of pure unity underlying all diversity and the need to experience it directly. For the *jīva* who does not know that it is *paramātman,* of what use are the Vedas? There are many who perform the Vedic rites merely to obtain heavenly rewards, but such rewards are only temporary.[92] A finite action produces a finite result, and any enjoyment earned in this way will eventually run out. Superficial acquaintance with the sacred word is profitless. We must realize here and now the deepest truth of the holy teachings, the truth of our very being.[93] Those who know that are transformed; they alone abide in the permanence and infinite joy of the Self.

9

छन्दांसि यज्ञाः क्रतवो व्रतानि
भूतं भव्यं यच्च वेदा वदन्ति ।
अस्मान् मायी सृजते विश्वमेत-
त्तस्मिंश्चान्यो मायया सन्निरुद्धः ॥ ९ ॥

chandāṁsi yajñāḥ kratavo vratāni bhūtaṁ bhavyaṁ yac ca vedā vadanti / asmān māyī sṛjate viśvam etat tasmiṁś cānyo māyayā sanniruddhaḥ //

9. The sacred verses, the sacrifices, the rituals, the observances, what has been, and what will be, and what the Vedas declare, [all these abide in this syllable]. From this the lord of *māyā* sends forth all this world in which the soul is confined by *māyā*.

Still inspired by the wonder surrounding him and believing that the world should be celebrated as a manifestation of divinity, Śvetāśvatara elaborates on the preceding *mantra*. He reminds us that the realm of our ordinary experience emanates from Brahman. All aspects of the Vedas, from the resounding verses to the wide range of ritual practices and spiritual observances they enjoin, originate in the syllable *Oṁ*. The seer declares with relish that whatever has been in the past and will be in the future and everything of which the Vedas speak—nothing short of the entire cosmos—reverberates with divine consciousness. There is nothing that is not divine, for *Oṁ* is Brahman, and Brahman alone is. In reality the phenomenal universe is nothing but consciousness.[94]

As the lord of *māyā* (*māyī*), the creator projects out of himself (*sṛjate*) the plurality of this entire world in which the objectified soul, literally "the other" (*anyaḥ*), remains confined by the limitations of *māyā*. The difference between God and the human soul is not one of essence—for both are the same consciousness—but one of conditioning. The Lord is *māyā's* master, but the individual soul (*jīvātman*) remains *māyā's* captive.

10

मायां तु प्रकृतिं विद्यान्मायिनं च महेश्वरम् ।
तस्यावयवभूतैस्तु व्याप्तं सर्वमिदं जगत् ॥ १० ॥

māyāṁ tu prakṛtiṁ vidyān māyinaṁ ca maheśvaram /
tasyāvayavabhūtais tu vyāptaṁ sarvam idaṁ jagat //

10. One should know nature surely to be *māyā* and the Great Lord to be the lord of *māyā*, but also this whole world to be filled with beings who are his parts.

On the surface this often quoted *mantra* appears to equate *prakṛti* with *māyā*. One modern translator takes it as an attempt to reconcile the philosophical views of Sāṁkhya and Vedānta,[95] but that comment invites further inquiry.

To recapitulate the historical data, the Śvetāśvataropaniṣad can be reasonably dated to the sixth or fifth century BCE.[96] Kapila, the traditional founder of the Sāṁkhya system, is said to have lived a century or two earlier, but his historicity is questionable.[97] Early references to Sāṁkhya in the Mokṣadharma portion of the Mahābhārata (12.168–353), datable to some time between the fifth century BCE and the first century CE, name Sāṁkhya as one of five established doctrinal systems, but the multiple descriptions of its principles and terminology vary considerably, indicating that Sāṁkhya was still in a developmental stage.[98] It would not reach its definitive, classical form until the appearance of Īśvarakṛṣṇa's *Sāṁkhyakārikā* some time between the third and fifth centuries CE, and by then it appears to have absorbed a number of Buddhist and Jain influences.[99] As for Vedānta, in Śvetāśvatara's time the term simply meant the Upaniṣads as the culmination of Vedic knowledge. Śvetāśvatara had no knowledge of the philosophical system known as Vedānta that would develop many centuries later. Historically speaking, it is untenable to suggest that the seer is attempting here to reconcile the positions of two philosophical schools that did not yet exist.

What, then, does he mean when he appears to equate *prakṛti* and *māyā*? Later schools of thought tend to treat these terms, along with *śakti*, as synonymous,[100] but if that had been true in Śvetāśvatara's time, his statement would have been unnecessary. In the sense that he intended them, these terms must have carried some distinction.

Prakṛti has a broad range of meaning. It can signify the primal substance, the original condition of something, physical nature as a whole, or (in the Sāṁkhya sense) matter as distinct from spirit.[101] It can also mean "that which brings forth."[102] Interestingly, the word *prakṛti*, apart from this occurrence in the present *mantra*, is unknown in the principal Upaniṣads. In the broader Upaniṣadic literature it occurs only once more in the later Maitryupaniṣad (6.10), where it has the simple connotation of physical nature. The rarity of this term in the Upaniṣads provides little context for interpretation, but since its later usage in the Maitrī indicates physical nature, it is more than likely that Śvetāśvatara uses it in the same sense. Reasonably, *prakṛti* here signifies the totality of all things existing in time and space, the whole of creation in its manifest form.

We are to know that the whole of nature, which the seer celebrates so eloquently and joyfully, is *māyā*. What, then, is *māyā?* In the long history of Sanskrit literature, this word has meant different things at different times. At first it meant "art," "wisdom," "extraordinary power," "supernatural power," or "magic." Over time it acquired some less than positive connotations: "sorcery," "trick," "deception," "fraud," "illusion," "unreality." Eventually *māyā* came to signify the cosmic principle that is the source of the visible universe and therefore the cause of bondage.

Like *prakṛti, māyā* is a word rarely used in the Upaniṣads. The earliest occurrence is in the Bṛhadāraṇyakopaniṣad (2.5.19), where it appears in a passage quoted from the Ṛgvedasaṁhitā (6.47.18) extolling the supreme God: "Indra, by his magical powers (*māyābhiḥ*), goes about in many forms (*pururūpa īyate*)." Commenting on this Upaniṣad, Śaṁkara rightly takes *māyābhiḥ* in the older Vedic sense and explains that "by his wisdom" Indra "manifests himself."[103] Recent scholars in the West, also sensitive to the historical context, have translated *māyābhiḥ* in this passage as "by his wizardry"[104] or "by his magical powers."[105] On the other hand, translators inclined toward *māyāvāda* render this same passage as "on account of false notions the Supreme Being is perceived as manifold"[106] or as "the Lord (Indra), through His māyās, appears manifold." A footnote to the latter translation explains that multiplicity results from ignorance and that *māyās* are the false superimpositions of created beings.[107] Considering that the principal Upaniṣads have no idea of the later Vedantic doctrine of superimposition,[108] we can reasonably conclude that Śvetāśvatara understands *māyā* to be a cosmic power producing something rather more magical than the later philosophers' dour cosmic illusion.[109] A more positive reading conforms not only to Śvetāśvatara's obvious celebration of the world but also to Śaṁkara's own interpretation of *māyā* in his commentary on the Bṛhadāraṇyakopaniṣad.

After the Śvetāśvatara, the term *māyā* occurs in only one other major Upaniṣad, the Prāśna (1.16), where it signifies deception as a *human* shortcoming. Still later, it figures in the Maitryupaniṣad (4.2), a work that quotes frequently from the classical Upaniṣads and presents an admixture of Sāṁkhya and Buddhist influences in portraying phenomena as momentary and the world as illusory. Here the word *māyā* clearly has the sense of illusion and anticipates the later Vedantic *māyāvāda*.[110] In contrast, the late Kaivalyopaniṣad, a brief text of only twenty-five verses, exhibits a distinctly Śaiva character. Here the Self, enchanted by *māyā* (*māyāparimohita*), becomes embodied and in the waking state enjoys the pleasures of sex, food, and drink (verse 12). The combined nuances of the word *parimohita* convey the idea that under the alluring spell of *māyā* the soul becomes bewitched and experiences perplexity or a loss of full awareness.[111] At once bedazzled and deluded, it mistakes the appearance for the reality and devotes its waking life to running after the things of this world. In the dream state the soul experiences happiness and sorrow in worlds created by its own *māyā* (*svamāyayā*) (verse 13). When all things vanish in the darkness of dreamless sleep, it enjoys a more profound happiness (verse 14). Finally it goes beyond the three states to know itself as Brahman (verse 15). Three verses later comes this first-person utterance: "Whatever appears in the three states of consciousness as the experienced, the experiencer, and the experience—from them I am distinct; I am the witness—pure consciousness, the eternal Śiva (*sadāśivaḥ*)" (verse 18). The eternal Śiva is none other than Brahman: "From me everything is born; in me everything is established; into me everything dissolves; I am that Brahman without a second" (*tad brahmādvayam asmy aham*) (verse 19). While extolling unitary consciousness as the supreme reality, the Kaivalyopaniṣad assigns to *māyā* a role that points to its position in the later nondualistic Śaivism of Kashmir—that of a veiling or limiting principle but not necessarily a negative one.

Looking at the present *mantra* again, we can reasonably conclude that Śvetāśvatara portrays the whole of nature as a magical display. The world as we know it can be enchanting in a positive sense, or bewildering, perplexing, and stupefying. Nothing that we perceive through the five senses or infer with the mind is exactly what it seems to be. In our state of *māyā*-constricted awareness we can only know the appearance and not the full reality behind it.

It is that full reality to which the seer now draws our attention. Understanding *māyā* in much the same way as the Bṛhadāraṇyakopaniṣad does, Śvetāśvatara says that the magic has a master and that the magician (*māyin*) is none other than the Great Lord (*maheśvara*). Similar vocabulary appears two or three centuries later in the tenth book of the Taittirīyāraṇyaka (the Mahānārāyaṇopaniṣad) and still later in the *Pāśupatasūtra*. Both texts declare that *māyā* is Brahman's power, and both texts designate Brahman as *māyin*.[112]

Śvetāśvatara's term *devātmaśakti* (1.3) has already made clear that the creative power is the power of the supreme Self. Again in the present *mantra* the power of *māyā* and the wielder of that power (*māyin*) are said to be inseparable. Recalling the seer's earlier statements that the experiential triad of *bhoktṛ-bhogya-preritṛ* is none other than Brahman, it follows that all living beings are parts of the supreme Lord. On this point the seer is particularly emphatic. He conveys his insistence by the correlative use of the particle *tu*. The first *tu* means "surely" or "certainly." One must know *surely* that *prakṛti* is *māyā*, that the whole of the natural world is a magical appearance. The second *tu* means "but also." One must know *also* that every living being that inhabits this world is a part of the whole, a part of Maheśvara, the Great Lord. Each soul is a tiny wave on the limitless ocean of consciousness. A wave rises up and then subsides, momentarily has form, yet never ceases to be part of the ocean, never ceases to be of the same substance as the ocean, never ceases to be water. In the same way, every *jīva* has a temporal existence that is only a transient expression of its essential nature, the consciousness that is Śiva. As the Trikaśāstra puts it, Paramaśiva is the supreme experient (*parapramātṛ*), who through his *māyā* obscures his own infinitude; thereupon the absolute unity of his divine nature appears fragmented as countless limited experients who mistakenly perceive the world as distinct from themselves[113] rather than as Śiva's own self-expressive expansion (*svarūpaprasāra*). Reality is both being and becoming, and in Śvetāśvatara's view they are not inimical. Contrary to the tenet of *māyāvāda*, "this whole world … filled with beings that are his parts" cannot be explained away as a valueless superimposition (*adhyāsa*) of illusion on reality, like the snake misperceived in the rope.[114] According to the Trikaśāstra the world-appearance (*ābhāsa*) is a magical creation of a magician, and magic is meant for enjoyment.[115] Śvetāśvatara's positive assessment of *māyā* and *māyin* finds restatement later in the opening verse of Abhinavagupta's *Parātrīśikāvivaraṇa,* wherein the philosopher-saint observes that "Śakti surely should not be considered as distinct from Śiva" (*na hi śaktiḥ śivāt bhedam āmarśayet*). As the Śaivas put it, Śakti without Śiva has no being, and Śiva without Śakti has no expression.

11

यो योनिं योनिमधितिष्ठत्येको
यस्मिन्निदं सं च वि चैति सर्वम्।
तमीशानं वरदं देवमीड्यं
निचाय्येमां शान्तिमत्यन्तमेति ॥ ११ ॥

yo yoniṁ yonim adhitiṣṭhaty eko yasminn idaṁ saṁ ca vi caiti sarvam /
tam īśānaṁ varadaṁ devam īḍyaṁ nicāyyemāṁ śāntim atyantam eti //

11. The One in whom all this world comes together and dissolves, the One who dwells in every kind of being—realizing that beneficent, resplendent, and praiseworthy Lord, one fully and forever goes to peace.

Having proclaimed that all the creatures who fill this world are parts of Maheśvara, the Great Lord, the seer now pours out a litany of adoration for this nondual consciousness-bliss in whom all this world comes together and dissolves (*idaṁ saṁ ca vi caiti sarvam*). It is this God who inhabits every kind of living being. Śvetāśvatara lauds the ruling Lord (*īśānam*) as shining, luminous, resplendent (*devam*), as worthy of praise (*īḍyam*), and as the beneficent granter of boons (*varadam*). Realizing him through direct knowledge, one attains supreme beatitude.

Several of the Sanskrit terms used here can be understood in more than one way. In the clause "the One who dwells in every kind of being" the verb *adhitiṣṭhati* can be translated as "rules over,"[116] "presides over,"[117] or "dwells in."[118] Either sense, that of governing or inhabiting, is possible, and either appears valid here; but in the light of the previous verse, "dwells in" seems preferable.

Dwells in what? The word *yonim* can signify a physical womb,[119] or more abstractly a source[120] or cause[121] or nature[122] in the sense of *prakṛti*,[123] but there is another definition that fits the context even better: *yoni* can also signify the form of existence or station fixed by birth, and it applies to humans, animals, and all other living creatures.[124] The doubling, *yoniṁ yonim,* is a simple grammatical device that implies *every kind* of living being. To say that God dwells in every kind of creature conforms to the idea expressed in the previous verse that all beings are his parts. It is a straightforward reading without the forced complexity of some later interpretations, which take *yoniṁ yonim* to indicate the primary and secondary aspects of *prakṛti*—primal nature in its unevolved (*avyakta*) state and manifest nature evolved into the elements of creation.[125] The text suggests no such distinction.

"Realizing him, one fully and forever goes to peace." This fourth quarter is identical to the corresponding *pāda* of Kaṭhopaniṣad 1.1.17. Realizing (*nicāyya*) implies direct experience, a knowledge unmediated by sense perception, cognition, or intellectual processes. Realizing the God whom Śvetāśvatara has just extolled in glowing terms, one attains peace. The Sanskrit reads "this peace" (*imāṁ śāntim*) to indicate its nearness. "This peace" is nothing foreign to the experiencer, because it already lies close at hand, in fact at the core of everyone's being, merely waiting to be recognized. *Realizing* is qualified by the adverb *atyantam,* translated here as "fully and forever." The dictionary definitions—"exceedingly," "in perpetuity," "absolutely," "completely"[126]—fall woefully short of conveying the flavor of this word, which literally means "in a manner that is beyond limit" in space and time. What a wonderful way to describe the experience of the infinite Self!

12

यो देवानां प्रभवश्चोद्भवश्च
विश्वाधिपो रुद्रो महर्षिः ।
हिरण्यगर्भं पश्यत जायमानं
स नो बुद्ध्या शुभया संयुनक्तु ॥ १२ ॥

yo devānāṁ prabhavaś codbhavaś ca viśvādhipo rudro maharṣiḥ /
hiraṇyagarbhaṁ paśyata jāyamānaṁ sa no buddhyā śubhayā saṁyunaktu //

12. He who is the source and substance of the gods is Rudra, lord of the universe and great seer. He saw Hiraṇyagarbha being born. May he endow us with clear understanding!

Except for a slight variation, this verse is identical to *mantra* 3.4. The only difference is in the third quarter, where the earlier verse reads, "in the beginning he brought forth Hiraṇyagarbha" (*hiraṇyagarbhaṁ janayāmāsa pūrvam*) and this one reads "he saw Hiraṇyagarbha being born" (*hiraṇyagarbhaṁ paśyata jāyamānam*).

To summarize the earlier commentary (see pp. 208–211), Rudra is at once the highest reality, the source of the creation, its cause and creator. The word *prabhava* conveys all those meanings. Yet even while the supreme, nondual Rudra remains ever in repose as consciousness-in-itself, through the inherent dynamism of consciousness (*devātmaśakti*) he is also the process by which the gods, meaning the outgoing sensory faculties, become manifest. He is their coming forth as well as their very existence. Those meanings belong to the word *udbhava*. The phrase *prabhavaś codbhavaś ca* implies that consciousness is at once the eternal, immutable, nondual reality and its temporal manifestation as diversity. Rudra is the essence, the process, and the product all at once, the triad (*traya*).

The essence is the immutable light of consciousness, the Rudra of eternal being, who witnesses the process of cosmic manifestation from its first stirring (*hiraṇyagarbha*) to its end product, the world of our experience. Put another way, consciousness-in-itself is essential to the experience of its own content, the ever-changing display (*ābhāsa*) that is the world. As Abhinavagupta explains, the light of consciousness has no form other than its own. If transformed into anything else, it would no longer be the light of consciousness, and in its absence the experience of the world would be impossible. Consciousness has to remain in its own essence to be the substratum of its own self-expression. Conversely, if the world were anything other than the light of consciousness, even though reflected in itself or dimmed by *māyā*, how could that world even appear to us? As Śvetāśvatara will declare later (6.14), "He alone shining, everything shines after him. By his light all this universe shines."

We experience the world and our own existence only through the light of consciousness. Each individual experiences the world through a particular set of limitations, but Rudra as the universal ruler (*viśvādhipaḥ*) and great seer of unlimited vision (*maharṣiḥ*) enjoys it as divine universality (see pp. 58–59). Śvetāśvatara prays, "May he endow us with clear understanding!" May we too have that divine experience. May we, through the grace of God, attain the state of perfect knowledge, fully realizing our true being.

13

यो देवानामधिपो
यस्मिंल्लोका अधिश्रिताः ।
य ईशे अस्य द्विपदश्चतुष्पदः
कस्मै देवाय हविषा विधेम ॥ १३ ॥

yo devānām adhipo yasmiṁl lokā adhiśritāḥ /
ya īśe asya dvipadaś catuṣpadaḥ kasmai devāya haviṣā vidhema //

13. He who is the ruler of the gods, in whom the worlds rest, he who rules over the two-footed and the four-footed creatures—what [other] god shall we worship with oblation?

The seer continues, now citing extracts from much older sacred texts: "He who rules over the two-footed and the four-footed creatures"—over human beings, birds, and animals—is a quotation of Ṛgveda 10.121.3c and Vājasaneyisaṁhitā 20.20.32b. From Ṛgveda 10.121.3d comes the most interesting of the citations: "What god shall we worship with oblation?"

This question forms the constant refrain of the Ṛgvedic hymn addressed not to any particular god or gods, but simple to Who? (*kaḥ*). Each of the ten verses extols the powers of the glorious creator god and ruler of all, called Hiraṇyagarbha at the hymn's beginning and Prajāpati at the end. Every verse but the last concludes, as if awestruck, with the rhetorical question, "What god shall we worship with oblation?" The implication is, "What god other than the One shall we worship with oblation?"[127] This understanding is borne out elsewhere in the Ṛgveda with the proclamation that "truth is One; the wise call it by various names" (1.164.46). By whatever name the Supreme Being is called—be it Mitra, Indra, Varuṇa, Agni, or any other, there is one God, and that God is the nondual reality.

In the previous *mantra* Śvetāśvatara says that Rudra witnessed the birth of Hiraṇyagarbha. This is a mythological way of saying that the Absolute witnessed within itself the initial stirring of manifestation, known in the Trika philosophy as *icchāśakti*. The Ṛgvedic hymn to Who? equates that same Hiraṇyagarbha with the Absolute. Again, the Divine and its causal potency are one. The hymn extols Hiraṇyagarbha, also called Prajāpati, as "the gods' one spirit" (10.121.7) and "the God of gods with none beside him" (10.121.8). Whether spelled out in philosophical language or expressed poetically, the meaning is the same: the ultimate truth is pure nonduality.

14

सूक्ष्मातिसूक्ष्मं कलिलस्य मध्ये
विश्वस्य स्रष्टारमनेकरूपम् ।
विश्वस्यैकं परिवेष्टितारं
ज्ञात्वा शिवं शान्तिमत्यन्तमेति ॥ १४ ॥

sūkṣmātisūkṣmaṁ kalilasya madhye viśvasya sraṣṭāram anekarūpam /
viśvasyaikaṁ pariveṣṭitāraṁ jñātvā śivaṁ śāntim atyantam eti //

14. He is subtler than the subtlest, in the midst of the unformed the creator of everything, assuming many forms. He alone encompasses the universe; knowing that auspicious being, one fully and forever goes to peace.

Continuing to extol the supreme divinity, this *mantra* declares him to be subtler than the subtlest, in other words the Absolute beyond the mind's ability to grasp. At the same time, in relation to the world this same Rudra acts as the author of the universe by bringing order to the primordial chaos (*kalila*). This idea of order from chaos represents an ancient and widespread view of creation found in many religious traditions. What Śvetāśvatara means is that the Lord brings form out of the unformed or imposes conditioning (*vikṛti*) on the unconditioned, primordial *prakṛti*.

By knowing the auspicious (*śivaṁ*) Rudra, whose forms are multiple and diverse (*anekarūpam*) and whose indissoluble unity at the same time embraces and pervades the entire universe (*viśvasyai-kaṁ pariveṣṭitāram*), "one fully and forever goes to peace" (*śāntim atyantam eti*). Śvetāśvatara repeats this utterance from *mantra* 4.11 (see p. 298) to impress that the knowledge of the unity underlying all diversity is the highest realization and that spiritual illumination is a state of transcendental beatitude.

15

स एव काले भुवनस्य गोप्ता
विश्वाधिपः सर्वभुतेषु गूढः ।
यस्मिन् युक्ता ब्रह्मर्षयो देवताश्च
तमेवं ज्ञात्वा मृत्युपाशांश्छिनत्ति ॥ १५ ॥

sa eva kāle bhuvanasya goptā viśvādhipaḥ sarvabhuteṣu gūḍhaḥ / yasmin yuktā brahmarṣayo devatāś ca tam evaṁ jñātvā mṛtyupāśāṁś chinatti //

15. He is surely the protector of the world in time, the lord of the universe, in all beings hidden, in whom the seers and gods are absorbed in meditation. Knowing him alone, one cuts through the bonds of death.

The world "in time" (*kāle*) refers to the universe during a period of cosmic manifestation. Here the Supreme Being, whom the previous *mantra* calls benevolent or auspicious (*śiva*), rules over his creation as its protector (*goptā*) and universal lord (*viśvādhipaḥ*). We must remember that during a period of cosmic manifestation, the infinite glory of the divine reality remains hidden in all beings (*sarvabhuteṣu gūḍhaḥ*). As Śvetāśvatara said early on (1.3), the causal potency of the supreme Self (*devātmaśakti*) remains hidden by its own effects (*svaguṇair nigūdhām*). The world of our experience is composed of *māyā's* five limiting veils (*kañcukas*), which include the fabric of time and space. The human mind (*antaḥkaraṇa*), being a part of this cosmos and functioning within it, is likewise restricted by those same five limitations (see pp. 116–120). Concerning time and space, the mind cannot possibly conceive a thought or express it except in temporal or spatial terms.

Being a product of *māyā,* the mind cannot reach beyond it but can only function within its realm. Any mental conception of God is necessarily tinged with *māyā's* limitations. As Advaita Vedānta puts it, the highest idea of divinity conceivable by the human mind is Īśvara. And what is Īśvara? It is *saguṇa* Brahman, Brahman in association with its *māyā.* The finite mind cannot wrap itself around the Infinite. It is as simple as that.

When we think of divinity, we often conceive of it in terms of rulership, just as this *mantra* does when it refers to God as "the lord of the universe." Who or what is the lord of the universe? Advaita Vedānta says it is Īśvara. Here nondualistic Śaivism takes a different position. Whereas Advaita Vedānta considers rulership (*aiśvarya*) to be an attribute of *saguṇa* Brahman owing to its association with *māyā,* the Trikaśāstra considers *aiśvarya* (also known as *svātantryaśakti* or *vimarśaśakti*) to be the inherent nature of Paramaśiva. In the *Tantrāloka* Abhinavagupta equates this supreme power of universal consciousness with *anuttara,* the Ultimate beyond which there is nothing else.[128] In the Śaiva definition, enlightenment is liberation (*mokṣa*), and liberation is absolute freedom (*svātantrya* or *aiśvarya*). Long before the formulation of the Trika teaching, Lakulīśa articulated this very view, and before him Śvetāśvatara declared the same in *mantra* 1.11. In the Trika scheme of things, *svātantrya,* also called *śaktitattva,* is the second *tattva,* identical to the first, called *śivatattva.* These two, consciousness and its power, are the essential nature (*svarūpaśakti*) of the nondual Divine, its eternal being anterior to and superior to any manifestation of *māyā,* which is the sixth *tattva.*

Everything that manifests from what we call Rudra, Śiva, or

Brahman exists in a state of finitude, but in that finitude is the implicit infinitude of the source. Here we must be careful not to entertain the mistaken idea that the Infinite is the sum total of all that is manifest. Finite parts, however many, cannot constitute an infinite whole. The Infinite is of an entirely different order of reality, beyond perception, cognition, and conception. Although surpassing his own manifestation, the supreme Rudra is never separate from it, and because his indivisible pervasiveness is hidden in all beings (*sarvabhuteṣu gūḍhaḥ*), the entire universe exists within him.

Abhinavagupta expresses this idea with the word *sampuṭīkṛti* ("encapsulation"). In the *Tantrāloka* (3.207) he writes of the whole universe shining in consciousness and from the same universe consciousness shining forth. The absolute reality is present in every finite state, and everything finite exists in the infinite Absolute.[129]

Just as the knowers of Brahman become absorbed (*yuktāḥ*) in the divine reality through meditation, every aspiring human being can attain that same experience. To know that reality is to recognize our own eternal nature. Then we no longer falsely identify with what exists in time: with a body that is born, grows, matures, declines, and dies, or with the mind's kaleidoscopically changing thoughts and moods. Knowing the Self beyond time, we cut through the bonds of death, the very ties that paradoxically bind us to what we call life—our phenomenal existence in the realm of *māyā*. The knowledge of the eternal, imperishable Self is what sets us free.

16

घृतात् परं मण्डमिवातिसूक्ष्मं
ज्ञात्वा शिवं सर्वभुतेषु गूढम् ।
विश्वस्यैकं परिवेष्टितारं
ज्ञात्वा देवं मुच्यते सर्वपाशैः ॥ १६ ॥

ghṛtāt paraṁ maṇḍam ivātisūkṣmaṁ jñātvā śivaṁ sarvabhuteṣu gūḍham /
viśvasyaikaṁ pariveṣṭitāraṁ jñātvā devaṁ mucyate sarvapāśaiḥ //

16. Knowing the auspicious one hidden in all beings like the most subtle essence of clarified butter, knowing that effulgent being who alone encompasses the universe, one is freed from all fetters.

Śvetāśvatara continues to express his joyful astonishment (*camatkāra*) at the divine essence shining forth through the manifold beauties of the created universe. To ordinary eyes the light of consciousness remains heavily veiled by the cloaks of *māyā,* but to the eye of the spirit, it reveals its glory.

Even when hidden, divinity is ever present and all-pervading. The seer gives the illustration of clarified butter. When heated, it releases a subtle essence (*maṇḍam*), which forms a delicious film on the surface. In the same way, when human consciousness is "heated" by intense concentration (*tapas*), the divine presence within the whole of creation rises to the surface, so to speak. It becomes apparent and transfigures the vision of life.

Put another way, when right understanding enables us to penetrate the world-appearance, we discover its delightful essence, the bliss of the infinite Brahman.[130] With this glorious vision of the divine reality before us, we are able to let go of the nonessentials—the false notions of I and mine and the rest of *māyā's* encumbrances. We discover that the real essence of the many is the One, and that the One is our very Self. Realizing our identity with the Infinite, we attain absolute freedom and joy.

17

एष देवो विश्वकर्मा महात्मा
सदा जनानां हृदये सन्निविष्टः ।
हृदा मनीषा मनसाऽभिक्लृप्तो
य एतद् विदुरमृतास्ते भवन्ति ॥ १७ ॥

eṣa devo viśvakarmā mahātmā sadā janānāṁ hṛdaye sanniviṣṭaḥ /
hṛdā manīṣā manasā 'bhikḷpto ya etad vidur amṛtās te bhavanti //

17. This god, the maker of all things, the great Self, is ever established in the hearts of living beings, corresponding within to the heart, intelligence, and mind. They who know this become immortal.

The supreme reality, Rudra, through his causal potency, becomes the creator, the maker of all things (*viśvakarmā*) whom the Ṛgveda lauds as the divine smith or architect of the universe. Projecting the creation, he embodies himself as the world and all living creatures. Even so, he remains the indivisible great Self (*mahātmā*), the ever present light of awareness at the heart (*hṛdaye*) or center of every sentient being.

The word *heart* occurs twice in this *mantra*, each time in a different technical sense. Throughout the history of Indian religion the heart (*hṛd*) has been a richly nuanced symbol of spiritual reality. It has long been considered the seat of feelings, emotions, thought, and intellectual operations.[131] The Ṛgveda speaks of its diverse functions as "seeing" what the eye cannot see, putting humans in touch with the gods, enabling one to penetrate the deepest mysteries and to fashion the inner visions into words, effecting purification and clarification, and connecting the individual soul with the transcendental reality.[132] In the Bṛhadāraṇyakopaniṣad (4.1.7) the venerable Yājñavalkya tells King Janaka that the heart is the abode and the support of all beings; truly it is the supreme Brahman. Later, in the Kaṭhopaniṣad (2.3.9), Yama, the king of death, teaches the young Naciketas that the heart is the dwelling place of the all-pervading, attributeless supreme Self (*puruṣo vyāpako 'liṅga*), invisible to the eye. It is in this sense as the center of awareness that Śvetāśvatara first uses *heart*.

The word takes on a different significance in the *mantra's* third quarter, which qualifies "this effulgent supreme Self" (*eṣa devo mahātmā*) as "corresponding within to the heart, intelligence, and mind" (*hṛdā manīṣā manasā 'bhikḷptaḥ*). To understand this second meaning, where *heart* is related to *intelligence* and *mind*, we need to trace the evolution of this grouping. An earlier version of *hṛdā manīṣā manasā* occurs in the Ṛgvedasaṁhitā (1.51.2), where a seer named Nodhas mentions that *ṛṣis* of old adorned their praise of Indra "with heart and mind and spirit" (*hṛdā manasā manīṣā*).[133] Perhaps he meant with feeling, thought, and enthusiastic deed. His phrase, with the second and third words reversed, found its way into the third quarter of Kaṭhopaniṣad 2.3.9, a passage identical to the corresponding part of Śvetāśvatara's *mantra*. Commenting on the Kaṭhopaniṣad, Śaṁkara takes *hṛdā manīṣā manasābhiklptaḥ* to mean "apprehended by heart, by thought, by mind" and explains that the way to knowledge of Brahman is through the concentrated effort and purification of these internal faculties.[134] The heart, as the center of awareness, is more than the dwelling-place of the supreme Self—the subjective consciousness that expresses itself through emotion, intellectual functioning, and interaction with the objective world; for Śaṁkara the heart is also the instrument for Self-realization.[135]

Śvetāśvatara, although quoting the third quarter verbatim from the Kaṭhopaniṣad, places it in a new context and imbues its words with somewhat different implications. In the Kaṭhopaniṣad the first half of the verse (2.3.9) expresses an utterly transcendental divine reality, but the first half of Śvetāśvatara's *mantra* presents a simultaneously transcendent and immanent and more personal divinity, suggestive of the Trikaśāstra's nondual Lord.

According to Śvetāśvatara, the divine consciousness that is Rudra is present in all living beings, corresponding internally (*abhiklptaḥ*) to the heart (*hṛdā*), the intelligence (*manīṣā*), and the mind (*manasā*). This triad at once recalls a seminal idea of the Taittirīyopaniṣad and looks ahead to the later philosophy of the Trikaśāstra. According to the Taittirīyopaniṣad (2.6.1) Brahman first desired (*akāmayata*) to be many, then deliberated (*atapyata*), and then emitted (*asṛjata*) the entire cosmos (*idaṁ sarvam*). Śaṁkara's commentary on this verse equates the performance of austerity with the exercise of knowledge and concludes that Brahman willed, thought, and created (see pp. 114–115). When Śvetāśvatara speaks of the heart, intelligence, and mind, he is clearly referring to the three powers of will (*icchā*), knowledge (*jñāna*), and action (*kriyā*) that Trika thinking attributes to the supreme Śiva.

At the level of universal experience (*śuddhādhvan*), *icchāśakti* is the will of the One to become many—the initial, potentially dynamic urge for self-expression. As it grows more active, stirring as the power of ideation, it is known as *jnānaśakti*. When it reaches the state of readiness to implement, it is called *kriyāśakti*. Above the level of *māyā*, these three facets of *śakti* are divine capacities. Below the level of *māyā*—within *prakṛti*—these same three powers of will, knowledge, and action correlate with how the individual soul experiences its own existence. In the higher state these powers characterize the *sadāśiva, īśvara,* and *sadvidyā tattvas* and constitute the Lord's threefold capacity of manifestation. In the phenomenal realm these same divine capacities express themselves as the human abilities to feel, to think, and to act. Thus diversified, the ultimately singular power of divine consciousness lies at the heart of all our experience. As Śvetāśvatara explains, this effulgent great Self (*eṣa devo mahātmā*), who is the single and ever present knowing principle at the heart or center (*hṛdaye*) of all experience, corresponds internally (*abhikḷptaḥ*) to the individual's emotional and willing capacity (*hṛdā*), determinative intelligence (*manīṣā*), and cognitive ability (*manasā*), which interact with the objective world. This triad of heart, intelligence, and mind constitutes the inner instrument (*antaḥkaraṇa*). What Śvetāśvatara means is that the indwelling Self, the supreme Rudra, experiences his play of creation through the individual's faculties of personal selfhood (*ahaṁkāra*), determinative intelligence (*buddhi*), and cognition (*manas*). The fundamental components of the human experience are feeling, thinking, and acting, and they are but limited versions of the higher powers of divine consciousness. There is an intrinsic connection between the individual soul and the supreme Lord, and in the highest state of realization, this connection becomes identity. As Śvetāśvatara has often said, "They who know this become immortal" (see p. 234).

18

यदाऽतमस्तन्न दिवा न रात्रिः
न सन्नचासच्छिव एव केवलः ।
तदक्षरं तत् सवितुर्वरेण्यं
प्रज्ञा च तस्मात् प्रसृता पुराणी ॥ १८ ॥

yadā 'tamas tan na divā na rātriḥ na san na cāsac chiva eva kevalaḥ /
tad akṣaraṁ tat savitur vareṇyaṁ prajñā ca tasmāt prasṛtā purāṇī //

18. When the darkness of ignorance is no more, then there is neither day nor night, neither existence nor nonexistence, only the auspicious One alone. That is the imperishable, that is the glory of Savitṛ, and from that the ancient wisdom has come forth.

The seer began his fourth discourse by saying that the effulgent God who is One and without color expands into the diverse universe of many colors. In the first ten *mantras* he celebrated the glories of the natural world, and from the eleventh through the seventeenth he shifted our attention to the immanent face of God, to the auspicious creator and protector who is established in every heart. Twice in the course of his rapturous outpouring (4.1, 4.12), he has uttered the prayer, "May he endow us with clear understanding!" (*sa no buddhyā śubhayā saṁyunaktu*).

When the light of Self-knowledge dispels the darkness of ignorance, all appearance of duality vanishes. Nondual consciousness, here called nondarkness (*atamas*), is spiritual illumination wherein no limitation of objectivity remains, no relativities such as day and night, light and darkness, heat and cold, good and evil. Not even the concept of existence (*sat*) and nonexistence (*asat*) remains, for those states are only relative to each other and mutually dependent—not absolute. What does remain is the changeless unity of the divine Self, described here as auspicious (*śivaḥ*) and alone (*kevalaḥ*). Śvetāśvatara describes the imperishable reality of consciousness-in-itself as the glory of Savitṛ (*tat savitur vareṇyam*), and Savitṛ represents the unity of consciousness and its power (see pp. 157–158).

The seer's main point is that the state of Self-realization, enlightenment, or liberation is the unconditioned state of nonduality. He expresses this with the phrase "only the auspicious One alone" (*śiva eva kevalaḥ*). Here the adjective *kevala* warrants further attention. Of the principal Upaniṣads the Śvetāśavatara is the only one to use it, and it occurs three times (1.11, 4.18, 6.11). *Kevala,* in the sense of "alone," "sole," and "excluding others," can be found in the Saṁhitā portions of the Ṛgveda and Atharvaveda and in the Yajurveda's Taittirīyasāṁhitā as well. In the Śatapathabrāhmaṇa *kevala* acquires the additional connotations of "not connected with anything else," "uncompounded," "pure," "isolated," "absolute," and by the time of the Mahābhārata, it can also mean "entire" or "whole."[136]

The adjective *kevala* and the substantive *kaivalya* ("isolation") figure in several schools of Indian thought. In the Jain religion, contemporary with Buddhism and representing the revival of an ancient ascetic (*śramaṇa*) tradition, the term *kevalajñāna* signifies the absolute knowledge in which the sentient soul (*jīva*) is isolated from the insentient constituent of the universe (*ajīva*). The liberated soul (*kevalin*), thus separated, is freed from *karma* and rebirth and remains unlimited and complete in its original state. Jain doctrine, along with Vedic ideas, probably played a role in the formation of the Sāṁkhya system,[137] but how and when the Sāṁkhya doctrine of *kaivalya* evolved is unclear. The oldest surviving Sāṁkhya text, the *Sāṁkhya-kārikā,* already presents the fully developed classical formulation. In the Sāṁkhya and the closely related Yoga system, *kaivalya* signifies the state of liberation in which the *puruṣa* is completely isolated or disentangled from *prakṛti* and restored to the experience of its true, original nature. In contrast, Lakulīśa's *dvaitādvaita* Śaivism rejects the dualistic Jain and Sāṁkhya definition of *kaivalya* as liberation. The distinction between *jīva* and *ajīva* or between *puruṣa* and *prakṛti* represents a certain state of spiritual attainment, to be sure, but falls short of eradicating the fundamental impurity (*mala*) of the bound soul, which is the sense of limited individuality (*paśutva*). In the Śaiva definition *puruṣa* is individualized subjectivity coexistent with objectivity (*prakṛti*). The *Pāśupatasūtra* maintains that as long as the soul has not recognized its omniscience and omnipotence, it has not achieved union (*sāyujya*) with the Lord.[138] Following Lakulīśa, the nondualistic Trika Śaivism similarly does not define *kaivalya* as the state of highest realization but only as the state in which finite subjectivity (*puruṣa*) is experienced as completely apart from the mental and physical apparatus of its *prakṛti.*[139] The aspirant has not yet penetrated the six *tattvas* of *māyā* to reach the universal experience of the divine Self.

Śvetāśvatara's usage of *kevala* is best understood in the historical context, which is pre-Jain and pre-Sāṁkhya and conforming to the usage of older Vedic texts. For Śvetāśvatara the word is simply an unequivocal expression of Upaniṣadic nondualism, a way of saying that the supreme Self is One without a second. This is the same understanding articulated in Sadānanda Yogīndra's *Vedāntasāra,* a late treatise on Advaita Vedānta that employs *kaivalya* to signify absolute unity.

The phrase *tat savitur vareṇyam,* quoted here in the third quarter, forms part of the Ṛgveda's most sacred verse, the Gāyatrī *mantra* (3.62.10). Literally, *vareṇyam* means "[that which is] to be wished for," "desirable," "excellent." What is more desirable than the infinite splendor of the self-effulgent, all-illuminating divine consciousness? Immanent in every heart, this light leads the aspirant to ever higher states of spiritual awareness by inspiring or bringing forth the ancient wisdom (*prajñā purāṇī*), the eternal knowledge of the ultimate Self.

19

नैनमूर्ध्वं न तिर्यञ्चं न मध्ये परिजग्रभत्।
न तस्य प्रतिमा अस्ति यस्य नाम महद् यशः ॥ १९ ॥

nainam ūrdhvaṁ na tiryañcaṁ na madhye parijagrabhat /
na tasya pratimā asti yasya nāma mahad yaśaḥ //

19. Not above, not across, not in the middle has anyone fully grasped him; there is no measure of him whose name is great glory.

This *mantra* is a quotation from the Vājasaneyisaṁhitā, consisting of the second half of verse 32.2 and the first half of the following verse. Śvetāśvatara incorporates five quotations from this older text in the course of his fourth discourse (in 4.2, 4.13c, 4.13d, 4.19, 4.22). *Mantra* 4.2, identical to Vājasaneyisaṁhitā 32.1, acknowledges the divine power visible in the natural forces of sun, moon, wind, water, and light and equates it with the ineffable deity, called simply "that" (*tat*). *Mantra* 4.13 poses a powerful rhetorical question, first found in the Ṛgvedic hymn addressed to Who? (10.121.3) and repeated in the Vājasaneyisaṁhitā (32.6): "What God shall we worship with oblation?" What is that ungraspable reality behind all graspable appearances, and how shall we worship it? Now, reciting Vājasaneyisaṁhitā 32.2cd and 32.3ab, Śvetāśvatara again addresses the divine ineffability.

How can one fully grasp that which is both nonmaterial and undifferentiated? The answer is simple: one cannot. Because the absolute Brahman is unbounded by physicality, no one has ever been able to take hold of it in the sense of height or breadth or anything in between. In Sanskrit and English alike, the word *grasping* means more than physical apprehension; it signifies mental apprehension as well. Can anyone *understand* what Brahman truly is? One cannot, but Śvetāśvatara is talking about even more than understanding. The verb *parigrah* indicates not just taking hold of something either physically or mentally, but *fully, completely, all inclusively* taking hold. No one has ever been able to wrap the mind around the divine being who is limitless consciousness, simply because the finite cannot embrace the Infinite.

The Infinite is beyond measure (*pratimā*). That is what the text suggests here, even though the usual and equally valid reading of *pratimā* is "likeness,"[140] "image,"[141] "equal,"[142] or "parallel."[143] The Absolute is indescribable[144] and cannot be fully represented by any material object, natural or man-made, or by any intellectual concept either. Any image, be it a statue or picture or symbol, exists in time and space and consists of physical elements and limiting attributes. A material image in turn represents a mental image or a conceptual abstraction, but even thought is subject to the limitations of *māyā*. A thought construct (*vikalpa*) arises as a finite modification in the undifferentiated wholeness of consciousness itself, which is by nature beyond thought (*nirvikalpa*). Any likeness, material or mental, is made of parts and is necessarily the product of differentiation and fragmentation. How can such a thing possibly represent the glorious wholeness of the One who is without a second? Even the most exalted thought can at best be only a dim suggestion of the divine reality.

The immeasurable glory of God that "fills all quarters and pervades everything,"[145] appears at the human level of experience as an innumerable multitude of creatures and objects with countless forms and qualities. Each one reflects some small measure of divine glory, but none can lay claim to being its single likeness.[146] Furthermore, a likeness of anything implies a separation from the reality it represents. What could possibly be separate from that which is One without a second? Finally the text makes clear that divine glory is not God's attribute but his essence: "There is no measure of him whose name is great glory" (*na tasya pratimā asti yasya nāma mahad yaśaḥ*). Reciting these ancient words, spoken long before his time, Śvetāśvatara affirms once again that consciousness and its power, the Divine and its self-expression, are one.

20

न संदृशे तिष्ठति रूपमस्य
न चक्षुषा पश्यति कश्चनैनम् ।
हृदा हृदिस्थं मनसा य एनमे-
वं विदुरमृतास्ते भवन्ति ॥ २० ॥

na saṁdṛśe tiṣṭhati rūpam asya na cakṣuṣā paśyati kaścanainam /
hṛdā hṛdistham manasā ya enam evaṁ vidur amṛtās te bhavanti //

20. His form stands not in the range of sight; no one sees him with the eye. They who with the heart and mind know him as abiding in the heart, they become immortal.

The first half of this *mantra*, identical to the first half of Kaṭhopaniṣad 2.3.9, declares that God's supreme form (*rūpam*) is in reality formlessness, invisible to the eye and by implication standing outside the full range of sense perception and all other means of mediate knowledge. Because the finite cannot comprehend the Infinite, the instruments of the lower, or relational, knowledge (*aparāvidyā*) are incapable of revealing the Absolute. The divine reality can only be realized through the higher, unmediated experience (*aparokṣānubhūti*), which is God-realization or Self-realization (see pp. 234–238).

That knowledge alone can confer immortality. On this point the Upaniṣad is insistent: "They who know this (or him, or the Lord) become immortal" is a pronouncement already met with in *mantras* 3.1, 3.7, 3.10, 3.13, and 4.17. As previously explained, "to become immortal" does not mean to live forever in finite form but to realize the identity of the indwelling Self (*ātman*) and the transcendent

Brahman. The recognition of our true, original nature, the knowledge of our own boundlessness and imperishability, confers ultimate freedom, even from the constraint of death.

21

अजात इत्येवं कश्चिद्भीरुः प्रपद्यते ।
रुद्र यत् ते दक्षिणं मुखं तेन मां पाहि नित्यम् ॥ २१ ॥

ajāta ity evaṁ kaścid bhīruḥ prapadyate /
rudra yat te dakṣiṇaṁ mukhaṁ tena māṁ pāhi nityam //

21. Because you are unborn, one who is fearful takes refuge in you. O Rudra, that which is your benevolent face—by that protect me always!

Coming after the previous *mantra's* mention of immortality, the word *bhīruḥ* ("fearful") here refers specifically to existential fear, founded on the impermanence of human life. This context takes us back to the opening verse of the Upaniṣad, where the seer asks on what our permanence (*sampratiṣṭhā*) rests in [life's course through] happiness and all the rest (*sukhetareṣu*)." For those who grow attached to the pleasant or merely to the comfortably familiar things in life, there inevitably arises the aching regret that all this shall pass away. Stronger than that may be the fear of death itself. Accordingly the word *bhīru* can also mean "dreading the beyond or the hereafter."[147] Depending on one's understanding of life, existential fear can encompass a wide range of emotion from resigned acceptance to chronic distress, reflected in the various renderings of *bhīru* as "afraid,"[148] "trembling,"[149] "frightened by death"[150] "frightened [by birth and death],"[151] or "terror-stricken."[152]

Given the specific context of this *mantra* and the overall context of the Upaniṣad, *bhīru* is best understood as representing any degree of existential discomfort (*duḥkha*), and for this Śvetāśvatara proposes a simple solution. One who is fearful of impermanence should take refuge (*prapadyate*) in that which is perpetual, hence unborn. Because

Rudra, the supreme Self, is unborn (*ajāta*), he (or it) is eternal being without beginning or end. Being eternal (*nitya*), it is constant (also *nitya*), inherent (another meaning of *nitya*), and one's very own (yet another meaning of *nitya*). As the seer says repeatedly, knowing—experiencing—one's true being, one is freed from all fetters and becomes immortal. *Fearful* thus describes the embodied soul, which experiences a broad array of existential distress, not least the primal fear rooted in the impermanence of all that it holds dear. What refuge can there be from the inevitable decay of everything in human experience? The only possible refuge is the imperishable divine reality, the immortal Rudra, who rests unborn—ever untouched by phenomenality.

The second line of this *mantra* is a prayer for divine grace and protection, but it implies much more. Representative translations read: "O Rudra, let thy gracious face protect me for ever!"[153] "O Rudra, may Thy benign face protect me for ever!"[154] "Rudra, with that propitious face of yours / Protect me always."[155] These give the impression that God's face is an auspicious one, but they fail to pay close attention to the original Sanskrit. A more faithful translation reads: "O Rudra, that face of thine which is propitious—with that do thou protect me ever!"[156] Śvetāśvatara's distinctive phrasing allows the possibility that Rudra has more than one face.

That should come as no surprise, given that the earliest hymns to Rudra, found in the Ṛgvedasaṁhitā, portray him as the powerful god of storms and as a gracious healer as well. He is at once destructive and benevolent, wrathful and protective, wise and compassionate, sovereign and blissful (see p. 35). The present translation—"O Rudra, that which is your benevolent face—by that protect me always!"—preserves the original syntax along with its implication that Rudra's faces are many.

A series of *mantras* in the tenth book of the Taittirīyāraṇyaka (10.43–47), also known as the Mahānārāyaṇopaniṣad (sections 17–21 in the Āndhra recension), portray Mahādeva (Rudra-Śiva) as five-faced (*pañcavaktra*) and give the names and attributes of each divine aspect. The text, composed two or three centuries after the Śvetāśvataropaniṣad, marks the oldest known occurrence of the five names together but already shows a fixed order and a definitive formulation that must have evolved over a period of time.[157] The names are Sadyojāta, Vāmadeva, Aghora, Tatpuruṣa, and Īśāna.

Among them the most widely attested is Īśāna. As an adjective ("owning," "possessing," "wealthy," "reigning") and as a noun ("ruler," "master," "lord"), it is one of the older designations of Rudra, found in the Ṛgveda, the Vājasaneyisaṁhitā, the Śatapathabrāhmaṇa, and the Atharvaveda. In those texts *īśāna* often designates a deity's might and authority, and it can apply to various gods, including Indra, Agni, Varuṇa, and Mitra. In the Taittirīyabrāhmaṇa (1.5.5.2), it signifies an individual god as lord and master.[158] One verse of the Bṛhadāraṇyakopaniṣad (1.4.11) names Īśāna as a specific god of the Vedic pantheon, but another (4.4.15) has him as the universal lord of what has been and what will be (*īśāno bhūtabhavyasya*), a characterization that reappears in the Kaṭhopaniṣad (2.1.12) and the Śvetāśvataropaniṣad (3.15). Significantly, Śvetāśvatara's *mantra* is a quotation from the Ṛgveda's Puruṣasūkta, and that verse (10.90.2) demonstrates that even in the early Vedic period *īśāna* could indicate the singular Supreme Being. Calling him "the lord of immortality" (*amṛtatvasyeśānaḥ*), the verse proclaims, "The [universal] Person is truly all this—what has been and what will be" (*puruṣa evedaṁ sarvaṁ yad bhūtaṁ yac ca bhavyam*).

As for the other names, the usage of *Sadyojāta* in the Taittirīyasaṁhitā and Vājasaneyisaṁhitā indicates a deity who is present or apparent in the very moment, a palpable reality. *Vāmadeva* is a fairly common name given to various *ṛṣis,* kings, and other persons, but the Vedic texts also identify him with Prajāpati, while the Purāṇas speak of a Vāmadeva who is clearly meant to be Śiva.[159] Information on *Aghora* is scarcer, but the name probably began as an attribute. A verse common to the Rudrādhyāya (Taittirīyasaṁhitā 4.5.1.1) and Śatarudrīya (Vājasaneyisaṁhitā 16.2) and quoted by Śvetāśvatara (3.5) invokes Rudra in his auspicious (*śiva*) and reassuring (*aghora*) form. Finally, one can surmise that *Tatpuruṣa,* as a name of Rudra, derives ultimately from the Puruṣasūkta and indicates the original or supreme spirit.

The five aspects of Rudra-Mahādeva named in the *mantras* of the Taittirīyāraṇyaka face the four cardinal directions and upward, the totality of five symbolizing divine omnipresence. The first *mantra* begins, "I take refuge in Sadyojāta," and then salutes the Lord's westward face, said to effect the evolution of the cosmos out of unconditioned potentiality. The devotee asks to be taken beyond every condition of finitude and then concludes with a salutation to that deity whose manifestation is this state of becoming (*bhavodbhavāya namaḥ*). It is the same Lord who binds and sets free. Cosmic evolution (*sṛṣṭi*) takes place when Sadyojāta's face is turned outward (*pratyagvṛtti*), and the world-process (*saṁsāra*) ends when it is turned inward (*prāgvṛtti*).[160]

The second *mantra* begins with salutation to Vāmadeva, the northward face, followed by a series of additional salutations (eight, nine, or ten, depending on the recension) directed to various expressions of his awe-inspiring power. The name *Vāmadeva* conveys the idea of an effulgent divine being whose qualities are beauty, splendor, and nobility.[161]

The *mantra* of the southern face, Aghora, acknowledges that all forms are Rudra's embodiment, whether auspicious (*aghora*), terrible (*ghora*), or surpassingly terrible (*ghoratara*). The Vedic commentator Sāyaṇa equates the three forms with the predominance, in turn, of *sattva, rajas,* and *tamas.*[162] In any case, this *mantra* acknowledges the dualities of human existence, expressed in the contrast of divine power as both gentle (*saumya*) and fierce (*ugra*), manifesting as death and fertility, illness and recovery, evil and deliverance from evil. The name *Aghora* ("not inspiring dread") emphasizes divine benevolence and restraint from doing harm.[163] Aghora is also known as Dakṣiṇāmūrti,[164] the form of Śiva whom Śaṁkara extols in his ten-part hymn, *Dakṣiṇāmūrtistotra,* as the compassionate, all-encompassing Lord who instructs humankind in the unity of the individual self and the supreme Self.

The name *Tatpuruṣa* may have evolved from a Śaiva variant of the Gāyatrī *mantra,* which also occurs earlier as Taittirīyāraṇyaka 10.1.23 (Mahānārayaṇopaniṣad 1.23): "May we know the [supreme] Person; may we meditate on the Great God; may Rudra inspire our thought" (*tatpuruṣāya vidmahe mahādevāya dhīmahi / tan no rudraḥ pracodayāt*). The prayer appeals to the primordial spirit, conceived as the universal soul.[165] *Puruṣa, Mahādeva,* and *Rudra* are all names for the one Supreme Being, each with a particular nuance. *Puruṣa* implies the immanence of the ultimate conscious principle as the Self of all.[166] *Mahādeva* conveys unrivaled greatness and resplendence, and *Rudra* represents the supreme reality presiding over all knowledge and wisdom.[167] As Rudra's eastern face, Tatpuruṣa is associated with the sun god Savitṛ, a connection made clear in Śvetāśvatara's second discourse (2.1–4, 7, 18). Tatpuruṣa, the indwelling light of consciousness, is the divine Self who inspires our contemplation and impels us to the higher knowledge.

Associated with liberation,[168] Īśāna, the upward-looking face (*ūrdhvavaktra*), is Rudra's supreme aspect. The fifth *mantra* proclaims him the possessor of all forms of knowledge (*īśānaḥ sarvavidyānām*) and the sovereign of all beings (*īśvaraḥ sarvabhūtānām*), higher than Hiraṇyagarbha, as Śvetāśvatara also notes (3.4, 4.12). Identifying him as the supreme Brahman, the *mantra* concludes with a prayer: "To me may he be auspicious, the ever auspicious one" (*śivo me astu sadāśivaḥ—Oṁ*).

Rudra's five faces play an important role in the *Pāśupatasūtra,* a text traditionally ascribed to the Śaiva reformer Lakulīśa, who lived in the first half of the second century CE. Possibly dating from before Lakulīśa's time, the *Pāśupatasūtra* draws on the Taittirīyāraṇyaka while showing some textual variations in the quoted passages.[169] The *mantras* denominating Śiva's five faces (*suvaktramantrāḥ* or *pañcabrahmamantrāḥ*) provide the philosophical basis of Lakulīśa's systematic *yoga* (*sādhanāmārga*). Like Patañjali's later *yoga,* Lakulīśa's is also eight-limbed (*aṣṭāṅga*) but with minor differences in the order and definition of the steps (see p. 33). The eight steps are subsumed under five stages, and the practice of each stage rests on repetition (*japa*) and meditation focused on one of the five Rudra *mantras* and the divine aspect it embodies, beginning with Sadyojāta and culminating with Īśāna.

According to the *Pāśupatasūtra,* contemplation of Sadyojāta, if focused to the exclusion of all else, leads the meditator beyond the created effect (*sūtras* 53–54), the *kārya,* which consists of the soul's individuality (*paśu*), its sentience (*vidyā*), and the objects it perceives (*kalā*) (see p. 45). Once established in the initial stage of complete dedication, the *yogin* becomes worthy of divine grace. Contemplating Vāmadeva as the all-powerful controller of everything that transpires in this world of cause and effect, the *yogin* develops the conviction that everything depends on divine will (*sūtra* 57). Next, as the cause of this world with its array of opposing effects, the Lord is understood to have diverse forms—peaceful (*aghora*), dread–inspiring (*ghora*), and confounding (*ghoratara*); everything exists in him alone (*sūtras* 89–90). Because his powers are beginningless and endless and present in every state from the finite to the infinite, nothing can be considered as different from him (*na śakyam bheda-*

darśanam). As Tatpuruṣa the Lord reveals unity in multiplicity (*bhedābheda*); he is the One in many forms (*sūtra* 107). Finally, as Īśāna, the Lord is supreme, ruling over every aspect of human existence and every sentient being. Yet as their source (*brahman*) he remains ever beyond them. Being free of all *duḥkha* and abiding in his own eternal, inherent freedom, he is ever auspicious (*sadāśiva*) (*sūtras* 144–146). Yet even as the ultimate Unmanifest, undifferentiated and without parts (*niṣkala*), he never ceases to be omniscient and omnipotent (*sūtra* 128),[170] a distinctively Śaiva point of view also voiced by Śvetāśvatara (1.11).

Along with their influential role in shaping Lakulīśa's Pāśupata doctrine, the five facets of Śiva delineated in the *pañcavaktra mantras* are traditionally held to be the source of the large body of sacred texts known as the Śaivāgama. These texts began to appear around Lakulīśa's time, probably after several centuries of oral transmission and evolution. For Śaivas the Āgamas carry the same weight of spiritual authority as the Vedas do for followers of the six orthodox *darśanas* that include the Sāṁkhya and the Vedānta. The ninety-two Āgamas fall into three groups that represent the entire spectrum of Indian philosophical thought from duality to absolute nonduality. For Śaivas the Āgamas are divine revelation that streams downward to the human level through Śiva's five faces. The ten *dvaita* Āgamas are revealed through Īśāna, Tatpuruṣa, and Sadyojāta, and the eighteen *dvaitādvaita* Āgamas flow through Vāma and Aghora. The sixty-four *advaita* Āgamas are said to proceed directly from the unity of Śiva and Śakti. Each of the ninety-two texts reflects a separate preceptorial lineage[171] and a specific stage of spiritual outlook from the purely dual to the absolutely nondual.[172] The *advaita* Āgamas and those others that lend themselves to nondualistic interpretation form the primary scriptural basis of the Trikaśāstra. Affirming this in the *Tantrāloka* (36.13–17), Abhinavagupta at the same time makes note of Lakulīśa's important contribution to the Śaivāgama.[173]

In the *Parātrīśikālaghuvṛtti* [Short commentary on the thirty verses on the Supreme] (verses 5–9), Abhinavagupta correlates Śiva's five faces and his five divine powers (*pañcaśakti*). Those powers belong to the pure, nondual order of creation (*śuddhādhvan*) that is the Divine's own universal, *māya*-transcending experience. Their sum total as the *śuddhādhvan* constitutes the divine emissional power (*visargaśakti*) intermediate (*parāpara*) between the unmanifest Absolute and the phenomenal universe.[174] In ascending order Abhinavagupta identifies Sadyojāta with the *sadvidyātattva* and *kriyāśakti,* the divine power of action; Vāmadeva with the *īśvaratattva* and *jñānaśakti,* the divine power of knowledge; Aghora with the *sadāśivatattva* and *icchāśakti,* the divine urge for self-expression; Tatpuruṣa with the *śaktitattva* and *ānandaśakti,* the divine power of bliss; and Īśāna with the *śivatattva* and *cicchakti,* the luminous power of consciousness itself.

Besides that connection, the five faces can be correlated with Śiva's five inherent activities or processes (*pañcakṛtya*). According to one reckoning, Sadyojāta (whose name, we recall, means "present or apparent in the very moment") represents *sṛṣṭi,* the emanation of the phenomenal world from unmanifest possibility. Vāmadeva represents *sthiti,* its sustenance. *Aghora* is tied to *saṁhāra,* the universal dissolution, but should be thought of as not frightening; through the dawning of true knowledge it dispels the ignorance of limitation and marks the resorption into divine unity. Tatpuruṣa represents *nigraha,* the power of self-concealment, whereby the Divine obscures its unity by expressing itself as multiplicity. Recall here Śvetāśvatara's statement that the ultimate cause (*devātmaśakti*) is hidden by its own effects (1.3). Finally, Īśāna is *anugraha,* self-revelation, otherwise known as grace. These five functions emanate from that supreme *niṣkala* Śiva, who is partless, formless, and unmanifest—the *parabrahman* of Advaita Vedānta.[175]

Over time Śiva's five faces came to be associated with any number of pentads, including the fivefold *prāṇa,* the five sensory faculties (*jñānendriyas*), the five organs of action (*karmendriyas*), the five subtle elements (*tanmātras*), and the five gross elements (*mahābhūtas*). The associations affirm that everything in the universe consists of things that are Śiva's parts, as Śvetāśvatara has already stated (4.10). Through his five faces Maheśvara, the Great Lord who is the supreme unity and the essence of all this universe, gives expression to every name and form and living creature. All appearances to the contrary, reality is a seamless whole, pulsating from inconceivable oneness to inconceivable multiplicity and back again. So great is the divine glory, whether at rest in its own bliss or overflowing in the joy of self-expression. Throughout his fourth discourse the seer has celebrated this conviction of a God identified with the world and a world identified with God.

22

मा नस्तोके तनये मा न आयुषि
मा नो गोषु मा न अश्वेषु रीरिषः ।
वीरान् मा नो रुद्र भामितो
वधीर्हविष्मन्तः सदमित् त्वा हवामहे ॥ २२ ॥

mā nas toke tanaye mā na āyuṣi mā no goṣu mā na aśveṣu rīriṣaḥ /
vīrān mā no rudra bhāmito vadhīr haviṣmantaḥ sadam it tvā havāmahe //

22. Harm us not in respect to our children and grandchildren, our lives, our cattle, our horses. Slay not our heroes in anger, O Rudra. Bearing oblations, we invoke you always!

Śvetāśvatara opened his fourth discourse with the ecstatic vision of a world pervaded by the divine presence. More than merely pervaded by that divinity, the world is the self-expression of that greater reality that lies hidden in everything even while transcending everything. In his outpouring of wonder, the seer has taken us from the dazzling outward appearance to the ineffable unity of the formless, all-pervading, indwelling God who is the source and support of all forms.

To close this discourse the seer quotes once more from the Ṛgveda (1.114.8). As the *mantra* appears here, it is identical to the older text except in one small detail. Additional variations arise in the versions also quoted in the Taittirīyasaṁhitā (4.5.10.3) and the Vājasaneyisaṁhitā (16.16), but Śvetāśvatara's citation indicates a more faithful transmission. Even though the verse is obviously designed to ward off misfortune, it originally occurs in a context that emphasizes Rudra's healing powers and reaffirms the goodness of creation. But because the world of duality contains an inescapable thread of imperfection, the supplicant finds it necessary to appeal to the creator not to withhold his protection and blessing from our lives. Lest we forget the supreme reality at the heart of all appearances, abiding in its own perfection beyond all happiness and misery, we consecrate our lives at every moment through unceasing recollection of that divinity, the great Rudra-Śiva, shining in and through all things.

पञ्चमोऽध्यायः

CHAPTER FIVE

1

द्वे अक्षरे ब्रह्मपरे त्वनन्ते
विद्याविद्ये निहिते यत्र गूढे ।
क्षरं त्वविद्या ह्यमृतं तु विद्या
विद्याविद्ये ईशते यस्तु सोऽन्यः ॥ १ ॥

dve akṣare brahmapare tv anante vidyāvidye nihite yatra gūḍhe /
kṣaraṁ tv avidyā hy amṛtaṁ tu vidyā vidyāvidye īśate yas tu so 'nyaḥ //

1. In the imperishable, infinite, and absolute Brahman, wherein both knowledge and ignorance lie hidden, surely ignorance is the perishable and knowledge is the immortal; but he who presides over knowledge and ignorance is [yet] another.

In the previous discourse Śvetāśvatara made the point that God, the divine reality, takes shape as the world around us, appearing as the multicolored display of natural phenomena and every kind of living being. The whole panorama of existence is nothing other than Rudra's own self-expression. But as wondrous as the creation may appear, how immeasurably more glorious is the resplendent and praiseworthy reality that is its source and substance, its sovereign and protector.

From focus on the manifest world and the immanent God who produces and pervades it, the seer now seeks in his fifth discourse to direct our attention increasingly toward the unity underlying and transcending the diversity (*mantras* 1–6). Though infinite and ineffable, Brahman, when possessed of qualities, appears as the cosmos and as the soul (*jīva* or *paśu*), subject to *karma* and rebirth. So prodigious is his power of *māyā* that it appears to limit the illimitable! As the individual soul, the infinite Lord appears infinitesimally small. Even so, this woefully restricted self partakes of infinity, being in essence free of any quality or conditioning (*mantras* 7–12). Beyond name and form and unfettered by the smallness of individuality, the true Self is immortal and eternally free (*mantras* 13–14).

Śvetāśvatara begins his fifth discourse by contrasting the Absolute and the relative. In the absolute Brahman (*brahmapare*) the duality of knowledge and ignorance (*dve vidyāvidye*) lies hidden, or latent.[1] Śvetāśvatara pairs knowledge and ignorance in a single grammatical compound, implying that they exist together in a mutually contrasting relationship. As long as we speak of knowledge (*vidyā*) and ignorance (*avidyā*), we remain immersed in the experience of duality. Relatively speaking, knowledge and ignorance differ from each other, but in one way they are alike. Ignorance is not the absence of awareness but only its fragmentation, limitation, and beclouding (see pp. 121–122). Strictly speaking, the lower or relative knowledge (*aparāvidyā*) falls under the heading of ignorance. It is superior to what we generally call ignorance, to be sure. Moreover, it is relative knowledge that helps to conquer relative ignorance. Still, as knowledge of the phenomenal world, relative knowledge is neither infinite nor absolute. The goal of spiritual life is to go beyond the duality of ignorance (*avidyā*) or lower knowledge (*aparāvidyā*) and to attain the supreme, nondual knowledge (*parāvidyā*), which is the experience of Brahman, the true Self. That is why Śvetāśvatara says that Brahman, who presides over both knowledge and ignorance, is yet another (*vidyāvidye īśate yas tu so 'nyaḥ*), something of an entirely different order.

In a broader and deeper sense *avidyā* refers here to the human condition, to the soul's state of embodied existence in the phenomenal world of time, space, and causality. Nothing in our existence is permanent, and Śvetāśvatara equates even our ignorance with impermanence (*kṣaraṁ tv avidyā*). We have forgotten our true being and in our not-knowing have identified ourselves with qualities and objects that are evanescent and fleeting. But knowledge of our true being is undying (*hy amṛtaṁ tu vidyā*), for it is the recognition that our essence is the immutable light of consciousness itself.

Nothing exists outside of the reality of this single, boundless consciousness—not even knowledge and ignorance. What are they, other than different modes of the one divine consciousness? As its modifications both are only partial forms of awareness, each manifesting the light to a greater or lesser degree but never in its unbounded fullness. As used here *vidyā* is the knowledge of the One that leads to liberation, and *avidyā* is the awareness of the many, which keeps us tied to the ever-changing, perishable material realm.[2] Śrī Rāmakṛṣṇa often used a prosaic example to illustrate their relative nature. A man, feeling his foot pierced by a thorn, uses another thorn to extract the first one and then throws both away.[3] The painful condition of having a thorn in one's foot represents the state of ignorance in which the *jīva* exists, perceiving the multiplicity of creation that hides the awareness of the Divine. To remove the thorn of ignorance, one employs the thorn of knowledge. This knowledge is the awareness that God dwells in all beings[4] and within reach. But then Śrī Rāmakṛṣṇa taught his disciples that the ultimate realization lies beyond both ignorance and knowledge. Knowing the many is ignorance (*ajñāna*), having the unwavering conviction of the divine presence in all beings is knowledge (*jñāna*), but knowing fully that God is beyond ignorance and knowledge is a superior knowledge (*vijñāna*)[5] resulting from direct, intuitive experience.[6]

Experience of what? As Śvetāśvatara explains, beyond knowledge and ignorance is "another" (*anyaḥ*), something inconceivably different—the supreme Brahman.[7] Whereas knowledge and ignorance are modifications of consciousness, Brahman is consciousness itself, free of any modification. Knowledge and ignorance are limited, definable forms of awareness, but the supreme Brahman is unlimited and indefinable in any way. *Vijñāna* is for Śrī Rāmakṛṣṇa the ultimate, unitive knowledge of the One beyond even the relative and the Absolute, "the realization that God alone has become the universe and all living beings."[8] That is what Abhinavagupta calls the supreme nonduality (*parādvaita*).

2

यो योनिं योनिमधितिष्ठत्येको
विश्वानि रूपाणि योनीश्च सर्वाः ।
ऋषिं प्रसूतं कपिलं यस्तमग्रे
ज्ञानैर्बिभर्ति जायमानं च पश्येत् ॥ २ ॥

yo yonim̐ yonim adhitiṣṭhaty eko viśvāni rūpāṇi yonīś ca sarvāḥ /
ṛṣim̐ prasūtam̐ kapilam̐ yas tam agre jñānair bibharti jāyamānam̐ ca paśyet //

2. The One who dwells in every kind of being, in all visible forms and in all their sources, is he who in the beginning contains the red-gold seer, begotten by his thoughts, and witnesses him being born.

The supreme Brahman inhabits and presides over (*adhitiṣṭhati*) every kind of living being (*yonim̐ yonim*). These words are identical to the first quarter of *mantra* 4.11. Moreover, the supreme reality, which Śvetāśvatara refers to as "this very God" (*eṣa devaḥ*) in the next verse, pervades and rules over all outward appearances (*viśvāni rūpāṇi*) as well as every subtle or causal aspect behind the visible forms. Now the seer wants to direct our attention away from the outwardly observable world and toward its subtler dimensions, from the world of the many to the inner reality of the One who is the ultimate source and the ultimate being.

The second line tells us that Brahman is the unchanging witness, who through his own knowledge or thought (*jñānaiḥ*) begets the creator, known variously as Hiraṇyagarbha, Prajāpati, or Brahmā (see pp. 190–191). The word *jñāna* appears not in the singular, which would indicate the supreme consciousness-in-itself, but in the instrumental plural (*jñānaiḥ*), which suggests a differentiating movement within consciousness. In the Trika teaching this is the initial triad of the *sadāśiva, īśvara,* and *sadvidyā tattvas,* the modalities of divine will (*icchāśakti*), knowledge (*jñānaśakti*), and action (*kriyāśakti*) through which the process of manifestation begins to unfold.

The word *kapila*, modifying the begotten seer (*prasūtam ṛṣim*) does not refer to the sage Kapila,[9] the reputed founder of the Sāṁkhya philosophy. Here *kapila* is not a proper name but an adjective meaning "reddish," "tawny," or "brown," literally "monkey-colored" (from *kapi*, "monkey").[10] Some translators render it as "fiery,"[11] or "of golden colour,"[12] because *kapi* also means "sun."[13] Like the red-gold light of the rising sun, the dawn of creation emerges with the appearance of Hiraṇyagarbha, the "golden womb" of the cosmos, thought-begotten of the supreme Brahman.

3

एकैकं जालं बहुधा विकुर्व-
न्नस्मिन् क्षेत्रे संहरत्येष देवः ।
भूयः सृष्ट्वा पतयस्तथेशः
सर्वाधिपत्यं कुरुते महात्मा ॥ ३ ॥

ekaikaṁ jālaṁ bahudhā vikurvann asmin kṣetre saṁharaty eṣa devaḥ /
bhūyaḥ sṛṣṭvā patayas tatheśaḥ sarvādhipatyaṁ kurute mahātmā //

3. Spreading out every single net, each one differently, into this field of action, this God [then] gathers them in. Moreover, having issued forth [all this by acting as] the lords of creation, thus the Lord, the great Self, holds sovereignty over all.

The seer has already taught that the entire play of creation, manifest as the knowable universe in all its immensity and diversity, ultimately springs from one uncaused cause, the supreme reality called Brahman or Rudra, which is self-luminous consciousness endowed with an inherent power of self-expression (*devātmaśakti*). The Taittirīyopaniṣad (2.6.1) and the Trikaśāstra agree that within consciousness itself the process of differentiation begins with the threefold expression of God's power to will, to envision, and to enact. From those initial stirrings the universe evolves methodically according to a cosmic blueprint, with each stage or degree of manifestation (*tattva*) unfolding from the potentiality inherent in the preceding stage, all the way back to the primary, uncaused cause.

The present verse has been described as "extremely difficult,"[14] "rather abstruse,"[15] or "syntactically confusing and possibly corrupt."[16] The complications arise from its metaphorical character and slightly awkward syntax as well as from the variance of two words in the early manuscripts.[17]

Śvetāśvatara speaks of God (*eṣa devaḥ*) as casting multiple nets into "this field" (*asmin kṣetre*). Each net is unique (*ekaikaṁ jālam*) and varied in its own way (*bahudhā*). This seeming case of mixed metaphors—casting a net into a field—has elicited a number of equally confusing interpretations. The net (*jāla*) has been taken to indicate *saṁsāra*,[18] *māyā*,[19] a "net [of illusion],"[20] or even possibly "the rays of the sun which are spread out in the morning and gathered in at night."[21] Another interpretation, following Nārāyaṇa Sarasvatī's *Śvetāśvataropaniṣaddīpikā* (an eighteenth-century commentary on the *Vṛtti*), understands the net as *karma*, the bondage of the individual soul to the consequences of its past actions.[22] Yet another opinion holds that the individual nets signify the adjuncts of the not-self—body, senses, mind, and other constituents of individuality that entangle the soul in the play of worldly existence.[23]

The word for "field" (*kṣetra*) likewise has more than one interpretation. It has been taken to mean the world,[24] *prakṛti* or *māyā*,[25] or *saṁsāra*.[26] Translating it as "ground," one author likens it to the soil from which vegetation springs up, only to decay, leaving the ground barren once again. The imagery suggests the cyclical nature of creation.[27] Besides these meanings, the word *kṣetra* can also signify any sphere of action or the physical body as the field of experience for the indwelling soul.[28]

The first half of the verse portrays God as "spreading out every single net," casting into "this field of action"—into this world—a multitude of souls, each with its own distinct web of individual experiences. At the time of liberation this same God gathers them in, one by one. The *paśu's* individualized awareness, transcending the limitations and obscurations of *māyā*, returns to its pristine, undifferentiated perfection.

The third quarter of the verse (*bhūyaḥ sṛṣṭvā patayas tatheśaḥ*) is the source of greatest confusion. Often the attempts to resolve its syntactical difficulties collide with the attempts to explain its meaning. Most translators render the second line as something like "having further created the lords, the Lord, the great Self, exerts his lordship over all."[29] "The lords" (*patayaḥ*) signify the secondary agents of creation. The problem, grammatically speaking, is that the lords cannot be the direct object, because the word is in the nominative case, as is "the Lord" (*īśaḥ*), the final word of the third *pāda*. This problematical translation follows the example of the *Śvetāśvataropaniṣadvṛtti*, which proposes that the clause is ungrammatical and that the nominative *patayaḥ* should be read as the accusative plural *patīn*.[30]

Alone among the translators, Paul Deussen understood *patayaḥ* to be in apposition to *īśaḥ*.[31] That construction violates no rules of syntax and allows us to understand the second line as reading, "Moreover (*bhūyaḥ*), having issued forth (*sṛṣṭvā*) [all this by acting as] the lords of creation (*patayaḥ*), thus (*tathā*) the Lord (*īśaḥ*), the great Self (*mahātmā*), holds sovereignty over all (*sarvādhipatyaṁ kurute*).

Why would the author of the *Vṛtti* suggest that the appositive to the subject (*patayaḥ*) be read as a direct object (*patīn*)? It appears he did so for doctrinal reasons. According to Advaita Vedānta Brahman in itself does not act; the Absolute can have no direct relationship with the relative. In the Vedantic view, Brahman, through an inexpressible (*anirvacanīya*) "association" with *māyā*, appears as the qualified Īśvara, and from Īśvara proceeds Hiraṇyagarbha, the first-born in the cosmogonic process. Hiraṇyagarbha's subtle body is the universal mind or cosmic intelligence (*mahātattva*), and his gross body is the physicality of the universe. According to Dharmarāja's *Vedāntaparibhāṣā* (verse 7), it is Parameśvara (the supreme Īśvara) who manifests Hiraṇyagarbha's subtle and gross bodies and the subtle bodies of all individual souls (*jīvas*) (see p. 191). All subsequent creation—including the physical bodies of living beings and all other material forms—is effected secondarily through Hiraṇyagarbha's agency.

That view can claim some support in what Śvetāśvatara says in the present *mantra*, which indeed speaks of secondary "agents of creation,"[32] "assistants,"[33] "controllers,"[34] "lords,"[35] "rulers,"[36] "presiding deities,"[37] or "demiurges"[38]—all readings of *patayaḥ*.

However, there is a more important point. The apposition of

patayaḥ and *īśaḥ*, which the indeclinable past participle (*sṛṣṭvā*) indicates, also demands that these two be identical to the agent of the main clause. This means that the Lord (*īśaḥ*), even acting as the secondary lords (*patayaḥ*), is none other than the great Self (*mahātmā*). This statement anticipates the uncompromising view of nonduality defined later by the Trikaśāstra. That system, as already explained, rejects Advaita Vedānta's doctrine of an utterly inactive Brahman (*śāntabrahmavāda*) in favor of its own doctrine of the Lord's nonduality (*īśvarādvayavāda*). Divine consciousness and its power are a single reality that is free to act even while its essence remains the eternally immutable radiance of awareness itself (*prakāśa*).

One more point remains regarding the plural lords. We can take them at face value as the mythological Marīci and other superhuman progenitors presented in the earlier Vedic texts,[39] or we can understand them as metaphors for the diversified powers of consciousness. In the Ṛgveda and the Atharvaveda the term *marīci* refers to "a particle of light, [a] shining mote or speck in the air."[40] According to the Vedantic view the universe is populated by countless individual centers of awareness, "from Hiraṇyagarbha to the mosquito," each one controlling its own domain. As the universal mind, Hiraṇyagarbha is foremost among them, ruling over every human mind and every speck of consciousness embodied in every living creature, great or small.[41]

But again, or moreover (*bhūyaḥ*), Śvetāśvatara affirms that consciousness truly is One, whether active or at rest: "having issued forth [all this by acting as] the lords of creation, thus the Lord, the great Self, holds sovereignty over all."

4

सर्वा दिश ऊर्ध्वमधश्च तिर्यक्

प्रकाशयन् भ्राजते यद्वनड्वान् ।

एवं स देवो भगवान् वरेण्यो

योनिस्वभावानधितिष्ठत्येकः ॥ ४ ॥

sarvā diśa ūrdhvam adhaś ca tiryak prakāśayan bhrājate yadv anaḍvān /
evaṁ sa devo bhagavān vareṇyo yonisvabhāvān adhitiṣṭhaty ekaḥ //

4. Just as the sun shines above, below, and across, illuminating all directions, so the glorious God, worthy of worship, presides as One over all his manifestations.

Not for the first time does this Upaniṣad draw a connection between the physical sun—the great luminary of the universe—and the divine reality lying at the heart of all creation. Just as the physical sun fills this world with its light, thereby making visible and knowable every created thing, so the effulgent God (*sa devaḥ*), who is the light of consciousness, presides over everything, majestically pervading and directing all the phenomena that he has projected out of his own essential unity.

Śvetāśvatara tells us that the world is not separate from the Divine. That divinity dwells in and presides over (both are meanings of *adhitiṣṭhati*) every manifest thing—over everything "whose own essential nature (*svabhāva*) is the source (*yoni*) itself." Whatever the one God pervades and rules over partakes of the divine essence that is its source; the whole of creation, proceeding from Brahman, has the nature of Brahman. The world shines with the light of consciousness, the light of the glorious Lord (*bhagavān*) who is to be sought after and adored (*vareṇyaḥ*).

5

यच्च स्वभावं पचति विश्वयोनिः
पाच्यांश्च सर्वान् परिणामयेद् यः ।
सर्वमेतद् विश्वमधितिष्ठत्येको
गुणांश्च सर्वान् विनियोजयेद् यः ॥ ५ ॥

yac ca svabhāvaṁ pacati viśvayoniḥ pācyāṁś ca sarvān pariṇāmayed yaḥ /
sarvam etad viśvam adhitiṣṭhaty eko guṇāṁś ca sarvān viniyojayed yaḥ //

5. And just as he who is the source of everything develops his own nature and transforms all that is potential, he it is who presides as One over this entire universe and distributes all its [diverse] qualities.

The world of our experience is nothing other than God's own self-expression. Brahman, the universal source (*viśvayoniḥ*) from which everything springs, develops (*pacati*) its own nature (*svabhāvam*), bringing to manifestation the possibilities that lie latent in the divine mind. Creation (*sṛṣṭi*) is not the making of something out of nothing (see pp. 206–207) but merely a change of state, a transformation of potentialities into the actualities of our day-to-day existence.

Presiding over our mundane lives, this same Brahman is the one God whom Śvetāśvatara extols. It is God who apportions and distributes (*viniyojayet*) all diversity, woven of unimaginably complex patterns of the *guṇas*' interaction, and over it he remains sovereign. Still, underlying the ever shifting patterns of color, form, sound, and other sensory impressions, underlying every possible experience of life, there remains the ever unchanging unity of Brahman.

6

तद् वेदगुह्योपनिषत्सु गूढं
तद् ब्रह्मा वेदते ब्रह्मयोनिम् ।
ये पूर्वं देवा ऋषयश्च तद् विदु-
स्ते तन्मया अमृता वै बभूवुः ॥ ६ ॥

tad vedaguhyopaniṣatsu gūḍhaṁ tad brahmā vedate brahmayonim /
ye pūrvaṁ devā ṛṣayaś ca tad vidus te tanmayā amṛtā vai babhūvuḥ //

6. That [Brahman] is hidden in the Upaniṣads, which among the Vedas are to be kept secret; Brahmā knows it as the source of expansion. The gods and seers of old who knew it became absorbed in it and truly immortal.

Here Śvetāśvatara refers to Brahman simply as "that" (*tat*), the neuter pronoun frequently employed by seers to denote the inexpressible divinity. Accounts of their direct experience of Brahman form those portions of the Vedas known as the Upaniṣads. The teaching they contain is to be kept secret (*guhya*), because the highest knowledge is not meant for everyone. As the Kaṭhopaniṣad (1.2.7) points out, "It is not given to many even to hear of him [Brahman, the Self], and many, hearing of him, do not understand." Amid the vast array of sacred instruction contained in the Vedas, the most profound and subtle teaching, having to do with the nature of the Self, is not only difficult to grasp but liable to misunderstanding. For that reason it is intended only for those who are ready to receive it. At the end of the Muṇḍakopaniṣad (3.2.10) the seer Aṅgiras declares that only those who are disciplined, well versed in the Vedas, devoted to Brahman, and purified by the faithful observance of Vedic rites should be taught the knowledge of Brahman.

With the idea of cosmic evolution still in mind, Śvetāśvatara informs us that Brahmā—meaning Hiraṇyagarbha, the first manifestation of the Absolute—knows Brahman to be the source of growth, expansion, evolution, or development. That is the literal meaning of the compound *brahmayonim* and the one that best fits the present context. Early and later commentators have tried to read different and more elaborate meanings into this admittedly ambiguous phrase, but none works so well as this simplest of readings. As the first-born, the creator god Brahmā understands that the absolute Brahman is the single and ultimate source of all manifestation.

According to Vedic tradition, Brahmā received this knowledge directly and imparted it in turn to the gods, who passed it along to the *ṛṣis*.[42] This higher knowledge of the One is different from the lower, or empirical, forms of knowledge of the many, which are relational and dependent on a threefold division of knower, knowing, and known. This higher knowledge (*parāvidyā*) results from the attainment of unitary consciousness. Here Śvetāśvatara alludes to a long line of spiritual forebears, observing that those who experienced Brahman in former times became absorbed in it, made one in substance with it, identical to it (*tanmayāḥ*), and thus immortal (*amṛtāḥ*). As the *ṛṣi* Aṅgiras says in the Muṇḍakopaniṣad (3.2.9), "Whoever knows the supreme Brahman becomes Brahman." Thus it was, is, and ever will be.

7

गुणान्वयो यः फलकर्मकर्ता
कृतस्य तस्यैव स चोपभोक्ता ।
स विश्वरूपस्त्रिगुणस्त्रिवर्त्मा
प्राणाधिपः सञ्चरति स्वकर्मभिः ॥ ७ ॥

guṇānvayo yaḥ phalakarmakartā kṛtasya tasyaiva sa copabhoktā /
sa viśvarūpas triguṇas trivartmā prāṇādhipaḥ sañcarati svakarmabhiḥ //

7. [But when] possessed of qualities, he who becomes the doer of action that bears fruit experiences the results of whatever he has done. That soul, of manifold form and three qualities and three paths, roams about according to his own deeds.

The primary message of all the Upaniṣads is the ultimate identity of the individual soul and the divine Self. In the present discourse the first six *mantras* have dealt with the divine Self, Brahman, as both the all-transcending reality and as the universal creator and sovereign. Now attention shifts to the individual soul, poetically called "the lord of the vital force" (*prāṇādhipaḥ*).[43]

When the supreme Lord becomes involved with the energies or qualities of creation (*guṇānvaḥ*) and experiences conditioned existence as the individual self, he becomes the doer of actions that bear fruit (*phalakarmakartā*). In the later language of the Trikaśāstra, when Śiva assumes a state of limitation as the living individual (*jīva*), his absolutely free and spontaneous action (*kriyā*) becomes reduced to the ordinary human action that binds (*karma*). Thus entangled in the web of cause and effect (which Śvetāśvatara elsewhere calls *jāla*), the individual soul becomes the experiencer (*upabhoktā*) of the consequences of whatever it has done (*kṛtasya tasyaiva*).

Nevertheless, it is important to remember that it is the Divine that experiences through the individual. The Kaṭhopaniṣad (1.3.4) confirms that those who rightly understand call the Self (*ātman*) the enjoyer (*bhoktā*) when it is united with the body, mind, and senses.

The Kaṭhopaniṣad echoes a far older view found in the the Bṛhadāraṇyakopaniṣad (2.5.19), where the *ṛṣi* Dadhyac Ātharvaṇa quotes in turn a verse from the most ancient part of the Ṛgveda-saṁhitā (6.47.18): "He [the Supreme Lord] assumed the likeness of every form (*rūpaṁ rūpaṁ pratirūpo babhūva*), each form of his meant for revealing him (*tad asya rūpaṁ praticakṣaṇāya*). [The Lord] Indra, through his magical powers goes about in many forms (*indro māyābhiḥ pururūpa īyate*); for to him are yoked ten hundred steeds (*yukta hy asya harayaḥ śatā daśa*)." On this passage Dadhyac then expounds, "He is the steeds, ten times a thousand, many [more], and without end. This Brahman is without before (*apūrvam*) or after (*anaparam*), without inside (*anantaram*) or outside (*abāhyam*). This Brahman is the Self that experiences everything (*ayam ātmā brahma sarvānubhūḥ*). This is the teaching (*ity anuśāsanam*)."

By "this is the teaching," Dadhyac makes clear that what he has just explained is already well established knowledge. This ancient teaching of the Ṛgveda describes a Supreme Being, variously called Indra, Puruṣa, and Brahman, who experiences a world wrought by his own powers (*māyābhiḥ*). It presents a positive view, and in the *Bṛhadāraṇyakopaniṣadbhāṣya* Śaṁkara accordingly interprets *māyābhiḥ* not in any illusory sense but in the sense of *prajñābhiḥ,* meaning "wisdom."[44] Moreover, the Supreme Being experiences his creation in multiple ways. Śaṁkara understands *harayaḥ* ("steeds") as a metaphor for *indriyāṇi,* the ten sensory and motor organs,[45] which in turn are multiplied by the multitudes that possess them. But amid this diverse display of consciousness assuming form with the intention of being seen (*tad asya rūpaṁ praticakṣaṇāya*) and enjoyed, consciousness nevertheless remains itself, the all-illumining light of awareness beyond the conditioning of time and space—and utterly untouched by cause and effect (*apūrvam anaparam*).

Śvetāśvatara similarly explains that the Lord, appearing as the individual soul, is of manifold form (*viśvarūpaḥ*), no longer cognizant of its divine nature and essential unity. In assuming form—in fact many forms over many lifetimes—the soul necessarily associates itself with an inexhaustible array of qualities and conditions that arise from the intricate interweavings of *sattva, rajas,* and *tamas.* That is why Śvetāśvatara describes the living soul (*prāṇādhipaḥ*) as *triguṇaḥ,* characterized by these three fundamental energies and all that they entail. He also describes the soul as *trivartmā* ("having three paths or courses"), a reference to the three different roads mentioned in the first chapter (1.4) that stretch out before each human soul. These are the paths of righteousness (*dharma*), unrighteousness (*adharma*), and knowledge (*jñāna*). The choice of one over the others would seem a simple matter but for the binding power of *karma,* which in large part determines the course of every life. Each soul roams about (*sañcarati*) according to its own deeds (*svakarmabhiḥ*), caught in a web of cause and effect.

The word *karma* (properly *karman*) basically means any action, either mental or physical. By extension it also means the consequence of any action as well as the cumulative potential effects of one's actions in totality. The antiquity of the doctrine of *karma* is revealed by a passage in the Bṛhadāraṇyakopaniṣad (4.4.5–6) belonging to a conversation between King Janaka and Yājñavalkya. The *ṛṣi* begins by saying that the individual self is truly Brahman (*sa va ayam ātmā brahma*), identified with intellect, mind, life-breath, sensory faculties, physical elements, emotions, virtue, nonvirtue, the perceptible, and the inferred. He continues, "As one acts (*yathākārī*), as one behaves (*yathācārī*), so does one become (*tathā bhavati*). The doer of good becomes good (*sādhukārī sādhur bhavati*), the doer of evil becomes evil (*pāpakārī pāpo bhavati*). One becomes virtuous through virtuous action, bad through bad action (*puṇyaḥ puṇyena karmaṇā bhavati pāpaḥ pāpena*)." Now indeed, Yājñavalkya adds, it is a person's desire that prompts the will, the will that leads to the deed, and the deed that bears the consequences.

Then to indicate that this teaching was established well before his time, the seer quotes an older verse and comments on it. In short, the individual self whose awareness is dominated by attachment becomes caught up in the cycle of desire and deed. But the one who becomes free of desire, whose only desire is for the Self (*ātmakāmaḥ*), no longer experiences the outward motion of awareness (*tasya prāṇā na utkrāmanti*). Being Brahman itself, the individual self merges into Brahman (*brahmaiva san brahmāpyeti*).

Abhinavagupta, speaking from the position of Śaiva nondualism, draws a contrast between God and the individual soul in a way that bears out both Yājñavalkya's and Śvetāśvatara's teachings. He explains that the consciousness of individuality, which results from the association with body, mind, and senses, is ignorance (*ajñāna*), forgetfulness of one's true, original nature. The divine reality,

Maheśvara ("the Great Lord"), manifests himself throughout the objectified multiplicity of creation (*idam*) but ever remains a single, undivided awareness (*aham*) that experiences the whole of his manifestation as reflected in himself and not externally.

Whereas the Supreme Being experiences blissful infinitude and absolute freedom as his very nature, the individual soul has an experience of a very different sort. The soul has forgotten its divine identity, which nevertheless remains at its heart, no matter how heavily veiled. Instead of the supreme, divine enjoyment (*paramabhoga*), the individual has a lesser experience (*bhoga*) of mixed pleasure, pain, and insentience, arising from the threefold differentiation and interaction of *sattva, rajas,* and *tamas.* For the human being, the "this" (*idam*) of the divine experience fractures into the "these" of the phenomena that fill the universe, now mistaken as separate from oneself and exterior.[46]

8

अङ्गुष्ठमात्रो रवितुल्यरूपः
सङ्कल्पाहङ्कारसमन्वितो यः ।
बुद्धेर्गुणेनात्मगुणेन चैव
आराग्रमात्रोप्यपरोऽपि दृष्टः ॥ ८ ॥

aṅguṣṭamātro ravitulyarūpaḥ saṅkalpāhaṅkārasamanvito yaḥ /
buddher guṇenātmaguṇena caiva ārāgramātropyaparo 'pi dṛṣṭaḥ //

8. He who is the size of a thumb and brilliant like the sun becomes endowed with intention and a sense of individuality. Through the attributes of mind and body as well is he seen as distinct, in fact as no larger than the point of an awl.

Continuing to distinguish between the infinite Self and the individual *jīva*, this *mantra* begins with the reminder that the great Lord is of "the size of a thumb" (*aṅguṣṭamātraḥ*), the same description found in *mantra* 3.13. Here, as before, it is not to be taken literally but as a symbol of the indwelling divinity (see p. 233). "Brilliant like the sun" (*ravitulyarūpaḥ*) recalls *mantra* 3.12, which extols the great Lord or innermost Person as "the imperishable light" (*jyotir avyayaḥ*). Present in the heart of every creature, he is consciousness itself, inherently luminous and ever pure.

When conditioned, that consciousness appears as the individual soul. In the previous *mantra* Śvetāśvatara spoke of the association with qualities as the reason for entanglement in the web of cause and effect. Now he names those factors that distinguish the *jīva* from the supreme Lord. They are intention (*saṁkalpa*), the ego-sense (*ahaṁkāra*), and those *tattvas* that constitute the mind and body.

Saṁkalpa denotes limited human intention. According to the Trikaśāstra it is a dim reflection of the divine will (*icchā*). The divine impulse for self-expression, found in the Upaniṣads as the primal utterance "let me be many" (*bahu syām*), is the initial volition necessary for cosmic evolution. In this first movement of consciousness, differentiation is only potential and not yet actualized. The ultimate I (*aham*) wills this (*idam*) within its own nonduality. As the volitional energy "descends," it becomes conditioned by *māyā*, and in the phenomenal world it is no longer the expression of divine omnipotence and utter freedom (*svātantrya*). *Icchā* appears instead as *saṁkalpa*, the finitized, unenlightened volition of the individual *jīva*.

It is important to note that the stirring of divine will (*icchāśakti*) is the first stage in the threefold manifestation of divine power; it precedes the functions of conceptualization (*jñānaśakti*) and actualization (*kriyāśakti*). Thus the divine *icchā*, which represents Śiva's absolute and unconditioned freedom, is preconceptual, whereas the human *saṁkalpa* is a "conception or idea or notion formed in the mind or heart, ... [a] definite intention or determination" directed toward the attainment of a specific purpose.[47]

The *jīva's* will or intention is inevitably intertwined with *karma*. It is ever conditioned by internal, accumulated tendencies as well as by external circumstances. Although we may believe that we are endowed with free will, our intentions are always contingent on something else. Even the individual preferences by which we assert our seemingly complete freedom of choice rest on our already established likes and dislikes, our character traits, and our previously imprinted patterns of behavior. Conversely the divine *icchā* is the spontaneous joy of self-expression, arising from the overflow of the all-transcending divine fullness (*pūrṇatva*). In contrast *saṁkalpa* is a specific intent arising from a particular need for fulfillment within the limitations of phenomenal existence, and it is often accompanied by some degree of anxiety over a successful outcome.

The need for fulfillment arises from the ego-sense, and that is why Śvetāśvatara mentions *saṁkalpa* and *ahaṁkāra* in the same breath. Both are limitations—the first of will, the second of selfhood. Accordingly the seer draws a distinction between the higher, divine Self and the lower, human self. The Trikaśāstra elaborates on this distinction, explaining that Śiva-consciousness is the experience of absolute perfection. But when concealed, this transcendental Self-experience, this state of nondual consciousness without an object,[48] this divine *pūrṇāhaṁtā* (literally "I-ness in full"), assumes a lesser, egocentric identity based on limiting factors. The Divine's own pure experience of infinite Self (*svaparāmarśa*),[49] of absolute subjectivity, becomes reduced to a lessened sense of objectified self-awareness based on identification with some (and separation from other) definable and defining qualities.

Because the individual self is by far a lesser version of the supreme Self, Śvetāśvatara describes it as no larger than the point of an awl—a remark designed to startle. In the next *mantra* he will continue to provoke well beyond that point before startling us again in an opposite way.

9

वालाग्रशतभागस्य शतधा कल्पितस्य च ।
भागो जीवः स विज्ञेयः स चानन्त्यायकल्पते ॥ ९ ॥

vālāgraśatabhāgasya śatadhā kalpitasya ca /
bhāgo jīvaḥ sa vijñeyaḥ sa cānantyāya kalpate //

9. The individual soul should be recognized as a fraction of the hundredth part of the tip of a hair, again divided a hundred times—yet it partakes of infinity.

In the process of cosmic manifestation, the supreme Lord becomes identified with all the attributes of individuality—with mind, personality, body, and then with all their associated qualities and the circumstances of their interaction with the surrounding world. As the infinite Self (*ātman*) identifies with factors that are not-self (*anātman*), human life becomes the experience of I in a sphere of otherness. The process is effected through the limiting, differentiating, and veiling powers of *māyā*. Through these five principles of subjective limitation the divine Self appears fragmented. It appears diminished in the power of agency by *kalā*, restricted in the power of knowing by *vidyā*, cast into insufficiency and want by *rāga*, reduced to mortality by *kāla*, and subjected to the way the world works by *niyati*. Compared to the infinite, all-powerful, all-knowing divine Self, the *jīva* is infinitesimal and powerless; yet the delusion of ego has each of us convinced of our own self-importance, paradoxically tied to identification with the finite and ephemeral.

Now, unexpectedly, Śvetāśvatara turns us from thoughts of the infinitesimal and inferior by reminding us that the individual self is to be recognized (*vijñeyaḥ*) for what it truly is. *Anantyāya kalpate*—it is fit for, capable of, and partaking of infinity. In essence the individual self is none other than the divine Self. *Ayam ātmā brahma.*

10

नैव स्त्री न पुमानेष न चैवायं नपुंसकः ।
यद्यच्छरीरमादत्ते तेन तेन स युज्यते ॥ १० ॥

naiva strī na pumān eṣa na caivāyaṁ napuṁsakaḥ /
yad yac charīram ādatte tena tena sa yujyate //

10. It is neither female nor male, nor is it even neuter; whatever body it assumes, with that is it associated.

In his fourth discourse (4.3) the seer quoted a passage from the Atharvaveda (10.8.27), saying, "You are woman, you are man, you are youth and maiden too; aged, you totter along with a staff; taking birth, you face in every direction." Now he claims that the Divine is in truth neither female nor male nor even neuter. Without contradiction he immediately adds that the unconditioned Self, beyond all attributes, becomes associated with the attributes of whatever body it assumes. Like water, which has no shape of its own yet takes the form of whatever contains it, the Self is both formless and capable of assuming any form.

As the preceding *mantra* reveals, the individual soul has an intrinsic connection to infinity; that means that its true nature is beyond any limitation or form. Now Śvetāśvatara presents the same idea from the opposite perspective: the infinite, formless Brahman has the ability to assume any form. The verb *yujyate* indicates that Brahman becomes yoked, connected to, fitted out with, or associated with any bodily form (*śarīra*) he (or it) chooses.

This idea brings to mind the Trika teaching that the particular (*viśeṣa*) has no existence apart from the universal (*sāmānya*).[50] At the same time the universal is not bound by the particular. To make that clear, Śvetāśvatara explains that the consciousness animating every living being is neither female nor male nor even neuter. To say that it is neither female nor male implies that it is genderless, and then to add that it is not even neuter negates even the quality of genderlessness. In other words, Brahman cannot be limited by any attribute or even by its absence. It is utterly beyond description.

Having intimated the ineffability of the Self, Śvetāśvatara goes on to say that it becomes identified with whatever body it takes on. The Supreme Being has become all this: man, woman, and all the rest; yet that identification exists only in the dualistic realm of time, space, and causality. Though seemingly fragmented into innumerable discrete centers of individualized awareness, the infinite Self ever remains a singular consciousness, even as the ocean's water, though appearing as waves, is nothing but water.

11

सङ्कल्पनस्पर्शनदृष्टिमोहै-

र्ग्रासाम्बुवृष्ट्यात्मविवृद्धिजन्म ।

कर्मानुगान्यनुक्रमेण देही
स्थानेषु रूपाण्यभिसम्प्रपद्यते ॥ ११ ॥

saṅkalpanasparśanadṛṣṭimohair grāsāmbuvṛṣṭyātmavivṛddhijanma /
karmānugāny anukrameṇa dehī sthāneṣu rūpāṇy abhisamprapadyate //

11. [As] the body lives and grows through an abundance of food and drink, [so] the dweller in the body, through its intentions, involvements, outlooks, and delusions, assumes a succession of forms and conditions according to its actions.

The seer now describes what happens when the infinite Self takes on an individual identity.

Understanding and translating this *mantra* is a daunting task in four respects. First, it appears that the seer is trying to pack a wealth of insight into a disconcerting thrift of words, assuming that his many ideas will be readily connectible by his hearers. Second, the laconic syntax demands that his concise expression be reshaped according to the thought patterns of English; a literal translation would be both stilted and unclear. Third, apart from the matter of syntax, several of the words employed are irreducible to satisfactory English equivalents, and adding to that complication, most of those terms have a wide range of meaning and can be made to serve a number of far-reaching interpretations. A comparison of several translations and commentaries illustrates just how widely opinions can differ. Fourth, if that were not enough, the verse has come down in variant versions, and even the early Indian commentators had to struggle with four instances of alternative wording.[51]

What can help us to reach a plausible understanding of this *mantra?* In a word, context. What is the literary context? How does this *mantra* fit in with the surrounding verses and with the text as a whole? What is the philosophical context? What is Śvetāśvatara's point of view? We know that his preceptorial lineage stems from the Yajurveda. Quite possibly the older texts within that tradition can help to dispel doubt over the specific interpretation of individual words and the concepts they embody—or at least help to narrow the field of possibilities.

To make sense of this challenging verse, it is advisable to start with the second *pāda*. The Śaṁkarācārya who wrote the *Vṛtti* takes it as an adverbial simile, beginning with an implied "just as" (*yathā*).[52] Just as physical existence (*janma*) depends on the growth and thriving (*vṛddhi*) of the body (*ātman*), which in turn depends on the nourishment of food and drink in abundance (*grāsāmbuvṛṣṭyā*), so does the embodied self (*dehin*) perpetuate its existence through subtler means. Just as an observable principle of causality operates at the level of physical nature and regulates how the world works, a subtler causal force operates at the nonmaterial level of human experience. That force, known as the law of *karma*, determines the conditions of birth and drives the circumstances of individual lives.

A similar distinction between material and nonmaterial causality appears in the Trika philosophy. There the term *niyati* denotes the natural physical law, also known as determinism. The term *karma*, in contrast, applies to the motivated human action that weaves its own entangling web. That said, it is a matter of observation that the two kinds of causality interact. Just as material conditions and outward events can shape our attitudes, personalities, and destinies, so can our inner mental and emotional processes shape the external events and circumstances of our lives.

The concept of *karma* as mental activity is already formulated in the Bṛhadāraṇyakopaniṣad (1.5.3). As the text sets out at length, everything depends on the mind's awareness: one might say, "I did not see," "I did not hear," or "I did not feel when I was touched on the back," because "my mind was elsewhere." Apart from physical perceptions, within the mind alone one experiences such feelings as desire, intention, doubt, conviction, lack of trust, repose, disquiet, shame, reflection, and fear. All these subtle, or nonphysical, activities are simply movements of the mind. Later in the same Upaniṣad (4.4.6) we find quoted an older verse, which declares that on whatever the mind is set, that determines the course of the individual's life. Every soul is the product of its own experiences.

Śvetāśvatara mentions four forms of mental activity in the first quarter of this *mantra*. They are *saṅkalpana, sparśana, dṛṣṭi,* and *moha.* Each term is rich in meaning and cannot be reduced to a single dictionary definition. Each calls for detailed consideration.

In the present context *saṅkalpana* has been translated variously as "thoughts,"[53] "thought,"[54] "idea or thinking,"[55] "imagination,"[56] "desires,"[57] "desire,"[58] or "intention."[59] Every one of these is, paradoxically, insufficiently focused and insufficiently broad! *Saṅkalpana* is best defined as the mental process of forming a specific purpose or intention aimed at fulfilling a particular need or desire. The seer wants us to recognize that a stream of such intentions flows unabated through ordinary human awareness, directed outward toward the fulfillment of one purpose after another.

Next, *sparśana* has been rendered as "touching,"[60] "touch,"[61] or "contact,"[62] but the word hints at much more. The process of mentally "touching" refers to the activity of the mind in cognizing the exterior world through the five avenues of sense perception. Thus, *sparśana* indicates a sensory interaction with the exterior world.

Translations of *dṛṣṭi* include "seeing,"[63] "sight,"[64] "vision,"[65] "looking,"[66] and "attachment."[67] The Sanskrit word can mean seeing or viewing in a general sense but also beholding with the mind's eye.[68] This last definition implies a process of envisioning, conceiving, and forming some sort of opinion, attitude, or understanding. Even today in English, one often says, "I see," meaning "I understand." Perhaps the word *outlook* best conveys the broader sense that *dṛṣṭi* implies here.

The last term, *moha,* makes a qualitative judgment on the foregoing activities of the mind. Previous translators have rendered it as "passions,"[69] "passion,"[70] "illusion,"[71] "delusion,"[72] and "attachment."[73] One translator accepts the variant *homa* in place of *moha* and understands it as the ritual action of offering oblations into the sacrificial fire.[74] The early commentator Vijñānabhagavat, likewise reading *homa,* understood it as symbolic of all physical action.[75] However, *moha,* and not *homa,* is the more widely accepted reading and the one that better fits the context of mental activity. *Moha* can connote a spectrum of mental dispositions that include distraction (forgetfulness of one's true nature), delusion (mistaking appearance for reality), misapprehension or error (straying from the truth), infatuation (loss of judgment owing to unreasoning attraction), confusion, and mental darkness. The word *moha* derives from a verbal root meaning "to lose consciousness," and every one of those definitions implies some lessening of awareness as the individual becomes increasingly involved with objective qualities or finite objects and identifies with them. This loss of the plenitude of true Self-awareness (*pūrṇāhaṁtā*) is what defines the condition of human individuality. By the word *moha* Śvetāśvatara wants to impress on us that the ideas, opinions, and attitudes we have formed about the world and ourselves are not necessarily correct. The world is not what we think it is, and we are not who we think we are. The *jīva*, believing itself to be this or that, forgets that it is greater than any identity based on what is finite, partial, and perishable. In fact its true nature is infinite, undivided, and everlasting. That is the crux of the matter; there is a difference between the eternal selfhood of the Divine and the temporary human identity it appears to assume.

That said, both divine *being* and human *existence* are the experience of consciousness. The light of consciousness is a singular reality, whether shining in full glory as Śiva or reflected dimly in the *jīva*. The divine experience is unconditioned consciousness-in-itself; the human experience is consciousness subject to various kinds of conditioning and limitation.

In the process of cosmic manifestation, as the Taittirīyopaniṣad explains, the One first feels a creative urge to become many, then formulates and projects the multiplicity. The Trika philosophy explains this process as the exercise of Śiva's complete freedom (*svātantrya*), expressed through the powers of spontaneous will (*icchāśakti*), creative ideation (*jñānaśakti*), and creative action (*kriyāśakti*). Having manifested the world, Śiva enters into it—that is, he experiences it through every sentient creature. In the embodied state, wherein subjective awareness becomes confused (literally "mixed up") with objective qualities, he forgets his true nature as the infinite One and falls into the delusion (*moha*) that he is the bound soul (*dehin*). The *dehin* then sees things as other than they really are. Its outlook (*dṛṣṭi*), based on its contact or interaction (*sparśana*) with a world that it views as separate from itself, perpetuates the deception. Even the seemingly free exercise of its own will (*saṅkalpana*) is ever circumscribed by some sort of conditioning or necessity.

In the embodied state, the freedom of divine activity (*kriyā*) is reduced to the binding power of human action (*karma*). As Śvetāśvatara explains, the embodied soul (*dehī*), according to its deeds and in due course (*karmānugāny anukrameṇa*), assumes various forms (*rūpāṇy abhisamprapadyate*) in a broad range of conditions (*sthāneṣu*)—"in happiness and all the rest" (*sukhetareṣu*), as he phrased it at the outset of his teaching (1.1). Now he reveals that the course of human life is a departure from the truth of our being.

12

स्थूलानि सूक्ष्माणि बहूनि चैव
रूपाणि देही स्वगुणैर्वृणोति ।
क्रियागुणैरात्मगुणैश्च तेषां
संयोगहेतुरपरोऽपि दृष्टः ॥ १२ ॥

sthūlāni sūkṣmāṇi bahūni caiva rūpāṇi dehī svaguṇair vṛṇoti /
kriyāguṇair ātmaguṇaiś ca teṣāṁ saṁyogahetur aparo 'pi dṛṣṭaḥ //

12. Indeed many forms, gross and subtle, does the embodied soul choose according to its own merits. Driven by its involvement with the effects of its actions and their particular qualities, it is seen as greatly inferior.

According to nondualistic Śaiva teaching the perfect I-consciousness (*pūrṇāhaṁtā*) of the supreme Lord rests in the infinite glory of his own perfection. Whereas that supreme consciousness is entirely nonrelational and absolutely free, the ego-based I-consciousness of the individual (*dehin*) is entangled in a complex network of restricting causal relationships. For this reason it is seen as greatly inferior (*aparo 'pi dṛṣṭaḥ*). The word *apara* can also mean "different," and another reading is that the individual soul, although having divine consciousness as its essence, nevertheless appears to be different and separate from its own higher nature.

This perceived inferiority refers not to the essence of the individual self, which is divine, but to the conditioned state with which it is erroneously identified. This state of ongoing birth, death, and rebirth is driven by *karma*. Although one often hears *karma* defined as a simple chain of cause and effect, Śvetāśvatara's image of a net or web (*jāla*) (3.1, 5.3) better conveys the vast complexity of the process. It is this principle of *karma* that weaves the intricate and elaborate web of unenlightened human existence that appears to us as the tapestries of individual lives and indeed as the entire panorama of human history.

As previously mentioned, the causal principles of *niyati* and *karma* are not the same. *Niyati* denotes the causality observable in the material universe. The laws of physics have been discovered through observation of phenomena and confirmed by scientific experiment. These laws order the workings of the physical universe. In contrast the law of *karma* deals with the workings of the ethical, moral, and psychological dimensions of human experience. Here too we begin with an assumed relationship of cause and effect, but how can any controlled experiment, which works so well with physical phenomena, confirm beyond doubt that a similar causality underlies the subtler mental and spiritual processes of human life? It cannot. *Karma,* being moral law, belongs not to the province of the physical sciences but to the purview of philosophy.

Philosophy tells us that *karma* is a purely human phenomenon. Even as it does not apply to physical matter, neither does it apply to the activities of animals, birds, and insects. Morality is a concept unknown to them, and their instinctual behavior belongs to the realm of natural process. *Karma* applies specifically to action arising from human volition.[76] In other words, it requires intention (*saṅkalpana*). The law of *karma* decrees that the embodied soul is responsible for its own choices and actions, both physical and mental, as well as for the consequences they bear and the destiny they create. That is exactly what Śvetāśvatara indicates here when he says, "Indeed many forms, gross and subtle, does the embodied soul (*dehī*) choose (*vṛṇoti*) according to its own merits," only to become "driven by its involvement with the effects of its actions and their particular qualities." Physical characteristics, life circumstances, mental and emotional dispositions, and even passing moods are manifestations (*rūpāṇi*) resulting from past and present choices.

Can we prove this? The proof is more elusive than the immediately observable confirmation of a scientific experiment. The web of human experience is far more subtle and infinitely complex. It is impossible for us to take a big enough step backward to view the whole picture. In all, *karma* is not only about what we do but about what happens to us as a result. Moreover, the actions of a single human being can have a profound bearing, directly or indirectly, on a host of other lives. Trying to trace the causal pattern of everything that happens is an impossible and futile pursuit and in the end a waste of time and effort. That said, there is a dimension of *karma* that is empirically verifiable. It shows itself when we consciously apply moral and spiritual principles to our thought and conduct and begin to witness a gradual transformation in ourselves.

A fuller understanding of this process emerges in the light of the general operations of *karma* as the philosophies of India have defined them. The word *karma* signifies any action, either physical, verbal, or mental, as well as its consequences and its cumulative effect. Because every action creates a mental impression (*saṁskāra*) and those impressions deepen into habitual tendencies, our actions determine what we become. *Karma* has four modes of operation that can be classified as *prārabdha, sañcita, āgāmin,* and *kriyamāṇa.*

Prārabdha ("commenced") signifies *karma* that has already been activated. *Prārabdha karma* consists of actions in a previous lifetime that determine the conditions into which the *jīva* is reborn, including its physical, mental, and emotional characteristics. Like an arrow that has already been shot, *prārabdha karma* is beyond one's control. Through the agency of other living beings and natural forces, it manifests externally to deliver the consequences of past actions. It operates internally by governing the habitual attitudes and patterns of behavior that keep the soul in bondage.

Sañcita ("stored up") denotes the *karma* that is the aggregate of latent impressions created either in the previous or present life. It remains in a dormant state, compared to that of an arrow resting in a quiver. Such an arrow may or may not be shot, and similarly *sañcita karma* may or may not come to fruition.

Āgāmī karma, that which is "coming up," comes to fruition as the result of actions performed in the present lifetime. Depending on the nature of the action and the situation, the consequences may be instantaneous or they may not play out until much later.

The terms *āgāmin* and *kriyamāṇa* ("being done") are sometimes used interchangeably, but there are technical distinctions between the two. *Kriyamāṇa karma* specifically refers to that which is done in the present moment. We can argue that *prārabdha karma* governs the present moment, and it is certainly true that any action is likely to be influenced, if not driven, by already established attitudes and behavioral patterns of our own making. But the present moment offers the freedom of choice either to yield to the existing impressions or to break with the force of habit. By cultivating better modes of thought and behavior in the present, we can redirect our destiny toward the ultimate goal of freedom. Śrī Rāmakṛṣṇa made exactly the same point as the Upaniṣadic seers when he declared that both bondage and freedom are of the mind.[77]

It is demonstrable that *kriyamāṇa karma* is not *karma* in the ordinary sense of binding action; rather it is the exercise of the freedom of choice which has the capacity to lead, if we so desire, to the rediscovery of our own intrinsic boundlessness. Śvetāśvatara has already said that the bound soul is capable of infinity and partakes of it (5.9), but as long as it remains driven by its passions and delusions and forgetful of its true autonomy, it is seen as decidedly inferior (*aparo 'pi dṛṣṭaḥ*).

13

अनाद्यनन्तं कलिलस्य मध्ये
विश्वस्य स्रष्टारमनेकरूपम्।
विश्वस्यैकं परिवेष्टितारं
ज्ञात्वा देवं मुच्यते सर्वपाशैः ॥ १३ ॥

anādyanantaṁ kalilasya madhye viśvasya sraṣṭāram anekarūpam /
viśvasyaikaṁ pariveṣṭitāraṁ jñātvā devaṁ mucyate sarvapāśaiḥ //

13. [But the Self is] without beginning or end, in the midst of the unformed the creator of everything, assuming many forms. He alone encompasses the universe; knowing that effulgent being, one is freed from all fetters.

Now attention returns to the supreme Self, described as having neither beginning (*anādi*) nor end (*ananta*). "Without beginning" is another way of saying uncreated and therefore self-existent. "Without end" means endless in every possible sense—untouched by any limitation of time, space, or causality.

After the opening phrase Śvetāśvatara crafts the rest of this *mantra* from phrases that he has spoken before. His purpose in repeating them is to impress their ideas firmly on the minds of his listeners. Part of the first *pāda* ("in the midst of the unformed") and the entire second *pāda* ("the creator of everything, assuming many forms") were first uttered in *mantra* 4.14. The third *pāda* ("he alone encompasses the universe") is common to *mantras* 3.7, 4.14, and 4.16, and the fourth *pāda* ("knowing that effulgent being, one is freed from all fetters") recurs five times in the course of the Upaniṣad (1.8, 2.15, 4.16, 5.13, 6.13), emphasizing the role of knowledge in liberation. Note that six additional verses end by stressing the same idea. Those *mantras* (3.1, 3.7, 3.10, 3.13, 4.17, 4.20) all affirm that they who *know* [the Self] become immortal.

In summary, the points that Śvetāśvatara wants to drive home are that the author of this universe brings the creation forth out of a primordial, unformed state. Through the ordering of form out of formlessness, the One expresses itself as the many, yet ever remains the ultimate reality of consciousness. This consciousness, extending forth as everything in the cosmos, is one, just as light radiating from the sun is an indissoluble unity that reveals, embraces, and pervades the entire world. Nevertheless, lighting and animating each soul, this awareness finds itself in the thrall of enjoyment and misery and thinks itself bound. Only when the impurities of smallness and separation vanish does the *jīvātman* truly recognize itself as *paramātman*. It has never been otherwise, and when all sense of difference (*bheda*) vanishes, the ultimate radiance reveals that, in truth, there never was any difference.

Śvetāśvatara could have ended the discourse here with his emphatic restatement of these important points. He could have left us thinking we know all we need to know about liberation. But the seer is wiser than his disciples, and lest we settle into complacency, he will in the chapter's final *mantra* direct our thoughts to further questions of knowledge and immortality.

14

भावग्राह्यमनीडाख्यं भावाभावकरं शिवम् ।
कलासर्गकरं देवं ये विदुस्ते जहुस्तनुम् ॥ १४ ॥

bhāvagrāhyam anīḍākhyaṁ bhāvābhāvakaraṁ śivam /
kalāsargakaraṁ devaṁ ye vidus te jahus tanum //

14. [The Self] who is to be grasped intuitively, who is called bodiless, the auspicious maker of existence and nonexistence, the effulgent being who brings forth the creation and its parts—they who know him lay aside the smallness of individuality.

The discourse comes to a close by emphasizing once again the role of knowledge in the transcendence of the human condition. The reality of Brahman, the supreme Self, is to be grasped (*grāhyam*)—understood—with the whole of one's awareness (*bhāva*). It cannot be grasped in the physical sense, because it is incorporeal (*anīḍa*, literally "without a nest, resting-place, or abode").[78] Confined neither to the body nor to any other place, not even to speech or thought, it can be known only intuitively. Effulgent (*devam*) and ever-auspicious (*śivam*), the one supreme Self brings forth from out of itself the duality of existence and nonexistence (*bhāvābhāva*) and the world that consists of a diversity of parts (*kalā*).

Those *jīvas* who have laid aside their sense of separate, individual selfhood attain liberation. The usual translation of the fourth *pāda* goes something like "they who know (*ye viduḥ*) give up (*te jahus*) the body (*tanum*)." The verb *jahuḥ* ordinarily means "they have left," "abandoned," "quitted," or "relinquished." In combination with a word for body (such as *śarīram* or *deham*) or for life-breath (such as *prāṇān* or *asūn*), it means "to die."[79] Although "they give up the body" in the sense of dying is a lexically valid reading, it is also an unfortunate one. Suggesting that physical death is either the precondition or outcome of enlightenment, it fails to convey the fuller meaning of this profound statement.

The key lies in the word *tanu*. "Body" is one of its meanings, but elsewhere in the text (3.5) and in other Upaniṣads (Praśnopaniṣad 2.12; Maitryupaniṣad 4.6, 5.2, 6.5–6), *tanu* is used in the technical sense of "form" or "manifestation" and specifically a form or manifestation emanating from the Divine. Other meanings of *tanu* include "person," or "self," but primarily the word refers to something that is small, minute, or attenuated.[80] *Tanu* derives from *tan*, which means "to extend," "to spread," "to stretch," "to diffuse (as light)," "to propagate," "to display," or "to manifest."[81] In *mantras* 5.8–9

Śvetāśvatara has dramatically illustrated that the individual soul is ever so small, whereas the supreme Self is immeasurably great. The soul is at*ten*uated (the syllable *ten* and the Sanskrit *tan* derive from a common source). The soul is diluted, weakened, and reduced to a fraction of the hundredth part of the tip of a hair, again divided a hundred times! The one Lord ex*ten*ds himself as countless souls that appear diminished, weakened, and subject to all kinds of limitations and afflictions. *Tanu* signifies *the sense of one's own individuality,* and to relinquish all the constraints of body, mind, and personality is to achieve the freedom of one's greater identity—the radiant fullness of the higher Self (*paramātman*).

On the matter of liberation (*mukti*) India's philosophies have produced a variety of opinions. Among Sāṁkhya, Advaita Vedānta, and Trika Śaivism, each has its own distinct ideas (see pp. 135–137). Sāṁkhya understands liberation as undoing the association (*saṁyoga*) or "mixing up" of consciousness (*puruṣa*) with insentient materiality (*prakṛti*). The liberated state is called *kaivalya* ("isolation" or "aloofness").

Advaita Vedānta defines liberation as transcending the inscrutable, world-producing *māyā* and knowing the self (*ātman*) to be Brahman. This view is traceable to the *mahāvākya* of the Bṛhadāraṇyakopaniṣad, "this self is Brahman" (*ayam ātmā brahma*), restated and elaborated by Śaṁkara as the formula "Brahman is real, the world is misleading, and the individual soul is none other than Brahman" (*brahma satyaṁ jagan mithyā jīvo brahmaiva nāparaḥ*).

Advaita Vedānta recognizes that human embodiment is not only a state of bondage resulting from ignorance but also a unique opportunity for transcendence. Among all sentient creatures only human beings have the capacity for Self-realization, because human consciousness alone is the field (*kṣetra*) of moral and discriminative action wherein the clashing dualities of right and wrong (*puṇya* and *pāpa*), the good and the pleasant (*śreyas* and *preyas*), and the real and the apparent (*sat* and *asat*) play out. This philosophy acknowledges degrees of illumination and beatitude through *kramamukti* ("gradual liberation") but also accepts that enlightenment may come suddenly. Either way, the ultimate state of illumination and freedom is one of identity with the impersonal Absolute, or *nirguṇa* Brahman.

There is an additional distinction between *videhamukti* ("discarnate liberation") and *jīvanmukti* ("liberation while living"). The first term defines liberation as complete only with the dropping off of the body. The second refers to liberation even while living in the embodied state. For the larger number of aspirants of lower qualification, the intense bliss of Self-knowledge in *nirvikalpa samādhi* is greater than the body can sustain, and for such souls the body quickly drops away.[82] That said, a few rare souls do not give up the body soon after *nirvikalpa samādhi* but return to life in the phenomenal world. Although still living in the body, they have overcome all limitation of individuality. They abide in constant identification with Brahman, ever aware that the Self is all and all is the Self. Then, having enjoyed the liberated state while living, they are not reborn after physical death.[83] According to the Muṇḍakopaniṣad (3.2.8–9), "Just as the flowing rivers, leaving behind their names and forms (*nāmarupe vihāya*), merge into the ocean, so does the knowing one (*vidvān*), freed from name and form (*nāmarūpād vimuktaḥ*), attain the all-transcending reality. Whoever knows the supreme Brahman becomes Brahman." That is the state of awareness free from any sort of conditioning, and that freedom is possible apart from either condition of embodiment or disembodiment.

For the most part the Trikaśāstra agrees with Advaita Vedānta but also holds some distinctive views of its own. These afford additional insight into Śvetāśvatara's teaching in the present *mantra.* Through the sense of individuality or attenuation, which the seer calls *tanu,* consciousness appears bound to phenomenal existence. Śiva as *jīva* appears deprived of power (*śaktidaridraḥ*), and the way back to freedom is to regain the inherent fullness of that divine power. *Mukti* is therefore the experience of the essential unity of Śiva and Śakti.[84] In the supreme state of Self-consciousness (*pūrṇāhaṁtā*), the liberated *jīva* realizes its true identity and experiences the fullness of infinite knowledge and the bliss of absolute freedom that are essential to the divine nature.

Abhinavagupta writes in the *Tantrāloka* (1.41) that the higher, liberating knowledge is not achieved through intellectual processes; rather it is natural, spontaneous, entirely independent, and self-supporting. It is nonconceptual, hence perfect (1.47). Such knowledge emerges only when the sense of individuality (Śvetāśvatara's *tanu*) melts away at the deepest level of one's being (Śvetāśvatara's *bhāva*), which is the "heart" or center of awareness. When consciousness (*saṁvid*) is experienced as pure, infinite, and free of all modification, one is liberated. Liberation can be either *jīvanmukti* or *videhamukti* (1.50).[85]

According to Trika teaching the enlightened living soul (*jīvanmukta*) is unaffected by any of the body's physical limitations or by any of the subtler restrictions of mind, ego, and intellect.[86] When awareness of the lower self dissolves in *samāveśa* ("absorption"), the *jīvanmukta* experiences the entire universe as an expression of its own highest Self.[87] All limitation of individuality has vanished, and what remains is the awareness of the unconditioned in the conditioned, of the infinite in the finite, of timelessness in time, of being in becoming.[88] This complete integration of the relative and the Absolute is the highest nonduality (*parādvaita*). The *Spandakārikā* (2.5) informs us, "One who truly realizes the identity of the universe and the Self, being united permanently with the universal consciousness, regards the whole world as the divine play and is liberated while living (*jīvanmuktaḥ*). Of this there is no doubt."[89]

The Trikaśāstra agrees with Advaita Vedānta that *jīvanmukti* follows the experience of transcendental consciousness (*turīya*) or *nirvikalpa samādhi*. In the *Tantrāloka* Abhinavagupta analyzes the experience of *turīya* (usually called *turya* in the Śaiva literature) as an ascent through seven stages. The first six are progressive degrees of *nimīlana* ("closed-eyed") *samādhi* or internal, subjective absorption.[90] The seventh and highest stage is called *unmīlana* ("open-eyed") *samādhi* or *jīvanmukti*.[91] Not all *yogins* attain *jīvanmukti*; only the most exceptional become established in that open-eyed bliss of universal consciousness (*jagadānanda*).[92] Then, whether awake, dreaming, or asleep, the *jīvanmukta* remains ever mindful of the true nature of subject and object, for such a soul has expanded beyond the three ordinary states of experience (*jāgrat, svapna,* and *suṣupti*) and abides in the knowledge of pure oneness. That universal bliss (*jagadānanda*) is absolute identification with Paramaśiva.[93]

Abhinavagupta's disciple Kṣemarāja observes further that a *jīvanmukta* enjoys liberation while in the body, but the body itself, being material, is still subject to *prārabdha karma*. The causal forces that have already been set in motion continue to operate until their effects are exhausted. Nevertheless, the conditions of embodiment no longer affect the liberated soul. And once the *prārabdha karma* is spent, the body drops off and the soul, already in permanent oneness with the supreme Lord, ever abides beyond time and space in its true being. With the death of the physical body *jīvanmukti* becomes *videhamukti.*[94]

The word *tanu* derives from the same verbal root as the word *tantra.* The Tantra teaches that the supreme Lord limits himself as the at*ten*uated human soul by ex*ten*ding himself as myriad *jīvas,* indeed as the whole of creation. In regard to liberation, the Kulārṇavatantra (9.14) describes *nirvikalpa samādhi* as the cessation of movement in the mind—the absence of all sensation and conceptualization. According to this text a soul thus absorbed in Śiva—one whose consciousness has reached the level of the *śivatattva*—is said to abide in ecstasy. But the text implies that *nirvikalpa samādhi* does not constitute liberation, because it excludes the external world and therefore retains a hint of distinction, a trace of duality. The *paramātman,* however, encompasses everything in its ineffable oneness; being consciousness itself, it includes every possible modification of itself. Only with the realization of the ultimate Paramaśiva, beyond even the *śivatattva,* is the soul absolutely free—so free that the question of bondage and freedom does not even arise (9.26).[95]

The teaching of the Kulārṇavatantra calls to mind the experience of Tota Puri, the wandering monk from Śaṁkara's Puri monastery, who instructed Śrī Rāmakṛṣṇa in the discipline of Advaita Vedānta. After only three days of practicing the Vedantic method of discriminative negation (*neti neti*), Śrī Rāmakṛṣṇa attained *nirvikalpa samādhi,* much to his preceptor's amazement. It had taken Tota Puri himself forty years of strenuous effort to reach that lofty state of nondual consciousness. Having brought his disciple to that same level, Tota Puri little suspected that his own spiritual perspective was about to be broadened through a series of sometimes painful but always instructive events. Śrī Rāmakṛṣṇa later commented that Tota Puri's strict adherence to the doctrine of Advaita Vedānta had not allowed him to accept Śakti, the power of Brahman, as a reality. As Śrī Rāmakṛṣṇa put it, Tota Puri would "trifle with Śakti" by viewing it as mere *māyā* and calling it false (*mithyā*). But during his eleven months with Rāmakṛṣṇa at Dakṣineśvar, the monk learned the greater truth of nonduality—that Brahman and Śakti are, in fact, identical.[96] In that state of realization, it is not the pleasure of the object that the *jīvanmukta* enjoys but the bliss of the Self,[97] for it abides in the constant knowledge that there is nothing but the Self.

षष्ठोऽध्यायः

CHAPTER SIX

1

स्वभावमेके कवयो वदन्ति
कालं तथान्ये परिमुह्यमानाः ।
देवस्यैष महिमा तु लोके
येनेदं भ्राम्यते ब्रह्मचक्रम् ॥ १ ॥

svabhāvam eke kavayo vadanti kālaṁ tathānye parimuhyamānāḥ /
devasyaiṣa mahimā tu loke yenedaṁ bhrāmyate brahmacakram //

1. Some thinkers speak of the inherent nature of things [as the cause of the universe]; others, of likewise muddled mind, speak of time. But it is the power and glory of the effulgent God here in the world by which this wheel of Brahman revolves.

Beginning his sixth and final discourse, Śvetāśvatara brings us full circle to the question that opened this Upaniṣad: What is the cause [of the universe]? He reminds us of immediately having dismissed seven possible causes, beginning with time (*kāla*) and the inherent nature of things (*svabhāva*) (1.2).

The seer has already intimated that the moments of time come into existence and quickly vanish like every other created thing. Time itself is an effect. Nor can the inherent nature of things be the primordial cause. The wetness of water, for example, has no existence apart from the water in which it inheres; how can the wetness precede the water as its cause? Any inherent quality is an observable and already manifest phenomenon—an effect. On similar grounds none of the other proposed causes offer tenable explanations (see pp. 87–91).

Reason alone cannot reveal the ultimate truth. The seer has already divulged that seekers of the truth, having entering into deep meditation (*dhyānayogānugatāḥ*), discover within themselves the power of the effulgent Self (*devātmaśaktim*) that lies hidden by its own effects (*svaguṇair nigūḍhām*) (1.3). Moreover, that Self is purely One (*ekaḥ*). The *Vivekacūḍāmaṇi* [The crest-jewel of discrimination], a late classic of Advaita Vedānta long attributed to Śaṁkara, makes the same point: "The crystal-clear truth of one's own Self (*svamamalaṁ tattvam*), hidden by *māyā's* effects (*māyākāryatirohitam*), is to be reached (*labhyate*) through the instruction of a knower of Brahman, [followed by] intensive reflection (*manana*), profound meditation (*dhyāna*), and other practices, and not through faulty reasoning (*na duryuktibhiḥ*) (verse 65). Abhinavagupta, in a previously cited passage from the *Tantrāloka*, also writes that the supreme truth is not reached through intellectual processes (1.41). It is a spontaneous knowledge—natural, self-evident, nonconceptual, and perfect (1.47). Such knowledge emerges only when the sense of individuality melts away at the deepest level of one's being, when consciousness is experienced as infinite and free of all modification. The great sages of the Upaniṣads, Advaita Vedānta, and the Trikadarśana agree that it is not reason but direct experience that reveals the answer to life's profoundest questions.

In the present *mantra* Śvetāśvatara divulges that the cause of the universe and of our existence in it is the power and glory of God (*devasya mahimā*). The word *mahiman* embraces the ideas of greatness, might, power, majesty, and glory. It also signifies "magnitude (as one of Śiva's attributes)" or "the magical power of increasing size at will."[1] Similarly the literal meaning of *brahman* is "growth," "expansion," "evolution," "development," "swelling of the spirit or soul."[2] The expansion of God takes form as the perceptible majesty and might of the universe. This expansion is possible only through the inherent power of divine consciousness, which is the seed of all possibility. This power of Brahman, here called *mahiman*, has yet another name—*śakti*—the same term that Śvetāśvatara himself has used in the compound *devātmaśakti* (1.3).

Now the seer tells us that those who accept man-made philosophies as rational explanations for our existence may appear to be thoughtful and learned men (*kavayaḥ*), but in truth they are confused. The term he uses (*parimuhyamānāḥ*) illustrates just how muddled they are in their thinking. Their minds are enveloped by the world's often alluring confusion. Though earnest enough, they do not recognize the divine glory that animates the world, nor do they consider that no experience of existence is even possible apart from the light and power of divine consciousness.

It is only the enlightened soul who can declare, "The entire universe is nothing other than the Divine, manifesting itself as all this diversity. I experience this through the eternal consciousness that is God's own awareness, reflected in the body-mind complex I call myself, but which is only a limitation of the Divine." This is more than a philosophical view; it is a deep experiential conviction that the cosmos is nothing other than eternal potentiality appearing as transient actuality.

Śrī Rāmakṛṣṇa affirmed this same idea. In a conversation with the Hindu reformer Keshab Sen, he expounded on the unity of being and becoming. He explained that what the follower of the path of knowledge (the *jñānin*) calls the Absolute (Brahman), the *yogin* calls the Self (*ātman*), and the devotee (the *bhakta*) calls the Lord (Bhagavān). The *jñānin*, practicing the discipline of negation (*neti neti*), attains knowledge of the Absolute (*brahmajñāna*) and thereafter has the unwavering conviction that Brahman alone is real and the world illusory. Then Śrī Rāmakṛṣṇa went on to say that the *bhakta* accepts all states of consciousness as real and the universe as a manifestation of God's power and glory. The sky, the stars, the moon, the sun, the mountains, the ocean, humans, birds, and animals—everything is the visible glory of God.[3] On another occasion he declared that the Absolute (*nitya*) and the relative (*līlā*) belong to the same reality, and that he himself accepted both. To explain away the world as *māyā* is to come up short in the totality of things.[4]

Finally, Śvetāśvatara refers again to the wheel of Brahman (*brahmacakra*), on which he expounded earlier in minute detail (1.4,

1.6). This cosmic wheel is a common symbol in later Śaiva texts, which offer deeper insight into its meaning and serve well to enhance our understanding of the present verse. As the "wheel of becoming,"[5] the *brahmacakra* represents the collective energies (*śaktis*) of the creation and the countless ways in which they manifest. Another name for it is *raśmicakra* ("wheel of the rays of light"). Found in Abhinavagupta's *Parātrīśikāvivaraṇa*, this term likens God and the whole of creation to the sun and its beams. In modern times Śrī Rāmakṛṣṇa employed the same image, saying that one cannot conceive of the sun (Brahman) without its rays (Śakti) or of the rays without the sun.[6] Analogous to the solar rays, the spokes of the wheel of Brahman represent the diversification of divine power through every possible form and function (see pp. 95–99). Whether thought of as sunbeams or spokes, these radiating energies stream from the center—from the very heart—of awareness.

For that reason Śiva's wheel of energy is also literally called the *śakticakra*. As it revolves, the universe first comes into existence and then dissolves. The wheel therefore exemplifies the cyclical nature of *saṁsāra*, with emanation (*sṛṣṭi*) and resorption (*saṁhāra*) ever succeeding each other. The Śaiva philosopher Kṣemarāja, commenting on the *Spandakārikā*, notes in his *Spandanirṇaya* [Determination of vibration] that manifestation and dissolution are the same energy of consciousness, appearing first in one way and then in another. Moreover, he adds that it is the same light of consciousness that shines on both what we take to be existent (*sat*) and what we take to be nonexistent (*asat*); the distinction is merely a conception of the human mind.[7]

Śvetāśvatara has already pointed out that the individual soul has its existence on the revolving part of the wheel: "On this vast wheel of Brahman (*brahmacakre*), wherein everything lives and dies, the soul revolves (*haṁso bhrāmyate*), thinking itself different from the animating force. Yet blessed by the knowledge of that very Brahman, it attains immortality" (1.6). Read literally, the verse conjures up the vivid image of a goose (*haṁsa*) fluttering frantically all over the wheel's spinning surface, unable to settle down.[8] Echoing Śvetāśvatara, Somānanda writes in the *Śivadṛṣṭi* that the bound soul, ignorant of its true identity, is caught up in the movement of the wheel, subject to the recurring cycle of birth, death, and rebirth. But the enlightened soul, having recognized its identity with the supreme Self, moves to the motionless center of the wheel and rests there, ever-blissful, at the heart of awareness.[9]

The Trikadarśana calls Śiva the "lord of the wheel" (*cakreśvara*). He remains the unmoved witness at the unmoving center. Śiva is the pure, ever-free I-consciousness that causes the emanation of the cosmos through the exercise of his own power. Immune to the thralldom of the wheel's turning, he is the serene watcher over all. Nothing escapes his omniscient gaze as he delights in the play, even while the bound soul, symbolized by the frantic goose, flutters about while the wheel spins.

When that bound soul (*haṁsa, jīva, paśu*) returns to the center—to the heart of awareness—all activity (*vṛtti*) of consciousness ceases. The *jīva* then realizes its supreme identity as Śiva. In the *Yogasūtra* (1.2) Patañjali speaks of the enlightened state as *yoga* and defines it as the cessation of all activity (*vṛttinirodhaḥ*) within the individual medium of consciousness (*citta*). Abhinavagupta also uses the term *nirodha* to indicate the state of absolute repose that results from the soul's recognition of its identity with the supreme Śiva–consciousness.[10] The author of the *Spandakārikā* (3.19) makes this same point, saying that one whose mind becomes firmly established in one place (*ekatra*), with its outward and inward movements restrained, attains the status of the true experient (*bhoktṛtām eti*) and becomes the lord of the wheel (*cakeśvaro bhavet*), resting in the bliss of universal I-consciousness.

2

येनावृतं नित्यमिदं हि सर्वं
ज्ञः कालकारो गुणी सर्वविद्यः ।
तेनेशितं कर्म विवर्ततेह
पृथिव्यप्तेजोनिलखानि चिन्त्यम् ॥ २ ॥

yenāvṛtaṁ nityam idaṁ hi sarvaṁ jñaḥ kālakāro guṇī sarvavidyaḥ / teneśitaṁ karma vivartate ha pṛthivyaptejonilakhāni cintyam //

2. Ever enveloping all this world, he is the intelligent maker of time, the omniscient possessor of the forces of creation. At his direction this work of creation surely unfolds. It is to be reflected upon as earth, water, fire, air, and space.

We have already seen that time is an effect and therefore has to have a cause or maker. And who, or what, is this maker of time (*kālakāraḥ*)? It is he who is the possessor and master of the energies of creation (*guṇī*), the source of the inherent qualities of every created thing. And who is this? The effulgent God (*deva*), now characterized as intelligent (*jñaḥ*), for his nature is consciousness itself. This eternal witness, the supreme Person, is the single reality that envelops all this world of our experience. Śvetāśvatara emphasizes "all *this* world" (*idaṁ hi sarvam*). This creation is God's own handiwork (*karma*) that expands, develops, and revolves (all meanings of *vivartate*) through his own conscious direction (*teneśitam*). This universe is to be reflected upon (*cintyam*) as earth, water, fire, air, and space.

The creation should be thought of as the glory of God, but its beauty and wonder should not be taken at face value. Ordinarily this *mantra* is thought to convey merely that the physical world is composed of the five gross elements, but commentators overlook the fact that if it were only a statement of cosmic evolution, the elements would logically be given in the reverse order—space, air, fire, water, and earth—for that is the order in which they emerge and become manifest. Here Śvetāśvatara gives a subtle clue that there is more to consider than earth's solid strength and fertility, than water's flowing purity, than fire's comforting warmth and revealing light, than the air that is our life's breath, than the space that contains them all and vibrates with the creative power of sound, the *praṇava*.

The enumeration of the five *tattvas* of physical matter implies the entire span of all the rest, all the way back to the ultimate cause. In saying that the elements of this world should be reflected upon in reverse order—as earth, water, fire, air, and space (*pṛthivyaptejonila-khāni*)—the seer is no longer speaking of the *evolution* of the universe, but of the mental *involution* that constitutes yogic practice. As miraculous as the world may appear to us, once it has become fully manifest, we are to try to rediscover its true nature, which is beyond miraculous. That is the essence of Śiva's divine play.

3

तत्कर्म कृत्वा विनिवर्त्य भूय-

स्तत्त्वस्य तत्त्वेन समेत्य योगम्।

एकेन द्वाभ्यां त्रिभिरष्टभिर्वा

कालेन चैवात्मगुणैश्च सूक्ष्मैः ॥ ३ ॥

tat karma kṛtvā vinivartya bhūyas tattvasya tattvena sametya yogam /
ekena dvābhyāṁ tribhir aṣṭabhir vā kālena caivātmaguṇaiś ca sūkṣmaiḥ //

3. After effecting the work of creation—having joined together with each stage of manifestation by one, two, three, or eight, and with time and the trifling qualities of mind and body—he again turns away from it.

This and the following *mantra* form a breathless utterance that one modern scholar calls "a mess with an impossible syntax."[11] The strategy in dealing with this sweeping passage is first to split it into two self-contained verses. The first, consisting entirely of dependent clauses, cannot stand on its own, but if the participle *vinivartya* ("having turned away") is rendered as a finite verb ("he turns away"), the *mantra* becomes a grammatically complete and manageable unit—without any change of meaning.

But syntax is the least of this passage's difficulties. Max Müller found these two verses "extremely obscure" and doubted that even the early Indian exegetes grasped the meaning of what Śvetāśvatara had uttered so many centuries before.[12] Their commentaries—the *Vivaraṇa* of Vijñānabhagavat, the *Dīpikā* of Śaṁkarānanda, and the *Vṛtti,* nominally by Śaṁkarācārya—differ widely among themselves.

What is the solution? In a word, context. There are several levels of context on which to draw: the context of the individual verse, of the surrounding verses, of the chapter, and of the Upaniṣad as a whole. Śvetāśvatara has left us clues in abundance. Beyond the text itself there are the contexts of the seer's preceptorial lineage, his religious affiliation, and his philosophical outlook.

To unlock the probable meaning of the present *mantra,* we shall examine it one quarter at a time, first considering the interpretations of others and then allowing the text to speak for itself.

With the minor syntactical adjustment already mentioned, the first quarter reads, "After effecting (*kṛtvā*) the work of creation (*tat karma*), he again turns away from it" (*vinivartya bhūyaḥ*). Simple enough, or so it would seem. Yet the author of the *Vṛtti,* along with three modern translators, thinks that this *mantra* refers to God and that *mantra* 6.4 refers to the *yogin.*[13] Vijñānabhagavat believes that both verses refer to the *yogin,*[14] a view shared by Śaṁkarānanda and one modern writer.[15] Most other translators take God as the subject of both verses.[16] But what is the context? There should be no question concerning the subject under discussion. The subject of the surrounding verses and of the bulk of this chapter is God. The first quarter of this *mantra* could not be much clearer: "After effecting the work of creation, he again turns away from it." *He* refers back to God (*deva*), already named in this chapter's opening *mantra* and then characterized in the next verse (6.2) as "the intelligent maker of time" (*jñaḥ kālakāraḥ*) and "the omniscient possessor of the forces of creation" (*guṇī sarvavidyaḥ*). It is God who engages in the creation and dissolution of the universe. The remaining three *pādas* of the present *mantra* will fill in the details of the manifestational process.

The second *pāda* (*tattvasya tattvena sametya yogam*) has also bred confusion. To what does the word *yoga* refer? Some translators take it as the joining of *puruṣa* and *prakṛti* that produces the phenomenal universe.[17] Others, following Vijñānabhagavat's commentary, think it signifies the union of the individual self with the supreme Self, meaning the liberation of the bound soul.[18] Śaṁkarānanda echoes that same opinion in writing of the union of the *yogin* with the reality behind appearances.[19] But is Śvetāśvatara speaking here of cosmic evolution or of liberation? The context should already have made the answer clear.

Additionally the second *pāda* offers another example of Śvetāśvatara's delight in wordplay, but the subtle undercurrent is lost in translation. "Having joined together (*sametya yogam*) with each stage of manifestation (*tattvasya tattvena*)" adequately conveys what the seer means to say but not how he says it. There is a tension playing out between two different meanings of the word *tattva,* which is the reason for their juxtaposition (*tattvasya tattvena*). *Tattva* signifies both a true or real state—truth or reality—as well as a particular principle or level of manifestation, which is a departure from the full reality. By joining together (*sametya yogam*) with [each] manifesting stage (*tattvena*) of [the greater] reality (*tattvasya*), God brings forth the panorama of creation, and that panorama is not the Divine-in-itself but the Divine as it appears to us.

The third *pāda* elaborates on the creative process. In the context of the preceding quarter, it should not be so cryptic as it has been made out to be. "By one, two, three, or eight" (*ekena dvābhyāṁ tribhir aṣṭabhir vā*) clearly elaborates on God's manifestation through the *tattvas*. The meaning of this cosmogonical shorthand probably would have been apparent to Śvetāśvatara's disciples, just as the colloquial expression "twenty-four seven" means "all the time" to present-day English speakers. But expressions change over time and meanings are lost. Even the medieval Indian commentators were mystified.

For the author of the *Vṛtti* "by one, by two, by three" indicates nothing more than the incremental steps contained in "by eight," which he interprets as the eight *tattvas* of earth, water, fire, air, space, mind, intellect, and ego.[20] But in a verse so densely packed with implications, how likely is it that "one," "two," and "three" are mere parts of "eight," with no significance of their own? Vijñānabhagavat, with characteristic emphasis on spiritual practice, takes "by one" to mean "by the *guru's* teaching"[21] or "by service to the *guru*."[22] Śaṁkarānanda thinks it means "by ignorance" (*avidyā*).[23] Some modern translators suggest that "one" signifies the *puruṣa* of Sāṁkhya,[24] but that flies in the face of Sāṁkhya's own doctrine that *puruṣas* are innumerable and only *prakṛti* is one. Two other translators hedge their bets with the option that "one" means either *puruṣa* or *prakṛti!*[25]

The meaning of "by two" (*dvābhyām*) is no less uncertain. Vijñānabhagavat proposes that the "two" are "love of the *guru* and love of God,"[26] while Śaṁkarānanda prefers "right and wrong" (*dharma* and *adharma*).[27] Other opinions are that "two" signifies either *puruṣa* and *prakṛti*,[28] or *prakṛti* in two states, the unmanifest (*avyakta*) and the manifest (*vyakta*).[29]

Vijñānabhagavat reads "by three" (*tribhiḥ*) as a reference to the spiritual discipline of *śravana, manana,* and *nididhyāsana*—hearing the truth from a qualified teacher, reflecting on it intellectually, and internalizing its transformative power through meditation.[30] Śaṁkarānanda and the writers who agree with him opt for the three *guṇas* as the intended meaning.[31] In an apparent departure from tradition, two modern translators take "by three" to signify the gross (*sthūla*), subtle (*sūkṣma*), and causal (*kāraṇa*) bodies.[32]

Only with "by eight" (*aṣṭabhiḥ*) do the scholars approach consensus. The dissenter is Vijñānabhagavat, who together with one modern sympathizer[33] takes this to mean the eight limbs of *yoga* as detailed in Patañjali's *Yogasūtra* (2.29). The problem is that the Śvetāśvataropaniṣad presents a more rudimentary formulation of yogic practice that predates Patañjali by some eight centuries! The general agreement is that "by eight" refers to the Sāṁkhya *prakṛtyaṣṭaka,* consisting of the five gross elements (*mahābhūtas*) plus mind (*manas*), intellect (*buddhi*), and ego (*ahaṁkāra*), a concept also expressed in the Bhagavadgītā (7.4) as the Lord's eightfold *prakṛti* (*prakṛtir aṣṭadhā*). That reading too is not without its problems.

Fanciful explanations aside, the immediate context of the *mantra* leaves no doubt that "by one, two, three, or eight" elaborates on the process of cosmic manifestation. The explanations based on the Sāṁkhya and Vedānta philosophies have failed to prove wholly satisfactory or in some instances even plausible. Beyond the Upaniṣad itself is there a still larger context that might prove illuminating? In view of the text's Śaiva leanings, is there anything in that tradition that can shed light on the numerical symbolism? There is. Closer in time and in spirit to this Upaniṣad than either classical Sāṁkhya or Advaita Vedānta is the Pāśupata doctrine of Lakulīśa. Its teachings appear to have been influenced by Śvetāśvatara and are confirmed to reflect the still older Taittirīya Vedic sphere to which Śvetāśvatara belongs (see pp. 46–47). Significantly Lakulīśa presents the evolution of the One into the many as a series of principles that manifest by one, two, three, and eight.

Concerning "by one" (*ekena*), the *Pāśupatasūtra* portrays Brahman as the eternal (*ādya*) reality, whose nature is pure being (*sat*). He is also called Rudra and Pati, the Lord. Because nothing can be understood as different from him (*na śakyam bhedadarśanam*), he rests by himself in his own unity.[34]

Cosmic emanation and dissolution depend on his playful will alone. When he manifests, there appears a twofold relationship of cause (*kāraṇa*) and effect (*kārya*). Significantly, Śvetāśvatara opens his first discourse with the question, What is the cause (*kiṁ kāraṇam*)?

Brahman, ever one in itself, abides as the uncaused cause, yet if he appears as the cause (*kāraṇa*), that necessarily presupposes an effect (*kārya*). As Lakulīśa puts it, Pati, the ruling Lord, has no meaning without *paśu*, the soul he rules over.[35] Here he echoes Śvetāśvatara, who speaks of Brahman as the sovereign Lord (*īśa*) and the soul as a not-sovereign entity (*anīśa*) (1.8). "By two" (*dvābhyām*) signifies the evolution of the single uncaused cause into the dual cause and effect.

Lakulīśa teaches that the effect, in turn, is threefold. "By three" (*tribhiḥ*) represents *kārya* diversifying into *vidyā, kalā,* and *paśu.* Consciousness, being primary, comes first. *Vidyā* is the subjective sentiency of the individual soul (*paśu*). *Kalā* is the objective insentiency of matter. Both *vidyā* and *kalā* account for the experience of the *paśu,* the individual subject, which includes awareness of both a subjective selfhood and the surrounding objective environment.[36]

"By eight" (*aṣṭabhiḥ*) refers to the further evolution of *vidyā,* or individual sentiency. There is only one constant in the life of an embodied soul—the awareness through which its existence is experienced. However diverse and however many the experiences may be, the light of consciousness is ever-present in its own unchanging singularity. Only in its activity (*vṛtti*) does consciousness appear to change, but any change belongs to its movements and not to its essence. *Vidyā* is the *paśu's* consciousness, conditioned only by the sense of individuality. At this stage there is no additional modification. But then *vidyā* assumes two further aspects. The first of these differentiates still further in three ways, and the second in two, bringing the total to eight.

Vidyā is first differentiated as *abodhasvabhāvā* ("nonilluminating") and *bodhasvabhāvā* ("illuminating"). These two are the subconscious and the conscious levels of mental experience. *Vidyā* is called nonilluminating when not actively engaged with any object, but that does not signal that it is free of content. As conditioned awareness, it indeed has content or modification, and that takes three forms, designated as *dharma, adharma,* and *saṁskāra. Dharma* here means the conditioning effects or colorations of righteous deeds; *adharma* means the conditioning of unrighteous deeds. *Saṁskāra* in this context is the repository of their accumulated impressions. Additionally *saṁskāra* is memory, the relational function of mind indispensable for interpreting empirical experience. *Dharma, adharma,* and *saṁskāra* are the characteristics of *abodhasvabhāvā vidyā*. In contrast, when human awareness is actively engaged with an object, it is called "illuminating" (*bodhasvabhāvā*), and its two forms are *vivekavṛtti* and *sāmānyavṛtti*. The word *vṛtti* signifies any movement or modification in the medium of consciousness. When human sentiency turns toward thoughts of the ultimate reality, it is deemed to be spiritually discriminating (*vivekavṛtti*). Without that discernment (*viveka*), it is deemed *sāmānyavṛtti*, a term describing general human awareness when engaged in the conduct of ordinary living. All empirical experience comes through the operation of *sāmānyavṛtti vidyā*.[37] But whatever form *vidyā* assumes, it signifies a subtle or mental stage of evolution rather than a gross or material one.

Before continuing on to the gross level of manifestation, which is the stage represented in the fourth *pāda*, there is another question to consider. Śvetāśvatara's point of view is nondualistic, but Lakulīśa's philosophy is one of unity-in-multiplicity (*dvaitādvaita*). Even while it serves admirably to explain Śvetāśvatara's symbolism here, is there possibly another interpretation? In fact it is possible to propose one that agrees in large part with Lakulīśa's ideas while drawing on the elegant simplicity of the later and uncompromisingly nondualistic Trikaśāstra. And historically speaking, even as Lakulīśa appears to have been strongly influenced by Śvetāśvatara, the great figures of Kashmir Śaivism from Vasugupta to Abhivanagupta acknowledged their indebtedness to Lakulīśa.

In the Trika view, the great Lord Śiva effects the work of creation by projecting countless mental and physical manifestations out of his own oneness and identifies with them for a time. After enjoying his divine play, he then withdraws back into his blissful, original being. The supreme oneness *beyond even one* is, of course, the ultimate Paramaśiva, who beyond the thirty-six *tattvas* transcends even the idea of the Absolute and the relative. "By one" cannot signify the ultimate (*anuttara*) or supremely nondual (*paramādvaita*) reality, because "one" here applies to the creative process.

Instead, "by one" means the state of unity called *purṇāhaṁtā* ("I-ness in full"), the identicality of the *śivatattva* (*prakāśa*) and the *śaktitattva* (*vimarśa*), the oneness of consciousness and its power. The self-existent light of consciousness and its reflective or self-referential capacity are one and the same.

At this level of unity arises the impulse "may I be many." This creative urge is the initial stirring of consciousness that will eventually flow "outward" through the succession of the remaining *tattvas*. "By two" indicates the first sign of differentiation, the awareness of subject-consciousness (*ahaṁtā*) and object-consciousness (*idaṁtā*), still in a potential state of "two-in-oneness."

"By three" signals the threefold differentiation into the powers of will, knowledge, and action (*icchāśakti, jñānaśakti,* and *kriyāśakti*). At this stage they too mark only a subtle modulation within the unity of the divine experience (*śuddhādhvan*). It is through *kriyāśakti* that the divine will to self-expression becomes implemented and the unity of consciousness appears as a plurality.

Each of the resulting centers of individual awareness (*puruṣa* in the Trika sense) becomes further defined as a subtle body. "By eight" signifies the aggregate of *manas, buddhi, ahaṁkāra* and the five subtle elements (*tanmātras*). This is known in the Trika system as *puryaṣṭaka* ("city of eight"). The subtle body is an important stage of evolution, because it accounts for the "deep structure" and continuity of the individual person from one lifetime to another.[38] Still, it is not the final stage. That arises only with the further development of the physical body specified in the fourth *pāda*.

The fourth *pāda* (*kalena caivātmaguṇaiś ca sūkṣmaiḥ*) is simple enough grammatically, but some of the words have various meanings, and some of the interpretations are as imaginative as this simple phrase is ambiguous. The author of the *Vṛtti* understands it as "by time and the subtle affections of the mind [such as] desire and so on" (*antaḥkaraṇaguṇaiḥ kāmādibhiḥ*).[39] Śaṁkarānanda also thinks that *ātmaguṇaiś ca sūkṣmaiḥ* means "and by the subtle affections of the mind."[40] The basic idea of subtle qualities of some kind is common to most renderings, but does *ātman* in this context really mean "mind"? Some writers think so,[41] but others propose that it means the body,[42] the individual self,[43] or God.[44] One translator takes *ātmaguṇaiḥ* to mean the inherent properties of *puruṣa* and *prakṛti* and relates this phrase to the principle of inherent nature (*svabhāva*) previously coupled with time (*kāla*) in *mantra* 6.1.[45] Vijñānabhagavat adds to the bewildering array of suppositions in treating *ātmaguṇaiḥ* and *sūkṣmaiḥ* as two distinct categories. *Ātmaguṇaiḥ,* he explains, means "by the soul's [cultivated] virtues"—compassion, charity, purity, benevolence, desirelessness, liberality, and the absence of malice. *Sūkṣmaiḥ* refers to good dispositions for knowledge, accumulated from the righteous actions of past births.[46] But this interpretation contradicts the *Vṛtti*'s position that *ātmaguṇaiḥ* means *kāmādibhiḥ*—desire or lust (*kāma*) along with the five other failings of anger (*krodha*), greed (*lobha*), pride (*mada*), jealousy (*mātsarya*), and delusion (*moha*).

Perhaps in this case a literal reading is the best. The first word, *kalena* ("by time" or "through time") poses no difficulty. Because the entire *mantra* details how the singular divine consciousness experiences itself as the multitude of individual souls, "by time" signals an entry into temporal limitation. Having already evolved to the level of the subtle body (*puryaṣṭaka*), the individual soul now becomes a physically embodied being (*dehin*), subject to human mortality through the relentless movement of time (*kalena*).

With the phrase *ātmaguṇaiḥ sūkṣmaiḥ* the fourth *pāda* indicates the last set of conditioning factors. The word *ātman* has many meanings, including supreme Self, life principle, individual self, intellect, mind, and body. In the context of the Vājasaneyisaṁhitā, from which Śvetāśvatara quotes frequently, *ātman* can indicate "the person or whole body considered as one and opposed to the separate members of the body."[47] This definition expresses a unity of disparate parts, a whole organism, which in the context of the present *mantra* is the human body-mind complex (*dehin* or *tanu*).

The compound *ātmaguṇa* affirms that the human organism has qualities or characteristics, and those are modified by the adjective *sūkṣma*. In philosophical discourse *sūkṣma* means "subtle," but its general meaning is "feeble," "trifling," or "insignificant."[48] God plays as the human being, whose capacities are woefully feeble in comparison to the fullness of divine power. Śvetāśvatara has already told us that the individual soul, "should be recognized as a fraction of the hundredth part of the tip of a hair, again divided a hundred times." In the grand scheme of the magnificent revolving wheel of Brahman, each life is surely trifling; yet, as the seer hastens to say, the human soul "partakes of infinity" (5.9).

One more point warrants discussion, and that concerns the words *vivartate* (6.2) and *vinivartya* (6.3). The proponents of Advaita Vedānta take these words to mean that the world is a false superimposition (*vivarta*) on the reality of Brahman, no more real than the snake misperceived in the rope.[49] The world appearance results from a wrong identification (*adhyāsa*). It is important to keep in mind that the doctrine of superimposition (*vivartavāda*) is a much later development, and that the illusory nature of the world suggested by it is for the most part foreign to the spirit of the Upaniṣads—that is, to the *vedānta* in its original definition.

In fact, the Chāṇḍogyopaniṣad (3.14.1) proclaims unequivocally, "All this is indeed Brahman" (*sarvaṁ khalv idaṁ brahma*). Elsewhere in the same text (6.8.6) the seer Uddālaka Āruṇi explains, "All creatures (*prajāḥ*) have being (*sat*) as their root, being as their abode, being as their resting place." In the still older Bṛhadāraṇyakopaniṣad (2.5.18), the seer Dadhyac Ātharvaṇa teaches: "There is nothing that is not enveloped by him [*puruṣa,* the Supreme Being], nothing that is not pervaded by him."

By *vivartate* Śvetāśvatara simply means "revolves." The wheel of Brahman revolves—the world turns. *Vivartate* expresses that simple fact without any judgment of reality or unreality. The interpretation is a matter of context. Two of the seer's frequently quoted ancient sources, the Vājasaneyisaṁhitā and the Taittirīyasaṁhitā, use the word *vivarta* ("the revolving one") to indicate the vast sky overhead, and with it the implication of time and its consequences. The meaning of *vivarta* can be extended to signify not only the physical turning of the globe but also the figurative turning of one thing into something else, a change from one state to another that unfolds in time. Only in later philosophy did *vivarta* acquire the sense of error, illusion, or unreality. Likewise, the related word *vinivartya* simply means "having turned away from" or "having ceased" the play of creation. Śvetāśvatara intends no judgment of truth or falsehood. His message is that it is God who expresses his power and glory through every detail of the creation, even through that which appears to us as insignificant (*sūkṣma*).

Sarvepalli Radhakrishnan sums up the world-view of the Upaniṣads in much the same way. The Aitareyopaniṣad, he notes, teaches that to know the One is not to deny the many. Similarly the Muṇḍakopaniṣad (1.1.3–4) speaks of a knowledge by which all else is known and hastens to add that there are two kinds of knowledge, the empirical (*aparā*) and the transcendental (*parā*). Both are to be cultivated (*dve vidye veditavye*), because it is the former that can direct one toward the supreme realization of Brahman. The Taittirīyopaniṣad (2.6.1) explains that the world is rooted in the consciousness that is Brahman, and the Kaṭhopaniṣad (2.3.1), with the sacred fig tree (*aśvattha*) as a metaphor for the world, repeats that its root cause is Brahman, the resplendently pure (*śukram*) and immortal (*amṛtam*). Logically the cause precedes the effect, and the effect depends on the cause. The world cannot exist apart from Brahman, so Brahman must be its essence.[50]

Radhakrishnan affirms that the universe is the self-limitation of the active Lord. The world and God are a single reality in two simultaneously present states. The finite is the active aspect of consciousness, and the infinite is consciousness in its ultimate purity. Because reality is One and One only, God does not *create* the world but *becomes* it. Something cannot be created out of nothing, say the Upaniṣads, so in their view creation can only be self-expression.[51] That said, God is the supreme Reality, and the world a series of lesser realities. Life in the cosmos is a mixture of the absolutely real and the relatively apparent, of the enduring and the transitory. It cannot be otherwise, for without the foundation of that consciousness by which all else is known, no experience of anything else would be possible. Rooted in the *being* of Brahman, the world process is a perpetual *becoming*, but one that is "by no means false."[52] The error is purely human and arises from regarding the world as independent of the Divine.[53]

In Radhakrishnan's assessment the Upaniṣadic world-view is closer to Abhinavagupta than to Śaṁkara. Even earlier than the Upaniṣads, the Ṛgveda puts forth a similar vision of God manifesting as the universe and the individual soul. Radhakrishnan observes that nowhere do the hymns of the Ṛgvedasaṁhitā suggest that the world of our experience is illusory.[54] The wonder-filled Nāsadīyasūkta [Hymn of creation] (10.129), portrays the nondual Supreme Being—besides which there is nothing else—as spontaneously generating the universe out of its own unconditioned perfection. Through its intrinsic power (*tapas*), the One (*tad ekam*), entirely free of qualities, first brings forth desire (*kāma*), an aspiring to determinate existence. Through this conscious act of self-definition—which means self-limitation—the One becomes the creator of the many and expresses itself through every created thing.[55] Elsewhere in the Ṛgveda, the Puruṣasūkta (10.90) observes that while the supreme Puruṣa indeed becomes the universe, the universe is only his partial expression and does not represent the wholeness of divine reality.[56] It is to that difference that the following *mantra* speaks.

4

आरभ्य कर्माणि गुणान्वितानि
भावांश्च सर्वान् विनियोजयेद् यः ।
तेषामभावे कृतकर्मनाशः
कर्मक्षये याति स तत्त्वतोऽन्यः ॥ ४ ॥

ārabhya karmāṇi guṇānvitāni bhāvāṁś ca sarvān viniyojayed yaḥ / teṣām abhāve kṛtakarmanāśaḥ karmakṣaye yāti sa tattvato 'nyaḥ //

4. He who undertakes the activities associated with conditions [again] undoes all the states of creation. When they are no more, what he has wrought is destroyed; when his handiwork perishes, he endures, different from it, in his true nature.

As the continuation of the previous *mantra,* this one is also subject to widely differing interpretations. The three ancient commentators read it as referring not to God but to the *yogin,* liberated from the consequences of his actions, but there is little agreement among their convoluted interpretations, and Śaṁkarānanda, even doubtful of his own first attempt, proceeds to suggest another![57]

Read in a straightforward way, the verse speaks simply of the qualified, limited states that God experiences as an individual soul even while his true being endures, ever the same, beyond all limitation.[58]

It is God who has undertaken (*ārabhya*) the activities of manifestation (*karmāṇi*). These activities or works are associated (*anvitāni*) with qualities or properties, with conditioning (*guṇa*). The finite universe and the individual souls that experience it are nothing more than the conditioning of the unconditioned, which arises when consciousness-at-rest (Brahman) is set in motion. The Divine ever remains the self-luminous reality, even while illuminating its own conditioned experience as the individual soul—the *haṁsa* on the revolving wheel of Brahman, the *jīva* interacting with the phenomenal world. When the play comes to an end, he who has wrought this universe through his own power then undoes all the conditioned states (*bhāvāṁś ca sarvān viniyojayet*) that account for existence as we know it. The word *bhāva* indicates a state of becoming or existing or appearing; it can mean universal continuance (*sthiti*) as opposed to cessation (*saṁhāra*); it can also refer to a *jīva's* continuity of existence from one lifetime to another.[59] When the divine handiwork perishes (*karmakṣaye*) and all expressions of diversity dissolve into oneness and are no more (*teṣām abhāve*), God continues on (*sa yāti*) according to his own true being (*tattvataḥ*),[60] different (*anyaḥ*) from all those states of becoming.

How is God's true nature different from that of his works, which include the individual soul? Śvetāśvatara answered that question in the previous discourse: "And just as he who is the source of everything develops his own nature and transforms all that is potential, he it is who presides as One over this entire universe and distributes all its [diverse] qualities (5.5). [But when] possessed of qualities, he who becomes the doer of action that bears fruit experiences the results of whatever he has done. That living soul, of manifold form and three qualities and three paths, roams about according to his own deeds. He who is the size of a thumb and brilliant like the sun becomes endowed with intention and a sense of individuality. Through the attributes of mind and body as well is he seen as distinct, in fact as no larger than the point of an awl. The individual soul should be recognized as a fraction of the hundredth part of the tip of a hair, again divided a hundred times—yet it partakes of infinity" (5.7–9).

Brahman is infinite; the individual self is finite, but both have consciousness as their essence. The difference is not qualitative but quantitative. The qualities (*guṇas*) of which Śvetāśvatara speaks arise from the limiting factors of *māya*. They only appear to us as qualitative differences. Divine omnipotence (*sarvakartṛtva*) and human capability are both the power to act; one is boundless, the other is severely circumscribed. The same is true of divine omniscience and human knowledge; both are awareness, but with a difference of degree. The same principle holds true all the way down to material phenomena. What we perceive as red and blue are the same phenomenon of light, vibrating at a slower or faster rate. Similarly, heat and cold, which we interpret as qualitative opposites, are merely a difference in the rate of molecular vibration, a quantitative difference. The physical universe is nothing but vibrating energy, and the differences of amplitude in space and frequency in time determine what we perceive as qualities with a vast range of distinction.

Water has no shape of its own but assumes the shape of the vessel that contains it. Sea water in a pot is no different in essence from the water of the limitless ocean; the qualities of form and volume belong only to the pot, not to the water that assumes them temporarily. In the same way, the appearance of the *jīva* belongs to the limiting factors that shape it, though its essence remains Śiva. Through his own power, the lord of *māyā* (*māyin*) creates the sense of difference (*bheda*) within his infinite oneness. But what is that difference? The word *bheda* fundamentally denotes a breaking, a splitting, a dividing, or a separating.

Let us recall that the summation of Śaṁkara's philosophy is contained in a single line of text: "Brahman is real, the world is misleading, and the individual soul is none other than Brahman" (*brahma satyaṁ jagan mithyā jīvo brahmaiva nāparaḥ*). If the middle clause is removed, what remains is "Brahman is real, and the individual soul is none other than Brahman." This is a slight elaboration of the Upaniṣadic equation *ayam ātmā brahma* ("this self is Brahman"). The human soul and the Divine are a single reality, but there is an added element in the longer statement that breaks the equation: *jagan mithyā* ("the world is misleading"). The individual soul does not recognize its true nature because the world intervenes.

Apart from the matter of "broken" unity or obscured identity, there is another idea here. *Jagat* literally means "that which moves." Śvetāśvatara has told us that the world turns (*vartate*), with all the attendant implications (see p. 372). *Jagat* is the sphere of activity for all manner of living creatures from plants to animals to humankind. *Jagat* is consciousness in motion; it is *being* in a constant state of *becoming*—in another word, impermanence. The things of the world come and go, and when we experience consciousness only as a parade of ever-changing phenomena, we lose sight of its immutable essence. At either end of the equation, surrounding this diversion of the world, we find the unchanging truth: the luminous core of our individual self-awareness is none other than the infinite consciousness that is Brahman.

The human being is an infinitesimal drop of divine consciousness, projected through the limitations of time and space. Because it is finite, it cannot simultaneously embrace the timeless and the temporal. As long as it remains enmeshed in the manifest manyness, it cannot know the pure unity that is its own source and true being. When that supreme knowledge dawns, the mystery is no longer unfathomable, but it remains ever inexpressible, for in the ultimate oneness, who remains to speak of what?

5

आदिः स संयोगनिमित्तहेतुः
परस्त्रिकालादकलोऽपि दृष्टः ।
तं विश्वरूपं भवभूतमीड्यं
देवं स्वचित्तस्थमुपास्य पूर्वम् ॥ ५ ॥

ādiḥ sa saṁyoganimittahetuḥ paras trikālād akalo 'pi dṛṣṭaḥ /
taṁ viśvarūpaṁ bhavabhūtam īḍyaṁ devaṁ svacittastham upāsya pūrvam //

5. When he who has the universe as his form, who is to be glorified as the essence of existence, has first been revered as the effulgent being abiding in one's own consciousness, he, the beginning and the conjoiner of elements, is himself seen as beyond the three times and without parts.

Only here does Śvetāśvatara allude to the *yogin* by tracing the whole range of awareness from the individual's perception of the world to the culminating nondual experience. One who aspires to spiritual knowledge is enjoined first to cultivate a sense of the sacred through worship (*upāsya pūrvam*). This involves revering the divine being whose form is the universe (*viśvarūpam*). He is to be glorified (*īḍyam*) as the essence of existence (*bhavabhūtam*) but also to be thought of as the effulgent God (*devam*) abiding in one's own awareness (*svacitta-stham*). *Citta* means the defined field of consciousness that is the individual soul. The term *stha* indicates not only the continuing presence but also the state of inner stillness. God is the illuminator and the unmoving witness of all activity (*karma* or *vṛtti*).

As the creator, he is the beginning (*ādiḥ*) that sets the process of cosmic evolution in motion; yet he remains eternal, beyond the differentiation of the three times (*paras trikālād*)—past, present, and future. He is the efficient cause (*nimittahetuḥ*) that brings the elements of creation into conjunction (*saṁyoga*); yet we cannot say that he fashions the world just as a potter (the efficient cause) forms the clay (the material cause) into a pot (the effect). That theory works with those philosophies that recognize an eternal distinction between the creator, the elements of creation, and the created. But what Śvetāśvatara now calls the efficient cause is the nondual Brahman itself, without any second.

The nondualistic view of causality finds poetic expression in the *Brahmajñānāvalīmālā,* a brief text that is the source of the dictum "Brahman is real, the world is misleading, and the individual soul is none other than Brahman." Verse 17 reads, "The seer and the seen are two principles that differ from each other; the seer is Brahman and the seen is *māyā.* So goes the drumbeat of the whole of Vedānta (*sarvavedāntaḍiṇḍimaḥ*)." Then, "A pot, a plastered wall, and all such things—the substance of each is surely clay. Likewise all the world is Brahman. So goes the drumbeat of Vedānta. Brahman is true, the world deceives, and the soul is none other than Brahman. By this the true teaching is to be known. So goes the drumbeat of Vedānta" (verses 19–20).

The seer and the seen (*drgdrśyau*) are two categories distinguishable from each other in only one sense: the seer (*dṛk*) is subject-consciousness and the seen (*drśya*) is object-consciousness. Both are of the nature of consciousness: an object can only be known *as the awareness of it.* To give a more graspable example, a pot, a plastered wall, or anything else made of clay is just that—clay. The forms come and go, but the substance endures. In the same way, anything apprehended by consciousness is necessarily made of consciousness; the entire world of our experience is the seen (*drśya*), and this exists only within the awareness of the seer (*dṛk*). In this way, the whole world is Brahman (*tadvad brahma jagat sarvam*). The *Brahmajñānāvalīmālā* presents its view of causality in these three verses. The efficient cause (Brahman) is also the material cause (the clay), and the effects (the objects made of clay). All appearances aside, Brahman is the enduring reality, and in truth there is nothing but Brahman. The world is false only in that we take it to be other than what it is. Our error is to mistake the modifications of consciousness for the essence of consciousness. "This is the drumbeat (*ḍiṇḍimaḥ*) of Vedānta"; this is the persistent assertion of the Upaniṣads.

Although the world appears to be composed of myriad parts, Śvetāśvatara says that God is seen as without parts (*akalo 'pi dṛṣṭaḥ*) and is perfect in his undifferentiated wholeness. Since there is no reality but Brahman, there can be nothing outside of Brahman from which to fashion the world. Similarly the Trika philosophy holds that the parts are appearances within the whole. Matter is a luminous display (*ābhāsa*) within consciousness, not a separate reality apart from it.

To repeat Śvetāśvatara's instruction, we must first cultivate reverence toward that divinity whose form is the universe (*viśvarūpam*) and constantly remind ourselves that this same effulgent being (*devam*) who is to be glorified (*īḍyam*) abides not only "out there" in the external world but also and ever at the heart of our own awareness (*svacittastham*). This light of consciousness is the true essence of our fleeting existence (*bhavabhūtam*). In it we find our permanance, but only with diligent contemplation and unbroken striving is its all-transcending grandeur fully revealed.

6

स वृक्षकालाकृतिभिः परोऽन्यो
यस्मात् प्रपञ्चः परिवर्ततेऽयम् ।
धर्मावहं पापनुदं भगेशं
ज्ञात्वाऽत्मस्थममृतं विश्वधाम ॥ ६ ॥

sa vṛkṣakālākṛtibhiḥ paro 'nyo yasmāt prapañcaḥ parivartate 'yam /
dharmāvahaṁ pāpanudaṁ bhageśaṁ jñātvā 'tmastham amṛtaṁ viśvadhāma //

6. When the lord of blessedness, who brings goodness and drives away evil, is known to abide in oneself as the immortal support of all, he by whom this expansive universe revolves is seen as higher and other than the parts of the world-tree and the aspects of time.

As long as one's awareness is tied to the outer world and the consciousness of duality, human life appears to be a mixture of happiness and misery. The individual interprets life's experiences in terms of good and bad, failing to apprehend the unity of being. When that is revealed in a flash of intuitive knowledge, all distinction of difference vanishes.[61] Until then we praise God as bringing good (*dharmāvaham*) and driving away evil (*pāpanudam*). In this aspect Śvetāśvatara calls him "the lord of blessedness" (*bhageśam*).

The word *bhaga* defies easy translation. Besides indicating general prosperity, good fortune, and well-being, it refers to a specific package of six divine glories: sovereignty (*aiśvarya*), righteousness (*dharma*), beauty (*yaśas*), splendor (*śrī*), wisdom (*jñāna*), and dispassion (*vairāgya*). Because Śvetāśvatara describes the lord of these divine powers as abiding in every soul, we can understand that they are ever at hand and always ours to use.

The epithet *bhageśa* is only one example of this *mantra's* dazzling imagery. Again Śvetāśvatara evokes the metaphorical world-tree (*vṛkṣa*), rooted in the unmanifest and branching out into all the diversity of creation (see pp. 222–224). He also refers to the universe as *prapañcaḥ,* meaning "expansion," "development," "manifestation," "diversity." The imagery suggests not a world that just *is,* but one that is alive and growing in a constant display of imaginative creativity. Paul Deussen translated *prapañca* poetically as "the unfolding panorama of the world."[62]

The word *prapañca* can be taken to consist of the prefix *pra-* ("forward") and *pañca* ("five"), perhaps suggesting originally the spreading out of the hand and later coming to symbolize any other form of fivefold diversification.[63] The cosmic principles (*tattvas*) common to Sāṁkhya, Vedānta, and Trika Śaivism include five sensory faculties (*jñānendriyas*), five capacities of action (*karmendriyas*), five subtle elements (*tanmātras*), and five gross elements (*mahābhūtas*). Those concepts are grounded in observation. Above them the Trikaśāstra speaks of the five limiting functions (*kañcukas*) of *māyā.* Still higher are Śiva's fivefold cosmic activity (*pañcakṛtya*) and fivefold power (*pañcaśakti*). His fivefold activity consists of emanation (*sṛṣṭi*), continuance (*sthiti*), resorption (*saṁhāra*), concealment (*nigraha*), and revelation or grace (*anugraha*). His fivefold power consists of the capacities of infinite awareness (*cicchakti*), bliss (*ānandaśakti*), the creative impulse (*icchāśakti*), creative ideation (*jñānaśakti*), and implementation (*kriyāśakti*).

Although experiencing this ever-turning, dualistic, chiaroscuro universe, an enlightened soul, established in the knowledge of the indwelling divinity, witnesses the self-luminous unity of the real beyond the apparent. Having recognized (*jñātvā*) the support and source of everything (*viśvadhāma*), one knows that the imperishable Self-awareness within one's own heart (*ātmastham amṛtam*) is no different from the transcendent Self, which is higher than (*paraḥ*) and different from (*anyaḥ*) any fleeting appearance.

7

तमीश्वराणां परमं महेश्वरं
तं देवतानां परमं च दैवतम् ।
पतिं पतीनां परमं परस्ता-
द्विदाम देवं भुवनेशमीड्यम् ॥ ७ ॥

tam īśvarāṇāṁ paramaṁ maheśvaraṁ taṁ devatānāṁ paramaṁ ca daivatam /
patiṁ patīnāṁ paramaṁ parastād vidāma devaṁ bhuvaneśam īḍyam //

7. May we know the effulgent lord of the world who is to be adored, the Great Lord supreme among lords, the God supreme among gods, the Sovereign supreme among sovereigns.

Śvetāśvatara exhorts us to aspire to the highest state of spiritual realization. The *sādhanā* he prescribes does not consist of halfway measures. He urges us not just to go beyond the perceptible world of our daily experience but to know intimately and fully the Great Lord

(Maheśvara) who is superior to all that he has made, who is higher even than the gods on high.

8

न तस्य कार्यं करणं च विद्यते
न तत्समश्चाभ्यधिकश्च दृश्यते ।
परास्य शक्तिर्विविधैव श्रूयते
स्वाभाविकी ज्ञानबलक्रिया च ॥ ८ ॥

na tasya kāryaṁ karaṇaṁ ca vidyate na tatsamaś cābhyadhikaś ca dṛśyate / parāsya śaktir vividhaiva śrūyate svābhāvikī jñānabalakriyā ca //

8. He has no need to act, nor any instrument of action; no one is seen as his equal or superior. It is heard that his supreme power is indeed manifold, a natural expression of his intelligence and might.

This outpouring of praise reveals a decidedly Śaiva point of view. The Supreme Being has no need to act, because for him there is nothing to be done (*na tasya kāryam*), nothing to be achieved. Complete and perfect in himself, God requires no instrument of action (*karaṇam*). Besides him there is nothing else—nothing, moreover, to which he can be compared and nothing that can surpass him.

God rests in his own natural freedom to act or not to act as he chooses. As the Trikaśāstra explains, should Śiva choose to act, his action arises spontaneously out of his joyful, unbounded autonomy (*svātantrya*) and has the nature of playful creativity, impelled neither by necessity nor by compulsion. Long before the Trika philosophy articulated this positive view of creation, Śvetāśvatara's spiritual forebears expressed a similar idea. In the Taittirīyopaniṣad (3.6.1), the seer Bhṛgu, following the instruction of his father Varuṇa, "knew that Brahman is joy (*ānando brahmeti vyajānāt*). For truly, from joy all beings are born (*ānandādd hy eva khalv imāni bhūtāni jāyante*); once born, by joy they live (*ānandena jātāni jīvanti*); toward joy they move, and into joy they merge (*ānandaṁ prayanti abhisaṁviśanti*)."

Now, for the fourth time in the course of his teaching, Śvetāśvatara employs the term *śakti*, a word absent from all the other principal Upaniṣads. He says that this *śakti* is heard (*śrūyate*) to be manifold (*vividhā*) and capable of expressing itself in countless ways. Some translators take the verb *śrūyate* as an allusion to the authority of the Vedas (the *śruti*, or revealed knowledge).[64] Others do not.[65]

It is significant that the word *śakti* is qualified with the adjective *parā* ("supreme"). The nondual Śaiva tradition defines *parāśakti* as the supreme power of consciousness. Devoid of thought constructs (*nirvikalpa*), it is the direct intuition of reality (*pratibhā*).[66] *Parāśakti* is synonymous with *citi*, a feminine form of *cit* implying dynamism. Whereas *cit* denotes the immutable principle underlying all change, *citi* or *parāśakti* is the vibratory awareness that brings about the world process.[67] Another name for this consciousness-as-power is *spanda*. Other Trika synonyms for *parāśakti* are *svātantrya* (the following of one's own free choice), *vimarśa* (the capacity of reflective self-awareness), *aiśvarya* ("sovereignty"), *kartṛtva* ("agency"), *sphurattā* (the natural, pulsating radiance of consciousness), *sāra* (the substance or essential part of anything), and *hṛdaya* ("the heart," meaning consciousness itself).[68] The Trikaśastra views the ultimate reality, Paramaśiva, as self-luminous consciousness, vibrant with its own power. *Cit* and *citi* are one essence. Consciousness *is* sentient energy, no matter what it is called. Because there is no difference between consciousness and its power, it can be said that Śiva *as* Śakti is the cause of the universe.

The *mantra* ends with the term *jñānabalakriyā*, a compound that further modifies *parā śakti*. It indicates that intelligence (*jñāna*) and vigorous strength (*bala*) form the expression (*kriyā*) of God's supreme power. The compounding of these three terms is also suggestive of the later Śaiva and Śākta triad of powers: *icchā*, *jñāna*, and *kriyā*—the creative intention, the formulative capacity, and the executive ability that drive cosmic manifestation.[69] Finally, the expression of intelligence and vigorous strength is entirely natural, because it is inherent (*svābhāvikī*) in the divine nature. The *mantra* that began by saying that God has no need to act ends by reinforcing this same idea—that cosmic manifestation springs spontaneously from the joy of divine freedom and fullness.

9

न तस्य कश्चित् पतिरस्ति लोके
न चेशिता नैव च तस्य लिङ्गम्।
स कारणं करणाधिपाधिपो
न चास्य कश्चिज्जनिता न चाधिपः ॥ ९ ॥

na tasya kaścit patir asti loke na ceśitā naiva ca tasya liṅgam /
sa kāraṇaṁ karaṇādhipādhipo na cāsya kaścij janitā na cādhipaḥ //

9. He has no master in the world nor ruler nor any distinctive mark. He is the cause, the Lord of the lord of the senses, and he has neither progenitor nor overlord.

The previous *mantra,* portraying God as unequaled and unsurpassable, at the same time asserts that divine consciousness and divine power are inseparable. Now Śvetāśvatara emphasizes the absolute sovereignty of the Supreme Being, who knows neither master (*patiḥ*), ruler (*īśitā*), nor lord (*adhipaḥ*). He is the self-existent One who rules over all that issues from him. As the ultimate cause (*kāraṇam*), he himself has no progenitor (*janitā*). Because he is the single, undivided reality, he is undifferentiated—without any distinguishing mark or characteristic (*liṅgam*).

The author of the *Vṛtti* takes *liṅgam* as the technical term used in logic to denote an invariable mark or sign that proves the existence of something through inference.[70] In the syllogism "where there is smoke, there is fire," smoke is the *liṅga,* the sign by which the presence of fire can be inferred. The *Vṛtti* argues that Brahman, having no ground of inference (*liṅga*), cannot be known through logic but only through direct revelation. One can rightly point out that inference is relational knowledge and Brahman is the Absolute beyond relation of any kind.[71]

The *Vṛtti*'s explanation works only to a point, however. Logically, if Brahman is One without a second, no secondary sign (*liṅga*) can exist.[72] But if we accept this interpretation of *liṇga,* we are asked to accept that where there is no smoke, there is nevertheless a fire—no effect, but a cause. Taken to its logical limit, this interpretation asks us to accept the reality of Brahman without the phenomenon of the world. We are asked to accept the absurdity of the cause (*kāraṇam*) being understood "in the sense of an unrelated substratum."[73] Such reasoning runs afoul of logic and counter to the spirit of the entire Upaniṣad, which declares that this world is evidence of divine glory and majesty. The point that Śvetāśvatara is perhaps trying to make is that logic simply does not apply here. In essence the *fullness* of divine glory is beyond the grasp of human thought and reason.

A simple reading of *liṅga* in a nontechnical sense avoids such complication. According to a Trika analogy, God in his transcendental aspect is absolutely undifferentiated and free of distinguishing marks, just like the clear fluid of the peahen's unfertilized egg. Once fertilization has occurred, the multicolored peacock develops and emerges in a glorious display of form and color. This reading accords well with the opening words of Śvetāśvatara's fourth discourse: "He who is One and without color brings forth many colors in many ways by his own power and by his own design" (4.1).

The word *loke* ("in the world") refers to the realm of our everyday experience. We know this world through the fivefold perception that comprises seeing, hearing, tasting, smelling, and touching. Each faculty is an instrument (*karaṇa*) of perceptual knowledge. The term *karaṇa* refers also to the five capacities of grasping, locomotion, speech, excretion, and reproduction. Together these ten faculties (*indriyas*) enable us to interact with the world, first by allowing information to enter into our awareness and then by empowering us to project our responses outward. The controller of these instruments (*karaṇādhipaḥ*) is the embodied *jīva*—a small, attenuated sovereign over only a finite sphere of influence. Śiva alone, the limitless One, is the lord of every *jīva (karaṇādhipādhipaḥ*), the Lord who guides every soul.

10

यस्तन्तुनाभ इव तन्तुभिः प्रधानजैः स्वभावतः ।
देव एकः स्वमावृणोत् स नो दधात् ब्रह्माप्ययम् ॥ १० ॥

yas tantunābha iva tantubhiḥ pradhānajaiḥ svabhāvataḥ /
deva ekaḥ svam āvṛṇot sa no dadhāt brahmāpyayam //

10. Like a spider with the filaments of its web, the one God surrounds himself with the things produced spontaneously from his unevolved nature. May he grant us entry into Brahman!

As in the fourth discourse, the seer once again draws on the imagery of the natural world to illustrate a subtler idea. Just as a spider spins its web out of its own body, the one God (*deva ekaḥ*) similarly surrounds himself with all the names, forms, and actions that are born or produced out of his own unmanifest state (*pradhānajaiḥ*). *Pradhāna,* a word virtually interchangeable with *prakṛti,* signifies the primary, undifferentiated, unevolved principle of materiality or nature which is the primordial germ of the visible universe.

The archaic language of this *mantra* indicates that as Śvetāśvatara speaks, he is alluding to an older teaching. The image of the spider occurs earlier in the Bṛhadāraṇyakopaniṣad (2.1.20), where King Ajātaśatru explains that just as a spider produces the filament of its web from out of its own body, and just as sparks go flying from a fire, so too with the same natural spontaneity and without extraneous help[74] there issue forth from this Self (*asmād ātmani*) all the vital forces (*sarve prāṇāḥ*), all worlds (*sarve lokāḥ*), all gods (*sarve devāḥ*), and all living creatures (*sarvāṇi bhūtāni*). The Self is the truth of the true (*satyasya satyam*), the supreme reality behind all lesser realities.

Earlier Śvetāśvatara spoke of Brahman as the efficient cause (*nimittahetu*) that conjoins the elements of creation (see p. 377), and now the analogy of the spider shows this same Brahman to be the material cause as well. We cannot take *pradhāna* (*prakṛti*) in the dualistic Sāṁkhya sense as one of two eternally independent and opposed realities. The intention here, as in the nondualistic systems of Advaita Vedānta and Trika Śaivism, is to recognize that reality is One. Hence Brahman is both the efficient and the material cause. As the Trikaśāstra maintains, consciousness (Śiva) and its capacity to manifest (Śakti) are one and the same reality. Although *pradhāna* may give the appearance (*ābhāsa*) of independent matter, it is in fact the active self-projection of consciousness within consciousness.[75]

Whatever makes up the world as we know it is produced or born spontaneously in accord with God's own nature (*svabhāvataḥ*).

The creation is a spontaneous action and not the result of any inner necessity or external compulsion.[76]

The comparison with the spider, which spins its web out of its own body, is rich with implications. First, the universe is part of God's own substance; there is nothing that is fundamentally not divine. Second, just as the spider surrounds itself with its web, God surrounds or conceals himself (*svam āvṛnot*) with all the interconnected objects and forces of the palpable universe. Third, just as the spider's web catches its prey, the multitudes of individual souls find themselves enmeshed in the web of *saṁsāra.*

Recognizing the bound state of humanity, Śvetāśvatara makes the fourth *pāda* a supplication for release. As is so often the case, the translation fails to capture the full import. *Apyaya* means a juncture with, an entry into, a vanishing into. More graphically, it denotes the pouring of a river into the sea.[77] With enlightenment, here called "entry into Brahman" (*brahmāpyayam*), the individual's contracted awareness meets the unlimited consciousness of the Absolute and flows into it like the water of a river disgorging into the sea. And just as that water is no longer identifiable as the river but merges into the vast ocean itself, so the *jīva* loses its separate, small identity in the immensity of its true being, the infinite ocean of consciousness.

The phrase *sa no dadhāt* (literally, "may he place us [in]") has a nuance lost in translation. The verb, in the archaic Vedic subjunctive, specifically exhorts the Divine but also suggests that God acts purely out of his own will. It implies that liberation comes through unconditional divine grace. And beyond that it conveys an idea of future inevitability—that this shall surely come to pass.

11

एको देवः सर्वभूतेषु गूढः
सर्वव्यापी सर्वभूतान्तरात्मा ।
कर्माध्यक्षः सर्वभूताधिवासः
साक्षी चेता केवलो निर्गुणश्च ॥ ११ ॥

eko devaḥ sarvabhūteṣu gūḍhaḥ sarvavyāpī sarvabhūtāntarātmā /
karmādhyakṣaḥ sarvabhūtādhivāsaḥ sākṣī cetā kevalo nirguṇaś ca //

11. The one God, hidden in all beings and pervading everything, is the soul of all creatures. Overseeing the universe, dwelling in all beings, he is the witness, the perceiver, and the Absolute devoid of qualities.

As in the previous *mantra,* the seer stresses the nondual nature of the Divine by repeating that he is the one God (*eko devaḥ*).

The singular, self-luminous divinity (*eko devaḥ*) lies hidden in every sentient creature (*sarvabhūteṣu gūḍhaḥ*), pervading all things (*sarvavyāpī*), presumably even seemingly insentient matter. Although everywhere, this divine presence remains covered by the veil of our unknowing in the same way that the sun's resplendence is momentarily concealed by a passing cloud.[78] This divinity is the innermost self of all beings (*sarvabhūtāntarātmā*), their essence and their reality.[79]

God is the overseer (*adhyakṣaḥ*) of the work (*karma*) that is his own creation. *Adhyakṣa* means either "supervisor" or "eyewitness," and both meanings can apply here.[80] In the former capacity, as Śvetāśvatara said earlier, God brings forth the multiplicity of creation by his own power and by his own design (4.1). Quoting from the Ṛgveda, the seer also praised God as Viśvakarman, the omnipresent "maker of everything," who is creative power personified as the architect of the universe (3.3). The imagery suggests a hands-on approach. Even so, the verse from the Ṛgveda introduces a note of detachment, suggesting the other definition of *adhyakṣa* as "eyewitness": the one God (*deva ekaḥ*) has eyes looking in all directions (*viśvataś cākṣuḥ*). Śvetāśvatara now adds that God is the witness (*sākṣī*). This term suggests a serene, detached observer, whereas *adhyākṣa* ("eyewitness") emphasizes the immediacy of the knowing, the intimacy of God with his creation.

In the original Sanskrit this verse consists of a string of epithets. Most are unambiguous, but one presents no small difficulty. Much uncertainty surrounds the word *cetā.* Max Müller notes that the manuscripts read *cetā* but that it could be a corruption of *cettā* ("attentive one," "guardian").[81] Monier-Williams's dictionary has no entry for *cetṛ* (the stem form of *cetā*), but Jacob's concordance lists the present *mantra* under the heading *cetṛ*.[82] How have translators dealt with this ambiguity? Among their renderings we find "perceiver,"[83] "thinker,"[84] "mere spirit,"[85] "pure consciousness,"[86] "animator,"[87] "knower,"[88] "bestower of intelligence,"[89] "bestower of consciousness,"[90] "spectator,"[91] "consciousness (in beings),"[92] and "watcher"[93] —hardly a consensus.

Since there is no agreement, perhaps a solution lies elsewhere. The word *cetṛ* occurs in one other Upaniṣad, the Maitrī, a later text belonging, like the Śvetāśvatara, to the Kṛṣṇa Yajurveda. There, translated as "perceiver,"[94] *cetā* is identified as "the self of one's self" (*ātmano 'tmā*) (6.7). This phrase is analogous to "the truth of the true" (*satyasya satyam*) found in the Bṛhadāraṇyakopaniṣad (2.1.20), where it indicates the supreme reality. Since the epithets of the present *mantra* proceed from the defined toward the absolutely unconditioned, it follows that by *cetā* Śvetāśvatara intends to indicate a state of awareness that surpasses that of an involved witness (*adhyakṣaḥ*) and even of a detached witness (*sākṣī*) to the play of creation—the state of divinity awakened to its own nondual nature.

The next word, *kevalaḥ*, bears that out. This term can mean "isolated" or "alone," and classical Sāṁkhya employs it to describe *puruṣa* when entirely dissociated from *prakṛti*. But that definition of liberation (*kaivalya*) rests on a nontheistic and dualistic conception of reality at odds with Śvetāśvatara's theistic nondualism. This *mantra* clearly states that God is all-pervasive and hidden in all beings as their innermost essence. No sense of separation can possibly be entertained here. Instead *kevalaḥ* means "alone" in the sense of "unique," of being One without a second. Not only is God absolute, but he is also unconditioned, devoid of all qualities or attributes (*nirguṇaḥ*). The one God is Brahman, the eternally changeless reality apart from the unfolding events of the created realm, yet constantly present in everything as its very essence.

This is not a matter of mere philosophical rumination but potentially a fact of one's own experience. If everything in the cosmos is the dwelling-place of Brahman, then everything deserves our respect.[95] Recognizing that God lives in us and that we live in God transforms our vision of the world, and the resultant wondrous joy awakens us to the higher ideals of spiritual living, which include reverence, appreciation, and compassion—in short, a sacred vision of life.

12

एको वशी निष्क्रियाणां बहूना-
मेकं बीजं बहुधा यः करोति ।
तमात्मस्थं येऽनुपश्यन्ति धीरा-
स्तेषां सुखं शाश्वतं नेतरेषाम् ॥ १२ ॥

eko vaśī niṣkriyāṇāṁ bahūnām ekaṁ bījaṁ bahudhā yaḥ karoti /
tam ātmasthaṁ ye 'nupaśyanti dhīrās teṣāṁ sukhaṁ śāśvataṁ netareṣām //

12. He who makes manifold the single seed is the one master of the actionless many. Steady are they who discover him abiding in themselves; to them belongs constant happiness and not to others.

In the first half of this *mantra* the subject is God; in the second half the emphasis shifts to individual souls. Keeping in mind that the overarching theme is the One and the many will help to clarify the difficulties plaguing the traditional reading of this verse.

Śvetāśvatara has already established that God is the single source of the cosmos, its one and only seed (*ekaṁ bījam*), and also its master (*vaśī*). The word *vaśin* ("ruler," "controller") also appears in the Bṛhadāraṇyakopaniṣad (4.4.22), where Yājñavalkya speaks of the great unborn Self (*mahān aja ātmā*) within the heart (*antarhṛdaye*) as the controller of all (*sarvasya vaśī*), the universal lord (*sarveśānaḥ*) and ruler (*sarvādhipatiḥ*). Śvetāśvatara uses the word *vaśī* similarly in *mantra* 3.18, where he describes God as "the master of the whole world" (*vaśī sarvasya lokasya*). Deriving from a verbal root meaning "to will," "to command," "to desire," "to wish," *vaśin* carries the inherent idea of divine will and suggests a voluntaristic philosophy. This idea is as old as the Ṛgvedasaṁhitā, where Viśvakarman's motivation also is will (see p. 206). The voluntaristic idea recurs in connection with Brahman in the Taittirīyopaniṣad's account of cosmic manifestation, where the One wills to become many (see pp. 114–115), and in Nandikeśvara's early system of nondualistic Śaivism as well (see pp. 40–41).

The present *mantra* speaks of God as the one controller (*vaśī*) of the actionless many (*niṣkriyāṇām bahūnām*), and it is this latter phrase that is the source of much confusion. *Niṣkriya* is translated as either "inactive"[96] or "actionless,"[97] either word meaning the same thing. But just what are the "inactive many"? Most translations indicate or imply that they are the individual *jīvas.*[98] Two translations take the phrase to mean insentient, material objects,[99] and two others are worded ambiguously enough to indicate either possibility or both.[100] Only Max Müller's translation, the earliest of the lot, expresses an implied uncertainty, rendering the first *pāda,* "He is the one ruler of the many who (seem to act, but really do) not act."[101]

The confusion arises from the *Vṛtti* attributed to Śaṁkarācārya, which explains that actions exist not in the Self (*sarvā hi kriyā nātmani*) but in the body and its faculties of perception and activity (*dehendriyeṣu*); the Self is ever inactive and unconditioned (*ātmā tu niṣkriyo nirguṇaḥ*).[102] Later commentators, following the *Vṛtti,* propose that created beings only appear to act, and that their actions and attributes are only a superimposition (*vivarta*) on the reality of Brahman.[103] One commentator suggests that *niṣkriya* refers both to the sentient *jīva* and to its attributes, such as body, mind, senses, and vital forces. Because these attributes are only modifications of insentient matter (*prakṛti*), they only appear to act, and their apparent activity must be ascribed to *māyā.* In reality they are actionless, and the *jīva* also, being essentially Brahman, is free of action.[104] This argument tries to have it both ways. Another explanation from the same tradition agrees that the individual *jīva* and matter are both inactive but adds that the powers of action seen in both belong to God and God alone; it makes no mention of *māyā.*[105] Yet another commentator observes that Brahman activates but does not act,[106] but is not activation itself an activity? Śvetāśvatara says unequivocally that God is the one ruler (*eko vaśī*) "who makes manifold the single seed." Ruling and creating hardly convey the idea of actionlessness. The Śaṁkarācārya who wrote the *Vṛtti* tried to impose on the text a much later doctrine of which Śvetāśvatara had no knowledge. In short, the interpretation based on *vivartavāda* does not work. Is there another way of reading *niṣkriyāṇāṁ bahūnām?*

There is, and as with previous instances of interpretative difficulties the solution is quite simple. We need look no farther than the text of the *mantra* itself. The actionless many are those steady souls who discover the Divine abiding within themselves (*tam ātmasthaṁ ye 'nupaśyanti dhīrāḥ*). In the context of this verse *niṣkriya* does not mean inactive in a general sense; it means exempt from outward religious obligations, free from a specific type of activity related to religious rites, ceremonies, or sacrifices (*kriyā*). God alone (*ekaḥ*) is the master, the guiding principle, of those souls whose high state of spiritual advancement no longer requires the performance of exterior ritual actions. They are exempt (*niṣkriya*), because they *discover, perceive,* and *reflect on* (all meanings of *anupaśyanti*) the divinity abiding in themselves (*tam ātmastham*). This higher knowledge has taken them beyond the level of conventional piety. Living in constant awareness of the divine presence, they become *dhīrāḥ*—steady, self-possessed, constant, and no longer affected by the changing conditions of life. Only they, and no others, abide in constant blessedness.

Is there any support for such a reading? In fact there is, in the Brahmopaniṣad. Although this late text is attached to the Atharvaveda and belongs to a lineage different from Śvetāśvatara's, in its fourth section it quotes five verses from the Śvetāśvataropaniṣad. It quotes *mantras* 1.14, 1.16, and 6.11 verbatim and 1.15 and 6.12 freely.[107] In its third section, where the term *niṣkriya* occurs, the text contrasts outer religious observances and inner spiritual experience, making the exact distinction Śvetāśvatara suggests here.

Until now the emphasis of the seer's sixth discourse has fallen on the nature of the Divine, but the second half of this *mantra* turns toward the aspiration of individual souls. Of course the two themes are intimately related, and a hint of that occurs in the first half of the verse: the second *pāda* reads, "he who makes manifold the single seed" (*ekaṁ bījaṁ bahudhā yaḥ karoti*). Clearly enough this refers to the evolution of the cosmos, but its wording also suggests a parallel to one of the great pronouncements of the Ṛgveda (1.164.46): "Truth is One; the wise call it by various names" (*ekaṁ sad viprā bahudhā vadanti*). This, conversely, refers to the experience of unity by those wise ones who are capable of knowing the divine reality. At the beginning of his fourth discourse Śvetāśvatara impressed on us that the manifestation of the cosmos and its dissolution are two phases of a single process (see pp. 261–262). The One expresses itself as the many, and then the many individual souls, upon enlightentment, merge back into the One. Attaining the state of actionlessless (*niṣkriyatā*) is part of the process.

How does one become actionless? Again the word *bīja* provides a clue. Śvetāśvatara uses the word to indicate the power of God that is the source of the universe—Śakti, the seed of all possibility. That same power of consciousness works in two ways—in God's manifestation of the universe and in the individual soul's return to divine unity. The Trikaśāstra can make our understanding of this verse all the more vivid. Exactly as Śvetāśvatara implies here, in the Śaiva definition *bīja* is the cause of the universe, the supreme energy of consciousness, whose essence is its own radiance (*viśvakāraṇaṁ sphurattātmā parāśaktiḥ*).[108]

The term *bīja* appears in *Śivasūtra* 3.15, which reads, succinctly, "Attentiveness to the seed" (*bījāvadhānam*). Commenting on this *sūtra,* Kṣemarāja explains that the *yogin* should cultivate full attentiveness to the source of the world. Kṣemarāja considers this source (*bīja*) to be the active light of consciousness, also known as *citi* or *parāśakti* or *parāvāc*—the terms are synonymous. He then quotes the Netratantra (7.40), which elaborates on *parāśakti* as the source of all the gods and of all subsequent, diversified powers. This Tantra teaches that the supreme power of consciousness (*parāśakti*), or consciousness-as-power (*citi*), is "of the nature of fire and moon" (*agnīsomātmikā*), meaning that it is the source of polarity from which all subsequent manifestation proceeds.[109] The word *avadhāna,* means not only "attention," "attentiveness," or "intentness" but a fully concentrated effort. It derives from the verb *avadhā,* meaning "to plunge into."[110] Real *sādhanā* calls for that kind of wholehearted commitment, a self-immersion into the awareness of the indwelling divinity, which is the blissful ocean of consciousness itself.

Vasugupta's next *sūtra* (3.16) reads, "Mentally established [in *parāśakti*], one is steeped (*nimajjati*) happily, with complete wellbeing (*sukham*), in the ocean [of immortality]." Again drawing on the Netratantra, Kṣemarāja notes that they who abide in constant awareness of the supreme source of the world-process (*viśvapravāha*) have no further need of any kind of lower or higher effortful practice, such as contemplation or meditation. Having relinquished all identification with the body-mind complex, they abide in the Self, steeped in bliss.[111] Vasugupta's text and Kṣemarāja's commentary clearly echo the content of Śvetāśvatara's *mantra:* "Steady are they [the actionless ones] who discover him abiding in themselves; to them belongs constant happiness and not to others."

Finally, this *mantra* is a variant of Kaṭhopaniṣad 2.2.12. Śvetāśvatara has modified the original first *pāda*, "the one master, the inner Self of all beings" (*eko vaśī sarvabhūtāntarātmā*), to "the one master of the actionless many" (*eko vaśī niṣkriyānām bahūnām*). Scholars explain that this change was designed to impart a more personal idea of God. As it stands in the Kaṭhopaniṣad, the verse extols the impersonal Brahman of the Vedānta. Śvetāśvatara's version better fits the Śaiva concept of the Absolute as the ultimate but *theistic* nondual reality.

13

नित्यो नित्यानां चेतनश्चेतनाना-
मेको बहूनां यो विदधाति कामान्।
तत्कारणं सांख्ययोगाधिगम्यं
ज्ञात्वा देवं मुच्यते सर्वपाशैः ॥ १३ ॥

nityo nityānāṁ cetanaś cetanānām eko bahūnāṁ yo vidadhāti kāmān /
tat kāraṇaṁ sāṁkhyayogādhigamyaṁ jñātvā devaṁ mucyate sarvapāśaiḥ //

13. He who fulfills all desires is the Eternal among the eternals, the Intelligent among the intelligent, the One among the many, the cause to be discovered through observing and directing the mind. Knowing that effulgent being, one is freed from all fetters.

This outpouring of superlatives attempts to express the inexpressible supremacy of the Divine and to show that he (or it) is the essence of everything that exists. Whatever appears eternal to us owes its eternality to the reality of Brahman. Whatever appears sentient owes its sentience to the light of consciousness shining forth, however dimly. In the case of the embodied creature, whose light of awareness is veiled, that light is still nothing but consciousness. The absolute One has the relative many as its countless individual expressions and avenues of experience.

Each of the three early Vedantic commentators attempts a specific philosophical interpretation for Śvetāśvatara's string of superlatives, but the end result is only disagreement over the details.[112] In the end, it is the poetry of this passage that conveys the vision of one eternal reality that alone is the conscious essence supporting and infusing all existence.

Will the God "who fulfills [all] desires" (*yo vidadhāti kāmān*) grant each of us everything we want in this life? No, because in our embodied state we are partial, fragmented, and incomplete, and no amount of grasping after the objects of our desire, which are also partial, fragmented, and incomplete, can reconstitute our original wholeness. The One who fulfills all desires is our own true being; knowing that alone, we experience divine fullness (*pūrṇatva*) wherein nothing could possibly be lacking. That is the ultimate fulfillment of which the seer spoke in his initial discourse (1.11).

Our true being is to be discovered, attained, and realized (all meanings of *adhigamyam*) through *sāṁkhya* and *yoga*. It is important to remember that these two associated terms did not mean to Śvetāśvatara's listeners what they mean today (see pp. 14–21 and 30–34). Those later definitions as orthodox Hindu *darśanas* still lay far off in the future. Nevertheless in the later catalog of the six classical *darśanas* Sāṁkhya is paired with the closely related Yoga system as codified by Patañjali. Just as a bird needs two wings to fly, the spiritual aspirant requires both theory (*sāṁkhya*) and method (*yoga*). We can surmise that Śvetāśvatara's pairing of these terms expresses a similar idea.

Because the word *sāṁkhya* appears in no older text of the Vedic canon than this one, there is no textual history on which to rely. Later it occurs several times in the Mahābhārata, usually in connection with the rational categorization of the constituents of nature or with reason in general.[113] As for *yoga*, the best indicator of what it means here comes from two earlier Upaniṣads. The Taittirīya is the first Vedic text to use the term. It defines *yoga* as the innermost state of conjunction or concentration, identical to the Self (2.4.1). The Kaṭhopaniṣad (2.3.10–11) presents *yoga* as the state in which the five sensory faculties together with the cognitive mind (*manas*) cease their normal activities and in which even the determinative faculty (*buddhi*) does not stir. This highest state (*paramāṁ gatim*), this steady control of the senses (*sthīrām indriyadhāraṇām*), is *yoga*.

In greater detail we also have Śvetāśvatara's own exposition of *yoga* in his second discourse. The first seven *mantras* present an overview of *yoga* from beginning to end. First the seer speaks of purifying the mind (*manas* in the general sense of *antaḥkaraṇa*) by joining it to holy thoughts (*dhiyaḥ*) (2.1). With the mind intent, one becomes open to divine inspiration (2.2). The next step is harnessing the naturally outgoing sensory faculties and turning their activity inward. With this reversal, consciousness turns back upon itself (2.3) and begins to perceive its own vibrant radiance (2.4). Individual awareness lessens and becomes attuned to the glory of Brahman (2.5). This experience gives rise to true understanding (2.6), and with the realization of the eternal One as the source of all, the soul is freed from bondage (2.7). Next the seer presents the method of *yoga,* describing the recommended posture for meditation (2.8), the control of the breath, the restraint of thought (2.9), and the conditions conducive to concentration (2.10). He speaks of signs of progress and degrees of attainment as way-stations along the road to realization (2.11–14). The inward journey culminates in the liberating knowledge of one's true identity as the Absolute (2.15). That ultimate reality is the supreme lord of the universe, existing simultaneously as his own infinite wholeness and as all created beings (2.16). Śvetāśvatara concludes the lesson by offering salutations to that effulgent God whose divine light pervades the whole of creation (2.17).

Given this context, the phrase *sāṁkhyayogādhigamyam* can be understood to mean that the Self is "to be discovered through observing and directing the mind," in other words, by managing our own awareness. Here *sāṁkhya* indicates a theoretical base that is rational and discriminative,[114] and *yoga* denotes its practical application.[115] For Śvetāśvatara *sāṁkhyayoga* means the examination of one's own consciousness—of how it is constituted and how it operates—and the practical use of that knowledge as a means of Self-realization.[116]

The *mantra's* final quarter is one that Śvetāśvatara utters five times in the course of this Upaniṣad (1.8, 2.15, 4.16, 5.13, 6.13), and its insistent repetition is meant to drive home its importance: "Knowing that effulgent being, one is freed from all fetters." Whatever form our practice may take, it is the knowledge—the experience—of the divine light of consciousness (*devam*) in and through and beyond all things that sets us free.

14

न तत्र सूर्यो भाति न चन्द्रतारकं
नेमा विद्युतो भान्ति कुतोऽयमग्निः ।
तमेव भान्तमनुभाति सर्वं
तस्य भासा सर्वमिदं विभाति ॥ १४ ॥

na tatra sūryo bhāti na candratārakaṁ nemā vidyuto bhānti kuto 'yam agniḥ /
tam eva bhāntam anubhāti sarvaṁ tasya bhāsā sarvam idaṁ vibhāti //

14. There the sun shines not, nor the moon and stars, nor does the lightning illumine, much less this earthly fire. He alone shining, everything shines after him. By his light all this universe shines.

The seer ended the previous *mantra* by stating for the fifth time that by knowing the effulgent One (*devam*) we are set free. Knowledge and light have a fundamental connection, and even though we may not give it much thought, it infuses even our colloquial speech. When we don't know something, we say that we are "in the dark." We may ask to be "enlightened" about something we don't fully understand. To understand something rightly is "to see the light."

By this same light everything in the world of our experience is known. The divine consciousness that we call God or Brahman illuminates all. Moreover, it is luminosity itself (*prakāśa*). It is not only the light that illumines in the physical sense[117] but also the light of understanding that pervades every sentient creature and makes all experience possible. Awareness itself cannot be illumined by any lesser light in the three worlds of heaven, atmosphere and earth—not by the sun, moon, and stars that shine in the heavenly realm, not by the lightning that flashes in the atmosphere, and not by the fire that casts its illumination on earth. None of these manifest forms of light shine *there*—in Brahman. Even the sun in all its brilliance does not shed its light on the Self; it is the Self that illumines everything that exists.[118]

The seer employs three verbs to express the nuanced aspects of shining. Divine consciousness shines in and of itself (*bhāti*). Our perception tells us that the sun, moon, stars, lightning, and fire that shine in their respective realms appear to shine of their own accord, but in regard to the Absolute, they do not shine (*na bhānti*). Apart from the supreme Self, all else (*sarvam*) merely shines after (*anubhāti*) or reflects him who alone truly shines (*tam eva bhāntam*).

In the final *pāda* Śvetāśvatara would have us understand that through God's own luminosity (*tasya bhāsā*), the whole universe (*sarvam idam*) becomes visible (*vibhāti*)[119] and shines forth diversely (*vibhāti*),[120] gleaming (*vibhāti*)[121] in splendor. God, the supreme Self, is pure consciousness—absolute, unconditioned, and self-luminous. It is not revealed by anything other than itself, and it alone reveals everything else. And what is everything else? Only its own reflection, existing as concept (*nāma*)[122] or ideation (*kalpanā*) in the divine mind (see pp. 272–273 and 285–286).

This wonderfully evocative *mantra,* found also in the Kaṭhopaniṣad (2.3.15) and the Muṇḍakopaniṣad (2.2.10), brought its influence to bear on a classic treatise on Advaita Vedānta, which discusses the nature of ultimate reality as consciousness, along with the means to its attainment. Quoted previously (see pp. 209–210), the penultimate verse of *Ātmabodha* appears clearly indebted to the present *mantra* and is no less beautiful: "Risen in the space of the heart, the Self, the sun of knowledge, dispels the darkness / pervading all and supporting all, it shines and causes everything to shine" (*hṛdākāśodito hy ātmā bodhabhānus tamopahṛt / sarvavyāpī sarvadhārī bhāti bhāsayate 'khilam*).

15

एको हंसः भुवनस्यास्य मध्ये
स एवाग्निः सलिले संनिविष्टः ।
तमेव विदित्वा अतिमृत्युमेति
नान्यः पन्था विद्यतेऽयनाय ॥ १५ ॥

eko haṁsaḥ bhuvanasyāsya madhye sa evāgniḥ salile saṁniviṣṭaḥ /
tam eva viditvā atimṛtyum eti nānyaḥ panthā vidyate 'yanāya //

15. The one supreme Self in the midst of this world, he alone is the fire submerged in water. Knowing him alone, one goes beyond death. There is no other way by which to go.

This poetic verse contains three words used metaphorically, and in them interpreters have discovered a breadth of meaning.

The word translated here as "supreme Self" is *haṁsa,* literally a swan, goose, or other aquatic bird. Often signifying the universal or the individual spirit, this term has a long history and a wealth of meaning (see pp. 109–110). The Vedic commentator Sāyaṇācārya analyzed *haṁsa* as a compound of [*a*]*haṁ* plus *sa,* yielding the inner meaning "I am that."[123] Alternatively, Vedantic commentators often cite traditional native etymology to explain that *haṁsa* means the supreme Self as the destroyer of the cause of bondage, namely ignorance (*hanty avidyādibandhakāraṇam iti haṁsaḥ*).[124]

Śvetāśvatara describes the supreme Self in the midst of this world as fire submerged in water (*agniḥ salile saṁniviṣṭaḥ*). Fire symbolizes the supreme Self, because Self-knowledge burns up ignorance just as fire consumes wood.[125] Both the swan (*haṁsa*) and fire (*agni*), equated here, signify right perception (*samyak darśana*)[126]—seeing things as they really are in the oneness of consciousness and not merely as the separate objects they appear to be.

The element of water (*salila*) has two traditional interpretations. According to the first, it represents the physical body, either by analogy to the similar sounding word *śarīra* ("body")[127] or because the body is composed in large part of water.[128] According to the second interpretation, water signifies the purified heart. A heart purified by worship, sacrifice, charitable acts, and other spiritual disciplines becomes as clear as water.[129] Because *haṁsa* in this verse represents the supreme Self, already perfect and in no need of purification, we can easily accept that "fire submerged in water" symbolizes the all-pervading supreme consciousness, intimately contained in or established in (*saṁniviṣṭaḥ*) the body. As for the heart, it should be sufficiently clear that divinity dwells in *every* heart, purified or not.

Perhaps this wonderful metaphor has still other meanings. Paul

Deussen, independent of any interpretive tradition, suggested that this phrase first underscores the difference between Brahman and the world and then, more abstractly, signifies the dichotomy of subject and object.[130] This reading is equally compatible with Advaita Vedānta and Trika Śaivism. For another commentator this figure of speech makes the point that pure spirit (*haṁsa*), although immanent in the world, is as different from it as fire is from water.[131] Besides meaning "water," *salila* signifies anything else that is flowing, surging, fluctuating, or unsteady.[132] If fire represents the eternal, steady light of consciousness, then water could stand for that which is ever in flux. Thus "fire submerged in water" becomes a powerful and poetic image to describe the Self as the limitless and constant amid a world seemingly marked by limitation and change.[133]

In the second half of this *mantra* Śvetāśvatara repeats the corresponding part of *mantra* 3.8, in turn a quotation from the Vājasaneyisaṁhitā (31.18): "Knowing him alone, one goes beyond death. There is no other way by which to go." Only by knowing the supreme Self—the truth of our being—do we go beyond death. To reach immortality is to realize the identity of *jīva* and Śiva.[134] It is as simple as that.

16

स विश्वकृद् विश्वविदात्मयोनि-
र्ज्ञः कालकारो गुणी सर्वविद्यः ।
प्रधानक्षेत्रज्ञपतिर्गुणेशः
संसारमोक्षस्थितिबन्धहेतुः ॥ १६ ॥

sa viśvakṛd viśvavid ātmayonir jñaḥ kālakāro guṇī sarvavidyaḥ /
pradhānakṣetrajñapatir guṇeśaḥ saṁsāramokṣasthitibandhahetuḥ //

16. He, the all-doing, the all-knowing, is the self-originated one; he is the intelligent maker of time, the omniscient possessor of the

forces of creation, the master of the natural world and the human soul. He is the cause of bondage to continuing existence and of release from the soul's wandering.

At the beginning of his first discourse, the seer asked his listeners to ponder the cause of the universe and the meaning of human existence (1.1). He swept aside a number of commonly held assumptions (1.2) and then declared that the cause of our existence is the self-luminous power of consciousness (*devātmaśakti*) lying hidden in everything (1.3). On the ever-turning wheel of the universe, the individual soul (*haṁsa*) revolves, living and dying, living and dying, thinking itself different from (and separate from) the animating force until, blessed by the knowledge of that very Brahman, it attains immortality (1.6). Realizing (*viditvā*) the infinite Brahman within, one becomes merged in it and freed from rebirth and its limitations (1.7). The present *mantra* summarizes those points.

That which is called Brahman, God, or Rudra is his own source (*ātmayoniḥ*); he is self-caused or self-originated.[135] An alternative reading takes *ātmayoniḥ* in the sense of *ātmanām yoniḥ,* "the source of [all] selves."[136] Either is grammatically valid and philosophically true, but the first seems marginally better here. It states explicitly that the Supreme Being is self-existent and has no creator. From this we can deduce that he never was not and never will not be. Though uncreated, he himself is all-creating (*sarvakṛt*) and all-knowing (*sarvavit*). These two terms convey the impression that God is a dynamic process rather than an inert abstraction.

As Śvetāśvatara said early on (1.2), time is not the cause of the universe as some have speculated. Now, in his final discourse, he is intent on emphasizing that time is always subordinate to the creator or cause (6.1–3, 6.5–6), whose very nature is eternity. For the seer this is an important point, important enough for him to reiterate the second *pāda* of *mantra* 6.2: "He is the intelligent maker of time (*jñaḥ kālakāraḥ*), the omniscient possessor of the forces of creation." God himself is the cause and the source of all temporal things.

His intelligence pervades the structure of every manifest phenomenon, be it the externally perceived universe or the sentient individual that perceives it internally. The emanation of phenomenality both as the macrocosm and the microcosm proceeds through the twenty-four cosmic principles (*tattvas*) from *prakṛti* to earth as delineated by Sāṁkhya and accepted also by Vedānta and Trika Śaivism, the latter expanding the total number to thirty-six. This systematic organization of the principles of mind and matter bespeaks a guiding intelligence. In reality, each of these *tattvas* is nothing but a modification of consciousness itself.

The intelligence that shapes and pervades the temporal realm belongs to the omniscient (*sarvavidyaḥ*) God who is the possessor of all sciences (another meaning of *sarvavidyaḥ*) and the possessor of the forces of creation as well. It is he, the *guṇin,* who controls the *guṇas,* the diversified expressions of divine energy that are the universal building blocks. As the controller of these energies (*guṇeśaḥ*), God is of course the master (*patiḥ*) of all that is made from them, the lord of the natural world (*pradhāna*) and of the sentient human soul (*kṣetrajña*) as well.

The term *kṣetrajña* appears here for the first time in Upaniṣadic literature. It is a distinctive expression associated with proto-Sāṁkhya. Just as the terms *puruṣa* and *ātman* are sometimes used interchangeably in earlier Sanskrit texts to denote either a cosmic or an individual person or self, *kṣetrajña* also can carry either of those meanings.[137] Here it means the individual soul, as it does also in the thirteenth chapter of the Bhagavadgītā (13.1–2, 26, 34). There the field (*kṣetra*) is identified as *prakṛti,* and the knower of the field (*kṣetrajñaḥ*) is called *puruṣa.* The field is the material body, and its knower is the conscious principle embodied within it—the awareness of subjectivity appearing as differentiated and limited by the conditioning of the *tattvas.* Although the term *kṣetrajña* was later displaced in classical Sāṁkhya by *puruṣa,*[138] its use continued on in Kashmir Śaivism to designate the individual subject.[139]

According to the Trikaśāstra, nothing happens but by divine will, and everything we witness in this earthly existence reflects one or another of Śiva's five cosmic activities (*pañcakṛtya*). Three of these processes are based on the observable fact that everything in the world of our experience has a beginning, a middle, and an end. The functions of emanation (*sṛṣṭi*), continuance (*sthiti*), and dissolution or resorption (*saṁhāra*) take place constantly at every level of manifestation. To these three processes, which are common to all schools of Indian thought, the Trika system adds two more divine activities; these are concealment (*nigraha*) and revelation or grace (*anugraha*). Through self-limitation Śiva conceals his true being as infinite consciousness-bliss (*cidānanda*) and contracts himself as the individual soul (*paśu*). Another name for this state of concealment is bondage (*paśutva*). When Śiva dissolves the limitation, allowing the individual's true nature to be recognized, his grace is called liberation. In speaking of the supreme Self as the cause (*hetuḥ*) both of bondage to this continuing existence (*sthitibandha*) and of liberation from the cycle of birth, death, and rebirth (*saṁsāramokṣa*), Śvetāśvatara expresses the same teaching embodied in the terms *nigraha* and *anugraha*.

17

स तन्मयो ह्यमृत ईशसंस्थो
ज्ञः सर्वगो भुवनस्यास्य गोप्ता ।
य ईशेऽस्य जगतो नित्यमेव
नान्यो हेतुर्विद्यत ईशनाय ॥ १७ ॥

sa tanmayo hy amṛta īśasaṁstho jñaḥ sarvago bhuvanasyāsya goptā /
ya īśe 'sya jagato nityam eva nānyo hetur vidyate īśanāya //

17. As such, he, the immortal, abiding as lord, is the all-knowing and everywhere-present guardian of this world; there is no other cause for his ruling [than he himself] who is the master of this world forever and ever.

"As such" (*tanmayaḥ*) refers to the previous *mantra's* assertion that the supreme Self is the cause of bondage to continuing existence and of release from the soul's wandering. Transcending his own play of creation, the Divine is *amṛtaḥ*—birthless, deathless, uncreated. His own freedom is the freedom of absolute sovereignty, conveyed here by the expression "abiding as lord" (*īśasaṁsthaḥ*).

Calling him the guardian, protector, or preserver (*goptā*) refers to the divine function of *stithi*, the maintenance of the cosmos. In this role God is everywhere present (*sarvagaḥ*) and all-knowing (*jñaḥ*). To underscore his unsurpassable glory, Śvetāśvatara restates poetically that he who rules over (*ya īśe*) this world, this realm of motion (*asya jagataḥ*) reigns forever and ever (*nityam eva*). Apart from his own nature there is no other cause (*nānyo hetuḥ vidyate*) for his sovereignty (*īśanāya*).

Here we recall the questions that opened this Upaniṣad. What is the cause (*kiṁ kāraṇam*)? By what do we live? What law governs us, whose lives run their course through happiness and all the rest? There is no cause or impulse or reason (*hetuḥ*) for the controlling (*īśanāya*) of this universe other than Brahman or God himself. Let us compare the two words Śvetāśvatara uses to express the idea of cause. *Kāraṇa* derives from the verbal root *kṛ* ("to do," "to make," "to perform," "to accomplish," "to cause"). *Hetu* derives from the verbal root *hi,* meaning "to send forth," "to set in motion," "to impel," "to urge on," "to stimulate," "to incite." Both words carry the idea of activity, dynamism, and energy. The ultimate cause—Brahman or Rudra—is the singular reality of consciousness itself, which is not different from its own power (*devātmaśakti*). Śvetāśvatara revealed that almost immediately—in *mantra* 1.3—and returned to that same theme in *mantras* 3.1, 4.1, and 6.8. His God is not a remote abstraction, divorced from the relative realities of our mundane existence, but is the supreme reality which is an active presence in and through every moment of our lives.

18

यो ब्रह्माणं विदधाति पूर्वं
यो वै वेदांश्च प्रहिणोति तस्मै ।
तं ह देवं आत्मबुद्धिप्रकाशं
मुमुक्षुर्वै शरणमहं प्रपद्ये ॥ १८ ॥

yo brahmāṇaṁ vidadhāti pūrvaṁ yo vai vedāṁś ca prahiṇoti tasmai /
taṁ ha devaṁ ātmabuddhiprakāśaṁ mumukṣur vai śaraṇam ahaṁ prapadye //

18. Longing for liberation, I take refuge in that very God who shines by his own intelligence, who creates Brahmā in the beginning and who indeed bestows on him the Vedas.

Speaking here as the aspirant, Śvetāśvatara describes the longing initially felt by the soul who has had an inkling of divine glory and senses that something greater lies beyond the limitation of individual selfhood—something self-luminous, vibrant, and scintillating throughout the whole of creation. That which the aspirant envisions as the source and support of the universe—as the Divine—extends the promise of unimaginable freedom and joy. Not surprisingly, it begins to exert an irresistible pull. The word *mumukṣu* denotes one who has this intense thirst for liberation. Why is this longing so potent? Because *mumukṣutva* is a nostalgic longing of the heart for something long forgotten, something once known so intimately that when the knowledge is regained, it comes as recognition (*pratyabhijñā*). Liberation (*mokṣa*) is the recognition of one's true, original nature.

Thus, "aspiring to freedom (*mumukṣuḥ*), I throw myself at the feet of God himself (*taṁ ha devaṁ prapadye*), taking refuge (*śaraṇam*) in him who shines by his own intelligence (*ātmabuddhiprakāśam*)." For those aspiring to freedom, this *mantra* is an injunction to direct their own awareness back upon itself, to recognize the unconditioned light of consciousness as God and Self and their own true being, to surrender the smallness of individuality to the all-dissolving radiance of infinity.

Within his luminous oneness Brahman first ideates the creator god, Brahmā or Hiraṇyagarbha, and to this first-born deity reveals the eternal Vedas. Between the cycles of cosmic manifestation, says orthodox tradition, the Vedas repose in their subtlest essence within divine consciousness, not yet materialized as the sacred texts we read or hear recited. In the Bṛhadāraṇkayopaniṣad (2.4.10) Yājñavalkya describes the Vedas as "the breath of the limitless reality" (*asya mahato bhūtasya niśvasitam*). They are the creative word (*vāc*) that is none other than *śakti,* the potency which transforms the causal into the subtle and the subtle into the gross.[140] This divine creativity that flows spontaneously and effortlessly, this undifferentiated word (*parāśakti*), manifests as distinct words and their inherent meanings to produce the abundant diversity of material nature, living creatures, and a multitude of activities. As the recipient and transmitter of the Vedas, Brahmā utters the words and shapes the worlds.[141]

19

निष्कलं निष्क्रियं शान्तं निरवद्यं निरञ्जनम् ।
अमृतस्य परं सेतुं दग्धेन्धनमिवानलम् ॥ १९ ॥

niṣkalaṁ niṣkriyaṁ śāntaṁ niravadyaṁ nirañjanam /
amṛtasya paraṁ setuṁ dagdhendhanam ivānalam //

19. [I take refuge in him], the supreme bridge to immortality, who is undivided, actionless, tranquil, faultless, and untainted, like a fire that has ceased its blazing.

Continuing, Śvetāśvatara extols the benevolent Lord as the supreme bridge to immortality (*amṛtasya paraṁ setum*). A bridge is a span between two sides of a divide. The divide in this case is the ignorance that lies between the infinite consciousness of the supreme Self and the finite awareness of the human soul. A span is a continuum, and for Śvetāśvatara, that continuum is the gracious deity himself, seamlessly flowing out of his own limitless perfection into human finitude and back again. Because consciousness is simultaneously transcendent and immanent, it is for the individual the means of traversing the constant distractions and occasional storms of life. Because the reality that supports and constitutes the entire universe is the reality at the heart of every human being, we live with the inherent and ever-present possibility of Self-recognition (*pratyabhijñā*), the same direct experience of our divine nature that the Vedānta calls *aparokṣānubhūti*. This identification of *ātman* and Brahman—this truth of all truths—is the bridge between the human beings we *think* we are and the divine being we come to *know* we are. When *thinking* stops and only *knowing* remains, the process of *becoming* yields to the pure unity of *being*. That is why Śvetāśvatara describes the reality of consciousness as without parts and undivided (*niṣkala*).

This state of undifferentiated wholeness is actionless (*niṣkriya*). Commentators of the Advaita Vedānta tradition take *niṣkriya* to mean that Brahman is static and devoid of activity, even to the point of being incapable of creative action, which they consider the province of *māyā*,[142] but that view is contradicted by everything else in this Upaniṣad. Brahman *is* the cause of this world, its creator, and its lord. Just three verses back Śvetāśvatara said, "He, the all-doing, the all-knowing, is the self-originated one; he is the intelligent maker of time, the omniscient possessor of the forces of creation, the master of the natural world and the human soul. He is the cause of bondage to continuing existence and of release from the soul's wandering." Hardly the description of an actionless reality! Yes, *niṣkriya* means "actionless," but in the sense of being at rest. When all empirical awareness—all experience of perceptual and conceptual thought—ceases, when all activity of consciousness (*cittavṛtti*) subsides, then consciousness itself shines forth in its essential nature. In the Trika definition this is Śiva in a state of repose (*viśrānti*). The description of the supreme Self as tranquil (*śānta*) also relates to the idea of being at rest. In practical terms tranquility means freedom from restlessness and discontent.[143] Philosophically it means freedom from modification.[144] Because all modification is based on difference and limitation, it is a descent from perfection. Its absence is a return to perfect wholeness, infinite freedom, and absolute peace.

To say that the Self is faultless (*niravadya*) is yet another way of expressing divine perfection. In truth nothing can touch the supreme Self, so Śvetāśvatara deems it taintless (*nirañjana*). That is hardly an adjective we would apply to our human selves. Whereas the divine powers of will, knowledge, and action are absolute and inviolable, we find our own hearts, minds, and bodies stained by the memories of bitter and painful experiences, bolstered by hopes, and saddled with the debts of past actions.

The finite soul is a contracted form of the infinite divinity, and in the Trikaśāstra contraction is called impurity (*mala*). A product of *māyā*, this impurity takes three forms depending on which aspect of divinity is reduced to its paltry human counterpart. As we have already learned, the impurity called *āṇavamala* is the consciousness of limited individuality: "I am small (*aṇu*) in my own sense of finitude, lack, and inferiority." This is the root impurity that gives rise to the other two. *Māyīyamala* is the impurity of duality or difference: "I live in the constant awareness of separation and otherness." *Kārmamala* is the impurity of action: "I act out of necessity or compulsion, driven by my own sense of want and bound to reap the favorable or unfavorable consequences of my actions."

As long as the *malas* function, either singly or in combination, they hold every finite being subject to their bondage. In contracting the divine power of action, *kārmamala* corresponds most strongly to the physical body. In forcing a separation between subject and object and limiting our understanding to duality, *māyīyamala* corresponds most strongly to the subtle body or mind. Both of these, in turn, derive from *āṇavamala,* the primal shrinking of universal selfhood into the semblance of a minute, defined entity (*aṇu*). With the removal of the obstructive *malas,* we transcend our bondage to the often fiery drama of human existence.

Śvetāśvatara compares the supreme Self to a fire that has ceased its blazing. Just as the crackling flames eventually consume every bit of the fuel, the brilliance of Self-recognition consumes the last vestiges of ignorance. Just as smoke no longer billows from the fire whose fuel is spent (*dagdhendhanam ivānalam*), the cloud of ignorance that once obscured the reality of the Self disperses in the clarity of purified awareness. Once the flames have subsided, the charcoal glows radiantly[145] in profound peace and fulfillment. The seer poetically likens the supreme Self resting in his own fullness to the contented afterglow of a fire.

20

यदा चर्मवदाकाशं वेष्टयिष्यन्ति मानवाः ।
तदा देवमविज्ञाय दुःखस्यान्तो भविष्यति ॥ २० ॥

yadā carmavad ākāśaṁ veṣṭayiṣyanti mānavāḥ /
tadā devam avijñāya duḥkhasyānto bhaviṣyati //

20. Apart from knowing the effulgent God, there will be an end to misery only when humankind can roll up the sky like a piece of leather.

At the beginning of the Upaniṣad Śvetāśvatara spoke of human life as running a course through "happiness and all the rest," through every possible circumstance we may find ourselves in and every possible reaction and mood of the mind. Human life embraces the entire spectrum of experience from pleasure and well-being (*sukha*) to gnawing discomfort and pain (*duḥkha*).

Now the seer says that any attempt to put an end to our existential unease short of knowing the effulgent, innermost Self will prove as futile as trying to roll up the sky as if it were a piece of leather! Is he suddenly seized with pessimism after his earlier and largely positive statements about the world as a manifestation of the Divine?

The answer lies in the same phrase that raises the question. Literally *duḥkhasyāntaḥ* means the "end (*antaḥ*) of misery,[146] sorrow,[147] or suffering"[148] (*duḥkhasya*). *Duḥkha* most broadly signifies the entire range of existential unease, the imperfection of the human condition. That experience is universal and inseparable from the smallness of individuality (*tanu*), which does not allow for complete and lasting fulfillment. That said, in order to appreciate the real flavor of the phrase *duḥkhasyāntaḥ,* we must recall that it is virtually identical to the compound *duḥkhānta* ("the end of *duḥkha*")—an early Śaiva term for liberation. With this context in mind we can discern the import of what Śvetāśvatara is trying to express. Lasting satisfaction comes only through liberation from the confines of the here and now. To seek infinite happiness in the finite world is as futile as trying to roll up the sky like a piece of leather. This bold image drives home the point that the seer has made many times already: only those souls who *know* the Divine go beyond the affliction of finitude. In the absence of right knowledge there can be no peace, no freedom, no immortality. To repeat a few of the seer's earlier pronouncements: "... [O]ne who is established in meditation knows the reality of Brahman as unborn [and ever being], constant, and untouched by anything within the creation; knowing that effulgent being, one is freed from all fetters" (2.15). "He is subtler than the subtlest, in the midst of the unformed the creator of everything, assuming many forms. He alone encompasses the universe; knowing that auspicious being, one fully and forever goes to peace" (4.14). "This is to be known as abiding eternally within oneself. Beyond this there is nothing further to be known ..." (1.12).

21

तपःप्रभावाद् देवप्रसादाच्च
ब्रह्म ह श्वेताश्वतरोऽथ विद्वान्।
अत्याश्रमिभ्यः परमं पवित्रं
प्रोवाच सम्यगृषिसङ्घजुष्टम्॥ २१॥

tapaḥprabhāvād devaprasādāc ca brahma ha śvetāśvataro 'tha vidvān /
atyāśramibhyaḥ paramaṁ pavitraṁ provāca samyagṛṣisaṅghajuṣṭam //

21. Śvetāśvatara, knowing Brahman itself by the power of his austerities and by the grace of God, thus imparted to the ascetics the highest means of purification, in which the multitude of seers rightly take delight.

Following Śvetāśvatara's emphatic and rather startling conclusion, the last three verses form an epilogue, possibly a later addition,[149] to the text. Here we find the Upaniṣad's only mention of the seer's name.

Like the opening words of the first chapter, addressed to a gathering of knowers of Brahman (*brahmavidaḥ*), the epilogue makes clear that Śvetāśvatara's teachings are intended for an audience of ascetics (*atyāśramibhyaḥ*) belonging to one of the Śaiva lineages of the time. The *Śvetāśvataropaniṣadvṛtti* takes the term *atyāśramin* to mean the highest sort of renunciant, one worthy of the designation *paramahaṁsa*,[150] but that explanation reflects the stratified monastic society that existed during the commentator's lifetime, a millennium and a half later. An *atyāśramin* may simply be a renunciant who has passed through or gone beyond (*ati*) the three stages (*āśramas*) of student life (*brahmacarya*), householder life (*gṛhastha*), and solitary retirement into the forest (*vānaprastha*) and has embraced the fourth stage (*saṁnyāsa*),[151] generally defined as the letting go of everything else for the sake of enlightenment. Of course, true *saṁnyāsa* is more than a socially constructed way of life or (in later times) the formality of monastic vows. True *saṁnyāsa* probes deep into the nature of human existence and requires the relinquishing of *tanu,* the sense of individuality, by stripping away everything until all that remains is the naked Self in all its unfettered glory.

This *mantra* extols the contents of the Upaniṣad as "the highest means of purification" (*paramaṁ pavitram*), once again to remind us of the importance of managing and directing our awareness by means of meditation and other spiritual practices so that the infinite and ever-perfect divine Self will shine forth.

Śvetāśvatara attained enlightenment through the combined power of his own austerities (*tapaḥprabhāvāt*) and the grace of God (*devaprasādāt*). In later centuries the Mahābhārata would define the highest *tapas* as the withdrawal of the mind and senses from unworthy objects (12.250.4), and Śaiva doctrine would teach that grace or self-revelation (*anugraha*) is one of Śiva's natural functions. But throughout his teaching Śvetāśvatara emphasizes the importance of both. The goal he lays out for us is to reunite with Rudra or Brahman, whom he glorifies as both the bestower of grace and the supreme truth of nonduality (3.11, 3.20).

As a knower of Brahman (*vidvān*)—notice again the emphasis on knowledge—Śvetāśvatara is an illumined soul, qualified to teach others. He joins other knowers of the Self before him, a succession of revered preceptors who, from the very inception of the Vedas, have handed down the sacred knowledge of Brahman from generation to generation.

22

वेदान्ते परमं गुह्यं पुराकल्पे प्रचोदितम् ।
नाऽप्रशान्ताय दातव्यं नाऽपुत्रायाशिष्याय वा पुनः ॥ २२ ॥

vedānte paramaṁ guhyaṁ purākalpe pracoditam /
nā 'praśāntāya dātavyaṁ na 'putrāyāśiṣyāya vā punaḥ //

22. The supreme secret, imparted in the Vedānta in a former age, is not to be given to one of unsubdued passions nor, again, to one who is neither a son nor a disciple.

Next the epilogue stipulates the qualifications of the student. The teaching of the Upaniṣads, known also as the Vedānta, is the supreme secret or highest mystery (*paramaṁ guhyam*).[152] Of knowledge (*veda*) it is the last word (*anta*). Here *vedānta* means simply the direct revelation of the supreme Self, experienced by the ancient seers whose teachings form the Upaniṣads. Earlier, Śvetāśvatara declared that "Brahman is hidden in the Upaniṣads, which among the Vedas are to be kept secret" (5.6). The epilogue reiterates that point. Esoteric knowledge is not meant for everyone, as Yama also tells Naciketas in the Kaṭhopaniṣad (1.2.7): "It is not given to many even to hear of him [Brahman, the Self]; and many, hearing of him, do not understand." Because this most profound teaching is not only extremely subtle but also liable to misunderstanding, it must be guarded. The teacher's duty is to test the prospective student repeatedly and to recognize the proper disposition and qualities in the one who is to be taught.[153] As Yama stipulates, the prospective disciple must be eager for wisdom and free of many distracting desires (1.2.4).

Anyone of unsubdued passions (*apraśāntaḥ*) is unfit to be a disciple. There are two more conditions. "One who is neither a son nor a disciple" echoes a passage in the Bṛhadāraṇyakopaniṣad (6.3.12), where Satyakāma Jābāla instructs that sacred lore should not be imparted to anyone else. That said, in the transmission of the knowledge of Brahman, the idea of worthiness takes precedence over biological relationship or gender, and the meaning of *son* can be extended to include any close relationship based on mutual trust and love.[154] We need only recall that one of the Upaniṣads' most memorable passages on the teaching of Self-knowledge concerns Yājñavalkya's instruction to his beloved wife Maitreyī, included not once but twice in the Bṛhadāraṇyakopaniṣad (2.4.1–13 and 4.5.1–15).

23

यस्य देवे परा भक्तिः यथा देवे तथा गुरौ ।
तस्यैते कथिता ह्यर्थाः प्रकाशन्ते महात्मनः ॥ २३ ॥
प्रकाशन्ते महात्मन इति ।

yasya deve parā bhaktiḥ yathā deve tathā gurau /
tasyaite kathitā hy arthāḥ prakāśante mahātmanaḥ //
prakāśante mahātmana iti /

23. To the one who has supreme devotion to God, and as to God so to the teacher, to that great-souled one shine forth these matters that have been related; to that great-souled one they shine forth!

The teacher is one who has attained the highest knowledge; the disciple is one who has been deemed fit to attain it.

Supreme devotion to God (*deve parā bhaktiḥ*) is the total commitment needed for spiritual illumination. Rudra is none other than Brahman, and Brahman is the supreme Self (*paramātman*). The devotion called for is the unwavering single-mindedness that culminates in direct experience of the identity of Brahman and *ātman.* Supreme devotion (*parā bhaktiḥ*) and supreme knowledge (*parā vidyā*) are one and the same. Whatever we may perceive as difference in the beginning of *sādhanā* converges in the ultimate unity of divine consciousness.

With complete trust and love, the disciple must look upon the *guru* as God himself in the form of an illumined human preceptor,[155] capable of transmitting the hidden truth of the Self (*paramaṁ guhyam*) in its full majesty. The disciple who is open to receiving it becomes a great and noble soul (*mahātman*), having gone beyond the limitation of the finite self. When the conditions are right, the truths related here (*ete kathitā hy arthāḥ*) naturally reveal themselves, become evident, and shine forth (*prakāśante*).[156] In the fullness of Self-realization the illumined soul can proclaim, "I am Brahman, I am Śiva; *ahaṁ brahmāsmi, śivo 'ham!*"

APPENDIX A
WORD-FOR-WORD TRANSLATION

1.1 ब्रह्मवादिनः those who discourse on sacred matters; expounders of the Vedas वदन्ति speak, discuss, say किम् what कारणम् cause, reason, source, origin [of the universe] ब्रह्म [is it] Brahman कुतः from where; why, how स्म ever, surely जाताः [are we] born जीवामः we live केन due to what, by what क्व where, in what place, whither च and सम्प्रतिष्ठा permanence, continuance / अधिष्ठिताः regulated, controlled, governed केन by what सुखेतरेषु in happiness [and in all the] rest वर्तामहे we live, exist, abide ब्रह्मविदः O knowers of Brahman व्यवस्थाम् law, rule, steadiness, constancy

1.2 कालः time स्वभावः inherent nature नियतिः law, fixed order, fate यदृच्छा chance, randomness, spontaneity, accident भूतानि elements योनिः womb, source, origin पुरुषः primeval universal soul, supreme being, personal animating principle, spirit, individualized consciousness इति thus चिन्त्या to be considered, thought about / संयोगः combination एषाम् of these न not तु even आत्मभावात् because of [their] own individual state आत्मा individual soul अपि also अनीशः not sovereign, powerless सुखदुःखहेतोः because of happiness [and] misery

1.3 ते they (the *brahmavādinaḥ*) ध्यानयोगानुगताः entered into deep meditation अपश्यन् saw, realized, experienced देवात्मशक्तिम् [the] luminous power of [the] Self स्वगुणैः by [its] own effects निगूढाम् hidden, concealed / यः who कारणानि

causes निखिलानि all तानि those कालात्मयुक्तानि associated with time [and the] self अधितिष्ठति controls, governs, presides over ऐकः [as] one

1.4 तम् him (who presides as one) एकनेमिम् with one rim त्रिवृतम् having three parts, triple षोडशान्तम् with sixteen ends शतार्धारम् with fifty spokes विंशतिप्रत्यराभिः with twenty counterspokes, wedges अष्टकैः षड्भिः with six sets of eight विश्वरूपैकपाशम् one tie, fetter, leather strap (that holds the wheel in place on the axle) of manifold forms त्रिमार्गभेदम् differentiating into three paths द्विनिमित्तैकमोहम् [whose] single delusion [has a] twofold cause

1.5 पञ्चस्रोतोम्बुम् containing five currents पञ्चयोन्युग्रवक्राम् [whose] sharp bends [are the] five sources पञ्चप्राणोर्मिम् [whose] waves [are the] five vital breaths पञ्चबुद्ध्यादिमूलाम् [whose] origin [is the] primordial root [of] fivefold perception / पञ्चावर्ताम् [having] five whirlpools पञ्चदुःखौघवेगाम् [whose] rapids [are the] five miseries पञ्चाशद्भेदाम् [having] fifty aspects पञ्चपर्वाम् [having] five obstacles अधीमः we think [of that one as a river]

1.6 सर्वाजीवे in which everything lives, is sustained सर्वसंस्थे in which everything rests, abides, merges बृहन्ते vast, great अस्मिन् in this हंसः [the] individual soul भ्राम्यते revolves, wanders, roams ब्रह्मचक्रे on [the] wheel of Brahman / पृथक् different आत्मानम् itself प्रेरितारम् from [the] inciter, moving force, impeller च and मत्वा knowing, considering जुष्टः blessed, favored ततः then तेन by [the knowledge of] that [Brahman] अमृतत्वम् immortality एति goes to, attains

1.7 उद्गीतम् sung; proclaimed, celebrated एतत् this परमम् supreme तु verily ब्रह्म Brahman तस्मिन् in it त्रयम् triad सुप्रतिष्ठा firm support, foundation अक्षरम् imperishable च and / अत्र here अन्तरम् within ब्रह्मविदः knowers of Brahman विदित्वा knowing, having known लीनाः merged ब्रह्मणि in Brahman तत्पराः intent on that as [their] highest goal योनिमुक्ताः released from birth

1.8 संयुक्तम् joined together, mutually associated एतत् this क्षरम् [the] perishable अक्षरम् [the] imperishable च and व्यक्ताव्यक्तम् [the] manifest [and the] unmanifest भरते supports, maintains विश्वम् universe ईशः [the] Lord / अनीशः devoid of lordship, not independent च and आत्मा [the individual] soul बध्यते is bound भोक्तृभावात् by [the state of] being [the] enjoyer, experiencer ज्ञात्वा knowing, realizing देवम् [the] effulgent being, God मुच्यते one is freed, released सर्वपाशैः from all fetters

1.9 ज्ञाज्ञौ [the] knowing [and the] not-knowing द्वौ two, both अजौ unborn, unproduced, uncaused, existing from all eternity ईशनीशौ (Vedic form of *īśānīśau*) [the] sovereign, ruler [and the] powerless, ruled अजा [there is] unborn हि because, surely एका one भोक्तृभोग्यार्थयुक्ता engaged in relating [the] enjoyer [and that which is] to be enjoyed / अनन्तः infinite च and आत्मा [the] Self विश्वरूपः [whose] form [is the] universe हि indeed अकर्ता [is a] non-agent त्रयम् triad यदा then विन्दते is discovered, realized [to be] ब्रह्मम् Brahman (Vedic form) एतत् this [triad]

1.10 क्षरम् [the] perishable [is] प्रधानम् primordial matter, nature अमृताक्षरम् [the] immortal [and] imperishable [is] हरः Hara क्षरात्मानौ perishable [matter and the individual] soul ईशते rules over देवः God एकः one / तस्य on him अभि-ध्यानात् by meditation योजनात् by being joined तत्त्वभावात् by becoming [that] reality भूयः again, repeatedly, constantly च and अन्ते in [the] end विश्वमायानिवृत्तिः cessation of all *māyā*

1.11 ज्ञात्वा knowing, having known देवम् God, [the] effulgent [one] सर्वपाशापहानिः [the] diminishing, vanishing, of all fetters क्षीणैः diminished, withered, wasted away क्लेशैः pains, afflictions, distresses जन्ममृत्युप्रहाणिः [the] cessation, disappearance, of birth [and] death / तस्य on him अभिध्यानात् by meditation तृतीयम् [a] third [state] देहभेदे in [the] distinction, breaking, destruction of [the] individual विश्वैश्वर्यम् universal sovereignty, lordship, supremacy केवले in [the] Absolute, [the sole] singularity आप्तकामः [whose] desires [are] fulfilled

1.12 एतत् this [realization] ज्ञेयम् [is] to be known नित्यम् eternally एव only आत्मसंस्थम् abiding in [one's own] self न not अतः this परम् beyond वेदितव्यम् to be known हि indeed किञ्चित् anything / भोक्ता [the] enjoyer, experiencer भोग्यम् [the] enjoyed, experienced प्रेरितारम् [the] inciter च and मत्वा having thought, known, understood सर्वम् all प्रोक्तम् declared, proclaimed त्रिविधम् threefold, triple, of three kinds ब्रह्मम Brahman (Vedic form) एतत् this

1.13 वह्नेः of fire यथा as योनिगतस्य lying [latent] in [its] source (wood) मूर्तिः [the] form (flame) न not दृश्यते is seen न not एव yet च and लिङ्गनाशः [the] destruction of [its] subtle form / सः it (the flame) भूयः again, repeated एव surely इन्धनयोनिगृह्यः perceptible upon [the] friction of [its] source (the kindling sticks) तत् वा likewise उभयम् both वै indeed, certainly प्रणवेन by means of [the] *praṇava* (*Oṁ*) देहे in [the] body

1.14 स्वदेहम् one's own body, individuality अरणिम् [the] lower kindling stick कृत्वा having made, making प्रणवम् [the] *praṇava* च and उत्तरारणिम् [the] upper kindling stick / ध्याननिर्मथनाभ्यासाद् by practicing [the] friction of constant meditation देवम् God पश्येत् one should see निगूढवत् as [the] hidden [fire]

1.15 तिलेषु in sesame seeds तैलम् oil दधिनि in [coagulated] milk इव just as सर्पिः butter आपः water स्रोतःसु in streams, currents, riverbeds अरणीषु in [the] kindling sticks च and अग्निः fire / एवम् in like manner आत्मा [the] Self आत्मनि in [the] self गृह्यते is grasped, realized, attained असौ this सत्येन

by truth एनम् this, it तपसा by heat, ardor, diligence, austerity यः who अनुपश्यति discerns, perceives, notices [intensely]

1.16 सर्वव्यापिनम् [the] all-pervading आत्मानम् Self क्षीरे in milk सर्पिः butter इव as अर्पितम् fixed upon / आत्मविद्यातपोमूलम् firmly fixed upon through ardor for Self-knowledge तत् that ब्रह्मोपनिषत् [is the] teaching concerning Brahman परम् supreme, highest

2.1 युञ्जानः uniting, joining, harnessing प्रथमम् first मनः [the] mind तत्त्वाय to reach [the] truth सविता Savitṛ धियः thoughts / अग्नेः of fire ज्योतिः [the] light निचाय्य perceiving पृथिव्याः [the] earth अधि out of आभरत् bore, conveyed

2.2 युक्तेन by [being] joined, engaged, intent upon, absorbed, concentrated, attentive मनसा with [the] mind वयम् we देवस्य of [the] effulgent [one] सवितुः of Savitṛ सवे in [the] sun, [the] impeller, [the] one who sets in motion / सुवर्गेयाय in order to lead to heaven, for [the] attainment of bliss शक्त्या by [his] power

2.3 युक्त्वाय yoking, harnessing, making ready मनसा with [the] mind देवान् [the] gods, [the] shining ones सुवर्यतः bliss-aspiring, reaching toward heaven धिया with thought, intelligence, meditation दिवम् to heaven / बृहज्ज्योतिः [the] bright-shining करिष्यतः [those who are] about to do सविता Savitṛ प्रसुवाति impels, incites, rouses, sets in motion तान् them

2.4 युञ्जते they yoke, harness, engage, concentrate मनः [the] mind उत and युञ्जते they yoke, harness, engage, concentrate धियः [the] thoughts विप्राः [the] wise, stirred, inspired [ones] विप्रस्य by [the] wise [one] बृहतः great, bright विपश्चितः all-knowing, learned, wise / वि दधे he creates, forms, establishes, puts into order, ordains (Vedic form) होत्राः [the] priestly functions, rites वयुनावित् learned in

[the] rules, path, way एकः one इत् alone, only, indeed (Vedic particle) मही great [be] देवस्य of [the] effulgent सवितुः Savitṛ परिष्टुतिः [the] praise

2.5 युजे I join, yoke वाम् you two ब्रह्म to Brahman पूर्व्यम् ancient, most excellent नमोभिः with reverential salutations, adoration वि एतु may go forth (Vedic form) श्लोकः praise, hymn of praise पथि on [the] path, course एव thus सूरेः of [the] sage / शृण्वन्तु may hear विश्वे all अमृतस्य of [the] immortal, of [the nectar of] immortality पुत्राः children आ तस्थुः ascended (Vedic form) ये they who धामानि to abodes, dwelling-places दिव्यानि divine, heavenly, celestial

2.6 अग्निः fire यत्र where अभिमथ्यते is kindled (by friction) वायुः air, wind, breath यत्र where अधिरुध्यते is restrained, controlled / सोमः *soma* यत्र where अतिरिच्यते overflows तत्र there सञ्जायते is born, emerges मनः understanding

2.7 सवित्रा by, through Savitṛ प्रसवेन [who is] setting in motion; [the] impulse जुषेत one should delight in ब्रह्म Brahman पूर्व्यम् ancient, most excellent, eternal / तत्र there (in Brahman) योनिम् [the] womb, source, origin; abode, home कृणवसे you should make, accomplish (Vedic subjunctive) न not हि at all ते you पूर्तम fulfilling, fulfillment; meritorious work अक्षिपत् attaches to, binds

2.8 त्रिरुन्नतम् with [the] three (chest, neck, and head) erect स्थाप्य causing to stand, fixing समम् steady, straight, aligned शरीरम् [the] body हृदि into [the] heart इन्द्रियाणि [the] sensory faculties मनसा with, by means of [the] mind सन्निवेश्य causing to enter / ब्रह्मोडुपेन [the] raft of Brahman प्रतरेत may one cross over विद्वान् [a] knower, seer, sage; one who is wise स्रोतांसि [the] currents, streams, rivers, torrents सर्वाणि all भयावहानि fear-bearing, fearful, dreadful

2.9 प्राणान् [the] vital forces प्रपीड्य having controlled इह here [in the body]

संयुक्तचेष्टः [whose] movement of [the] limbs [is] restrained क्षीणे in diminished प्राणे breath नासिकया through [the] nostrils उच्छ्वसीत should breath, should breath again / दुष्टाश्वयुक्तम् yoked to unruly horses इव like, as वाहम् [a] chariot एनम् this, that विद्वान् [the] knower, wise one मनः [the] mind धारयेत should hold, should restrain अप्रमत्तः careful, attentive, vigilant

2.10 समे in [a] level, even, smooth [place] शुचौ clean, pure, holy शर्करावह्निवालुकाविवर्जिते free of pebbles, fire, [and] sand शब्दजलाश्रयादिभिः from connection to sound [and] water / मनोनुकूले pleasing to [the] mind न not तु but चक्षुपीडने painful to [the] eye गुहानिवाताश्रयणे in seeking refuge [in a] hidden [place], cave, sheltered from wind प्रयोजयेत् one should concentrate

2.11 नीहार + धूम + अर्क + अनिल + अनलानाम् mist, smoke, sun, wind, fire खद्योत + विद्युत् + स्फटिक + शशीनाम् firefly, lightning, [quartz] crystal, [the] moon / एतानि these रूपाणि forms पुरःसराणि [are] precursors ब्रह्मणि of Brahman अभिव्यक्तिकराणि causing [the] manifestation योगे in yoga

2.12 पृथिवि + अप् + तेजः + अनिल + खे in earth, water, fire, air, [and] space समुत्थिते arising, appearing, becoming manifest पञ्चात्मके fivefold, consisting of five elements योगगुणे in [the] perception of yoga प्रवृत्ते [when these] emerge / न not तस्य his रोगः disease न not जरा old age न not मृत्युः death प्राप्तस्य he attains योगाग्निमयम् made of the fire of yoga शरीरम् [a] body

2.13 लघुत्वम् lightness [of body]; ease, facility आरोग्यम् freedom from disease; health अलोलुपत्वम् freedom from desire वर्णप्रसादः clarity of complexion स्वरसौष्ठवम् beauty of voice च and / गन्धः odor शुभः pleasant मूत्रपुरीषम् urine [and] feces अल्पम् small योगप्रवृत्तिम् progress in yoga प्रथमाम् first वदन्ति they say

2.14 यथा just इव as बिम्बम् [a] disc, mirror मृदया by dirt उपलिप्तम् covered, coated, smeared, dirtied तेजोमयम् brightly, as full of light भ्राजते shines, glitters, sparkles तत् that सुधान्तम् well-cleaned, purified (Vedic form of *sudhautam*) / तत् that वा very (in the same way, similarly) आत्मतत्त्वम् [the] true nature of [the] soul, reality of [the] Self प्रसमीक्ष्य having observed, perceived, seen देही [the] embodied being एकः one कृतार्थः fulfilled, having attained an object or accomplished [a] purpose भवते becomes वीतशोकः free from sorrow

2.15 यदा when आत्मतत्त्वेन by [the] reality of [the] Self तु very ब्रह्मतत्त्वम् [the] reality of Brahman दीप [a] lamp, light उपमेन like, resembling इह here, in this place (the heart) युक्तः [one who is] joined, established in meditation प्रपश्येत् should see, know, understand / अजम् unborn, birthless, ever being ध्रुवम् fixed, firm, constant, permanent, unchanging सर्वतत्त्वैः of all categories of existence विशुद्धम् completely cleaned, purified ज्ञात्वा knowing देवम् [the] effulgent being, God मुच्यते one is released सर्वपाशैः from all fetters

2.16 एषः this ह very, same देवः effulgent being, God प्रदिशः in all directions अनु one after another (referring to the cardinal points) सर्वाः all पूर्वः first ह very, same जातः born स he उ now, again गर्भे in [the] womb अन्तः within / स he एव alone जातः [is] born स he जनिष्यमाणः [is] to be born प्रत्यङ्ङ् turned toward, facing जनान् [all] beings तिष्ठति stands, remains, continues (in any condition or action), exists, is present सर्वतोमुखः facing in all directions

2.17 यः who देवः god, deity अग्नौ in fire यः who अप्सु in water यः who विश्वम् all भुवनम् [the] universe, creation आविवेश has entered / यः who ओषधीषु in [the] plants यः who वनस्पतिषु in [the] trees तस्मै to that देवाय god नमः salutation नमः salutation

3.1 यः who एकः one, alone, single, same जालवान् possessor of [the] net [of *māyā*] ईशते rules, commands, reigns ईशनीभिः by [his own] commandings सर्वान् all लोकान् worlds ईशते rules [over] ईशनीभिः by [his own] powers / यः who एव only, indeed, surely एकः one उद्भवे in birth, in springing forth, in becoming visible सम्भवे in existence, in being together with or contained in च and ये they who एतत् this विदुः know अमृताः immortal ते they भवन्ति become

3.2 एकः one हि for, because रुद्रः Rudra न not द्वितीयाय second तस्थुः they obey यः who इमान् these लोकान् worlds ईशते rules ईशनीभिः by [his] powers / प्रत्यङ्ङ् turned toward, facing जनान् people, living beings तिष्ठति stands, is present सञ्चुकोच withdraws, contracts अन्तकाले at [the] end of time संसृज्य having projected, partaken of विश्वा all भुवनानि worlds गोपाः guardian

3.3 विश्वतश्चक्षुः [whose] eyes [are] everywhere, on all sides उत and विश्वतोमुखः [whose] faces [are] everywhere, on all sides विश्वतोबाहुः [whose] arms, forearms [are] everywhere, on all sides उत and विश्वतस्पात् [whose] feet [are] everywhere, on all sides / सम् धमति blows, kindles (a fire by blowing), smelts, fuses, melts together (Vedic form) बाहुभ्याम् with [his two] arms संपतत्रैः with bellows (lit., wings, perhaps a kind of fan made of feathers) द्यावाभूमी heaven [and] earth जनयन् causing to be born देवः god एकः one

3.4 यः he who देवानाम् of [the] gods प्रभवः source, origin, cause च and उद्भवः generation, production, becoming visible, existence च and विश्वाधिपः lord of [the] universe रुद्रः Rudra महर्षिः great seer / हिरण्यगर्भम् Hiraṇyagarbha जन-यामास generated, begot, caused to be born, brought into being, projected पूर्वम् in [the] beginning सः he नः us बुद्ध्या with intelligence, reason, mind, intellect, understanding शुभया bright, fit, good, auspicious संयुनक्तु may endow

3.5 या which ते your रुद्र Rudra शिवा auspicious, propitious, gracious, kind, benevolent तनूः body, person, self, form, manifestation अघोरा not terrible, not terrifying अपापकाशिनी not evil-appearing, revealing virtue / तया by that नः us तनुवा form शन्तमया most beneficent, salutary गिरिशन्त mountain-dweller अभिचाकशीहि [do *or* always] look upon, illuminate [thoroughly]

3.6 याम् which इषुम् arrow गिरिशन्त mountain-dweller हस्ते in hand बिभर्षि you hold अस्तवे to shoot / शिवाम् propitious, beneficent गिरित्र mountain-protector ताम् that, it कुरु make मा not हिंसीः injure पुरुषम् man, human जगत् animal (lit., "the moving," in Vedic usage as distinct from a human being)

3.7 ततः परम् beyond that ब्रह्म Brahman परम् supreme बृहन्तम् vast, extended, bright (as a luminous body) यथानिकायम् according to [their] forms, like an assemblage सर्वभूतेषु in all beings गूढम् hidden / विश्वस्य of [the] universe एकम् one, alone परिवेष्टितारम् one who surrounds, encloses, encompasses, embraces ईशम् lord, master तम् that ज्ञात्वा having known, knowing अमृताः immortal भवन्ति they become

3.8 वेद know (Vedic perfect tense with present meaning) अहम् I एतम् this (indicating greatest degree of proximity to the speaker) पुरुषम् person, soul of [the] universe, spirit, conscious principle महान्तम् great, immense, supreme आदित्यवर्णम् sun-colored, effulgent like the sun तमसः darkness परस्तात् beyond / तम् him एव alone विदित्वा having known, by knowing अतिमृत्युम् overcoming death एति he goes न no, not अन्यः other पन्थाः path, way विद्यते there is अयनाय for going

3.9 यस्मात् than he परम् higher, superior, beyond न not अपरम् lower, inferior, different अस्ति there is किंचित् something, anything यस्मात् than he न not अणीयः more minute, smaller न not ज्यायः greater, larger अस्ति there is कश्चित् anyone / वृक्षः tree इव like स्तब्धः immovable, firmly fixed दिवि in [the] heaven, sky तिष्ठति stands एकः one तेन by whom इदम् this पूर्णम् filled पुरुषेण Person सर्वम् all

3.10 ततः than that यत् that which, what उत्तरतरम् still higher, further beyomd तत् that अरूपम् formless अनामयम् without disease / ये they who एतत् this [Brahman] विदुः know अमृताः immortal ते they भवन्ति become अथ but इतरे others, [the] rest दुःखम् suffering, pain, misery एव only, alone, indeed अपियन्ति go near, approach, encounter, enter into

3.11 सर्वाननशिरोग्रीवः having all faces, heads, [and] necks सर्वभूतगुहाशयः abiding in [the] heart (cave, hidden place) of all beings / सर्वव्यापी all-pervading सः he भगवान् [the] glorious Lord तस्मात् therefore सर्वगतः omnipresent, universally diffuse शिवः auspicious, propitious, gracious, benign, benevolent, kind

3.12 महान् great, immense, high, eminent प्रभुः master, lord; [the] excelling, mighty, powerful one वै indeed, truly, certainly पुरुषः Person, conscious principle सत्त्वस्य of mind, mental disposition, character, resolve, self-control एषः this (nearest) प्रवर्तकः acting, proceeding, setting in motion, producing, effecting / सुनिर्मलाम् absolutely pure इमाम् this प्राप्तिम् attainment, gain, occurrence ईशानः ruler, lord, controller; [the] reigning one, [the] ruling one ज्योतिः light अव्ययः imperishable, immutable

3.13 अङ्गुष्ठमात्रः of [the] size of [a] thumb पुरुषः Person अन्तरात्मा inner Self सदा always, ever जनानाम् of all living beings, men हृदये in [the] heart सन्निविष्टः present, established, contained / हृदा by [the] heart मन्वीशः [the]

ruler, lord, of humankind मनसा by [the] mind अभिक्लृप्तः inwardly corresponding to, arranged in accord with ये they who एतत् this विदुः know अमृताः immortal ते they भवन्ति become

3.14 सहस्रशीर्षा having [a] thousand heads, thousand-headed पुरुषः [the] Person, conscious principle सहस्राक्षः having [a] thousand eyes सहस्रपात् having [a] thousand feet / स he भूमिम् [the] earth, [the] world विश्वतस् on all sides, everywhere, all around वृत्वा having surrounded अत्यतिष्ठत् standing beyond, surpasses दशाङ्गुलम् by [the breadth of] ten fingers

3.15 पुरुषः [the] Person एव indeed इदम् this सर्वम् all ("all this," the world) यत् what, that which भूतम् has been यत् what च and भव्यम् will be / उत also, and, even अमृतत्वस्य of immortality ईशानः lord, ruler यत् what अन्नेन by [means of] food अतिरोहति grows beyond, ascends, rises out of, arises from

3.16 सर्वतः on all sides, everywhere पाणिपादम् having hands [and] feet तत् that [Brahman] सर्वतः on all sides, everywhere अक्षिशिरोमुखम् having eyes, heads, [and] faces / सर्वतः on all sides, everywhere श्रुतिमत् having ears लोके in [the] world सर्वम् all, everything आवृत्य having turned towards, enveloping, encompassing, pervading तिष्ठति stands, stations [itself], remains engaged in

3.17 सर्वेन्द्रियगुणाभासम् [whose] splendor, appearance, [is the] qualities [of] all sensory [and] motor faculties सर्वेन्द्रियविवर्जितम् removed, separated, from all [those] faculties / सर्वस्य of all प्रभुम् [the] power ईशानम् ruling सर्वस्य of all शरणम् [the] refuge बृहत् great

3.18 नवद्वारे nine-doored पुरे in [the] city देही [the] embodied [soul or spirit] हंसः soul, spirit (lit., a migratory bird) लेलायते moves to and fro, quivers, shakes

बहिः outside, outward / वशी ruler, lord, master सर्वस्य all लोकस्य of [the] world स्थावरस्य immovable, stationary, fixed चरस्य moving च and

3.19 अपाणिपादः without hands [and] feet जवनः quick, swift, fleet ग्रहीता taking, seizing पश्यति sees अचक्षुः without eyes सः he शृणोति hears अकर्णः without ears / सः he वेत्ति knows वेद्यम् what is to be known न not च and तस्य of him अस्ति there is वेत्ता knower तम him आहुः they call अग्र्यम् foremost पुरुषम् Person, conscious principle महान्तम् great

3.20 अणोः than small, fine, minute अणीयान् smaller, finer, more minute महतः than great महीयान् greater आत्मा [the] Self गुहायाम् in [the] heart, cave, hidden place निहितः [is] placed, laid, fixed. kept in अस्य of this जन्तोः creature, man (collectively, living beings) / तम् him अक्रतुम् [who is] free of, untouched by, desire पश्यति one sees वीतशोकः [becomes] freed from sorrow धातुः of [the] creator, establisher, supporter प्रसादात् by [the] grace महिमानम् greatness, might, majesty, power, glory ईशम् [that is the] Lord

3.21 वेद know (Vedic perfect tense with present meaning) अहम् I एतम् this अजरम् ageless, undecaying पुराणम् primordial, existing from [the] beginning सर्वात्मानम् Self of all सर्वगतम् omnipresent विभुत्वात् by reason of all-pervasiveness / जन्मनिरोधम् restraint of birth, birthlessness प्रवदन्ति declare, proclaim यस्य of whom ब्रह्मवादिनः expounders of Brahman हि indeed, therefore प्रवदन्ति declare नित्यम् eternal

4.1 यः who एकः [is] one अवर्णः colorless, without color बहुधा in many ways शक्तियोगात् by application of [his] power वर्णान् colors अनेकान् many, separate निहितार्थः by [his] set design, purpose दधाति brings forth, produces, creates / च and वि एति goes apart, dissolves, disappears (Vedic form) च and अन्ते in [the] end विश्वम् [the] universe, all आदौ in [the] beginning सः that देवः God, shining one सः he नः us बुद्ध्या with understanding शुभया clear संयुनक्तु may endow

4.2 तत् that, it एव indeed अग्निः Agni, fire तत् that आदित्यः Āditya, [the] sun तत् that वायुः Vāyu, wind तत् that उ also चन्द्रमास् Candramās, [the] moon / तत् that एव indeed शुक्रम् brightness तत् that ब्रह्म Brahman तत् that आपः [the primordial] waters तत् that प्रजापतिः Prajāpati, lord of creatures

4.3 त्वम् you [are] स्त्री woman त्वम् you पुमान् man असि are त्वम् you कुमारः youth उत and, also वा or कुमारी maiden / त्वम् you जीर्णः aged दण्डेन wth [a] staff वञ्चसि you totter about त्वम् you जातः born भवसि become विश्वतोमुखः having faces in all directions; facing everywhere

4.4 नीलः dark blue पतङ्गः butterfly हरितः green parrot लोहिताक्षः red-eyed तडिद्गर्भः thundercloud ऋतवः seasons समुद्राः seas / अनादिमत् without beginning त्वम् you विभुत्वेन by pervasiveness वर्तसे exist यतः from whom जातानि born भुवनानि worlds विश्वा all

4.5 अजाम् [an] unborn [female], she-goat एकाम् one, single लोहितशुक्लकृष्णाम् red, white, [and] black बह्वीः many प्रजाः offspring सृजमानाम् giving birth to, producing सरूपाः of [its] own kind, like itself / अजः [an] unborn [male], he-goat हि indeed एकः one जुषमाणः enjoying, delighting in, taking pleasure in अनुशेते lies beside जहाति gives up, refrains from, abstains from एनाम् her भुक्तभोगाम् [whose] purpose [is] enjoyment अजः unborn [male] अन्यः another

4.6 द्वा two (Vedic form) सुपर्णा having beautiful wings, birds सयुजा inseparable, united सखाया friends, companions समानम् [the] very same वृक्षम् tree परिषस्वजाते cling fast to / तयोः of [the] two अन्यः [the] one पिप्पलम् fruit of the pipal tree (*Ficus religiosa*) स्वादु sweet अत्ति eats अनश्नन् not eating अन्यः [the] other अभिचाकशीति looks on continuously

4.7 समाने very same वृक्षे in [the] tree पुरुषः [the individual] soul निमग्नः sunken, immersed in, plunged into, overwhelmed, fallen into, fixed, stuck अनीशया by powerlessness, impotence शोचति grieves मुह्यमानः deluded, bewildered, confounded / जुष्टम् pleased, propitious, contented यदा when पश्यति sees अन्यम् [the] other ईशम् lord, master, ruler अस्य his महिमानम् greatness, majesty, glory इति thus वीतशोकः freed from sorrow

4.8 ऋचः sacred verse (recited in praise of a deity) अक्षरे imperishable परमे highest, supreme व्योमन् heaven, sky, space यस्मिन् in which देवाः [the] gods अधि निषेदुः reside, repose (Vedic form) विश्वे all / यः he who तम् that, it न not वेद knows किम् what ऋचा with [the] sacred verse करिष्यति will do ये they who इत् alone, only, indeed (equivalent to classical Sanskrit *eva*) तत् that, it विदुः know ते they इमे these [very ones] समासते abide, are satisfied, remain fulfilled

4.9 छन्दांसि sacred verses, [Vedic] hymns, meters यज्ञाः sacrifices, offerings, acts of worship or devotion क्रतवः sacrificial rites, ceremonies, intentions व्रतानि vows, pious observances, religious practices भूतम् what has been, [the] past भव्यम् what will be, [the] future यत् what च and वेदाः [the] Vedas वदन्ति speak of, declare / अस्मात् from it (the *praṇava*) मायी [the] lord or ruler of *māyā* सृजते emits (from himself), projects, produces, creates विश्वम् all, [the] world, universe एतत् this तस्मिन् in it (the world) च and अन्यः [the] other (the *jīva*) मायया by *māyā* सन्निरुद्धः [is] held back, restrained, checked, confined

4.10 मायाम् *māyā* तु surely, indeed प्रकृतिम् nature विद्यात् one should know मायिनम् [the] lord of *māyā*, magician, conjurer च and महेश्वरम् [the] Great

Lord / तस्य his अवयवभूतैः by beings, living creatures, who are [his] parts तु but also व्याप्तम् [is] pervaded, filled सर्वम् all इदम् this जगत् world

4.11 यः he who योनिं योनिम् [every kind of] class, race, caste, living being; womb; source, cause अधितिष्ठति inhabits; rules over, presides over एकः one यस्मिन् in whom इदम् this [universe] सम् [एति] comes together च and वि एति dissolves, comes apart (Vedic forms) च and सर्वम् all / तम् him, that ईशानम् lord, ruler वरदम् giver of blessings, boon-granter देवम् shining, luminous; god ईड्यम् praiseworthy, worthy of adoration निचाय्य having realized इमाम् this शान्तिम् peace अत्यन्तम् exceedingly, perpetually, completely एति goes

4.12 यः he who देवानाम् of [the] gods प्रभवः source, origin, cause च and उद्भवः existence, generation, production, becoming visible च and विश्वाधिपः lord of [the] universe रुद्रः Rudra महर्षिः great seer / हिरण्यगर्भम् Hiraṇyagarbha पश्यत saw जायमानम् being born सः he नः us बुद्ध्या with intelligence, reason, intellect, understanding शुभया bright, fit, good, auspicious संयुनक्तु may endow

4.13 यः he who देवानाम् of [the] gods अधिपः ruler, regent, king, lord यस्मिन् in whom लोकाः [the] worlds अधिश्रिताः [are] placed; rest, reside / यः he who ईशे (Vedic form) rules अस्य this द्विपदः two-footed (human beings) चतुष्पदः four-footed (cattle and other animals) कस्मै what, which देवाय god हविषा with oblation विधेम are we to worship

4.14 सूक्ष्मातिसूक्ष्मम् subtler than [the] subtlest कलिलस्य of chaos, [the] unformed मध्ये in [the] middle विश्वस्य of everything, of [the] universe स्रष्टारम् [the] creator अनेकरूपम् having many forms / विश्वस्य of [the] universe एकम् one, alone परिवेष्टितारम् [the] encompasser ज्ञात्वा having known, knowing शिवम् [the] auspicious one शान्तिम् peace अत्यन्तम् beyond limit एति attains

4.15 सः he एव surely, indeed काले in time भुवनस्य of [the] world गोप्ता [the] protector विश्वाधिपः [the] lord of [the] universe सर्वभुतेषु in all beings गूढः hidden / यस्मिन् in whom युक्ताः joined, merged, absorbed ब्रह्मर्षयः seers of Brahman देवताः gods, deities च and तम् him एवम् thus ज्ञात्वा knowing, having, known मृत्युपाशान् [the] bonds, fetters, of death छिनत्ति one cuts through

4.16 घृतात् than clarified butter परम् finer, superior मण्डम् essence; the film on clarified butter or boiled grain इव like अतिसूक्ष्मम् exceedlingly subtle ज्ञात्वा having known, knowing शिवम् [the] auspicious [one] सर्वभुतेषु in all beings गूढम् hidden / विश्वस्य of [the] universe एकम् one, alone परिवेष्टितारम् [the] encompasser ज्ञात्वा having known, knowing देवम् [the] effulgent being मुच्यते one is freed, released सर्वपाशैः from all fetters

4.17 एषः this (nearest degree of proximity) देवः god विश्वकर्मा [the] maker of [the] universe महात्मा [the] great Self सदा always, ever जनानाम् of all living beings, creatures, men हृदये in [the] heart सन्निविष्टः present, established, contained / हृदा by [the] heart मनीषा by thought, reflection, wisdom, intelligence मनसा by [the] mind (by all mental powers) अभिक्लृप्तः inwardly corresponding to, arranged in accord with ये they who एतत् this विदुः know अमृताः immortal ते they भवन्ति become

4.18 यदा when अतमस् non-darkness, non-ignorance, knowledge तत् then न neither दिवा day न nor रात्रिः night न neither सत् existence न nor च as well as (emphatic particle) असत् nonexistence शिवः [the] auspicious [one] एव only, indeed केवलः alone, one, absolute / तत् that अक्षरम् imperishable तत् that सवितुः of Savitṛ वरेण्यम् [that which is] to be wished for, desirable, excellent प्रज्ञा wisdom, knowledge च and तस्मात् from that प्रसृता come forth, issued forth, proceeded पुराणी ancient

4.19 न not एनम् him ऊर्ध्वम् above न not तिर्यञ्चम् across न not मध्ये in [the] middle परिजग्रभत् one grasps fully / न not तस्य of him प्रतिमा likeness, image; measure अस्ति there is यस्य whose नाम name महत् great यशः glory

4.20 न not संदृशे in [the range of] sight तिष्ठति stands रूपम् form अस्य his न not चक्षुषा with [the] eye पश्यति sees कश्चन anyone एनम् him / हृदा with [the] heart हृदिस्थम् abiding in [the] heart मनसा with [the] mind ये they who एनम् him एवम् thus विदुः know अमृताः immortal ते they भवन्ति become

4.21 अजातः unborn, not yet developed इति thus, "as you know" एवम् surely कश्चित् someone भीरुः fearful प्रपद्यते takes refuge / रुद्र O Rudra यत् that [which is] ते your दक्षिणम् benevolent, propitious मुखम् face तेन by that माम् me पाहि protect नित्यम् always

4.22 मा [do] not (a particle expressing prohibition) नः us तोके in [respect to] children तनये in grandchildren मा not नः our आयुषि life, duration of life, health मा not नः our गोषु in cattle मा not नः our अश्वेषु in horses रीरिषः harm, injure / वीरान् heroes मा not नः our रुद्र O Rudra भामितः angered, enraged वधीः slay हविष्मन्तः possessing, bearing oblations सदम् always इत् thus त्वा you हवामहे we invoke, worship

5.1 द्वे two अक्षरे in [the] imperishable ब्रह्मपरे in [the] supreme Brahman तु and अनन्ते in [the] infinite विद्याविद्ये knowledge [and] ignorance निहिते [are] laid, placed, fixed, kept in यत्र wherein गूढे hidden, concealed, invisible / क्षरम् perishable तु surely अविद्या ignorance हि therefore अमृतम् immortal तु and विद्या knowledge विद्याविद्ये knowledge [and] ignorance ईशते rules over, controls यः he who तु but सः he अन्यः another

5.2 यः who योनिं योनिम् every kind of being अधितिष्ठति inhabits, presides over एकः one विश्वानि all रूपाणि forms, outward appearances, phenomena योनीः sources च and सर्वाः all / ऋषिम् seer, inspired poet or sage प्रसूतम् procreated, begotten, born, produced, sprung कपिलम् brown, tawny, reddish; sunlike यः he who तम् him अग्रे in [the] beginning ज्ञानैः by knowledge(s) बिभर्ति contains, holds, bears जायमानम् being born च and पश्येत् sees

5.3 एकैकम् one by one, every single one जालम् net, snare बहुधा variously, in many ways विकुर्वन् extending, spreading out अस्मिन् in this क्षेत्रे field संहरति withdraws, gathers in एषः this देवः god, effulgent being / भूयः moreover, besides, further, again सृष्ट्वा having projected, created पतयः [as the] lords तथा thus, likewise ईशः [the] Lord सर्वाधिपत्यम् lordship over all कुरुते does, exercises महात्मा [the] great Self

5.4 सर्वाः all दिशः directions ऊर्ध्वम् above अधः below च and तिर्यक् across प्रकाशयन् illumining भ्राजते shines यत् उ just as अनड्वान् [the] sun (lit., an ox or bull) / एवम् so, in that way सः that, the देवः god ("the shining one") भगवान् glorious वरेण्यः to be desired, worthy of adoration योनिस्वभावान् [those whose] true nature [is the] source अधितिष्ठति rules over, dwells in, inhabits एकः one

5.5 यत् just as च and स्वभावम् [its] own nature पचति develops, matures विश्वयोनिः [the] source of [the] universe पाच्यान् those things that are capable of being matured, which are potential च and सर्वान् all [things] परिणामयेत् transforms यः who / सर्वम् all एतत् this विश्वम् universe अधितिष्ठति presides over एकः one गुणान् qualities च and, yet सर्वान् all विनियोजयेत् distributes, apportions यः who

5.6 तत् that [Brahman] वेदगुह्योपनिषत्सु to be kept secret in [the] Upaniṣads of

[the] Vedas गूढम् hidden तत् that [Brahman] ब्रह्मा Brahmā वेदते knows ब्रह्मयोनिम् [to be the] source of expansion (or of Brahmā [himself], or of [the] Vedas) / ये who पूर्वम् formerly, of old देवाः [the] gods ऋषयः seers च and तत् that [Brahman] विदुः knew, realized ते they तन्मयाः made up of that, absorbed in that, identical to that अमृताः immortal वै truly, indeed बभूवुः became

5.7 गुणान्वयः having qualities, characterized by [the] *guṇas* यः he who फलकर्मकर्ता [the] doer of action that bears fruit कृतस्य of actions, deeds तस्य his एव indeed, surely सः he च and, but उपभोक्ता [the] enjoyer, experiencer / सः that विश्वरूपः manifold, assuming all (or various) forms त्रिगुणः "three-*guṇaed*," characterized by [the] three basic energies त्रिवर्त्मा "three-pathed," having three ways or courses प्राणाधिपः [the] master of [the] vital breath [the individual soul] सञ्चरति roams, wanders, moves about स्वकर्मभिः according to [his] own deeds

5.8 अङ्गुष्ठमात्रः of [the] size of [a] thumb रवितुल्यरूपः of sunlike appearance सङ्कल्पाहङ्कारसमन्वितः endowed with intent [and] individuality (volition and ego-sense) यः who / बुद्धेः of intelligence गुणेन by [the] attribute आत्मगुणेन by [the] attribute of the physical body च and एव as well, also आराग्रमात्रः of [the] size of [the] point of [an] awl अपि indeed अपरः distinct [from Brahman], lower, inferior अपि also दृष्टः [is] seen

5.9 वालाग्रशतभागस्य of [the] hundredth part of [the] tip of [a] hair शतधा [a] hundred times कल्पितस्य divided च and / भागः [as a] fraction जीवः individual soul सः the विज्ञेयः should be recognized, discerned, rightly known सः it च yet अनन्त्याय to (of) infinity कल्पते partakes, is capable

5.10 न neither एव surely, truly, indeed स्त्री woman न nor पुमान् man एषः this (the *jīva*) न not च and एव certainly अयम् this नपुंसकः neuter / यत् यत्

whatever शरीरम् body आदत्ते [it] assumes तेन तेन by that, with each सः he, it युज्यते is joined, connected, associated

5.11 सङ्कल्पन + स्पर्शन + दृष्टि + मोहैः by intention (purpose), touch (perception, interaction), sight (outlook, understanding), [and] delusion (misapprehension) ग्रास + अम्बु + वृष्ट्या by [the] raining (abundance, bounty) of food [and] drink आत्म + विवृद्धि + जन्म [are sustained] [the] life (longevity) [and] growth of [the] body / कर्मानुगानि according to [its] actions अनुक्रमेण successively देही [the] embodied [soul] स्थानेषु in [various] conditions रूपाणि forms अभिसम्प्रपद्यते assumes

5.12 स्थूलानि gross सूक्ष्माणि subtle बहूनि many च and एव indeed, surely रूपाणि forms देही [the] embodied being स्वगुणैः by [its] own merits वृणोति chooses (assumes) / क्रियागुणैः by [the] qualities of [its] actions आत्मगुणैः by [the] qualities of [their] individual character; च and तेषाम् their संयोगहेतुः impelled by [the] conjunction अपरः inferior, different अपि even, moreover दृष्टः [is] seen

5.13 अनाद्यनन्तम् without beginning or end, eternal कलिलस्य of confusion, disorder, primordial chaos मध्ये in [the] middle विश्वस्य of everything, of [the] universe स्रष्टारम् [the] creator अनेकरूपम् having many forms, having diverse forms / विश्वस्य of [the] universe एकम् one, alone परिवेष्टितारम् [the] encompasser ज्ञात्वा having known, knowing देवम् [the] effulgent being मुच्यते one is freed, released सर्वपाशैः from all fetters

5.14 अभावग्राह्यम् grasped, perceived, understood by [the] heart, mind अनीडाख्यम् called [the one] without [a] nest, resting-place, abode; called incorporeal भावाभावकरम् [the] maker of existence [and] nonexistence, of appearance [and] non-appearance शिवम् auspicious, beneficent / कलासर्गकरम्

[the] maker of creation [and its] parts (or elements) देवम् effulgent ये they who विदुः know ते they जहुः lay aside, give up तनुम् [the] small, [the] minute, [the] sense of individual personhood

6.1 स्वभावम् inherent nature एके some कवयः thinkers, knowing ones, learned ones वदन्ति speak of कालम् time तथा likewise अन्ये others परिमुह्यमानाः of bewildered mind; of confused thinking / देवस्य of God एषः this महिमा greatness, might, glory, majesty तु but लोके in [the] world येन by which इदम् this भ्राम्यते is turned ब्रह्मचक्रम् wheel of Brahman

6.2 येन by whom आवृतम् encompassed, surrounded, overspread नित्यम् always इदम् this हि therefore, indeed सर्वम् all ज्ञः knowing, intelligent, wise [the conscious principle] कालकारः [the] maker of time गुणी [the] possessor of qualities सर्वविद् all-knowing, omniscient यः who / तेन by him ईशितम् commanded, directed, ordained कर्म work, product, effect विवर्तते turns around, revolves, expands, develops ह indeed, assuredly, of course पृथिवी + अप् + तेजः + अनिल + खानि [as] earth, water, fire, air, [and] space (the five physical elements) चिन्त्यम् [is] to be thought about, reflected on, considered

6.3 तत् that कर्म work [of creation] कृत्वा having made, done विनिवर्त्य withdrawing, turning away भूयः again तत्त्वस्य of principle तत्त्वेन with principle समेत्य bringing about योगम् [the] joining / एकेन by one द्वाभ्याम् by two त्रिभिः by three अष्टभिः by eight वा and कालेन by time च and एव indeed आत्मगुणैः by [the] qualities of mind [and] body च and सूक्ष्मैः weak, feeble

6.4 आरभ्य having undertaken कर्माणि actions, works गुणान्वितानि associated with qualities भावान् conditions, states च and सर्वान् all विनियोजयेत् undoes, disjoins यः who / तेषाम् their अभावे in nonexisiting कृतकर्मनाशः [the]

destroyer of created works कर्मक्षये in [the] perishing of works याति continues, goes on सः he तत्त्वतः according to [his] own nature अन्यः other, different

6.5 आदिः beginning सः he संयोगनिमित्तहेतुः [the] efficient cause of conjunction परः beyond त्रिकालात् [the] three times (past, present, and future) अकलः without parts, entire अपि surely, even, also दृष्टः [is] seen / तम् him विश्वरूपम् [whose] form [is the] universe भवभूतम् [the] essence of existence ईड्यम् to be revered, praiseworthy देवम् [the] effulgent one, God स्वचित्तस्थम् abiding in one's own consciousness उपास्य having revered, worshiped पूर्वम् first

6.6 सः he वृक्ष + काल + आकृतिभिः [the] constituent parts, aspects, of [the] tree [and] time परः higher than, beyond अन्यः other than, different from यस्मात् because of whom प्रपञ्चः manifestation, expansion [of the universe], diversity परिवर्तते revolves, turns around अयम् this / धर्मावहम् bringing goodness, virtue पापनुदम् removing, driving away evil भगेशम् [the] lord of prosperity, blessedness ज्ञात्वा having known, knowing आत्मस्तम् abiding in [the] self अमृतम् immortal विश्वधाम [the] support, seat, of all

6.7 तम् that, the, him ईश्वराणाम् of lords परमम् supreme महेश्वरम् great lord तम् that, the, him देवतानाम् of gods, deities परमम् supreme च and दैवतम् god, deity / पतिम् sovereign, ruler, master पतीनाम् of sovereigns, rules, masters परमम् supreme परस्तात् beyond, over, above विदाम may we know देवम् [the] shining one, god भुवनेशम् [the] lord of prosperity, good fortune, well-being, divine glories ईड्यम् to be glorified, adored; praiseworthy

6.8 न not तस्य his, of him कार्यम् [something] to be made or done; duty; need; aim, purpose करणम् act of doing; instrument of action; organ of sense च and विद्यते exists न not तत्समः equal to him च and अभ्यधिकः superior;

surpassing च and दृश्यते is seen / परा supreme अस्य of this; his शक्तिः power, energy, force विविधा of various sorts, manifold, diverse एव indeed, truly श्रूयते is heard स्वाभाविकी of one's own being, natural, inherent ज्ञानबलक्रिया [the] doing of [his] intelligence [and] might च and

6.9 न not तस्य his, of him कश्चित् any पतिः master, ruler, lord अस्ति there is लोके in [the] world न not च and ईशिता master न and एव indeed, surely च and तस्य his, of him लिङ्गम् distinguishing sign, mark / सः he कारणम् [the] cause करणाधिपाधिपः [the] lord of [the] lord of [the] senses न not च not अस्य of this, his कश्चित् any जनिता progenitor न nor चाधिपः lord, ruler, master

6.10 यः who तन्तुनाभः [a] spider इव like तन्तुभिः with [its] threads, filaments, web प्रधानजैः with [the] products of [his] unevolved nature स्वभावतः naturally, spontaneously; by [his] inherent nature / देवः [the] god एकः one स्वम् himself आवृणोति surrounds, covers, conceals सः he नः us दधात् may put (Vedic subjunctive) ब्रह्माप्ययम् [into] entry into, union with, Brahman

6.11 एकः one देवः god सर्वभूतेषु in all beings गूढः hidden सर्वव्यापी all-pervading सर्वभूतान्तरात्मा [the] inner self (soul) of all creatures / कर्माध्यक्षः overseeing [the] work (the created universe) सर्वभूताधिवासः dwelling in all beings साक्षी witnessing चेता observer केवलः alone, isolated, absolute निर्गुणः without attributes, devoid of qualities च and

6.12 एकः one वशी lord, controller, ruler, master निष्क्रियाणाम् of [the] actionless (those exempt from the performance of ritual) बहूनाम् many एकम् one बीजम् seed बहुधा manifold यः who करोति makes / तम् him आत्मस्थम् abiding in themselves ये they who अनुपश्यन्ति perceive, discover, consider, reflect on धीराः steady, self-possessed, constant, composed, calm तेषाम्

theirs, of them सुखम् happiness शाश्वतम् eternal, perpetual, constant न not इतरेषाम् of others

6.13 नित्यः [the] eternal नित्यानाम् of eternals चेतनः [the] intelligent चेतनानाम् of [those that are] intelligent एकः [the] one बहूनाम् among [the] many यः who विदधाति fulfills कामान् desires / तत् that, the कारणम् cause सांख्ययोगाधिगम्यम् to be discovered through analysis [and] application ज्ञात्वा knowing, realizing देवम् [the] effulgent being, God मुच्यते one is freed, released सर्वपाशैः from all fetters

6.14 न not तत्र there सूर्यः [the] sun भाति shines न not चन्द्रतारकम् [the] moon [and] stars न not इमाः these विद्युतः lightnings भान्ति shine कुतस् much less अयम् this अग्निः [earthly] fire / तम् him एव alone, indeed, truly भान्तम् shining अनुभाति shines after सर्वम् all, everything तस्य his भासा light, brightness, splendor सर्वम् all इदम् this [universe] विभाति shines forth, appears

6.15 एकः one हंसः swan (the supreme Self) भुवनस्य world अस्य of this मध्ये in [the] midst सः he एव alone, indeed अग्निः fire सलिले in water संनिविष्टः submerged / तम् him एव alone विदित्वा having known, by knowing अतिमृत्युम् overcoming death एति he goes न no, not अन्यः other पन्थाः path, way विद्यते there is अयनाय for going

6.16 सः he विश्वकृत् all-doing, all-making विश्ववित् all-knowing आत्मयोनिः self-originated (or [the] source of souls) ज्ञः intelligent, knowing कालकारः maker of time गुणी possessor of qualities सर्वविद्यः omniscient, all-knowing / प्रधान + क्षेत्रज्ञ + पतिः [the] master of material nature [and the] individual soul गुणेशः [the] lord of the (three) universal energies or qualities संसार + मोक्ष + स्थिति +

बन्ध + हेतुः the cause of bondage to continuing existence [and] release from [the soul's] wandering

6.17 सः he तन्मयः identical with that (the cause of release from bondage to continuing existence and from transmigration) हि therefore अमृतः immortal ईशसंस्थः abiding as lord ज्ञः knowing सर्वगः omnipresent, all-pervading भुवनस्य of [the] world अस्य of this गोप्ता protector, guardian, preserver / यः he who ईशे is [the] master (Vedic form) अस्य of this जगतः of [the] world नित्यम् always, eternally एव indeed, surely न no अन्यः other हेतुः cause, impulse विद्यते there is ईशनाय for controlling

6.18 यः who ब्रह्माणम् Brahmā विदधाति creates, effects, produces, establishes पूर्वम् at first, in [the] beginning यः who वै indeed, surely वेदान् [the] Vedas च and प्रहिणोति bestows तस्मै on him / तम् [in] that ह very देवम् God आत्मबुद्धिप्रकाशम् shining by [his] own intelligence मुमुक्षुः desirous of liberation, strving for freedom वै surely, truly शरणम् refuge अहम् I प्रपद्ये take

6.19 निष्कलम् without parts, undivided निष्क्रियम् without action, actionless शान्तम् peaceful, tranquil निरवद्यम् faultless, blameless, beyond reproach निरञ्जनम् untainted, pure, simple, stainless / अमृतस्य of immortality परम् highest सेतुम् bridge दग्धेन्धनम् [whose] fuel (or blazing) [is] consumed इव like अनलम् fire

6.20 यदा when चर्मवत् like an animal skin, hide, piece of leather आकाशम् free or open space, sky वेष्टयिष्यन्ति will cause to roll up मानवाः men, people, human beings / तदा then देवम् God अविज्ञाय for [the] not knowing दुःखस्य of suffering, misery अन्तः end भविष्यति there will be

6.21 तपःप्रभावात् by [the] power of austerity देवप्रसादात् by [the] grace of God च and ब्रह्म Brahman ह that very (previously spoken of) श्वेताश्वतरः Śvetāśvatara अथ thus, here, now विद्वान् knowing / अत्याश्रमिभ्यः to those beyond [the] stages of life परमम् highest, supreme पवित्रम् means of purification प्रोवाच proclaimed, taught, imparted सम्यक् + ऋषि + सङ्घ + जुष्टम् rightly, correctly, delighted in [by the] multitude, host, company [of] seers

6.22 वेदान्ते in [the] Vedānta (the teaching of the Upaniṣads) परमम् [the] highest, supreme गुह्यम् secret, mystery पुराकल्पे in [a] former age, cycle प्रचोदितम् imparted, proclaimed, taught / न not अप्रशान्ताय to one of unsubdued passions दातव्यम् [is] to be given न nor अपुत्राय to [one who is] not [a] son अशिष्याय to [one who is] not [a] disciple वा or पुनः again

6.23 यस्य of whom देवे in God परा [the] highest, supreme भक्तिः devotion यथा as, in which way देवे in God तथा so, in that way गुरौ in [the] teacher / तस्य of whom एते these कथिताः related, spoken, told हि indeed अर्थाः matters, things, topics, subjects प्रकाशन्ते shine forth, become evident, become revealed महात्मनः to [the] great-souled [one], to [the] noble [one] / प्रकाशन्ते they shine forth महात्मन to [the] great-souled [one] इति thus

APPENDIX B
TEXTUAL CORRESPONDENCES

Dating Indian texts with any degree of precision is highly problematical. However, those listed below can generally be classified as either older or more recent than the Śvetāśvataropaniṣad. Older texts are the Ṛgvedasaṁhitā, Taittirīyasaṁhitā, Vājasaneyisaṁhitā, Atharvaveda (Books 1–13), Śatapathabrāhmaṇa, Taittirīyabrāhmaṇa, Taittirīyāraṇyaka (Books 1–9), Bṛhadāraṇyakopaniṣad, and Kaṭhopaniṣad. Texts composed after the Śvetāśvataropaniṣad are the Atharvaveda (Books 14–20), Muṇḍakopaniṣad, Mahānārāyanopaniṣad (Book 10 of the Taittirīyāraṇyaka), and Bhagavadgītā.

ABBREVIATIONS

AV	Atharvaveda	ṚV	Ṛgvedasaṁhitā
BhG	Bhagavadgītā	ŚB	Śatapathabrāhmaṇa
BṛU	Bṛhadāraṇyakopaniṣad	ŚU	Śvetāśvataropaniṣad
KaU	Kaṭhopaniṣad	TĀ	Taittirīyāraṇyaka
MnU	Mahānārāyaṇopaniṣad (Āndhra recension)	TB	Taittirīyabrāhmaṇa
		TS	Taittirīyasaṁhitā
MuU	Muṇḍakopaniṣad	VS	Vājasaneyisaṁhitā

TABLE 1
VERSES QUOTED FROM EARLIER SOURCES

References in Roman type are identical to the *mantras* of the Śvetāśvataropaniṣad shown in the first column; those in italics are variants. The letters *a, b, c,* and *d* designate the quarters (*pādas*) within a verse.

ŚU 2.1ad	TS 4.1.1.1ad	VS 11.1ad	ŚB 6.3.1.12–13ad
ŚU 2.1b	TS 4.1.1.1b	*VS 11.1b*	*ŚB 6.3.1.12–13b*
ŚU 2.1c	*TS 4.1.1.1c*	VS 11.1c	ŚB 6.3.1.12–13c
ŚU 2.2ab	TS 4.1.1.3	VS 11.2	ŚB 6.3.1.14
ŚU 2.2c	TS 4.1.1.3c	*VS 11.2*	*ŚB 6.3.1.14*

ŚU 2.3a	TS 4.1.1.2a	*VS 11.3*	*ŚB 6.3.1.15*	
ŚU 2.3bcd	TS 4.1.1.2	VS 11.3	ŚB 6.3.1.15	
ŚU 2.4	ṚV 5.81.1	TS 1.2.13.1	TS 4.1.1.4	VS 5.14
	VS 11.4	VS 37.2	ŚB 3.5.3.11	ŚB 6.3.1.16
ŚU 2.5ad	ṚV 10.13.1ad	TS 4.1.1.5ad	VS 11.5ad	ŚB 6.3.1.17ad
ŚU 2.5bc	ṚV 10.13.1bc	*TS 4.1.1.5bc*	VS 11.5bc	ŚB 6.3.1.17bc
ŚU 2.7c	*ṚV 6.16.17d*			
ŚU 2.7d	ṚV 6.16.18a			
ŚU 2.16	VS 32.4			
ŚU 2.17	*TS 5.5.9.3*	*AV 7.87*		
ŚU 3.1d	*BṛU 4.4.14c*			
ŚU 3.3	ṚV 10.81.3	*VS 17.19*	*TS 4.6.2.4*	*AV 13.2.26*
ŚU 3.5	TS 4.5.1.1	VS 16.2		
ŚU 3.6	TS 4.5.1.2	VS 16.3		
ŚU 3.8	VS 31.18			
ŚU 3.10cd	*BṛU 4.4.14cd*			
ŚU 3.13ab	KaU 2.3.17ab			
ŚU 3.13cd	*KaU 2.3.9cd*			
ŚU 3.13d	*BṛU 4.4.14c*			
ŚU 3.14	ṚV 10.90.1	VS 31.1	TĀ 3.12.1	
ŚU 3.15	ṚV 10.90.2	VS 31.2	TĀ 3.12.1	
ŚU 3.20	*KaU 1.2.20*			
ŚU 4.2	VS 32.1			
ŚU 4.3	AV 10.8.27			
ŚU 4.6	ṚV 1.164.20			
ŚU 4.8	ṚV 1.164.39	TB 3.10.9, 14	TĀ 2.11.1	AV 9.10.18
ŚU 4.11d	KaU 1.1.17			
ŚU 4.13c	VS 20.20.32b			
ŚU 4.13cd	ṚV 10.121.3cd			
ŚU 4.13d	VS 32.6d			
ŚU 4.17cd	KaU 2.3.9cd			
ŚU 4.17d	*BṛU 4.4.14c*			
ŚU 4.19	VS 32.2cd–3ab			
ŚU 4.20ab	KaU 2.3.9ab			
ŚU 4.20cd	*KaU 2.3.9cd*			
ŚU 4.22a	*ṚV 1.114.8a*	TS 4.5.10.3a	VS 16.16a	
ŚU 4.22b	ṚV 1.114.8b	TS 4.5.10.3b	VS 16.16b	
ŚU 4.22c	ṚV 1.114.8c	TS 4.5.10.3c	*VS 16.16c*	
ŚU 4.22d	ṚV 1.114.8d	*TS 4.5.10.3d*	VS 16.16d	
ŚU 6.12cd	KaU 2.2.12cd	*KaU 2.3.13cd*		
ŚU 6.13a	*KaU 2.2.13a*			
ŚU 6.13b	KaU 2.2.13b			
ŚU 6.14	KaU 2.2.15			
ŚU 6.15cd	VS 31.18cd			

TABLE 2
VERSES QUOTED IN LATER TEXTS

The asterisk indicates verses attested for the first time in the Śvetāśvataropaniṣad and apparently original to it. The unmarked verses come from older sources (as shown in Table 1) and appear also in later texts as shown here.

ŚU 2.5abc	*AV 18.3.39*
ŚU 3.4acd*	*MnU 12.12acd*
ŚU 3.4b*	MnU 12.12b
ŚU 3.9*	MnU 12.13
ŚU 3.14	AV 19.6.1
ŚU 3.15	AV 19.6.4
ŚU 3.16*	BhG 13.13
ŚU 3.17ab*	BhG 13.14ab
ŚU 3.20	MnU 12.1
ŚU 4.6	MuU 3.1.1
ŚU 4.7	MuU 3.1.2
ŚU 4.12ad*	*MnU 12.12ad*
ŚU 4.12bc*	MnU 12.12bc
ŚU 4.19	*MnU 1.10*
ŚU 4.20ab	MnU 1.11ab
ŚU 4.20cd	*MnU 1.11cd*
ŚU 6.14	MuU 2.2.10

TABLE 3
INTERNAL CORRESPONDENCES

ŚU 1.8d	2.15d	4.16d	5.13.d	6.13d
ŚU 2.15d	1.8d	4.16d	5.13.d	6.13d
ŚU 3.1d	3.10c	3.13d	4.17d	*4.20d*
ŚU 3.4ab	4.12ab			
ŚU 3.4c	*4.12c*			
ŚU 3.4d	4.1d	4.12d		
ŚU 3.7c	414c	4.16c	5.13c	
ŚU 3.8cd	6.15cd			
ŚU 3.10c	3.1d	3.13d	4.17d	*4.20d*
ŚU 3.13bd	4.17bd			
ŚU 3.13c	*4.17c*			
ŚU 3.13d	3.1d	3.10c	*4.20d*	
ŚU 4.1d	3.4d	4.12d		
ŚU 4.11a	5.2a			
ŚU 4.12ab	3.4ab			
ŚU 4.12c	*3.4c*			
ŚU 4.12d	3.4d	4.1d		
ŚU 4.14a	*5.13a*			

ŚU 4.14b	5.13b			
ŚU 4.14c	3.7c	4.16c	5.13c	
ŚU 4.16c	3.7c	4.14c	5.13c	
ŚU 4.16d	1.8d	2.15d	5.13d	6.13d
ŚU 4.17bd	3.13bd			
ŚU 4.17c	*3.13c*			
ŚU 4.17d	3.1d	3.10c	*4.20d*	
ŚU 4.20d	*3.1d*	*3.10c*	*3.13d*	*4.17d*
ŚU 5.2a	4.11a			
ŚU 5.13a	414.a			
ŚU 5.13b	4.14b			
ŚU 5.13c	3.7c	4.14c	4.16c	
ŚU 5.13d	1.8d	2.15d	4.16d	6.13d
ŚU 6.2b	6.16b			
ŚU 6.13d	1.8d	2.15d	4.16d	5.13.d
ŚU 6.15cd	3.8cd			
ŚU 6.16b	6.2b			

NOTES

INTRODUCTION: TEXT AND CONTEXT

1. F. Max Müller, trans., *The Upanishads, Part II* (Oxford: Clarendon Press, 1884), xxxii–xxxiii.
2. Ibid., xlii.
3. Paul Deussen, *Sixty Upaniṣads of the Veda,* trans. V. M. Bedeker and G. B. Palsule, 2 vols. (Delhi: Motilal Banarsidass, 1980), 1:301–302.
4. Ibid., 303.
5. Robert Ernest Hume, *The Thirteen Principal Upanishads* (London: Oxford University Press, 1921), 8–9.
6. Swāmī Tyāgīśānanda, *Śvetāśvatara Upaniṣad,* 7th ed. (Mylapore, Madras: Sri Ramakrishna Math, 1979), 4.
7. Swami Nikhilananda, trans., *The Upanishads,* 4 vols. (New York: Ramakrishna-Vivekananda Center, 1952), 2:37–39.
8. S. Radhakrishnan, trans. *The Principal Upaniṣads* (1953; reprint ed., New Delhi: HarperCollins India, 1994), 707.
9. Gerald James Larson, *Classical Sāṁkhya,* 2nd ed. (Delhi: Motilal Banarsidass, 1979), 200–202.
10. Swāmī Gambhīrānanda, *Śvetāśvatara Upaniṣad* (Calcutta: Advaita Ashrama, 1986), vi.
11. Swami Lokeswarananda, trans., *Śvetāśvatara Upaniṣad* (Calcutta: Ramakrishna Mission Institute of Culture, 1994), 7–8.
12. Patrick Olivelle, *Upaniṣads* (Oxford: Oxford University Press, 1996), 252.
13. Swami Vedananda, *The Svetasvatara Upanishad* (Gurnee, Illinois: Scars Publications, 2001), 8.
14. Valerie Roebuck, *The Upaniṣads,* rev. ed. (London: Penguin Books, 2003), 447–448.
15. Félix G. Ilárraz and Òscar Pujol, *La sabiduría del bosque* (Madrid: Editorial Trotta, 2003), 311.
16. Edwin Bryant, *The Quest for the Origins of Vedic Culture* (Oxford: Oxford University Press, 2001), 243–244.
17. William Dwight Whitney, *Sanskrit Grammar,* 2nd ed. (Cambridge: Harvard University Press, 1889), xv.
18. Manoranjan Basu, *Fundamentals of the Philosophy of Tantras* (Calcutta: Mira Basu Publishers, 1986), 20.
19. Bryant, 244–246.
20. Shrikant G. Talageri, *The Rigveda: A Historical Analysis* (New Delhi: Aditya Prakashan, 2000), 38.
21. S. P. Gupta, "The Sarasvatī and the Homeland of Early Ṛigvedic Ṛishis," in *In Search of Vedic-Harappan Relationship,* ed. Ashvini Agrawal (New Delhi: Aryan Books International, 2005), 59, 66.
22. Shivaji Singh, "Need of a New Paradigm," in *In Search of Vedic-Harappan Relationship,* ed. Agrawal, 156.

23. Ibid.
24. Ibid., 155–156.
25. Ibid.
26. Moti Lal Pandit, *The Trika Śaivism of Kashmir* (New Delhi: Munshiram Manoharlal, 2003), 50.
27. Narendra Nath Bhattacharyya, *History of the Tantric Religion* (New Delhi: Manohar, 1992), 174.
28. Jan Gonda, *Viṣṇuism and Śivaism: A Comparison* (New Delhi: Munshiram Manoharlal, 1970), 18.
29. Müller, xxxiv.
30. Ibid., xxxi.
31. Ibid., xxxiv–xxxv.
32. Ibid., xxxv.
33. Ibid., xli–xlii.
34. Deussen, 1:302–303.
35. Larson, 138–139.
36. Ibid., 64.
37. Ibid., 65.
38. Ibid., 71.
39. Ibid., 95.
40. Ibid., 154.
41. Ibid., 72.
42. Ibid., 98.
43. Ibid., 72.
44. Ibid., 113–117.
45. Ibid., 72.
46. Ibid., 172.
47. Moti Lal Pandit, *The Disclosure of Being* (New Delhi: Munshiram Manoharlal, 2006), 96.
48. Larson, 172–173.
49. M. L. Pandit, *Disclosure*, 96.
50. Larson, 155–156.
51. Ibid., 90–91.
52. Müller, xxxvi–xxxvii.
53. José Pereira, "Bādarāyaṇa," in *Great Thinkers of the Eastern World*, ed. Ian P. McGreal (New York: HarperCollins, 1995), 170.
54. Bina Gupta, "Gauḍapāda," in *Great Thinkers*, ed. McGreal, 207.
55. Nikhilananda, *Upanishads*, 2:205.
56. Gupta, "Gauḍapāda," 208–210.
57. Pasalapudi Victor, *Life and Teachings of Ādi Śaṅkarācārya* (New Delhi: D. K. Printworld, 2002), 19–30.
58. Ibid., 22.
59. Gambhīrānanda, *Śvetāśvatara Upaniṣad*, vi–vii.
60. Victor, 48–49.
61. Swami Satprakashananda, *The Universe, God, and God-Realization* (St. Louis: Vedanta Society of St. Louis, 1977), 111.
62. Ibid., 77.
63. Ibid., 111.
64. Larson, 152.
65. Nikhilananda, *Upanishads*, 2:39.
66. Gambhīrānanda, *Śvetāśvatara Upaniṣad*, vi.
67. Nikhilananda, *Upanishads*, 2:39.
68. Tyāgīśānanda, 102.
69. Swami Satprakashananda, *Methods of Knowledge according to Advaita Vedanta* (London: George Allen & Unwin, 1965), 325.
70. Swami Prabhavananda, *The Spiritual Heritage of India* (Hollywood: Vedanta Press, 1963), 285.
71. W. D. Whitney, "The Upanishads and their Latest Translation," *American Journal of Philology*, vol. 7 (1886): 1–26.
72. Shereen Ratnagar, *Understanding Harappa* (New Delhi: Tulika, 2001), 104.
73. Ibid., 113.
74. Bryant, 163.
75. Jonathan Mark Kenoyer, *Ancient Cities of the Indus Valley Civilization* (Karachi: Oxford University Press and American Institute of Pakistan Studies, 1998), 113–114.
76. Devadatta Kālī, *In Praise of the Goddess* (Berwick, Maine: Nicolas-Hays, 2003), 21.
77. Ralph T. H. Griffith, trans., *The Rig Veda* (1896; reprint ed., New York: Book-of-the-Month Club, 1992), 636–637.
78. John Bowker, ed., *The Oxford Dictionary of World Religions* (Oxford: Oxford University Press, 1997), 919.
79. Swāmī Gambhīrānanda, trans.,

Eight Upaniṣads. 2nd revised ed., 2 vols. (Calcutta: Advaita Ashrama, 1989), 1:334–335.
80. Larson, 96.
81. Ibid., 132.
82. Ibid.
83. Bowker, 1058.
84. Larson, 132.
85. Kanti Chandra Pandey, *An Outline of History of Śaiva Philosophy* (1954 reprint. Delhi: Motilal Banarsidass, 1999), 30.
86. Ibid., 140–143.
87. Sir Monier Monier-Willams, *A Sanskrit-English Dictionary* (Oxford: Oxford University Press, 1899), 883.
88. Ibid.
89. Griffith, 151–152.
90. Bowker, 905.
91. Monier-Williams, 883.
92. Jonathan Z. Smith, ed., *The Harper-Collins Dictionary of Religion* (San Francisco: HarperSanFrancisco, 1995), 976.
93. Deba Brata SenSharma, *The Philosophy of Sādhanā* (Albany: State University of New York Press, 1990), 7.
94. Gonda, 21.
95. Ibid., 47.
96. Pandey, 5.
97. Paul Eduardo Muller-Ortega, *The Triadic Heart of Śiva* (Albany: State University of New York Press, 1989), 27.
98. Pandey, 56–57.
99. Ibid., 56.
100. Ibid., 57.
101. Monier-Williams, 455, 938.
102. Basu, 26.
103. Pandey, 48.
104. Ibid., 50–51.
105. Ibid., 180.
106. Ibid., 181–182.
107. Ibid., 181.
108. Ibid., 182–183.
109. Kālī, 101.
110. Pandey, 184.
111. Ibid., 56.
112. Larson, 108.
113. Mark S. G. Dyczkowski, *The Canon of the Śaivāgama and the Kubjikā Tantras of the Western Kaula Tradition* (Albany: State University of New York Press, 1988), 19.
114. Pandey, 9.
115. Ibid., 65.
116. Ibid., 9–13.
117. Ibid., 57.
118. Ibid., 64–65.
119. Bhattacharyya, *Tantric Religion,* 34.
120. Pandey, 26–28.
121. Dyczkowski, *Canon,* 23.
122. Muller-Ortega, 31.
123. Bhattacharyya, *Tantric Religion,* 199.
124. Ibid., 50–51.
125. Dyczkowski, *Canon,* 21.
126. G. V. Tagare, *Śaivism* (New Delhi: D. K. Printworld, 1996), 31–34.
127. Pandey, 111.
128. Ibid., 120.
129. Bhattacharyya, *Tantric Religion,* 201.
130. Ibid.
131. Pandey, 125.
132. Bhattacharyya, *Tantric Religion,* 201–202.
133. Pandey, 140.
134. Bhattacharyya, *Tantric Religion,* 201–202.
135. Muller-Ortega, 32.
136. Bhattacharyya, *Tantric Religion,* 202.
137. Dyczkowski, *Canon,* 21–22.
138. Muller-Ortega, 32.
139. Dyczkowski, *Canon,* 26; Bhattacharyya, *Tantric Religion,* 266.
140. Bhattacharyya, *Tantric Religion,* 202.
141. Pandey, 114.
142. Ibid., 111.
143. Ibid., 145.
144. Ibid., 27–28.

145. Ibid., 120.
146. Ibid., 113.
147. Ibid., 114.
148. Ibid., 28.
149. Ibid., 116.
150. Ibid. 44–45.
151. Dyczkowski, *Canon,* 24.
152. Ibid., 25.
153. Pandey, 8.
154. Bhattacharyya, *Tantric Religion,* 50.
155. Pandey, 8.
156. Ibid., 2.
157. Ibid., 5–6.
158. Dyczkowski, *Canon,* 25.
159. Mark S. G. Dyczkowski, *The Doctrine of Vibration* (Albany: State University of New York Press, 1987), 229*n*69.
160. Dyczkowski, *Canon,* 25.
161. Muller-Ortega, 39.
162. Tagare, *Śaivism,* 77.
163. Pandey, 6–7.
164. Muller-Ortega, 17.
165. Dyczkowski, *Doctrine,* 13.
166. Muller-Ortega, 17–18.
167. Ibid., 45–46.
168. Dyczkowski, *Doctrine,* 9.
169. Ibid., 8, 17.
170. Natalia Isayeva, *From Early Vedanta to Kashmir Shaivism* (Delhi: Sri Satguru Publications, 1997), 137.
171. Dyczkowski, *Doctrine,* 17.
172. Jaideva Singh, *Pratyabhijñāhṛdayam* (Delhi: Motilal Banarsidass, 1982), 21–22.
173. Swami Sivananda, *Lord Siva and His Worship* (Shivanandanagar, U.P.: Divine Life Society, 1989), 87.
174. Ibid., 38–39.
175. Mahendranath Gupta [M.], *The Gospel of Sri Ramakrishna,* trans. Swami Nikhilananda (New York: Ramakrishna-Vivekananda Center, 1942), 134.
176. Ibid., 634–635.
177. Ibid., 835.
178. Satprakashananda, *Universe,* 111.
179. Singh, *Pratyabhijñāhṛdayam,* 23–24.
180. Ibid., 27-28.
181. M. Gupta, *Gospel,* 103–104, 271, 345, 417, 604, 708, 802, 811.
182. G. T. Deshpande, *Abhinavagupta* (New Delhi: Sahitya Akademi, 1989), 142–143.
183. Ibid., 150.
184. Ibid., 143.
185. Larson, 168.
186. Dyczkowski, *Doctrine,* 94.

CHAPTER ONE

1. Pandey, 64.
2. Ibid.
3. Ibid., 120.
4. Monier-Willams, 737–738.
5. Müller, 231.
6. Deussen, 1:305.
7. Hume, 394.
8. Tyāgīśānanda, 10.
9. Swami Prabhavananda and Frederick Manchester, trans., *The Upanishads* (Hollywood: Vedanta Press, 1947), 187.
10. Nikhilananda, *Upanishads,* 2:71.
11. Radhakrishnan, 709.
12. Gambhīrānanda, *Śvetāśvatara Upaniṣad,* 45.
13. Lokeswarananda, 10.
14. Olivelle, 253.
15. Vedananda, 36.
16. Roebuck, 295.
17. Larson, 155–156.
18. Bhattacharyya, *Tantric Religion,* 174–178.
19. Larson, 114.
20. Müller, 232; Deussen, 1:305; Nikhilananda, *Upanishads,* 2:71; Gambhīrānanda, *Śvetāśvatara Upaniṣad,* 47; Lokeswarananda, 12; Vedananda, 38.
21. Hume, 394; Tyāgīśānanda, 12; Prabhavananda and Manchester,

187; Radhakrishnan, 709; Olivelle, 253; Roebuck, 295; Ilárraz and Pujol, 312.
22. Hume, 394.
23. Tyāgīśānanda, 12.
24. Prabhavananda and Manchester, 187.
25. Radhakrishnan, 709.
26. Olivelle, 253.
27. Roebuck, 295.
28. Ilárraz and Pujol, 312.
29. Müller, 232; Radhakrishnan, 709.
30. Deussen, 1:305; Ilárraz and Pujol, 312.
31. Hume, 394.
32. Tyāgīśānanda, 12; Prabhavananda and Manchester, 187.
33. Nikhilananda, *Upanishads,* 2:71.
34. Gambhīrānanda, *Śvetāśvatara Upaniṣad,* 47; Vedananda, 36.
35. Lokeswarananda, 12.
36. Olivelle, 253.
37. Roebuck, 295.
38. Pandey, 124–125.
39. Tracy Pintchman, *The Rise of the Goddess in the Hindu Tradition* (Albany: State University of New York Press, 1994), 101; G. A. Jacob, *A Concordance to the Principal Upaniṣads and Bhagavad-gītā* (1891; reprint ed., Delhi: Motilal Banarsidass, 1985), 906.
40. Pintchman, 98–99.
41. Pandey, 4.
42. Ibid., 119.
43. Ibid., 9.
44. Gambhīrānanda, *Śvetāśvatara Upaniṣad,* 50.
45. Tyāgīśānanda, 19.
46. Müller, 232*n*6.
47. Gambhīrānanda, *Śvetāśvatara Upaniṣad,* 60–61.
48. Ibid., 62–63.
49. Ibid., 63–64.
50. Jacob, 134.
51. Gambhīrānanda, *Śvetāśvatara Upaniṣad,* 61*n*1; Basu, 39.
52. Tyāgīśānanda, 22.
53. Ilárraz and Pujol, 327*n*6.
54. Müller, 233; Deussen, 1:306; Hume, 394; Nikhilananda, *Upanishads,* 2:74; Radhakrishnan, 711; Olivelle, 253; Vedananda, 43; Roebuck, 296; Ilárraz and Pujol, 312.
55. Tyāgīśānanda, 20; Gambhīrānanda, *Śvetāśvatara Upaniṣad,* 59; Lokeswarananda, 18.
56. Müller, 232*n*6; Deussen, 1:306; Hume, 395; Nikhilananda, *Upanishads,* 2:74; Radhakrishnan, 712; Gambhīrānanda, *Śvetāśvatara Upaniṣad,* 65; Vedananda, 43.
57. Lokeswarananda, 22–23.
58. Tyāgīśānanda, 23; Ilárraz and Pujol, 327*n*6.
59. Olivelle, 385*n*4–5; Roebuck, 450*n*14.
60. Dyczkowski, *Doctrine,* 17.
61. Griffith, 3*n*12.
62. Tyāgīśānanda, 24.
63. Müller, 232*n*1.
64. Ibid., 234.
65. Radhakrishnan, 713.
66. Tyāgīśānanda, 24.
67. Nikhilananda, *Upanishads,* 2:76; Lokeswarananda, 25.
68. Müller, 234; Hume, 395; Tyāgīśānanda, 24.
69. Deussen, 1:306; Gambhīrānanda, *Śvetāśvatara Upaniṣad,* 66; Vedananda, 49.
70. Satprakashananda, *Universe,* 122–123.
71. Balajit Nath Pandit, *Specific Principles of Kashmir Shaivism* (New Delhi: Munshiram Manoharlal, 1997), 30–31.
72. Singh, *Pratyabhijñāhṛdayam,* 144–145.
73. Ibid., 146.
74. Gambhīrānanda, *Śvetāśvatara Upaniṣad,* 66.
75. Hume, 395; Tyāgīśānanda, 24; Radhakrishnan, 713; Roebuck, 450*n*20.
76. Müller, 234*n*1; Deussen, 1:306; Nikhilananda, *Upanishads,* 2:76;

Gambhīrānanda, *Śvetāśvatara Upaniṣad,* 67; Lokeswarananda, 26; Olivelle, 386*n*4–5; Vedananda, 50.
77. Swami Prabhavananda and Christopher Isherwood, trans., *How to Know God* (Hollywood: Vedanta Press, 1953), 116.
78. Gambhīrānanda, *Śvetāśvatara Upaniṣad,* 67.
79. Müller, 234*n*1; Deussen, 1:306; Olivelle, 384*n*4–5.
80. Tyāgīśānanda, 24.
81. Gonda, 44–46.
82. Pandey, 83.
83. Tagare, *Śaivism,* 31.
84. Gonda, 47.
85. Singh, *Pratyabhijñāhṛdayam,* 122*n*17.
86. Monier-Williams, 1286.
87. Bowker, 405.
88. Roebuck, 403*n*13.
89. Teun Goudriaan, "Imagery of the Self from Veda to Tantra" in *The Roots of Tantra,* ed. Katherine Anne Harper and Robert L. Brown (Albany: State University of New York Press, 2002), 182.
90. Jaideva Singh, *Śiva Sūtras* (Delhi: Motilal Banarsidass, 1979), 262.
91. Dyczkowski, *Doctrine,* 90.
92. Ibid.
93. Radhakrishnan, 449.
94. Gambhīrānanda, *Eight Upaniṣads,* 1:343–344.
95. Radhakrishnan, 548.
96. M. L. Pandit, *Trika Śaivism,* 73.
97. Nikhilananda, *Upanishads,* 2:80–81.
98. Singh, *Śiva Sūtras,* 240.
99. Kamalakar Mishra, *Kashmir Śaivism* (Delhi: Sri Satguru Publications, 1999), 172.
100. Ibid., 174.
101. Jaideva Singh, *Vijñānabhairava or Divine Consciousness* (Delhi: Motilal Banarsidass, 1979), 113.
102. Singh, *Pratyabhijñāhṛdayam,* 124.
103. Ibid.
104. B. N. Pandit, *Specific Principles,* 76.
105. Ibid.
106. M. L. Pandit, *Trika Śaivism,* 213.
107. Mishra, 175.
108. Ilárraz and Pujol, 328*n*15.
109. Müller, 235*n*5; Gambhīrānanda, *Śvetāśvatara Upaniṣad,* 81, 85.
110. Mishra, 197.
111. Müller, 235*n*7.
112. Nikhilananda, *Upanishads,* 2:81; Radhakrishnan, 714; Gambhīrānanda, *Śvetāśvatara Upaniṣad,* 84–85; Vedananda, 58.
113. Roebuck, 451*n*26.
114. Müller, 235*n*7.
115. Satprakashananda, *Methods,* 85.
116. Ibid., 102.
117. Ibid., 111.
118. M. L. Pandit, *Disclosure,* 23.
119. Balajit Nath Pandit, *History of Kashmir Shaivism* (Srinagar: Utpal Publications, 1989), 33–34.
120. Dyczkowski, *Doctrine,* 46.
121. B. N. Pandit, *Specific Principles,* x.
122. M. L. Pandit, *Trika Śaivism,* 27.
123. Deshpande, 47.
124. Singh, *Śiva Sūtras,* 56–57.
125. Ibid., 57.
126. Tyāgīśānanda, 33.
127. Müller, 236; Hume, 396; Nikhilananda, *Upanishads,* 2:83; Radhakrishnan, 716; Olivelle, 254.
128. Roebuck, 297.
129. Gambhīrānanda, *Śvetāśvatara Upaniṣad,* 87; Vedananda, 62.
130. Deussen, 1:308; Lokeswarananda, 40.
131. Tyāgīśānanda, 34.
132. Prabhavananda and Manchester, 189.
133. Monier-Williams, 496.
134. Ibid., 766.
135. Pandey, 10.
136. Ibid., 114–115.
137. Ibid., 145.
138. Ibid., 10.
139. Ibid., 140.

140. Singh, *Pratyabhijñāhṛdayam,* 24.
141. Ibid.
142. Mishra, 125.
143. Ibid., 123.
144. Satprakashananda, *Methods,* 301.
145. Müller, 236*n*2, Nikhilananda, *Upanishads,* 2:83; Lokeswarananda, 39–42; Vedananda, 62–63.
146. Nikhilananda, *Upanishads,* 2:83–84.
147. Vedananda, 62.
148. Radhakrishnan, 716.
149. Gambhīrānanda, *Śvetāśvatara Upaniṣad,* 88–89.
150. Monier-Williams, 906.
151. Satprakashananda, *Methods,* 291.
152. Sir John Woodroffe, *The Garland of Letters,* 9th ed. (Pondicherry: Ganesh & Company, 1989), 259.
153. Isayeva, 30–31*n*30.
154. Ibid., 95–96.
155. Ibid., 2.
156. Edward Craig, ed., *The Routledge Encyclopaedia of Philosophy,* 10 vols. (London and New York: Routledge, 1998), 1: 763.
157. Isayeva, 3–5.
158. Satprakashananda, *Universe,* 144.
159. Satprakashananda, *Methods,* 293.
160. M. Gupta, *Gospel,* 404, 416, 465, 653.
161. Satprakashananda, *Methods,* 296.
162. Tyāgīśānanda, 38.
163. Müller, 237; Deussen, 1:308.
164. Hume, 396; Nikhilananda, *Upanishads,* 2:86; Radhakrishnan, 718; Olivelle, 255.
165. Roebuck, 297; Ilárraz and Pujol, 314.
166. Lokeswarananda, 47.
167. Tyāgīśānanda, 38; Gambhīrānanda, *Śvetāśvatara Upaniṣad,* 98; Vedananda, 66.
168. Prabhavananda and Manchester, 190.
169. Radhakrishnan, 718.
170. Nikhilananda, *Upanishads,* 2:86.
171. Radhakrishnan, 153.

CHAPTER TWO

1. Müller, 238*n*1.
2. Tyāgīśānanda, 39–40.
3. Hume, 397; Radhakrishnan, 719.
4. Müller, 238; Olivelle, 255; Roebuck, 299.
5. Deussen, 1:309.
6. Tyāgīśānanda, 38; Prabhavananda and Manchester, 190; Ilárraz and Pujol, 314.
7. Gambhīrānanda, *Śvetāśvatara Upaniṣad,* 101; Nikhilananda, *Upanishads,* 2:87; Vedananda, 69.
8. Lokeswarananda, 51.
9. Tyāgīśānanda, 40.
10. Vedananda, 70.
11. Tyāgīśānanda, 40.
12. Prabhavananda and Manchester, 190.
13. Kālī, 57.
14. Müller, 238.*n*2.
15. Griffith, 537.
16. Monier-Williams, 737.
17. Richard Hughes Seager, ed., *The Dawn of Religious Pluralism* (La Salle, Illinois: Open Court, 1993), 425.
18. Ilárraz and Pujol, 328*n*27.
19. Gambhīrānanda, *Śvetāśvatara Upaniṣad,* 107.
20. Prabhavananda and Manchester, 191.
21. Bryant, 65.
22. Müller, 241.
23. Deussen, 1:309.
24. Nikhilananda, *Upanishads,* 2:90.
25. Gambhīrānanda, *Śvetāśvatara Upaniṣad,* 108–109.
26. Lokeswarananda, 62.
27. Vedananda, 77.
28. Hume, 398.
29. Roebuck, 300.
30. Olivelle, 255.
31. Radhakrishnan, 790.
32. Ilárraz and Pujol, 315.
33. Tyāgīśānanda, 46.
34. Prabhavananda and Manchester, 191.

35. Müller, 241.
36. Deussen, 1:309.
37. Hume, 398.
38. Tyāgīśānanda, 46.
39. Prabhavananda and Manchester, 191.
40. Nikhilananda, *Upanishads,* 2:91; Radhakrishnan, 720.
41. Gambhīrānanda, *Śvetāśvatara Upaniṣad,* 108.
42. Lokeswarananda, 62.
43. Olivelle, 255.
44. Vedananda, 77.
45. Roebuck, 300.
46. Ilárraz and Pujol, 315.
47. Monier-Williams, 642.
48. Ibid.
49. Larson, 150.
50. M. L. Pandit, *Disclosure,* 75–76.
51. Muller-Ortega, 65.
52. Swāmī Swāhānanda, *The Chāndogya Upaniṣad,* 6th ed. (Mylapore, Madras: Sri Ramakrishna Math, 1984), 549–553.
53. Muller-Ortega, 73.
54. Singh, *Vijñānabhairava,* x.
55. Ibid., 45.
56. Kālī, 94.
57. Tyāgīśānanda, 48.
58. Gambhīrānanda, *Eight Upaniṣads,* 1:163–168; Radhakrishnan, 623–625.
59. Singh, *Pratyabhijñāhṛdayam,* 95*n*1.
60. Gambhīrānanda, *Śvetāśvatara Upaniṣad,* 117.
61. Lokeswarananda, 71.
62. Vedananda, 83.
63. Satprakashananda, *Universe,* 119.
64. Satprakashananda, *Methods,* 50–51*n*48.
65. Ibid.
66. Satprakashananda, *Universe,* 120. 67. Satprakashananda, *Methods,* 51*n*49.
68. Ibid., 51.
69. Nikhilananda, *Upanishads,* 2:93–94.
70. Gambhīrānanda, *Śvetāśvatara Upaniṣad,* 118.
71. Vedananda, 84.
72. Prabhavananda and Isherwood, 70–71.
73. Nikhilananda, *Upanishads,* 2:94.
74. Tyāgīśānanda, 55.
75. Ibid., 55.
76. Vedananda, 87.
77. M. L. Pandit, *Disclosure,* 17–20.
78. Ibid., 23.
79. Singh, *Śiva Sūtras,* 163–164.
80. Monier-Williams, 1299.
81. Prabhavananda, *Spiritual Heritage,* 289.
82. Satprakashananda, *Universe,* 110.
83. Ibid., 118.
84. Ibid.
85. Ibid., 128.
86. Ibid., 118.
87. M. Gupta, *Gospel,* 134.
88. Ibid., 634–635.
89. Ibid., 835.
90. M. L. Pandit, *Trika Śaivism,* 250.
91. Mishra, 274–275.
92. Monier-Williams, 1124.
93. Gonda, 47.
94. Mishra, 325.
95. Swami Lakshmanjoo, *Kashmir Shaivism* (Culver City: Universal Shaiva Fellowship, 2002), 8–9.
96. Mishra, 167.
97. Ibid., 166.
98. Ibid.
99. André Padoux, *Vāc,* trans. Jacques Gontier (1990; reprint ed. (Delhi: Sri Satguru Publications, 1992), 77.
100. Mishra, 327.
101. Ibid., 166.
102. Lakshmanjoo, 9.
103. Mishra, 166.
104. Roebuck, 453*n*14.

CHAPTER THREE

1. Jacob, 218.
2. Monier-Williams, 171.
3. Tyāgīśānanda, 58; Radhakrishnan, 725; Gambhīrā-

nanda, *Śvetāśvatara Upaniṣad,* 123; Lokeswarananda, 81; Vedananda, 91.
4. Roebuck, 453*n*1.
5. Pintchman, 98–99.
6. Monier-Williams, 1048.
7. Pintchman, 98–99.
8. Ibid., 99.
9. Swami Nikhilananda, trans., *Self-Knowledge* (New York: Rama–krishna-Vivekananda Center, 1946), 56.
10. Tyāgīśānanda, 59.
11. Nikhilananda, *Upaniṣads,* 2:96.
12. Narendra Nath Bhattacharyya, *History of the Śākta Religion,* 2nd rev. ed. (New Delhi: Munshiram Manoharlal, 1996), 213.
13. Mishra, 142, 144.
14. Tyāgīśānanda, 59.
15. Lokeswarananda, 82.
16. Muller-Ortega, 126.
17. Singh, *Vijñānabhairava,* 138.
18. Muller-Ortega, 126.
19. Gambhīrānanda, *Śvetāśvatara Upaniṣad,* 123.
20. Bowker, 905.
21. Stephan Schuhmacher and Gert Woerner, eds., *The Encyclopedia of Eastern Philosophy and Religion* (Boston: Shambhala, 1989), 389.
22. Tyāgīśānanda, 60; Olivelle, 389*n*3.
23. Griffith, 591*n*1.
24. Bowker, 997.
25. Lokeswarananda, 83–84.
26. Ibid.
27. Ibid., 84.
28. Kālī, 214.
29. Griffith, 592*n*7.
30. Roebuck, 453*n*3.
31. Dyczkowski, *Doctrine,* 87.
32. Müller, 245; Tyāgīśānanda, 62; Prabhavananda and Manchester, 194.
33. Lokeswarananda, 86.
34. Deussen, 1:312.
35. Hume, 400; Nikhilananda, *Upaniṣads,* 2:98.
36. Radhakrishnan, 726; Ilárraz and Pujol, 317.
37. Gambhīrānanda, *Śvetāśvatara Upaniṣad,* 126.
38. Olivelle, 257.
39. Vedananda, 94.
40. Roebuck, 302.
41. Radhakrishnan, 623.
42. Ibid., 628.
43. Monier-Williams, 1054.
44. Ibid., 1055.
45. Nikhilananda, *Upanishads,* 2:99.
46. Tyāgīśānanda, 64–65.
47. Ibid., 65.
48. Monier-Williams, 408.
49. Tyāgīśānanda, 65–66.
50. Padoux, 80.
51. G. V. Tagare, *The Pratyabhijñā Philosophy* (Delhi: Motilal Banarsidass, 2002), 16.
52. B. N. Pandit, *Specific Principles,* xviii.
53. M. Gupta, *Gospel,* 103–104, 271, 345, 417, 604, 708, 802, 811.
54. Monier-Williams, 648.
55. Ibid., 637.
56. B. N. Pandit, *Specific Principles,* 77.
57. Müller, 245.
58. Deussen, 1:312.
59. Hume, 400.
60. Tyāgīśānanda, 66.
61. Prabhavananda and Manchester, 195.
62. Nikhilananda, *Upanishads,* 2:99.
63. Radhakrishnan, 727.
64. Gambhīrānanda,*Śvetāśvatara Upaniṣad,* 130.
65. Lokeswarananda, 94.
66. Olivelle, 257.
67. Vedananda, 100.
68. Roebuck, 303.
69. Ilárraz and Pujol, 317.
70. Arthur A. Macdonell, *A Vedic Grammar for Students* (Oxford: Oxford University Press, 1971), 295.
71. Schuhmacher and Woerner, *Encyclopedia,* 282.
72. Mishra, 150.

73. Griffith, 602*n*1.
74. Mishra, 114.
75. Kenoyer, 105; Deo Prakash Sharma, "Early Harappan Ceramics," in *Early Harappans and Indus-Sarasvati Civilization*, ed. Deo Prakash and Madhuri Sharma, 2 vols. (New Delhi: Kaveri Books, 2006), 1:136.
76. D. P. Sharma, 136.
77. Kenoyer, 105–106.
78. Ibid., 105.
79. Ibid.
80. Lokeswarananda, 96.
81. Griffith, 14.
82. Ilárraz and Pujol, 330*n*44.
83. Lokeswarananda, 98.
84. Har Dutt Sharma, *Sāṁkhya-Kārikā* (Poona: Oriental Book Agency, 1933), 2.
85. Ibid.
86. Ibid.
87. Ibid.
88. Lokeswarananda, 97–98.
89. Ilárraz and Pujol, 317.
90. Deussen, 1:313*n*3.
91. H. H. Wilson, "Essays on the Religious Sects of the Hindus," *Asiatic Researches* 16 (1828), 11.
92. Woodroffe, 34.
93. Ibid., xi.
94. Monier-Williams, 743.
95. Radhakrishnan, 728.
96. Nikhilananda, *Upanishads*, 2:101.
97. Gambhīrānanda, *Śvetāśvatara Upaniṣad*, 133.
98. Nikhilananda, *Upanishads*, 2:101.
99. Mishra, 284.
100. M. L. Pandit, *Trika Śaivism*, 230.
101. Mishra, 289.
102. Ibid., 285.
103. Tyāgīśānanda, 70.
104. Singh, *Pratyabhijñāhṛdayam*, 95*n*1.
105. Mishra, 255.
106. Satprakashananda, *Universe*, 179.
107. M. L. Pandit, *Trika Śaivism*, 141–142.
108. Ibid., 145–146.
109. B. N. Pandit, *Specific Principles*, 45.
110. Dyczkowski, *Doctrine*, 110.
111. Satprakashananda,*Methods*, 35–36.
112. Larson, 9.
113. Satprakashananda, *Methods*, 36.
114. Ibid., 15.
115. Monier-Williams, 45.
116. Radhakrishnan, 38–39.
117. Swami Prabhavananda, *Vedic Religion and Philosophy* (Mylapore, Madras: Sri Ramakrishna Math, 1950), 35–36.
118. Radhakrishnan, 35–37.
119. Prabhavananda, *Vedic Religion*, 35.
120. Dyczkowski, *Doctrine*, 165.
121. B. N. Pandit, *Specific Principles*, 7–8.
122. Ilárraz and Pujol, 330*n*51; Tyāgīśānanda, 73; Prabhavananda and Manchester, 196.
123. Boris Marjanovic, trans. *Abhinavagupta's Commentary on the Bhagavad Gita (Gītārtha-saṁgraha)* (Varanasi: Indica Books, 2002), 273–275.
124. Madhusūdhana Saraswati, *Bhagavad-Gītā with the Annotation* Gūḍhārtha-Dīpikā, trans. Swāmī Gambhīrānanda (Calcutta: Advaita Ashrama, 1998), 724–725; Swāmī Vireśwarānanda, trans., *Śrīmad Bhagavad Gītā with the Gloss of Śrīdhara Swāmī* (Mylapore, Madras: Sri Ramakrishna Math, 1948), 377–378; A. G. Krishna Warrier, *Śrīmad Bhagavad Gītā Bhāṣya of Śrī Saṁkarācārya* (Mylapore, Madras: Sri Ramakrishna Math, 1983), 435–436; Gambhīrānanda, *Śvetāśvatara Upaniṣad*, 136–137; Nikhilananda, *Upanishads*, 2:103; Vedananda, 109–110.
125. B. N. Pandit, *History*, 45.
126. Monier-Williams, 755–756.

127. Padoux, 452.
128. Mishra, 92.
129. Ibid., 67.
130. M. L. Pandit, *Trika Śaivism*, 189.
131. Padoux, 452.
132. B. N. Pandit, *Specific Principles*, 153.
133. Ibid., xxi.
134. Padoux, 82*n*141.
135. Ibid., 250*n*72.
136. Ibid., 141.
137. Goudriaan, 182.
138. Singh, *Vijñānabhairava*, 140–144.
139. Goudriaan, 182.
140. Lokeswarananda, 115.
141. Ibid., 115–116.
142. Radhakrishnan, 585.
143. Ibid., 225.
144. Nikhilananda, *Upanishads*, 2:104.
145. Ibid.
146. Ibid.
147. Mishra, 330–331.
148. Ibid., 332–333.
149. Radhakrishnan, 730.
150. Swami Sarvadevananda, informal conversation (Santa Barbara, California, 28 May 2006).
151. Vedananda, 122.

CHAPTER FOUR

1. Müller, 249*n*3.
2. Olivelle, 390*n*1.
3. Ibid.
4. Ibid., 259.
5. Müller, 249; Deussen, 1:315.
6. Tyāgīśānanda, 77, Nikhilananda, *Upanishads*, 2:106; Gambhīrānanda, *Śvetāśvatara Upaniṣad*, 141; Vedananda, 116, Roebuck, 305.
7. Monier-Williams, 1004.
8. Dyczkowski, *Doctrine*, 21.
9. Ibid., 85–86.
10. Ibid., 77.
11. Hume, 402; Nikhilananda, *Upanishads*, 2:106; Radhakrishnan, 731; Roebuck, 305.
12. Tyāgīśānanda, 77; Gambhīrānanda, *Śvetāśvatara Upaniṣad*, 141; Illáraz and Pujol, 319.
13. Lokeswarananda, 124.
14. Vedananda, 116.
15. Müller, 249.
16. Deussen, 1:315.
17. Nikhilananda, *Upanishads*, 2:106.
18. Gambhīrānanda, *Śvetāśvatara Upaniṣad*, 141.
19. Radhakrishnan, 731.
20. Vedananda, 116.
21. Müller, 249.
22. Deussen, 1:315.
23. Monier-Williams, 564.
24. Müller, 249*n*1.
25. Satprakashananda, *Universe*, 113.
26. Ibid., 77.
27. Ibid., 111.
28. Ibid.
29. Padoux, 174.
30. Dyczkowski, *Doctrine*, 25.
31. Mishra, 191.
32. Ibid., 98.
33. Ibid., 92–93.
34. Ibid., 203.
35. Dyczkowski, *Doctrine*, 46.
36. Mishra, 202.
37. B. N. Pandit, *Specific Principles*, 24.
38. Ibid.
39. Dyczkowski, *Doctrine*, 25.
40. B. N. Pandit, *Specific Principles*, 25.
41. Padoux, 92.
42. B. N. Pandit, *Specific Principles*, x.
43. Mishra, 197.
44. Ibid., 418*n*6.
45. Ibid., 195.
46. Ibid., 178.
47. Ibid., 191–192.
48. Ibid., 203–204.
49. Ibid., 206.
50. SenSharma, 25.
51. Padoux, 80.
52. Ibid., 92.
53. Dyczkowski, *Doctrine*, 89.
54. Ibid., 136–137.
55. Ibid., 40.
56. Ibid.
57. Ibid., 41.
58. Ibid.

59. M. Gupta, *Gospel*, 345–346.
60. Ibid., 366; 490.
61. Ibid., 634–635.
62. Ibid., 835.
63. M. L. Pandit, *Trika Śaivism*, 56.
64. Müller, 250*n*2.
65. Nikhilananda, *Upanishads*, 2:109.
66. Chatterjee, Satischandra and Datta, Dhirendramohan, *An Introduction to Indian Philosophy*, 6th ed. (Calcutta: University of Calcutta, 1960), 391–392.
67. Roebuck, 455*n*6.
68. Monier-Williams, 767.
69. Ibid., 759.
70. Ibid., 1296.
71. Pandey, 123.
72. Ibid., 124.
73. Griffith, 111*n*22.
74. Nikhilananda, *Upanishads*, 2:110.
75. B. N. Pandit, *Specific Principles*, 19.
76. M. L. Pandit, *Trika Śaivism*, 188–189.
77. Radhakrishnan, 733.
78. Griffith, 111*n*20.
79. Nikhilananda, *Upanishads*, 2:110.
80. Vedananda, 121.
81. Tyāgīśānanda, 83.
82. Gambhīrānanda, *Śvetāśvatara Upaniṣad*, 146.
83. Swami Prabhavananda, *The Eternal Companion*, 3rd ed. (Hollywood: Vedanta Press, 1970), 5.
84. Tyāgīśānanda, 84; Prabhavananda and Manchester, 199; Nikhilananda, *Upanishads*, 2:111; Radhakrishnan, 733; Gambhīrānanda, *Śvetāśvatara Upaniṣad*, 146; Olivelle, 259.
85. Müller, 251; Deussen, 1:316; Hume, 403; Ilárraz and Pujol, 320; Lokeswarananda, 138; Roebuck, 306.
86. Vedananda, 122–123.
87. Nikhilananda, *Upanishads*, 2:111.
88. Griffith, 113*n*39.
89. Müller, 251*n*2.
90. Ibid.
91. Isayeva, 98–99.
92. Vedananda, 123.
93. Tyāgīśānanda, 86.
94. Nikhilananda, *Upanishads*, 2:113.
95. Radhakrishnan, 734.
96. M. L. Pandit, *Trika Śaivism*, 50.
97. Larson, 138–139.
98. Ibid., 113–117.
99. Ibid., 92–95.
100. M. L. Pandit, *Disclosure*, 85.
101. Monier-Williams, 654.
102. M. L. Pandit, *Disclosure*, 85.
103. Radhakrishnan, 208.
104. Olivelle, 132.
105. Roebuck, 39.
106. Swāmī Mādhavānanda, ed., *The Bṛhadāraṇyaka Upaniṣad*, 2nd ed. (Mylapore, Madras: Sri Ramakrishna Math, 1951), 178.
107. Nikhilananda, *Upanishads*, 2:194.
108. Mishra, 384.
109. Olivelle, 391*n*9–10.
110. Radhakrishnan, 793.
111. Monier-Williams, 599.
112. Pandey, 27–28, 113.
113. SenSharma, 37.
114. Nikhilananda, *Upanishads*, 2:113–114; Gambhīrānanda, *Śvetāśvatara Upaniṣad*, 151–152; Lokeswarananda, 146–147; Vedananda, 125–126.
115. Mishra, 212–213.
116. Müller, 252; Radhakrishnan, 735; Gambhīrānanda, *Śvetāśvatara Upaniṣad*, 152.
117. Tyāgīśānanda, 87–88; Olivelle, 260; Vedananda, 126.
118. Nikhilananda, *Upanishads*, 2:114.
119. Prabhavananda and Manchester, 200; Olivelle, 260; Roebuck, 306.
120. Radhakrishnan, 735.
121. Müller, 252; Ilárraz and Pujol, 320.
122. Vedananda, 126.
123. Tyāgīśānanda, 87–88; Nikhilananda, *Upanishads*, 2:114; Gambhīrānanda, *Śvetāśvatara Upaniṣad*, 152.
124. Monier-Williams, 858.

125. Tyāgīśānanda, 88; Nikhilananda, *Upanishads,* 2:114; Gambhīrānanda, *Śvetāśvatara Upaniṣad,* 152.
126. Monier-Williams, 160.
127. Griffith, 628*n*1.
128. B. N. Pandit, *Specific Principles,* 181–182.
129. Muller-Ortega, 135–136.
130. Vedananda, 131.
131. Monier-Williams, 1302.
132. Muller-Ortega, 65.
133. Griffith, 40.
134. Radhakrishnan, 644.
135. Muller-Ortega, 70.
136. Monier-Williams, 309–310.
137. Larson, 93.
138. Pandey, 133–134.
139. B. N. Pandit, *Specific Principles,* 161.
140. Deussen, 1:318; Hume, 405; Nikhilananda, *Upanishads,* 2:118; Radhakrishnan, 737; Gambhīrānanda, *Śvetāśvatara Upaniṣad,* 162; Olivelle, 261; Roebuck, 307.
141. Müller, 253.
142. Tyāgīśānanda, 97; Prabhavananda and Manchester, 201.
143. Vedananda, 134.
144. Loswarananda, 166.
145. Nikhilananda, *Upanishads,* 2:118.
146. Vedananda, 134.
147. Monier-Williams, 758.
148. Tyāgīśānanda, 98; Radhakrishnan, 308.
149. Müller, 254.
150. Lokeswarananda, 170.
151. Nikhilananda, *Upanishads,* 2:119.
152. Gambhīrānanda, *Śvetāśvatara Upaniṣad,* 164.
153. Müller, 254.
154. Nikhilananda, *Upanishads,* 2:119.
155. Roebuck, 308.
156. Hume, 405.
157. Gonda, 42.
158. Ibid., 35.
159. Ibid., 42–43.
160. Swami Vimalananda, trans., *Mahānārāyanopaniṣad* (Mylepore, Madras: Sri Ramakrishna Math, 1957), 206–207.
161. Ibid., 207–209.
162. Pandey, 116.
163. Gonda, 43.
164. Vimalananda, 209.
165. Gonda, 44.
166. Vimalananda, 47–48.
167. Ibid., 46.
168. Gonda, 48.
169. Pandey, 120.
170. Ibid., 120–123.
171. Tagare, *Śaivism,* 77.
172. Pandey, 6–7.
173. Dyczkowski, *Doctrine,* 229*n*69.
174. M. L. Pandit, *Trika Śaivism,* 76; Muller-Ortega, 131.
175. Gonda, 47–48.

CHAPTER FIVE

1. Deussen, 1:319.
2. Radhakrishnan, 738.
3. M. Gupta, *Gospel,* 780–781.
4. Ibid., 404.
5. Ibid., 899–900.
6. Ibid., 781.
7. Tyāgīśānanda, 102.
8. M. Gupta, *Gospel,* 288.
9. Radhakrishnan, 738.
10. Monier-Williams, 250.
11. Radhakrishnan, 738; Müller, 255.
12. Tyāgīśānanda, 102.
13. Monier-Williams, 250.
14. Müller, 255*n*11.
15. Nikhilananda, *Upanishads,* 2:122.
16. Roebuck, 456*n*3.
17. Müller, 255*n*8.
18. Ibid., 255*n*9; Radhakrishnan, 739; Gambhīrānanda, *Śvetāśvatara Upaniṣad,* 169.
19. Vedananda, 142.
20. Hume, 406.
21. Olivelle, 392*n*3.
22. Gambhīrānanda, *Śvetāśvatara Upaniṣad,* 169; Lokeswarananda, 179; Vedananda, 143.
23. Nikhilananda, *Upanishads,* 2:122.

24. Müller, 255*n*9; Hume, 406; Radhakrishnan, 739; Lokeswarananda, 179; Olivelle, 261.
25. Tyāgīśānanda, 103; Nikhilananda, *Upanishads,* 2:122; Gambhīrānanda, *Śvetāśvatara Upaniṣad,* 169.
26. Vedananda, 142.
27. Tyāgīśānanda, 103.
28. Monier-Williams, 332.
29. Müller, 255; Hume, 406; Tyāgīśānanda, 103; Nikhilananda, *Upanishads,* 2:122; Radhakrishnan, 739; Gambhīrānanda, *Śvetāśvatara Upaniṣad,* 169; Lokeswarananda, 180, Ilārraz and Pujol, 322.
30. Müller, 255*n*8.
31. Deussen, 1:320*n*1.
32. Tyāgīśānanda, 103.
33. Deussen, 1:320.
34. Nikhilananda, *Upanishads,* 2:122.
35. Radhakrishnan, 739.
36. Gambhīrānanda, *Śvetāśvatara Upaniṣad,* 169.
37. Lokeswarananda, 180.
38. Ilárraz and Pujol, 322.
39. Müller, 256; Tyāgīśānanda, 103; Gambhīrānanda, *Śvetāśvatara Upaniṣad,* 169.
40. Monier-Williams, 790.
41. Nikhilananda, *Upanishads,* 2:122.
42. Ibid., 124.
43. Monier-Williams, 706.
44. Radhakrishnan, 208.
45. Deussen, 1:442.
46. Deshpande, 80.
47. Monier-Williams, 1126.
48. Georg Feuerstein, *Tantra: The Path of Ecstasy* (Boston: Shambhala, 1998), 77.
49. SenSharma, 32–33.
50. M. L. Pandit, *Disclosure,* 269.
51. Müller, 257*n*6.
52. Ibid.
53. Ibid., 257.
54. Radhakrishnan, 741; Gambhīrānanda, *Śvetāśvatara Upaniṣad,* 176; Lokeswarananda, 197.
55. Deussen, 1:321.
56. Hume, 407.
57. Nikhilananda, *Upanishads,* 2:126.
58. Tyāgīśānanda, 109; Vedananda, 152.
59. Olivelle, 262; Roebuck, 310.
60. Müller, 257.
61. Deussen, 1:321; Hume, 407; Radhakrishnan, 741; Gambhīrānanda, *Śvetāśvatara Upaniṣad,* 176; Lokeswarananda, 197; Olivelle, 262; Vedananda, 152; Roebuck, 310.
62. Tyāgīśānanda, 109; Nikhilananda, *Upanishads,* 2:126.
63. Müller, 257.
64. Deussen, 1:321; Hume, 407; Tyāgīśānanda, 109; Radhakrishnan, 741; Olivelle, 262: Roebuck, 310.
65. Gambhīrānanda, *Śvetāśvatara Upaniṣad,* 176.
66. Lokeswarananda, 197.
67. Nikhilananda, *Upanishads,* 2:126; Vedananda, 152.
68. Monier-Williams, 492.
69. Müller, 258; Radhakrishnan, 741.
70. Roebuck, 310.
71. Deussen, 1:321.
72. Hume, 407; Tyāgīśānanda, 109; Nikhilananda, *Upanishads,* 2:126; Gambhīrānanda, *Śvetāśvatara Upaniṣad,* 176; Vedananda, 152.
73. Lokeswarananda, 197.
74. Olivelle, 262.
75. Müller, 257*n*6.
76. Satprakashananda, *Methods,* 211–212.
77. M. Gupta, *Gospel,* 539.
78. Monier-Williams, 31.
79. Ibid., 1296.
80. Ibid., 435.
81. Ibid.
82. SenSharma, 169.
83. Satprakashananda, *Universe,* 290–291.
84. *Studies on the Tantras* (Calcutta: Ramakrishna Mission Institute of Culture, 1989), 55.
85. M. L. Pandit, *Disclosure,* 232.
86. Ibid., 66.

87. Singh, *Śiva Sūtras*, 244; Tagare, *Pratyabhijñā Philosophy*, 97–98.
88. M. L. Pandit, *Disclosure*, 66.
89. Jaideva Singh, *Spanda-Kārikās* (Delhi: Motilal Banarsidass, 1980), 119.
90. Lakshmanjoo, 114.
91. Ibid.; Feuerstein, 255–256.
92. Lakshmanjoo, 120.
93. Ibid., 114.
94. Dyczkowski, *The Aphorisms of Śiva* (New Delhi: Indica, 1998), 140.
95. Feuerstein, 258–259.
96. Swami Prabhananda, *First Meetings with Sri Ramakrishna* (Mylapore, Madras: Ramakrishna Math, 1987), 36.
97. Mishra, 298.

CHAPTER SIX

1. Monier-Williams, 803.
2. Ibid., 737.
3. M. Gupta, *Gospel*, 133.
4. Ibid., 652.
5. M. L. Pandit, *Disclosure*, 23.
6. M. Gupta, *Gospel*, 134.
7. Dyczkowski, *Doctrine*, 121–122.
8. Olivelle, 253; Roebuck, 296.
9. Dyczkowski, *Doctrine*, 122.
10. Abhinavagupta, *Parā–trīśikā–Vivaraṇa*, trans. Jaideva Singh (Delhi: Motilal Banarsidass, 1988), 32.
11. Olivelle, 394*n*3–4.
12. Müller, 260*n*7.
13. Ibid.; Gambhīrānanda, *Śvetāśvatara Upaniṣad*, 182; Lokeswarananda, 211; Vedananda, 162.
14. Müller, 260*n*7.
15. Nikhilananda, *Upanishads*, 2:130–131.
16. Müller, 260; Deussen, 1:322; Radhakrishnan, 743; Roebuck, 312; Olivelle, 263; Ilárraz and Pujol, 324.
17. Müller, 260*n*7; Hume, 408; Tyāgīśānanda, 115.
18. Nikhilananda, *Upanishads*, 2:130.
19. Müller, 260*n*7.
20. Gambhīrānanda, *Śvetāśvatara Upaniṣad*, 182; Vedananda, 162.
21. Müller, 260*n*7.
22. Nikhilananda, *Upanishads*, 2:130.
23. Tyāgīśānanda, 115; Vedananda, 165.
24. Deussen, 1:322; Hume, 409; Radhakrishnan, 744; Ilárraz and Pujol, 332*n*80
25. Olivelle, 263; Roebuck, 312.
26. Nikhilananda, *Upanishads*, 2:130.
27. Lokeswarananda, 211.
28. Radhakrishnan, 744; Ilárraz and Pujol, 332*n*80.
29. Deussen, 1:322; Hume, 409; Olivelle, 394*n*3; Roebuck, 457*n*1.
30. Nikhilananda, *Upanishads*, 2:130.
31. Deussen, 1:332*n*3; Hume, 409; Radhakrishnan, 744; Olivelle, 394*n*3–4; Roebuck, 457*n*1; Ilárraz and Pujol, 332*n*80.
32. Tyāgīśānanda, 115; Lokeswarananda, 211.
33. Nikhilananda, *Upanishads*, 2:130.
34. Pandey, 122.
35. Ibid., 124–125.
36. Ibid., 125.
37. Ibid., 127–128.
38. Torella, Raffaele Torella, *The Īśvarapratyabhijñākārikā of Utpaladeva: with the Author's Vṛtti* (Delhi: Motilal Banarsidass, 2002), 204*n*24.
39. Radhakrishnan, 743–744.
40. Müller, 260*n*7.
41. Ibid., 260; Gambhīrānanda, *Śvetāśvatara Upaniṣad*, 182; Lokeswarananda, 211;Vedananda, 162.
42. Olivelle, 263.
43. Hume, 408; Radhakrishnan, 743; Roebuck, 312.
44. Deussen, 1:322.
45. Tyāgīśānanda, 117.
46. Müller, 260*n*7; Nikhilananda, *Upanishads*, 2:130–131.
47. Monier-Williams, 135.
48. Ibid., 1240.

49. Tyāgīśānanda, 114; Gambhīrānanda, *Śvetāśvatara Upaniṣad,* 181; Lokeswarananda, 209–10; Nikhilananda, *Upanishads,* 2:129–130; Vedananda, 160–161.
50. Radhakrishnan, 80–81.
51. Ibid., 81–82.
52. Ibid., 90.
53. Ibid., 80–81.
54. Ibid., 41.
55. Ibid., 35–37.
56. Ibid., 38–39.
57. Müller, 260*n*7.
58. Radhakrishnan, 744.
59. Monier-Williams, 754.
60. Ibid., 433.
61. Lokeswarananda, 219.
62. Deussen, 1:323.
63. Roebuck, 457–458*n*4.
64. Müller, 263; Hume, 409; Tyāgīśānanda, 121; Nikhilananda, *Upanishads,* 2:134; Radhakrishnan, 745; Lokeswarananda, 221; Vedananda, 172.
65. Gambhīrānanda, *Śvetāśvatara Upaniṣad,* 188; Olivelle, 264: Ilárraz and Pujol, 324.
66. Dyczkowski, *Doctrine,* 152.
67. Singh, *Śiva Sūtras,* 248.
68. Singh, *Spanda-Kārikās,* xvii–xviii.
69. C. Mackenzie Brown, *The Devī Gītā—The Song of the Goddess* (Albany: State University of New York Press, 1998), 96–97*n*6.
70. Radhakrishnan, 746.
71. Tyāgīśānanda, 122.
72. Nikhilananda, *Upanishads,* 2:135.
73. Ibid.
74. Mādhavānanda, 128.
75. Mishra, 180–181.
76. Nikhilananda, *Upanishads,* 2:135.
77. Monier-Williams, 55–56.
78. Nikhilananda, *Upanishads,* 2:136.
79. Gambhīrānanda, *Śvetāśvatara Upaniṣad,* 191.
80. Olivelle, 394*n*11.
81. Müller, 264*n*1.
82. Jacob, 361.
83. Müller, 264.
84. Hume, 409.
85. Deussen, 1:324.
86. Tyāgīśānanda, 123.
87. Nikhilananda, *Upanishads,* 2:136.
88. Radhakrishnan, 746; Ilárraz and Pujol, 325.
89. Gambhīrānanda, *Śvetāśvatara Upaniṣad,* 190.
90. Lokeswarananda, 226.
91. Olivelle, 264.
92. Vedananda, 175.
93. Roebuck, 313.
94. Deussen 1:350; Radhakrishnan, 821.
95. Lokeswarananda, 227–228.
96. Deussen, 1:324; Hume, 409; Tyāgīśānanda, 124; Radhakrishnan, 746; Gambhīrānanda, *Śvetāśvatara Upaniṣad,* 191; Lokeswarananda, 230; Olivelle, 264; Roebuck, 313; Ilárraz and Pujol, 325.
97. Nikhilananda, *Upanishads,* 2:137; Vedananda, 176.
98. Müller, 264; Deussen, 1:324; Nikhilananda, *Upanishads,* 2:137; Radhakrishnan, 746; Gambhīrānanda, *Śvetāśvatara Upaniṣad,* 192; Lokeswarananda, 230; Olivelle, 264; Vedananda, 176.
99. Tyāgīśānanda, 124; Ilárraz and Pujol, 325.
100. Hume, 409; Roebuck, 313.
101. Müller, 264.
102. Ibid., 264*n*3; Gambhīrānanda, *Śvetāśvatara Upaniṣad,* 192; Radhakrishnan, 746.
103. Gambhīrānanda, *Śvetāśvatara Upaniṣad,* 192; Lokeswarananda, 230.
104. Nikhilananda, *Upanishads,* 2:137.
105. Tyāgīśānanda, 124.
106. Lokeswarananda, 230.
107. Deussen, 2:729–730.
108. Singh, *Śiva Sūtras,* 250–251.
109. Ibid., 162.
110. Monier-Williams, 99.
111. Singh, *Śiva Sūtras,* 163–165.
112. Müller, 264*n*4.

113. Larson, 3.
114. Monier-Williams, 1199.
115. Ibid., 856.
116. Tyāgīśānanda, 125; Radhakrishnan, 747; Olivelle, 394*n*13.
117. Tyāgīśānanda, 126.
118. Lokeswarananda, 235.
119. Monier-Williams, 977.
120. Gambhīrānanda, *Eight Upaniṣads,* 2:141.
121. Monier-Williams, 977.
122. Gambhīrānanda, *Eight Upaniṣads,* 2:141.
123. Monier-Williams, 1286.
124. Müller, 265*n*2; Tyāgīśānanda, 127; Nikhilananda, *Upanishads,* 2:139; Radhakrishnan, 747; Gambhīrānanda, *Śvetāśvatara Upaniṣad,* 195; Lokeswarananda, 237–238; Vedananda, 180–181.
125. Nikhilananda, *Upanishads,* 2:139.
126. Vedananda, 181.
127. Monier-Williams, 1189.
128. Lokeswarananda, 238.
129. Nikhilananda, *Upanishads,* 2:139.
130. Deussen, 1:325*n*2.
131. Tyāgīśānanda, 127.
132. Monier-Williams, 1189.
133. Tyāgīśānanda, 127.
134. Nikhilananda, *Upanishads,*2:139.
135. Müller, 265; Deussen, 1:325; Hume, 410; Tyāgīśānanda, 128; Radhakrishnan, 747; Lokeswarananda, 239; Olivelle, 264.
136. Nikhilananda, *Upanishads,* 2:140; Vedananda, 182; Roebuck, 314.
137. Larson, 115.
138. Ibid., 168.
139. Dyczkowski, *Doctrine,* 94.
140. Satprakashananda, *Universe,* 241–242.
141. Ibid., 242.
142. Nikhilananda, *Upanishads,* 2:141.
143. Lokeswarananda, 245.
144. Gambhīrānanda, *Śvetāśvatara Upaniṣad,* 199.
145. Nikhilananda, *Upanishads,* 2:141.
146. Müller, 266; Tyāgīśānanda, 131, Prabhavananda and Manchester, 203, Nikhilananda, *Upanishads,* 2:141.
147. Deussen, 1:326, Radhakrishnan, 748; Gambhīrānanda, *Śvetāśvatara Upaniṣad,* 200; Vedananda, 188; Roebuck, 315.
148. Lokeswarananda, 247; Olivelle, 265; Ilárraz and Pujol, 326.
149. Müller, xxxiv.
150. Ibid., 266*n*6; Radhakrishnan, 749.
151. Lokeswarananda, 249–250; Olivelle, 395.
152. Gambhīrānanda, *Śvetāśvatara Upaniṣad,* 205.
153. Ibid.
154. Vedananda, 192.
155. Nikhilananda, *Upanishads,* 2:143.
156. Lokeswarananda, 253–254.

BIBLIOGRAPHY

Abhinavagupta. *Parā-trīśikā-Vivaraṇa: The Secret of Tantric Mysticism.* Translated by Jaideva Singh. Delhi: Motilal Banarsidass, 1988.

Agrawal, Ashvini, ed. *In Search of Vedic-Harappan Relationship.* New Delhi: Aryan Books International, 2005.

Basu, Manoranjan. *Fundamentals of the Philosophy of Tantras.* Calcutta: Mira Basu Publishers, 1986.

Bhattacharyya, Narendra Nath. *History of the Śākta Religion.* 2nd rev. ed. New Delhi: Munshiram Manoharlal, 1996.

———. *History of the Tantric Religion: A Historical, Ritualistic and Philosophical Study.* New Delhi: Manohar, 1992.

Bowker, John, ed. *The Oxford Dictionary of World Religions.* Oxford: Oxford University Press, 1997.

Brant, Edwin. *The Quest for the Origins of Vedic Culture: The Indo-Aryan Migration Debate.* Oxford: Oxford University Press, 2001.

Brown, C. Mackenzie. *The Devī Gītā—The Song of the Goddess: A Translation, Annotation, and Commentary.* Albany: State University of New York Press, 1998.

Chatterjee, Satischandra, and Datta, Dhirendramohan, *An Introduction to Indian Philosophy,* 6th ed. Calcutta: University of Calcutta, 1960.

Craig, Edward, ed. *The Routledge Encyclopaedia of Philosophy.* 10 vols. London and New York: Routledge, 1998.

Deshpande, G. T. *Abhinavagupta.* New Delhi: Sahitya Akademi, 1989.

Deussen, Paul. *Sixty Upaniṣads of the Veda.* Translated by V. M. Bedekar and G. B. Palsule. 2 vols. 1897. Reprint. Delhi: Motilal Banarsidass, 1997.

Dvivedi, M. N. *The Yoga-Sūtras of Patañjali.* 1890. Reprint. Delhi: Sri Satguru Publications, 2001.

Dyczkowski, Mark S. G. *The Aphorisms of Śiva: The* Śiva Sūtra *with Bhāskara's Commentary, the* Vārttika. New Delhi: Indica Books, 1998.

———. *The Canon of the Śaivāgama and the Kubjikā Tantras of the Western Kaula Tradition.* Albany: State University of New York Press, 1988.

———. *The Doctrine of Vibration: An Analysis of the Doctrines and Practices of Kashmir Shaivism.* Albany: State University of New York Press, 1987.

Eggeling, Julius, trans. *The Satapatha Brahmana, Part III.* Sacred Books of the East, Vol. 41. Oxford: Clarendon Press, 1894.

Feuerstein, Georg. *Tantra: The Path of Ecstasy.* Boston: Shambhala, 1998.

Gambhīrānanda, Swāmī, trans. *Brahma-Sūtra-Bhāṣya of Śrī Śaṅkarācārya.* 2nd. ed. Calcutta: Advaita Ashrama, 1972.

———. *Eight Upaniṣads: With the Commentary of Śaṅkarācārya.* 2 vols. 2nd revised ed. Calcutta: Advaita Ashrama, 1989.

———. *Śvetāśvatara Upaniṣad: With the Commentary of Śaṅkarācārya.* Calcutta: Advaita Ashrama, 1986.

Gonda, Jan. *Viṣṇuism and Śivaism: A Comparison.* 1970. Reprint. New Delhi: Munshiram Manoharlal, 1976.

Goudriaan, Teun. "Imagery of the Self from Veda to Tantra" in *The Roots of Tantra,* edited by Katherine Anne Harper and Robert L. Brown. Albany: State University of New York Press, 2002.

Griffith, Ralph T. H., trans. *The Rig Veda.* 1896. Reprint. New York: Book-of-the-Month Club, 1992.

Grimes, John. *A Concise Dictionary of Indian Philosophy: Sanskrit Terms Defined in English.* Albany: State University of New York Press, 1989.

Gupta, Bina. "Gauḍapāda." In *Great Thinkers of the Eastern World,* edited by Ian P. McGreal. New York: HarperCollins, 1995.

———. "Shankara." In *Great Thinkers of the Eastern World,* edited by Ian P. McGreal. New York: HarperCollins, 1995.

———. "Sureshvara." In *Great Thinkers of the Eastern World,* edited by Ian P. McGreal. New York: HarperCollins, 1995.

Gupta, Mahendranath [M.]. *The Gospel of Sri Ramakrishna.* Translated by Swami Nikhilananda. New York: Ramakrishna-Vivekananda Center, 1942.

Gupta, S. P. "The Sarasvatī and the Homeland of Early Ṛigvedic *Ṛishis:* In the Light of Recent Scientific Researches." In *In Search of Vedic-Harappan Relationship,* edited by Ashvini Agrawal. New Delhi: Aryan Books International, 2005.

Hume, Robert Ernest. *The Thirteen Principal Upanishads: Translated from the Sanskrit with an Outline of the Philosophy of the Upanishads.* London: Oxford University Press, 1921.

Ilárraz, Fīlix G., y Pujol, Òscar. *La sabiduría del bosque: Antología de las principales upaniṣáds.* Madrid: Editorial Trotta, 2003.

Isayeva, Natalia. *From Early Vedanta to Kashmir Shaivism: Gaudapada, Bhartrhari, and Abhinavagupta.* Delhi: Sri Satguru Publications, 1997.

Jacob, G. A. *A Concordance to the Principal Upaniṣads and Bhagavadgītā.* 1891. Reprint. Delhi: Motilal Banarsidass, 1985.

Kālī, Devadatta. *In Praise of the Goddess: The Devīmāhātmya and Its Meaning.* Berwick, Maine: Nicolas-Hays, 2003.

Kenoyer, Jonathan Mark. *Ancient Cities of the Indus Valley Civilization.* Karachi: Oxford University Press and American Institute of Pakistan Studies, 1998.

Lakshmanjoo, Swami. *Kashmir Shaivism: The Supreme Secret.* Edited by John Hughes. Culver City, California: Universal Shaiva Fellowship, 2002.

———. *Shiva Sutras: The Supreme Awakening.* Edited by John Hughes. Culver City, California: Universal Shaiva Fellowship, 2002.

Larson, Gerald James. *Classical Sāṁkhya: An Interpretation of Its History and Meaning.* 2nd rev. ed. Delhi: Motilal Banarsidass, 1979.

Lokeswarananda, Swami, trans. *Śvetāśvatara Upaniṣad.* Calcutta: Ramakrishna Mission Institute of Culture, 1994.

Macdonell, Arthur A. *A Vedic Grammar for Students.* 1916. Reprint. Oxford: Oxford University Press, 1971.

Mādhavānanda, Swāmī, trans. *The Bṛhadāraṇyaka Upaniṣad.* 2nd ed. Mylapore, Madras: Sri Ramakrishna Math, 1951.

———. *Vivekacūḍāmaṇi of Śrī Śaṅkarācārya.* 2nd ed. Calcutta: Advaita Ashrama, 1926.

Mahadevan, T. M. P., trans. *Self Knowledge (Ātma-bodha) of Śrī Śaṅkarācārya.* New Delhi: Arnold-Heinemann, 1975.

Marjanovic, Boris, trans. *Abhinavagupta's Commentary on the Bhagavad Gita (Gītārtha-saṁgraha).* Varanasi: Indica Books, 2002.

McGreal, Ian P., ed. *Great Thinkers of the Eastern World.* New York: HarperCollins, 1995.

Mishra, Kamalakar. *Kashmir Śaivism: The Central Philosophy of Tantrism.* Delhi: Sri Satguru Publications, 1999.

Monier-Williams, Monier. *A Sanskrit-English Dictionary.* Oxford: Oxford University Press, 1899.

Müller, F. Max, trans. *The Upanishads, Part II.* Sacred Books of the East, vol. 15. Oxford: Clarendon Press, 1884.

Muller-Ortega, Paul Eduardo. *The Triadic Heart of Śiva: Kaula Tantricism of Abhinavagupta in the Non-Dual Shaivism of Kashmir.* Albany: State University of New York Press, 1989.

Nikhilananda, Swami, trans. *Self-Knowledge (Ātmabodha).* New York: Ramakrishna-Vivekananda Center, 1946.

———. *The Upanishads: A New Translation.* 4 vols. New York: Ramakrishna-Vivekananda Center, 1952.

Olivelle, Patrick. *Upaniṣads.* Oxford: Oxford University Press, 1996.

Padoux, André. *Vāc: The Concept of the Word in Selected Hindu Tantras.* Translated by Jacques Gontier. 1990. Reprint. Delhi: Sri Satguru Publications, 1992.

Pandey, Kanti Chandra. *An Outline of History of Śaiva Philosophy.* 1954. Reprint. Delhi: Motilal Banarsidass, 1999.

Pandit, Balajit Nath. *History of Kashmir Shaivism.* Srinagar, Kashmir: Utpal Publications, 1989.

———. *Specific Principles of Kashmir Shaivism.* New Delhi: Munshiram Manoharlal, 1997.

Pandit, Moti Lal. *The Disclosure of Being: A Study of Yogic and Tantric Methods of Enstasy.* New Delhi: Munshiram Manoharlal, 2006.

———. *The Trika Śaivism of Kashmir.* New Delhi: Munshiram Manoharlal, 2003.

Pereira, José. "Bādarāyaṇa." In *Great Thinkers of the Eastern World,* edited by Ian P. McGreal. New York: HarperCollins, 1995.

Pintchman, Tracy. *The Rise of the Goddess in the Hindu Tradition.* Albany: State University of New York Press, 1994.

Powell, Barbara. *Windows into the Infinite: A Guide to the Hindu Scriptures.* Fremont, California: Asian Humanities Press, 1996.

Prabhananda, Swami. *First Meetings with Sri Ramakrishna.* Mylapore, Madras: Sri Ramakrishna Math, 1987.

Prabhavananda, Swami. *The Eternal Companion: Brahmananda, Teachings and Reminiscences.* 3rd ed. Hollywood: Vedanta Press, 1970.

———. *The Spiritual Heritage of India.* Hollywood: Vedanta Press, 1963.

———. *Vedic Religion and Philosophy.* Mylapore, Madras: Sri Ramakrishna Math, 1950.

Prabhavananda, Swami, and Isherwood, Christopher. *How to Know God: The Yoga Aphorisms of Patanjali.* Hollywood: Vedanta Press, 1953.

Prabhavananda, Swami, and Manchester, Frederick, trans. *The Upanishads: Breath of the Eternal.* Hollywood: Vedanta Press, 1947.

Radhakrishnan, S., trans. *The Principal Upaniṣads.* 1953. Reprint. New Delhi: HarperCollins India, 1994.
Ratnagar, Shereen. *Understanding Harappa: Civilization in the Greater Indus Valley.* New Delhi: Tulika, 2001.
Roebuck, Valerie J., trans. *The Upanishads.* London: Penguin Books, 2003.
Śaṅkarācārya. *Vivekacūḍāmaṇi.* Translated by Swāmī Madhāvānanda. 2nd ed. Calcutta: Advaita Ashrama, 1926.
Saraswati, Madhusūdhana. *Bhagavad-Gītā with the Annotation* Gūḍhārtha-Dīpikā. Translated by Swāmī Gambhīrānanda. Calcutta: Advaita Ashrama, 1998.
Satprakashananda, Swami. *Meditation: Its Process, Practice, and Culmination.* St. Louis: The Vedanta Society of St. Louis, 1976.
———. *Methods of Knowledge according to Advaita Vedanta.* London: George Allen & Unwin, 1965.
———. *The Universe, God, and God-Realization: From the Viewpoint of Vedanta.* St. Louis: The Vedanta Society of St. Louis, 1977.
Seager, Richard Hughes, ed. *The Dawn of Religious Pluralism: Voices from the World's Parliament of Religions, 1893.* La Salle, Illinois: Open Court, 1993.
SenSharma, Deba Brata. *The Philosophy of Sādhanā: With Special Reference to the Trika Philosophy of Kashmir.* Albany: State University of New York Press, 1990.
Sharma, Deo Prakash. "Early Harappan Ceramics." In *Early Harappans and Indus-Sarasvati Civilization,* edited by Deo Prakash Sharma and Madhuri Sharma. New Delhi: Kaveri Books, 2006.
Sharma, Deo Prakash, and Sharma, Madhuri, eds. *Early Harappans and Indus-Sarasvati Civilization.* 2 vols. New Delhi: Kaveri Books, 2006.
Sharma, Har Dutt. *The Sāṁkhya-Kārikā: Īśvara Kṛṣṇa's Memorable Verses on Sāṁkhya Philosophy with the Commentary of Gauḍapādācārya.* Poona: Oriental Book Agency, 1933.
Sheridan, Daniel P. "Īshvarakrishna." In *Great Thinkers of the Eastern World,* edited by Ian P. McGreal. New York: HarperCollins, 1995.
Schuhmacher, Stephan, and Woerner, Gert, eds. *The Encyclopedia of Eastern Philosophy and Religion.* Boston: Shambhala, 1989.
Singh, Jaideva. *Pratyabhijñāhṛdayam: The Secret of Self-Recognition.* 4th rev. ed. Delhi: Motilal Banarsidass, 1982.
———. *Śiva Sūtras: The Yoga of Supreme Identity.* Delhi: Motilal Banarsidass, 1979.
———. *Spanda-Kārikās: The Divine Creative Pulsation.* Delhi: Motilal Banarsidass, 1980.
———. *Vijñānabhairava or Divine Consciousness: A Treasury of 112 Types of Yoga.* Delhi: Motilal Banarsidass, 1979.
Singh, Shivaji. "Need of a New Paradigm: Ascertaining Vedic-Harappan Relationship." In *In Search of Vedic-Harappan Relationship,* edited by Ashvini Agrawal, 154–182. New Delhi: Aryan Books International, 2005.
Sivananda, Swami. *Lord Siva and His Worship.* Shivanandanagar, U.P.: Divine Life Society, 1989.
Smith, Jonathan Z., ed. *The HarperCollins Dictionary of Religion.* San Francisco: HarperSanFrancisco, 1995.
Studies on the Tantras. Calcutta: Ramakrishna Mission Institute of Culture, 1989.
Swāhānanda, Swāmī, trans. *The Chāndogya Upaniṣad.* 6th ed. Mylapore, Madres: Sri Ramakrishna Math, 1984.
———. *Pañcadaśī of Sri Vidyaranya Swami.* Mylapore, Madras: Sri Ramakrishna Math, 1967.

Tagare, G. V. *The Pratyabhijñā Philosophy*. Delhi: Motilal Banarsidass, 2002.
———. *Śaivism*. New Delhi: D. K. Printworld, 1996.
Talageri, Shrikant G. *The Rigveda: A Historical Analysis*. New Delhi: Aditya Prakashan, 2000.
Thibaut, George, trans. *The Vedānta Sūtras with the Commentary by Sankaracarya*, Pt. 1 Sacred Books of the East, edited by Max Müller, vol. 34. Oxford: Clarendon Press, 1890.
Torella, Raffaele. *The Īśvarapratyabhijñākārikā of Utpaladeva: with the Author's Vṛtti*. Corrected edition. Delhi: Motilal Banarsidass, 2002.
Tyāgīśānanda, Swāmī, trans. *Śvetāśvatara Upaniṣad*. 7th ed. Mylapore, Madras: Sri Ramakrishna Math, 1979.
Vedananda, Swami. *The Svetasvatara Upanishad: Swami Bhaskareshwarananda's Elucidation of Shankaracharya's Commentary on the Upanishad*. Gurnee, Illinois: Scars Publications, 2001.
Victor, Pasalapudi George. *Life and Teachings of Ādi Śaṅkarācārya*. New Delhi: D. K. Printworld, 2002.
Vimalananda, Swami, trans. *Mahānārāyaṇopaniṣad*. Āndhra recension. Mylapore, Madras: Sri Ramakrishna Math, 1957.
Vireśwarānanda, Swāmī, trans. *Śrīmad Bhagavad Gītā with the Gloss of Śrīdhara Swāmī*. Mylapore, Madras: Sri Ramakrishna Math, 1948.
Warrier, A. G. Krishna. *Śrīmad Bhagavad Gītā Bhāṣya of Śrī Śaṁkarācārya*. Mylapore, Madras: Sri Ramakrishna Math, 1983.
Whitney, William Dwight. *Sanskrit Grammar: Including both the Classical Language, and the older Dialects, of Veda and Brahmana*. 2nd ed. Cambridge: Harvard University Press, 1889.
———. "The Upanishads and their Latest Translation," *American Journal of Philology* 7 (1886): 1–26.
Wilson, H. H. "Essays on the Religious Sects of the Hindus," *Asiatic Researches* 16 (1828): 11.
Woodroffe, Sir John [Arthur Avalon]. *The Garland of Letters: Studies in the Mantra-Śāstra*. 9th ed. Pondicherry: Ganesh & Company, 1989.

INDEX

Sanskrit terms and their English definitions are cross-referenced, with the main entry under the Sanskrit. For a fuller explanation of any Sanskrit term the reader is referred to the text.

ŚVETĀŚVATAROPANIṢAD THEMATIC INDEX
(by verse)

Two books by Devadatta Kālī from Nicolas-Hays

In Praise of the Goddess: The Devīmāhātmya and Its Meaning

A new translation, with commentary, of the sacred Hindu scripture and its eight Angas

by Devadatta Kālī

About 16 centuries ago, an unknown Indian author or authors gathered together the diverse threads of already ancient traditions and wove them into a verbal tapestry that today is still the central text for worshippers of the Hindu Devi, the Divine Mother. This spiritual classic, the *Devimahatmya,* addresses the perennial questions of the nature of the universe, humankind, and divinity. How are they related, how do we live in a world torn between good and evil, and how do we find lasting satisfaction and inner peace?

These questions and their answers form the substance of the *Devīmāhātmya.* Its narrative of a dispossessed king, a merchant betrayed by the family he loves, and a seer whose teaching leads beyond existential suffering sets the stage for a trilogy of myths concerning the all-powerful Divine Mother, Durga, and the fierce battles she wages against throngs of demonic foes. In these allegories, her adversaries represent our all-too-human impulses toward power, possessions, and pleasure. The battlefields symbolize the field of human consciousness on which our lives' dramas play out in joy and sorrow, in wisdom and folly.

The *Devīmāhātmya* speaks to us across the ages of the experiences and beliefs of our ancient ancestors. We sense their enchantment at nature's bounty and their terror before its destructive fury, their recognition of the good and evil in the human heart, and their understanding that everything in our experience is the expression of a greater reality, personified as the Divine Mother.

2003 • ISBN: 0-89254-080-X • 416 Pages, 6 x 9 • Paperback • $22.95

The Veiling Brilliance: A Journey to the Goddess

by Devadatta Kālī

The Veiling Brilliance tells the tale of three men—a king, a merchant, and a seer— but at its core is a revelation about the central tenets of goddess worship within an ancient religion. A humiliated king, Suratha, and a down-on-his-luck merchant, Samadhi, find themselves at the ashram of the seer Medhas. There, they receive the support and teaching they need to return successfully to the world at large, but each in a manner based on his own individual need. This fascinating novel of attainment and redemption allows readers a rare glimpse into the world of traditional Hindu goddess worship, not from a pedantic, evangelical, or proselytizing approach, but through the gentle, almost incidental teaching form 0f fiction. Follow the three main characters as they bond with each other and grow together in a quest for enlightenment which will allow the two students to emerge back into the world, healed and ready for the vicissitudes of secular life.

Based on the ancient Hindu scripture, the *Devīmāhātmya, The Veiling Brilliance* includes wisdom found in many other Hindu classics such as the Rigveda Samhita, the Upanishads, the Bhagavadgita, the Yogasutra of Patanjali, and traditional tantric works. In fact, the title refers directly to that essence of Shakti, and Hindu worship of the goddess—although hidden or veiled from the eyes of those caught up in everyday life, the brilliance of her wisdom cannot be kept from those who seek it out.

Some other titles From Ibis Press/ Nicolas-Hays

Tantric Temples: Eros and Magic in Java

by Peter Levenda

Tantra is one of the most misunderstood of the esoteric disciplines. This book illustrates the history of Tantrism in Java with more than a hundred full-color photographs of temples, statues and iconography—some rarely seen before, including the recently-excavated "white temple" of Yogyakarta—and accounts of contemporary practices in the shrines, cemeteries and secret schools of Java. In the process, we will learn how this esoteric philosophy has affected the everyday lives of the most populous Muslim country in the world.

We will also learn that an important Tibetan teacher of the eleventh century studied at the feet of a Tantric master in Java and brought back with him to Tibet the sacred—and secret—teachings that are important to Tibetan Buddhist practice today.

Hindu influences are equally at play in this dynamic tradition. Sacred sexuality is alive and well in Java, where the Sultans still pay homage to the Goddess of the Southern Sea in a colorful and arcane ritual, and where Muslim men and women meet at secret shrines to marry a stranger before having intercourse in a sacred cemetery in order to obtain supernatural favors. The relationship between sexuality, religion, and power is clear and unequivocal.

It was this Tantra —the real Tantra—that has influenced secret societies, mystics, alchemists, Kabbalists and magicians for hundreds if not thousands of years. This book tells the story of how human sexuality became a metaphor and a template for both spiritual transformation and the manipulation of reality; how various sexual acts and psycho-biological states became the basis for a comprehensive cosmology that incorporates every aspect of human experience.

2011 • ISBN 978-0-89254-169-0 • 352 pages, 7.5 x 10.5 • Hardcover • $69.00

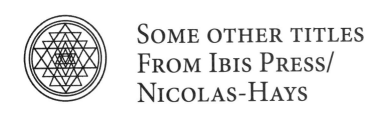

Kali: The Black Goddess of Dakshineswar
by Elizabeth U. Harding

A devotee's guide to the Goddess Kali in her temple in Calcutta, where the saint, Ramakrishna, received enlihtenment. The daily ritual of the temple, how worship is handled, life in the temple, and stories of Ramakrishna are explained in this one-of-a-kind volume.

"Never before in print have I seen Her brought to life with such passion and truth." —Ma Jaya, spiritual teacher, author of The River.

"This book will help clear the misunderstanding about the Hindu goddess Kali. The author's rational and devotional approach made her work authentic and inspiring." —Swami Chetanananda, The Vedanta Society of St. Louis.

1993 • ISBN: 0-89254-025-7 • 352 Pages, 5 ⅜ x 8 ¼ • paperback • $18.95

The Diamond Sutra: The Prajna Paramita
Translated by William Gemmell

First published in 1912, William Gemmell's translation of *The Diamond Sutra* was one of the first books to introduce general readers in the West to Buddhism. It still stands as a refreshing, easy-to-understand look at an ancient and enduring tradition.

The Diamond Sutra, a sacred Buddhist text, recounts the Buddha's discourse to one of his disciples. It discusses fundamental Buddhist practices, including how food is to be consumed, begging for alms, and monastic vows. Gemmell's fully annotated translation presents important information from the Asia experts of his day. The annotation also provides still-relevant parallels between Buddhist principles and Western spirituality.

William Gemmell's simple, elegant translation of *The Diamond Sutra* remains one of the best general introductions to Buddhism.

2003 • ISBN: 0-89254-075-3 • 160 Pages, 5 x 7 • Paperback • $14.95

Dervish Yoga for Health and Longevity
Samadeva Gestural Euphony: The Seven Major Arkanas
by Idris Lahore, Ennea Griffith, & Emma Thyloch

Just about every kid has experienced the euphoria of spinning around, arms outstretched. The Sufi dervishes harnessed this joyful movement in their ecstatic celebration of and union with the divine. Thanks to Idris Lahore, the art, philosophy, and science of the movements of Samadeva, as they have been taught and practiced by the dervishes in their secret brotherhood since ancient times, are now available to westerners.

Dervish Yoga for Health and Longevity details the seven fundamental arkana, or sacred exercises, of Samadeva, which are similar to the movements of yoga, T'ai Chi Ch'uan, and dance. The exercises are simple and extraordinarily revitalizing. They rebalance the psyche, slow down the aging process, regenerate the spirit, and fortify the body, bringing it health, energy, suppleness, and harmony. Each arkana corresponds to one of the major energy centers, or chakras, in the body, and the authors include extensive information about each chakra and the effects of the exercises upon them. Illustrated by numerous detailed photographs, these exercises can be easily learned in just ten minutes a day.

2007 • ISBN: 0-89254-131-8 • 200 Pages, 7 x 10 • Paperback • $16.95

Asteroid Goddesses
The Mythology, Psychology, and Astrology of the Re-emerging Feminine
by Demetra George & Douglas Bloch

This new edition of a beloved classic includes updated ephemerides from 1930–2050. It studies the sixteen asteroid Goddesses—including Ceres, Pallas, Juno, and Vesta, and the Moon and Venus—which comprise the full expression of the feminine principle. Describes the effects and influences of asteroids in the signs, houses, and in aspect.

Demetra George is a professional astrologer and author specializing in archetypal mythology and ancient techniques. She leads pilgrimages to the sacred sites in the Mediterranean and India with Ancient Oracle Tours, and mentors private students through Thema: Foundations in Astrology.

2003 • ISBN: 978-0892540822 • 368 Pages, 5½" x 8½". Paperback •$18.95

Astrology and the Authentic Self
by Demetra George

This ground-breaking book provides a model for the practicing astrologer to analyze a client's life purpose as indicated through the natal chart. It addresses significant concerns, such as relationship and vocation and provides methods for determining current timing movements. Ms. George gives the methods to communicate this complex information in a concise and professional manner within the context of an astrological counseling session. She provides an excellent introduction to the doctrines of ancient astrology concerning how to determine the condition of a planet and its capacity to be effective and produce favorable outcomes. She outlines how to follow these traditional guidelines, but interprets them within a modern context, adding the insights of more contemporary approaches.

2008 • ISBN: 0-89254-149-2 • 316 Pages, 6 x 9 • Paperback• $24.95

Stress Elimination Handbook
A holistic Self-Help Program to restore health, achieve balance and promote well-being.

by Grandmaster Adrian Simon Lowe

Includes large full-color wall chart illustrating 38 Lion's Tail Qi Gong positions

The epidemic of our times, stress has its roots in the very essence of life and has caused more suffering and diminishment of the human spirit than any other form of affliction. Stress is the root cause of imbalance and dis-ease. Its causes can be identified as Acute and Chronic. Acute stressful factors include: financial problems, fear, family disharmony, noise, sleep disturbances, crowd activity, pedestrian and motorized traffic, isolation, physical hunger and severe temperature changes. Chronic stressful factors include: vibratory, parasitic, prolonged and/or serious illness, political or religious dogma, marriage/divorce, poverty, death, employment issues and/or work environment and media fear mongering.

The text includes detailed text and charts to illustrate the medical and scientific aspects of the effects of stress on our immune system and overall health. The importance of proper breathing and of enhancing Qi with nutrition, water and architectural design are also discussed. LAMAS Qi Gong is an ancient art that can help to conquer and reduce stress on all levels, while preventing damage to mind, body and spirit. Qi Gong techniques will also boost the immune system and help one achieve a more balanced lifestyle, improved health and an increased sense of wellbeing.

Grandmaster Lowe travels extensively worldwide to teach Qi Gong and heal others. He is an empath, medical intuitive, spiritual Qi healer, and the leading authority in the field of Qi Gong.

2010 • ISBN: 978-0892541621 • 176 pages, 7x10 • Sewn paperback • $21.95 • Includes 35 pages of color photos detailing postures in addition to the Wall Chart

Soul-Centered Astrology: A Key to Your Expanding Self
by Alan Oken

This is a groundbreaking sourcebook influenced by Theosophical philosophy, Alice Bailey, and the Ancient Wisdom Teachings. Alan Oken describes the evolutionary process of spiritual self-development with the twelve astrological signs and their soul-centered planetary rulers and the esoteric significance of the planets in the signs. The book features an elevation of the spiritual importance of the ascendant, the incarnational relevance of cardinal, fixed, and mutable crosses, and the correlation between astrology and the Seven Rays. Revealing the soul's path to inner enlightenment and outer fulfillment, it offers a complete course for the serious student of the stars that encompasses and goes beyond birth signs and natal charts.

2008 • ISBN: 0-89254-134-2 • 429 Pages. 6 x 9 • Paperback • $22.95

Your Secret Self: Illuminating the Mysteries of the Twelfth House
by Tracy Marks, M.A.

The Twelfth House in astrology is home to creative inspiration, spirituality, and compassion. It is also where we will find our demons: self-defeating patterns, escapism and the most hidden parts of our shadow self. Tracy Marks provides penetrating insights into the inner workings of both the hidden weaknesses and strengths of the Twelfth House, and provides practical and easy-to-use worksheets to support the process.

Tracy Marks, M.A., is a licensed mental health counselor, astrologer, writer, instructor, and nature photographer. Her transformational astrology books, including *Astrology of Self-Discovery* and *The Art of Chart Interpretation,* have been translated into nine languages and have sold over 150,000 copies.

2010 • ISBN: 978-0-89254-161-4 • 272 pages, 6 x 9 • Paperback • $24.95

Pythagoras: His Life and Teachings

By Thomas Stanley; Preface by Manly P. Hall; Introduction by Henry L. Drake; Edited by James Wasserman; With a Study of Greek Sources by J. Daniel Gunther

An invaluable compendium of ancient sources on the life and teachings of Pythagoras—the Father of Philosophy and Founder of the Western Esoteric Tradition. The timeless brilliance of this exhaustive survey of the best classical writers of antiquity on Pythagoras was first published in 1687 in Thomas Stanley's massive tome, *The History of Philosophy.* It remains as contemporary today as it was over three hundred years ago.

The text of the 1687 book has been reset and modernized to make it more accessible to the modern reader. Spelling has been regularized, obsolete words not found in a modern dictionary have been replaced, and contemporary conventions of punctuation have been used.

Biographical sketches of Thomas Stanley and Pythagoras by Manly Palmer Hall, founder of the Philosophical Research Society, have been included, along with a profound overview of Pythagorean philosophy by Platonic scholar Dr. Henry L. Drake. The extensive Greek language references throughout the text have been corrected and contextualized, and reset in a modern Greek font. Each quotation has been verified with the source document in Greek. An extensive annotated appendix of these classical sources is included. A complete bibliography details all the reference works utilized, and a small Glossary defines a number of terms, especially those from musical theory, which may be unfamiliar to the non-technical reader.

Thomas Stanley (1625–1678) was the first English historian of philosophy. He gained distinction during his own lifetime as a poet and a translator.

2010 • ISBN: 978-089254-160-7 • 416 pages, 6 x 9 • Paperback • $24.95